A Textbook of Belief Dynamics

APPLIED LOGIC SERIES

VOLUME 11

Managing Editor

Dov M. Gabbay, *Department of Computer Science, King's College, London, U.K.*

Co-Editor

Jon Barwise, *Department of Philosophy, Indiana University, Bloomington, IN, U.S.A.*

Editorial Assistant

Jane Spurr, *Department of Computer Science, King's College, London, U.K.*

SCOPE OF THE SERIES

Logic is applied in an increasingly wide variety of disciplines, from the traditional subjects of philosophy and mathematics to the more recent disciplines of cognitive science, computer science, artificial intelligence, and linguistics, leading to new vigor in this ancient subject. Kluwer, through its Applied Logic Series, seeks to provide a home for outstanding books and research monographs in applied logic, and in doing so demonstrates the underlying unity and applicability of logic.

The titles published in this series are listed at the end of this volume.

A Textbook of Belief Dynamics

Theory Change and Database Updating

by

SVEN OVE HANSSON
Department of Philosophy,
Uppsala University

KLUWER ACADEMIC PUBLISHERS
DORDRECHT / BOSTON / LONDON

A C.I.P. Catalogue record for this book is available from the Library of Congress.

ISBN 978-90-481-5125-7

Published by Kluwer Academic Publishers,
P.O. Box 17, 3300 AA Dordrecht, The Netherlands.

Sold and distributed in North, Central and South America
by Kluwer Academic Publishers,
101 Philip Drive, Norwell, MA 02061, U.S.A.

In all other countries, sold and distributed
by Kluwer Academic Publishers,
P.O. Box 322, 3300 AH Dordrecht, The Netherlands.

Printed on acid-free paper

EDITORIAL PREFACE

The editors are happy to present Professor Hansson's book on Belief Dynamics.

Belief revision and dynamics is another central area of pure and applied logic now addressed by our series. It has serious applications not only in philosophy (philosophy of science, conditional logic) but also in computer science (database updates, agent theory).

There is every indication that this area is going to be a unifying theme for many related applications of logic.

THE EDITORS

CONTENTS

PREFACE

The primary purpose of this book is to serve as a textbook in the rapidly growing interdisciplinary field of theory change and database updating. Its subject can be summarized in two questions: What does it mean to change one's beliefs in a rational way? When can a computer program be said to revise its database in a rational way? The tools used to shed some light on these issues are formal models of beliefs and belief changes. In these models, states of belief are represented by sets of sentences, and changes in belief are represented by various operations that modify these sets.

The book is divided into discursive and formal sections; the latter are marked with '+'. The sections not marked with '+' are as informal as I feel that a textbook in a formalized discipline can be. In these sections, the emphasis is on the intuitive interpretation of various postulates and constructions in belief dynamics. Numerous examples of belief change are given to make this discussion concrete. Formal theorems are stated and explained in these sections, but the proofs are deferred to the + sections.

The + sections are quite different in character. Their principal purpose is to introduce to the reader the major proof methods that are used in formal work in this field. The + sections contain proofs of the theorems from the discursive sections. They also contain additional formal results, mostly of a somewhat more technical nature. Each + section is followed by exercises.

Solutions to the exercises are available in a separate volume.

It is possible to read the discursive sections without reading the + sections. However, I hope that most readers will follow me into at least some of the + sections. (Some suitable selections are suggested on p. 1.)

I also hope that some of those readers who plunge deeper into the logical aspects of the subject will feel tempted to have a try at some of the unsolved problems listed in Chapter 6^{+}. There is still a lot of work to be done in this area.

Many colleagues have helped me by commenting on the various manuscripts that have led up to this book. I could not have written it without having learnt so much from conversations and correspondence with the late Carlos Alchourrón and with John Cantwell, Eduardo Fermé, André Fuhrmann, Peter Gärdenfors, Isaac Levi, Sten Lindström, David Makinson, Abhaya Nayak, Erik Olsson, Maurice Pagnucco, Wlodek Rabinowicz, Dietmar Rager, Hans Rott, Tor Sandqvist, Krister

Segerberg, and Mary-Anne Williams. Special thanks go to Jane Spurr for taking care of the typesetting so well.

Sven Ove Hansson
Uppsala, March 1996

SUGGESTED COURSES

Introductory level A

(Requires very little background in logic.)
1:1–9
2:1–11
3:1–12
4:1–7
5:1–2
6

Introductory level B

1:1–9, $1{:}10^{+}$–13^{+}
2:1–11, $2{:}12^{+}$, $2{:}14^{+}$–15^{+}
3:1–12, $3{:}20^{+}$–22^{+}
4:1–7
5:1–2, $5{:}3^{+}$
6

Intermediate level

1:1–9, $1{:}10^{+}$–14^{+}
2:1–11, $2{:}12^{+}$–15^{+}, $2{:}19^{+}$, $2{:}22^{+}$, $2{:}24^{+}$
3:1–12, $3{:}13^{+}$–16^{+}, $3{:}19^{+}$–23^{+}
4:1–7, 4: 8^{+}–$4{:}11^{+}$, $4{:}14^{+}$–15^{+}
5:1–2, $5{:}3^{+}$
6

Graduate level

The whole book.

CHAPTER 1

HAVING BELIEFS

1 WHAT IS BELIEF DYNAMICS?

When was the last time that you changed your mind? I hope it was not long ago. The world around us changes all the time, and in order to cope with it we must constantly change our beliefs: acquire new ones and revise or give up old ones. If we wish computers to react sensibly to changing environments, then they too must be capable of revision.

This is a book about changes in the beliefs of minds and in the data of databases. It introduces a young field of research that was not recognized as a subject of its own until the middle of the 1980's. The new subject grew out of two converging research traditions.

One of these is computer science. Since the beginning of computing, programmers have constructed databases and procedures by which they can be updated. The development of artificial intelligence inspired computer scientists to construct more sophisticated models of database updating. The 'truth maintenance systems' developed by Jon Doyle in the late 1970's were important in this development [12]. One of the most significant theoretical contributions was a 1983 paper by Ronald Fagin, Jeffrey Ullman and Moshe Vardi, in which they introduced the notion of 'database priorities' [17].

The second of the two research traditions is philosophy. In a wide sense, belief change has been a subject of philosophical reflection since antiquity. In the twentieth century, philosophers have discussed the mechanisms by which scientific theories develop, and they have proposed criteria of rationality for revisions of probability assignments. Beginning in the 1970's a more focused discussion of the requirements of rational belief change has taken place in the philosophical community. Two milestones can be pointed out. The first was a series of studies conducted by Isaac Levi in the 1970's [70; 71]. Levi posed many of the problems that have since then been the major concerns of this field of research. He also provided much of the basic formal framework. William Harper's work from the same period has also had a lasting influence [64]. The next milestone was the AGM model, so called after its three originators, Carlos Alchourrón, Peter Gärdenfors, and David Makinson. Alchourrón and Makinson had previously cooperated in studies of changes in legal codes [2]. Gärdenfors's early work was concerned with the connections between belief change and conditional sentences (if-sentences) [29]. With combined forces the three wrote a paper that provided a new, much more general and versatile formal framework for studies of belief change [1]. Since the paper was published in 1985, its major concepts and constructions have been the subject of significant elaboration and development [35; 38; 116].

Presently, there is a strong tendency towards confluence of the traditions from philosophy and from computer research. Computer scientists have related their constructions to the demands on rational belief change developed by philosophers [11; 65; 98]. At the same time, philosophers have directed their efforts at more realistic models that can be implemented on actual computers [24; 51].

This is a flourishing field of research, with a high tempo of innovations and with a steady cross-fertilization from various disciplines. The field is so new that it does not even have a well-established name. 'Belief dynamics', that was chosen for the name of this book, is only one of several names that are being used. Some of the others are:

database updating
theory change
theory revision
belief change
belief revision

Is belief dynamics a useful discipline? Can it be of any help, apart from keeping philosophers and theoretical computer scientists busy? It is really too early to tell, but some of the latest developments may be useful to practical computing by providing criteria by which to judge whether a particular program revises its database in a rational and efficient way [58]. There is also hope that belief dynamics can be useful in cognitive psychology. It should be capable of providing models of learning and other mental processes.

Round the corner, other applications bide their time. Philosophers of science have use for more precise models of changes in scientific theories and worldviews [89]. Legal theorists need models of changes in legal systems. Economists wishing to develop realistic models of the economy have use for formal representations of the changing beliefs of economic agents. There is no lack of potential applications for belief dynamics.

2 ANSWER MODES AND DOXASTIC ATTITUDES

It is commonly assumed in belief dynamics that a computer and a human mind perform changes in very much the same way. In this and the following few sections, we are going to use a simple hypothetical computer as an example, but the major ideas are equally applicable to models of human beliefs.

Let us assume that we are communicating with a database that contains information on some particular subject, such as the physical characteristics of seabirds. The machine can answer questions about the 'beliefs' of its database:

Do you believe that the male mallard has a green head?
Yes.
Do you believe that the guillemot has a yellow beak?
No.
Do you believe that the whooper swan has black wings?
Yes.

(Whoops, the database needs updating!)

In this way, we get to know what beliefs are represented in the database, but we will not learn how they are represented. This is a common and useful level of abstraction in studies of belief dynamics. The nuts and bolts will not concern us, only the beliefs that are represented (by whatever nuts and bolts).

We are going to study the properties of databases in general, i.e., those properties that do not depend on the subject-matter of a particular database. We do not want to be bothered by the intricacies of ornithology, or for that matter, any other particular subject-matter. Instead, we are interested in the general pattern of answers to question such as

Do you believe that ...?,

where '...' stands for any sentence. Sentential logic, the logic of sentences, will be used as a means to abstract from the contents of particular sentences. To begin with, let us assume that there are sentences $p, q, r, \ldots$ that the database may contain beliefs about. It answers questions such as the following:

Do you believe that p?
Yes.
Do you believe that q?
No.

The usual truth-functional connectives are used to form negated or combined sentences: $\neg$ ('not'), & ('and'), $\vee$ ('or'), $\rightarrow$ ('if ... then'), and $\leftrightarrow$ ('if and only if').

The computer should be able to answer questions that refer to negated sentences, such as

Do you believe that $\neg r$?
No.

For the most part, we will be interested in systems that answer questions in a consistent way. We do not want to endure conversations such as the following:

Do you believe that p?
Yes.

Do you believe that $\neg p$?
Yes.

A belief system that has belief in both a sentence and its negation is *logically inconsistent*, which a rational being should not be. On the other hand, there is nothing wrong with the following dialogue:

Do you believe that p?
No.
Do you believe that $\neg p$?
No.

A rational being may very well believe in neither a sentence nor its negation, perhaps because she does not have sufficient information.

In summary, there are three attitudes that a consistent believer can have with respect to a sentence p and its negation $\neg p$.

1. Believe that p is true (belief, acceptance)
2. Believe that p is false (disbelief, rejection)
3. Neither believe that p is true nor that it is false (suspension of belief)

We can now choose to communicate with our database with a somewhat less awkward phrase than 'Do you believe that p?' Instead we can ask:

Is it the case that p?

to which the system answers 'yes' if it believes p to be true, 'no' if it believes it to be false, and 'I do not know' if it believes neither. These are the three *basic answer modes* of our simple database system. With a philosophical term, they are the three *doxastic attitudes* that we are going to take into account. ('Doxastic' means related to belief. Another common term is 'epistemic attitude'. 'Epistemic' means related to knowledge.)

Clearly the three basic doxastic attitudes do not cover all the attitudes that one may have with respect to the truth or falsity of a sentence. You can also have doxastic attitudes such that you:

Assign the probability 5 per cent to p.
Believe it to be impossible that p is true.
Believe it to be almost certain that p is false.

In many AI applications, we may want the program to have answer modes other than the three basic ones. Dialogues such as the following can then be possible:

How probable is it that p is true?
72 per cent.
Is it impossible that q?
No, but it is almost impossible.

The use of non-basic answer modes (doxastic attitudes) adds realism to a model of belief change. At the same time it makes the model more complicated. It is therefore a good research strategy to squeeze out as much as possible from models with the three basic answer modes before introducing more complex models. Indeed, this has been the strategy of most researchers in belief dynamics. In this book, we will be almost exclusively concerned with the basic answer modes. Only in Chapter 5 will moderate extensions of the scope of answer modes be considered.

3 INPUTS

Since we judge a database by the way it answers questions, a natural way to change it is to instruct it to answer questions in a new way. For this, we only need two types of instructions, 'Believe that . . . !' and 'Do not believe that . . . !' Changes should be successful, as in the following two dialogues.

Do you believe that p?
No.
Believe that p!
Do you believe that p?
Yes.

Do you believe that q?
Yes.
Do not believe that q!
Do you believe that q?
No.

In the first case, the instruction (input) leads the computer to *incorporate* a belief into its database. In the second case, the instruction leads it to *contract* (remove) a belief.

In models with non-basic answer modes, other types of inputs will be needed. For instance, if we want to update probability assignments, then we may have to give instructions such as 'assign to q the probability 50 per cent'. However, since we will be primarily concerned with the basic answer modes, we have good reasons to be content with the two simple input modes that result in the presence or the absence of a specified belief:

incorporation: the result is that a belief is accepted
contraction: the result is that a belief is not accepted

Belief changes in real life are often much more complex than (single) incorporations or contractions. It is a fundamental assumption in belief dynamics—introduced by Isaac Levi [70]—that complex changes can be analyzed as sequences of changes of the two simple types:

> *Decomposition principle* [22] (*first version*):
> Every legitimate belief change is decomposable into a sequence of incorporations and contractions.

The decomposition principle should not be read as a requirement that you actually change your beliefs in this stepwise fashion, one incorporation or contraction at a time. All that is needed is that the outcomes of your complex belief changes are the same *as if* you had performed them in this way.

The models of belief change that we are going to study are all *input-assimilating*. They describe how a subject or a computer transforms its state of belief upon receipt of an input or an instruction. Between the inputs, the state of belief is assumed to be constant. Therefore, the following dialogue is not possible:

> Do you believe that p?
> Yes.
> Do you believe that p?
> No.

Actual subjects change their minds as a result of deliberations that are not induced by new inputs. The idealized belief states of belief dynamics only change as a direct result of new inputs.

Furthermore, the models that we shall study will be *deterministic* in the way they assimilate inputs. This means that given a belief state and an input (such as 'Do not believe that p!'), the next belief state is well-determined. Chance has no role in the selection of the new belief state. Clearly, this is not a realistic feature, but it makes our models much simpler and easier to handle, not least from a computational point of view. Studies of *indeterministic* belief change (with more than one admissible result of subjecting a specified belief state to a specified input) tend to confirm most of the major results from deterministic models [13; 28; 79].

Our framework is *sentential* in the sense that the factual information of both inputs (instructions) and question-answer dialogues is conveyed by sentences. This is by no means unproblematic. Actual epistemic agents are moved to change their beliefs largely by non-linguistic inputs, such as sensory impressions. Sentential models of belief change (tacitly) assume that all inputs can, in terms of their effects on belief states, be adequately represented by sentences. When I see a hen on the roof (a sensory input), I am assumed to adjust my belief state *as if* I modified it to include the sentence 'There is a hen on the roof' (a linguistic input) [54].

We will occasionally allow for one (moderate) modification of the sentential framework: the simultaneous incorporation or contraction of several sentences. Thus, inputs such as the following will be permitted:

> Believe in all of the sentences p, q, and r!
> Do not believe in any of the sentences s, t, u, or v!

The simultaneous contraction (incorporation) of several sentences was originally called 'batch operations' [16], but André Fuhrmann's term 'multiple operations' is now generally accepted [24]. It is important to distinguish between *multiple* contraction, in which several sentences are retracted at a swoop and *iterated* (repeated) contraction, in which they are retracted one at a time.

4 BELIEF STATES AND BELIEF SETS

When talking about change we have been assuming that there is something that changes. This something, the object of change, is the *belief state.* We can develop various constructions to be used as models of the belief state. Alternatively, we can treat it as a 'black box'. After receiving certain inputs, it answers questions in certain ways. Its internal mechanisms for doing this need not concern us.

Irrespective of whether we have a constructive or a 'black box' approach to the belief state, its most prominent feature is the set of sentences in which it avows belief. This set is called the set of beliefs or (more commonly) the *belief set.* To be more precise, a sentence p is in the belief set if and only if the question

Do your believe that p?

is answered 'Yes' by the system. Every belief state has a belief set. In other words, there is a function s that assigns a belief set to every belief state. This function is called the *support function* since it sorts out the sentences that are supported by the belief set [47]. Let $\mathcal{K}$ be a belief state. Then $s(\mathcal{K})$ is the belief set that is associated with $\mathcal{K}$.

A fully rational person should believe in the logical consequences of her own beliefs. The same applies to artificially intelligent systems. They should not behave as follows:

Do your believe that p?
Yes.
Do you believe that q?
Yes.
Do you believe that p and q?
No.

In other words, if both p and q are elements of $s(\mathcal{K})$, then $p\&q$ (p and q) is also an element of $s(\mathcal{K})$. More generally, everything that follows logically from the belief set is an element of the belief set. In other words, the belief set is *closed under logical consequence.*

To express logical closure in the formal language, we are going to use the *consequence operator* Cn. For any set A of sentences, $\mathrm{Cn}(A)$ is the set of sentences that follow logically from A. Thus, $\alpha \in \mathrm{Cn}(A)$ is another way of saying that α

follows logically from A. As an alternative notation, we will also sometimes write $A \vdash \alpha$ to denote this. $A \vdash \alpha$ and $\alpha \in \mathrm{Cn}(A)$ are interchangeable notations.

A set A is closed under logical consequence if and only if it contains all its own logical consequences, i.e., if and only if $\mathrm{Cn}(A)$ is a subset of A. Since everything follows logically from itself, A is always a subset of $\mathrm{Cn}(A)$. Therefore, the criterion for A to be closed under logical consequence can be reformulated:

$$A = \mathrm{Cn}(A),$$

which is the conventional formulation. We have postulated that for every belief state, its belief set is closed under logical consequence, i.e., that for every belief state $\mathcal{K}$:

$$s(\mathcal{K}) = \mathrm{Cn}(s(\mathcal{K}))$$

Logical closure, as applied to our logical language with its truth-functional connectives, has some seemingly counter-intuitive consequences. For any two sentences α and β, $\alpha \vee \beta$ is a logical consequence of α, so that if α is in the belief set, then so is $\alpha \vee \beta$. Likewise, both $\beta \rightarrow \alpha$ and $\neg\alpha \rightarrow \beta$ follow from α, so that they are both elements of all belief sets that contain α. Furthermore, all logically true sentences, such as mathematical theorems, are logical consequences of any set of sentences (including the empty set). Therefore, all belief sets contain all logical truths.

Examples

1. I believe that dolphins are mammals. Therefore, I believe that dolphins are either mammals or gods.
2. I believe that the sun is a star. Therefore, I believe that if the moon is made of cheese, then the sun is a star.
3. I believe that Robespierre was a lawyer. Therefore, I believe that if Robespierre was not a lawyer, then the Reign of Terror never took place.
4. Since all mathematical truths follow logically from my belief set, I believe in all mathematical truths.

In order to make sense of examples like these, we must be careful to remember that 'and', 'or', and 'if' are used in the truth- functional sense, that only corresponds in a skeletal fashion to the richer meanings of these words in ordinary English. In particular, the if-sentence of the second example is believed only because everything implies a truth, and that of the third example only because a falsehood implies everything. These sentences should not be confounded with conditional sentences about what would have been the case if the moon was made of cheese or if Robespierre had not been a lawyer.

The fourth example illustrates another reason why logical closure is not satisfied by actual doxastic agents: We are unable to make all the inferences and draw all the conclusions that would be required in order to believe in all the consequences of our beliefs. Isaac Levi has clarified this by pointing out that a belief set consists of the sentences that someone is *committed to believe*, not those that she actually believes in [70; 73]. According to Levi, you are doxastically committed to believe in all the logical consequences of your beliefs, but typically your performance does not fulfil this commitment.

Levi's clarification, in the 1970's, of the formal notion of a belief set provided one of the conceptual ground-pillars on which studies in belief dynamics have since then been built. Levi's original term for a belief set was 'corpus'. Other synonyms are 'knowledge set' and 'theory'. The latter term is often used by logicians, since 'theory' is an established logical term for a set that is closed under logical consequence. The belief set is often denoted by a boldface **K**. (**K** originally stands for 'knowledge'. Many authors in this field use 'knowledge' as a synonym for 'belief'. This usage is unfortunate, since a statement must be true in order to be known but not in order to be believed.)

Belief sets are—and must be—central in any account of belief dynamics that is restricted to the basic answer modes. The simplest and most obvious representation of belief states is therefore to represent them by their respective belief sets. Each belief state is then identified with its respective belief set, and operations of change are performed on the belief set, rather than on some underlying belief state from which it can be derived. This is the approach of Isaac Levi, the AGM trio, and several other researchers—in particular philosophers and logicians.

The identification of belief states with belief sets simplifies our notation. Let $\div$ denote the operation of contraction. If this operation is performed on a belief state $\mathcal{K}$, then the new set of beliefs that results after contraction by α is denoted by $s(\mathcal{K} \div \alpha)$. If we instead assume that contraction take place directly on the belief set **K**, then the new belief set can be denoted by $\mathbf{K} \div \alpha$. The support function can be dispensed with. In the next two sections, we are going to take a first look at operations of contraction and incorporation, as applied in this way directly to a belief set.

5 CHOOSING WHAT TO BELIEVE

Contraction is the operation of removing a specified belief from the belief set. The format for this operation, as applied directly to the belief set, is:

$$\mathbf{K} \div \alpha = \mathbf{K}' \text{ ('}\mathbf{K}\text{ contracted by alpha is equal to }\mathbf{K}\text{ prime')}$$

where **K** is the old belief set, α the sentence to be removed and $\mathbf{K}'$ the new (contracted) belief set. In most cases, many more sentences than α itself must be removed in order to get rid of α. No sentence that implies α is allowed to be retained, and if a set of sentences together imply α, then at least one of them will have to go.

Example
I previously believed that Mary is a musician. In order to remove this belief from my belief set, I must also remove—among others—my belief that Mary plays the cello in the local symphony orchestra.

Not only do we have to remove several beliefs, there may be many alternative ways to do this.

Example
I believed both that John has a cat (α) and that he has a dog (β). Then I heard him saying 'I would never dream of keeping both a dog and a cat'. This leads me to contract my belief set by the sentence $\alpha\&\beta$, i.e., to replace it by a new belief set that does not contain $\alpha\&\beta$.
But how should I do this? Should I give up my belief that John has a cat (α), while retaining my belief that he has a dog (β)? Should I do it the other way around? Or should I give up both α and β?

In most studies of belief contraction, it has been assumed that contraction should be minimal in the sense of leading to the loss of as few previous beliefs as possible. We should give up beliefs only when forced to do so, and then we should give up as few of them as possible. This principle has several names, such as 'conservatism' [63; 104], 'conservativity' [35], 'minimum mutilation' [103], and 'minimal change'[112].

If we wish to apply the principle of conservatism uncompromisingly, then the contracted belief set $\mathbf{K} \div \alpha$ should be as large a subset of $\mathbf{K}$ as it can be without implying α. As was indicated in our last example, however, there will in general be more than one such maximal subset of $\mathbf{K}$.

In order to express this more precisely, we can use the notion of a *remainder set*. For any set A and any sentence α, the remainder set of A by α, $A\perp\alpha$, is the set of maximal subsets of A that do not imply α. In other words:

DEFINITION 1.1 (Alchourrón and Makinson [2]) *Let A be a set of sentences and α a sentence. The set $A\perp\alpha$ ('A less alpha' [82]) is the set such that $B \in A\perp\alpha$ if and only if:*

1. $B \subseteq A$
2. $\alpha \notin \mathrm{Cn}(B)$
3. *There is no set B' such that $B \subset B' \subseteq A$ and $\alpha \notin \mathrm{Cn}(B)$.*

If conservatism is strictly applied, then the outcome of contracting $\mathbf{K}$ by α should be an element of $\mathbf{K}\perp\alpha$:

$$\mathbf{K} \div \alpha \in \mathbf{K}\perp\alpha.$$

An operation $\div$ that satisfies this property is a *maxichoice contraction* (originally called 'choice contraction') [3]. Since $\mathbf{K}\perp\alpha$ typically has many elements, we need a *selection mechanism* to choose between them. The most general selection mechanism for this purpose is a *selection function* that for every remainder set $\mathbf{K}\perp\alpha$ selects exactly one element of $\mathbf{K}\perp\alpha$ (unless $\mathbf{K}\perp\alpha$ is empty; more on that shortly). Following convention we will denote selection functions by the Greek letter γ (gamma). The selected element from $\mathbf{K}\perp\alpha$ is written $\gamma(\mathbf{K}\perp\alpha)$ ('the selection from **K** less alpha'). The general format for maxichoice contraction is therefore:

$$\mathbf{K} \div \alpha = \gamma(\mathbf{K}\perp\alpha).$$

By what criteria does γ select among the elements of $\mathbf{K}\perp\alpha$? Most researchers in this field follow the lead of Isaac Levi, who asserted that the criteria for doxastic choice are not directly correlated with probabilities. Instead, they express degrees of corrigibility or vulnerability to change, that are more closely related to informational value or explanatory power than to probability [70; 73].

Maxichoice contraction was soon found to be unsatisfactory since it does not allow the believer to contract cautiously. In the cat-and-dog example, a cautious person who does not know which of α and β to give up may choose to withdraw both of them.

This procedure can be generalized: If we cannot choose between the various elements of $\mathbf{K}\perp\alpha$, then only such sentences should be included that are accepted in all the elements of $\mathbf{K}\perp\alpha$. In other words, $\mathbf{K}\div\alpha$ should be equal to the intersection of all the elements of $\mathbf{K}\perp\alpha$:

$$\mathbf{K} \div \alpha = \bigcap(\mathbf{K}\perp\alpha).$$

(If you are unaccustomed to this use of the intersection sign, just note that for any set S, $\bigcap S$ is the intersection of the elements of S. Thus, $\bigcap\{X, Y\} = X \cap Y$.)

This operation is called *full meet contraction* (originally 'meet contraction') [3]. Unfortunately, it has the opposite disadvantage: it forces the agent to be cautious in all situations. In our example, there may very well be good reasons to retain belief in α but not in β. At any rate, it would be unwise to disallow all doxastic behaviour that is not as completely cautious as full meet contraction. We seem to need some procedure that is intermediate between the extreme caution of full meet contraction and the extreme incautiousness of maxichoice contraction.

The intermediate solution is to use a selection function, as in maxichoice contraction, but allow it to choose several elements of $\mathbf{K}\perp\alpha$. The outcome of the contraction of **K** by α is then identified with the intersection of the selected elements of $\mathbf{K}\perp\alpha$. This is *partial meet contraction*, the major innovation in the classic 1985 paper by Carlos Alchourrón, Peter Gärdenfors, and David Makinson [1]. The formal definition is as follows:

DEFINITION 1.2 (AGM [1]) *Let A be a set of sentences. A* selection function *for A is a function γ such that for all sentences α:*

1. *If $A\perp\alpha$ is non-empty, then $\gamma(A\perp\alpha)$ is a non-empty subset of $A\perp\alpha$, and*
2. *If $A\perp\alpha$ is empty, then $\gamma(A\perp\alpha) = \{A\}$.*

DEFINITION 1.3 (AGM [1]) *Let A be a set of sentences and γ a selection function for A. The* partial meet contraction *on A that is generated by γ is the operation $\sim_\gamma$ such that for all sentences α:*

$$A\sim_\gamma\alpha = \bigcap\gamma(A\perp\alpha).$$

An operation $\div$ on A is a partial meet contraction if and only if there is a selection function γ for A such that for all sentences α : $A \div \alpha = A\sim_\gamma\alpha$.

These definitions do not require the set A to be logically closed, but in the AGM model partial meet contraction is applied to a logically closed belief set. (In Section 1.7, the same definition will be applied to sets that are not logically closed.)

In the principal case, (1) in Definition 1.2, the outcome of partial meet contraction by a sentence α is equal to the intersection of the set of selected maximal subsets of the original set that do not imply α.

Case (2) is applicable only when $A\perp\alpha$ is empty, i.e., when there is no maximal subset of A that does not imply α. With reasonable demands on the logic, this is true if and only if α is logically true (a tautology). In conjunction with Definition 1.3, clause (2) tells us that if α is logically true, then A is unchanged after contraction by α. (Note that $\bigcap\{A\} = A$.) The reason why this clause has been adopted is that if α is a logically true sentence, then α follows from any set of sentences (including the empty set). Therefore, there can be no belief set that does not contain α. When instructed to take away something that cannot be taken away, we should let everything be as it was.

Definitions 1.2 and 1.3 follow the classic AGM paper in which partial meet contraction was introduced. Hans Rott has proposed an alternative pair of definitions [116]: Clause (2) of the first definition is changed so that $\gamma(A\perp\alpha) = \emptyset$ when $A\perp\alpha = \emptyset$. In the second definition, an extra clause is added to ensure that $A\sim_\gamma\alpha = A$ when $\gamma(A\perp\alpha) = \emptyset$. Rott's variant of the definitions simplifies the treatment of selection functions, since they will satisfy the very reasonable property $\gamma(A\perp\alpha) \subseteq A\perp\alpha$. However, since Definitions 1.2 and 1.3 are the standard definitions used in most of the belief revision literature, they will be used here as well.

For any selection function γ, '$\sim_\gamma$' denotes the partial meet contraction generated by γ. The symbol '$\div$' is used for operations of contraction in general, irrespective of whether or not they are partial meet contractions.

Maxichoice and full meet contraction can now be reintroduced as special cases of partial meet contraction:

DEFINITION 1.4 (AGM [1]) *Let $\div$ be an operator for a set A. Then:*

1. *$\div$ is an operator of* maxichoice contraction *if and only if it coincides with a partial meet contraction $\sim_\gamma$ such that for all sentences $\alpha, \gamma(A\bot\alpha)$ has exactly one element.*
2. *$\div$ is an operator of* full meet contraction *if and only if it coincides with a partial meet contraction $\sim_\gamma$ such that for all sentences α, if $A\bot\alpha$ is non-empty, then $\gamma(A\bot\alpha) = A\bot\alpha$.*

The symbol '$\sim$' is used for full meet contraction.

There is only one operation of full meet contraction on a given set A. This is the reason why the selection function can be dropped. $A \sim \alpha$ is the full meet contraction of A by α.

Partial meet contraction has played a central role in the development of belief dynamics. This is not because of computational simplicity—to the contrary, selection functions are quite demanding from a computational point of view. Instead, this is because of the nice properties of partial meet contraction (more about that later) and of its generality. As we shall see in Chapter 2, several other interesting operations of contraction can be shown to be subcases of partial meet contraction.

6 YOU CANNOT BELIEVE IN EVERYTHING

By incorporation is meant a process of changing a belief set $\mathbf{K}$ to make it include a specified sentence α. The simplest way to incorporate α into $\mathbf{K}$ is to add it set-theoretically: $\mathbf{K} \cup \{\alpha\}$. This is, however, a bit too simple, since $\mathbf{K} \cup \{\alpha\}$ is not in general logically closed. In the dynamics of belief sets, we want to preserve logical closure. This can be achieved by taking the outcome of the operation to be $\mathrm{Cn}(\mathbf{K}\cup\{\alpha\})$ instead of merely $\mathbf{K}\cup\{\alpha\}$. In this way, we have defined the operation of *expansion* of a belief set, that was first introduced by Levi:

DEFINITION 1.5 (Isaac Levi [70]) *Let $\mathbf{K}$ be a belief set and α a sentence. $\mathbf{K}+\alpha$ ('$\mathbf{K}$ expanded by α'), the* (closing) expansion *of $\mathbf{K}$ by α, is defined as follows:*

$$\mathbf{K} + \alpha = \mathrm{Cn}(\mathbf{K} \cup \{\alpha\}).$$

It is easy to verify that if $\alpha \in \mathbf{K}$, then $\mathbf{K} + \alpha$ is equal to $\mathbf{K}$. This is as it should be. To incorporate a belief that is already in the belief set is a redundant operation, that should lead to no change at all.

Something quite different happens when we perform the expansion $\mathbf{K} + \alpha$ on a belief set $\mathbf{K}$ such that $\neg\alpha \in \mathbf{K}$. In that case, the resulting belief set will be logically inconsistent (contradictory).

That, one might say, is not at all unrealistic. Probably most of us have contradictory beliefs, but we are nevertheless able to get along well and (at least sometimes) behave quite rationally. There should be nothing seriously wrong, either, with a computer accepting two contradictory sentences, if this does not lead to the propagation of inconsistencies to other parts of its database. This is all true, but it cannot be applied if we use belief sets as models of belief states.

The reason for this is that everything follows from an inconsistent set. This you can check with truth-tables. If both α and $\neg\alpha$ are elements of the belief set, then so is $\alpha\&\neg\alpha$. It is a truth-functional tautology (logical truth) that $\alpha\&\neg\alpha\rightarrow\beta$ for any arbitrary sentence β, so that β follows logically from $\alpha\&\neg\alpha$. Therefore, if both α and $\neg\alpha$ are elements of the belief set, then so is every sentence β. If you have inconsistent beliefs, then you (are committed to) believe everything. Inconsistent belief sets contain all sentences. They cannot be used for making any distinctions at all.

It follows from this that there is only one inconsistent belief set. It consists of all sentences of the language. It is usually denoted $\mathbf{K}_\perp$ (where '$\perp$' stands for contradiction), and it is identical to $\text{Cn}(\{\alpha\&\neg\alpha\})$. It is often called the 'absurd belief set' [35].

Since we wish to avoid the absurd belief set, expansion is not a useful method to incorporate beliefs that contradict previous beliefs into a belief set. For such *belief-contravening* incorporations, we need a consistency-preserving operation. Such an operation should add the new belief to the belief set, but remove enough of the original belief set to ensure that the outcome is a *consistent* belief set that contains the new belief. An operation that does this is called an operation of *revision*.

In the AGM model, the revision of a belief set takes place in two steps. In order to revise $\mathbf{K}$ by α:

1. contract $\mathbf{K}$ by $\neg\alpha$
2. expand the resulting belief set by α.

In the first step, enough of $\mathbf{K}$ is removed to ensure that it no longer contradicts α (which a belief set does if and only if it contains $\neg\alpha$). After that, α can be added through expansion, which is done in the second step.

Letting $*$ stand for revision, this procedure can be summarized in the form of an equation:

$$\mathbf{K} * \alpha = (\mathbf{K} \div \neg\alpha) + \alpha.$$

This is the *Levi identity* [3; 30]. In the AGM model, operators of revision are derived from operators of partial meet contraction via the Levi identity:

DEFINITION 1.6 (AGM [1]) *The operator $*$ on a belief set* $\mathbf{K}$ *is an operator of (*closing*)* partial meet revision *if and only if there is some operator $\sim_\gamma$ of partial meet contraction on* $\mathbf{K}$ *such that for all sentences α:*

$$\mathbf{K} * \alpha = (\mathbf{K}\sim_\gamma\neg\alpha) + \alpha.$$

We now have two operations of incorporation, namely expansion and revision. Since revision is definable in terms of contraction and expansion, we can—if we accept the Levi identity—express the decomposition principle from Section 1.3 in a somewhat stronger and more precise way:

> *Decomposition principle (second version):*
> Every legitimate belief change is decomposable into a sequence of expansions and contractions.

Most of the logicians and philosophers who have studied belief dynamics have focused their work on operators of contraction, whereas computer scientists have been primarily interested in operators of revision. The Levi identity, and the decomposition principle, provide a firm connection between the two approaches.

In the literature on belief dynamics, the word 'revision' is commonly used in two distinct senses. First, it is used for consistency-preserving incorporation, as defined above. Secondly, it is used as a synonym of change, and the whole field of research is often called 'theory revision' or 'belief revision'. In this book, 'revision' is only used in the first sense, but in most of the research literature it is used freely in both senses.

7 BELIEF BASES

In spite of its simplicity, the identification of belief states with belief sets has non-negligable disadvantages, in particular from a computational point of view. A belief set is a very large entity. As we have already seen, for any two sentences α and β, if α is in a belief set, then so are both $\alpha\vee\beta$ and $\alpha\vee\neg\beta$, since they are logical consequences of α. Therefore, if the language is sufficiently rich, the belief set will contain myriads of sentences that the believer has never thought of.

> **Example**
> The sentence 'I have ten fingers' is in my belief set. Therefore, I believe that either I have ten fingers, or Alan Turing was born on a Monday. For the same reason, I believe that either I have ten fingers, or Alan Turing was not born on a Monday.

Indeed, if the language contains an infinite number of sentences, then so does the belief set.

It seems unnatural for changes to be performed on such large entities as belief sets, that contain all kinds of irrelevant and never-thought-of sentences. It is more natural to think of the belief state as represented by a limited number of sentences that may (roughly) correspond to the explicit beliefs. Changes can operate on this smaller set, rather than directly on the belief set. Such a model is much closer to the workings of actual human minds and actual computers.

This leads us to represent belief states by sets of sentences that are *not* closed under logical consequence. Such sets are called *belief bases*, and the formal definition is as follows:

DEFINITION 1.7 *Any set A of sentences is a* belief base.

Let **K** *be a belief set. Then a set A of sentences is a belief base for* **K** *if and only if* $\mathbf{K} = \mathrm{Cn}(A)$.

Belief bases are not required by definition to be finite, but in all realistic applications they will be so.

In a belief base approach, the criterion for a sentence α to be believed is that it is a consequence of the belief base, $\alpha \in \mathrm{Cn}(A)$. The elements of the belief base are the *basic beliefs*, and the elements of its logical closure that are not elements of the belief base itself are the (merely) *derived beliefs*. In set-theoretical language:

α is a belief if and only if $\alpha \in \mathrm{Cn}(A)$
α is a basic belief if and only if $\alpha \in A$
α is a (merely) derived belief if and only if $\alpha \in \mathrm{Cn}(A)\setminus A$.

(For any two sets X and Y, $X\setminus Y$ is the set of elements of X that are not elements of Y.)

In computer science, belief bases were the original approach, naturally suggesting themselves from the way computers work. In philosophy, the original approach was to apply operations of change directly to the belief set, but in the last few years there has been a growing interest in belief bases among philosophers.

In this approach, changes are performed on the belief base. Derived beliefs are changed only as a result of changes of the base. Although we (are committed to) believe the logical consequences of our basic beliefs, these consequences are subject only to exactly those changes that follow from changes of the basic beliefs. The underlying intuition is that the merely derived beliefs are not worth retaining for their own sake. If one of them loses the support that it had in basic beliefs, then it will be automatically discarded.

Example [43]
I believe that Paris is the capital of France (α). I also believe that there is milk in my fridge (β). Therefore, I believe that Paris is the capital of France if and only if there is milk in my fridge ($\alpha\leftrightarrow\beta$). I open the fridge and find it necessary to replace my belief in β with belief in $\neg\beta$ ('not β'). I cannot then, on pain of inconsistency, retain both my belief in α and my belief in $\alpha\leftrightarrow\beta$.

Belief set approach: Both α and $\alpha\leftrightarrow\beta$ are elements of the belief set. When I open my fridge and find no milk, I make a choice between retaining α and retaining $\alpha\leftrightarrow\beta$. The retraction of $\alpha\leftrightarrow\beta$ does not follow automatically. It has to be ensured by a selection mechanism (such as a selection function) that chooses between α and $\alpha \leftrightarrow \beta$.

Belief base approach: Whereas β is a basic belief, $\alpha \leftrightarrow \beta$ is a merely derived belief. When β is removed, $\alpha \leftrightarrow \beta$ disappears automatically. The option of retaining it will not even arise.

Example [43]

Let α denote that I have money on my bank account, and β that I own a large fortune in stocks and shares. For good reasons, I believe that α is true and β is false. As a consequence of my belief in α, I also believe that $\alpha \vee \beta$ is true. One morning, I receive a telephone call from the bank, telling me that my account is empty. I therefore lose my belief in α. If I am a sensible person, I will then also lose my belief in $\alpha \vee \beta$.

Belief set approach: The retraction of $\alpha \vee \beta$ has to be ensured by the use of a selection mechanism that determines (among other things) whether to retain $\alpha \vee \beta$ or $\alpha \vee \neg \beta$.

Belief base approach: $\alpha \vee \beta$ is automatically lost when it is no longer implied by the belief base.

Thus, when elements of a belief base are removed, all beliefs are lost that depended on the removed elements. This process has been called 'disbelief propagation' [90].

Partial meet contraction is equally applicable to belief bases as to belief sets. The operator of expansion, on the other hand, must be modified. Instead of Definition 1.5 that was framed for belief sets ($\mathbf{K} + \alpha = \text{Cn}(\mathbf{K} \cup \{\alpha\})$), we should use the simpler definition $A + \alpha = A \cup \{\alpha\}$.

DEFINITION 1.8 *Let A be a belief base and α a sentence. $A + \alpha$ ('A expanded by α'), the* (non-closing) expansion *of A by α, is defined as follows:*

$$A + \alpha = A \cup \{\alpha\}.$$

In order to limit the number of symbols, the same symbol ('+') will be used for both closing and non-closing expansions. It will be clear from the context which of the two operations is intended.

The Levi identity can be applied to belief bases, but non-closing expansion must be employed. In this way, partial meet revision can be defined for belief bases:

DEFINITION 1.9 *The operator $*$ on a belief base A is an operator of* (non-closing) partial meet revision *if and only if there is some operator $\sim_\gamma$ of partial meet contraction on A such that for all sentences α:*

$$A * \alpha = (A \sim_\gamma \neg \alpha) + \alpha$$

where + is non-closing expansion.

Contrary to operations on belief sets, operations on belief bases can reflect the common human experience of giving up only one single belief.

Example [43]
I previously believed that my nephew was born in 1981 (α). When I gave up that belief, I considered myself to give up exactly one previous belief.

Belief set approach: For every sentence β in the language, my original belief set contained both $\alpha \vee \beta$ and $\alpha \vee \neg \beta$. Since these two sentences together logically imply α, at least one of them must go when α is lost. Therefore, I will give up at least as many beliefs as there are sentences in the language.

Belief base approach: Provided that α is in the belief base, and is not implied by the rest of the elements of the belief base, it is the only belief that I give up when contracting by α.

For every belief base A, there is a belief set $\mathrm{Cn}(A)$ that represents the beliefs held according to A. On the other hand, one and the same belief set can be represented by different belief bases. In this sense, belief bases have more expressive power than belief sets. As an example, the two belief bases $\{\alpha, \beta\}$ and $\{\alpha, \alpha \leftrightarrow \beta\}$ have the same logical closure, since $\mathrm{Cn}(\{\alpha, \beta\}) = \mathrm{Cn}(\{\alpha, \alpha \leftrightarrow \beta\})$. Nevertheless, these belief bases are not identical. They are *statically equivalent*, in the sense of representing the same beliefs. On the other hand, the following example shows that they are not *dynamically equivalent* in the sense of behaving in the same way under operations of change [45]. They can therefore be taken to represent different ways of holding the same beliefs.

Example
Let α denote that the Liberal Party will support the proposal to subsidize the steel industry, and let β denote that Ms Smith, who is a liberal MP, will vote in favour of that proposal.

Abe has the basic beliefs α and β, whereas Bob has the basic beliefs α and $\alpha \leftrightarrow \beta$. Thus, their beliefs (on the belief set level) with respect to α and β are the same.

Both Abe and Bob receive and accept the information that α is false, and they both revise their belief states to include the new belief that $\neg \alpha$. After that, Abe has the basic beliefs $\neg \alpha$ and β, whereas Bob has the basic beliefs $\neg \alpha$ and $\alpha \leftrightarrow \beta$. Now, their belief sets are no longer the same. Abe believes that β whereas Bob believes that $\neg \beta$.

In the AGM approach, cases like these are taken care of by assuming that although Abe's and Bob's belief states are represented by the same belief set, this belief set is associated with different selection mechanisms in the two cases [36]. Abe has a selection mechanism that gives priority to β over $\alpha\leftrightarrow\beta$, whereas Bob's selection mechanism has the opposite priorities.

In Section 1.6, we observed that there is only one inconsistent belief set. In other words, if $\mathbf{K}$ and $\mathbf{K}'$ are two inconsistent belief sets, then $\mathbf{K} = \mathbf{K}'$. The corresponding property does not hold for belief bases. The following two belief bases:

$$A = \{p, \neg p, q_1, q_2, q_3, q_4\} \text{ and}$$
$$B = \{p, \neg p, \neg q_1, \neg q_2, \neg q_3, \neg q_4\}$$

are both inconsistent, but they are not identical. They are statically equivalent, since $\text{Cn}(A) = \text{Cn}(B) = \mathbf{K}_\perp$. However, they are not dynamically equivalent since, by any reasonable operator of contraction:

$$A \div p = \{\neg p, q_1, q_2, q_3, q_4\} \text{ and}$$
$$B \div p = \{\neg p, \neg q_1, \neg q_2 \neg q_3 \neg q_4\}$$

so that $\text{Cn}(A \div p) \neq \text{Cn}(B \div p)$.

This is a valuable property of belief bases. You can easily think of two persons who both have inconsistent beliefs. It does not make much sense to say that their states of belief must therefore be the same. Similarly, a database that contains inconsistent information does not have to be beyond repair. It should be possible to remove the inconsistency, while keeping the information that is not affected by contradiction. This can be done if the inconsistent belief state is represented by a belief base. On the other hand, once we have arrived at an inconsistent belief set, all distinctions are lost, and they cannot be so easily regained by operations performed directly on the belief set.

8 WHICH BELIEFS ARE BASIC?

The use of belief bases has the advantage of allowing for more distinctions, but it gives rise to troublesome questions on how these distinctions should be drawn. A proponent of belief bases should be capable of answering the question: Which beliefs are basic, and which are not?

The ultimate criterion for a belief to be an element of the belief base is that it is 'self-sustained', i.e., worth retaining for its own sake (even if it is not implied by some other belief that is worth retaining). In a sense, however, this is a reformulation of the question rather than an answer. The next question is: Which beliefs are self-sustained in this sense?

The most clear examples are beliefs that are directly based on memories [53]. For instance, I believe that I saw a pheasant from my kitchen window yesterday. I believe this on the only ground that I remember it to have happened. In a belief base representation of my belief state, this belief should be represented by a sentence that is included in the belief base.

However, not all basic beliefs are directly based on memories. There are also other beliefs that must, for all practical purposes, be treated as self-sustained. In particular, previously derived beliefs may become basic when we lose track of their justifications. 'Paris is the capital of France' is a possible example. There is a long list of reasons why I believe Paris to be the capital of France. I have, however, lost track of most or perhaps even all of these reasons. Therefore, this belief stands on its own, just like beliefs that are directly based on memories. It provides the justification for other beliefs, such as 'Either Paris or Nice is the capital of France', but it is not (any longer) itself derived from other beliefs.

'Frogs are vertebrates' and 'Someone has climbed the top of Mount Everest' are other possible examples of beliefs that may stand on their own, just like beliefs that are directly based on memories. These two examples illustrate that generalizations and existential beliefs may, just like particular beliefs, be treated as basic.

The difference between belief bases and belief sets has often been related to the distinction between 'foundationalist' and 'coherentist' viewpoints in the theory of knowledge [14; 36]. According to a foundationalist view of belief, 'every piece of knowledge stands at the apex of a pyramid that rests on stable and secure foundations whose stability and security does not derive from the upper stories or sections' [121]. Belief bases have been taken to represent the foundations of a foundationalist belief system. According to a coherentist view, 'a body of knowledge is a free-floating raft every plank of which helps directly or indirectly to keep all the others in place, and no plank of which would retain its status with no help from the others' [121]. Belief sets are said to represent such a coherentist structure.

Although there may some truth in the claim that bases are more akin to foundationalism and belief sets to coherentism, the analogy should not be pushed too far. In belief base models, the relation between the belief base and the belief set is a simple relationship of logical consequence, that does no justice at all to the complex relations of justification in a reasonable version of foundationalism. The belief set model does not either fit in exactly with the coherentist view. Although coherentists typically claim that *all* beliefs contribute to the justification of other beliefs, they hardly mean this to apply to merely derived beliefs such as 'either Paris or Nice is the capital of France', that I believe only because I believe Paris to be the capital of France [61].

Belief bases have often been taken to consist of the beliefs that have independent justification. This is only a very rough approximation. Independently justified beliefs are worth retaining for their own sake, but they are not necessarily the only beliefs that are worth retaining for their own sake. This will be clear from the following example:

Example [42]
I originally believed, for good and independent reasons, both that Andy is the mayor's son (α) and that Bob is the mayor's son (β). Then I hear the mayor say in a public speech: 'I certainly have nothing against our youth studying abroad. My only son did it for three years'.

Upon hearing this, I contract my belief state by $\alpha \& \beta$. As a result of this I lose both my belief in α and my belief in β. However, I retain my belief that $\alpha \vee \beta$, i.e., that either Andy or Bob is the son of the mayor.

In this case, we may assume that $\alpha \vee \beta$ had no independent justification. It was believed only as a consequence of my beliefs in α and β. If the belief base was $\{\alpha, \beta\}$, then $\alpha \vee \beta$ cannot be an element of the contracted belief base. It seems reasonable, however, in this and many other cases, to retain belief in the disjunction of two independently justified beliefs, when they can no longer coexist and one cannot choose between them.

If we wish to make this into a general pattern of belief change, then we should postulate that if both α and β are worth retaining for their own sake, then so is $\alpha \vee \beta$. This is another way of saying that if both α and β satisfy the requirements for being elements of the base, then so does $\alpha \vee \beta$. Such a belief base will be *closed under disjunction*. The formal definition is as follows:

DEFINITION 1.10 *Let A be a set of sentences. Then $\mathcal{V}(A)$, the* disjunctive closure *of A, is the set of sentences that are either elements of A or disjunctions of elements of A.*

A set A is closed under disjunction if and only if $A = \mathcal{V}(A)$.

Disjunctively closed bases may be seen as intermediates between belief bases *simpliciter* and logically closed belief sets. If a belief base A is not disjunctively closed, then we have:

$$A \subset \mathcal{V}(A) \subset \mathrm{Cn}(A).$$

Disjunctively closed belief bases do not share the immediate intuitive appeal of bases *simpliciter*. They are based on a more complex intuition, namely that a belief is worth retaining for its own sake if and only if it is either independently justified or the disjunction of some independently justified beliefs. This intuition is questionable, and as Hans Rott has pointed out it contradicts the common requirement that the elements of a belief base should be fundamental or explicit beliefs [117]. Disjunctive closure should be seen as an interesting special case rather than as a mandatory property of plausible belief bases.

9 BELIEF SETS OR BELIEF BASES?

Belief bases have more expressive power than belief sets. Furthermore, in order to achieve computational tractability, we must have a finite representation of the belief state, such as a (finite) belief base. It might therefore be tempting to concentrate our efforts entirely on belief bases, and give up belief sets altogether. However, belief sets cannot be so easily discarded.

In an influential 1982 paper, Allen Newell postulated the existence in artificial intelligence of a *knowledge level* [100]. In the traditional hierarchy of system levels, beginning with the device level and the circuit level, the knowledge level is positioned immediately above the symbol level (program level). The knowledge level is specified entirely in terms of the contents of the knowledge (beliefs). There is no distinction on this level between information that is explicitly available and information that is implied by available information [8]. It should be possible to predict and understand what an agent does on the knowledge level, without referring to the symbol level, in much the same way as the symbol level should allow for prediction and understanding without reference to the lower levels of the system.

Mukesh Dalal has formulated the principle of *irrelevance of syntax* for databases, that may be seen as an application of knowledge level analysis [11; 65]. According to that principle, the outcome of an operation that changes a database should not depend on the syntax (representation) of either the old or the new information. It seems to follow from this that the outcome should not depend on which belief base we use to represent a belief state.

The idea of a knowledge level has a strong intuitive appeal. Clearly, belief sets are knowledge level entities. More precisely put, changes on belief sets represent on the knowledge level 'what an ideal reasoner would or should do when forced to reorganize his beliefs', thus indicating what people and computers should do 'if they were not bounded by limited logical reasoning capabilities' [40].

We are thus faced with a dilemma. On the one hand, we wish to be able to describe and analyze epistemic behaviour on the knowledge level. This would lead us to use belief sets as models of belief states. On the other hand, we need models that have a finite representation and are suitable for actual computing. This leads us to use finite belief bases, rather than belief sets, to represent belief states. In Chapter 4, we are going to see how these two *desiderata* can be combined. Before we are ready for that, however, we need to take a much closer look at the operations of contraction and revision, as applied to both belief bases and belief sets.

CHAPTER 1+

BASIC TOOLS

The 'plus' chapters of the book are devoted to the formal aspects of belief dynamics. This chapter introduces some of the basic formal tools that will be used in the later 'plus' chapters.

10+ LOGICAL CONSEQUENCE

We are going to make free use of classical sentential logic, with its symbols:

$\neg$	not ...	(negation)
$\vee$	... or ...	(disjunction)
&	... and ...	(conjunction)
$\rightarrow$	if ... then ...	(implication)
$\leftrightarrow$	... if and only if ...	(equivalence)

It will be assumed that the reader is acquainted with sentential logic, and in particular with the truth-table method for checking truth-functional formulas. We will use the symbol $\top$ to represent an arbitrary tautology and $\bot$ to represent an arbitrary contradictory sentence ('falsum').

All belief sets and belief bases are subsets of a language $\mathcal{L}$ that is closed under truth-functional operations. (Thus, if $\alpha \in \mathcal{L}$, then $\neg\alpha \in \mathcal{L}$. If $\alpha \in \mathcal{L}$ and $\beta \in \mathcal{L}$, then $\alpha\vee\beta \in \mathcal{L}$, etc. for all the truth-functional operations.) The language may be either finite or infinite.

The language may (but need not) be based on atomic sentences. If it is, then there is a set of logically independent atomic sentences $p, q, r \ldots$, such that all sentences in the language can be formed from these atomic sentences by the truth-functional operations.

Lower-case Greek letters $\alpha, \beta, \ldots$ range over sentences, whereas lower-case Latin letters $p, q, r \ldots$ represent atomic sentences. Capital Latin letters, $A, B, C \ldots$ represent sets of sentences. (Boldface **K** is reserved for logically closed sets.)

Sets of sentences will be subjected to the common set-theoretical operations. The conventional set-theoretical notation will be used, namely:

$\alpha \in A$	α is an element of A
$A \subseteq B$	A is a subset of B
$A \subset B$	A is a proper subset of B (A is a subset of B, but not equal to B)
$A \cup B$	the union of A and B (elements of A or B or both)
$A \cap B$	the intersection of A and B (elements of both A and B)
$A \backslash B$	the difference between A and B (elements of A but not of B)
$\emptyset$	the empty set (has no elements)

The symbols $\in$, $\subseteq$, and $\subset$ are negated by over-crossing, thus $\notin$ stands for 'is not an element of', and similarly $\not\subseteq$ negates $\subseteq$ and $\not\subset$ negates $\subset$.

The symbols for union and intersection will also be applied to sets of sets, so that $\bigcap S$ denotes the intersection of the elements of S, and $\bigcup S$ the union of the elements of S. (Thus, $\bigcap\{D, E, F\} = D \cap E \cap F, \bigcup\{D, E, F\} = D \cup E \cup F$, and $\bigcap\{D\} = \bigcup\{D\} = D$.)

The major purpose of this section is to introduce the *consequence operator* Cn. This operator takes us from a set to all its logical consequences. Thus, Cn(A) is the set of logical consequences of A, and $\alpha \in \text{Cn}(A)$ holds if and only if α is a logical consequence of A. A sentence α follows logically from another sentence β if and only if $\alpha \in \text{Cn}(\{\beta\})$ (often abbreviated $\alpha \in \text{Cn}(\beta)$). A sentence α is logically true (tautological) if and only if it can be concluded without any premises, i.e. from the empty set of premises: $\alpha \in \text{Cn}(\emptyset)$.

Consequence operators were introduced by Alfred Tarski in the 1930s. According to the standard definition, a consequence operator has three defining properties:

DEFINITION 1.11 (Alfred Tarski [123]) A consequence operation *on $\mathcal{L}$ is a function* Cn *that takes each subset of $\mathcal{L}$ to another subset of $\mathcal{L}$, such that:*

i. $A \subseteq \text{Cn}(A)$ *(inclusion)*

ii. If $A \subseteq B$, *then* $\text{Cn}(A) \subseteq \text{Cn}(B)$ *(monotony)*

iii. $\text{Cn}(A) = \text{Cn}(\text{Cn}(A))$ *(iteration)*

We are going to assume that logical consequence includes classical truth-functional consequence. Furthermore, the standard properties of deduction and compactness will be assumed to hold.

POSTULATE 1.12 Cn *satisfies the following three properties:*

iv. If α can be derived from A by classical truth-functional logic, then $\alpha \in \text{Cn}(A)$. *(supraclassicality)*

v. $\beta \in \text{Cn}(A \cup \{\alpha\})$ *if and only if* $(\alpha \rightarrow \beta) \in \text{Cn}(A)$. *(deduction)*

vi. If $\alpha \in \text{Cn}(A)$, *then* $\alpha \in \text{Cn}(A')$ *for some finite subset* $A' \subseteq A$. *(compactness)*

The deduction property establishes the common relationship between truth-functional implication and logical consequence. Compactness ensures that all logical deductions have a finite set of premises.

It follows from supraclassicality that if two sentences α and α' are truth-functionally equivalent, then for all sets A of sentences, $\alpha \in \mathrm{Cn}(A)$ if and only if $\alpha' \in \mathrm{Cn}(A)$. To see this, let $\alpha \in \mathrm{Cn}(A)$. Since $\alpha \rightarrow \alpha'$ is logically true, supraclassicality yields $\alpha \rightarrow \alpha' \in \mathrm{Cn}(A)$. We therefore have $\{\alpha, \alpha \rightarrow \alpha'\} \subseteq \mathrm{Cn}(A)$, thus by monotony $\mathrm{Cn}(\{\alpha, \alpha \rightarrow \alpha'\}) \subseteq \mathrm{Cn}(\mathrm{Cn}(A))$ and by iteration $\mathrm{Cn}(\{\alpha, \alpha \rightarrow \alpha'\}) \subseteq \mathrm{Cn}(A)$. If follows from supraclassicality that $\alpha' \in \mathrm{Cn}(\{\alpha, \alpha \rightarrow \alpha'\})$, and thus $\alpha' \in \mathrm{Cn}(A)$. It can be proved in the same way that if $\alpha' \in \mathrm{Cn}(A)$ then $\alpha \in \mathrm{Cn}(A)$.

Since truth-functionally equivalent sentences are interchangeable in this respect, it will often be practical to treat them as identical. As an example of this, we may proceed as if $p \rightarrow q$ and $\neg p \vee q$ were the same sentence. This practice is admissible in contexts that abstract from the linguistic forms of sentences. It substantially simplifies notation.

Next, a few observation statements will be proved, that introduce important properties of Cn. In the rest of the 'plus' chapters, these elementary properties of Cn will be used without explicit reference.

OBSERVATION 1.13 $\mathrm{Cn}(A \cup B) = \mathrm{Cn}(A \cup \mathrm{Cn}(B))$.

Proof. The best way to prove that two sets are identical is often to prove separately that each is a subset of the other.

Part I: In order to prove that $\mathrm{Cn}(A \cup B) \subseteq \mathrm{Cn}(A \cup \mathrm{Cn}(B))$, we can use inclusion to establish that $A \cup B \subseteq A \cup \mathrm{Cn}(B)$. It follows from monotony that $\mathrm{Cn}(A \cup B) \subseteq \mathrm{Cn}(A \cup \mathrm{Cn}(B))$.

Part II. In order to show that $\mathrm{Cn}(A \cup \mathrm{Cn}(B)) \subseteq \mathrm{Cn}(A \cup B)$, we can use inclusion to get $A \cup \mathrm{Cn}(B) \subseteq A \cup B \cup \mathrm{Cn}(B) \subseteq \mathrm{Cn}(A \cup B) \cup \mathrm{Cn}(B)$. By monotony, $\mathrm{Cn}(B) \subseteq \mathrm{Cn}(A \cup B)$, so that $\mathrm{Cn}(A \cup B) \cup \mathrm{Cn}(B) = \mathrm{Cn}(A \cup B)$. We therefore have $A \cup \mathrm{Cn}(B) \subseteq \mathrm{Cn}(A \cup B)$. By monotony, $\mathrm{Cn}(A \cup \mathrm{Cn}(B)) \subseteq \mathrm{Cn}(\mathrm{Cn}(A \cup B))$. By iteration, $\mathrm{Cn}(\mathrm{Cn}(A \cup B)) = \mathrm{Cn}(A \cup B)$, so that $\mathrm{Cn}(A \cup \mathrm{Cn}(B)) \subseteq \mathrm{Cn}(A \cup B)$, thus concluding the proof. ■

OBSERVATION 1.14 *If* $A \subseteq B \subseteq \mathrm{Cn}(A)$, *then* $\mathrm{Cn}(A) = \mathrm{Cn}(B)$.

Proof. Let $A \subseteq B \subseteq \mathrm{Cn}(A)$. It follows from $A \subseteq B$, by monotony, that $\mathrm{Cn}(A) \subseteq \mathrm{Cn}(B)$. Furthermore, it follows from $B \subseteq \mathrm{Cn}(A)$, by monotony, that $\mathrm{Cn}(B) \subseteq \mathrm{Cn}(\mathrm{Cn}(A))$. By iteration, $\mathrm{Cn}(\mathrm{Cn}(A)) = \mathrm{Cn}(A)$, so that $\mathrm{Cn}(B) \subseteq \mathrm{Cn}(A)$. From $\mathrm{Cn}(A) \subseteq \mathrm{Cn}(B)$ and $\mathrm{Cn}(B) \subseteq \mathrm{Cn}(A)$ we may conclude that $\mathrm{Cn}(A) = \mathrm{Cn}(B)$. ■

OBSERVATION 1.15 *If* $\beta \in \mathrm{Cn}(X \cup \{\alpha_1\})$ *and* $\beta \in \mathrm{Cn}(X \cup \{\alpha_2\})$, *then* $\beta \in \mathrm{Cn}(X \cup \{\alpha_1 \vee \alpha_2\})$. *(introduction of disjunction into the premises)*

Proof. Suppose that $\beta \in \text{Cn}(X \cup \{\alpha_1\})$ and $\beta \in \text{Cn}(X \cup \{\alpha_2\})$. By deduction, $\alpha_1 \rightarrow \beta \in \text{Cn}(X)$ and $\alpha_2 \rightarrow \beta \in \text{Cn}(X)$. We therefore have $\{\alpha_1 \rightarrow \beta, \alpha_2 \rightarrow \beta\} \subseteq \text{Cn}(X)$. By truth-functional logic, $\alpha_1 \vee \alpha_2 \rightarrow \beta$ follows from $\alpha_1 \rightarrow \beta$ and $\alpha_2 \rightarrow \beta$, so that by supraclassicality: $\alpha_1 \vee \alpha_2 \rightarrow \beta \in \text{Cn}(\{\alpha_1 \rightarrow \beta, \alpha_2 \rightarrow \beta\})$.

Since $\{\alpha_1 \rightarrow \beta, \alpha_2 \rightarrow \beta\} \subseteq \text{Cn}(X)$, monotony yields $\text{Cn}(\{\alpha_1 \rightarrow \beta, \alpha_2 \rightarrow \beta\}) \subseteq \text{Cn}(\text{Cn}(X))$. By iteration, $\text{Cn}(\text{Cn}(X)) = \text{Cn}(X)$, so that $\text{Cn}(\{\alpha_1 \rightarrow \beta, \alpha_2 \rightarrow \beta\}) \subseteq \text{Cn}(X)$. From this and $\alpha_1 \vee \alpha_2 \rightarrow \beta \in \text{Cn}(\{\alpha_1 \rightarrow \beta, \alpha_2 \rightarrow \beta\})$ we may conclude that $\alpha_1 \vee \alpha_2 \rightarrow \beta \in \text{Cn}(X)$. It follows by deduction that $\beta \in \text{Cn}(X \cup \{\alpha_1 \vee \alpha_2\})$. This finishes the proof. ■

OBSERVATION 1.16 *If* $\beta \in \text{Cn}(X \cup \{\alpha\})$ *and* $\beta \in \text{Cn}(X \cup \{\neg\alpha\})$, *then* $\beta \in \text{Cn}(X)$.

Proof. Suppose that $\beta \in \text{Cn}(X \cup \{\alpha\})$ and $\beta \in \text{Cn}(X \cup \{\neg\alpha\})$. It follows from Observation 1.15 that $\beta \in \text{Cn}(X \cup \{\alpha \vee \neg\alpha\})$. By deduction, $(\alpha \vee \neg\alpha) \rightarrow \beta \in \text{Cn}(X)$. Since $(\alpha \vee \neg\alpha) \rightarrow \beta$ is truth-functionally equivalent with β, we therefore have $\beta \in \text{Cn}(X)$, as desired. ■

OBSERVATION 1.17 $\text{Cn}(\{\alpha \vee \beta\}) = \text{Cn}(\{\alpha\}) \cap \text{Cn}(\{\beta\})$.

Proof. Let us prove the two inclusions separately.

Part I: In order to prove that $\text{Cn}(\{\alpha \vee \beta\}) \subseteq \text{Cn}(\{\alpha\}) \cap \text{Cn}(\{\beta\})$, let $\delta \in \text{Cn}(\{\alpha \vee \beta\})$. We are first going to show that $\delta \in \text{Cn}(\{\alpha\})$.

By deduction, it follows from $\delta \in \text{Cn}(\{\alpha \vee \beta\})$ that $\alpha \vee \beta \rightarrow \delta \in \text{Cn}(\emptyset)$, i.e. $\{\alpha \vee \beta \rightarrow \delta\} \subseteq \text{Cn}(\emptyset)$. Since $\alpha \rightarrow \delta$ follows truth-functionally from $\alpha \vee \beta \rightarrow \delta$, we have $\alpha \rightarrow \delta \in \text{Cn}(\{\alpha \vee \beta \rightarrow \delta\})$. By monotony, it follows from $\{\alpha \vee \beta \rightarrow \delta\} \subseteq \text{Cn}(\emptyset)$ that $\text{Cn}(\{\alpha \vee \beta \rightarrow \delta\}) \subseteq \text{Cn}(\text{Cn}(\emptyset))$. By iteration, $\text{Cn}(\text{Cn}(\emptyset)) = \text{Cn}(\emptyset)$, so that $\text{Cn}(\{\alpha \vee \beta \rightarrow \delta\}) \subseteq \text{Cn}(\emptyset)$. It follows from this and $\alpha \rightarrow \delta \in \text{Cn}(\{\alpha \vee \beta \rightarrow \delta\})$ that $\alpha \rightarrow \delta \in \text{Cn}(\emptyset)$. By deduction, $\delta \in \text{Cn}(\{\alpha\})$.

It can be shown in exactly the same way that $\delta \in \text{Cn}(\{\beta\})$. It follows by set theory (the definition of intersection) that $\delta \in \text{Cn}(\{\alpha\}) \cap \text{Cn}(\{\beta\})$. Thus, if $\delta \in \text{Cn}(\{\alpha \vee \beta\})$, then $\delta \in \text{Cn}(\{\alpha\}) \cap \text{Cn}(\{\beta\})$, i.e. $\text{Cn}(\{\alpha \vee \beta\}) \subseteq \text{Cn}(\{\alpha\}) \cap \text{Cn}(\{\beta\})$. This finishes the first part of the proof.

Part II: Next, let us assume that $\delta \in \text{Cn}(\{\alpha\}) \cap \text{Cn}(\{\beta\})$. Our task is to prove that $\delta \in \text{Cn}(\{\alpha \vee \beta\})$. Since $\delta \in \text{Cn}(\{\alpha\})$, deduction yields $\alpha \rightarrow \delta \in \text{Cn}(\emptyset)$. Similarly, $\delta \in \text{Cn}(\{\beta\})$ yields $\beta \rightarrow \delta \in \text{Cn}(\emptyset)$. We therefore have $\{\alpha \rightarrow \delta, \beta \rightarrow \delta\} \subseteq \text{Cn}(\emptyset)$. By monotony, $\text{Cn}(\{\alpha \rightarrow \delta, \beta \rightarrow \delta\}) \subseteq \text{Cn}(\text{Cn}(\emptyset))$. By iteration, $\text{Cn}(\text{Cn}(\emptyset)) = \text{Cn}(\emptyset)$, so that $\text{Cn}(\{\alpha \rightarrow \delta, \beta \rightarrow \delta\}) \subseteq \text{Cn}(\emptyset)$.

Since $\alpha \vee \beta \rightarrow \delta$ follows from $\alpha \rightarrow \delta$ and $\beta \rightarrow \delta$, supraclassicality yields $\alpha \vee \beta \rightarrow \delta \in \text{Cn}(\{\alpha \rightarrow \delta, \beta \rightarrow \delta\})$. Since $\text{Cn}(\{\alpha \rightarrow \delta, \beta \rightarrow \delta\}) \subseteq \text{Cn}(\emptyset)$, we have $\alpha \vee \beta \rightarrow \delta \in \text{Cn}(\emptyset)$. By deduction, $\delta \in \text{Cn}(\{\alpha \vee \beta\})$, as desired. This finishes the proof. ■

OBSERVATION 1.18 $\text{Cn}(A \cup \{\alpha, \beta\}) = \text{Cn}(A \cup \{\alpha \& \beta\})$.

Proof. Let us prove the two inclusions separately.

Part I, proof that $\text{Cn}(A \cup \{\alpha,\beta\}) \subseteq \text{Cn}(A \cup \{\alpha\&\beta\})$: It follows by supraclassicality that both α and β are elements of $\text{Cn}(A \cup \{\alpha\&\beta\})$. Thus, $\{\alpha,\beta\} \subseteq \text{Cn}(A \cup \{\alpha\&\beta\})$. By inclusion and monotony, $A \subseteq \text{Cn}(A \cup \{\alpha\&\beta\})$, so that $A \cup \{\alpha,\beta\} \subseteq \text{Cn}(A \cup \{\alpha\&\beta\})$. By monotony, $\text{Cn}(A \cup \{\alpha,\beta\}) \subseteq \text{Cn}(\text{Cn}(A \cup \{\alpha\&\beta\}))$. By iteration, $\text{Cn}(\text{Cn}(A \cup \{\alpha\&\beta\})) = \text{Cn}(A \cup \{\alpha\&\beta\})$. We therefore have $\text{Cn}(A \cup \{\alpha,\beta\}) \subseteq \text{Cn}(A \cup \{\alpha\&\beta\})$, as desired.

Part II, proof that $\text{Cn}(A \cup \{\alpha\&\beta\}) \subseteq \text{Cn}(A \cup \{\alpha,\beta\})$: It follows by supraclassicality that $\alpha\&\beta \in \text{Cn}(A \cup \{\alpha,\beta\})$, i.e. $\{\alpha\&\beta\} \subseteq \text{Cn}(A \cup \{\alpha,\beta\})$. By inclusion and monotony, $A \subseteq \text{Cn}(A \cup \{\alpha,\beta\})$, so that $A \cup \{\alpha\&\beta\} \subseteq \text{Cn}(A \cup \{\alpha,\beta\})$. By monotony, $\text{Cn}(A \cup \{\alpha\&\beta\}) \subseteq \text{Cn}(\text{Cn}(A \cup \{\alpha,\beta\}))$. By iteration, $\text{Cn}(\text{Cn}(A \cup \{\alpha,\beta\})) = \text{Cn}(A \cup \{\alpha,\beta\})$. We therefore have $\text{Cn}(A \cup \{\alpha\&\beta\}) \subseteq \text{Cn}(A \cup \{\alpha,\beta\})$, which finishes the proof. ■

It follows by repeated use of Observation 1.18 that if A is a finite set, then $\text{Cn}(A)$ is identical to the set of consequences of the conjunction of the elements of A:

$$\text{Cn}(\{\alpha_1,\alpha_2,\ldots,\alpha_n\}) = \text{Cn}(\{\alpha_1\&\alpha_2\&\ldots\&\alpha_n\}).$$

Letting $\&A$ denote the conjunction of all the elements of A, we can therefore write:

$$\text{Cn}(A) = \text{Cn}(\{\&A\}).$$

This notation can be extended to cover infinite sets that have finite representations:

DEFINITION 1.19 *A set A is* finite-based *if and only if there is some finite set A' such that* $\text{Cn}(A) = \text{Cn}(A')$.

If A is non-empty and finite-based, then $\&A$ denotes the conjunction of all elements of some finite set A' such that $\text{Cn}(A) = \text{Cn}(A')$.

For this definition to be adequate, so that $\&A$ is well-determined, it must be the case that for any set A, if A' and A'' are non-empty finite sets such that $\text{Cn}(A) = \text{Cn}(A') = \text{Cn}(A'')$, then $\&A'$ and $\&A''$ are logically equivalent. In order to show that this is the case, suppose that it is not. Then $\text{Cn}(A') = \text{Cn}(A'')$ but $\&A'$ and $\&A''$ are not logically equivalent. It follows that at least one of $\&A'$ and $\&A''$ does not logically imply the other. Without loss of generality, we may assume that $\&A'$ does not logically imply $\&A''$, i.e. that $\&A'' \notin \text{Cn}(\{\&A'\})$. However, we have $\text{Cn}(\{\&A''\}) = \text{Cn}(A'')$ by repeated use of Observation 1.18. By inclusion, $\{\&A''\} \subseteq \text{Cn}(\{\&A''\})$, i.e. $\&A'' \in \text{Cn}(\{\&A''\})$. Since $\text{Cn}(\{\&A''\}) = \text{Cn}(A'') = \text{Cn}(A')$, this contradicts $\&A'' \notin \text{Cn}(\{\&A'\})$. This contradiction shows that our assumptions were inconsistent, and this was all that was required for the proof.

A set A of sentences is *logically consistent* according to the logic represented by Cn if and only if it is impossible to derive both a sentence and its negation from A. In formal language:

DEFINITION 1.20 *A set A is* inconsistent *if and only if there is some sentence α such that both $\alpha \in \text{Cn}(A)$ and $\neg\alpha \in \text{Cn}(A)$. It is* consistent *if and only if it is not inconsistent.*

As has already been indicated, inconsistencies in classical logic are always global.

OBSERVATION 1.21 *Let A be an inconsistent set and let β be any sentence. Then $\beta \in \text{Cn}(A)$.*

Proof. Since A is inconsistent, there is some α such that $\{\alpha, \neg\alpha\} \subseteq \text{Cn}(A)$. By monotony this yields $\text{Cn}(\{\alpha, \neg\alpha\}) \subseteq \text{Cn}(\text{Cn}(A))$. By iteration, $\text{Cn}(\text{Cn}(A)) = \text{Cn}(A)$, so that $\text{Cn}(\{\alpha, \neg\alpha\}) \subseteq \text{Cn}(A)$. Since β follows truth-functionally from α and $\neg\alpha$, we have $\beta \in \text{Cn}(\{\alpha, \neg\alpha\})$ and thus $\beta \in \text{Cn}(A)$. This concludes the proof. ■

Alternatively, we may define a set A to be inconsistent if and only if $\text{Cn}(A) = \mathcal{L}$. Since our logic is supra-classical, the two definitions are equivalent. (In non-classical logic, they may differ.)

It is often convenient to use the symbol $\vdash$ for implication of single sentences:

DEFINITION 1.22 *For any set A and sentence α:*
$A \vdash \alpha$ ('A implies alpha') if and only if $\alpha \in \text{Cn}(A)$.
$\alpha \vdash \beta$ is an abbreviation of $\{\alpha\} \vdash \beta$.
$\vdash \beta$ is an abbreviation of $\emptyset \vdash \beta$.
$A \nvdash \alpha$ denotes that $A \vdash \alpha$ is not the case.

The properties of $\vdash$ can readily be obtained from the properties of Cn, as will be seen from the following example:

OBSERVATION 1.23 *$X \vdash \neg\alpha$ if and only if $X \cup \{\alpha\} \vdash \bot$.*

Proof. The two directions of the equivalence will be proved separately.

Part I. Suppose that $X \vdash \neg\alpha$, i.e. $\neg\alpha \in \text{Cn}(X)$. Since $\neg\alpha$ is logically equivalent with $\alpha \rightarrow \bot$, we have $\alpha \rightarrow \bot \in \text{Cn}(X)$, and by deduction $\bot \in \text{Cn}(X \cup \{\alpha\})$, i.e. $X \cup \{\alpha\} \vdash \bot$.

Part II. Suppose that $X \cup \{\alpha\} \vdash \bot$, i.e. $\bot \in \text{Cn}(X \cup \{\alpha\})$. By deduction we have $\alpha \rightarrow \bot \in \text{Cn}(X)$, i.e. $\neg\alpha \in \text{Cn}(X)$, i.e. $X \vdash \neg\alpha$. ■

Exercises

1. Does the following property hold for all subsets A of $\mathcal{L}$?:
   If $\alpha \vee \beta \in \text{Cn}(A)$ then either $\alpha \in \text{Cn}(A)$ or $\beta \in \text{Cn}(A)$.
2. Show that $\text{Cn}(\{\alpha \vee \neg\alpha\}) = \text{Cn}(\emptyset)$.

3. Show that $\text{Cn}(\{\alpha\rightarrow\beta\}) = \text{Cn}(\{\neg\alpha\}) \cap \text{Cn}(\{\beta\})$.
4. Show that $\text{Cn}(\{\alpha\rightarrow\beta\}) \cap \text{Cn}(\{\beta\rightarrow\alpha\}) = \text{Cn}(\emptyset)$.
5. Show that if $A \subseteq D \subseteq B \subseteq \text{Cn}(A)$ then $\text{Cn}(D) = \text{Cn}(B)$.
6. Show that if $A \subseteq \text{Cn}(B)$, then $\text{Cn}(A \cup B) \subseteq \text{Cn}(B)$.
7. Show that $\text{Cn}(B) = \text{Cn}(D)$ if and only if $B \subseteq \text{Cn}(D)$ and $D \subseteq \text{Cn}(B)$.
8. [129] Show that Cn is a consequence operator if and only if it satisfies:
   $X \subseteq \text{Cn}(\text{Cn}(X)) \subseteq \text{Cn}(X) \subseteq \text{Cn}(X \cup Y)$.
9. [129] Let Cn and Cn′ be two consequence operators that satisfy deduction and compactness. Show that Cn = Cn′ if and only if $\text{Cn}(\emptyset) = \text{Cn}'(\emptyset)$.
10. Let Cn be any supraclassical operator of consequence, and Cn_0 the operator such that $\text{Cn}_0(X)$ consists exactly of the truth-functional consequences of X. Show that:
    If $\text{Cn}_0(X) \subseteq \text{Cn}_0(Y)$, then $\text{Cn}(X) \subseteq \text{Cn}(Y)$.
11. [45] Let Cn_0 be the truth-functional consequence operator. For any subset T of $\mathcal{L}$, let Cn_T be the operation on subsets of $\mathcal{L}$ such that for all sets A of sentences:
    $\text{Cn}_T(A) = \text{Cn}_0(T \cup A)$.
    Prove that Cn_T is a consequence operator and that it satisfies supraclassicality, deduction and compactness.
12. Let Cn be any consequence operator, and let Cn′ be the operator such that for for all sentences α and sets A of sentences:
    $\alpha \in \text{Cn}'(A)$ if and only if $\alpha \in \text{Cn}(\{\beta\})$ for some $\beta \in A$.
    Show that Cn′ is a consequence operator.
13. Prove that $\alpha \vdash \beta$ if and only if $\vdash \alpha\rightarrow\beta$.
14. Prove that if $\alpha \vdash \beta$ and $\beta \vdash \delta$, then $\alpha \vdash \delta$. (transitivity of $\vdash$)
15. Prove that if $\alpha \vdash \beta$ and $\beta \vdash \alpha$, then $\alpha \vdash \delta$ if and only if $\beta \vdash \delta$. (reciprocity)
16. Prove that if $X \vdash \alpha$ and $X \cup \{\alpha\} \vdash \beta$, then $X \vdash \beta$.
17. Let X be a set such that $X \nvdash \alpha\vee\beta$. Let $A = X \cup \{\beta\rightarrow\alpha\}$. Show that:
    (a) $A \nvdash \alpha$
    (b) $A \cup \{\alpha\vee\beta\} \vdash \alpha$.

11+ CLOSURE PROPERTIES

In belief dynamics, sets that are closed under logical consequence are called belief sets. In logical terminology, they are called theories.

DEFINITION 1.24 *A set A is* logically closed *(*closed under logical consequence*) if and only if $A = \text{Cn}(A)$.*

We will make frequent use of two closely related properties of logically closed sets, that both pertain to intersections. The first of these is that *logical closure is preserved under intersection.*

OBSERVATION 1.25 *If A and B are logically closed, then so is $A \cap B$.*

Proof. Let A and B be logically closed, and let $\alpha \in \text{Cn}(A \cap B)$. Since $A \cap B \subseteq A$ it follows by monotony that $\text{Cn}(A \cap B) \subseteq \text{Cn}(A)$, so that $\alpha \in \text{Cn}(A)$. Since A is logically closed, $\alpha \in A$. In the same way we can prove that $\alpha \in B$. It follows from $\alpha \in A$ and $\alpha \in B$ that $\alpha \in A \cap B$. ■

The second property is that Cn *distributes over the intersection of logically closed sets.*

OBSERVATION 1.26 *If A and B are logically closed, then*

$$\text{Cn}(A \cap B) = \text{Cn}(A) \cap \text{Cn}(B).$$

Proof. It follows from Observation 1.25 that $A \cap B = \text{Cn}(A \cap B)$. Since A and B are logically closed, we also have $A \cap B = \text{Cn}(A) \cap \text{Cn}(B)$. ■

For logically closed sets, set membership ($\in$) and logical consequence ($\vdash$) are interchangeable, i.e. if A is logically closed, then

$A \vdash \alpha$ if and only if $\alpha \in A$, and
$A \nvdash \alpha$ if and only if $\alpha \notin A$.

We will not require belief sets to be finite. For some purposes, however, it will be convenient to refer to finite examples of logically closed sets (belief sets). A simple way to obtain such models is to let the language consist only of the two atomic sentences p and q and their truth-functional combinations, and to let Cn be purely truth-functional. This language only contains 16 (atomic and molecular) logically distinct sentences, and is therefore quite manageable. We can easily list the elements of various belief sets, such as:

$$\text{Cn}(\{p\leftrightarrow q\}) = \{p\leftrightarrow q, p\rightarrow q, q\rightarrow p, \top\}$$
$$\text{Cn}(\{p\&q\}) = \{p\&q, p, p\leftrightarrow q, q, p\rightarrow q, p\vee q, q\rightarrow p, \top\}$$

Figure 1.1 depicts the elements of $\text{Cn}(\{p\&q\})$ and their logical relationships. Note that the diagram only applies to this diatomic language. If the language is larger, then $\text{Cn}(\{p\&q\})$ will contain more sentences than those shown in the diagram (such as $p\vee r$, $p\vee q\vee r$, etc.)

In the study of belief bases, a couple of weaker closure properties are useful. The most important of these is *relative closure*, that is defined as follows:

DEFINITION 1.27 ([44]) *For any two sets A and B of sentences, A is B-*closed *(logically closed relative to B) if and only if* $\text{Cn}(A) \cap B \subseteq A$.

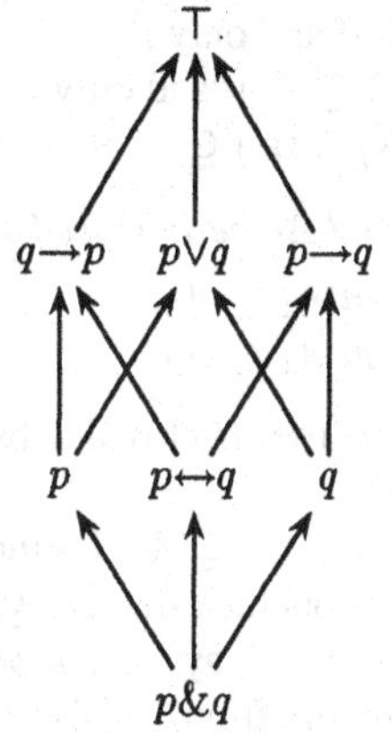

Figure 1.1. The elements of Cn({p&q}) in a language that consists of p, q, and their truth-functional combinations. Arrows denote logical implication.

Thus, for a set A to be B-closed, it must contain those of its own logical consequences that are also elements of B. As an example, $\{p\}$ is not logically closed relative to $\{p, q, q \rightarrow p\}$, since the latter set contains $q \rightarrow p$, that is a consequence of $\{p\}$ without being one of its elements.

Clearly, every set is logically closed relative to itself. As a limiting case, to say that a set is $\mathcal{L}$-closed is just another way of saying that it is logically closed.

Just like logical closure, relative closure is preserved under intersection:

OBSERVATION 1.28 *If A_1 and A_2 are B-closed, then so is $A_1 \cap A_2$.*

Proof. Let $\alpha \in \mathrm{Cn}(A_1 \cap A_2) \cap B$. We need to prove that $\alpha \in A_1 \cap A_2$.

Since $A_1 \cap A_2 \subseteq A_1$ it follows by monotony that $\mathrm{Cn}(A_1 \cap A_2) \subseteq \mathrm{Cn}(A_1)$. Since we have $\alpha \in \mathrm{Cn}(A_1 \cap A_2)$, we may conclude that $\alpha \in \mathrm{Cn}(A_1)$. We also have $\alpha \in B$, so that $\alpha \in \mathrm{Cn}(A_1) \cap B$. Since A_1 is B-closed, $\mathrm{Cn}(A_1) \cap B \subseteq A_1$, so that $\alpha \in A_1$. In the same way we can prove that $\alpha \in A_2$. It follows from $\alpha \in A_1$ and $\alpha \in A_2$ that $\alpha \in A_1 \cap A_2$. ■

The following three observations introduce some additional useful properties of relative closure:

OBSERVATION 1.29 *A is $B_1 \cup B_2$-closed if and only if A is both B_1-closed and B_2-closed.*

Proof. The observation follows by a simple set-theoretical argument:
$\mathrm{Cn}(A) \cap (B_1 \cup B_2) \subseteq A$ holds if and only if
$(\mathrm{Cn}(A) \cap B_1) \cup (\mathrm{Cn}(A) \cap B_2) \subseteq A$, if and only if
$(\mathrm{Cn}(A) \cap B_1) \subseteq A$ and $(\mathrm{Cn}(A) \cap B_2) \subseteq A$. ■

OBSERVATION 1.30 *Let A_1 and A_2 be B-closed subsets of B. Then:*

1. If $\mathrm{Cn}(A_1) \subseteq \mathrm{Cn}(A_2)$, then $A_1 \subseteq A_2$.
2. If $\mathrm{Cn}(A_1) \subset \mathrm{Cn}(A_2)$, then $A_1 \subset A_2$.

Proof. *Part 1*: Let A_1 and A_2 be two B-closed subsets of B such tha $\mathrm{Cn}(A_1) \subseteq \mathrm{Cn}(A_2)$.

By the B-closure of A_1, $\mathrm{Cn}(A_1) \cap B \subseteq A_1$. By inclusion, $A_1 \subseteq \mathrm{Cn}(A_1)$. Since we also have $A_1 \subseteq B$, we may conclude that $A_1 \subseteq \mathrm{Cn}(A_1) \cap B$. We therefore have $A_1 = \mathrm{Cn}(A_1) \cap B$. In the same way we can prove that $A_2 = \mathrm{Cn}(A_2) \cap B$.

It follows by elementary set theory from $\mathrm{Cn}(A_1) \subseteq \mathrm{Cn}(A_2)$ that $\mathrm{Cn}(A_1) \cap B \subseteq \mathrm{Cn}(A_2) \cap B$. By substituting A_1 for $\mathrm{Cn}(A_1) \cap B$ and A_2 for $\mathrm{Cn}(A_2) \cap B$, we obtain $A_1 \subseteq A_2$, as desired.

Part 2: Let A_1 and A_2 be B-closed subsets of B such that $\mathrm{Cn}(A_1) \subset \mathrm{Cn}(A_2)$. It follows from Part 1 of the present observation that $A_1 \subseteq A_2$. It follows from $\mathrm{Cn}(A_1) \subset \mathrm{Cn}(A_2)$ that $A_1 \neq A_2$. We can conclude from $A_1 \subseteq A_2$ and $A_1 \neq A_2$ that $A_1 \subset A_2$. ■

OBSERVATION 1.31 *If A_1 is an A_2-closed subset of A_2, and A_2 an A_3-closed subset of A_3, then A_1 is an A_3-closed subset of A_3.*

COROLLARY. *If A_1 is an A_2-closed subset of A_2, and A_2 is logically closed, then A_1 is logically closed.*

Proof. Suppose that A_1 is an A_2-closed subset of A_2, and that A_2 is an A_3-closed subset of A_3. It follows trivially that A_1 is a subset of A_3. Our remaining task is to show that A_1 is A_3-closed. Let $\alpha \in \mathrm{Cn}(A_1) \cap A_3$. We have to show that $\alpha \in A_1$.

Since $A_1 \subseteq A_2$ we have by monotony $\mathrm{Cn}(A_1) \subseteq \mathrm{Cn}(A_2)$ and by set theory $\mathrm{Cn}(A_1) \cap A_3 \subseteq \mathrm{Cn}(A_2) \cap A_3$. It follows from this and $\alpha \in \mathrm{Cn}(A_1) \cap A_3$ that $\alpha \in \mathrm{Cn}(A_2) \cap A_3$. Since A_2 is A_3-closed, i.e. $\mathrm{Cn}(A_2) \cap A_3 \subseteq A_2$, we may conclude that $\alpha \in A_2$. It follows from this and $\alpha \in \mathrm{Cn}(A_1)$ that $\alpha \in \mathrm{Cn}(A_1) \cap A_2$. Since A_1 is A_2-closed, we have $\mathrm{Cn}(A_1) \cap A_2 \subseteq A_1$, so that $\alpha \in A_1$. This concludes the proof. ■

The corollary is obtained by substituting $\mathcal{L}$ for A_3 in the observation. (Remember that $\mathcal{L}$-closure and logical closure are two names of the same property.)

The property of disjunctive closure was introduced in Section 1.8. A set A is *disjunctively closed (closed under disjunction)* if and only if for all sentences α and β: if $\alpha \in A$ and $\beta \in A$, then $\alpha \vee \beta \in A$.

Just like logical closure, disjunctive closure is preserved under intersection:

OBSERVATION 1.32 *If A and B are disjunctively closed, then so is $A \cap B$.*

Proof. Suppose that A and B are disjunctively closed. Let α and β be elements of $A \cap B$. Then $\alpha \in A$ and $\beta \in A$, and by the disjunctive closure of A, $\alpha \vee \beta \in A$. In the same way it follows that $\alpha \vee \beta \in B$. From $\alpha \vee \beta \in A$ and $\alpha \vee \beta \in B$ we may conclude that $\alpha \vee \beta \in A \cap B$. ■

The following observation parallels the result for logical closure that was obtained as a corollary to Observation 1.31:

OBSERVATION 1.33 *If A_1 is an A_2-closed subset of A_2, and A_2 is disjunctively closed, then A_1 is disjunctively closed.*

Proof. Let A_2 be disjunctively closed, and let A_1 be an A_2-closed subset of A_2. We need to show that if α and β are elements of A_1, then so is $\alpha \vee \beta$.

Suppose that $\alpha \in A_1$ and $\beta \in A_1$. Then $\alpha \vee \beta \in \mathrm{Cn}(A_1)$. Since $A_1 \subseteq A_2$, we have $\alpha \in A_2$ and $\beta \in A_2$. By the disjunctive closure of A_2, $\alpha \vee \beta \in A_2$. We therefore have $\alpha \vee \beta \in \mathrm{Cn}(A_1) \cap A_2$. By the A_2-closure of A_1, $\alpha \vee \beta \in A_1$. ■

Cn does not distribute over the intersection of disjunctively closed sets, i.e. it does not hold in general that if A and B are disjunctively closed, then $\mathrm{Cn}(A \cap B) = \mathrm{Cn}(A) \cap \mathrm{Cn}(B)$. To see this, just let $A = \{p\}$ and $B = \{q\}$. Then $\mathrm{Cn}(A \cap B) = \mathrm{Cn}(\emptyset)$ and $\mathrm{Cn}(A) \cap \mathrm{Cn}(B) = \mathrm{Cn}(\{p \vee q\})$. However, a related but weaker distributive property can be obtained:

OBSERVATION 1.34 ([49]) *Let D be a disjunctively closed set of sentences, and let A and B be D-closed subsets of D. Then* $\mathrm{Cn}(A \cap B) = \mathrm{Cn}(A) \cap \mathrm{Cn}(B)$.

Proof. The proof that $\mathrm{Cn}(A \cap B) \subseteq \mathrm{Cn}(A) \cap \mathrm{Cn}(B)$ is trivial. For the other direction, let $\delta \in \mathrm{Cn}(A) \cap \mathrm{Cn}(B)$. By compactness, there is a finite subset A' of A such that $\delta \in \mathrm{Cn}(A')$ and a finite subset B' of B such that $\delta \in \mathrm{Cn}(B')$. Then we have $\&A' \vdash \delta$ and $\&B' \vdash \delta$. It follows that

$$(\&A') \vee (\&B') \vdash \delta.$$

By truth-functional logic, $(\&A') \vee (\&B')$ is equivalent with

$$\&\{\alpha \vee \beta \mid (\alpha \in A') \& (\beta \in B')\}.$$

(To verify this is a tedious but fairly straight-forward exercise.) We therefore have

$$\&\{\alpha \vee \beta \mid (\alpha \in A') \& (\beta \in B')\} \vdash \delta$$

from which it follows that

$$\{\alpha \vee \beta \mid (\alpha \in A') \& (\beta \in B')\} \vdash \delta.$$

It follows by $A' \subseteq A \subseteq D$, $B' \subseteq B \subseteq D$, and the disjunctive closure of D that

$$\{\alpha \vee \beta \mid (\alpha \in A')\&(\beta \in B')\} \subseteq D.$$

We also have

$$\{\alpha \vee \beta \mid (\alpha \in A')\&(\beta \in B')\} \subseteq \mathrm{Cn}(A),$$

so that

$$\{\alpha \vee \beta \mid (\alpha \in A')\&(\beta \in B')\} \subseteq \mathrm{Cn}(A) \cap D.$$

Since A is D-closed, we may conclude from this that

$$\{\alpha \vee \beta \mid (\alpha \in A')\&(\beta \in B')\} \subseteq A.$$

In the same way, it can be shown that

$$\{\alpha \vee \beta \mid (\alpha \in A')\&(\beta \in B')\} \subseteq B.$$

We therefore have

$$\{\alpha \vee \beta \mid (\alpha \in A')\&(\beta \in B')\} \subseteq A \cap B.$$

Since $\{\alpha \vee \beta \mid (\alpha \in A')\&(\beta \in B')\} \vdash \delta$, it follows that $A \cap B \vdash \delta$, i.e.

$$\delta \in \mathrm{Cn}(A \cap B).$$

which concludes the proof. ■

Exercises

18. Let $\mathcal{L}$ be the language that consists of p, q, and their truth-functional combinations. Let Cn represent truth-functional consequence. List the elements of the following sets:

    (a) $\mathrm{Cn}(\{p \vee q\})$
    (b) $\mathrm{Cn}(\{p \rightarrow q\})$
    (c) $\mathrm{Cn}(\{p\})$
    (d) $\mathrm{Cn}(\emptyset)$

19. Show that a set A is logically closed if and only if there is some B such that $A = \mathrm{Cn}(B)$.

20. Show that if A and B are logically closed, then $A \cup B$ is logically closed if and only if either $A \subseteq B$ or $B \subseteq A$.

21. Let p and q be atomic sentences. Which of the following sets are $\{p, p \vee q\}$-closed?

    (a) $\{p, q\}$
    (b) $\{q\}$

(c) $\{p \vee q\}$
(d) $\{\neg p, \neg q\}$
(e) $\emptyset$.

22. Let A be a finite set of sentences and let B_1 and B_2 be A-closed subsets of A. Show that $B_1 \subset B_2$ iff $\mathrm{Cn}(B_1) \subset \mathrm{Cn}(B_2)$.
23. Let A be a finite set of sentences and c a function such that for all subsets B of A, $c(B) = \{\&(X) \mid \emptyset \neq X \subseteq B\}$. (Thus, $c(B)$ is the closure under conjunction of B.) Show that for all A-closed subsets B_1 and B_2 of A: If $c(B_1) = c(B_2)$, then $B_1 = B_2$.
24. [48] Two sets A_1 and A_2 are *mutually closed* if and only if A_1 is A_2-closed and A_2 is A_1-closed. Show that if both A_1 and A_2 are B-closed subsets of B, then A_1 and A_2 are mutually closed.
25. [49] A set A is *closed under implication* if and only if for all α and β: if $\alpha \in A$ and $\beta \in A$, then $\alpha \rightarrow \beta \in A$. Show that closure under implication is preserved under intersection.

12+ REMAINDER SETS

Remainder sets were introduced in Section 1.5. For any set A and sentence α, $A \perp \alpha$ is the set of maximal subsets of A that do not imply α. In this section, we are going to use the original definition of the remainder operation, that was introduced by Carlos Alchourrón and David Makinson. This definition is somewhat more general since it allows α to be replaced by a set of sentences. For any two sets of sentences A and B, $A \perp B$ is the set of maximal subsets of A that do not imply any element of B.

DEFINITION 1.35 (Alchourrón and Makinson [2]) *For any two sets A and B of sentences, $A \perp B$, (A's)* remainder set *modulo B is the set such that $X \in A \perp B$ if and only if:*

i. $X \subseteq A$
ii. $\mathrm{Cn}(X) \cap B = \emptyset$
iii. There is no set X' such that $X \subset X' \subseteq A$ and $\mathrm{Cn}(X') \cap B = \emptyset$.

$A \perp \beta$ is an abbreviation of $A \perp \{\beta\}$.
If $X \in A \perp B$, then X is a remainder *(of A, by B)* [2]. *A will be called the* progenitor *and B the* rejector *of the remainder set $A \perp B$* [56].

The purpose of introducing sets, rather than single sentences, as rejectors is to make possible a logic of multiple contraction (contraction by several sentences at the same time). As a side-effect, Definition 1.35 allows us to use the empty set as a rejector. It follows from the definition that for all sets A:

$$A\bot\emptyset = \{A\}$$

In other words, if the rejector is empty, then nothing is rejected. If the progenitor is inconsistent, then rejection by the empty set does not produce consistent remainders. However, if the rejector is non-empty (and all interesting rejectors are), then all remainders are consistent, even if the progenitor is inconsistent. To see this, study condition (ii) of the definition. If B is non-empty, then it follows from $\mathrm{Cn}(X) \cap B = \emptyset$ that there is some sentence $\beta \in B$ such that $\beta \notin \mathrm{Cn}(X)$. Since inconsistent sets imply all sentences of the language, this is sufficient to prove that X is consistent.

It also follows from Definition 1.35 that if X and Y are elements of the same remainder set, then it cannot be the case that $X \subset Y$. (Otherwise, (iii) is violated for X, as can be verified by substituting Y for X' in the definition.) Therefore, if we are able to prove for two sets X and Y that $X \subseteq Y$ and $\{X, Y\} \subseteq A\bot B$, then we can conclude that $X = Y$.

OBSERVATION 1.36 ([44]) *If $X \in A\bot B$, then X is A-closed.*

Proof. Let $X \in A\bot B$. Suppose that X is not A-closed, i.e. that $\mathrm{Cn}(X) \cap A \not\subseteq X$. There is then some δ such that $\delta \in \mathrm{Cn}(X) \cap A$ and $\delta \notin X$. Let $Y = X \cup \{\delta\}$. We then have $X \subset Y \subseteq A$ and $\mathrm{Cn}(X) = \mathrm{Cn}(Y)$. It follows that $\mathrm{Cn}(Y) \cap B = \emptyset$, contrary to $X \in A\bot B$. We can conclude from this contradiction that X is A-closed. ■

It is a natural and very useful property of remainders that if there is, for two given sets A and B, some set X that satisfies (i) and (ii) of Definition 1.35, then there is some superset X' of X that satisfies all three conditions:

POSTULATE 1.37 (*upper bound property*, Alchourrón and Makinson [2]) *If $X \subseteq A$, and $\mathrm{Cn}(X) \cap B = \emptyset$, then there is some X' such that $X \subseteq X' \in A\bot B$.*

The upper bound property follows from compactness and Zorn's lemma, which is equivalent to the axiom of choice [2].) Since the axiom of choice holds for finite sets, the upper bound property is provable if the progenitor (A) is finite. For our present purposes, it is reasonable to accept the axiom of choice, and hence to accept the upper bound property as a postulate for infinite progenitors as well.

The upper bound property is needed for the proof of several elementary properties of remainders. One of these is that $A\bot B$ is non-empty unless B contains some logical truth:

OBSERVATION 1.38 (Alchourrón and Makinson [2]) *$A\bot B = \emptyset$ if and only if $B \cap \mathrm{Cn}(\emptyset) \neq \emptyset$.*

Proof. We are going to prove the following equivalent form of the observation:

$$A \perp B \neq \emptyset \text{ if and only if } B \cap \mathrm{Cn}(\emptyset) = \emptyset.$$

For one direction, suppose that $A \perp B \neq \emptyset$. Then there is some set X such that $X \in A \perp B$ and consequently $\mathrm{Cn}(X) \cap B = \emptyset$. It follows by monotony that $\mathrm{Cn}(\emptyset) \subseteq \mathrm{Cn}(X)$, and from this that $\mathrm{Cn}(\emptyset) \cap B \subseteq \mathrm{Cn}(X) \cap B$. From this and $\mathrm{Cn}(X) \cap B = \emptyset$ it follows that $\mathrm{Cn}(\emptyset) \cap B = \emptyset$.

For the other direction, let $B \cap \mathrm{Cn}(\emptyset) = \emptyset$. It follows by the upper bound property (letting $X = \emptyset$ in Postulate 1.37) that there is some Y such that $Y \in A \perp B$. ■

The upper bound property provides us with a necessary and sufficient condition for $A \perp B_1 = A \perp B_2$, namely that every subset of A implies some element of B_1 if and only if it implies some element of B_2:

OBSERVATION 1.39 *The following two conditions are equivalent:*

1. $A \perp B_1 = A \perp B_2$
2. *For all subsets D of A : $B_1 \cap \mathrm{Cn}(D) = \emptyset$ if and only if $B_2 \cap \mathrm{Cn}(D) = \emptyset$.*

Proof. (1) *implies* (2): Suppose that (2) does not hold. Without loss of generality, we may assume that there is some subset D of A such that $B_1 \cap \mathrm{Cn}(D) = \emptyset$ and $B_2 \cap \mathrm{Cn}(D) \neq \emptyset$. By the upper bound property there is then some set D' such that $D \subseteq D' \in A \perp B_1$. Since $B_2 \cap \mathrm{Cn}(D) \neq \emptyset$, $B_2 \cap \mathrm{Cn}(D') \neq \emptyset$ and thus $D' \notin A \perp B_2$. Thus $A \perp B_1 \neq A \perp B_2$, so that (1) does not hold.

(2) *implies* (1): Suppose that (1) does not hold, i.e. $A \perp B_1 \neq A \perp B_2$. Without loss of generality, we may assume that there is some $X \in A \perp B_1$ such that $X \notin A \perp B_2$. There are two cases:

First case, $B_2 \cap \mathrm{Cn}(X) \neq \emptyset$: Then we have $B_1 \cap \mathrm{Cn}(X) = \emptyset$ and $B_2 \cap \mathrm{Cn}(X) \neq \emptyset$, which is sufficient to show that (2) does not hold.

Second case, $B_2 \cap \mathrm{Cn}(X) = \emptyset$: Then by the upper bound property there is some X' such that $X \subset X' \in A \perp B_2$. It follows that $B_1 \cap \mathrm{Cn}(X') \neq \emptyset$ and $B_2 \cap \mathrm{Cn}(X') = \emptyset$, which shows that (2) does not hold. ■

The next observation shows that a sentence that implies an element of the rejector can be added to either the progenitor or the rejector, without changing the remainder set.

OBSERVATION 1.40 *If α implies some element of B, then:*

1. $(A \cup \{\alpha\}) \perp B = A \perp B$.
2. $A \perp (B \cup \{\alpha\}) = A \perp B$.

Proof. Suppose that α implies some element β of B. We need to prove:

1A. $(A \cup \{\alpha\}) \perp B \subseteq A \perp B$

1B. $A \perp B \subseteq (A \cup \{\alpha\}) \perp B$

2A. $A \perp (B \cup \{\alpha\}) \subseteq A \perp B$, and

2B. $A \perp B \subseteq A \perp (B \cup \{\alpha\})$.

Part 1A: In order to prove that $(A \cup \{\alpha\}) \perp B \subseteq A \perp B$, suppose that $X \in (A \cup \{\alpha\}) \perp B$. We are going to show that $X \in A \perp B$ by showing that the three conditions of Definition 1.35 are satisfied.

To show that (i) is satisfied, it is sufficient to observe that since X implies no element of B, $\alpha \notin X$. From this and $X \subseteq A \cup \{\alpha\}$ follows that $X \subseteq A$.

We already know from $X \in (A \cup \{\alpha\}) \perp B$ that X implies no element of B, i.e. that $\mathrm{Cn}(X) \cap B = \emptyset$, so that (ii) is satisfied.

In order to show that (iii) is satisfied, suppose to the contrary that there is some Y such that $X \subset Y \subseteq A$ and $\mathrm{Cn}(Y) \cap B = \emptyset$. It then follows from $X \subset Y \subseteq A \cup \{\alpha\}$ and $\mathrm{Cn}(Y) \cap B = \emptyset$, that $X \notin (A \cup \{\alpha\}) \perp B$, contrary to the conditions. This contradiction concludes the proof of (iii), and thereby Part 1A of the proof.

Part 1B. In this part of the proof, let us suppose that $X \in A \perp B$. We are going to show that $X \in (A \cup \{\alpha\}) \perp B$, again by verifying the three conditions of Definition 1.35.

It follows from $X \subseteq A$ that $X \subseteq A \cup \{\alpha\}$, so that (i) is satisfied.

We already know from $X \in A \perp B$ that X implies no element of B, i.e. that $\mathrm{Cn}(X) \cap B = \emptyset$, so that (ii) is satisfied.

In order to show that (iii) is satisfied, suppose to the contrary that there is some Y such that $X \subset Y \subseteq A \cup \{\alpha\}$ and $\mathrm{Cn}(Y) \cap B = \emptyset$. It follows from $\mathrm{Cn}(Y) \cap B = \emptyset$ that $\alpha \notin Y$, so that $Y \subseteq A$. We therefore have $X \subset Y \subseteq A$ and $\mathrm{Cn}(Y) \cap B = \emptyset$, contrary to $X \in A \perp B$. This contradiction concludes the proof of (iii), and thereby Part 1B of the proof.

Part 2A: Let $X \in A \perp (B \cup \{\alpha\})$. We are going to show that $X \in A \perp B$, i.e. that the three conditions of Definition 1.35 are satisfied.

It follows directly from $X \in A \perp (B \cup \{\alpha\})$ that $X \subseteq A$ and that X implies no element of B, so that (i) and (ii) are satisfied.

In order to show that (iii) is satisfied, suppose to the contrary that there is some Y such that $X \subset Y \subseteq A$ and $\mathrm{Cn}(Y) \cap B = \emptyset$. It follows from $\mathrm{Cn}(Y) \cap B = \emptyset$ and $\alpha \vdash \beta$ that $\alpha \notin \mathrm{Cn}(Y)$. It follows from this and $\mathrm{Cn}(Y) \cap B = \emptyset$ that $\mathrm{Cn}(Y) \cap (B \cup \{\alpha\}) = \emptyset$, contrary to $X \subset Y \subseteq A \cup \{\alpha\}$ and $X \in A \perp (B \cup \{\alpha\})$.

Since this contradiction was derived from our assumption that $X \subset Y \subseteq A$ and $\mathrm{Cn}(Y) \cap B = \emptyset$, we can conclude that there is no Y with this property, i.e. that (iii) is satisfied.

Part 2B: Let $X \in A \perp B$. We are going to show that $X \in A \perp (B \cup \{\alpha\})$, once again by showing that the three conditions of Definition 1.35 are satisfied.

That $X \subseteq A$ follows from $X \in A \bot B$. Thus, (i) is satisfied.

It follows from $X \in A \bot B$ that X implies no element of B. Suppose that $X \vdash \alpha$. Then it follows from $\alpha \vdash \beta$ that $X \vdash \beta$, but since $\beta \in B$ this contradicts $X \in A \bot B$. We can conclude that X implies no element of $B \cup \{\alpha\}$, i.e. that $\mathrm{Cn}(X) \cap (B \cup \{\alpha\}) = \emptyset$, so that (ii) is satisfied.

For (iii), suppose to the contrary that there is some Y such that $X \subset Y \subseteq A$ and $\mathrm{Cn}(Y) \cap (B \cup \{\alpha\}) = \emptyset$. It follows by set theory that $\mathrm{Cn}(Y) \cap B = \emptyset$. We therefore have $X \subset Y \subseteq A$ and $\mathrm{Cn}(Y) \cap B = \emptyset$, contrary to $X \in A \bot B$. This contradiction show that there can be no Y with the given properties, i.e. that (iii) is satisfied. ■

The following four observations provide us with additional procedures that extend progenitors or rejectors:

OBSERVATION 1.41

1. *If $X \in A \bot \beta$, then $X \cup \{\neg\beta\} \in (A \cup \{\neg\beta\}) \bot \beta$.*
2. *If $\neg\beta \notin A$, then $X \in A \bot \beta$ if and only if $\neg\beta \notin X$ and $X \cup \{\neg\beta\} \in (A \cup \{\neg\beta\}) \bot \beta$.*

Proof. *Part 1:* It follows from $X \in A \bot \beta$ that $X \subseteq A$ and consequently that $X \cup \{\neg\beta\} \subseteq A \cup \{\neg\beta\}$. Thus condition (i) of Definition 1.35 is satisfied.

To show that $X \cup \{\neg\beta\} \nvdash \beta$, suppose to the contrary that $X \cup \{\neg\beta\} \vdash \beta$. Then it follows from the deduction property that $X \vdash \neg\beta \rightarrow \beta$ or equivalently $X \vdash \beta$, contrary to $X \in A \bot \beta$. We can conclude that $X \cup \{\neg\beta\} \nvdash \beta$. Thus condition (ii) is satisfied.

We are going to prove (iii) by showing that if $\varepsilon \in (A \cup \{\neg\beta\}) \backslash (X \cup \{\neg\beta\})$, then $X \cup \{\neg\beta\} \cup \{\varepsilon\} \vdash \beta$. Let $\varepsilon \in (A \cup \{\neg\beta\}) \backslash (X \cup \{\neg\beta\})$. Then $\varepsilon \in A \backslash X$. Since $X \in A \bot \beta$, it follows that $X \cup \{\varepsilon\} \vdash \beta$ and thus $(X \cup \{\neg\beta\}) \cup \{\varepsilon\} \vdash \beta$.

Part 2: Let $\neg\beta \notin A$. For one direction, let $X \in A \bot \beta$. It then follows from $X \subseteq A$ that $\neg\beta \notin X$ and from Part 1 that $X \cup \{\neg\beta\} \in (A \cup \{\neg\beta\}) \bot \beta$.

For the other direction, let $\neg\beta \notin X$ and $X \cup \{\neg\beta\} \in (A \cup \{\neg\beta\}) \bot \beta$. We are going to show that $X \in A \bot \beta$.

It follows from $\neg\beta \notin A$, $\neg\beta \notin X$, and $X \cup \{\neg\beta\} \subseteq A \cup \{\neg\beta\}$ that $X \subseteq A$. Thus, (i) is satisfied.

Suppose that $X \vdash \beta$. Then we have $X \cup \{\neg\beta\} \vdash \beta$, contrary to $X \cup \{\neg\beta\} \in (A \cup \{\neg\beta\}) \bot \beta$. We can conclude from this that $X \nvdash \beta$. Thus, (ii) is satisfied.

Finally, we are going to prove (iii) by showing that if $\varepsilon \in A \backslash X$, then $X \cup \{\varepsilon\} \vdash \beta$. Let $\varepsilon \in A \backslash X$. Then $\varepsilon \in (A \cup \{\neg\beta\}) \backslash (X \cup \{\neg\beta\})$, and it follows from $X \cup \{\neg\beta\} \in (A \cup \{\neg\beta\}) \bot \beta$ that $X \cup \{\neg\beta\} \cup \{\varepsilon\} \vdash \beta$, i.e. by the deduction property $X \cup \{\varepsilon\} \vdash \neg\beta \rightarrow \beta$, or equivalently $X \cup \{\varepsilon\} \vdash \beta$, as desired. This completes the proof of the observation. ■

OBSERVATION 1.42 *If* $X \in A \perp B$ *and* $X \nvdash \alpha$, *then* $X \in A \perp (B \cup \{\alpha\})$.

Proof. Let $X \in A \perp B$ and $X \nvdash \alpha$. We are going to prove that $X \in A \perp (B \cup \{\alpha\})$ by showing that the three conditions of Definition 1.35 are satisfied.

We already have $X \subseteq A$, so that (i) is satisfied. It follows from $X \in A \perp B$ and $X \nvdash \alpha$ that X implies no element of $B \cup \{\alpha\}$, so that (ii) is satisfied. For (iii), let Y be any set such that $X \subset Y \subseteq A$. Then it follows from $X \in A \perp B$ that $\text{Cn}(Y) \cap B \neq \emptyset$. From this it follows by set theory that $\text{Cn}(Y) \cap (B \cup \{\alpha\}) \neq \emptyset$, so that (iii) is satisfied. ■

OBSERVATION 1.43 *If* $X \in A \perp B$, *then there is some set* Y *such that* $X \subseteq Y \in (A \cup \{\alpha\}) \perp B$.

Proof. Since the observation is trivially true if $\alpha \in A$, we can assume that $\alpha \notin A$. We can distinguish between two cases:

Case 1, $X \cup \{\alpha\}$ implies some element of B: It follows from this and $X \in A \perp B$ that X is a maximal subset of $A \cup \{\alpha\}$ that does not imply any element of B. Let $Y = X$, and we directly have $Y \in (A \cup \{\alpha\}) \perp B$.

Case 2, $X \cup \{\alpha\}$ does not imply any element of B: Let $Y = X \cup \{\alpha\}$. Then Y is a subset of $A \cup \{\alpha\}$ that does not imply any element of B. To prove that $Y \in (A \cup \{\alpha\}) \perp B$ it remains to be shown that there is no Y' such that $Y \subset Y' \subseteq A$ and $\text{Cn}(Y') \cap B = \emptyset$. Suppose to the contrary that there is some Y' with this property. Let $X' = Y' \setminus \{\alpha\}$. Then $X \subset X' \subseteq A$, and we may also conclude from $\text{Cn}(Y') \cap B = \emptyset$ that $\text{Cn}(X') \cap B = \emptyset$. This contradicts $X \in A \perp B$. The contradiction shows that there can be no set Y' with the given properties, and this is sufficient to show that $Y \in (A \cup \{\alpha\}) \perp B$. ■

OBSERVATION 1.44 *If* $X \in A \perp (B \cup \{\alpha\})$, *then there is some set* Y *such that* $X \subseteq Y \in A \perp B$.

Proof. It follows from $X \in A \perp (B \cup \{\alpha\})$ that X is a subset of A that does not imply any element of B. The observation follows directly from the upper bound property. ■

We can use these properties to clarify the relationship between the remainder sets $A \perp \{\alpha, \beta\}$ and $A \perp \{\alpha \vee \beta\}$.

Since both α and β imply $\alpha \vee \beta$, we can add both of them to the rejector of $A \perp \{\alpha \vee \beta\}$ (Observation 1.40). In this way we obtain:

$$A \perp \{\alpha \vee \beta\} = A \perp \{\alpha, \beta, \alpha \vee \beta\}.$$

It follows from Observation 1.44 that:

If $X \in A\bot\{\alpha, \beta, \alpha\vee\beta\}$, then there is some Y such that $X \subseteq Y \in A\bot\{\alpha, \beta\}$.

Combining these two results, we obtain:

If $X \in A\bot\{\alpha\vee\beta\}$, then there is some Y such that $X \subseteq Y \in A\bot\{\alpha, \beta\}$.

This is a more elaborate way of saying that in order to get rid of $\alpha\vee\beta$, we must get rid of both α and β. However, the converse is not true. We can get rid of both α and β without getting rid of $\alpha\vee\beta$. For instance, $\{p\vee q\}$ is an element (indeed the only element) of $\{p, q, p\vee q\}\bot\{p, q\}$.

The relations between $A\bot(\alpha\&\beta)$, $A\bot\alpha$, and $A\bot\beta$ are important in belief dynamics. We will therefore often have use for the following observation:

OBSERVATION 1.45 $A\bot(\alpha\&\beta) \subseteq A\bot\alpha \cup A\bot\beta$.

Proof. Let $X \in A\bot(\alpha\&\beta)$. We are going to show that $X \in A\bot\alpha \cup A\bot\beta$. It follows from $X \in A\bot(\alpha\&\beta)$ that $X \nvdash \alpha\&\beta$, and consequently that either $X \nvdash \alpha$ or $X \nvdash \beta$.

First suppose that $X \nvdash \alpha$. It follows from $X \nvdash \alpha$ and $X \in A\bot(\alpha\&\beta)$, by Observation 1.42 that $X \in A\bot\{\alpha, \alpha\&\beta\}$. Since $\alpha\&\beta \vdash \alpha$, we obtain $A\bot\{\alpha, \alpha\&\beta\} = A\bot\alpha$ from Observation 1.40. We can therefore conclude that $X \in A\bot\alpha$.

Next, suppose that $X \nvdash \beta$. It follows in exactly the same way that $X \in A\bot\beta$.

In summary, we have shown that either $X \nvdash \alpha$ or $X \nvdash \beta$ and that in the first case, $X \in A\bot\alpha$, and in the second case $X \in A\bot\beta$. This is sufficient to prove that $X \in A\bot\alpha \cup A\bot\beta$. ■

Set inclusion cannot in general be strengthened to identity in Observation 1.45. In other words, it does not hold in general that $A\bot(\alpha\&\beta) = A\bot\alpha \cup A\bot\beta$. To see this, it is sufficient to observe that there are cases in which $X \in A\bot\alpha, Y \in A\bot\beta$ and $X \subset Y$. (For a simple example, let $A = \{p\}$. Then $\emptyset \in A\bot p, \{p\} \in A\bot(p\&\neg p)$ and $\emptyset \subset \{p\}$.) In such cases, it cannot hold that $A\bot(\alpha\&\beta) = A\bot\alpha \cup A\bot\beta$, since this would require that both X and Y are elements of $A\bot(\alpha\&\beta)$. As was noted above, if $X \subset Y$, then X and Y cannot be elements of the same remainder set. Interestingly enough, however, it can be shown that $A\bot(\alpha\&\beta) = A\bot\alpha \cup A\bot\beta$ holds in all cases in which there is no $X \in A\bot\alpha$ and $Y \in A\bot\beta$ such that $X \subset Y$ or $Y \subset X$.

OBSERVATION 1.46 ([51]) $A\bot(\alpha\&\beta) = A\bot\alpha \cup A\bot\beta$ *holds if and only if* $X \not\subset Y \not\subset X$ *for all* $X \in A\bot\alpha$ *and* $Y \in A\bot\beta$.

Proof. *Part I:* For one direction, suppose that $A\bot(\alpha\&\beta) = A\bot\alpha \cup A\bot\beta$. We need to show that $X \not\subset Y \not\subset X$ for all $X \in A\bot\alpha$ and $Y \in A\bot\beta$. Suppose to the contrary that this is not the case. Then there is some $X \in A\bot\alpha$ and some $Y \in$

$A\perp\beta$ such that either $X \subset Y$ or $Y \subset X$. In both cases, $\{X, Y\} \subseteq A\perp(\alpha\&\beta)$. This is impossible since an element of a remainder set cannot be a proper subset of another element of the same remainder set. This contradiction concludes Part I of the proof.

Part II: For the other direction, suppose that $X \not\subset Y \not\subset X$ for all $X \in A\perp\alpha$ and $Y \in A\perp\beta$. Our task is now to show that $A\perp(\alpha\&\beta) = A\perp\alpha \cup A\perp\beta$. It was shown in Observation 1.45 that $A\perp(\alpha\&\beta) \subseteq A\perp\alpha \cup A\perp\beta$, so it only remains to show that $A\perp\alpha \cup A\perp\beta \subseteq A\perp(\alpha\&\beta)$.

Let $X \in A\perp\alpha$. We are going to prove that $X \in A\perp(\alpha\&\beta)$ by showing that the three conditions of Definition 1.35 are satisfied.

We already have $X \subseteq A$, so that (i) is satisfied. It follows from $X \in A\perp\alpha$ that $X \nvdash \alpha$, and consequenctly $X \nvdash (\alpha\&\beta)$, so that (ii) is satisfied.

In order to show that (iii) is satisfied, suppose to the contrary that this is not the case. Then there is some W such that $X \subset W \subseteq A$ and $W \nvdash (\alpha\&\beta)$. It follows from $X \subset W \subseteq A$ and $X \in A\perp\alpha$ that $W \vdash \alpha$. With $W \nvdash (\alpha\&\beta)$ this yields $W \nvdash \beta$, from which it follows by the upper bound property that $W \subseteq Y$ for some $Y \in A\perp\beta$. Since $X \subset Y$, this contradicts our assumption that $X \not\subset Y \not\subset X$ for all $X \in A\perp\alpha$ and $Y \in A\perp\beta$. This contradiction is sufficient to show that (iii) is satisfied. We have proved that $X \in A\perp(\alpha\&\beta)$.

In the same way it follows that if $X \in A\perp\beta$ then $X \in A\perp(\alpha\&\beta)$. We can conclude that $A\perp\alpha \cup A\perp\beta \subseteq A\perp(\alpha\&\beta)$. ■

To conclude this section, we are going to show that remainders of multiple rejectors can in a sense be 'reduced' to remainders of singleton rejectors. Every remainder of a multiple rejector is an intersection of a set of remainders of singleton rejectors:

OBSERVATION 1.47 *If $X \in A\perp B$ and $B \neq \emptyset$, then*

$$X = \bigcap\{Y \mid X \subseteq Y \in A\perp\beta \textit{ for some } \beta \in B\}.$$

Proof. Let $S = \{Y \mid X \subseteq Y \in A\perp\beta \text{ for some } \beta \in B\}$. Since $X \in A\perp B$, we can use the upper bound property to conclude that S is non-empty. It follows directly that $X \subseteq \bigcap S$.

In order to prove that $\bigcap S \subseteq X$, suppose to the contrary that there is some δ such that $\delta \in \bigcap S$ and $\delta \notin X$. It follows from $\delta \in \bigcap S$ that $\delta \in A$. We can conclude from $\delta \in A$, $\delta \notin X$, and $X \in A\perp B$ that there must be some $\varepsilon \in B$ such that $X \cup \{\delta\} \vdash \varepsilon$.

Since $X \subseteq A$ and $X \nvdash \varepsilon$, it follows by the upper bound property that there is some Z such that $X \subseteq Z \in A\perp\varepsilon$. By the definition of S, $Z \in S$.

Since $\delta \in \bigcap S$, it follows from $Z \in S$ that $\delta \in Z$. It follows from $X \subseteq Z, \delta \in Z$ and $X \cup \{\delta\} \vdash \varepsilon$ that $Z \vdash \varepsilon$, contrary to our assumption that $Z \in A\perp\varepsilon$. This contradiction concludes our proof that $\bigcap S \subseteq X$. ■

Exercises

26. Let p, q, r, and s be (logically independent) atomic sentences, and let Cn be purely truth-functional. Identify the following remainder sets:
    (a) $\{p, q\}\bot p\&q$
    (b) $\{p, q, r\}\bot p\&q$
    (c) $\{q\}\bot p\&q$
    (d) $\{p, q\lor r, q\lor\neg r\}\bot p\&q$
    (e) $\{p\&q, p\&\neg p\}\bot p\&q$
    (f) $\{p\lor r, p\lor\neg r, q\&s, q\&\neg s\}\bot p\&q$
    (g) $\{p\lor q, p\leftrightarrow q\}\bot p\&q$
    (h) $\{p\lor q, p\rightarrow q, q\rightarrow p\}\bot p\&q$
    (i) $\emptyset\bot p\&q$
    (j) $\emptyset\bot(p\lor\neg p)$
    (k) $\{p\&q\}\bot\{p, q\}$
    (l) $\{p\lor q\}\bot\{p, q\}$
    (m) $\{q, r\}\bot\{p, q\}$
    (n) $\{p\lor r, p\lor\neg r\}\bot\{p, q\}$
    (o) $\{p\lor q, p\rightarrow q, q\rightarrow p\}\bot\{p, q\}$
    (p) $\{p, q, r\}\bot\emptyset$
    (q) $\{p, \neg p\}\bot\emptyset$
    (r) $\{p, \neg p\}\bot\{r\}$
    (s) $\emptyset\bot\emptyset$.
27. Show that if $X \in A\bot(\alpha\lor\beta)$ then $\alpha \notin \text{Cn}(X)$.
28. Show that $A\bot B_1 \cap A\bot B_2 \subseteq A\bot(B_1 \cup B_2)$.
29. Show that $A\bot\alpha \cap A\bot\beta \subseteq A\bot(\alpha\&\beta)$.
30. Show that if $\vdash \alpha\rightarrow\beta$, $X \in A\bot\alpha$ and $Y \in A\bot\beta$, then $X \not\subset Y$.
31. Show that if $\emptyset \in A\bot B$, then $\{\emptyset\} = A\bot B$.
32. Show that for all finite sets X and Y, $X\bot Y = (\bigcup(X\bot Y))\bot Y$.
33. [43] Show that $X \in (A \cup \{\alpha\})\bot\neg\alpha$ holds if and only if $\alpha \in X \in (A \cup \{\alpha\})\bot\bot$.
34. Let α and β be two sentences such that $\alpha \vdash \beta$. Show that if $X \in A\bot\beta$, then there is some Y such that $X \subseteq Y \in A\bot\alpha$.
35. Show that if $A\bot\alpha = A\bot\beta$, then $A\bot\alpha = A\bot(\alpha\&\beta)$.
36. Show that for all sets A and B: $A\bot B = (A\backslash B)\bot(\text{Cn}(A) \cap B)$.
37. [25] The *choice remainder* operator is defined as follows: $X \in A\angle B$ if and only if:
    (i′) $X \subseteq A$
    (ii′) $B \not\subseteq \text{Cn}(X)$
    (iii′) There is no set X' such that $X \subset X' \subseteq A$ and $B \not\subseteq \text{Cn}(X')$.
    a. Prove that for all β, $A\angle\{\beta\} = A\bot\{\beta\}$.
    b. Show that it does not hold for all sets B that $A\angle B = A\bot B$.
    c. Show that if B is finite, then there is a sentence β such that $A\angle B = A\bot\{\beta\}$.

13⁺ REMAINDERS OF CLOSED PROGENITORS

In this section, we are going to apply the remainder operator to logically closed progenitors. This will give rise to new and stronger properties, that are particularly useful in the AGM model of belief change. In that model, selection functions are applied to sets of the form $A\perp\alpha$, where the progenitor A is logically closed and the rejector α is a single sentence.

Remainders of logically closed progenitors are themselves logically closed.

OBSERVATION 1.48 ([1]) *If A is logically closed and $X \in A\perp B$, then X is logically closed.*

Proof. Let A be logically closed, and let $X \in A\perp B$. It follows from Observation 1.36 that X is A-closed. We can conclude from the corollary of Observation 1.31 that X is logically closed. ■

By combining Observation 1.48 with Observation 1.25, that showed logical closure to be preserved under intersection, we obtain the important result that if S is a non-empty subset of $A\perp B$, then $\bigcap S$ is logically closed. It follows from this that the outcome of partial meet contraction of a logically closed set is itself logically closed.

Another important property of a remainder of a logically closed set is that it contains a disjunction of two elements of the progenitor if and only if it contains at least one of the disjuncts. The following observation proves a more general property, that holds for disjunctively closed sets, but it is the corollary on logically closed sets that we will have most use for.

OBSERVATION 1.49 *Let A and B be disjunctively closed sets, and let $X \in A\perp B$. Then it holds for all $\alpha_1, \alpha_2 \in A$ that $\alpha_1 \vee \alpha_2 \in X$ if and only if either $\alpha_1 \in X$ or $\alpha_2 \in X$.*

COROLLARY ([1]) Let $X \in A\perp\beta$ for some logically closed set A such that $\alpha_1, \alpha_2 \in A$. Then $\alpha_1 \vee \alpha_2 \in X$ if and only if either $\alpha_1 \in X$ or $\alpha_2 \in X$.

Proof. For one direction, let $\alpha_1 \vee \alpha_2 \in X$ and suppose to the contrary that $\alpha_1 \notin X$ and $\alpha_2 \notin X$. It follows from $\alpha_1 \in A, \alpha_1 \notin X$ and $X \in A\perp B$ that there is some $\beta_1 \in B$ such that $X \cup \{\alpha_1\} \vdash \beta_1$. In the same way we can see that there is some $\beta_2 \in B$ such that $X \cup \{\alpha_2\} \vdash \beta_2$.

It follows by the deduction property of Cn that $\alpha_1 \rightarrow \beta_1 \in \mathrm{Cn}(X)$ and $\alpha_2 \rightarrow \beta_2 \in \mathrm{Cn}(X)$. Since $\alpha_1 \rightarrow \beta_1$ and $\alpha_2 \rightarrow \beta_2$ together imply $\alpha_1 \vee \alpha_2 \rightarrow \beta_1 \vee \beta_2$, we then have $\alpha_1 \vee \alpha_2 \rightarrow \beta_1 \vee \beta_2 \in \mathrm{Cn}(X)$ and consequently by the deduction property $\beta_1 \vee \beta_2 \in \mathrm{Cn}(X \cup \{\alpha_1 \vee \alpha_2\})$. Since $\alpha_1 \vee \alpha_2 \in X$, this is equivalent to $\beta_1 \vee \beta_2 \in \mathrm{Cn}(X)$.

However, since B is closed under disjunction, this means that X implies an element of B, contrary to $X \in A \bot B$. We can conclude from this contradiction that either $\alpha_1 \in X$ or $\alpha_2 \in X$.

The other direction follows from Observation 1.36. ∎

To see how the corollary follows from the observation, just note that since A is logically closed and $\{\beta\}$ is a singleton, they are both disjunctively closed.

The following observation will turn out to be useful in several of the proofs:

OBSERVATION 1.50 *Let A be a logically closed set such that $\alpha\&\beta \in A$. If $X \in A\bot(\alpha\&\beta)$, then exactly one of α, β, and $\alpha \leftrightarrow \beta$ is an element of X.*

Proof. We are first going to show that at least one of α, β, and $\alpha \leftrightarrow \beta$ is an element of X. Suppose that $\alpha \notin X$ and $\beta \notin X$. Our task is to show that $\alpha \leftrightarrow \beta \in X$.

It follows from $X \in A\bot(\alpha\&\beta)$ and $\alpha \notin X$ that $X \cup \{\alpha\} \vdash \alpha\&\beta$. By the deduction property we obtain $X \vdash \alpha \rightarrow \alpha\&\beta$, that is truth-functionally equivalent to $X \vdash \alpha \rightarrow \beta$.

Similarly, it follows from $X \in A\bot(\alpha\&\beta)$ and $\beta \notin X$ that $X \cup \{\beta\} \vdash \alpha\&\beta$. By the deduction property we obtain $X \vdash \beta \rightarrow \alpha\&\beta$, that is equivalent to $X \vdash \beta \rightarrow \alpha$.

It follows from $X \vdash \alpha \rightarrow \beta$ and $X \vdash \beta \rightarrow \alpha$ that $X \vdash \alpha \leftrightarrow \beta$. By the logical closure of X (Observation 1.48), $\alpha \leftrightarrow \beta \in X$.

It remains to be proved that no more than one of the three is an element of X. If more than one of α, β, and $\alpha \leftrightarrow \beta$ is an element of X, then one of the three sets $\{\alpha, \beta\}$, $\{\alpha, \alpha \leftrightarrow \beta\}$, and $\{\beta, \alpha \leftrightarrow \beta\}$, is a subset of X. Since each of these sets implies $\alpha\&\beta$, this contradicts $X \in A\bot(\alpha\&\beta)$. The contradiction concludes the proof. ∎

The following is a direct consequence of Observation 1.50:

OBSERVATION 1.51 (Alchourrón and Makinson [3]) *If A is a logically closed set such that $\alpha \in A$ and $X \in A\bot\alpha$, then for all sentences β: either $\alpha \vee \beta \in X$ or $\alpha \vee \neg\beta \in X$.*

Proof. Since α is logically equivalent to $(\alpha\vee\beta)\&(\alpha\vee\neg\beta)$, it follows from Observation 1.50 that either $\alpha\vee\beta$, $\alpha\vee\neg\beta$ or $\alpha\vee\beta \leftrightarrow \alpha\vee\neg\beta$ is an element of X. Since $\alpha\vee\beta \leftrightarrow \alpha\vee\neg\beta$ is logically equivalent to α, it can be concluded from $X \in A\bot\alpha$ that $\alpha\vee\beta \leftrightarrow \alpha\vee\neg\beta$ is not an element of X. We can therefore conclude that either $\alpha\vee\beta \in X$ or $\alpha\vee\neg\beta \in X$. ∎

One of the most important differences between the remainder sets of closed and non-closed progenitors is that the following observation holds only for the former:

OBSERVATION 1.52 (Recovery Lemma [42]) *Let A be a logically closed set and B a finite-based set. If $X \in A\bot B$ and $\beta \in A$ then $X \cup B \vdash \beta$.*

COROLLARY (Alchourrón and Makinson [3]) *Let A be a logically closed set. If $X \in A\perp\alpha$, and $\beta \in A$, then $\alpha\rightarrow\beta \in X$.*

Proof. If $B = \emptyset$, then $X = A$, from which $X \cup B \vdash \beta$ follows directly. For the principal case, when $B \neq \emptyset$, let $S = \{Y \mid X \subseteq Y \in A\perp\alpha$ for some $\alpha \in B\}$.

It follows from Observation 1.47 that $X = \bigcap S$.

Next, let $Y \in A\perp\alpha$ for some $\alpha \in B$. We are going to prove that $\alpha\rightarrow\beta \in Y$. Suppose to the contrary that $\alpha\rightarrow\beta \notin Y$. Since $\beta \in A$, it follows by the logical closure of A that $\alpha\rightarrow\beta \in A$. It follows from $\alpha\rightarrow\beta \in A$, $\alpha\rightarrow\beta \notin Y$, and $Y \in A\perp\alpha$ that $Y \cup \{\alpha\rightarrow\beta\} \vdash \alpha$. By deduction, $Y \vdash (\alpha\rightarrow\beta)\rightarrow\alpha$, which is truth-functionally equivalent to $Y \vdash \alpha$. This contradicts $Y \in A\perp\alpha$, and we may conclude that $\alpha\rightarrow\beta \in Y$.

Since $\&B\rightarrow\alpha$ is logically true, it follows from $\alpha\rightarrow\beta \in Y$ that $\&B\rightarrow\beta \in \text{Cn}(Y)$. By the logical closure of Y (Observation 1.48), $\&B\rightarrow\beta \in Y$.

We have proved that $\&B\rightarrow\beta \in Y$ holds for all $Y \in S$. It follows that $\&B\rightarrow\beta \in \bigcap S$. Since $X = \bigcap S$, we have $\&B\rightarrow\beta \in X$. It follows by deduction from $X \vdash \&B\rightarrow\beta$ that $X \cup \{\&B\} \vdash \beta$, and consequently $X \cup B \vdash \beta$, as desired. ■

The corollary to Observation 1.52 was proved by Carlos Alchourrón and David Makinson in 1982. This result had a central role in the development of the AGM model. (The full force of Observation 1.52 is needed in studies of multiple contraction of logically closed sets.)

In the course of preparing their classic 1985 paper, the AGM trio discovered a lemma with which they could substantially shorten several of their proofs. Between themselves, they called it the 'yellow lemma', since a yellow pen was used by one of the authors to mark the parts of the proofs that could be replaced by reference to the lemma. This is the 'yellow lemma':

OBSERVATION 1.53 (AGM [1]) *Let A be a logically closed set. If $X \in A\perp\alpha$, then $X \in A\perp\beta$ for all $\beta \in A\backslash X$.*

Proof. Let A be a logically closed set, and let $X \in A\perp\alpha$ and $\beta \in A\backslash X$. We are going to show that $X \in A\perp\beta$. This will be done in the usual way, i.e. by showing that the three conditions of Definition 1.35 are satisfied. We have $X \subseteq A$ from $X \in A\perp\alpha$, so that (i) is satisfied.

Since X is logically closed, it follows from $\beta \notin X$ that $\beta \notin \text{Cn}(X)$, so that (ii) is satisfied.

For (iii), suppose to the contrary that there is some Y such that $X \subset Y \subseteq A$ and $Y \nvdash \beta$. It follows from $X \subset Y \subseteq A$ and $X \in A\perp\alpha$ that $Y \vdash \alpha$. It follows by Observation 1.52 (the recovery lemma) from $X \in A\perp\alpha$ and $\beta \in A$ that $\alpha\rightarrow\beta \in X$, and from $X \subset Y$ that $Y \vdash \alpha\rightarrow\beta$. From $Y \vdash \alpha$ and $Y \vdash \alpha\rightarrow\beta$ we obtain $Y \vdash \beta$, contrary to the definition by which Y was introduced. It follows that there can be no Y such that $X \subset Y \subseteq A$ and $Y \nvdash \beta$, i.e. that (iii) is satisfied. ■

One might wish to generalize Observation 1.53 by replacing α by a set of sentences. This, however, cannot be done. For a simple counter-example, let the language consist of the atomic sentences p and q and their truth-functional combinations, and let Cn be purely truth-functional. Let $A = \text{Cn}(\{p\&q\})$ and $X = \{p\vee q, \top\}$ It is an easy exercise to verify that $X \in A\bot\{p, q\}$. We also have $p \in A\backslash X$. However, $X \in A\bot\{p\}$ does not hold. Condition (iii) of Definition 1.35 is not satisfied, as can be seen from $X \subset \{q, p\vee q, \top\} \subseteq A$ and $\{q, p\vee q, \top\} \nvdash p$.

Observation 1.53 can be used to prove the following:

OBSERVATION 1.54 *Let A be a logically closed set and let $\alpha \in A$ and $\beta \in A$. Then: $A\bot\alpha \subseteq A\bot\beta$ if and only if $\vdash \beta\rightarrow\alpha$.*

Proof. For one direction, let $A\bot\alpha \subseteq A\bot\beta$. Suppose to the contrary that $\nvdash \beta\rightarrow\alpha$. Since $\beta\rightarrow(\beta\rightarrow\alpha)$ is equivalent with $\beta\rightarrow\alpha$, we then have $\nvdash \beta\rightarrow(\beta\rightarrow\alpha)$. It follows (by the deduction property of Cn) that $\{\beta\} \nvdash \beta\rightarrow\alpha$. From this, and $\{\beta\} \subseteq A$, it follows by the upper bound property that there is some set Z such that $\{\beta\} \subseteq Z \in A\bot(\beta\rightarrow\alpha)$. Since α logically implies $\beta\rightarrow\alpha$, $\alpha \notin Z$, and we obtain from Observation 1.53 that $Z \in A\bot\alpha$. Since $\beta \in Z$ we also have $Z \notin A\bot\beta$, so that $A\bot\alpha \nsubseteq A\bot\beta$, contrary to the conditions. We can conclude from this contradiction that $\vdash \beta\rightarrow\alpha$.

For the other direction, suppose that $\vdash \beta\rightarrow\alpha$, and let $X \in A\bot\alpha$. Then $\beta \notin X$ (since otherwise X would imply α), and we can conclude from Observation 1.53 that $X \in A\bot\beta$. ■

We now have enough tools to prove the following results on remainder sets with closed progenitors and conjunctive or disjunctive restrictors:

OBSERVATION 1.55 (AGM [1]) *Let A be a logically closed set and let α and β be elements of A. Then: $A\bot(\alpha\&\beta) = A\bot\alpha \cup A\bot\beta$.*

Proof. It follows from Observation 1.45 that $A\bot(\alpha\&\beta) \subseteq A\bot\alpha \cup A\bot\beta$. Furthermore, it follows from Observation 1.54 that $A\bot\alpha \subseteq A\bot(\alpha\&\beta)$ and $A\bot\beta \subseteq A\bot(\alpha\&\beta)$. It follows set-theoretically that $A\bot(\alpha\&\beta) = A\bot\alpha \cup A\bot\beta$. ■

OBSERVATION 1.56 (Hans Rott [116]) *Let A be a logically closed set and let α and β be elements of A. Then $A\bot(\alpha\vee\beta) = A\bot\alpha \cap A\bot\beta$.*

Proof. It follows from Observation 1.55 that $A\bot(\alpha\vee\beta) \subseteq A\bot\alpha \cap A\bot\beta$. In order to show that $A\bot\alpha \cap A\bot\beta \subseteq A\bot(\alpha\vee\beta)$, let $Y \in A\bot\alpha \cap A\bot\beta$. According to Observation 1.55, $Y \in A\bot(\alpha\&\beta)$.

It follows by Observation 1.50 from $Y \in A\bot(\alpha\&\beta)$ and $\alpha\&\beta \in A$ that one of the sentences α, β, and $\alpha\leftrightarrow\beta$ is an element of Y. Since $Y \in A\bot\alpha$, $\alpha \notin Y$. Since $Y \in A\bot\beta$, $\beta \notin Y$. We may conclude that $\alpha\leftrightarrow\beta \in Y$.

Next, suppose that $\alpha\vee\beta \in Y$. It would then follow truth-functionally from $\alpha\leftrightarrow\beta \in Y$ and $\alpha\vee\beta \in Y$ that $\alpha\&\beta \in \mathrm{Cn}(Y)$. This contradicts our assumption that $Y \in A\perp\alpha$ (and likewise our assumption that $Y \in A\perp\beta$). We can therefore conclude that $\alpha\vee\beta \notin Y$.

It follows from $\alpha \in A$, by the logical closure of A, that $\alpha\vee\beta \in A$. We now have $Y \in A\perp\alpha$ and $\alpha\vee\beta \in A\setminus Y$. It follows from Observation 1.53 that $Y \in A\perp(\alpha\vee\beta)$. Since this holds for all $Y \in A\perp\alpha \cap A\perp\beta$, we have completed our proof that $A\perp\alpha \cap A\perp\beta \subseteq A\perp(\alpha\vee\beta)$. ■

Exercises

38. Let the language consist of the atomic sentences p and q and their truth-functional combinations, and let Cn be purely truth-functional. (Cf. Section 1.11^{+} and Figure 1.1.) Let $A = \mathrm{Cn}(\{p\&q\})$. Identify the following remainder sets:

    (a) $A\perp(p\&q)$
    (b) $A\perp p$
    (c) $A\perp(p\leftrightarrow q)$
    (d) $A\perp(q\rightarrow p)$
    (e) $A\perp(p\vee q)$
    (f) $A\perp\{p, p\vee q\}$
    (g) $A\perp\{p, q\}$
    (h) $A\perp\{p\leftrightarrow q, p\vee q\}$
    (i) $A\perp\{p, q, p\leftrightarrow q\}$

39. Let A be a logically closed set and let $\alpha \in A$ and $\beta \in A$. Show that $A\perp(\alpha\vee\beta) \subseteq A\perp(\alpha\&\beta)$.

40. Show that if A is a logically closed set, $\alpha \in A$, and $X \in A\perp\alpha$, then $A = \mathrm{Cn}(X \cup \{\alpha\})$.

41. Let A be a logically closed set and let $X \in A\perp\alpha$. Show that if $\beta \in A\setminus X$, then $\mathrm{Cn}(X \cup \{\neg\alpha\}) \subseteq \mathrm{Cn}(X \cup \{\neg\beta\})$.

42. Let A be a logically closed set, and let $X \in A\perp\alpha$ and $X \subset Y \subset A$. Show that $Y \neq \mathrm{Cn}(Y)$.

43. Let A be a logically closed set, such that $\alpha, \beta \in A$. Furthermore, let $X \in A\perp\alpha$. Show that $\beta \in X$ if and only if $\alpha\vee\beta \in X$.

44. Let $\alpha \in A = \mathrm{Cn}(\{\kappa\})$. Show that $X \in A\perp\alpha$ if and only if $\alpha \notin X \in A\perp\kappa$.

45. The corollary of Observation 1.52 can be proved in a much simpler way if we prove it directly, without the more general result of the observation. Show how.

46. Show that if A is logically closed, then there are no sets B_1 and B_2 and sentences α and β such that $B_1 \subset B_2$, $B_1 \in A\perp\alpha$, and $B_2 \in A\perp\beta$.

47. Show that if B is logically closed, then $A\perp B = \emptyset$.

14+ REMAINDERS OF THE LANGUAGE

The largest progenitor from which we can construct remainders is the language itself. Remainders of the language by single sentences, i.e. sets X such that $X \in \mathcal{L}\perp\alpha$ for some α, do not represent plausible sets of beliefs, but they are useful as tools of logic. As will be seen in this section, they have nice properties that make them simple to work with.

Since the language is logically closed, all the properties of remainders with closed progenitors apply to remainders of the language. As a simple example of this, if $X \in \mathcal{L}\perp\alpha$ then X is logically closed.

If $X \in \mathcal{L}\perp\alpha$ for some α, then $X \nvdash \perp$. It follows from Observation 1.53 that $X \in \mathcal{L}\perp\perp$. Therefore

$$\mathcal{L}\perp\perp = \{X \mid X \in \mathcal{L}\perp\alpha \text{ for some } \alpha\},$$

and we can refer to $\mathcal{L}\perp\perp$ as the set of remainders (by single sentences) of the language. The following observation introduces some of the most important properties of the elements of $\mathcal{L}\perp\perp$.

OBSERVATION 1.57 *Let $X \in \mathcal{L}\perp\perp$. Then for all sentences α and β:*

1. *Either $\alpha \in X$ or $\neg\alpha \in X$.*
2. *$\alpha \notin X$ if and only if: $\neg\alpha \in X$.*
3. *$\alpha\vee\beta \in X$ if and only if: either $\alpha \in X$ or $\beta \in X$.*
4. *$\alpha\rightarrow\beta \in X$ if and only if: if $\alpha \in X$, then $\beta \in X$.*

Proof. (1–2) Since $\perp$ is equivalent to $\alpha\&\neg\alpha$ it follows from Observation 1.50 that exactly one of α, $\neg\alpha$ and $\alpha\leftrightarrow\neg\alpha$ is an element of X. Since $\alpha\leftrightarrow\neg\alpha$ is equivalent to $\perp$, the third alternative is excluded. Hence, exactly one of $\alpha \in X$ and $\neg\alpha \in X$ holds.
(3) From Observation 1.49 (the corollary).
(4) Since $\alpha\rightarrow\beta$ is logically equivalent with $\neg\alpha\vee\beta$, it follows from Part 3 that $\alpha\rightarrow\beta$ $\in X$ holds if and only if either $\neg\alpha \in X$ or $\beta \in X$, thus according to Part 2 if and only if either $\alpha \notin X$ or $\beta \in X$, thus if and only if: if $\alpha \in X$, then $\beta \in X$. ■

In ordinary logical parlance, the elements of $\mathcal{L}\perp\perp$ are called *maximal consistent sets* or *possible worlds*. They are the largest consistent sets that the logic allows for; if $X \in \mathcal{L}\perp\perp$, then for every set Y: if $X \subset Y$, then Y is inconsistent.

As a direct consequence of the foregoing observation, we obtain the following:

OBSERVATION 1.58 *$X \in \mathcal{L}\perp\alpha$ if and $\neg\alpha \in X \in \mathcal{L}\perp\perp$.*

Proof. For one direction, suppose that $X \in \mathcal{L}\perp\alpha$. Then it follows that $\alpha \notin X$ and from Observation 1.57, Part 2, that $\neg\alpha \in X$. It follows from Observation 1.53 that $X \in \mathcal{L}\perp\perp$.

For the other direction, let $\neg\alpha \in X \in \mathcal{L}\perp\perp$. It follows from the consistency of X that $\alpha \notin X$, and then from Observation 1.53 that $X \in \mathcal{L}\perp\alpha$. ■

Two important connections make maximal consistent sets useful in belief dynamics. One of these is a connection between consistent logically closed sets (belief sets) and sets of maximal consistent sets. To introduce it, we need the following notation:

DEFINITION 1.59 *For any set A of sentences, $[A] = \{X \mid A \subseteq X \in \mathcal{L}\perp\perp\}$. $[\alpha]$ is an abbreviation of $[\{\alpha\}]$.*

Thus, $[A]$ is the set of maximal consistent sets that contain A.

OBSERVATION 1.60 *Let A be a consistent set of sentences. Then $\bigcap[A] = \mathrm{Cn}(A)$.*

COROLLARY *If A is consistent and logically closed, then $\bigcap[A] = A$.*

Proof. For one direction, let $\alpha \in \bigcap[A]$. Suppose that $\alpha \notin \mathrm{Cn}(A)$. Then $A \cup \{\neg\alpha\}$ is consistent, and it follows by the upper bound property that there is some X such that $A \cup \{\neg\alpha\} \subseteq X \in \mathcal{L}\perp\perp$. It follows that $X \in [A]$. Since $\alpha \notin X$ it then follows that $\alpha \notin \bigcap[A]$, contrary to the conditions. We can conclude from this contradiction that $\alpha \in \mathrm{Cn}(A)$.

For the other direction, let $\alpha \in \mathrm{Cn}(A)$. For each $Y \in [A]$ it follows from $A \subseteq Y$ that $\mathrm{Cn}(A) \subseteq \mathrm{Cn}(Y)$. Since Y is logically closed, we have $\alpha \in \mathrm{Cn}(A) \subseteq \mathrm{Cn}(Y) = Y$. This holds for all $Y \in [A]$, and consequently $\alpha \in \bigcap[A]$. ■

The corollary provides us with a one-to-one correspondence (bijection) between on the one hand sets that are consistent and logically closed, and on the other hand subsets of $\mathcal{L}\perp\perp$, i.e. sets of maximal consistent sets. The only logically closed set that is not covered by this correspondence is the only set that is inconsistent and logically closed, i.e. $\mathcal{L}$ itself. By letting $\bigcap\emptyset = \mathcal{L}$, we can obtain a full correspondence for all logically closed sets. (Note that $[\mathcal{L}] = \emptyset$.) This correspondence has nice properties:

OBSERVATION 1.61 *Let A and B be logically closed sets. Then:*

1. $[A] = [B]$ *iff* $A = B$.
2. $[A] \subseteq [B]$ *iff* $B \subseteq A$.
3. $[A] \subset [B]$ *iff* $B \subset A$.

4. $[A \cup B] = [A] \cap [B]$.

Proof. *Part 1:* If $[A] = [B]$ then $\bigcap[A] = \bigcap[B]$, and it follows from Observation 1.60 that $A = \bigcap[A] = \bigcap[B] = B$. The other direction is trivial.

Part 2: For one direction, suppose that $[A] \subseteq [B]$. It then follows from set theory that $\bigcap[B] \subseteq \bigcap[A]$, i.e. from Observation 1.60, $B \subseteq A$.

For the other direction, let $B \subseteq A$, and let $X \in [A]$, i.e. $A \subseteq X \in \mathcal{L}\bot^{\bot}$. It follows that $B \subseteq X \in \mathcal{L}\bot^{\bot}$, i.e. $X \in [B]$.

Part 3: This follows from Part 2: $[A] \subset [B]$ iff $([A] \subseteq [B])\&\neg([B] \subseteq [A])$ iff $(B \subseteq A)\&\neg(A \subseteq B)$ iff $B \subset A$.

Part 4: $[A \cup B] = \{X \mid A \cup B \subseteq X \in \mathcal{L}\bot^{\bot}\}$
$= \{X \mid A \subseteq X \in \mathcal{L}\bot^{\bot}\} \cap \{X \mid B \subseteq X \in \mathcal{L}\bot^{\bot}\} = [A] \cap [B]$. ■

The other connection that was promised above is a bijection between elements of $A\bot\alpha$ and elements of $\mathcal{L}\bot\alpha$. This connection was discovered by Adam Grove [41]. Let $X \in A\bot\alpha$. Then $X \subset A$, and by Observation 1.61, $[A] \subset [X]$. Due to the maximality of the remainder X, $[X]$ should be the outcome of a smallest possible addition to $[A]$ to ensure that the resulting set X does not imply α. Thus, we should expect that $[X] = [A] \cup W$ for some $W \in [\neg\alpha]$ (i.e. equivalently: for some $W \in \mathcal{L}\bot\alpha$). It is not difficult to prove that this is indeed correct:

OBSERVATION 1.62 (Adam Grove [41]) *Let A be a logically closed set and let $\alpha \in A$. Then $X \in A\bot\alpha$ if and only if there is some $W \in \mathcal{L}\bot\alpha$ such that* $[X] = [A] \cup W$.

Proof. *For one direction*, let $X \in A\bot\alpha$. Then $X \subset A$, and (by Observation 1.61) $[A] \subset [X]$. Suppose that there is some logically closed set Y such that $[A] \subset [Y] \subset [X]$. Then $X \subset Y \subset A$. This can be shown to be impossible, as follows: Let $\beta \in Y \backslash X$. Then $\beta \in A \backslash X$, and it follows from Observation 1.53 that $X \in A\bot\beta$, and thus from Observation 1.52 (the recovery lemma) that $\text{Cn}(X \cup \{\beta\}) = A$. Since $X \cup \{\beta\} \subseteq Y = \text{Cn}(Y))$ we obtain $A = \text{Cn}(X \cup \{\beta\}) \subseteq \text{Cn}(Y) = Y$, contrary to $Y \subset A$. It follows from this contradiction that there is no set Y with the desired properties. From this it can be concluded that $[X] = [A] \cup W$ for some $W \in \mathcal{L}\bot^{\bot}$.

It remains to be shown that $W \in \mathcal{L}\bot\alpha$. Suppose not. Then (by Observation 1.57) $\alpha \in W$. Since $\alpha \in A = \bigcap[A]$ it would follow that $\alpha \in \bigcap([A] \cup W)$, i.e. $\alpha \in \bigcap[X] = X$, contrary to $X \in A\bot\alpha$. We can conclude from this contradiction that $W \in \mathcal{L}\bot\alpha$.

For the other direction, let $W \in \mathcal{L}\bot\alpha$ and $[X] = [A] \cup W$. We then have $X = \bigcap[X] = \bigcap([A] \cup W) = (\bigcap[A]) \cap W = A \cap W$. It remains to be shown that $A \cap W \in A\bot\alpha$. This is done, as usual, by showing that the three conditions of Definition 1.35 are satisfied. We have (i) $A \cap W \subseteq A$, and (ii) $A \cap W \nvdash \alpha$

(since $W \nvdash \alpha$). For (iii), let $\beta \in A \backslash (A \cap W)$. Suppose that $\beta \to \alpha \notin A \cap W$. We then have $\beta \notin W$ and (since $\alpha \in A$ so that $\beta \to \alpha \in A$) also $\beta \to \alpha \notin W$. It follows from Observation 1.57, Part 2, that $\neg\beta \in W$ and $\neg(\beta \to \alpha) \in W$, contrary to the logical consistency of W. We can conclude that $\beta \to \alpha \in A \cap W$. Hence, if $\beta \in A \backslash (A \cap W)$, then $(A \cap W) \cup \{\beta\} \vdash \alpha$. The proof that $A \cap W \in A \perp \alpha$ is completed. ■

This result can be further strengthened to a bijection (one-to-one) correspondence) between remainders with A and $\mathcal{L}$, respectively, as progenitors. The following notation can be used to state the bijection:

DEFINITION 1.63 ([25]) $A \Delta B = \{X \mid X \in A \perp \beta$ *for some* $\beta \in B\}$
$A \Delta B$ *is a* subremainder set, *and its elements are the* subremainders *of* A.

In particular, note that:

$$A \Delta A = \{X \mid X \in A \perp \alpha \text{ for some } \alpha \in A\}$$
$$\mathcal{L} \Delta A = \{X \mid X \in \mathcal{L} \perp \alpha \text{ for some } \alpha \in A\}$$

Grove's bijection can be expressed as a bijection between $A \Delta A$ and $\mathcal{L} \Delta A$.

OBSERVATION 1.64 (Grove's bijection [41]) *Let A be a logically closed set. Then there is a bijection (one-to-one correspondence) g_A from $A \Delta A$ to $\mathcal{L} \Delta A$ such that*
(I) for all $X \in A \Delta A$ and $\alpha \in A$: $X \in A \perp \alpha$ iff $g_A(X) \in \mathcal{L} \perp \alpha$.
(II) for all $Y \in \mathcal{L} \Delta A$: $g_A^{-1}(Y) = Y \cap A$.

Proof. For all $X \in A \Delta A$, let $g_A(X) = \text{Cn}(X \cup \{\neg\alpha\})$ for some $\alpha \in A \backslash X$. We need to show (1) that g_A is well-defined, (2) that (I) holds, (3) that g_A is a bijection, and (4) that (II) holds.

Part 1: We first have to show g_A is well-defined, i.e. that if $\alpha_1, \alpha_2 \in A \backslash X$, then $\text{Cn}(X \cup \{\neg\alpha_1\}) = \text{Cn}(X \cup \{\neg\alpha_2\})$. Let $\alpha_1, \alpha_2 \in A \backslash X$. Then it follows from Observation 1.53 that $X \in A \perp \alpha_1$. It follows from $\alpha_1 \in A \backslash X$ by Observation 1.52 (the recovery lemma) that $A \subseteq \text{Cn}(X \cup \{\alpha_1\})$ and consequently $\alpha_2 \in \text{Cn}(X \cup \{\alpha_1\})$. It follows by the deduction property of Cn that $\alpha_1 \to \alpha_2 \in \text{Cn}(X)$, which is equivalent to $\neg\alpha_2 \to \neg\alpha_1 \in \text{Cn}(X)$. By one more application of the deduction property, we obtain $\neg\alpha_1 \in \text{Cn}(X \cup \{\neg\alpha_2\})$, from which follows $\text{Cn}(X \cup \{\neg\alpha_1\}) \subseteq \text{Cn}(X \cup \{\neg\alpha_2\})$. In the same way we can show that $\text{Cn}(X \cup \{\neg\alpha_2\}) \subseteq \text{Cn}(X \cup \{\neg\alpha_1\})$. We thus have $\text{Cn}(X \cup \{\neg\alpha_1\}) = \text{Cn}(X \cup \{\neg\alpha_2\})$, which is what we needed to show that g_A is well- defined.

Part 2: For one direction, let $X \in A \perp \alpha$. We need to show that $\text{Cn}(X \cup \{\neg\alpha\}) \in \mathcal{L} \perp \alpha$. As usual, this will be done by showing that the three conditions of Definition 1.35 are satisfied. Clearly $\text{Cn}(X \cup \{\neg\alpha\}) \subseteq \mathcal{L}$, so that (i) is satisfied.

For (ii), suppose to the contrary that $\text{Cn}(X \cup \{\neg\alpha\}) \vdash \alpha$. Then $X \cup \{\neg\alpha\} \vdash \alpha$, and it follows by the deduction property that $X \vdash \neg\alpha \to \alpha$, or equivalently $X \vdash \alpha$, contrary to $X \in A\bot\alpha$. We may conclude that $\mathrm{Cn}(X \cup \{\neg\alpha\}) \nvdash \alpha$, so that (ii) holds.

For (iii), suppose that it does not hold. Then there must be some sentence β such that $\beta \notin \mathrm{Cn}(X \cup \{\neg\alpha\})$ and $\mathrm{Cn}(X \cup \{\neg\alpha, \beta\}) \nvdash \alpha$.

It follows from Observation 1.51 that either $\alpha\vee\beta \in X$ or $\alpha\vee\neg\beta \in X$. However, neither of these is possible. It follows from $\alpha\vee\beta \in X$ that $\beta \in \mathrm{Cn}(X \cup \{\neg\alpha\})$, contrary to the conditions for β. Similarly, it follows from $\alpha\vee\neg\beta \in X$ that $\alpha \in \mathrm{Cn}(X \cup \{\neg\alpha, \beta\})$, also contrary to the conditions for β. We can conclude that (iii) is satisfied, and in summary that $\mathrm{Cn}(X \cup \{\neg\alpha\}) \in \mathcal{L}\bot\alpha$.

For the other direction, let X be an element of $A\Delta A$ such that $g_A(X) \in \mathcal{L}\bot\alpha$. It follows from $X \in A\Delta A$ that there is some $\beta \in A$ such that $X \in A\bot\beta$. Thus $\beta \in A\backslash X$, and it follows from Part 1 of the present proof that $g_A(X) = \mathrm{Cn}(X \cup \{\neg\beta\})$. It follows from $\mathrm{Cn}(X \cup \{\neg\beta\}) \in \mathcal{L}\bot\alpha$ that $X \nvdash \alpha$. Using Observation 1.53, we can conclude from $X \in A\bot\beta, \alpha \in A$, and $\alpha \notin X$ that $X \in A\bot\alpha$.

Part 3: To show that g_A is a bijection, we need to show that for all X and Y in $A\Delta A$: if $X \neq Y$, then $g_A(X) \neq g_A(Y)$.

Let $X, Y \in A\Delta A$. Then $X \in A\bot\alpha$ and $Y \in A\bot\beta$ for some $\alpha, \beta \in A$. Let $X \neq Y$. Then there is some δ such that $\delta \in X\backslash Y$. It follows that $\delta \in A\backslash Y$. Using Part 1 of the present proof, we can conclude that $g_A(Y) = \mathrm{Cn}(Y \cup \{\neg\delta\})$. Furthermore, it follows from $\delta \in X$ that $\delta \in \mathrm{Cn}(X \cup \{\neg\alpha\}) = g_A(X)$. By Part 2 of the present proof, $g_A(X)$ and $g_A(Y)$ are both consistent, and we may conclude from $\delta \in g_A(X)$ and $\neg\delta \in g_A(Y)$ that $g_A(X) \neq g_A(Y)$.

Part 4. Let $Y \in \mathcal{L}\Delta A$. We need to show that $g_A(Y \cap A) = Y$, i.e. that if $\alpha \in A\backslash(Y \cap A)$, then $\mathrm{Cn}((Y \cap A) \cup \{\neg\alpha\}) = Y$.

For one direction, note that $\neg\alpha \in Y$ can be concluded from $\alpha \notin Y$. (Observation 1.57.) Since Y is logically closed, it follows that $\mathrm{Cn}((Y \cap A) \cup \{\neg\alpha\}) \subseteq Y$.

For the other direction, let $\beta \in Y$. Since $\alpha \in A$ we then have $\alpha\vee\beta \in Y \cap A$, hence $\beta \in \mathrm{Cn}(\{\neg\alpha, \alpha\vee\beta\}) \subseteq \mathrm{Cn}((Y \cap A) \cup \{\neg\alpha\})$. We can conclude that $Y \subseteq \mathrm{Cn}((Y \cap A) \cup \{\neg\alpha\})$. ■

Grove's bijection can be used to prove properties of remainder sets with closed progenitors in a simpler and more straight-forward way than what would otherwise be possible. It enables us to use the strong and simple properties of maximal consistent sets in the proofs, as can be seen from the following example:

OBSERVATION 1.65 (Hans Rott [116]) *Let A be a theory and let $\alpha, \beta \in A$. Then $A\bot(\beta\rightarrow\alpha) = (A\bot\alpha)\backslash(A\bot\beta)$.*

Proof. *Case 1*, $\beta\rightarrow\alpha \in \mathrm{Cn}(\emptyset)$: In this case, $A\bot(\beta\rightarrow\alpha) = \emptyset$. It follows from Observation 1.54 that $A\bot\alpha \subseteq A\bot\beta$, i.e. that $(A\bot\alpha)\backslash(A\bot\beta) = \emptyset$.

Case 2, $\beta\rightarrow\alpha \notin \mathrm{Cn}(\emptyset)$: We can use Grove's bijection:
$X \in A\bot(\beta\rightarrow\alpha)$

iff $g_A(X) \in \mathcal{L}\bot(\beta\rightarrow\alpha)$ (Grove's bijection)
iff $\neg(\beta\rightarrow\alpha) \in g_A(X)$ (Observation 1.58)
iff $(\beta\&\neg\alpha) \in g_A(X)$
iff $\beta \in g_A(X)$ and $\neg\alpha \in g_A(X)$
iff $\neg\beta \notin g_A(X)$ and $\neg\alpha \in g_A(X)$ (Observation 1.57)
iff $g_A(X) \notin \mathcal{L}\bot\beta$ and $g_A(X) \in \mathcal{L}\bot\alpha$ (Observation 1.58)
iff $X \notin A\bot\beta$ and $X \in A\bot\alpha$ (Grove's bijection)
iff $X \in (A\bot\alpha)\setminus(A\bot\beta)$. ■

Finally, the following compactness property for remainders can now be easily obtained:

OBSERVATION 1.66 (Remainder Compactness, Hans Rott [116]) *Let A be a logically closed set. Let α be a non-tautological element of A and let B be a subset of A, such that each element of B is non-tautological. If $A\bot\alpha \subseteq A\Delta B$, then there is some finite subset B' of B such that $A\bot\alpha \subseteq A\Delta B'$.*

Proof. Let $A\bot\alpha \subseteq A\Delta B$.

We are first going to show that $B \vdash \alpha$. Suppose that $B \nvdash \alpha$. It follows from the upper bound property that there is some W such that $B \subseteq W \in A\bot\alpha$. Then for all $\beta \in B$ we have $W \notin A\bot\beta$, hence $W \notin A\Delta B$ so that $A\bot\alpha \not\subseteq A\Delta B$. We can conclude from this contradiction that $B \vdash \alpha$.

It follows from compactness that there is a finite subset B' of B such that $B' \vdash \alpha$. Now let $X \in A\bot\alpha$. Then, since B' implies α, $B' \not\subseteq X$. Thus there is some $\beta \in B'$ such that $\beta \notin X$. It follows from Observation 1.53 that $X \in A\bot\beta$. Since this holds for all $X \in A\bot\alpha$, the proof is completed. ■

Exercises

48. Show that if $X \in \mathcal{L}\bot\bot$, then for all sentences α and β: $\alpha\leftrightarrow\beta \in X$ if and only if either $\alpha\&\beta \in X$ or $\neg\alpha\&\neg\beta \in X$.
49. Show that $[\alpha] = \mathcal{L}\bot\neg\alpha$.
50. Show that if $\alpha \in A = \mathrm{Cn}(A)$ and $X \in \mathcal{L}\bot\alpha$, then $A \cap X \in A\bot\alpha$.
51. For any finite and non-empty set B, let $n(B)$, the sentential negation of B, be the disjunction of the negated elements of B, i.e. if $B = \{\beta_1, \ldots, \beta_n\}$, then $n(B) = \neg\beta_1\vee\ldots\vee\neg\beta_n$. Show that $[B] = \mathcal{L}\bot n(B)$.
52. Show that:

    (a) $[\alpha] \subseteq [\beta]$ iff $\vdash \alpha\rightarrow\beta$.
    (b) $[\neg\alpha] = (\mathcal{L}\bot\bot)\setminus[\alpha]$.
    (c) $[\alpha\&\beta] = [\alpha] \cap [\beta]$.
    (d) $[\alpha\vee\beta] = [\alpha] \cup [\beta]$.

(e) $[\alpha \rightarrow \beta] = (\mathcal{L}\bot^{\bot})\backslash([\alpha]\backslash[\beta])$.

53. [116] Let A be a logically closed set and let $\alpha, \beta \in A\backslash\mathrm{Cn}(\emptyset)$. Use Grove's bijection in the same way as in Observation 1.65 to show:

(a) $A\bot(\alpha\&\beta) = A\bot\alpha \cup A\bot\beta$.

(b) $A\bot(\alpha\vee\beta) = A\bot\alpha \cap A\bot\beta$.

54. Does the following condition hold in general for subsets A and X of $\mathcal{L}$? If $X \in \mathcal{L}\bot A$, then for all $\delta \in \mathcal{L}$, either $\delta \in x$ or $\neg\delta \in X$.

55. Show that if A is logically closed and B is finite, then $A\Delta B = A\bot(\&B)$.

56. Let A be logically closed, and let $B \subseteq A$ and $D \subseteq A$. Show that if B is finite and $A\Delta B \subseteq A\Delta D$, then $A\Delta B \subseteq A\Delta D'$ for some finite subset D' of D.

15+ REMAINDER EQUATIONS

In some applications, we will need to construct, for two sets A and B, a rejector X such that $A \in B\bot X$. In doing this, we solve the 'equation' $A \in B\bot X$. The first question that one should ask when confronted with an equation is whether it does at all have a solution. The following observation provides a necessary and sufficient condition for this type of equation to have a solution, and it also provides a solution.

OBSERVATION 1.67 ([56]) *Let A be a consistent set of sentences and B any set of sentences. Then:*

1. If A is a B-closed subset of B, then $\{A\} = B\bot(B\backslash A)$.

2. The following three conditions are equivalent:

(a) A is a B-closed subset of B,

(b) There is some X such that $A \in B\bot X$, and

(c) There is some X such that $\{A\} = B\bot X$.

COROLLARY. *If there is some X such that $A \in B\bot X$, then there is some Y such that $\{A\} \in B\bot Y$.*

Proof. *Part 1*: Let A be a B-closed subset of B. We are first going to show that $A \in B\bot(B\backslash A)$, and after that we will show that A is the only element of $B\bot(B\backslash A)$. To show that $A \in B\bot(B\backslash A)$, we have to prove that the three conditions of Definition 1.35 are satisfied. We have $A \subseteq B$ by the conditions, so that (i) is satisfied.

For (ii), suppose to the contrary that A implies some element β of $B\backslash A$. Then $\beta \in \mathrm{Cn}(A)$. By the conditions, A is B-closed, i.e. $\mathrm{Cn}(A) \cap B \subseteq A$. Since $\beta \in \mathrm{Cn}(A)$ and $\beta \in B$, we may conclude that $\beta \in A$, contrary to the assumption that $\beta \in B\backslash A$. This contradiction is sufficient to prove (ii).

For (iii), suppose to the contrary that there is some set Y such that $A \subset Y \subseteq B$ and $\text{Cn}(Y) \cap (B \backslash A) = \emptyset$. It follows set-theoretically from $A \subset Y \subseteq B$ that $Y \cap (B \backslash A) \neq \emptyset$, so that by monotony $\text{Cn}(Y) \cap (B \backslash A) \neq \emptyset$. From this contradiction we may conclude that (iii) holds.

It remains to be shown that A is the only element of $B \perp (B \backslash A)$. Let $Z \in B \perp (B \backslash A)$. We are going to show that $Z = A$.

It follows from $Z \in B \perp (B \backslash A)$ that $Z \subseteq B$ and that $Z \cap (B \backslash A) = \emptyset$. From this it follows set- theoretically that $Z \subseteq A$. It follows from $Z \in B \perp (B \backslash A)$ and $A \in B \perp (B \backslash A)$ that $Z \not\subset A$, and we can conclude that $Z = A$.

Part 2: It follows from Part 1 of this observation that (a) implies (c). Clearly, (c) implies (b). That (b) implies (a) follows from Observation 1.36. We can conclude that the three conditions are equivalent. ■

Our equation can be generalized by replacing A by two sets A_1 and A_2, and requiring that

$$\{A_1, A_2\} = B \perp X,$$

or at least

$$\{A_1, A_2\} \subseteq B \perp X.$$

It is not difficult to see that even if both A_1 and A_2 are B-closed subsets of B, these equations do not always have a solution. If $A_1 \subset A_2$, then $\{A_1, A_2\} \subseteq B \perp X$ cannot hold. The equation is therefore insolvable if either (1) A_1 or A_2 is not a consistent B-closed subset of B, or (2) $A_1 \subset A_2$ or $A_2 \subset A_1$. The following observation shows that it is sufficient to exclude these two cases; in all other cases the equation is solvable.

OBSERVATION 1.68 ([48]) *Let A_1 and A_2 be consistent sets, and B a set of sentences. Then:*

1. *If A_1 and A_2 are B-closed subsets of B such that $A_1 \not\subset A_2 \not\subset A_1$, then $\{A_1, A_2\} = B \perp \{\beta_1 \& \beta_2 \mid (\beta_1 \in B \backslash A_1) \& (\beta_2 \in B \backslash A_2)\}$.*
2. *The following three conditions are equivalent:*
   - *(a) A_1 and A_2 are B-closed subsets of B such that $A_1 \not\subset A_2 \not\subset A_1$.*
   - *(b) There is some X such that $\{A_1, A_2\} \subseteq B \perp X$.*
   - *(c) There is some X such that $\{A_1, A_2\} = B \perp X$.*

Proof. *Part 1*. The case when $A_1 = A_2$ was proved in Observation 1.67, and we can therefore assume that $A_1 \neq A_2$. Let

$$X = \{\beta_1 \& \beta_2 \mid (\beta_1 \in B \backslash A_1) \& (\beta_2 \in B \backslash A_2)\}.$$

We are first going to show that $A_1 \in B \perp X$. To do this, we need to show that conditions (i)–(iii) of Definition 1.35 are satisfied. We already have $A_1 \subseteq B$, so that (i) is satisfied. For (ii), suppose to the contrary that A_1 implies some element of X. Since every element of X is a conjunction with an element of $B\backslash A_1$ as one of its conjuncts, this means that A_1 implies some element β of $B\backslash A_1$. We then have $\beta \in \mathrm{Cn}(A_1)$ and $\beta \in B\backslash A_1$. This, however, contradicts the B-closure of A_1. We can conclude that (ii) is satisfied.

For (iii), suppose to the contrary that it does not hold. Then there is a sentence $\delta \in B\backslash A_1$ such that $A_1 \cup \{\delta\}$ does not imply any element of X. It follows from the construction of X that for all $\beta_2 \in B\backslash A_2$, $A_1 \cup \{\delta\}$ does not imply $\delta \& \beta_2$, hence $A_1 \nvdash \beta_2$. Since this holds for all $\beta_2 \in B\backslash A_2$, we have $\mathrm{Cn}(A_1) \cap (B\backslash A_2) = \emptyset$. From this and $A_2 \subseteq B$ it follows set-theoretically that $\mathrm{Cn}(A_1) \cap B \subseteq A_2$. Since $A_1 \subseteq \mathrm{Cn}(A_1) \cap B$ it follows that $A_1 \subseteq A_2$, contrary to the conditions. From this contradiction it follows that (iii) is satisfied.

We have now proved that $A_1 \in B \bot X$. The proof that $A_2 \in B \bot X$ is similar. In order to prove that $\{A_1, A_2\} = B \bot X$ it remains to be shown that if $Z \in B \bot X$, then either $Z = A_1$ or $Z = A_2$.

Let $Z \in B \bot X$. It follows from Observation 1.36 that Z is a B-closed subset of B. Suppose that $Z \nsubseteq A_1$ and $Z \nsubseteq A_2$. Then there is some $\beta_1 \in Z$ such that $\beta_1 \in B\backslash A_1$ and some $\beta_2 \in Z$ such that $\beta_2 \in B\backslash A_2$. It follows from the construction of X that $\beta_1 \& \beta_2 \in X$. Since $Z \vdash \beta_1 \& \beta_2$, this contradicts $Z \in B \bot X$. We may conclude from this contradiction that either $Z \subseteq A_1$ or $Z \subseteq A_2$. Since an element of a remainder set cannot be a proper subset of another element of the same remainder set, we have $Z \not\subset A_1$ and $Z \not\subset A_2$. It follows from this that either $Z = A_1$ or $Z = A_2$, and we are done.

Part 2. Clearly, (c) implies (b). That (b) implies (a) follows from Observation 1.36. It follows from Part (1) that (a) implies (c). ■

Another interesting variation of our equation $A \in B \bot X$ is to require that X is a singleton (set with exactly one element). We then have the equation $A \in B \bot \xi$. It is not solvable for all sets A and B such that $A \in B \bot X$ can be solved. In other words, for two sets A and B it may be the case that there is some X such that $A \in B \bot X$, but no single sentence ξ such that $A \in B \bot \xi$.

In order to see this, let the language consist of the atomic sentences p and q and their truth-functional combinations, and let Cn represent purely truth-functional consequence. Furthermore, let $A = \{p \vee q\}$ and $B = \{p, q, p \vee q\}$. Then A is a B-closed subset of B. There is no difficulty in finding a set X such that $A \in B \bot X$: just let $X = \{p, q\}$.

On the other hand there is no sentence ξ such that $A \in B \bot \xi$. To see this, suppose to the contrary that ξ has this property. It then follows from $\{p \vee q\} \in \{p, q, p \vee q\} \bot \xi$, by Part (iii) of Definition 1.35, that $\{p \vee q, p\} \vdash \xi$. Since p logically implies $p \vee q$, this is equivalent to $\{p\} \vdash \xi$, and by the deduction theorem we obtain $\vdash p \rightarrow \xi$. It follows in the same way that $\vdash q \rightarrow \xi$. By truth-functional logic we may conclude from $\vdash p \rightarrow \xi$ and $\vdash q \rightarrow \xi$ that $\vdash p \vee q \rightarrow \xi$. By the deduction theorem,

$\{p \vee q\} \vdash \xi$, contrary to $\{p \vee q\} \in \{p, q, p \vee q\} \perp \xi$. This contradiction is sufficient to show that there is no ξ such that $A \in B \perp \xi$.

In order to adopt Observation 1.67 to singleton rejectors, we must strengthen the conditions. The following property can be used for that purpose:

DEFINITION 1.69 ([56]) *For any two sets A and B of sentences, A is detachably B-closed (detachably logically closed relative to B) if and only if for all sets W:*
If $W \subseteq B$ and $\bigvee(W) \in \mathrm{Cn}(A)$, then $W \cap A \neq \emptyset$,
where $\bigvee(W)$ is the disjunction of the elements of W.

Detachable B-closure implies B-closure. This can be seen by letting W be a singleton $\{\varepsilon\}$. We then obtain:

$$\text{If } \varepsilon \in B \text{ and } \varepsilon \in \mathrm{Cn}(A), \text{ then } \varepsilon \in A$$

which is the defining formula for B-closure.

Another immediate consequence of the definition is that if A is detachably B-closed for some (consistent or inconsistent) set B, then A is consistent. This can be seen by letting $W = \emptyset$ in the definition, and observing that $\bigvee(\emptyset) = \perp$.

OBSERVATION 1.70 ([56]) *Let A and B be two finite sets of sentences. Then:*

1. *If A is a detachably B-closed subset of B, then $\{A\} = B \perp (\bigvee(B \setminus A))$*
2. *The following three conditions are equivalent:*
   - *(a) A is a detachably B-closed subset of B,*
   - *(b) There is some ξ such that $A \in B \perp \xi$, and*
   - *(c) There is some ξ such that $\{A\} = B \perp \xi$.*

COROLLARY ([51]) *If $A \in B \perp \alpha$ and B is finite, then $\{A\} = B \perp \bigvee(B \setminus A)$.*

Proof. *Part 1*: Let A be a detachably B-closed subset of B. There are two cases, according to whether or not $B \setminus A = \emptyset$.

Case 1, $B \setminus A = \emptyset$: Then $A = B$ and $\bigvee(B \setminus A) = \perp$. Since A is detachably B-closed, it is consistent. We therefore have $\{A\} = B \perp \perp = B \perp (\bigvee(B \setminus A))$.

Case 2, $B \setminus A \neq \emptyset$: We are first going to show that $A \in B \perp (\bigvee(B \setminus A))$ by showing that the three conditions of Definition 1.35 are satisfied.

We have $A \subseteq B$ by the conditions, so that (i) is satisfied.

For (ii), suppose to the contrary that $A \vdash \bigvee(B \setminus A)$. We then have $B \setminus A \subseteq B, \bigvee(B \setminus A)) \in \mathrm{Cn}(A)$ and $(B \setminus A) \cap A = \emptyset$, contrary to the detachable B-closure of A. We can conclude from this contradiction that (ii) is satisfied.

For (iii), suppose to the contrary that there is some Y such that $A \subset Y \subseteq B$ and $Y \nvdash \bigvee(B \setminus A)$. This is clearly impossible, since it would follow from $A \subset Y \subseteq B$

that Y contains some element of $B\backslash A$ and consequently $Y \vdash \bigvee(B\backslash A)$. Thus, (iii) is satisfied.

We have now shown that $A \in B\perp(\bigvee(B\backslash A))$. Let $W \in B\perp(\bigvee(B\backslash A))$, in order to show that $\{A\} = B\perp(\bigvee(B\backslash A))$. Since all elements of $B\backslash A$ imply $\bigvee(B\backslash A)$, it follows from $W \in B\perp(\bigvee(B\backslash A))$ that $W \cap (B\backslash A) = \emptyset$. Since A and W are subsets of B, it follows set-theoretically that $W \subseteq A$. Since W and A are elements of the same remainder set, we have $W \not\subset A$, and consequently $W = A$. This concludes Part 1 of the proof.

Part 2: It follows from Part 1 that (a) implies (c), and it is obvious that (c) implies (b). In order to show that the three conditions are all equivalent, it is sufficient to show that (b) implies (a).

Suppose to the contrary that (b) holds but not (a). Then there are A, B and ξ such that $A \in B\perp\xi$ and A is not a detachably B-closed subset of B. There is then some W such that $W \subseteq B$, $\bigvee(W) \in \text{Cn}(A)$, and $W \cap A = \emptyset$. Let $W = \{\varepsilon_1, \ldots, \varepsilon_n\}$. For each ε_k it can be concluded from $A \in B\perp\xi$ and $\varepsilon_k \in B\backslash A$ that $A \cup \{\varepsilon_k\} \vdash \xi$. Thus, $A \vdash \varepsilon_k \rightarrow \xi$ for all ε_k. It follows truth-functionally that $A \vdash \varepsilon_1 \vee \ldots \vee \varepsilon_n \rightarrow \xi$, i.e. $A \vdash \bigvee(W) \rightarrow \xi$, and thus by the deduction property, $A \cup \{\bigvee(W)\} \vdash \xi$. Since $\bigvee(W) \in \text{Cn}(A)$, this is equivalent to $A \vdash \xi$, which contradicts $A \in B\perp\xi$. This contradiction concludes the proof. ■

OBSERVATION 1.71 ([51]) *If $A \in B\perp\alpha$ and B is finite, then:*
$\{A\} = B\perp(\bigvee(B\backslash A)) = B\perp(\alpha \vee \bigvee(B\backslash A)$.

The proof of Observation 1.71 is left to the reader as an exercise.

Finally, we are going to generalize the equation $A \in B\perp\xi$ by replacing A by a finite set of sets.

OBSERVATION 1.72 ([56]) *Let $A_1, \ldots, A_n$ and B be finite sets of sentences. Then:*

1. *If $A_1, \ldots, A_n$ are detachably B-closed subsets of B, such that $A_k \not\subset A_m \not\subset A_k$ for all $1 \leq k \leq m \leq n$, then:*
   $\{A_1, \ldots, A_n\} = B\perp((\bigvee(B\backslash A_1))\& \ldots \&(\bigvee(B\backslash A_n)))$.
2. *The following three conditions are equivalent:*
   - *(a) $A_1, \ldots, A_n$ are detachably B-closed subsets of B, and such that $A_k \not\subset A_m \not\subset A_k$ for all $1 \leq k \leq m \leq n$,*
   - *(b) There is some ξ such that $\{A_1, \ldots, A_n\} \subseteq B\perp\xi$, and*
   - *(c) There is some ξ such that $\{A_1, \ldots, A_n\} = B\perp\xi$.*

Proof. *Part 1*: Suppose that $A_1, \ldots, A_n$ are detachably B-closed subsets of B, such that $A_k \not\subset A_m \not\subset A_k$ for all $1 \leq k \leq m \leq n$. It follows from Observation 1.70 that $\{A_k\} = B\perp(\bigvee(B\backslash A_k))$ for all A_k. By repeated use of Observation 1.46, we obtain $\{A_1, \ldots, A_n\} = B\perp((\bigvee(B\backslash A_1))\& \ldots \&(\bigvee(B\backslash A_n)))$.

Part 2: It follows from Part 1 that (a) implies (c). Clearly, (c) implies (b). It only remains to be shown that (b) implies (a). Suppose that (b) is satisfied. It follows from Observation 1.70 that $A_1, \dots, A_n$ are all detachably B-closed. Furthermore, since $A_1, \dots, A_n$ are members of the same remainder set, $A_k \not\subseteq A_m \not\subseteq A_k$ holds for all A_k, A_m in $\{A_1, \dots, A_n\}$. This completes the proof. ■

Exercises

57. Given the sets A and B, provide a necessary and sufficient condition

    (a) for the existence of a set X such that $\{A\} = X \perp B$.

    (b) for the existence of a set X such that $A \in X \perp B$.

58. Given a set A, provide a necessary and sufficient condition

    (a) for the existence of sets X and Y such that $A \in X \perp Y$,

    (b) for the existence of sets X and Y such that $\{A\} = X \perp Y$.

59. Let the language be finite. Show that the following two conditions are equivalent:

    (a) There is some Y such that $\{A, \dots, A_n\} = (A_1 \cup \dots \cup A_n) \perp Y$

    (b) There are X and Y such that $\{A_1, \dots, A_n\} = X \perp Y$.

60. Given two sets A and B, provide a necessary and sufficient condition for the existence of two sets X and Y such that $\{A, B\} \subseteq X \perp Y$.

61. Let B be a finite set. Show that if $A_1 \in B \perp \alpha_1$ and $A_2 \in B \perp \alpha_2$, and $A_1 \not\subseteq A_2 \not\subseteq A_1$, then there is some β such that $\{A_1, A_2\} = B \perp \beta$.

62. [51] Prove Observation 1.71.

CHAPTER 2

GIVING UP BELIEFS

In this chapter, we are going to study operations of *contraction*. What does it mean to give up a belief in a rational way?

Belief sets are special cases of belief bases. Historically, formal results on belief sets have in most cases preceded corresponding results on belief bases. In this survey, however, since belief bases are the more general case, they provide the starting-point, and belief sets will be treated as an (important) special case.

The first section is devoted to the problem of finding good examples of belief contraction. In Sections 2.2–2.6 we are going to have a closer look at partial meet contraction. After that, some alternative approaches to contraction are introduced: Levi's saturatable and value-based contractions (2.7), kernel contraction and its important variant safe contraction (2.8–2.9), and contraction guided by a relation of epistemic entrenchment (2.10). Finally, in Section 2.11, we are going to investigate how the various approaches to belief contraction can cope with the problems of repeated contraction.

1 PURE AND IMPURE CONTRACTION

Can you give an example of belief contraction? At first, this seems to be a simple task. It is easy to come up with examples in which beliefs have been lost:

> **Example**
> When I came home yesterday, I believed that my copy of Rousseau's *The Social Contract* was on the kitchen table. When I saw the empty kitchen table, I gave up that belief.

Although a belief is given up in this example, this is not a case of belief contraction (in the common technical sense of that term). Seeing the table, I realized that the book was not there. This new belief replaced the old belief to the contrary. This is revision, not contraction. In 'pure' contraction, a belief should be given up without being replaced by any new belief.

Examples

1. I previously believed that the dinosaurs died out due to sudden climatic change (α). Then I was told by a geologist that this is only one out of several competing hypotheses. I have therefore given up my belief in α, but I do not believe in $\neg\alpha$ either.
2. 'The Johnsons must be at home', I said to David. 'The lights are on in their house.'—'They always leave the lights on when they leave the house, in order to ward off burglars', he said. I then gave up my belief that the Johnsons are at home.

In both these cases a belief is rejected, without its negation being accepted instead. Strictly speaking, however, neither of them is a case of pure contraction. In the first example a new belief was acquired to the effect that there are several competing scientific hypotheses on the extinction of the dinosaurs. In the second case, rejection was caused by the new belief that the Johnsons leave the lights on when they go away.

It is, indeed, difficult to find an example of *pure* contraction, in which no new belief is accepted. When we give up a belief, this is typically because we have learnt something new that forces the old belief out. In the literature on belief dynamics, examples such as the last two ones are often interpreted as referring to (pure) contraction. The new belief that gave rise to contraction is neglected, and is not included in the (idealized) new belief set. This is an imprecise but convenient convention, that makes it much easier to find examples of contraction.

A certain type of hypothetical belief change has often been taken to exemplify pure contraction.

Example

'You do not share my belief that there will be an economic recession next year. For the sake of argument, let us assume that we do not know whether that is true or not...'

We sometimes hypothetically give up a belief in order to give a contradictory belief a hearing. Such *contractions for the sake of argument* have sometimes been taken to be pure contractions [24; 25; 73]. However, their value as examples is controversial, since these contractions are not seriously undertaken by the agent.

The evasiveness of pure contraction should not lead us to believe that contraction is unimportant. Contraction is an essential element of rational belief change. It typically occurs as a part of more complex changes that involve both losses and acquisitions of information. For the formal analysis, it is useful to develop models of pure contraction, i.e. contraction that is not accompanied by any incorporation of new beliefs. In order to guide the formal analysis we need to find as good intuitive examples as possible of pure contraction. Since the contractive parts of complex belief changes cannot be perfectly isolated, some amount of idealization is necessary.

2 SOME BASIC POSTULATES

Contraction should be successful, i.e. the result of contracting a belief base A by a sentence α should be a new belief base that does not imply α. As a first approximation, an operator $\div$ of contraction for A should satisfy the condition that for all sentences α:

$$\alpha \notin \mathrm{Cn}(A \div \alpha)$$

This is, however, a too strong requirement. Let α be a tautology. Then $\alpha \in \mathrm{Cn}(B)$ holds for every set B (including the empty set). It follows that $\alpha \notin \mathrm{Cn}(A \div \alpha)$ cannot hold. We can only require that $\alpha \notin \mathrm{Cn}(A \div \alpha)$ if α is not logically true, i.e. if it is not an element of $\mathrm{Cn}(\emptyset)$. The success postulate (as proposed by Peter Gärdenfors) is therefore conditional on α not being logically true.

Success: [31]
If $\alpha \notin \mathrm{Cn}(\emptyset)$, then $\alpha \notin \mathrm{Cn}(A \div \alpha)$.

The success postulate prohibits implausible operations such as:

$$\{p, q\} \div p = \{p, q\}$$

There are other implausible candidates for contraction that the success postulate does not exclude, such as:

$$\{p, q\} \div p = \{q, r\}$$

This is not a case of (pure) contraction, since a new belief (r) has been added. In general, we want the contracted set to be a subset of the original one:

Inclusion: [31]
$A \div \alpha \subseteq A$.

Together, success and inclusion signify that the outcome of a contraction is a *subset of the original set that does not, if this can be avoided, imply the sentence to be contracted.* These two basic properties provide a convenient demarcation of contractions from other types of belief change:

DEFINITION 2.1 *An operator $\div$ for a set A is an operator of* contraction *if and only if it satisfies success and inclusion.*

Next, let us consider two limiting cases (extreme cases) of contraction. The first of these is the case when α is logically true. (We have already made an exemption from the success postulate for this case.) The conventional treatment of this case follows the maxim: When demanded to do the impossible, do nothing. In other words, if required to take away something that cannot be taken away, then we should leave the original set unchanged. This idea is codified in the following postulate:

Failure: [25]
If $\alpha \in \text{Cn}(\emptyset)$, then $A \div \alpha = A$.

In the other limiting case, the sentence to be contracted is not implied by the original belief set, e.g.:

$$\{p, q\} \div r$$

What should we do when required to take away something that is not there? A sensible answer is that such an operation should leave the original set unchanged. If you do not believe that reindeer are rodents, then the contraction of your belief base (or belief set) by that belief involves no change at all. Such contractions are idle (vacuous) operations. In our example:

$$\{p, q\} \div r = \{p, q\}$$

More generally, the following is a credible property of belief contraction:

Vacuity: [30]
If $\alpha \notin \text{Cn}(A)$, then $A \div \alpha = A$.

Let us now turn to the principal case of belief contraction, namely when the sentence α to be contracted from A is a non-tautological element of $\text{Cn}(A)$. According to the success postulate, enough of A is given up to ensure that $A \div \alpha$ does not imply α. However, belief change should not only be successful, it should also be minimal. (Cf. Section 1.5.) We need to make sure that we do not give up too much.

The following is one way to give precision to the rather vague notion of 'not giving up too much': The beliefs that we give up in order to contract A by α should all be such that they contributed to the fact that A, but not $A \div \alpha$, implies α. More precisely, for β to be deleted in the process of forming $A \div \alpha$ from A, there should be some order in which the elements of A can be removed, such that the removal of β is the crucial step through which α ceases to be logically implied. Thus, contractions such as

$$\{p, q, p \leftrightarrow q, r\} \div p = \{q\}$$

should not be accepted. This can be seen by trying out the six possible ways of going stepwise from $\{p, q, p \leftrightarrow q, r\}$ to $\{q\}$:

$$\begin{array}{lll}
\{p,q,p\leftrightarrow q,r\} & \{p,q,p\leftrightarrow q,r\} & \{p,q,p\leftrightarrow q,r\} \\
\{q,p\leftrightarrow q,r\} & \{q,p\leftrightarrow q,r\} & \{p,q,r\} \\
\{q,r\} & \{q,p\leftrightarrow q\} & \{q,r\} \\
\{q\} & \{q\} & \{q\}
\end{array}$$

$$\begin{array}{lll}
\{p,q,p\leftrightarrow q,r\} & \{p,q,p\leftrightarrow q,r\} & \{p,q,p\leftrightarrow q,r\} \\
\{p,q,r\} & \{p,q,p\leftrightarrow q\} & \{p,q,p\leftrightarrow q\} \\
\{p,q\} & \{q,p\leftrightarrow q\} & \{p,q\} \\
\{q\} & \{q\} & \{q\}
\end{array}$$

In none of these was the deletion of r the step in which the set ceased to imply p. This shows that r does not in any way contribute to the fact that $\{p,q,p\leftrightarrow q,r\}$ but not $\{q\}$ implies p. It therefore seems to have been deleted without good reason.

For another example, let us consider the contraction:

$$\{p,p\leftrightarrow q,q\}\div(p\&q)=\emptyset.$$

There are six routes from $\{p,p\leftrightarrow q,q\}$ to $\emptyset$:

$$\begin{array}{lll}
\{p,p\leftrightarrow q,q\} & \{p,p\leftrightarrow q,q\} & \{p,p\leftrightarrow q,q\} \\
\{p\leftrightarrow q,q\} & \{p\leftrightarrow q,q\} & \{p,q\} \\
\{q\} & \{p\leftrightarrow q\} & \{q\} \\
\emptyset & \emptyset & \emptyset
\end{array}$$

$$\begin{array}{lll}
\{p,p\leftrightarrow q,q\} & \{p,p\leftrightarrow q,q\} & \{p,p\leftrightarrow q,q\} \\
\{p,q\} & \{p,p\leftrightarrow q\} & \{p,p\leftrightarrow q\} \\
\{p\} & \{p\leftrightarrow q\} & \{p\} \\
\emptyset & \emptyset & \emptyset
\end{array}$$

In the first and sixth route, $p\&q$ ceased to be implied when $p\leftrightarrow q$ was deleted. In the second and fourth route, it ceased to be implied when q was deleted, and in the third and fifth route when p was deleted. Thus, all three deleted elements contribute to the fact that $\{p,p\leftrightarrow q,q\}$, but not $\emptyset$ implies $p\&q$. This contraction passed our test.

The formulation of the test in terms of various routes from A to $A\div\alpha$ is illustrative but cumbersome. In what follows we are going to use a more compact formulation, thas is based on the following postulation:

> An element β of A contributes to the fact that A but not $A\div\alpha$ implies α if and only if there is some set A' such that:

1. $A \div \alpha \subseteq A' \subseteq A$,
2. A' does not imply α, and
3. $A' \cup \{\beta\}$ implies α.

Using this criterion, we can now formulate a formal postulate that ensures that nothing is removed for no reason:

> *Relevance:* [42; 45]
> If $\beta \in A$ and $\beta \notin A \div \alpha$, then there is a set A' such that $A \div \alpha \subseteq A' \subseteq A$ and that $\alpha \notin \mathrm{Cn}(A')$ but $\alpha \in \mathrm{Cn}(A' \cup \{\beta\})$.

There is an obvious way to weaken the postulate of relevance: Instead of requiring A' to be interposed between $A \div \alpha$ and A, we may content ourselves with requiring that it be a subset of A:

> *Core-retainment:* [44]
> If $\beta \in A$ and $\beta \notin A \div \alpha$, then there is a set A' such that $A' \subseteq A$ and that $\alpha \notin \mathrm{Cn}(A')$ but $\alpha \in \mathrm{Cn}(A' \cup \{\beta\})$.

Core-retainment requires of an excluded sentence β that it in some way contributes to the fact that A implies α. (Relevance requires that it contributes to the fact that A, but not $A \div \alpha$, implies α.) The name has been chosen since the elements of A that do not at all contribute to making A imply α may be called the *α-core* of A. Core-retainment requires that for every sentence α, the α-core is left undisturbed in contraction by α.

When performing contraction on a belief base, we want the outcome to be a new belief base. Similarly, when contracting a belief set, we want to obtain a new belief set. The first of these conditions follows directly from the postulate of inclusion. All sets of sentences are belief bases, and inclusion guarantees that the outcome of contraction is a set of sentences (namely a subset of the original belief base). It is less self-evident, however, that the outcome of contracting a belief set will be a belief set. Contractions such as

$$\mathrm{Cn}(\{p, q\}) \div p = \{q\}$$

should not be accepted. (It would be more sensible to let the outcome be $\mathrm{Cn}(\{q\})$ in this case.) We can avoid this by postulating that logical closure be preserved under contraction:

> *Closure:* [30]
> If A is logically closed, then so is $A \div \alpha$ for all α.

It would not make sense to require that $A \div \alpha$ be logically closed except when A is so. Such a requirement would conflict with the postulate of inclusion. For let

$A = \{p\}$. Then if $A \div p$ is logically closed, it must contain $q \vee \neg q$. However, since $q \vee \neg q \notin A$, it follows by inclusion that $q \vee \neg q \notin A \div p$.

There is, however, a weaker closure postulate that is plausible for belief bases as well. To see that, let us consider a contraction operator $\div$ such that:

$$\{p, q, p \vee q\} \div p = \{q\}.$$

This does not seem to be a plausible outcome of contracting by p. q is retained in the contracted set, and q implies $p \vee q$. Therefore, it was unnecessary to remove $p \vee q$, that is anyhow implied by the contracted set. More generally, original beliefs that are implied by the contracted set should be elements of the contracted set:

Relative closure: [44]
$A \cap \mathrm{Cn}(A \div \alpha) \subseteq A \div \alpha$.

We have already tacitly assumed that logically equivalent formulae are treated alike. Thus, since $\neg\delta \vee \varepsilon$ and $\delta \rightarrow \varepsilon$ are logically equivalent, the outcome of contracting a belief base (or a belief set) by one of these sentences should be the same as that of contracting it by the other. In the formal language, we can express the logical equivalence of two sentences α and β by saying that $\alpha \leftrightarrow \beta$ is logically true. A sentence is logically true if and only if it can be derived from the empty set of premises. In other words, α and β are logically equivalent if and only if $\alpha \leftrightarrow \beta \in \mathrm{Cn}(\emptyset)$. The following postulate ensures that contractions by logically equivalent sentences yield the same result:

Extensionality: [31]
If $\alpha \leftrightarrow \beta \in \mathrm{Cn}(\emptyset)$, then $A \div \alpha = A \div \beta$.

A logic is extensional if it allows logically equivalent sentences to be freely substituted for each other. Our postulate of extensionality guarantees that the logic of contraction is extensional in this sense. (This postulate has also been called 'preservation', since it guarantees that logical equivalence is preserved [1].)

Extensionality rules out patterns such as the following (note that p and $p \& (q \vee \neg q)$ are logically equivalent):

$$\{r, r \rightarrow p\} \div p = \{r\}$$
$$\{r, r \rightarrow p\} \div (p \& (q \vee \neg q)) = \{r \rightarrow p\}.$$

On the other hand, extensionality does not prohibit the following pattern:

$$\{r, r \rightarrow p\} \div p = \{r\}$$
$$\{r, r \rightarrow p\} \div (p \vee q) = \{r \rightarrow p\}.$$

Nevertheless, this last pattern of contraction may seem strange. Although p and $p \vee q$ are not logically equivalent, they are 'equivalent' in terms of being implied by

$\{r, r \rightarrow p\}$ and its subsets. Any subset of $\{r, r \rightarrow p\}$ implies p if and only if it implies $p \vee q$. It does not seem unreasonable to require that p and $p \vee q$ should therefore be treated alike under contraction from $\{r, r \rightarrow p\}$. For the same reason, the following two contractions:

$$\{p, q\} \div q$$
$$\{p, q\} \div (p \rightarrow q)$$

should have the same outcome. (A subset of $\{p, q\}$ implies q if and only if it implies $p \rightarrow q$.) More generally, if two sentences α and β are implied by exactly the same subsets of A, then the outcomes of contracting by α and by β should be identical:

> *Uniformity:* [45]
> If it holds for all subsets A' of A that $\alpha \in \mathrm{Cn}(A')$ if and only if $\beta \in \mathrm{Cn}(A')$, then $A \div \alpha = A \div \beta$.

All the ten postulates that we have now introduced are satisfied by partial meet contraction. Indeed, the relationship works both ways: If an operation $\div$ on a set A satisfies these conditions, then it is a partial meet contraction. In formal language:

THEOREM 2.2 ([45]) *The operator $\div$ is an operator of partial meet contraction for a set A if and only if it satisfies the postulates of success, inclusion, relevance, and uniformity.*
[Proof: p. 125.]

This is a *representation theorem.* It shows that partial meet contraction represents the four listed postulates. To say that an operator $\div$ satisfies the four postulates is (logically speaking) the same as to say that it is a partial meet contraction (based on some selection function γ).

Representation theorems are also called *axiomatic characterizations*, since they characterize an operation (in this case partial meet contraction) in terms of axioms or postulates.

It was pointed out in Section 1.4 that we can choose between a 'constructive' and a 'black box' approach to belief dynamics. In a constructive approach to contraction, a mechanism for contraction is explicitly constructed. In a black box approach, we instead specify the properties that an operator should have (irrespective of how it is constructed). Representation theorems unite the two approaches, thereby improving our understanding both of the constructions and of the postulates.

We should not be surprised, though, if an operation constructed in some other way than partial meet contraction turns out to satisfy the four postulates of Theorem 2.2. This only shows that the same operation could also have been constructed as a partial meet contraction.

Of the ten postulates introduced in this section, only four were used in the representation theorem. The reason for this is that the remaining six postulates follow from these four:

OBSERVATION 2.3 *Let $\div$ be an operation on A. Then:*

1. *If $\div$ satisfies relevance, then it satisfies relative closure and core-retainment.*
2. *If $\div$ satisfies inclusion and core-retainment, then it satisfies failure and vacuity.*
3. *If $\div$ satisfies inclusion and relative closure, then it satisfies closure.*
4. *If $\div$ satifies uniformity, then it satisfies extensionality.*

[Proof: p. 112.]

Uniformity is stronger than extensionality, i.e. it implies extensionality, but is not implied by it. For logically closed sets, however, the two conditions are equivalent in the presence of vacuity.

OBSERVATION 2.4 *If an operator $\div$ for a logically closed set A satisfies extensionality and vacuity, then it satisfies uniformity.*
[Proof: p. 113.]

3 THEORY-CONTRACTION AND THE RECOVERY POSTULATE

One of the simplest sequences of changes is that of first giving up and then regaining one and the same belief:

Example
I believed that I had my latchkey on me (α). Then I felt in my left pocket, where I usually keep it, and did not find it. I lost my belief in α (but without starting to believe in $\neg\alpha$ instead). Half a second later, I found the key, and regained my belief in α.

The example roughly corresponds to a sequence of first contracting by a sentence α, and then expanding by the same sentence α. In this case, it seems reasonable to expect that this sequence leaves the belief state unchanged. In other words, expansion by α recovers what was lost when α was contracted. This property is called 'recovery', and has a central role in the AGM model of belief change.

Recovery: [31]
$A \subseteq \text{Cn}((A\div\alpha) \cup \{\alpha\})$.

Recovery does not hold in general for partial meet contraction of (non-closed) belief bases. To see this, let $A = \{p\&q\}$. Then it holds for any operator $\sim_\gamma$ of partial meet contraction that $A \sim_\gamma p = \emptyset$. Clearly, $p \& q \notin \text{Cn}(\emptyset \cup \{p\})$. We can conclude that $A \not\subseteq \text{Cn}((A \sim_\gamma p) \cup \{p\})$, so that recovery does not hold.

For partial meet contraction of belief sets, however, recovery is satisfied:

OBSERVATION 2.5 (AGM [1]) *Let A be a (logically closed) belief set and* $\sim_\gamma$ *an operator of partial meet contraction for A. Then for all sentences* $\alpha \in A$*:*
$A \subseteq \text{Cn}((A \sim_\gamma \alpha) \cup \{\alpha\})$,
i.e. recovery is satisfied.
[Proof: p. 123.]

Just like relevance, recovery serves to prevent unwarranted losses from the original belief set. According to recovery, so much is retained that everything can be recovered by reinstatement of the contracted sentence. As the following observation shows, relevance implies recovery, and in the presence of the postulates of closure, inclusion, and vacuity, the two conditions are equivalent:

OBSERVATION 2.6 ([25]) *Let A be a (logically closed) belief set and* $\div$ *an operator for A. Then:*

1. *If* $\div$ *satisfies relevance, then it satisifes recovery.*
2. *If* $\div$ *satisfies closure, inclusion, vacuity, and recovery, then it satisfies relevance.*

[Proof: p. 114.]

Recovery can be used instead of relevance in a representation theorem for partial meet contraction of belief sets:

THEOREM 2.7 (AGM [1]) *The operator* $\div$ *is an operator of partial meet contraction for a belief set A if and only if it satisfies the postulates of closure, inclusion, vacuity, success, extensionality, and recovery.*
[Proof: 131.]

This theorem is one of the central results of the AGM model. The six postulates referred to in the theorem are commonly called the *basic Gärdenfors postulates* (or basic AGM postulates).

How plausible is the postulate of recovery? Peter Gärdenfors has claimed that 'it is reasonable to require that we get all of the beliefs in A back again after first contracting and then expanding with respect to the same belief' [31]. On the other hand, another member of the AGM trio, David Makinson, has emphasized that recovery is the only of the six Gärdenfors postulates that is 'open to query from the point of view of acceptability under its intended reading' [83]. Several authors have argued against the recovery postulate as a general principle of belief contraction [24; 44; 49; 73; 79; 101]. The following two examples have been offered to show that recovery does not hold:

Example [44; 87]
I believe that 'Cleopatra had a son' (ϕ) and that 'Cleopatra had a daughter' (ψ), and thus also that 'Cleopatra had a child' ($\phi \vee \psi$, briefly κ). Then I receive information that makes me give up my belief in κ, and contract my belief set accordingly, forming $A \div \kappa$. Soon afterwards I learn from a reliable source that Cleopatra had a child. It seems perfectly reasonable for me to then add κ (i.e. $\phi \vee \psi$) to my set of beliefs without also reintroducing either ϕ or ψ.

Example [57]
I previously entertained the two beliefs 'George is a criminal (α) and 'George is a mass murderer' (β). When I received information that induced me to give up the first of these beliefs (α), the second (β) had to go as well (since α would otherwise follow from β).
I then received new information that made me accept the belief 'George is a shoplifter' (δ). The resulting new belief set is the expansion of $A \div \alpha$ by δ, $(A \div \alpha) + \delta$. Since α follows from δ, $(A \div \alpha) + \alpha$ is a subset of $(A \div \alpha) + \delta$. By recovery, $(A \div \alpha) + \alpha$ includes β, from which follows that $(A \div \alpha) + \delta$ includes β.
Thus, since I previously believed George to be a mass murderer, I cannot any longer believe him to be a shoplifter without believing him to be a mass murderer.

Due to the problematic character of the recovery postulate, David Makinson proposed a wider category of operators on belief sets. He defined a *withdrawal* as an operator that satisfies the other five basic Gärdenfors postulates, but not necessarily recovery:

DEFINITION 2.8 (David Makinson [83]) *An operator* $\div$ *on a belief set A is a* withdrawal *if and only if it satisfies closure, inclusion, vacuity, success, and extensionality.*

Clearly, all partial meet contractions on belief sets are withdrawals, but there are also withdrawals that are not partial meet contractions. As a rather extreme example, the operation defined as follows:

$$\text{If } \alpha \notin A, \text{ then } A \div \alpha = A$$
$$\text{If } \alpha \in A, \text{ then } A \div \alpha = \mathrm{Cn}(\emptyset)$$

is also a withdrawal. This is a truly annihilating operation. Whenever a belief is removed, all other non-tautological beliefs have to go with it. This is almost as far away from minimal contraction as we can get.

If we are not content with the recovery postulate, then just to give it up does not seem to be a satisfactory solution. It should be replaced by a weaker postulate that serves to prevent too drastic losses of previous beliefs.

Relevance would be an obvious candidate. However, as we saw above (Observation 2.6), a withdrawal on a logically closed set satisfies relevance if and only if it satisfies recovery. Perhaps surprisingly, core-retainment, the weakened version of relevance, cannot either be used to define a category of withdrawals that is distinct from partial meet contraction:

OBSERVATION 2.9 ([44]) *Let A be a belief set and $\div$ an operation on A. If $\div$ satisfies core-retainment, then it satisfies recovery.*
[Proof: p. 114.]

Since we already know that partial meet contraction satisfies core-retainment, it follows from this observation that a withdrawal on a logically closed set satisfies core-retainment if and only if it satisfies recovery (i.e. if and only if it is a partial meet contraction). This result is indeed disturbing, since it is not easy to find a weaker formalization than core-retainment of the intuition that beliefs that do not in any way contribute to the fact that A implies α should be retained in $A{\div}\alpha$. If a withdrawal satisfies this (seemingly weak) intuition, then it must—or at least so it seems—satisfy the intuitively much stronger postulate of recovery. This *pertinacity of the recovery postulate* is an important feature of the AGM framework. It can be used as an argument in favour of the recovery postulate: Since recovery follows from six highly plausible postulates (closure, inclusion, vacuity, success, extensionality, and core-retainment), recovery should be accepted 'as an emerging property, rather than as a fundamental postulate, of belief set contraction' [62].

The recovery issue will be taken up again in Chapter 4.

4 TWO LIMITING CASES

In Section 1.5, when first introducing partial meet contraction, we defined two limiting cases: full meet contraction and maxichoice contraction.

Full meet contraction is the case when the selection function is actually redundant, since for all non-tautological α, $\gamma(A\perp\alpha)$ is identical to $A\perp\alpha$. Full meet contraction represents an extremely cautious epistemic behaviour.

Extreme caution can also be expressed in terms of *cores*, as defined in Section 2.2: The α-core of a set A is the set of sentences in A that do not at all contribute to making A imply α. (A sentence β in A is an element of the α-core of A if and only if there is no subset A' of A such that A' does not imply α but $A'\cup\{\beta\}$ implies α.) An extremely cautious way to contract A by α is to give up everything in A except its α-core:

Core identity:
$\beta \in A \div \alpha$ if and only if $\beta \in A$ and there is no $A' \subseteq A$ such that $\alpha \notin \text{Cn}(A')$ and $\alpha \in \text{Cn}(A' \cup \{\beta\})$.

As can be seen from the following observation, core identity is a very powerful postulate. Single-handedly, it ensures that the operation is identical to full meet contraction.

OBSERVATION 2.10 *An operation $\div$ for a set A is an operation of full meet contraction if and only if it satisfies core identity.*
[Proof: p. 124.]

For (logically closed) belief sets, an alternative axiomatic characterization can be obtained with a simpler but less powerful postulate:

Meet identity: [1]
If $\alpha, \beta \in A$, then $(A \div \alpha) \cap (A \div \beta) = A \div (\alpha \& \beta)$.

Meet identity has also been called 'intersection' [1]. By adding it to the six basic Gärdenfors postulates, we obtain an axiomatic characterization of full meet contraction on belief sets:

THEOREM 2.11 (AGM [1]) *The operator $\div$ is an operator of full meet contraction for a belief set A if and only if it satisfies the postulates of closure, inclusion, vacuity, success, extensionality, recovery, and meet identity.*
[Proof: p. 133.]

Meet identity holds for full meet contraction of (logically closed) belief sets, but not for belief bases in general. This can be seen from the following example: Let $A = \{p, p \leftrightarrow q, p \vee q\}$, and let $\sim$ denote full meet contraction. We then have:

$$A \sim (p \rightarrow q) = \bigcap(A \perp (p \rightarrow q)) = \bigcap\{\{p, p \vee q\}\} = \{p, q \vee q\}$$
$$A \sim (q \rightarrow p) = \bigcap(A \perp (q \rightarrow p)) = \bigcap\{\{p \vee q\}\} = \{p \vee q\}$$
$$A \sim (p \leftrightarrow q) = \bigcap(A \perp (p \leftrightarrow q)) = \bigcap\{\{p, p \vee q\}\} = \{p, p \vee q\}$$

so that

$$(A \sim (p \rightarrow q)) \cap (A \sim (q \rightarrow p)) \neq (A \sim (p \leftrightarrow q)),$$

contrary to meet identity.

The following example shows that meet identity is not a plausible property of belief contraction:

Example
'To which classes of vertebrates do elephants and dolphins belong?' asked the biology teacher.
'Elephants are mammals, and dolphins are mammals too', said John. She looked at him as if waiting for him to correct his answer. This made him uncertain. However, he was quite sure that elephants are mammals, so he only doubted that dolphins are mammals.

Let α denote that elephants are mammals and β that dolphins are mammals. Under the influence of the teacher's nerve-racking behaviour, John contracted $\alpha\&\beta$ from his set of beliefs. However, when doing this he retained his belief in α. Thus $\alpha \in A{\div}(\alpha\&\beta)$. On the other hand, it follows from the success postulate that $\alpha \notin A{\div}\alpha$, and consequently (by set theory) that $\alpha \notin (A{\div}\alpha) \cap (A{\div}\beta)$. We therefore have $(A{\div}\alpha) \cap (A{\div}\beta) \neq A{\div}(\alpha\&\beta)$, so that meet identity does not hold.

The implausibility of full meet contraction on belief sets is further corroborated by the following formal result:

OBSERVATION 2.12 (Alchourrón and Makinson [3]) *Let A be a logically closed set and $\sim$ the operator of full meet contraction for A. Then for all sentences $\alpha \in A$:*

$$A \sim \alpha = A \cap \mathrm{Cn}(\{\neg\alpha\}).$$

[Proof: p. 125.]

It can be seen from this that full meet contraction, as applied to belief sets, is quite a drastic operation. It sacrifices beliefs that are, in an intuitive sense, completely unrelated to the belief to be contracted.

Example
Mary previously believed both that her husband is faithful (α) and that London is the capital of Great Britain (β). After losing her belief in α, she still believed that β.

Any reasonable account of belief change must be compatible with a pattern such as this. However, full meet contraction of belief sets is not. Since β is not a logical consequence of $\neg\alpha$, it cannot be retained after full meet contraction by α.

We now have ample evidence that full meet contraction, as applied to belief sets, is quite implausible. What about the other limiting case, maxichoice contraction?

Maxichoice contraction on a set A is defined as partial meet contraction by a selection function γ such that for all sentences α, $\gamma(A\perp\alpha)$ is a singleton (set with exactly one element). Maxichoice contractions are as conservative as contractions can be, i.e. they retain as much of the original belief set as is possible without violating *success*. The following condition can be used for an axiomatic characterization of maxichoice contraction:

Fullness: [1]
If $\beta \in A$ and $\beta \notin A \div \alpha$,
then $\alpha \notin \mathrm{Cn}(A \div \alpha)$ and $\alpha \in \mathrm{Cn}((A \div \alpha) \cup \{\beta\})$.

Fullness is essentially a strengthened version of relevance. If we replace relevance by fullness in the axiomatic characterization of partial meet contraction (Theorem 2.2), then we obtain a characterization of maxichoice contraction:

THEOREM 2.13 *The operator $\div$ is an operator of maxichoice contraction for a set A if and only if it satisfies the postulates of success, inclusion, fullness, and uniformity.*
[Proof: p. 128.]

For maxichoice contraction of a (logically closed) belief set, the following result can be obtained:

OBSERVATION 2.14 (Alchourrón and Makinson [3]) *Let A be a (logically closed) belief set and $\sim_\gamma$ an operator of maxichoice contraction for A. Then it holds for all sentences α in A and all sentences β that either $\neg\alpha \rightarrow \beta \in A \sim_\gamma \alpha$ or $\neg\alpha \rightarrow \neg\beta \in A \sim_\gamma \alpha$.*
[Proof: p. 124.]

Note that the sentence β in this observation does not have to be an element of the original belief set A. It is not difficult to find examples of belief changes that violate this property of maxichoice contraction:

> **Example**
> I used to believe that Neptune is closer to the sun than Uranus (α). I had no idea whether or not Alpha Centauri has a planet with intelligent life (β). Then I gave up my belief in α. After that, I did not believe that if Neptune is not closer to the sun than Uranus, then Alpha Centauri has a planet with intelligent life. Neither did I believe that if Neptune is not closer to the sun than Uranus, then Alpha Centauri does not have a planet with intelligent life.

In this case, both $\neg\alpha \rightarrow \beta$ and $\neg\alpha \rightarrow \neg\beta$ are elements of the original belief set A, since they follow logically from its element α. (Observe that $\neg\alpha \rightarrow \beta$ is equivalent to $\alpha \vee \beta$ and $\neg\alpha \rightarrow \neg\beta$ to $\alpha \vee \neg\beta$.) However, there is no obvious reason why any of them should be an element of $A \div \alpha$. It seems to be an unavoidable conclusion that maxichoice contraction, as applied to a logically closed belief set, is not at all a plausible operation.

David Makinson has defended maxichoice contraction, maintaining that the problem originates in the 'misapplication' of maxichoice contraction to belief sets. In his view, maxichoice contraction should instead be applied to belief bases, to which it is much better suited [83].

5 HOW TO GIVE UP CONJUNCTIONS

Several of the most useful postulates for belief contraction refer to the contraction of conjunctions.

In order to give up a conjunction $\alpha\&\beta$, you must relinquish your belief in α or your belief in β (or both). Suppose that when contracting by $\alpha\&\beta$ you lose your belief in α, i.e. that $\alpha \notin \mathrm{Cn}(A\div(\alpha\&\beta))$. We can then argue as follows: If δ needs to be removed in order to remove α, and α needs to be removed in order to remove $\alpha\&\beta$, then δ needs to be removed in order to remove $\alpha\&\beta$. Hence, if $\delta \notin A\div\alpha$, then $\delta \notin A\div(\alpha\&\beta)$. This argument (that originates with Abhaya Nayak [94]), supports the following postulate:

Conjunctive inclusion: [1]
If $\alpha \notin \mathrm{Cn}(A\div(\alpha\&\beta))$, then $A\div(\alpha\&\beta) \subseteq A\div\alpha$.

Conjunctive inclusion has also been called 'conjunction' [23].

Another fairly reasonable principle for contraction by a conjunction is that it should overlap the common part of the contractions by the conjuncts. In other words, whatever is an element of both $A\div\alpha$ and $A\div\beta$ should also be an element of $A\div(\alpha\&\beta)$.

Example
I was invited to a neighbourhood garden party. Before I went to the party, I believed that everybody in our block was invited (ε). I also believed that Alice would be there (α) and that Bob would be there (β). Alice and Bob are a married couple who live in our block, two houses away.

Case 1: When I came to the party, I was unable to find Alice. I therefore gave up my belief that she was there (α). However, I still believed that everybody in the neighbourhood had been invited (ε).

Case 2: At the party, I could not see Bob anywhere. I gave up my belief that he was there (β). However, I still believed that everybody in the neighbourhood had been invited (ε).

Case 3: On my way to the party, I saw that Alice's and Bob's front door was open. This made me give up my belief that they were both at the party ($\alpha\&\beta$). Did I still believe that everybody in the neighbourhood had been invited (ε)?

It would seem strange to answer this question in the negative. In order to cease believing $\alpha\&\beta$ one must either cease believing α or cease believing β. Since neither the expulsion of α nor that of β requires that ε is given up, we can expect that the expulsion of $\alpha\&\beta$ should not do so either. This principle has the following formal definition:

Conjunctive overlap:
$(A \div \alpha) \cap (A \div \beta) \subseteq A \div (\alpha\&\beta)$.

This postulate has also been called 'intersection' [23]. It seems to hold in most of the examples that readily come to mind. However, counter-examples are not impossible to construct:

Example
I believe that Accra is a national capital (α). I also believe that Bangui is a national capital (β). As a (logical) consequence of this, I also believe that either Accra or Bangui is a national capital ($\alpha \vee \beta$).

Case 1: 'Give the name of an African capital' says my geography teacher.

'Accra' I say, confidently.

The teacher looks angrily at me without saying a word. I lose my belief in α. However, I still retain my belief in β, and consequently in $\alpha \vee \beta$.

Case 2: I answer 'Bangui' to the same question. The teacher gives me the same wordless response. In this case, I lose my belief in β, but I retain my belief in α and consequently my belief in $\alpha \vee \beta$.

Case 3: 'Give the names of two African capitals' says my geography teacher.

'Accra and Bangui' I say, confidently.

The teacher looks angrily at me without saying a word. I lose confidence in my answer, that is, I lose my belief in $\alpha\&\beta$. Since my beliefs in α and in β were equally strong, I cannot choose between them, so I lose both of them.

After this, I no longer believe in $\alpha \vee \beta$.

Let A be the original belief set in this example. Then $\alpha \vee \beta$ is an element both of $A \div \alpha$ and $A \div \beta$, and consequently an element of $(A \div \alpha) \cap (A \div \beta)$, but it is not an element of $A \div (\alpha\&\beta)$. The example shows that conjunctive overlap does not always hold for contraction of belief sets.

In belief base representation, conjunctive overlap can be defended against this counterexample in the following way: Let A be the original belief base. Then $\alpha \vee \beta \in \mathrm{Cn}(A \div \alpha)$, but $\alpha \vee \beta$ is not a basic belief so it is not an element of $A \div \alpha$. (Similarly, $\alpha \vee \beta \in \mathrm{Cn}(A \div \beta)$, but $\alpha \vee \beta \notin A \div \beta$.) Therefore, $\alpha \vee \beta$ is not an element of $(A \div \alpha) \cap (A \div \beta)$, so the fact that $\alpha \vee \beta \notin A \div (\alpha\&\beta)$ does not contradict conjunctive overlap.

When we contract a set A by a non-tautological conjunctive sentence $\alpha\&\beta$, there are three options:

1. give up α, but retain β
2. give up β, but retain α
3. give up both α and β.

In the first case, it would seem reasonable to expect that $A\div(\alpha\&\beta) = A\div\alpha$, and in the second case that $A\div(\alpha\&\beta) = A\div\beta$. In the third case, when both α and β are given up, we may expect that exactly those beliefs are lost that one would lose either in order to give give up α or in order to give up β, in other words: $A\div(\alpha\&\beta) = (A\div\alpha) \cap (A\div\beta)$. This leads us to the following condition:

> *Conjunctive factoring:* [1]
> Either $A\div(\alpha\&\beta) = A\div\alpha$, $A\div(\alpha\&\beta) = A\div\beta$, or $A\div(\alpha\&\beta) = (A\div\alpha) \cap (A\div\beta)$.

Conjunctive factoring has also been called 'ventilation' [1].

Finally, let us consider contractions by conjunctions with three conjuncts, such as $A\div(\alpha\&\beta\&\delta)$. Roughly speaking, there are three ways to ensure that a set does not imply $\alpha\&\beta\&\delta$, namely to see to it that it does not imply α, that it does not imply β, or that it does not imply δ. The first two of these are also the two ways to make it not imply $\alpha\&\beta$. Let us consider the cases in which $\alpha \in A\div(\alpha\&\beta)$. In these cases it follows from the success postulate that $\beta \notin A\div(\alpha\&\beta)$. Since β but not α was removed, it is better (more information-economical) to exclude β from A than to exclude α. Now, what about $A\div(\alpha\&\beta\&\delta)$ in a case like this? As we have already observed, there are three ways to get rid of $\alpha\&\beta\&\delta$: to exclude α, to exclude β, and to exclude δ. We have just concluded from $\alpha \in A\div(\alpha\&\beta)$ that it is better to exclude β from A than to exclude α. Since there is at least one way to get rid of $\alpha\&\beta\&\delta$ that is better than to exclude α, we should not exclude α. (Whether we should exclude β, δ, or both, cannot be concluded from $\alpha \in A\div(\alpha\&\beta)$.) This amounts to the following postulate:

> *Conjunctive trisection:* [49; 115]
> If $\alpha \in A\div(\alpha\&\beta)$, then $\alpha \in A\div(\alpha\&\beta\&\delta)$.

We now have four postulates for contraction of conjunctions: conjunctive inclusion, conjunctive overlap, conjunctive factoring, and conjunctive trisection. For partial meet contraction of (logically closed) belief sets, we can restrict our attention to two of them:

OBSERVATION 2.15 *Let A be a (logically closed) belief set, and let $\div$ be an operation on A that satisfies closure, inclusion, vacuity, success, extensionality, and recovery. Then:*

1. *(Hans Rott* [115]*) Conjunctive overlap is satisfied if and only if conjunctive trisection is satisfied.*
2. *(AGM* [1]*) Conjunctive factoring is satisfied if and only if both conjunctive overlap and conjunctive inclusion are satisfied.*

[Proof: p. 118.]

Of the four properties, conjunctive overlap and conjunctive inclusion are the ones most commonly referred to. They were introduced by Peter Gärdenfors as postulates for contractions of belief sets, to supplement his six basic postulates. They are commonly called *Gärdenfors's supplementary postulates* for belief contraction.

6 MORE ORDERLY CONTRACTIONS

A selection function for a set A should, for all sentences α, select those elements of $A\perp\alpha$ that are 'best', or most worth retaining. However, the definition of a selection function is very general, and allows for quite disorderly selection functions that do not in any sensible way select the best among the elements of a remainder set. For example, consider the set

$$A = \{p\vee q, p\rightarrow q, q\rightarrow p\},$$

where p and q are logically independent sentences. It has the subsets

$$\begin{aligned} B_1 &= \{p\vee q, p\rightarrow q\} \\ B_2 &= \{p\vee q, q\rightarrow p\} \\ B_3 &= \{p\rightarrow q, q\rightarrow p\} \end{aligned}$$

We have

$$\begin{aligned} A\perp(p\leftrightarrow q) &= \{B_1, B_2\} \\ A\perp(p\&q) &= \{B_1, B_2, B_3\} \end{aligned}$$

Now suppose that the selection function makes the following selections:

$$\begin{aligned} \gamma(A\perp(p\leftrightarrow q)) &= \{B_1\} \\ \gamma(A\perp(p\&q)) &= \{B_2\} \end{aligned}$$

In the first case, the selection function 'prefers' B_1 to B_2. In the second case, it 'prefers' B_2 to B_1. This seems strange, since we expect the selection function to express what the doxastic agent or the database prefers to retain. If an element B_1 of $A\perp\alpha$ is included in $\gamma(A\perp\alpha)$, whereas another element B_2 of $A\perp\alpha$ is not, then B_1 should be in some sense preferred to B_2. If the selection function is orderly, then such preferences should be consistent, i.e. independent of the sentence to be contracted.

Preferences can be expressed in formal terms by a binary relation. Let $\sqsubseteq$ be a relation on subsets of A, such that $A_1 \sqsubseteq A_2$ holds if and only if A_2 is at least as good (at least as much worth retaining) as A_1. Then for a selection function γ to be *based* on $\sqsubseteq$ it must be the case that for every remainder set $A \perp \alpha$, γ selects those elements of $A \perp \alpha$ that are 'best' according to $\sqsubseteq$. More precisely, a set $B \in A \perp \alpha$ should be an element of $\gamma(A \perp \alpha)$ if and only if it holds for all elements C of $A \perp \alpha$ that B is at least as much worth retaining as C. A selection function that is based on a relation in this way is called *relational*:

DEFINITION 2.16 (AGM [1]) *A selection function γ for a set A is* relational *if and only if there is a relation $\sqsubseteq$ such that for all sentences α, if $A \perp \alpha$ is non-empty, then $\gamma(A \perp \alpha) = \{B \in A \perp \alpha \mid C \sqsubseteq B$ for all $C \in A \perp \alpha\}$.*

An operator of partial meet contraction is relational if and only if it is based on a relational selection function.

The formula of Definition 2.16 is called the *marking-off identity*[1], since it marks off the preferred elements of the remainder set. For analogous reasons, $\sqsubseteq$ will be called the *marking-off relation*.

It is convenient to have a notation for the 'strict part' of the marking-off relation. The symbol $\sqsubset$ will be used for that purpose, i.e. $A_1 \sqsubset A_2$ will denote that A_2 is more worth retaining than A_1. The formal definition is as follows:

$$A_1 \sqsubset A_2 \leftrightarrow (A_1 \sqsubseteq A_2) \& \neg(A_2 \sqsubseteq A_1).$$

A selection function that reflects underlying doxastic preferences should be relational. Furthermore, a well-behaved preference relation should satisfy the fundamental rationality postulates for preferences, in particular transitivity.

Transitivity:
If $A \sqsubseteq B$ and $B \sqsubseteq C$, then $A \sqsubseteq C$.

We can (for a change) illustrate transitivity with a non-epistemic example. Consider three wines: Château Impérial, Buffalo Valley, and Alsace Inférieur. If Buffalo Valley is better than Alsace Inférieur, and Château Impérial is better than Buffalo Valley, then Château Impérial is better than Alsace Inférieur.

One of our basic assumptions is that losses of previous beliefs should, if possible, be avoided. As a consequence of this, a relation of doxastic preference, such as $\sqsubseteq$, should put more value on a set than on any of its proper subsets. Thus, the marking-off relation should have the following property:

Maximizing property: [48]
If $A \subset B$, then $A \sqsubset B$.

A selection function (and its corresponding operator of contraction) will be called *maximizingly relational* if and only if it is based on some maximizing relation.

As the following observation shows, the maximizing property, taken alone, is devoid of impact on the contraction operator.

OBSERVATION 2.17 *Let A be a belief base and $\sim_\gamma$ an operator of partial meet contraction for that base. Then $\sim_\gamma$ is relational if and only if it is maximizingly relational.*
[Proof: p. 151.]

This does not mean, however, that the maximizing property is always redundant. We may also require of a marking-off relation that it be both maximizing and transitive. A selection function (and the contraction that it gives rise to) is *transitively, maximizingly relational* (TMR) if and only if it is relational by a marking-off relation that is both transitive and maximizing. When combined with transitivity, the maximizing property is not in general redundant [48]. To see this, let $A = \{p, q, q \rightarrow p\}$. We then have:

$$A \perp (p\&q) = \{\{q\}, \{p, q \rightarrow p\}\}$$
$$A \perp p = \{\{q\}, \{q \rightarrow p\}\}$$

Let:

$$\gamma(A \perp (p\&q)) = \{\{q\}\}$$
$$\gamma(A \perp p) = \{\{q \rightarrow p\}\}$$

Let $\sqsubseteq$ be a marking-off relation for γ. It must then be the case that $\{p, q \rightarrow p\} \sqsubseteq \{q\}$ and $\{q\} \sqsubseteq \{q \rightarrow p\}$.

Suppose that $\sqsubseteq$ is transitive. It then follows from $\{p, q \rightarrow p\} \sqsubseteq \{q\}$ and $\{q\} \sqsubseteq \{q \rightarrow p\}$ that $\{p, q \rightarrow p\} \sqsubseteq \{q \rightarrow p\}$.

Next, suppose that $\sqsubseteq$ is maximizing. It then follows from $\{q \rightarrow p\} \subset \{p, q \rightarrow p\}$ that $\{q \rightarrow p\} \sqsubset \{p, q \rightarrow p\}$. Since $\{p, q \rightarrow p\} \sqsubseteq \{q \rightarrow p\}$ and $\{q \rightarrow p\} \sqsubset \{p, q \rightarrow p\}$ cannot both hold, $\sqsubseteq$ cannot be both maximizing and transitive. The example shows that a selection function can be transitively relational without being transitively maximizingly relational. The maximizing property is not redundant, after all.

Note the distinction: All transitively relational partial meet contractions are maximizingly relational (Observation 2.17). They are relational by some transitive relation, and also relational by some maximizing relation. However, some of them are not relational by any relation that is both transitive and maximizing, i.e. they are not transitively maximizingly relational.

The set A used in this example is not a belief set, i.e. it is not logically closed. This is an essential feature of the example. Indeed, no example of this kind can be constructed for a logically closed set. In other words, it is only for non-closed belief bases that there is a difference between transitively relational and transitively maximizingly relational partial meet contraction.

OBSERVATION 2.18 ([49]) *Let A be a (logically closed) belief set and* $\sim_\gamma$ *an operator of partial meet contraction for A. Then* $\sim_\gamma$ *is transitively maximizingly relational if and only if it is transitively relational.*
[Proof: p. 163.]

There are strong connections between the properties that we have now imposed on selection functions and the postulates for conjunctions that were introduced in Section 2.5:

OBSERVATION 2.19 *Let A be a set of sentences and* $\sim_\gamma$ *an operator of transitively, maximizingly relational partial meet contraction on A. Then:*

1. [50] $\sim_\gamma$ *satisfies conjunctive overlap.*
2. *If A is finite and disjunctively closed, then* $\sim_\gamma$ *satisfies conjunctive inclusion and conjunctive factoring.*
3. [1; 115] *If A is logically closed, then* $\sim_\gamma$ *satisfies conjunctive inclusion, conjunctive factoring, and conjunctive trisection.*

[Proof: p. 152.]

Conjunctive overlap holds for all relational partial meet contractions of belief sets:

OBSERVATION 2.20 (AGM [1]) *Let A be a (logically closed) belief set and* γ *a relational selection function for A. Then* $\sim_\gamma$ *satisfies conjunctive overlap.*
[Proof: p. 148.]

Furthermore, and more importantly, conjunctive overlap and conjunctive inclusion are necessary and sufficient conditions for partial meet contraction on a belief set to be transitively relational. We therefore have the following representation theorem:

THEOREM 2.21 (AGM [1]) *Let A be a (logically closed) belief set and* $\div$ *an operation for A. Then* $\div$ *is a transitively relational partial meet contraction if and only if it satisfies closure, inclusion, vacuity, success, extensionality, recovery, conjunctive overlap, and conjunctive inclusion.*
[Proof: p. 163.]

In summary, the six basic Gärdenfors postulates axiomatically characterize partial meet contraction on belief sets. If the two supplementary Gärdenfors postulates (conjunctive overlap and conjunctive inclusion) are added, then we obtain an axiomatic characterization of transitively relational partial meet contraction. These two results (our Theorems 2.7 and 2.21) were the peak achievements with respect to contraction in the 1985 paper by the AGM trio.

7 LEVI'S CONTRACTION OPERATORS

Remainders from logically closed sets have the following somewhat surprising property:

DEFINITION 2.22 (Isaac Levi [73]) *A set X of sentences is* α-saturatable *if and only if:*

1. $X = \mathrm{Cn}(X)$, *and*
2. $\mathrm{Cn}(X \cup \{\neg\alpha\}) \in \mathcal{L}\bot\bot$.

OBSERVATION 2.23 (Alchourrón and Makinson [3]) *Let A be logically closed, and let $\alpha \in A$. Then it holds for all $X \in A\bot\alpha$ that X is α-saturatable.*
[Proof: p. 159.]

Thus, an α-saturatable set is a logically closed set such that the addition of $\neg\alpha$ is sufficient to make the closure of the resulting set maximally consistent.

The elements of $A\bot\alpha$ are all α-saturatable, but they are not all the subsets of A that have this property. This can be seen from the following example [73]. Let $\mathcal{L}$ be the language containing only the truth-functional combinations of the logically independent sentences p and q. Let $A = \mathrm{Cn}(\{p, q\})$. Then $\mathrm{Cn}(\{p\leftrightarrow q\})$ and $\mathrm{Cn}(\{q\})$ are elements of $A\bot p$. It is easy to show that they are both p-saturatable:

$$\mathrm{Cn}(\mathrm{Cn}(\{p\leftrightarrow q\}) \cup \{\neg p\}) = \mathrm{Cn}(\{\neg p, \neg q\}) \in \mathcal{L}\bot\bot.$$
$$\mathrm{Cn}(\mathrm{Cn}(\{q\}) \cup \{\neg p\}) = \mathrm{Cn}(\{\neg p, q\}) \in \mathcal{L}\bot\bot$$

There are also two other p-saturatable subsets of A, namely $\mathrm{Cn}(\{q\rightarrow p\})$ and $\mathrm{Cn}(\{\neg q\rightarrow p\})$:

$$\mathrm{Cn}(\mathrm{Cn}(\{q\rightarrow p\}) \cup \{\neg p\}) = \mathrm{Cn}(\{\neg p, \neg q\}) \in \mathcal{L}\bot\bot.$$
$$\mathrm{Cn}(\mathrm{Cn}(\{\neg q\rightarrow p\}) \cup \{\neg p\}) = \mathrm{Cn}(\{\neg p, q\}) \in \mathcal{L}\bot\bot.$$

However, neither $\mathrm{Cn}(\{q\rightarrow p\})$ nor $\mathrm{Cn}(\{\neg q\rightarrow p\})$ is an element of $A\bot p$. This we can see, in the case of $\mathrm{Cn}(\{q\rightarrow p\})$, from the fact that $\mathrm{Cn}(\{q\rightarrow p\}) \subset \mathrm{Cn}(\{p\leftrightarrow q\}) \subseteq A$ and $\mathrm{Cn}(\{p\leftrightarrow q\}) \nvdash p$.

The following notation will be used for saturatable sets:

DEFINITION 2.24 (Isaac Levi [73]) *Let A be a logically closed set and α a sentence. Then: $X \in S(A, \alpha)$ if and only if*

1. $X \subseteq A$
2. $X = \mathrm{Cn}(X)$
3. $\mathrm{Cn}(X \cup \{\neg\alpha\}) \in \mathcal{L}\bot\bot$.

$S(A,\alpha)$ is the α-saturatable family *of A. Its elements are the* α-saturatable subsets *of A.*

It follows directly from Observation 2.23 that $A\perp\alpha \subseteq S(A,\alpha)$ for all belief sets A and sentences α.

Partial meet contraction of A by α is based on a selection among the elements of $A\perp\alpha$. Isaac Levi has proposed that an operator of contraction should instead be based on a selection among the elements of $S(A,\alpha)$. For a formal development of this proposal, we need to widen the scope of selection functions, so that they take saturatable families as arguments. In this section, by a selection function for A will be meant a function γ such that for all sentences α, $\gamma(S(A,\alpha))$ is a non-empty subset of $S(A,\alpha)$ unless the latter is empty, in which case $\gamma(S(A,\alpha)) = \{A\}$. Levi's contraction operators can then be defined as follows:

DEFINITION 2.25 ([60; 73]) *Let A be a logically closed set. Then $\div$ is a* Levi-contraction *for A if and only if there exists a selection function γ for A such that for all $\alpha \in \mathcal{L}$:*

1. *if $\alpha \in A$ then $A{\div}\alpha = \bigcap\gamma(S(A,\alpha))$, and*
2. *if $\alpha \notin A$ then $A{\div}\alpha = A$.*

This definition is slightly more complicated than that of partial meet contraction. The definition of partial meet contraction has no counterpart to the second clause, since $A{\div}\alpha = \bigcap\gamma(A\perp\alpha)$ holds for all α. (It would make no difference to add such a clause, though, since if $\alpha \notin A$, then $\bigcap\gamma(A\perp\alpha) = A$.) The reason why the second clause has been included in Definition 2.25 is that otherwise, vacuity would not be satisfied, as can be seen from the following example: Let $\mathcal{L}$ be the language consisting of all truth-functional combinations of p and q. Let $A = \text{Cn}(\{p,q\})$, and let $A' = \text{Cn}(\{p\})$. Clearly, $\neg q \notin A$. It is easy to show that both A and A' are elements of $S(A,\neg q)$. We can construct a selection function γ such that $\gamma(S(A,\neg q)) = \{A, A'\}$, and thus $\bigcap\gamma(S(A,\neg q)) = \bigcap\{A,A'\} = A'$. Since A' is a proper subset of A, vacuity would not be satisfied in this example without clause (2). By adding clause (2), we ensure that vacuity always holds.

If α is logically true, then $S(A,\alpha)$ is empty, and hence $\gamma(S(A,\alpha)) = \{A\}$, so that $A{\div}\alpha = A$, just as for partial meet contraction.

Levi-contraction can be axiomatically characterized as follows:

THEOREM 2.26 ([60]) *Let A be a logically closed set. Then the operator $\div$ is a Levi-contraction for A if and only if it satisfies closure, inclusion, success, vacuity, extensionality, and failure.*
[Proof: p. 165.]

Levi-contractions do not in general satisfy recovery. For a direct demonstration of this, again let the language consist of p, q, and their truth-functional combinations, and let $A = \mathrm{Cn}(\{p, q\})$. Then, as we saw above, $\mathrm{Cn}(\{q \rightarrow p\}) \in S(A, p)$, and we can therefore construct a Levi-contraction $\div$ that is based on a selection function γ such that $\gamma(S(A, p)) = \{\mathrm{Cn}(\{q \rightarrow p\})\}$. Then $A \div p = \mathrm{Cn}(\{q \rightarrow p\})$. It follows that $\mathrm{Cn}((A \div p) \cup \{p\}) = \mathrm{Cn}(\{p\})$, which is a proper subset of A, so that recovery is not satisfied.

According to Levi, not all information is of value to the inquiring agent. When a person contracts her belief set ('corpus' in Levi's terminology), she should aim at retaining as much as possible of the valuable information. Instead of minimizing the loss of information, she should minimize the loss of informational value. This may be compatible with losses of information that are large enough to induce violations of the postulate of recovery.

In order to express informational value, we can use a measure V on the set of logically closed subsets of A, viz. a function V that assigns a real number to each logically closed subset of A. Thus, $V(X) \leq V(Y)$ means that X has at most as much informational value as Y, and $V(X) = V(Y)$ means that the two sets have equal informational value. (Alternatively, and with essentially the same result, a transitive and connected preference relation on the set of logically closed subsets of A can be used.)

Levi distinguishes between two monotonicity requirements on V [73]:

If $X \subset Y$, then $V(X) < V(Y)$ (*strong monotonicity*)
If $X \subset Y$, then $V(X) \leq V(Y)$ (*weak monotonicity*)

According to weak (and strong) monotonicity, a set can never have a lower informational value than any of its proper subsets. Thus, we can never increase the informational value of a belief set by contracting it. On the other hand, weak (but not strong) monotonicity allows a belief set to have the same value as one of its proper subsets. Hence, it may be the case that $X \subset Y$ and $V(X) = V(Y)$. Then the elements of $Y \backslash X$ can be thought of as beliefs in Y with no informational value.

The type of contraction that Levi argues for can be based on a *weakly* monotonic measure of informational value:

DEFINITION 2.27 ([60; 73]) *Let A be a logically closed set. Then the operator $\div$ is an operator of* value-based Levi-contraction *on A if and only if it is based on a selection function γ that is generated from a weakly monotonic value-measure V on the logically closed subsets of A, such that for all α:*
$\gamma(S(A, \alpha)) = \{X \in S(A, \alpha) \mid V(Y) \leq V(X)$ *for all* $Y \in S(A, \alpha)\}$.

Value-based Levi-contraction satisfies both of Gärdenfors's supplementary postulates:

OBSERVATION 2.28 ([60]) *Let A be a logically closed set and $\div$ a value-based Levi-contraction on A. Then $\div$ satisfies conjunctive overlap and conjunctive inclusion.*
[Proof: p. 168.]

Hence, value-based Levi-contraction satisfies all the Gärdenfors postulates except recovery.

8 KERNEL CONTRACTION

Partial meet contraction is based on a selection among subsets of A that do not imply α. Another possible approach is to select the sentences to be discarded, in other words to base the operator of contraction on a selection among the elements of A that contribute to make it imply α. This approach was proposed by Carlos Alchourrón and David Makinson. In an important paper that was published in 1985 they introduced the operation of 'safe contraction' [4]. A more general variant of the same approach, 'kernel contraction', was introduced much later [52]. For systematic reasons, we are going to study the more general construction first.

The sentences that we remove in order to contract A by α should be sentences that contribute to making A imply α. For example, let p, q, and r be logically independent sentences, and let

$$A = \{p, q, p \rightarrow q, q \rightarrow p, r\}$$

We are going to contract $p\&q$ from A. Consider the following three subsets of A:

$$\{p, q\}$$
$$\{p, p \rightarrow q\}$$
$$\{q, q \rightarrow p\}$$

Each of these sets implies $p\&q$. Each of them is also *minimal* in the sense that it does not have a proper subset that implies $p\&q$. These are all the sets there are with these properties. They are the ***inclusion-minimal subsets*** of A that imply $p\&q$. In short, they will be called the ***$p\&q$-kernels*** of A.

A sentence in A contributes to make A imply $p\&q$ if and only if it is an element of some $p\&q$-kernel of A. Therefore, when selecting what elements to exclude from $A \div (p\&q)$, we should choose among those sentences that are elements of some $p\&q$-kernel.

A subset of A implies a sentence α if and only if it contains some α-kernel. We want to construct a contraction $A \div \alpha$ that satisfies the success postulate. Therefore, no α-kernel should be included in $A \div \alpha$. In other words: Among the sentences selected for removal there must be at least one element from each α-kernel in A. This is a necessary and sufficient condition for success to be satisfied.

In order to express this in the formal language, it is convenient to use a notation for kernels that is analogous to that for remainders:

DEFINITION 2.29 ([52]) *Let $A \subseteq \mathcal{L}$ and $\alpha \in \mathcal{L}$. Then $A \perp\!\!\!\perp \alpha$ is the set such that $X \in A \perp\!\!\!\perp \alpha$ if and only if:*

1. $X \subseteq A$
2. $X \vdash \alpha$, *and*
3. *If* $Y \subset X$, *then* $Y \not\vdash \alpha$.

$A \perp\!\!\!\perp \alpha$ *is a* kernel set, *and its elements are the* α-kernels *of* A.

Kernels have also been called 'entailment sets' [24]. In our example:

$$A \perp\!\!\!\perp (p\&q) = \{\{p, q\}, \{p, p \rightarrow q\}, \{q, q \rightarrow p\}\}.$$

The function that selects sentences to be removed will be called an *incision function* since it makes an incision into every α-kernel. It is defined as follows:

DEFINITION 2.30 ([52]) *An* incision function σ *for* A *is a function such that for all* α:

1. $\sigma(A \perp\!\!\!\perp \alpha) \subseteq \bigcup(A \perp\!\!\!\perp \alpha)$
2. *If* $\emptyset \neq X \in A \perp\!\!\!\perp \alpha$, *then* $X \cap \sigma(A \perp\!\!\!\perp \alpha) \neq \emptyset$.

An incision function selects sentences to be discarded. The outcome of a contraction should consist of all elements of the original set not selected for removal by the incision function, i.e. if $\div$ is based on the incision function σ, then $A \div \alpha = A \backslash \sigma(A \perp\!\!\!\perp \alpha)$. The symbol $\approx_\sigma$ will be used to denote the operator of contraction that is based on σ:

DEFINITION 2.31 ([52]) *Let* σ *be an incision function for* A. *The* kernel contraction $\approx_\sigma$ *for* A *is defined as follows:*

$$A \approx_\sigma \alpha = A \backslash \sigma(A \perp\!\!\!\perp \alpha)$$

An operator $\div$ *for* A *is a kernel contraction if and only if there is some incision function* σ *for* A *such that* $A \div \alpha = A \approx_\sigma \alpha$ *for all sentences* α.

In the limiting case when α is logically true, $A \perp\!\!\!\perp \alpha = \{\emptyset\}$, and it follows from Definition 2.30 that $\sigma(A \perp\!\!\!\perp \alpha) = \emptyset$. In the other limiting case, when $\alpha \notin \mathrm{Cn}(A)$, $A \perp\!\!\!\perp \alpha = \emptyset$, and again it follows that $\sigma(A \perp\!\!\!\perp \alpha) = \emptyset$. In both cases, it follows from $\sigma(A \perp\!\!\!\perp \alpha) = \emptyset$ that $A \div \alpha = A$. Thus, both limiting cases are treated in the same way as in partial meet contraction (and the postulates of failure and vacuity are satisfied).

The following representation theorem has been obtained for kernel contraction:

THEOREM 2.32 ([52]) *The operator* $\div$ *for* A *is a kernel contraction if and only if it satisfies success, inclusion, core-retainment, and uniformity.*
[Proof: p. 172.]

This theorem should be compared to Theorem 2.2, in which partial meet contraction was characterized by the four postulates success, inclusion, relevance, and uniformity. By replacing relevance by the weaker postulate of core-retainment, we obtained kernel contraction instead of partial meet contraction. It follows from the two axiomatic characterizations that *all partial meet contractions are kernel contractions*. We may see kernel contraction as a generalization of partial meet contraction.

Kernel contraction is a very general class of operations, and it is easy to find examples of it that are not at all intuitively plausible. Let p and q be logically independent sentences, and let:

$$A = \{p, p\vee q, p\leftrightarrow q\}$$

We then have:

$$A \perp\!\!\!\perp (p\&q) = \{\{p, p\leftrightarrow q\}, \{p\vee q, p\leftrightarrow q\}\}$$

Now let σ be an incision function such that:

$$\sigma(A \perp\!\!\!\perp (p\&q)) = \{p\vee q, p\leftrightarrow q\}$$

It gives rise to an operator of contraction such that:

$$A \approx_\sigma (p\&q) = \{p\}.$$

It does not seem sensible for $p\vee q$ to be given up here. Since p was not given up, $p\vee q$ is implied by the contracted set $A\approx_\sigma(p\&q)$. The exclusion of $p\vee q$ was unnecessary, and violates the basic principle of minimality of belief change: nothing should be given up without reason. (Core-retainment is too weak to offer protection against such breaches of minimality.) The property that is lacking is relative closure ($A \cap \mathrm{Cn}(A\div\alpha) \subseteq A\div\alpha$). Since partial meet contraction satisfies relative closure, this example also shows that some kernel contractions are not partial meet contractions.

What is needed to ensure that an operator of kernel contraction satisfies relative closure? The following definition introduces a condition on incision functions and the ensuing theorem shows that this condition does the job, i.e. it is exactly what is required to ensure that a kernel contraction satisfies relative closure.

DEFINITION 2.33 ([52]) *An incision function σ for a set A is* smooth *if and only if it holds for all subsets B of A that if $B \vdash \beta$ and $\beta \in \sigma(A \perp\!\!\!\perp \alpha)$, then $B \cap \sigma(A \perp\!\!\!\perp \alpha) \neq \emptyset$.*

A kernel contraction is smooth if and only if it is based on a smooth incision function.

THEOREM 2.34 ([52]) *The operator $\div$ for A is a smooth kernel contraction if and only if it satisfies success, inclusion, core-retainment, uniformity, and relative closure.*
[Proof: p. 175.]

There is another, perhaps simpler way to achieve relative closure. Instead of restricting what kind of incision function to be used, we may perform contraction by any incision function, and *afterwards* obtain relative closure. This is done by adding those $A\div\alpha$-implied elements of A that were dropped by the incision function. The process of reintroducing the elements that were unnecessarily removed will be called *saturation*, and the operation that it gives rise to is *saturated kernel contraction.*

DEFINITION 2.35 ([52]) *Let σ be an incision function for A. The* saturated kernel contraction $\hat{\approx}_\sigma$ *for A that it gives rise to is defined as follows:*

$$A\hat{\approx}_\sigma\alpha = A\cap \mathrm{Cn}(A\approx_\sigma\alpha)$$

An operator $\div$ for A is a saturated kernel contraction if and only if there is some incision function σ for A such that $A\div\alpha = A\hat{\approx}_\sigma\alpha$ for all sentences α.

Fortunately, it makes no difference which of the two methods to obtain relative closure that we choose. The following theorem shows that saturated and smooth kernel contractions are just two different ways to construct the same class of operations.

THEOREM 2.36 ([52]) *An operator $\div$ for a set A is a saturated kernel contraction if and only if it is a smooth kernel contraction.*
[Proof: p. 176.]

We have already seen an example showing that some kernel contractions are not partial meet contractions. The following example confirms the stronger claim that *some smooth kernel contractions are not partial meet contractions*: Let p, q, and r be logically independent sentences, and let $A = \{p, q, r\}$. We then have

$$A\perp\!\!\!\perp(p\&(q\vee r)) = \{\{p,q\},\{p,r\}\}$$

Let σ be such that

$$\sigma(A\perp\!\!\!\perp(p\&(q\vee r))) = \{p,r\}.$$

It can straightforwardly be verified that a function σ with this property can be a smooth incision function for A. It follows that

$$A\approx_\sigma(p\&(q\vee r)) = \{q\}.$$

To see that $\approx_\sigma$ cannot be a partial meet contraction, consider the relevant remainder set:

$$A\perp(p\&(q\vee r)) = \{\{p\},\{q,r\}\}.$$

A selection function γ for A must select a non-empty subset of $A\perp(p\&(q\vee r))$, i.e. $\gamma(A\perp(p\&(q\vee r)))$, is either $\{\{p\}\}$, $\{\{q,r\}\}$, or $\{\{p\},\{q,r\}\}$. It follows that $A\sim_\gamma(p\&(q\vee r))$ is either $\{p\}$, $\{q,r\}$, or $\emptyset$. It cannot be $\{q\}$.

How plausible is an operation such as this? The following example serves to show that it is not entirely implausible:

> **Example** [44]
> A: Last summer I saw a three-toed woodpecker just outside my window. I could clearly see its red forehead and its red rump.
> B: You must be mistaken. The three-toed woodpecker does not have a red forehead or a red rump.
> A: You make me uncertain. Thinking about it, the only thing I am certain of is that the bird had a red forehead.

A's original beliefs were that the bird was a three-toed woodpecker (p), that it had a red forehead (q), and that it had a red rump (r). She contracted $p\&(q \vee r)$ that had been denied by B, and retained only q. As we have just seen, such a contraction can be a smooth kernel contraction, but it cannot be a partial meet contraction. It is not evident that such contractions are at all events irrational.

Our interpretation of this example referred to a belief base. No analogous example can be found for belief sets, since the difference between smooth kernel contractions and partial meet contractions disappears when the set to be contracted is a belief set:

THEOREM 2.37 ([52]) *Let A be a belief set. Then an operation $\div$ is a smooth kernel contraction for A if and only if it is a partial meet contraction for A.* *[Proof: p. 177.]*

Thus, for belief bases, smooth (or saturated) kernel contraction is an interesting generalization of partial meet contraction. For belief sets, it coincides with partial meet contraction.

9 SAFE CONTRACTION

The task of an incision function is to select sentences to be discarded. This can also be done by a selection function that selects at least one element from each kernel. Let s be a function such that for each element X of $A \perp\!\!\!\perp \alpha$, $s(X)$ is a subset of X that is non-empty if X is nonempty. Given such a selection function, let $\sigma(A \perp\!\!\!\perp \alpha)$ be the union of all sets $s(X)$ such that $X \in A \perp\!\!\!\perp \alpha$. It can be seen from Definition 2.30 that σ is an incision function. Since it cumulates the selections of s, it may be called the *cumulation* of s.

DEFINITION 2.38 A kernel selection function *for A is a function s such that for all $X \in \{X \mid X \in A \perp\!\!\!\perp \alpha$ for some $\alpha\}$:*

1. $s(X) \subseteq X$
2. $s(X) \neq \emptyset$ *if* $X \neq \emptyset$.

DEFINITION 2.39 *Let s be a kernel selection function. Then the function σ is the* cumulation *of s if and only if for all α:*

$$\sigma(A \perp\!\!\!\perp \alpha) = \bigcup\{s(X) \mid X \in A \perp\!\!\!\perp \alpha\}.$$

An incision function σ for A is cumulative *if and only if it is the cumulation of some kernel selection function for A. An operator of kernel contraction is cumulative if and only if it is based on a cumulative incision function.*

Not all kernel contractions are cumulative. To see this, let p and q be logically independent sentences and let $A = \{p, p \rightarrow q, q \rightarrow p\}$. We then have:

$$A \perp\!\!\!\perp q = \{\{p, p \rightarrow q\}\}$$
$$A \perp\!\!\!\perp (p \leftrightarrow q) = \{\{p, p \rightarrow q\}, \{p \rightarrow q, q \rightarrow p\}\}$$

A kernel contraction for A may very well be based on an incision function σ such that $\sigma(A \perp\!\!\!\perp q) = \{p \rightarrow q\}$ and $\sigma(A \perp\!\!\!\perp (p \leftrightarrow q)) = \{p, q \rightarrow p\}$. However, this is not a cumulative kernel contraction. To see this, suppose to the contrary that σ is the cumulation of some kernel selection function s. It then follows from $\sigma(A \perp\!\!\!\perp q) = \{p \rightarrow q\}$ that $s(\{p, p \rightarrow q\}) = \{p \rightarrow q\}$, and since $\{p, p \rightarrow q\} \in A \perp\!\!\!\perp (p \leftrightarrow q)$ this requires that $p \rightarrow q \in \sigma(A \perp\!\!\!\perp (p \leftrightarrow q))$, contrary to the definition of σ.

Intuitively, the kernel selection function s can be thought of as selecting for deletion the least valuable elements of each kernel. It is therefore reasonable to let s be based on a binary relation that represents comparative epistemic value. Let $\prec$ be that relation. Intuitively, $\alpha \prec \beta$ means that α should be discarded rather than β if we have to give up one of them. It can be read 'α is less safe than β'.

A kernel selection function s can be based on a relation $\prec$ in the following sense:

DEFINITION 2.40 *A kernel selection function s for A is* based *on a relation $\prec$ if and only if for all $X \in A \perp\!\!\!\perp \alpha$:*

$\beta \in s(X)$ if and only if $\beta \in X$ and there is no $\delta \in X$ such that $\delta \prec \beta$.

An incision function is based on a relation $\prec$ if and only if it is the cumulation of some kernel selection function that is based on $\prec$.

In other words, $s(X)$ consists of all those elements of X that are 'worst' in the sense of not being epistemically 'better' than any other element.

Not every relation $\prec$ can be used to construct a kernel selection function. For a simple counter-example, let $\prec$ be a reflexive relation and let α be a non-tautological element of A. Then $\{\alpha\} \in A \perp\!\!\!\perp \alpha$. Since $\alpha \prec \alpha$, if s is based on $\prec$ in the manner of Definition 2.40, then $s(\{\alpha\}) = \emptyset$, so that s cannot be a kernel selection function.

The following definition provides us with a sufficient condition for a relation $\prec$ to be serviceable as a basis for a kernel selection function:

DEFINITION 2.41 *Let* A *be a set of sentences and* $\prec$ *a relation on* A. *Then* $\prec$ *satisfies acyclicity if and only if for all positive integers* n: *If* $\{\alpha_1, \ldots, \alpha_n\} \subseteq A$, *then it is* not *the case that* $\alpha_1 \prec \alpha_2 \prec \ldots \prec \alpha_n \prec \alpha_1$.

It follows from the definition that if $\prec$ is acyclic, then it is also *irreflexive*, i.e. $\alpha \prec \alpha$ does not hold for any α.

OBSERVATION 2.42 *Let* $\prec$ *be a relation on* A *that satisfies acyclicity. Then the function* s *that is based on* $\prec$ *in the manner of Definition 2.40 is a kernel selection function.*
[Proof: p. 180.]

We will assume that $\prec$ treats logically equivalent sentences alike. An acyclic relation over a set A that does this will be called a *hierarchy* over A.

DEFINITION 2.43 (Alchourrón and Makinson [4]) *A relation* $\prec$ *over a set* A *is a* hierarchy *over* A *if and only if:*

1. *it is acyclic*
2. *if* $\alpha \leftrightarrow \alpha' \in \text{Cn}(\emptyset)$ *and* $\beta \leftrightarrow \beta' \in \text{Cn}(\emptyset)$, *then* $\alpha \prec \beta$ *holds if and only if* $\alpha' \prec \beta'$.

We can now define the notion of safe contraction (that historically preceded kernel contraction).

DEFINITION 2.44 (Alchourrón and Makinson [4]) *Let* $\prec$ *be a hierarchy over* A. *Let* σ *be the incision function that is based on* $\prec$. *Then* $\tilde{\approx}_\sigma$, *the saturation of the kernel contraction based on* σ, *is the* safe contraction *based on* $\prec$.

The original definition of safe contraction was phrased in terms of 'safe elements' of A. An element β of A is *safe with respect to* α if and only if it is not an element of $\sigma(A \perp\!\!\!\perp \alpha)$, i.e. if and only if it is not an element of $s(X)$ for any $X \in A \perp\!\!\!\perp \alpha$, i.e. (and now follows the original formulation) if and only if for all $X \in A \perp\!\!\!\perp \alpha$, either $\beta \notin X$ or there is some $\delta \in X$ such that $\delta \prec \beta$. Let A/α be the set of elements of A that are safe with respect to α. Then $A \tilde{\approx}_\sigma \alpha = A \cap \text{Cn}(A/\alpha)$.

Since safe contraction is a variant of kernel contraction, some of its basic properties follow directly from what we already know about kernel contraction. In particular, since saturated kernel contractions on logically closed sets (belief sets) are partial meet contractions, *safe contractions on (logically closed) belief sets are partial meet contractions* [4].

Interesting results can be obtained by imposing additional requirements on the hierarchy $\prec$. It would be natural to require that $\prec$ satisfies transitivity (i.e. that if $\alpha \prec \beta$ and $\beta \prec \delta$, then $\alpha \prec \delta$.) If you are more willing to give up α than to give up

β, and also more willing to give up β than to give up δ, then you can be expected to be more willing to give up α than to give up δ.

Next, let us consider cases when $\mathrm{Cn}(\{\beta\}) \subset \mathrm{Cn}(\{\alpha\})$, i.e. when β is logically weaker than α (implied by α but not equivalent to α). In such cases, we can give up α without giving up β, but we cannot give up β without giving up α.

Example
I believe that John Dewey was born in Burlington (α), and also that he was born in the U.S.A. (β). I can give up α without giving up β, but I cannot give up β without giving up α.

In cases like this we are, from a formal point of view, more willing to give up α than to give up β, and thus $\alpha \prec \beta$.

Strict dominance:
If $\mathrm{Cn}(\{\beta\}) \subset \mathrm{Cn}(\{\alpha\})$, then $\alpha \prec \beta$.

The following two properties are satisfied by all hierarchies that satisfy transitivity and strict dominance:

Continuing-up: [4]
If $\alpha \prec \beta$ and $\beta \vdash \delta$, then $\alpha \prec \delta$.

Continuing-down: [4]
If $\alpha \vdash \beta$ and $\beta \prec \delta$, then $\alpha \prec \delta$.

Examples

1. I believe that bumble-bees are hymenoptera (α). I also believe that salamanders are amphibians (β) and that salamanders are vertebrates (δ). Since I am more willing to give up α than to give up β, and β implies δ, I am more willing to give up α than δ. (*continuing-up*)
2. I believe that John Dewey was born in Burlington (α), that he was born in the U.S.A. (β), and that he spent most of his life in the U.S.A. (δ). Since α implies β, and I am more willing to give up β than to give up δ, I am more willing to give up α than δ. (*continuing-down*)

Continuing-up and continuing-down have turned out to be extremely useful properties in studies of safe contraction. Each of them is sufficient to make sure that *conjunctive overlap* ($(A{\div}\alpha) \cap (A{\div}\beta) \subseteq A{\div}(\alpha\&\beta)$) is satisfied.

OBSERVATION 2.45 (Alchourrón and Makinson [4]) *Let $\prec$ be a hierarchy over the logically closed set A, and let $\div$ be the safe contraction that is based on $\prec$. Then:*

1. *If $\prec$ satisfies continuing-up, then $\div$ satisfies conjunctive overlap.*

2. *If $\prec$ satisfies continuing-down, then $\div$ satisfies conjunctive overlap.*
[Proof: p. 181 and p. 183.]

Connectivity $((\alpha \prec \beta) \vee (\beta \prec \alpha))$ implies $\alpha \prec \alpha$, that violates acyclicity. Therefore, a hierarchy cannot satisfy connectivity. However, a hierarchy can satisfy the following related property:

Virtual connectivity:
If $\alpha \prec \beta$ then either $\alpha \prec \delta$ or $\delta \prec \beta$.

Continuing-up, continuing-down and virtual connectivity are the three properties of hierarchies that are most commonly referred to. A hierarchy that satisfies both continuing-up and continuing-down is called a *regular* hierarchy.

In the presence of virtual connectivity, continuing-up and continuing-down are interchangeable.

OBSERVATION 2.46 (Alchourrón and Makinson [4]) *If a hierarchy is virtually connected, then it satisfies continuing-up if and only if it satisfies continuing-down.*
[Proof: p. 179.]

The most advanced formal result that has been obtained for safe contraction is the following representation theorem. (The case when the language is finite was proved by Alchourrón and Makinson [5], and the general case by Hans Rott.)

THEOREM 2.47 (Hans Rott [114]) *Let A be a logically closed set and $\div$ an operation on A. Then $\div$ is a safe contraction, based on a regular and virtually connected hierarchy, if and only if it satisfies both the basic and the supplementary Gärdenfors postulates (i.e. closure, inclusion, vacuity, success, extensionality, recovery, conjunctive overlap, and conjunctive inclusion).*
[Proof: p. 185.]

It follows from Theorems 2.21 and 2.47 that an operator $\div$ on a belief set is a safe contraction, based on a regular and virtually connected hierarchy, if and only if it is a transitively relational partial meet contraction.

10 EPISTEMIC ENTRENCHMENT

When forced to give up previous beliefs, we should give up beliefs that have as little explanatory power and overall informational value as possible. As an example of this, if we can choose between giving up beliefs in natural laws and beliefs in single factual statements, we should in most cases retain our beliefs in the natural laws, that have much higher explanatory power. This was the basic idea behind Peter Gärdenfors's proposal that contraction of beliefs should be ruled by an ordering of *epistemic entrenchment*. In Gärdenfors's own words:

> 'Even if all sentences in a belief set are accepted or considered as facts (so that they are assigned maximal probability), this does not mean that all sentences are of equal value for planning or problem-solving purposes. Certain pieces of our knowledge and beliefs about the world are more important than others when planning future actions, conducting scientific investigations, or reasoning in general. We will say that some sentences in a belief system have a higher degree of *epistemic entrenchment* than others... The guiding idea for the construction is that when a belief set A is revised or contracted, the sentences in A that are given up are those having the lowest degrees of epistemic entrenchment.' [37]

The formal tool introduced by Gärdenfors to express epistemic entrenchment is a binary relation. Let α and β be two elements of the belief set. 'β is more entrenched than α' means that β is more useful in inquiry or deliberation, or has more 'epistemic value' than α. (Observe that there is no simple connection between entrenchment or epistemic value on the one hand, and probabilities on the other.) At least ideally, it should be possible to determine the comparative degree of entrenchment of various sentences prior to (and without reference to) the operator of contraction or any other operator of change [35]. When we perform belief contraction, the beliefs with the lowest entrenchment should turn out to be the ones that are given up.

For this to be a valid analysis, the two notions of epistemic value and vulnerability to change must be inversely related in an exact manner, so that they can be adequately represented by one and the same binary relation. Only under this assumption—which is of course open to philosophical debate—can the formal results to be reported in this section be interpreted as originally intended by Gärdenfors. Another, less demanding interpretation is to regard epistemic entrenchment as 'just another word for comparative retractability'. Then 'ϕ is less entrenched than ψ' means that 'it is easier to discard ϕ than to discard ψ', and no connection to an independent notion of epistemic value is postulated [111].

The following symbols will be used for epistemic entrenchment:

$\alpha \leq \beta$ α is at most as entrenched as β
$\alpha < \beta$ α is less entrenched than β
$\alpha \equiv \beta$ α and β are equally entrenched.

$<$ and $\equiv$ can be defined in terms of $\leq$:

$$\alpha < \beta \text{ if and only if } (\alpha \leq \beta)\&\neg(\beta \leq \alpha)$$
$$\alpha \equiv \beta \text{ if and only if } (\alpha \leq \beta)\&(\beta \leq \alpha)$$

Gärdenfors has proposed five postulates for epistemic entrenchment. First, epistemic entrenchment is transitive:

Transitivity:
If $\alpha \leq \beta$ and $\beta \leq \delta$, then $\alpha \leq \delta$.

Thus, if you are at most as willing to give up α as to give up β and also at most as willing to give up β as to give up δ, then you should be at most as willing to give up α as to give up δ. (This postulate can also be paraphrased in terms of epistemic value: If α has at most as much epistemic value as β and β at most as much as δ, then α also has at most as much epistemic value as δ.)

The next postulate compares two sentences, one of which logically implies the other. Let α be a sentence that logically implies β. If you are forced to give up β, then you will also have to give up α (since α cannot be retained without its logical consequence β also being retained). Therefore, you will appear to be at least as willing to give up α as to give up β; or in other words: α should be at most as entrenched as β:

Dominance: [35]
If $\alpha \vdash \beta$, then $\alpha \leq \beta$.

Next, let us compare the sentences α and β to their conjunction $\alpha\&\beta$. In order to give up $\alpha\&\beta$ you must give up either α or β. In the first case, the loss incurred by giving up $\alpha\&\beta$ should be the same as that from giving up α. In the second case it should be the same as that from giving up β. Thus:

$$\text{Either } \alpha\&\beta \equiv \alpha \text{ or } \alpha\&\beta \equiv \beta.$$

Since $\alpha\&\beta$ logically implies α, it follows already from dominance that $\alpha\&\beta \leq \alpha$. In the same way, since $\alpha\&\beta$ logically implies β, it follows that $\alpha\&\beta \leq \beta$. If we wish to avoid unnecessary redundancies in the list of postulates, it is therefore better to postulate:

Conjunctiveness: [35]
Either $\alpha \leq \alpha\&\beta$ or $\beta \leq \alpha\&\beta$.

In the way already indicated it follows from conjunctiveness and dominance that either $\alpha\&\beta \equiv \alpha$ or $\alpha\&\beta \equiv \beta$. Furthermore, it follows from the three postulates that we have now introduced that for all sentences α and β, either $\alpha \leq \beta$ or $\beta \leq \alpha$ (or equivalently: either $\alpha < \beta, \beta < \alpha$, or $\alpha \equiv \beta$):

Connectivity:
Either $\alpha \leq \beta$ or $\beta \leq \alpha$.

OBSERVATION 2.48 (Gärdenfors and Makinson [38]) *If the relation $\leq$ (of epistemic entrenchment) satisfies transitivity, dominance, and conjunctiveness, then it satisfies connectivity.*
[Proof: p. 187.]

The three postulates already given provide us with most of the properties that are needed for epistemic entrenchment. (In particular, conjunctiveness has a surprising strength in formal derivations.) In order to complete Gärdenfors's list of postulates, it only remains to add two postulates that treat the two limiting cases: sentences outside of the belief set and sentences that are logically true.

First, let us consider the sentences that are not elements of the belief set. Since these sentences have been 'given up' from the beginning, they are clearly the sentences that the subject is most willing to give up. Thus, they should be less entrenched than any sentence in the belief set. Furthermore, since all of these sentences are as vulnerable to contraction as any sentence can be, they should all have the lowest possible degree of entrenchment. Therefore, they should all be equally entrenched. (In terms of epistemic value, we can say that they should all have the lowest possible epistemic value.) This is implied by the postulate of *minimality*, so named since it identifies those sentences that have minimal entrenchment.

Minimality: [35]
If the belief set A is consistent, then $\alpha \notin A$ if and only if $\alpha \leq \beta$ for all β.

OBSERVATION 2.49 *If the belief set A is consistent and* $\leq$ *satisfies transitivity, connectivity, and minimality, then:*

1. *if* $\alpha \notin A$ *and* $\beta \in A$. *then* $\alpha < \beta$
2. *if* $\alpha \notin A$ *and* $\beta \notin A$, *then* $\alpha \equiv \beta$.

[Proof: p. 187.]

Since any belief set contains all logical truths (tautologies), logical truths can never be given up. They must therefore have the highest degree of entrenchment. This can easily be shown to follow from dominance. Let α be a logical truth. Then it holds for all sentences β that $\vdash \beta \rightarrow \alpha$ (every sentence implies every logical truth). Therefore, according to dominance, it holds for all sentences β that $\beta \leq \alpha$. This is another way of saying that α has the highest degree of entrenchment.

However, this is not all that we have to say about the highest degree of entrenchment. Another reasonable requirement is that the logical truths should be the only sentences that have the highest degree of entrenchment. In other words, all other sentences should be possible to give up. This does not follow from the four postulates introduced so far. It follows from the fifth and last of Gärdenfors's postulates for entrenchment:

Maximality: [35]
If $\beta \leq \alpha$ for all β, then $\vdash \alpha$.

Transitivity, dominance, conjunctiveness, minimality, and maximality will be referred to as *the standard postulates for entrenchment*. A relation that satisfies all of them will be called a *standard entrenchment ordering* for the belief set A. It is important to observe that one of these postulates, namely minimality, explicitly refers to the belief set. Therefore, a standard entrenchment ordering is always an entrenchment ordering *for a specified belief set*. It cannot be used for any other set of beliefs than the one that it is intended for.

Given the standard postulates, our next task is to connect the entrenchment ordering with an operator of contraction. This can be done in two directions. We can (1) given an operator of contraction define an entrenchment ordering, or (2) given an entrenchment ordering define a contraction operator.

To begin with, let us construct an entrenchment ordering out of an operator of contraction. The guiding principle for this construction has already been indicated: $\alpha \leq \beta$ should hold if and only if, in the choice between giving up α and β, the former is given up. A choice between giving up α and giving up β arises when we contract by the conjunction $\alpha\&\beta$. Therefore $\alpha \leq \beta$ should hold if and only if $\alpha \notin A\div(\alpha\&\beta)$.

However, there is an exception to this rule: If $\alpha\&\beta$ is a tautology, then both α and β are also tautologies. Therefore, they are both elements of $A\div(\alpha\&\beta)$, so that neither $\alpha \notin A\div(\alpha\&\beta)$ nor $\beta \notin A(\alpha\&\beta)$ can hold. We must make a special proviso to see to it that $\alpha \equiv \beta$ holds in this case. Due to the symmetry of the formula, it is sufficient to postulate that $\alpha \leq \beta$ holds if $\alpha\&\beta$ is a tautology. (It follows by substitution of β for α and vice versa that $\beta \leq \alpha$ holds as well in this case, and thus $\alpha \equiv \beta$.) We arrive at the following definition:

$$(\mathrm{C}\leq) \quad \alpha \leq \beta \text{ if and only if } \alpha \notin A\div(\alpha\&\beta) \text{ or } \alpha\&\beta \in \mathrm{Cn}(\emptyset).$$

The other, more interesting task is to define contraction in terms of an entrenchment ordering. Gärdenfors proposed the following definition:

Gärdenfors's entrenchment-based contraction:
$(\mathrm{G}\div)$ $\beta \in A\div\alpha$ if and only if $\beta \in A$ and either $\alpha < (\alpha\vee\beta)$ or $\alpha \in \mathrm{Cn}(\emptyset)$.

It is not immediately obvious why $\alpha < (\alpha\vee\beta)$ appears in this definition. The following argument [38] for the use of $\alpha < (\alpha\vee\beta)$ has the disadvantage of depending on the controversial assumption that $\div$ should satisfy recovery. (There does not seem to be any good argument for $\alpha < (\alpha\vee\beta)$ that does not appeal to this postulate.)

If $\div$ satisfies recovery, then it holds for all $\beta \in A$ that $\alpha\rightarrow\beta \in A\div\alpha$. Since $\alpha\rightarrow\beta$ and $\alpha\vee\beta$ together imply β, it follows that if $\alpha\vee\beta \in A\div\alpha$, then $\beta \in A\div\alpha$. Furthermore, if $\beta \in A\div\alpha$, then $\alpha\vee\beta \in A\div\alpha$. Thus, in order to determine whether or not a sentence β is in $A\div\alpha$, we can instead determine whether or not $\alpha\vee\beta$ is in $A\div\alpha$. We can see from (C$\leq$) (excluding the limiting cases) that:

$$\alpha\vee\beta \notin A\div((\alpha\vee\beta)\&\alpha) \text{ if and only if } (\alpha\vee\beta) \leq \alpha.$$

Using extensionality, we obtain:

$$\alpha\vee\beta \notin A\div\alpha \text{ if and only if } (\alpha\vee\beta) \leq \alpha.$$

It remains to negate both sides of the equivalence (making use of the connectivity of $\leq$) to obtain:

$$\alpha\vee\beta \in A\div\alpha \text{ if and only if } \alpha < (\alpha\vee\beta).$$

Since we have shown $\alpha\vee\beta \in A\div\alpha$ to be equivalent to $\beta \in A\div\alpha$ (given recovery), we finally obtain:

$$\beta \in A\div\alpha \text{ if and only if } \alpha < (\alpha\vee\beta).$$

Hans Rott has pointed out that the comparison $\alpha < (\alpha\vee\beta)$ in this definition is not the one that should intuitively be expected [110]. He has investigated the following alternative definition:

Rott's entrenchment-based contraction [110]:
$(R\div)$ $\beta \in A\div\alpha$ if and only if $\beta \in A$ and either $\alpha < \beta$ or $\alpha \in \mathrm{Cn}(\emptyset)$.

Thus, when contracting a set A by a non-tautological sentence α, we retain, with this operation, exactly those sentences that are more entrenched than α.

Gärdenfors's entrenchment-based contraction is exactly characterized by the six basic and two supplementary Gärdenfors postulates (namely closure, inclusion, vacuity, success, extensionality, recovery, conjunctive overlap, and conjunctive inclusion). Hence, this construction of contraction is equivalent to that which is based on transitively relational selection functions.

THEOREM 2.50 (Peter Gärdenfors [35; 38]) *1. Let $\leq$ be a standard entrenchment ordering on the consistent belief set A. Furthermore, let $\div_G$ be Gärdenfors's entrenchment-based contraction on A, based on $\leq$. Then $\div_G$ satisfies the six basic and two supplementary Gärdenfors postulates, as well as ($C\leq$).*

2. Let $\div$ be an operation on the consistent belief set A that satisfies the six basic and two supplementary Gärdenfors postulates. Furthermore, let $\leq$ be the relation that is derived from $\div$ through ($C\leq$). Then $\leq$ satisfies the standard entrenchment postulates, and it also satisfies ($G\div$).
[Proof: p. 188.]

Rott's entrenchment-based contraction can be shown to satisfy all the (basic and supplementary) Gärdenfors postulates for contraction except one, namely recovery:

OBSERVATION 2.51 (Hans Rott [110]) *Let $\leq$ be a standard entrenchment ordering on a belief set A, and let $\div_R$ be Rott's entrenchment-based contraction on A, based on $\leq$. Then:*

1. *$\div_R$ satisfies closure, inclusion, vacuity, success, extensionality, conjunctive overlap, and conjunctive inclusion.*
2. *$\div_R$ does not in general satisfy recovery.*

[Proof: p. 192.]

As we saw in Section 2.3, recovery is the most controversial among the Gärdenfors postulates, and quite plausible counter-examples have been put forward. At first glance, Rott's entrenchment-based contraction may therefore seem to be more plausible than Gärdenfors's. Unfortunately, however, it has other questionable properties not shared by Gärdenfors's operation:

Expulsiveness:
If $\nvdash \alpha$ and $\nvdash \beta$, then either $\alpha \notin A \div \beta$ or $\beta \notin A \div \alpha$.

OBSERVATION 2.52 *Let $\leq$ be a standard entrenchment ordering on a belief set A, and let $\div_R$ and $\div_G$ be Rott's and Gärdenfors's entrenchment-based contractions, based on $\leq$. Then:*

1. *$\div_R$ satisfies expulsiveness, but*
2. *$\div_G$ does not in general satisfy expulsiveness.*

[Proof: p. 193.]

According to expulsiveness, for any two non-tautological elements α and β of the belief set, either α is expelled when β is contracted, or β when α is contracted. This is a highly implausible property of belief contraction, since it does not allow unrelated beliefs to be undisturbed by each other's contraction.

Example
I believe that my car is parked in front of the house (α). I also believe that Shakespeare wrote the Tempest (β). Should I give up the first of these beliefs, I would still retain the second. Should I give up the second, I would retain the first.

Rott himself regards $\div_R$ as an interesting limiting case rather than as a plausible operation in itself.[1]

[1] *Note added in proof*: Recently, Maurice Pagnucco and Hans Rott have axiomatically characterized Rott's entrenchment-based contraction. This can be done with closure, inclusion, success, extensionality, vacuity, failure, conjunctive inclusion, and the following postulate: If $\alpha \notin \mathrm{Cn}(\emptyset)$, then $A \div \alpha \subseteq A \div (\alpha \& \beta)$. For details, see Pagnucco's thesis (*The Role of Abductive Reasoning within the Process of Belief Revision*, University of Sydney, 1996), and a forthcoming joint paper by Rott and Pagnucco.

Lindström and Rabinowicz [79] have proposed that a realistic entrenchment-based contraction operator should be posited between Rott's and Gärdenfors's operators, i.e. that if $\div$ is a reasonable operator, then for all α:

$$A{\div}_{R}\alpha \subseteq A{\div}\alpha \subseteq A{\div}_{G}\alpha.$$

It can be shown that, given some of the more plausible postulates of contraction, this must indeed be the case:

OBSERVATION 2.53 *Let $\div$ be an operator of contraction for the belief set A. Let $\leq$ be the relation defined from $\div$ via (C$\leq$). Furthermore, let $\div_G$ and $\div_R$ be Gärdenfors's and Rott's (entrenchment-based) contractions, based on $\leq$. Then:*

1. *If $\div$ satisfies inclusion, closure, success, and extensionality, then $A{\div}\alpha \subseteq A{\div}_{G}\alpha$ for all α.*
2. *If $\div$ satisfies closure, failure, and conjunctive inclusion, then $A{\div}_{R}\alpha \subseteq A{\div}\alpha$ for all α.*

[Proof: p. 195.]

Epistemic entrenchment has been defined for belief sets, not belief bases. It is no simple matter to transfer the same construction to belief bases. One of the reasons for this is a philosophical problem that applies not only to entrenchment but to all selection mechanisms that are based on a relation among the *elements* of a belief base [43]. (This includes safe contraction, but not relational partial meet contraction, that is based on a relation among the *subsets* of the base). Let us consider a belief base $A = \{\alpha, \beta, \delta\}$. A choice between β and δ may very well depend on whether or not α is retained. For example, $\{\alpha, \beta\}$ may be epistemically preferred to $\{\alpha, \delta\}$ (as the result of some contraction), although $\{\delta\}$ is epistemically preferred to $\{\beta\}$ (as the result of some other contraction). This can easily be expressed with a relation on subsets of A, but it cannot be expressed with a relation on elements of A.

This problem does not apply to selection mechanisms that operate on (logically closed) belief sets. Let us instead consider the belief set $\mathrm{Cn}(A)$. It contains conjunctions such as $\alpha\&\beta$ and $\alpha\&\delta$ that can be used to express what we could not express with reference to elements of A. We can have an entrenchment ordering on $\mathrm{Cn}(A)$ such that $\beta < \delta$ and $\alpha\&\delta < \alpha\&\beta$ (but no relation on the elements of A can express this).

Probably the most successful application to belief bases of the ideas behind entrenchment is the theory of *ensconcement relations*, that has been developed by Mary-Anne Williams [124; 125; 126]. She defines an ensconcement relation $\preccurlyeq$ on a set A (with the strict part $\prec$) as a transitive and connective relation that satisfies the following three conditions:

1. If $\beta \in A\backslash\mathrm{Cn}(\emptyset)$, then $\{\alpha \in A \mid \beta \ll \alpha\} \nvdash \beta$
2. If $\nvdash \alpha$ and $\vdash \beta$, then $\alpha \ll \beta$.
3. If $\vdash \alpha$ and $\vdash \beta$, then $\alpha \leqslant\!\!\!\!\ll \beta$.

According to the first of these conditions, the formulas that are strictly more ensconced than α do not (even conjointly) imply α. According to last two conditions, if there are any tautologies in a belief base A, then they are its most ensconced formulas.

Given an ensconcement relation $\leqslant\!\!\!\!\ll$ and a formula α, the *proper cut* for α is the set $\mathtt{cut}_{\ll}(\alpha)$ obtained by cutting off the lower-ensconced parts until what remains does not imply α. In formal terms:

$$\beta \in \mathtt{cut}_{\ll}(\alpha) \text{ if and only if } \beta \in A \text{ and } \{\delta \in A \mid \beta \leqslant\!\!\!\!\ll \delta\} \nvdash \alpha.$$

The cut operation can be used to construct an operator $\div_{W}$ of contraction as follows:

$$\begin{array}{l}\beta \in A \div_{W} \alpha \text{ if and only if} \\ \beta \in A \text{ and either (i) } \alpha \in \mathrm{Cn}(\emptyset) \text{ or (ii) } \mathtt{cut}_{\ll}(\alpha) \vdash \alpha \vee \beta.\end{array}$$

Williams has shown that for every ensconcement-based contraction on a belief base A, there is an entrenchment-based contraction $\div_{G}$ on the corresponding belief set $\mathrm{Cn}(A)$ such that for all sentences α:

$$A \div_{W} \alpha = (\mathrm{Cn}(A) \div_{G} \alpha) \cap A.$$

In other words, a formula is retained after ensconcement-based contraction if and only if it is a member of the belief base and it would have been retained after the corresponding entrenchment-based contraction.

11 REPEATED CONTRACTION

Up to now, we have only been concerned with contractions from one and the same belief base or belief set. We have defined our operators of contraction to be specific for one particular set. For example, an operator of partial meet contraction is defined as a contraction operator for a specified set A. It is not applicable to any other set than A. Therefore, we are not able to perform a sequence of operations such as $A \div \alpha \div \beta$.

This is clearly a severe limitation, not least from a computational point of view. It does not seem worthwhile to build a computer model that can only contract its database (belief state) once, after which it is left without means for further contractions. A realistic and useful model of belief contraction should allow for repeated (iterated) contractions, and for chains of contractions and expansions such as $A \div \alpha \div \beta + \delta + \varepsilon \div \xi \ldots$. In other words, we need an operator that can contract any set by any sentence. Such operators are called *global*, in contrast to *local* operators that are defined only for contractions of a single specified set.

In spite of the importance of repeated contraction, relatively few formal results are available on global operators. Arguably, this is excusable in view of the youth of this research field and of the need to first settle the fundamental issues that arise even for local operators. In this section, we are going to see how partial meet, kernel, safe, and entrenchment-based contraction can be extended to global operations.

Partial meet contraction: The simplest way to obtain a global operator of partial meet contraction, one might think, would be to use the same selection function for all sets to be contracted. However, this is not possible, due to the way selection functions treat the empty set.

The way we have defined selection functions, if $A \bot \alpha = \emptyset$, then $\gamma(A \bot \alpha) = \{A\}$. As a consequence of this, if γ is a selection function for A, and $A \neq B$, then γ is not a selection function for B. For let $A \bot \alpha = B \bot \alpha = \emptyset$. For γ to be a function it must be the case that $\gamma(A \bot \alpha) = \gamma(B \bot \alpha)$. For γ to be a selection function for $A, \gamma(A \bot \alpha) = \{A\}$ must hold, and in order for γ to be a selection function for B it must satisfy $\gamma(B \bot \alpha) = \{B\}$. Since $A \neq B$, this is impossible.

Therefore, a global operator of partial meet contraction must apply different selection functions to different belief bases (belief sets). A convenient way to achieve this is to introduce two-place selection functions. A two-place selection function γ has two argument places, one for the belief base (belief set) and one for the remainder set. $\gamma(A, A \bot \alpha)$ is a subset of $A \bot \alpha$ if the latter is non-empty, and similarly $\gamma(B, B \bot \beta)$ is a subset of $B \bot \beta$, etc. $\gamma(A, A \bot \alpha)$ can also be written $\gamma_A(A \bot \alpha)$, and for every set A, γ_A should be a (one-place) selection function for A. In formal terms:

DEFINITION 2.54 ([45; 50]) *A* two-place selection function *is a function γ such that for each subset A of $\mathcal{L}, \gamma(A, \ ) = \gamma_A(\ )$ is a one-place selection function for A.*

Each two-place selection function gives rise to an operator of global partial meet contraction $\sim_\gamma$ *such that for all sets A and sentences α: $A \sim_\gamma \alpha = \bigcap \gamma_A(A \bot \alpha)$.*

Two-place selection functions can be applied either to belief sets or to belief bases. In the former case, the belief set completely determines the outcome of contraction (or revision) by a specified sentence. ‘If I know your beliefs, then I know how you would change them.’ As a direct consequence of this, we have *path-independence with respect to belief sets*: Once you have arrived at a certain belief set, your future belief changes are not influenced by how you arrived at it. These properties are far from realistic, and some authors maintain that the application of two-place selection functions to belief sets is not even useful as a first approximation [7; 43].

The same construction fares somewhat better when applied to belief bases. Then it is the belief *base* that uniquely determines the outcome of contraction, and we have path-independence with respect to belief bases. But, as we saw in Section 1.7, two belief bases with the same logical closure may represent dynamically different ways to hold the same beliefs. Therefore, two belief states may be statically equivalent (support the same beliefs) without being dynamically equivalent (behave in the same way under operations of change).

As a special case of Definition 2.54, we may wish to make a two-place selection function for belief bases unified in the sense that it acts according to the same epistemic priorities when applied to different belief bases. Since it was only the limiting case of contraction by logical truths that prevented us from using one and the same one-place selection function for all belief bases (belief sets), we can construct a two-place selection function that is 'almost one-place', where 'almost' means with the exception of this limiting case.

DEFINITION 2.55

1. [50] *A two-place selection function* γ *is* unified *if and only if for all subsets* A *and* B *of* $\mathcal{L}$ *and all elements* α *and* β *of* $\mathcal{L}$*:*
   If $A{\perp}\alpha = B{\perp}\beta \neq \emptyset$, *then* $\bigcap\gamma_A(A{\perp}\alpha) = \bigcap\gamma_B(B{\perp}\beta)$.
2. (Hans Rott) *A two-place selection function* γ *is* perfectly unified *if and only if for all subsets* A *and* B *of* $\mathcal{L}$ *and all elements* α *and* β *of* $\mathcal{L}$*: If* $A{\perp}\alpha = B{\perp}\beta \neq \emptyset$, *then* $\gamma_A(A{\perp}\alpha) = \gamma_B(B{\perp}\beta)$.
3. *A two-place selection function is relational (transitively relational, transitively maximizingly relational) if and only if all the one-place selection functions that it gives rise to are relational (etc.) by one and the same relation.*

The following theorem provides an axiomatic characterization of unified and perfectly unified partial meet contraction on belief bases. It turns out to make no difference if we require the selection function to be perfectly unified or just unified:

THEOREM 2.56 *The following three conditions on a global operator* $\div$ *are equivalent:*

1. [50] *It is an operator of partial meet contraction that is based on a unified selection function.*
2. (Hans Rott) *It is an operator of partial meet contraction that is based on a perfectly unified selection function.*
3. [50] *It satisfies success, inclusion, relevance, uniformity, and in addition the following:*
   If $\alpha \notin \mathrm{Cn}(\emptyset)$, *and each element of* Z *implies* α, *then:* $A{\div}\alpha = (A \cup Z){\div}\alpha$. *(redundancy).*

[Proof: p. 130.]

According to redundancy, the prior addition to A of one or several sentences that each implies α does not change the outcome of contraction by α. Such sentences are redundant in the sense that if success is satisfied, they cannot be members of $A{\div}\alpha$. Therefore, it is reasonable that they should have no influence on the choice that a selection mechanism makes among the rest of the elements of A. As an example, *redundancy* requires that:

$$\{p\vee q, \neg p\vee q, q\&r\}{\div}\{q\} = \{p\vee q, \neg p\vee q\}{\div}\{q\}.$$

Finally, it should be remembered that (as was mentioned in Section 1.5) partial meet contraction can also be constructed with a modified version of selection functions, that differs from the standard definition only in the limiting case when $A\bot\alpha$ is empty. In that case, the alternative definition sets $\gamma(A\bot\alpha)$ equal to $\emptyset$ instead of A. (This requires that an extra clause is added to the definition of $\sim_\gamma$ to ensure that $A\sim_\gamma\alpha = A$ when $A\bot\alpha$ is empty, i.e. when α is logically true.) With this construction (that is favoured by Hans Rott) we can use a one-place selection function instead of a perfectly unified two-place selection function to construct the global operators characterized in Theorem 2.56.

Kernel contraction: Kernel contraction does not have the problem that partial meet contraction has in the treatment of contraction by logical truths. If α is a logical truth, then $A\perp\!\!\!\perp\alpha = \{\emptyset\}$, and $\sigma(A\perp\!\!\!\perp\alpha) = \emptyset$, i.e. $\sigma(\{\emptyset\}) = \emptyset$. (This yields $A\approx_\sigma\alpha = A$, so that the postulate of failure is satisfied just as for partial meet contraction.) Since the condition $\sigma(\{\emptyset\}) = \emptyset$ does not mention A, the limiting case does not prevent σ from being an incision function for contraction of several—or indeed all—subsets of the language. The formal definition of global kernel contraction is therefore quite straight-forward (and there is no need to introduce two-place incision functions):

DEFINITION 2.57 ([52]) *A* global incision function *is a function σ such that for all sets A of sentences and all sentences α:*

i. $\sigma(A\perp\!\!\!\perp\alpha) \subseteq \bigcup(A\perp\!\!\!\perp\alpha)$

ii. If $\emptyset \neq X \in A\perp\!\!\!\perp\alpha$, *then* $X \cap \sigma(A\perp\!\!\!\perp\alpha) \neq \emptyset$.

To each global incision function σ is associated a global kernel contraction $\approx_\sigma$ *such that for all sets A of sentences and sentences α:*

$$A\approx_\sigma\alpha = A\setminus\sigma(A\perp\!\!\!\perp\alpha).$$

An operator $\div$ is a global kernel contraction if and only if there is some incision function σ such that $A{\div}\alpha = A\approx_\sigma\alpha$ for all A and α.

Finitely global incision functions *and* finitely global kernel contractions *are defined in the same way, but restricted to the case when A is a finite set of sentences.*

An axiomatic characterization has been obtained for finitely global kernel contraction:

THEOREM 2.58 ([52]) *The finitely global operator* $\div$ *is an operator of finitely global kernel contraction if and only if it satisfies success, inclusion, core-retainment, uniformity, and:*

> *If* $(A\div\alpha)+\beta \neq (A+\beta)\div\alpha$, *then there is some* δ *such that* $A\div\delta \nvdash \alpha$ *and* $(A\div\delta)+\beta \vdash \alpha$. *(permutation)*

where $+$ *denotes non-closing expansion* $(A+\beta = A\cup\{\beta\})$.
[Proof, p. 174.]

According to permutation, if expansion by β and contraction by α are not permutable, this must be because expansion by β contributes to make A imply α.

Safe contraction: The results just reported for kernel contraction are equally valid for safe contraction. Let $\prec$ be a hierarchy that is defined for the whole language ($\mathcal{L}$). Then $\prec$ can, at least from a formal point of view, be used to contract any set of sentences. This formal advantage of safe contraction was noted by Alchourrón and Makinson already in their 1985 paper in which safe contraction was introduced [4]. The subject does not seem to have been taken up since then, and the properties of repeated safe contraction are still insufficiently explored.

Although safe (and kernel) contraction can be transferred to a global setting in a more straightforward way than conventionally defined partial meet contraction, it does not necessarily follow that global safe contraction on belief sets is more intuitively plausible. In global safe contraction, just like global partial meet contraction, the belief set will completely determine the outcome of contraction by a specified sentence. In neither case can we have static equivalence without dynamic equivalence.

Epistemic entrenchment: Contrary to the hierarchies of safe contraction (but just like the selection functions of partial meet contraction) entrenchment orderings are relative to a belief set. One of the entrenchment postulates, namely that of *minimality*, explicitly mentions the belief set. Therefore, epistemic entrenchment does not share the formal advantages of safe contraction in studies of repeated belief change.

Nevertheless, epistemic entrenchment has other advantages that make it one of the more promising approaches to repeated belief change. Two different methods to apply entrenchment repeatedly have been studied.

The first of these methods is to introduce a function that assigns an entrenchment ordering to each belief set. Several such constructions have been explored [114; 115; 118; 119]. Probably the most promising of these was proposed by Hans Rott, who introduced a relation $\lhd$ over the language, and defined $<_A$ (the strict part of the entrenchment ordering for the belief set A) as follows:

> $\alpha <_A \beta$ if and only if there is a subset Y of A such that $Y \vdash \beta$ and that for every subset X of A, if $X \vdash \alpha$, then: (1) $X \neq \emptyset$ and (2) for every $\psi \in Y$ there is some $\chi \in X$ such that $\chi \lhd \psi$. [40; 114]

If $\lhd$ is transitive and virtually connected, then this definition provides us, for each belief set A, with an entrenchment ordering $\leq_A$ for A, that satisfies the five standard postulates for entrenchment [114]. With this construction static equivalence will, of course, imply dynamic equivalence.

The second of the two approaches makes use of what may be called the *self-sufficiency* of entrenchment orderings. Given an entrenchment ordering $\leq$ for a belief set A, we can 'recover' A from $\leq$ via the simple identity:

$$A = \{\delta \mid \beta < \delta \text{ for some } \beta\}.$$

Instead of contracting and revising belief sets, we can therefore contract and revise entrenchment orderings. Thus, given a belief set A and an entrenchment ordering $\leq$ for A, when contracting by a sentence α the outcome should be a new entrenchment ordering $\leq'$. We are then automatically provided with a new belief set, namely the set $\{\delta \mid \beta <' \delta \text{ for some } \delta\}$. If the operation has been successful, then this new belief set should not contain α.

This approach was first discovered by Hans Rott, who has investigated various ways to contract an entrenchment ordering by a sentence to arrive at a new entrenchment ordering [113]. Abhaya Nayak has proposed an interesting further modification of this approach, namely to let inputs (as well as belief states) be represented by entrenchment relations. Hence, belief change will consist in the incorporation of an entrenchment relation (the input) into a prior entrenchment relation (the original belief state) to arrive at a new entrenchment relation (the new belief state). This framework is very general, and depending on the properties of the input, such an operation of change may be a contraction, a revision, or some other form of belief change. Nayak and his colleagues have investigated some revision-like operations, but contraction does not yet seem to have been investigated in this framework [95; 96; 97]. Nevertheless, this seems to be one of the more promising models of iterated belief change.

In Nayak's model, there will be many ways to contract (or revise) a given belief set by a given sentence. This increased complexity may be a price that has to be paid for a realistic modelling of iterated change [128].

CHAPTER 2^{+}

THE LOGIC OF CONTRACTION

In this chapter, we are going to have a closer look at the constructions and postulates from Chapter 2. The theorems and observations from that chapter will be proved, and some additional properties of the constructions will be introduced. We are also going to have a look at multiple contraction (Section 2.16^{+}).

Whereas Chapter 2 was organized according to the intuitive interpretations of various concepts and results, Chapter 2^{+} is organized according to proof methods and other considerations of formal development.

12^{+} RELATIONS BETWEEN THE BASIC POSTULATES

Through representation theorems, postulates for belief contraction can be connected to various constructive approaches to contraction. However, it can also be instructive to study the interrelations between the postulates without connecting them to any particular construction. In this and the following section, such a 'free-floating' approach to the postulates will be adopted. Let us first have a fresh look at the basic postulates that were introduced in Sections 2.2 and 2.3:

Success: If $\alpha \notin \mathrm{Cn}(\emptyset)$, then $\alpha \notin \mathrm{Cn}(A \div \alpha)$.
Inclusion: $A \div \alpha \subseteq A$.
Failure: If $\alpha \in \mathrm{Cn}(\emptyset)$, then $A \div \alpha = A$.
Vacuity: If $\alpha \notin \mathrm{Cn}(A)$, then $A \div \alpha = A$.
Relevance: If $\beta \in A$ and $\beta \notin A \div \alpha$, then there is a set A' such that $A \div \alpha \subseteq A' \subseteq A$ and that $\alpha \notin \mathrm{Cn}(A')$ but $\alpha \in \mathrm{Cn}(A' \cup \{\beta\})$.
Core-retainment: If $\beta \in A$ and $\beta \notin A \div A$, then there is a set A' such that $A' \subseteq A$ and that $\alpha \notin \mathrm{Cn}(A')$ but $\alpha \in \mathrm{Cn}(A' \cup \{\beta\})$.
Closure: If A is logically closed, then so is $A \div \alpha$ for all α.
Relative closure: $A \cap \mathrm{Cn}(A \div \alpha) \subseteq A \div \alpha$.
Extensionality: If $\alpha \leftrightarrow \beta \in \mathrm{Cn}(\emptyset)$, then $A \div \alpha = A \div \beta$.
Uniformity: If it holds for all subsets A' of A that $\alpha \in \mathrm{Cn}(A')$ if and only if $\beta \in \mathrm{Cn}(A')$, then $A \div \alpha = A \div \beta$.
Recovery: $A \subseteq \mathrm{Cn}((A \div \alpha) \cup \{\alpha\})$.

In Observation 2.3, a number of logical connections between these properties were given. Most of the proofs are fairly simple.

If $\div$ satisfies *inclusion* and *core-retainment*, then it satisfies *failure*. [Part of Observation 2.3.]

Proof. Let $\div$ be an operator for A that satisfies *inclusion* and *core-retainment*. In order to prove *failure*, let $\alpha \in \text{Cn}(\emptyset)$. We need to prove that $A \div \alpha = A$.

Suppose to the contrary that $A \div \alpha \neq A$. By *inclusion*, $A \div \alpha \subseteq A$, so it follows from $A \div \alpha \neq A$ that $A \div \alpha \subset A$. There is therefore at least one sentence β such that $\beta \in A$ and $\beta \notin A \div \alpha$. It follows by *core-retainment* that there is a set A' such that $A' \subseteq A$ and that $\alpha \notin \text{Cn}(A')$ but $\alpha \in \text{Cn}(A' \cup \{\beta\})$. However, this is impossible since it follows from $\alpha \in \text{Cn}(\emptyset)$ that $\alpha \in \text{Cn}(A')$. We may conclude from this contradiction that $A \div \alpha = A$. ■

If $\div$ satisfies *inclusion* and *core-retainment*, then it satisfies *vacuity*. [Part of Observation 2.3.]

Proof. Let $\div$ be an operator for A that satisfies *inclusion* and *core-retainment*. In order to prove *vacuity*, let $\alpha \notin \text{Cn}(A)$. Again, we need to show that $A \div \alpha = A$. The proof is quite similar to the preceding one.

Suppose that $A \div \alpha \neq A$. By *inclusion*, $A \div \alpha \subseteq A$, so that $A \div \alpha \subset A$. There must be some sentence β such that $\beta \in A$ and $\beta \notin A \div \alpha$. It follows by *core-retainment* that there is a set A' such that $A' \subseteq A$ and that $\alpha \notin \text{Cn}(A')$ but $\alpha \in \text{Cn}(A' \cup \{\beta\})$. (So far we have just repeated what we did in the previous proof. Now for the part that differs:)

Since $A' \cup \{\beta\}$ is a subset of A, it clearly follows from $\alpha \notin \text{Cn}(A)$ that $\alpha \notin \text{Cn}(A' \cup \{\beta\})$. We may conclude from this contradiction that $A \div \alpha = A$. ■

If $\div$ satisfies *relevance*, then it satisfies *core-retainment* and *relative closure*. [Part of Observation 2.3.]

Proof. Let $\div$ be an operator for A that satisfies *relevance*. It can be seen directly from the definitions that it satisfies *core-retainment*. In order to prove that *relative closure* holds, i.e. that $A \cap \text{Cn}(A \div \alpha) \subseteq A \div \alpha$, we are going to let $\beta \notin A \div \alpha$ and show that $\beta \notin A \cap \text{Cn}(A \div \alpha)$. (This is often the simplest way to prove set-theoretical inclusion.)

If $\beta \notin A$, then it follows trivially that $\beta \notin A \cap \text{Cn}(A \div \alpha)$. (It is mostly a good idea to get rid of simple extreme cases before taking up the principal case.) In the remaining case, we have $\beta \in A$ and $\beta \notin A \div \alpha$. It follows from *relevance* that there is a set A' such that $A \div \alpha \subseteq A' \subseteq A$ and that $\alpha \notin \text{Cn}(A')$ but $\alpha \in \text{Cn}(A' \cup \{\beta\})$.

Next, we are going to show that $\beta \notin \text{Cn}(A')$. Suppose to the contrary that $\beta \in \text{Cn}(A')$. Then it follows that $\text{Cn}(A') = \text{Cn}(A' \cup \{\beta\})$, contrary to $\alpha \notin \text{Cn}(A')$ and $\alpha \in \text{Cn}(A' \cup \{\beta\})$. We can conclude that that $\beta \notin \text{Cn}(A')$.

It follows from $A \div \alpha \subseteq A'$ that $\text{Cn}(A \div \alpha) \subseteq \text{Cn}(A')$, and then from $\beta \notin \text{Cn}(A')$ that $\beta \notin \text{Cn}(A \div \alpha)$. From this follows $\beta \notin A \cap \text{Cn}(A \div \alpha)$, as desired. ■

If $\div$ satisfies *inclusion* and *relative closure*, then it satisfies *closure*.
[Part of Observation 2.3.]

Proof. Let $\div$ be an operator for a logically closed set A that satisfies *inclusion* and *relative closure*. In order to prove that *closure* holds, we must show that $A\div\alpha = \text{Cn}(A\div\alpha)$. Since $A\div\alpha \subseteq \text{Cn}(A\div\alpha)$ holds trivially, it remains to be shown that $\text{Cn}(A\div\alpha) \subseteq A\div\alpha$.

By *inclusion* we have $A\div\alpha \subseteq A$, and consequently $\text{Cn}(A\div\alpha) \subseteq \text{Cn}(A)$. Since A is logically closed, we may conclude that $\text{Cn}(A\div\alpha) \subseteq A$ so that (by set theory) $A \cap \text{Cn}(A\div\alpha) = \text{Cn}(A\div\alpha)$.

By *relative closure*, $A\cap\text{Cn}(A\div\alpha) \subseteq A\div\alpha$. Combining this with $A\cap\text{Cn}(A\div\alpha) = \text{Cn}(A\div\alpha)$ that we have just proved, we obtain $\text{Cn}(A\div\alpha) \subseteq A\div\alpha$, as desired. ■

If $\div$ satisfies *uniformity*, then it satisfies *extensionality*.
[Part of Observation 2.3.]

Proof. This should not detain us long. Let $\div$ be an operator for A that satisfies *uniformity*. In order to prove *extensionality*, let $\alpha\leftrightarrow\beta \in \text{Cn}(\emptyset)$. It follows from this that if a set A' implies α, then it implies β, and vice versa. By *uniformity* we then have $A\div\alpha = A\div\beta$. ■

Interesting alternative formulations of relevance and core-retainment have been proposed by Hans Rott. Excepting the limiting case when $\alpha \in \text{Cn}(\emptyset)$, if success holds, then relevance is equivalent with:

$$A\div\alpha = \bigcap\{X \in A\perp\alpha \mid A\div\alpha \subseteq X\}.$$

(Cf. Exercise 70.) Excepting the same limiting case, core- retainment is equivalent to:

$$\bigcap(A\perp\alpha) \subseteq A\div\alpha.$$

(Cf. Exercise 69.) These reformulations are more transparent in the sense of showing how relevance and core-retainment relate to the construction of partial meet contraction.

Next, we are going to derive some results that hold only for logically closed sets. These results establish that for such sets: (1) extensionality and uniformity are interchangeable in the presence of vacuity, and (2) relevance, core-retainment, and recovery are interchangeable in the presence of closure, inclusion, and vacuity.

If an operator $\div$ for a logically closed set A satisfies *extensionality* and *vacuity*, then it satisfies *uniformity*.
[Observation 2.4.]

Proof. Let A be a logically closed set and $\div$ an operator for A that satisfies *extensionality* and *vacuity*. In order to prove that *uniformity* is satisfied, let α and β be two sentences such that for all subsets A' of A, A' implies α if and only if it implies β. We are going to show that $A \div \alpha = A \div \beta$.

First, let us treat the case when $\alpha \notin A$. Since $A = \text{Cn}(A)$, it then follows by *vacuity* that $A \div \alpha = A$. Since A is a subset of itself, it follows from $\alpha \notin \text{Cn}(A)$ that $\beta \notin \text{Cn}(A)$. By *vacuity*, $A \div \beta = A$, so that $A \div \alpha = A \div \beta$.

Next, let us treat the principal case, in which $\alpha \in A$. Since $A = \text{Cn}(A)$, we then have $\text{Cn}(\{\alpha\}) \subseteq A$. Since $\text{Cn}(\{\alpha\})$ is a subset of A that implies α, it implies β, so that we have $\beta \in \text{Cn}(\{\alpha\})$. It follows from $\beta \in \text{Cn}(\{\alpha\})$, $\alpha \in A$, and $A = \text{Cn}(A)$ that $\beta \in A$. From this it follows in exactly the same way that $\alpha \in \text{Cn}(\{\beta\})$. From $\beta \in \text{Cn}(\{\alpha\})$ and $\alpha \in \text{Cn}(\{\beta\})$ it follows that $\alpha \leftrightarrow \beta \in \text{Cn}(\emptyset)$, and we may conclude by *extensionality* that $A \div \alpha = A \div \beta$. ■

> If an operator $\div$ for a logically closed set A satisfies *core-retainment*, then it satisfies *recovery*.
> [Observation 2.9.]

Proof. Let $\div$ be an operator for the logically closed set A that satisfies *core-retainment*. In order to show that $A \subseteq \text{Cn}((A \div \alpha) \cup \{\alpha\})$, let $\beta \notin \text{Cn}((A \div \alpha) \cup \{\alpha\})$. We need to show that $\beta \notin A$.

First, we are going to show that $\alpha \rightarrow \beta \notin A$. Suppose to the contrary that $\alpha \rightarrow \beta \in A$. It follows from $\beta \notin \text{Cn}((A \div \alpha) \cup \{\alpha\})$, by the deduction property of Cn, that $\alpha \rightarrow \beta \notin \text{Cn}(A \div \alpha)$. It then follows by *core-retainment* from $\alpha \rightarrow \beta \in A$ and $\alpha \rightarrow \beta \notin A \div \alpha$ that there is some set A' such that $A' \subseteq A$ and that $\alpha \notin \text{Cn}(A')$ but $\alpha \in \text{Cn}(A' \cup \{\alpha \rightarrow \beta\})$. The latter expression is equivalent to $(\alpha \rightarrow \beta) \rightarrow \alpha \in \text{Cn}(A')$, and thus, by truth- functional logic, to $\alpha \in \text{Cn}(A')$. Since we also have $\alpha \notin \text{Cn}(A')$, a contradiction has been derived. It follows that $\alpha \rightarrow \beta \notin A$.

Since $\alpha \rightarrow \beta$ follows logically from β, it follows directly from $\alpha \rightarrow \beta \notin A$, by the logical closure of A, that $\beta \notin A$. This finishes our proof. ■

Since relevance logically implies core-retainment, we obtain the following as a corollary:

> If an operator $\div$ for a logically closed set A satisfies *relevance*, then it satisfies *recovery*.
> [Part of Observation 2.6.]

Conversely, we can obtain relevance (and core-retainment) from recovery, but for this result a few auxiliary postulates are needed:

> If an operator $\div$ for a logically closed set A satisfies *closure, inclusion, vacuity*, and *recovery*, then it satisfies *relevance*.
> [Part of Observation 2.6.]

Proof. Let A be logically closed, and let $\div$ be an operator that satisfies *closure, inclusion, vacuity*, and *recovery*. We need to show that if $\beta \in A$ and $\beta \notin A\div\alpha$, then there is some A' such that $A\div\alpha \subseteq A' \subseteq A$, $A' \nvdash \alpha$ and $A' \cup \{\beta\} \vdash \alpha$.

If $\alpha \notin A$, then it follows, since A is logically closed, that $\alpha \notin \mathrm{Cn}(A)$, and then by *vacuity* that $A = A\div\alpha$. Thus, there can be no β such that $\beta \in A$ and $\beta \notin A\div\alpha$, and we are done.

For the principal case, when $\alpha \in A$, let β be a sentence such that $\beta \in A$ and $\beta \notin A\div\alpha$. We are going to show that the desired conclusion holds for the set $A' = (A\div\alpha) \cup \{\beta\rightarrow\alpha\}$. We need to show (1) $A' \subseteq A$, (2) $A' \nvdash \alpha$ and (3) $A' \cup \{\beta\} \vdash \alpha$.

(1). By *inclusion* $A\div\alpha \subseteq A$. Since $\beta\rightarrow\alpha$ is a logical consequence of α, it follows from $\alpha \in A$ and the logical closure of A that $\beta\rightarrow\alpha \in A$. We can conclude from $A\div\alpha \subseteq A$ and $\beta\rightarrow\alpha \in A$ that $(A\div\alpha) \cup \{\beta\rightarrow\alpha\} \subseteq A$, i.e. $A' \subseteq A$.

(2). In order to prove that $A' \nvdash \alpha$, suppose to the contrary that $A' \vdash \alpha$, i.e. $(A\div\alpha) \cup \{\beta\rightarrow\alpha\} \vdash \alpha$. This is logically equivalent to $A\div\alpha \vdash (\beta\rightarrow\alpha)\rightarrow\alpha$, i.e. $A\div\alpha \vdash \alpha\vee\beta$.

Since $\beta \in A$ it follows from *recovery* that $A\div\alpha \vdash \alpha\rightarrow\beta$. Since β is a logical consequence of $\alpha\vee\beta$ and $\alpha\rightarrow\beta$, we can now conclude that $A\div\alpha \vdash \beta$. However, it follows from $\beta \notin A\div\alpha$, by *closure*, that $A\div\alpha \nvdash \beta$. We can conclude from this contradiction that $A' \nvdash \alpha$.

(3). That $A' \cup \{\beta\} \vdash \alpha$ follows directly from $\{\beta\rightarrow\alpha\} \subseteq A'$. This concludes the proof. ■

Exercises

63. [101] Let $\div$ be an operator for the logically closed set A. Show that if $\div$ satisfies *closure* and *recovery*, then the following postulates hold:
    (a) If $\alpha \in A$, then $\beta\rightarrow\alpha \in A\div(\alpha\vee\beta)$.
    (b) If $\alpha \in A$, then $\alpha \in A\div(\alpha\rightarrow\beta)$.

64. Let $\div$ be an operator for A. Show that if *inclusion, relative closure*, and *recovery* are satisfied, then so is *failure*.

65. Let $\div$ be an operator for the logically closed set A, such that *closure* and *recovery* are satisfied. Show that for all $\alpha, \beta \in A$:
    $\alpha\vee\beta \in A\div\alpha$ if and only if $\beta \in A\div\alpha$.

66. Let $\div$ be an operator for the logically closed set A, that satisfies *recovery*.
    (a) Show that for all α, $A \cap \mathrm{Cn}(\{\neg\alpha\}) \subseteq \mathrm{Cn}(A\div\alpha)$.
    (b) Show that $A{\sim}\alpha \subseteq \mathrm{Cn}(A\div\alpha)$, where $\sim$ is full meet contraction.

67. Let A be a logically closed set, and let $\div$ be an operation for A that satisfies *closure, success*, and *fullness*. (Fullness is as follows: If $\beta \in A$ and $\beta \notin A\div\alpha$, then $\alpha \notin \mathrm{Cn}(A\div\alpha)$ and $\alpha \in \mathrm{Cn}((A\div\alpha) \cup \{\beta\})$.) Show that the following condition is satisfied:
    If $\alpha_1 \in A$ and $\alpha_2 \in A$, then either $\alpha_1 \in A\div(\alpha_1\&\alpha_2)$, $\alpha_2 \in A\div(\alpha_1\&\alpha_2)$, or $(\alpha_1\leftrightarrow\alpha_2) \in A\div(\alpha_1\&\alpha_2)$.

68. Let A be a set and $\div$ an operation on that set. Show that if $\div$ satisfies *core-retainment*, then it also satisfies:
If $\alpha \in A$, then $\alpha \in A \div \neg\alpha$. (*negation-retainment*).

69. (Hans Rott)

   (a) Let A be a set of sentences, and let $\alpha \in \mathcal{L}$ and $\beta \in A$. Show that the following two conditions are equivalent:

      i. There is some X such that $X \subseteq A$, $X \nvdash \alpha$, and $X \cup \{\beta\} \vdash \alpha$.
      ii. There is some X such that $\beta \notin X \in A \bot \alpha$.

   (b) Show that, excepting the case when α is logically true, *core-retainment* is equivalent to $\bigcap(A \bot \alpha) \subseteq A \div \alpha$.

70. (Hans Rott)

   (a) Let A and B be sets of sentences, and let $\alpha \in \mathcal{L}$ and $\beta \in A$. Show that the following two conditions are equivalent:

      i. There is some X such that $B \subseteq X \subseteq A$, $X \nvdash \alpha$, and $X \cup \{\beta\} \vdash \alpha$.
      ii. There is some X such that $B \subseteq X \in A \bot \alpha$ and $\beta \notin X$.

   (b) Show that, excepting the limiting case when α is logically true, if *success* holds, then *relevance* is equivalent to $A \div \alpha = \bigcap\{X \in A \bot \alpha \mid A \div \alpha \subseteq X\}$.

71. In indeterministic belief revision, contraction of A by α has several alternative outcomes. (Cf. Section 1.3.) Let $AC_\alpha B$ denote that B is a possible outcome of contracting α from A. How would you transfer to this framework the following postulates:

   (a) success,
   (b) inclusion, and
   (c) extensionality?

13+ RELATIONS BETWEEN THE CONJUNCTIVE POSTULATES

In this section, we are going to investigate the interrelations between the four conjunctive postulates from Section 2.5. To begin with, let us recapitulate the postulates:

Conjunctive inclusion: If $\alpha \notin \mathrm{Cn}(A \div (\alpha \& \beta))$ then
$A \div (\alpha \& \beta) \subseteq A \div \alpha$.
Conjunctive overlap: $(A \div \alpha) \cap (A \div \beta) \subseteq A \div (\alpha \& \beta)$.
Conjunctive factoring: Either $A \div (\alpha \& \beta) = A \div \alpha$, $A \div (\alpha \& \beta) = A \div \beta$, or $A \div (\alpha \& \beta) = (A \div \alpha) \cap (A \div \beta)$.
Conjunctive trisection: If $\alpha \in A \div (\alpha \& \beta)$ then $\alpha \in A \div (\alpha \& \beta \& \delta)$.

To simplify some of the proofs, we are going to introduce a fifth property:

Partial antitony: [1]
$A{\div}\alpha \cap \mathrm{Cn}(\{\alpha\}) \subseteq A{\div}(\alpha\&\beta)$.

The word 'antitony' [1] is an abbreviation of 'anti-monotony'. Full antitony, $A{\div}\alpha \subseteq A{\div}(\alpha\&\beta)$, does not hold for any sensible operator of contraction. Partial antitony is much more plausible, and can be shown to be equivalent to conjunctive trisection, provided only that extensionality holds.

OBSERVATION 2.59 (Hans Rott [115]) *Let $\div$ be an operator for A. Then:*

1. *If $\div$ satisfies partial antitony, then it satisfies conjunctive trisection.*
2. *If $\div$ satisfies extensionality and conjunctive trisection, then it satisfies partial antitony.*

Proof. *Part 1*: Suppose that $\div$ satisfies *partial antitony*. Let $\alpha \in A{\div}(\alpha\&\beta)$. We are going to show that $\alpha \in A{\div}(\alpha\&\beta\&\delta)$.

Clearly, $\alpha \in \mathrm{Cn}(\{\alpha\&\beta\})$. Thus, $\alpha \in (A{\div}(\alpha\&\beta)) \cap \mathrm{Cn}(\{\alpha\&\beta\})$. It follows directly by *partial antitony* that $\alpha \in A{\div}(\alpha\&\beta\&\delta)$.

Part 2: Let $\div$ satisfy *extensionality* and *conjunctive trisection*. Let $\varepsilon \in A{\div}\alpha \cap \mathrm{Cn}(\{\alpha\})$. We are going to show that $\varepsilon \in A(\alpha\&\beta)$.

Since $\varepsilon \in \mathrm{Cn}(\{\alpha\})$, $\alpha\&\varepsilon$ is logically equivalent to α, and it follows by *extensionality* that $A{\div}(\alpha\&\varepsilon) = A{\div}\alpha$. We therefore have $\varepsilon \in A{\div}(\alpha\&\varepsilon)$. It follows by *conjunctive trisection* that $\varepsilon \in A{\div}(\alpha\&\varepsilon\&\beta)$. Since ε follows logically from α, $\alpha\&\varepsilon\&\beta$ is logically equivalent to $\alpha\&\beta$, and *extensionality* yields $A{\div}(\alpha\&\varepsilon\&\beta) = A{\div}(\alpha\&\beta)$. We therefore have $\varepsilon \in A{\div}(\alpha\&\beta)$, as desired. ■

Note that Observation 2.59 holds even if A is not logically closed. Most of the other results that have been obtained on the conjunctive properties only apply to logically closed sets.

The following observation establishes that for logically closed sets, partial antitony and conjunctive overlap are interchangeable in the presence of the basic postulates.

OBSERVATION 2.60 (AGM [1]) *Let A be logically closed and let $\div$ be an operator for A.*

1. *If $\div$ satisfies closure, inclusion, vacuity, extensionality, recovery, and conjunctive overlap, then it satisfies partial antitony.*
2. *If $\div$ satisfies closure, inclusion, recovery, and partial antitony, then it satisfies conjunctive overlap.*

Proof. *Part 1*: Let A be logically closed, and let $\div$ be an operation for A that satisfies *closure, inclusion, vacuity, extensionality, recovery*, and *conjunctive overlap*. Let $\varepsilon \in (A{\div}\alpha) \cap \mathrm{Cn}(\{\alpha\})$. We need to show that $\varepsilon \in A{\div}(\alpha\&\beta)$.

If either $\alpha \notin A$ or $\beta \notin A$, then we have $\alpha\&\beta \notin A$. It follows from *vacuity* that $A\div(\alpha\&\beta) = A$. It follows by *inclusion* from $\varepsilon \in A\div\alpha$ that $\varepsilon \in A$, and we have $\varepsilon \in A = A\div(\alpha\&\beta)$, as desired.

In the principal case, $\alpha \in A$ and $\beta \in A$. By *extensionality*, we have $A\div(\alpha\&\beta) = A\div(\alpha\&(\alpha\rightarrow\beta))$. (Observe the trick of 'reorganizing' $\alpha\&\beta$ into the equivalent form $\alpha\&(\alpha\rightarrow\beta)$, thus allowing for a different application of a conjunctive postulate.) By *conjunctive overlap*, $(A\div\alpha) \cap (A\div(\alpha\rightarrow\beta)) \subseteq A\div(\alpha\&\beta)$. Therefore, if we can prove that $\varepsilon \in (A\div\alpha) \cap (A\div(\alpha\rightarrow\beta))$, then we are done.

By our assumption, $\varepsilon \in A\div\alpha$. In order to prove $\varepsilon \in A\div(\alpha\rightarrow\beta)$, we can use *recovery* to obtain $A \subseteq \text{Cn}((A\div(\alpha\rightarrow\beta)) \cup \{\alpha\rightarrow\beta\})$. Since $\alpha \in A$, we obtain $\alpha \in \text{Cn}((A\div(\alpha\rightarrow\beta)) \cup \{\alpha\rightarrow\beta\})$, and by the deduction property of Cn, $(\alpha\rightarrow\beta)\rightarrow\alpha \in \text{Cn}(A\div(\alpha\rightarrow\beta))$. Since $(\alpha\rightarrow\beta)\rightarrow\alpha$ is logically equivalent to α, it follows by *closure* that $\alpha \in A\div(\alpha\rightarrow\beta)$. Since, by our assumption, $\varepsilon \in \text{Cn}(\{\alpha\})$, we can apply *closure* once more and obtain $\varepsilon \in A\div(\alpha\rightarrow\beta)$.

Part 2: Let A be a logically closed set and $\div$ an operation for A that satisfies *closure, inclusion, recovery*, and *partial antitony*. Let $\varepsilon \in (A\div\alpha) \cap (A\div\beta)$. We are going to show that $\varepsilon \in A\div(\alpha\&\beta)$. This can be done by showing that $\varepsilon\vee\alpha$, $\varepsilon\vee\beta$ and $(\alpha\&\beta)\rightarrow\varepsilon$ are elements of $A\div(\alpha\&\beta)$.

1. It follows by *closure* from $\varepsilon \in A\div\alpha$ that $\varepsilon\vee\alpha \in A\div\alpha$. Since $\varepsilon\vee\alpha \in \text{Cn}(\{\alpha\})$, it follows by *partial antitony* that $\varepsilon\vee\alpha \in A\div(\alpha\&\beta)$.
2. It follows in exactly the same way from $\varepsilon \in A\div\beta$ that $\varepsilon\vee\beta \in A\div(\alpha\&\beta)$.
3. By *recovery*, $A \subseteq \text{Cn}((A\div(\alpha\&\beta)) \cup \{\alpha\&\beta\})$. It follows by *inclusion* from $\varepsilon \in A\div\alpha$ that $\varepsilon \in A$, so that $\varepsilon \in \text{Cn}((A\div(\alpha\&\beta)) \cup \{\alpha\&\beta\})$. By the deduction property of Cn, $\alpha\&\beta\rightarrow\varepsilon \in \text{Cn}((A\div(\alpha\&\beta))$, and by *closure* $\alpha\&\beta\rightarrow\varepsilon \in A\div(\alpha\&\beta)$.

Since ε follows logically from $\varepsilon\vee\alpha$, $\varepsilon\vee\beta$, and $\alpha\&\beta\rightarrow\varepsilon$, we can conclude that $\varepsilon \in \text{Cn}(A\div(\alpha\&\beta))$, and by *closure* that $\varepsilon \in A\div(\alpha\&\beta)$. This concludes the proof. ■

Observations 2.59 and 2.60 can be combined to the following:

> Let A be logically closed and let $\div$ be an operator for A that satisfies *closure, inclusion, vacuity, extensionality*, and *recovery*. Then it satisfies *conjunctive trisection* if and only if it satisfies *conjunctive overlap*. [Observation 2.15, Part 1.]

Next, we are going to show that conjunctive factoring is (in the presence of the basic postulates) equivalent to the conjunction of conjunctive overlap and conjunctive inclusion. The proof will be divided into two parts, one for each direction of the equivalence.

Let A be a logically closed set and $\div$ an operation for A. If $\div$ satisfies *closure, inclusion, success, failure, recovery, conjunctive inclusion*, and *conjunctive overlap*, then it satisfies *conjunctive factoring*. [Observation 2.15, one direction of Part 2.]

Proof. [1] Let $\div$ be an operation for the logically closed set A that satisfies the listed postulates.

In the limiting case in which $\vdash \alpha\&\beta$ we also have $\vdash \alpha$ and $\vdash \beta$. It follows by *failure* that $A\div(\alpha\&\beta) = A\div\alpha = A\div\beta = A$, so that *conjunctive factoring* holds.

In the principal case, in which $\nvdash \alpha\&\beta$, suppose that $A\div(\alpha\&\beta) \neq A\div\alpha$ and $A\div(\alpha\&\beta) \neq A\div\beta$. We need to show that $A\div(\alpha\&\beta) = (A\div\alpha)\cap(A\div\beta)$. By set theory, this holds if and only if (1) $(A\div\alpha)\cap(A\div\beta) \subseteq A\div(\alpha\&\beta)$, (2) $A\div(\alpha\&\beta) \subseteq A\div\alpha$, and (3) $A\div(\alpha\&\beta) \subseteq A\div\beta$.

(1) follows from *conjunctive overlap*.

(2) and (3): We are first going to show that at least one of these two conditions holds, and after that that if one of them holds, then so does the other.

It follows from *success* that $\alpha\&\beta \notin \text{Cn}(A\div(\alpha\&\beta))$. From this it follows that either $\alpha \notin \text{Cn}(A\div(\alpha\&\beta))$ or $\beta \notin \text{Cn}(A\div(\alpha\&\beta))$. In the first case, it follows from *conjunctive inclusion* that $A\div(\alpha\&\beta) \subseteq A\div\alpha$, and in the second case that $A\div(\alpha\&\beta) \subseteq A\div\beta$. We have now showed that at least one of these two conditions holds. It remains to show that if one of them holds, then so does the other.

Suppose that $A\div(\alpha\&\beta) \subseteq A\div\alpha$. In order to show that $A\div(\alpha\&\beta) \subseteq A\div\beta$, suppose to the contrary that $A\div(\alpha\&\beta) \nsubseteq A\div\beta$. It follows from *conjunctive inclusion* and *closure* that $\beta \in A\div(\alpha\&\beta)$.

By our initial conditions, $A\div(\alpha\&\beta) \neq A\div\alpha$. It can be concluded from this and $A\div(\alpha\&\beta) \subseteq A\div\alpha$ that there is some sentence ε such that $\varepsilon \in A\div\alpha$ and $\varepsilon \notin A\div(\alpha\&\beta)$. Since by *closure*, $A\div(\alpha\&\beta)$ is logically closed, it follows from $\varepsilon \notin A\div(\alpha\&\beta)$ and $\beta \in A\div(\alpha\&\beta)$ that $\beta\rightarrow\varepsilon \notin A\div(\alpha\&\beta)$. From this it follows by *conjunctive overlap* that either $\beta\rightarrow\varepsilon \notin A\div\alpha$ or $\beta\rightarrow\varepsilon \notin A\div\beta$.

This, however can easily be shown to be impossible. Since $\beta\rightarrow\varepsilon$ follows logically from ε, it also follows from $\varepsilon \in A\div\alpha$, by *closure*, that $\beta\rightarrow\varepsilon \in A\div\alpha$. And it follows by *inclusion* from $\varepsilon \in A\div\alpha$ that $\varepsilon \in A$. From this we may conclude by *recovery* that $\varepsilon \in \text{Cn}((A\div\beta) \cup \{\beta\})$. By the deduction property of Cn, $\beta\rightarrow\varepsilon \in \text{Cn}(A\div\beta)$, and by *closure*, $\beta\rightarrow\varepsilon \in A\div\beta$.

We have shown a contradiction to follow from our assumption that $A\div(\alpha\&\beta) \nsubseteq A\div\beta$. We can therefore conclude that $A\div(\alpha\&\beta) \subseteq A\div\beta$. This was proved under the assumption that $A\div(\alpha\&\beta) \subseteq A\div\alpha$. By an exactly similar proof (just exchange α and β), we can prove that if $A\div(\alpha\&\beta) \subseteq A\div\beta$, then $A\div(\alpha\&\beta) \subseteq A\div\alpha$. Thus, if one of the two conditions holds, then so does the other. This is what we needed to complete the proof. ∎

Let A be a logically closed set and $\div$ an operation for A. If $\div$ satisfies *closure, inclusion, vacuity, extensionality, recovery*, and *conjunctive factoring*, then it satisfies *conjunctive inclusion* and *conjunctive overlap*.
[Observation 2.15, one direction of Part 2.]

Proof. [1] *Conjunctive overlap* follows directly from *conjunctive factoring*. It remains to be shown that *conjunctive inclusion* holds. Let $\alpha \notin \mathrm{Cn}(A\div(\alpha\&\beta))$. We are going to show that $A\div(\alpha\&\beta) \subseteq A\div\alpha$.

In the limiting case when $A \nvdash \alpha$, *vacuity* yields $A\div\alpha = A$, and *inclusion* yields $A\div(\alpha\&\beta) \subseteq A = A\div\alpha$, as desired.

In the principal case, when $A \vdash \alpha$, we are going to use (just as in the proof of Observation 2.60) the logical equivalence between $\alpha\&\beta$ and $\alpha\&(\alpha\rightarrow\beta)$. It follows from *extensionality* that $A\div(\alpha\&\beta) = A\div(\alpha\&(\alpha\rightarrow\beta))$. By applying *conjunctive factoring*, we can conclude that $A\div(\alpha\&\beta)$ is identical to one of the three expressions $A\div\alpha$, $A\div(\alpha\rightarrow\beta)$, and $(A\div\alpha)\cap(A\div(\alpha\rightarrow\beta))$. In the first and last of these three cases, it follows directly that $A\div(\alpha\&\beta) \subseteq A\div\alpha$. In order to complete our proof, it is sufficient to prove that the second case, i.e. $A\div(\alpha\&\beta) = A\div(\alpha\rightarrow\beta)$, is impossible.

By *recovery*, $A \subseteq \mathrm{Cn}((A\div(\alpha\rightarrow\beta)) \cup \{\alpha\rightarrow\beta\})$. By the logical closure of A, it follows from $A \vdash \alpha$ that $\alpha \in A$, so that $\alpha \in \mathrm{Cn}((A\div(\alpha\rightarrow\beta)) \cup \{\alpha\rightarrow\beta\})$. By the deduction property of Cn we then have $(\alpha\rightarrow\beta)\rightarrow\alpha \in \mathrm{Cn}(A\div(\alpha\rightarrow\beta))$. Since $(\alpha\rightarrow\beta)\rightarrow\alpha$ is logically equivalent to α, it follows by *closure* that $\alpha \in A\div(\alpha\rightarrow\beta)$. By our initial condition, $\alpha \notin A\div(\alpha\&\beta)$. It follows that $A\div(\alpha\&\beta) \neq A\div(\alpha\rightarrow\beta)$, which is what we needed to complete the proof. ∎

Exercises

72. Let $\div$ be an operator for the logically closed set A. Show that if $\div$ satisfies *closure* and *partial antitony*, then it satisfies:
If $\delta \in A\div\alpha$, then $\alpha\vee\delta \in A\div(\alpha\&\beta)$.

73. Let $\div$ be an operation for A (that is not necessarily logically closed). Show that if *success, failure*, and *conjunctive inclusion* hold, then:

    (a) [1] Either $A\div(\alpha\&\beta) \subseteq A\div\alpha$ or $A\div(\alpha\&\beta) \subseteq A\div\beta$. (*conjunctive covering*)

    (b) [116] $A\div(\alpha\&\beta) \subseteq \mathrm{Cn}((A\div\alpha)\cup(A\div\beta))$ (*weak conjunctive inclusion*).

    (c) If A is logically closed and *closure* holds, then: If $\alpha \notin A\div\beta$, then $A\div(\alpha\&\beta) \subseteq A\div\alpha$.

74. Provide a direct proof (i.e. not with partial antitony as an intermediate) that in the presence of the basic postulates, *conjunctive overlap*, as applied to a logically closed set, implies *conjunctive trisection*. (Hint: Note that $\alpha\&\beta\&\delta$ is logically equivalent to $(\alpha\&\beta)\&(\alpha\&\beta\rightarrow\delta)$.)

75. [115] Consider the following three conditions:
(1) If $\beta \in A\div(\alpha\&\beta)$, then $A\div(\alpha\&\beta) \subseteq A\div\alpha$.
(2) If $\beta \in A\div(\alpha\&\beta)$, then $A\div\alpha \subseteq A\div(\alpha\&\beta)$.
(3) If $\alpha\rightarrow\beta \in A\div\beta$ and $\beta\rightarrow\alpha \in A\div\alpha$, then $A\div\alpha = A\div\beta$. (*reciprocity*)

   (a) Show that if *success, failure*, and *conjunctive inclusion* are satisfied, then so is (1).
   (b) Show that if A is logically closed and *inclusion, closure, recovery*, and *conjunctive overlap* are satisfied, then so is (2). (Hint: Show that if $\varepsilon \in A\div\alpha$, then $\beta\rightarrow\varepsilon \in (A\div\alpha)\cap(A\div\beta)$.)
   (c) Show that if *extensionality*, (1), and (2) hold, then so does the following condition:
   If $\alpha\rightarrow\beta \in A\div\beta$, then $A\div\beta = A\div(\alpha\vee\beta)$.
   (Hint: Note that β is equivalent to $(\alpha\rightarrow\beta)\&(\alpha\vee\beta)$.)
   (d) Show that if A is logically closed, then in the presence of *closure* and *extensionality*, (3) holds if and only if both (1) and (2) hold.

14+ PROPERTIES OF PARTIAL MEET CONTRACTION

In this section, we are going to show that partial meet contraction has the basic properties that were introduced in Sections 2.2 and 2.3. To begin with, let us verify that it satisfies the four postulates that were used in the axiomatic characterization of Theorem 2.2, namely *success*, *inclusion*, *relevance*, and *uniformity*.

Partial meet contraction satisfies *success*.
[Part of Theorem 2.2.]

Proof. Let γ be a selection function for A, and let $\nvdash \alpha$. We need to show that $\bigcap\gamma(A\perp\alpha) \nvdash \alpha$.

Since $\nvdash \alpha$, $A\perp\alpha$ is nonempty. Therefore, by the definition of a selection function, $\gamma(A\perp\alpha)$ is a nonempty subset of $A\perp\alpha$. Let $X \in \gamma(A\perp\alpha)$. It follows from $X \in A\perp\alpha$ that $X \nvdash \alpha$. It follows from $X \in \gamma(A\perp\alpha)$, by set theory, that $\bigcap\gamma(A\perp\alpha) \subseteq X$. We can conclude from $\bigcap\gamma(A\perp\alpha) \subseteq X$ and $X \nvdash \alpha$ that $\bigcap\gamma(A\perp\alpha) \nvdash \alpha$, as desired. ■

Partial meet contraction satisfies *inclusion*.
[Part of Theorem 2.2.]

Proof. Let γ be a selection function for A. We need to show that for all α, $\bigcap\gamma(A\perp\alpha) \subseteq A$. There are two cases, both of which are quite simple:

Case 1, $\vdash \alpha$. Then $A\perp\alpha$ is empty. It follows by the definition of a selection function that $\gamma(A\perp\alpha) = \{A\}$, so that $\bigcap\gamma(A\perp\alpha) = A$ and we are done.

Case 2, $\nvdash \alpha$. Then $\gamma(A\perp\alpha)$ is a nonempty subset of $A\perp\alpha$. Since every element of $A\perp\alpha$ is a subset of A, so is every element of $\gamma(A\perp\alpha)$, and so is $\bigcap\gamma(A\perp\alpha)$. ■

Partial meet contraction satisfies *relevance*.
[Part of Theorem 2.2.]

Proof. Let γ be a selection function for A. We need to show that for all α, if $\beta \in A$ and $\beta \notin \bigcap\gamma(A\bot\alpha)$, then there is some A' such that $\bigcap\gamma(A\bot\alpha) \subseteq A' \subseteq A$ and $\alpha \notin \text{Cn}(A')$ but $\alpha \in \text{Cn}(A' \cup \{\beta\})$. Again, there are two cases, according to whether or not α is logically true.

Case 1, $\vdash \alpha$: Then $A\bot\alpha$ is empty. It follows that $\gamma(A\bot\alpha) = \{A\}$, so that $\bigcap\gamma(A\bot\alpha) = A$. From this follows that there can be no β such that $\beta \in A$ and $\beta \notin \bigcap\gamma(A\bot\alpha)$. We can conclude that *relevance* is satisfied in this case. (It is satisfied 'vacuously', i.e. because its initial conditions are not satisfiable.)

Case 2, $\nvdash \alpha$: Then $\gamma(A\bot\alpha)$ is a nonempty subset of $A\bot\alpha$. It follows from $\beta \notin \bigcap\gamma(A\bot\alpha)$ that there is some element A' of $\gamma(A\bot\alpha)$ such that $\beta \notin A'$. It follows from $A' \in A\bot\alpha$ that $\alpha \notin \text{Cn}(A')$. Furthermore, since $A' \in A\bot\alpha$ it follows from $A' \subset A' \cup \{\beta\} \subseteq A$ that $\alpha \in \text{Cn}(A' \cup \{\beta\})$. (Cf. Definition 1.35.) We can also see from $A' \in \gamma(A\bot\alpha)$ that $\bigcap\gamma(A\bot\alpha \subseteq A' \subseteq A$. Thus, *relevance* is satisfied in this case, as well. ■

The above proof makes use of the *maximality* of remainders, i.e. of the fact that if $X \in A\bot\alpha$ and $X \subset Y \subseteq A$, then $Y \vdash \alpha$. This is a standard method that will be used in many other proofs in this and the following sections.

Partial meet contraction satisfies *uniformity*.
[Part of Theorem 2.2.]

Proof. Let γ be a selection function for A. Let α and β be two sentences such that it holds for all subsets A' of A that $\alpha \in \text{Cn}(A')$ if and only if $\beta \in \text{Cn}(A')$. It follows from Observation 1.39 that $A\bot\alpha = A\bot\beta$. From this, we can conclude that $\bigcap\gamma(A\bot\alpha) = \bigcap\gamma(A\bot\beta)$. ■

Note that the proof of uniformity makes essential use of the fact that selection functions have been defined on remainder sets of the form $A\bot\alpha$, not on pairs of the form $\langle A, \alpha\rangle$. If we had instead defined selection functions as follows:

$\gamma(A, \alpha)$ is a non-empty subset of $\gamma(A\bot\alpha)$ if $A\bot\alpha$ is non-empty;
$\gamma(A, \alpha) = \{A\}$ if $A\bot\alpha$ is empty,

then $\bigcap\gamma(A, \alpha)$ would have been an operation very similar to partial meet contraction in other respects, but it would have been possible for $\gamma(A, \alpha) \neq \gamma(A, \beta)$ to hold if $A\bot\alpha = A\bot\beta$, which the standard definition does not allow. In what follows, we will stick to the standard definition.

In summary, we have shown that partial meet contraction satisfies *success, inclusion, relevance*, and *uniformity*. We can now combine this result with Observation 2.3 to conclude that partial meet contraction also satisfies *failure, closure, relative closure, core-retainment, vacuity,* and *extensionality.* In the same way, it follows from Observation 2.6 that partial meet contraction on a logically closed set satisfies *recovery.* This is a central result in the theory of partial meet contraction. It can also be proved in a more direct and perhaps more lucid way:

> Let A be a logically closed set and $\sim_\gamma$ an operator of partial meet contraction for A. Then $\sim_\gamma$ satisfies *recovery.*
> [Observation 2.5.]

Proof. [1] Let $\sim_\gamma$ be an operator of partial meet contraction for the logically closed set A. We are going to show that $A \subseteq \text{Cn}((A\sim_\gamma\alpha) \cup \{\alpha\})$, i.e. that for all β, if $\beta \in A$, then $\beta \in \text{Cn}((A\sim_\gamma\alpha) \cup \{\alpha\})$. There are three cases.

Case 1, $\alpha \notin A$: Then, since A is logically closed, $\alpha \notin \text{Cn}(A)$. It follows that $A\bot\alpha = \{A\}$, and thus $A\sim_\gamma\alpha = A$, from which the desired conclusion follows immediately.

Case 2, $\alpha \in \text{Cn}(\emptyset)$: We then have $A\bot\alpha = \emptyset$ and $\gamma(A\bot\alpha) = \{A\}$, and thus $A\sim_\gamma\alpha = A$, from which the desired conclusion follows immediately.

Case 3, $\alpha \in A$ and $\alpha \notin \text{Cn}(\emptyset)$: This is the principal case. We are first going to show that if $\beta \in A$ and $X \in A\bot\alpha$, then $\alpha\rightarrow\beta \in X$.

Suppose that this is not the case. There are then a set X and a sentence β such that $\beta \in A, X \in A\bot\alpha$ and $\alpha\rightarrow\beta \notin X$. Since $\alpha\rightarrow\beta$ is a logical consequence of β, it follows from $\beta \in A$ that $\alpha\rightarrow\beta \in A$. It follows from this and $\alpha\rightarrow\beta \notin X \in A\bot\alpha$ that $\alpha \in \text{Cn}(X \cup \{\alpha\rightarrow\beta\})$. It follows by the deduction property of Cn that $(\alpha\rightarrow\beta)\rightarrow\alpha \in \text{Cn}(X)$, and since α is logically equivalent to $(\alpha\rightarrow\beta)\rightarrow\alpha$, we have $\alpha \in \text{Cn}(X)$. This contradicts $X \in A\bot\alpha$. We have derived a contradiction from $\alpha\rightarrow\beta \notin X$. From this contradiction, we can conclude that $\alpha\rightarrow\beta \in X$ (given that $\beta \in A$ and $X \in A\bot\alpha$).

The rest of the proof is straight-forward. Let $\beta \in A$. Then $\alpha\rightarrow\beta \in X$ holds for all $X \in A\bot\alpha$. Since $\gamma(A\bot\alpha)$ is a non-empty subset of $A\bot\alpha$, it follows by set theory that $\alpha\rightarrow\beta \in \bigcap\gamma(A\bot\alpha)$, i.e. $\alpha\rightarrow\beta \in A\sim_\gamma\alpha$. From this it follows that $\beta \in \text{Cn}((A\sim_\gamma\alpha) \cup \{\alpha\})$, which finishes the proof. ■

Just like the proof for relevance, the proof for recovery makes use of the maximality of remainders. Here it was combined with the deduction property of Cn in a way that will reappear in several of the proofs to follow.

Next, we are going to study the properties of partial meet contraction in the two limiting cases, maxichoice contraction and full meet contraction. First we are going to show that *fullness* holds for maxichoice contraction.

> If $\sim_\gamma$ is a maxichoice contraction for A, then it satisfies *fullness*, i.e.:
> For all $\beta \in A$ such that $\beta \notin A\sim_\gamma\alpha$, it holds that $\alpha \notin \text{Cn}(A\sim_\gamma\alpha)$ and $\alpha \in \text{Cn}((A\sim_\gamma\alpha) \cup \{\beta\})$.
> [Part of Theorem 2.13.]

Proof. If $\vdash \alpha$, then $A \sim_\gamma \alpha = A$, so that $\beta \in A$ and $\beta \notin A \sim_\gamma \alpha$ cannot hold, and fullness is vacuously satisfied.

If $\nvdash \alpha$, then $A \sim_\gamma \alpha$ is an element of $A \perp \alpha$, and $\alpha \notin \mathrm{Cn}(A \sim_\gamma \alpha)$. It follows, by the definition of a remainder set, from $A \sim_\gamma \alpha \subset (A \sim_\gamma \alpha) \cup \{\beta\} \subseteq A$ that $\alpha \in \mathrm{Cn}((A \sim_\gamma \alpha) \cup \{\beta\})$. ■

This proof was unusually short, since the properties of maxichoice contraction follow rather directly from the properties of remainders. The same applies to the proof of the following property of maxichoice contraction:

> Let A be logically closed and $\sim_\gamma$ a maxichoice contraction for A. Then it holds for all $\alpha \in A$ and all β that either $\neg\alpha \rightarrow \beta \in A \sim_\gamma \alpha$ or $\neg\alpha \rightarrow \neg\beta \in A \sim_\gamma \alpha$.
> [Observation 2.14.]

Proof. Case 1, $\vdash \alpha$: Then $\vdash \neg\alpha \rightarrow \beta$. By *closure* (we may use the properties of partial meet contraction shown above!) we then have $\neg\alpha \rightarrow \beta \in A \sim_\gamma \alpha$ (and similarly $\neg\alpha \rightarrow \neg\beta \in A \sim_\gamma \alpha$, but we only need one of them for the proof).

Case 2, $\nvdash \alpha$: Then $A \sim_\gamma \alpha \in A \perp \alpha$. It follows from Observation 1.51 that either $\neg\alpha \rightarrow \beta \in A \sim_\gamma \alpha$ or $\neg\alpha \rightarrow \neg\beta \in A \sim_\gamma \alpha$. (Note that $\alpha \vee \beta$ is equivalent with $\neg\alpha \rightarrow \beta$, and $\alpha \vee \neg\beta$ with $\neg\alpha \rightarrow \neg\beta$.) ■

For *full meet* contraction, we have introduced the postulate of *core identity*:

> *Core identity*:
> $\beta \in A \div \alpha$ if and only if $\beta \in A$ and there is no $A' \subseteq A$ such that $\alpha \notin \mathrm{Cn}(A')$ and $\alpha \in \mathrm{Cn}(A' \cup \{\beta\})$.
>
> An operation $\div$ for a set A is an operation of full meet contraction if and only if it satisfies *core identity*, i.e.
> $A \sim \alpha = \bigcap (A \perp \alpha)$
> $= \{\beta \in A \mid \text{if } A' \subseteq A \text{ and } A' \nvdash \alpha, \text{ then } A' \cup \{\beta\} \nvdash \alpha\}$.
> [Observation 2.10.]

Proof. Core identity is an equivalence, and for the proof we can divide it into its two implications:

1. If $\beta \in A \sim \alpha$, then $\beta \in A$ and there is no $A' \subseteq A$ such that $\alpha \notin \mathrm{Cn}(A')$ and $\alpha \in \mathrm{Cn}(A' \cup \{\beta\})$.
2. If $\beta \in A$ and there is no $A' \subseteq A$ for which it holds that $\alpha \notin \mathrm{Cn}(A')$ and $\alpha \in \mathrm{Cn}(A' \cup \{\beta\})$, then $\beta \in A \sim \alpha$.

(2) can be seen to be equivalent to *core-retainment*, that we know to hold for partial meet contraction (including full meet contraction). It remains to be shown that (1) holds.

Let $\beta \in A{\sim}\alpha$. It follows directly from the construction of full meet contraction that $\beta \in A$. The remaining task is to show that there is no $A' \subseteq A$ such that $\alpha \notin \text{Cn}(A')$ and $\alpha \in \text{Cn}(A' \cup \{\beta\})$. Suppose to the contrary that there is some A' with this property. It follows by the upper bound property from $A' \subseteq A$ and $\alpha \notin \text{Cn}(A')$ that there is some A'' such that $A' \subseteq A'' \in A \bot \alpha$. Clearly, $\alpha \notin \text{Cn}(A'')$. Since $A' \subseteq A''$ and $\alpha \in \text{Cn}(A' \cup \{\beta\})$ we may conclude that $\beta \notin A''$. Since $A'' \in A \bot \alpha$, it follows that $\beta \notin \bigcap(A \bot \alpha) = A{\sim}\alpha$. This contradiction concludes the proof. ■

The previous proof illustrates an important proof method for partial meet contraction. In order to show that a sentence β is not an element of $A{\sim}_{\gamma}\alpha$, it is sufficient to provide an element X of $\gamma(A \bot \alpha)$ such that $\beta \notin X$. The rest follows by set theory from $A{\sim}_{\gamma}\alpha = \bigcap \gamma(A \bot \alpha)$. In the case of full meet contraction, $\gamma(A \bot \alpha) = A \bot \alpha$, which simplifies this type of proof.

The same method can be used for proving another strong result on full meet contraction:

> If A is logically closed, $\alpha \in A$ and $\sim$ is full meet contraction, then $A{\sim}\alpha = A \cap \text{Cn}(\{\neg\alpha\})$.
> [Observation 2.12.]

Proof. *One direction*: In order to prove that $A{\sim}\alpha \subseteq A \cap \text{Cn}(\{\neg\alpha\})$, suppose to the contrary that $A{\sim}\alpha \not\subseteq A \cap \text{Cn}(\{\neg\alpha\})$, i.e. that there is some ε such that $\varepsilon \in A{\sim}\alpha$ and $\varepsilon \notin A \cap \text{Cn}(\{\neg\alpha\})$. It follows from $\varepsilon \in A{\sim}\alpha$, by the construction of full meet contraction, that $\varepsilon \in A$. From this and $\varepsilon \notin A \cap \text{Cn}(\{\neg\alpha\})$ it follows that $\varepsilon \notin \text{Cn}(\{\neg\alpha\})$, i.e. (by the deduction property of Cn) $\nvdash \neg\alpha \rightarrow \varepsilon$, or equivalently $\nvdash \neg\varepsilon \rightarrow \alpha$, i.e. (again using the deduction property) $\neg\varepsilon \nvdash \alpha$. It follows from this that $\alpha \vee \neg\varepsilon \nvdash \alpha$. Since $\alpha \in A$ and A is logically closed, we have $\alpha \vee \neg\varepsilon \in A$. It follows from $\{\alpha \vee \neg\varepsilon\} \subseteq A$ and $\{\alpha \vee \neg\varepsilon\} \nvdash \alpha$, by the upper bound property, that there is some set X such that $\{\alpha \vee \neg\varepsilon\} \subseteq X \in A \bot \alpha$. Since $\{\alpha \vee \neg\varepsilon, \varepsilon\} \vdash \alpha$, we can conclude that $\varepsilon \notin X$. It follows from $\varepsilon \notin X \in A \bot \alpha$ that $\varepsilon \notin \bigcap(A \bot \alpha)$. (This is where the proof method referred to above was used.) We thus have $\varepsilon \notin A{\sim}\alpha$, contrary to the conditions. This is sufficient for this direction of the proof.

The other direction: For the proof that $A \cap \text{Cn}(\{\neg\alpha\}) \subseteq A{\sim}\alpha$, we need to distinguish between two cases, according to whether or not $\vdash \alpha$.

Case 1, $\vdash \alpha$: Then $A{\sim}\alpha = A$, from which $A \cap \text{Cn}(\{\neg\alpha\}) \subseteq A{\sim}\alpha$ follows directly.

Case 2, $\nvdash \alpha$: Let $\beta \in A \cap \text{Cn}(\{\neg\alpha\})$. We are going to show that $\beta \in A{\sim}\alpha$. Suppose to the contrary that $\beta \notin A{\sim}\alpha$. There must then be some set Y such that $\beta \notin Y \in A \bot \alpha$. Since $\beta \in A$, it follows that $\alpha \in \text{Cn}(Y \cup \{\beta\})$. By the deduction property of Cn, $Y \vdash \beta \rightarrow \alpha$, We also have $\beta \in \text{Cn}(\{\neg\alpha\})$, which by the deduction property yields $\vdash \neg\alpha \rightarrow \beta$, or equivalently $\vdash \neg\beta \rightarrow \alpha$. Since $\beta \rightarrow \alpha$ and $\neg\beta \rightarrow \alpha$ together imply α, we get $Y \vdash \alpha$, contrary to $Y \in A \bot \alpha$. Since this contradiction was obtained from our assumption that $\beta \notin A{\sim}\alpha$, we can conclude that $\beta \in A{\sim}\alpha$, which finishes the proof. ■

The identity $A{\sim}\alpha = A \cap \mathrm{Cn}(\{\neg\alpha\})$ only holds if A is logically closed. The same applies to the postulate of *meet identity*:

> Let A be a logically closed set and $\sim$ full meet contraction for A. Then $\sim$ satisfies:
> If $\alpha, \beta \in A$, then $(A{\sim}\alpha) \cap (A{\sim}\beta) = A{\sim}(\alpha\&\beta)$. (*meet identity*)
> [Part of Theorem 2.11.]

Proof. Let A be a logically closed set and let $\alpha, \beta \in A$. It follows from Observation 1.55 that
$A{\perp}\alpha \cup A{\perp}\beta = A{\perp}(\alpha\&\beta)$. It follows by set theory that
$\bigcap(A{\perp}\alpha \cup A{\perp}\beta) = \bigcap(A{\perp}(\alpha\&\beta))$
$\bigcap(A{\perp}\alpha) \cap \bigcap(A{\perp}\beta) = \bigcap(A{\perp}(\alpha\&\beta))$
$(A{\sim}\alpha) \cap (A{\sim}\beta) = A{\sim}(\alpha\&\beta)$. ■

Exercises

76. Let the language consist of the atomic sentences p and q and their truth-functional combinations. Let $A = \{p, q, p{\vee}q\}$. Let $\sim$ be full meet contraction, and perform the following contractions:

    (a) $A{\sim}(p\&q)$
    (b) $A{\sim}p$
    (c) $A{\sim}q$
    (d) $A{\sim}(p{\vee}q)$
    (e) $A{\sim}(p{\rightarrow}q)$

77. Let p, q, and r be logically independent sentences. Using Theorem 2.2, explain why an operator $\div$ cannot be a partial meet contraction if:

    (a) $\{p, q{\rightarrow}p\}{\div}(q{\rightarrow}p) = \{p\}$
    (b) $\{p, q\}{\div}(p\&q) = \{p{\vee}q\}$
    (c) $\{p, q{\rightarrow}p\}{\div}p = \emptyset$

78. Let γ be a selection function for a set A (not necessarily logically closed). Furthermore, let α be a sentence such that $\vdash \alpha$ and $\alpha \in A$. Show that it holds for all $\beta \in A$ that $\alpha \in A{\sim}_{\gamma}\beta$.

79. Let A be logically closed, and let α and β be elements of A. Furthermore, let γ be a selection function for A. Show that:
    If $\alpha{\vee}\beta \in A{\sim}_{\gamma}\alpha$, then $\beta \in A{\sim}_{\gamma}\alpha$.

80. [1] Let $\sim$ be full meet contraction, and let $\div$ be an operation (not necessarily partial meet contraction) such that $A{\sim}\alpha \subseteq A{\div}\alpha$ for all α. Show that $\div$ satisfies *recovery*.

81. Let A be an inconsistent and logically closed set, and let $\sim$ be full meet contraction. Show that for any sentence α, $(A\sim\alpha) \cap (A\sim\neg\alpha) = \text{Cn}(\emptyset)$.

82. Let $\sim$ be full meet contraction, and let $A = \text{Cn}(\{\alpha\})$.
    (a) Show that $A\sim\alpha = \text{Cn}(\emptyset)$
    (b) Show that if $\beta \in A$, then $A\sim\beta = \text{Cn}(\{\beta\rightarrow\alpha\})$.

83. [1] Show that maxichoice contraction satisfies the following condition:
If $\beta \in A, \delta \in A$ and $\beta\vee\delta \in A\div\alpha$, then either $\beta \in A\div\alpha$ or $\delta \in A\div\alpha$. (*primeness*).

84. [18] Eduardo Fermé has proposed the following way to construct a contraction operator for belief sets that does not satisfy *recovery*: Let A be a belief set, and let $\sim_\gamma$ be an operation of partial meet contraction on A. Furthermore, let f be a function such that (1) for all $\alpha \in A\backslash\text{Cn}(\emptyset) : f(\alpha) \in A\backslash(A\sim_\gamma\alpha)$, and (2) for all $\alpha, \beta \in A\backslash\text{Cn}(\emptyset)$: if $\alpha\leftrightarrow\beta \in \text{Cn}(\emptyset)$, then $f(\alpha) = f(\beta)$.
Let $\div$ be an operation on A such that
(I) if $\alpha \in A\backslash\text{Cn}(\emptyset)$, then $A\div\alpha = A\sim_\gamma\alpha \cap A\sim_\gamma(\alpha\rightarrow f(\alpha))$, and
(II) otherwise, $A\div\alpha = A\sim_\gamma\alpha$.
    (a) Show that $\div$ satisfies *closure, inclusion, vacuity, success, extensionality*, and *failure*.
    (b) Show that if $\alpha \in A\backslash\text{Cn}(\emptyset)$ and $f(\alpha) \notin \text{Cn}(\{\alpha\})$, then $A \neq \text{Cn}((A\div\alpha) \cup \{\alpha\})$.

85. [49] Let A be a set that is closed under implication, i.e. such that if $\alpha_1 \in A$ and $\alpha_2 \in A$, then $\alpha_1\rightarrow\alpha_2 \in A$. Let γ be a selection function for A. Show that for all $\alpha_1, \ldots, \alpha_n \in A$:
$A \subseteq \text{Cn}(A\sim_\gamma(\alpha_1\&\ldots\&\alpha_n) \cup \{\alpha_1\&\ldots\&\alpha_n\})$.
(This is a strengthened form of *recovery*.)

15+ PROVING REPRESENTATION THEOREMS

A representation theorem (an axiomatic characterization) is a theorem that connects a *construction* with a *set of postulates*, showing that the former is exactly characterized by the latter. For example, let us consider our representation theorem for maxichoice contraction:

> The operator $\div$ is an operator of maxichoice contraction for a set A if and only if it satisfies the postulates of *success, inclusion, fullness*, and *uniformity*.

A proof of a representation theorem has two parts. In the *construction-to-postulates* part, it is shown that the construction specified in the theorem (here: maxichoice contraction) satisfies the given postulates (here: success, inclusion, fullness, and uniformity). In the *postulates-to-construction* part, it is shown that if an operation satisfies the given postulates, then that operation can be constructed in the way specified in the theorem (here: constructed as a maxichoice contraction). This is often the trickiest part of a representation theorem. It requires that we can find a construction that works.

In the case of maxichoice contraction, a fairly obvious construction is available for the proof. For $\div$ to be a maxichoice contraction, it must be the case that $A{\div}\alpha \in A{\perp}\alpha$ for all non-tautological α. Given this, we can construct our maxichoice contraction by just letting $\gamma(A{\perp}\alpha) = \{A{\div}\alpha\}$.

> The operator $\div$ is an operator of maxichoice contraction for a set A if and only if it satisfies the postulates of *success, inclusion, fullness*, and *uniformity*.
> [Theorem 2.13.]

Proof. *Construction-to-postulates*: This part of the proof has already been given in Section 2.14$^+$.

Postulates-to-construction: Let $\div$ be an operation for A that satisfies *success, inclusion, fullness*, and *uniformity*. Let γ be such that:

$$\gamma(A{\perp}\alpha) = \{A{\div}\alpha\}.$$

We need to show, (1) that γ is a (well-defined) function, (2) that γ is a maxichoice selection function, and (3) that for all α, $\bigcap\gamma(A{\perp}\alpha) = A{\div}\alpha$.

Part 1: In order for γ to be a function, it must be the case that for all α_1 and α_2, if $A{\perp}\alpha_1 = A{\perp}\alpha_2$, then $\gamma(A{\perp}\alpha_1) = \gamma(A{\perp}\alpha_2)$. Suppose that $A{\perp}\alpha_1 = A{\perp}\alpha_2$. It then follows from Observation 1.39 that any subset of A implies α_1 if and only if it implies α_2. By *uniformity*, $A{\div}\alpha_1 = A{\div}\alpha_2$. It follows from the definition of γ that $\gamma(A{\perp}\alpha_1) = \gamma(A{\perp}\alpha_2)$.

Part 2: For γ to be a maxichoice selection function, it must satisfy two conditions (cf. Definition 1.4): (A) if $A{\perp}\alpha$ is non-empty, then $\gamma(A{\perp}\alpha)$ is a set containing exactly one element of $A{\perp}\alpha$, and (B) if $A{\perp}\alpha$ is empty, then $\gamma(A{\perp}\alpha) = \{A\}$.

Part 2A: Since we have defined $\gamma(A{\perp}\alpha) = \{A{\div}\alpha\}$, what we need to show is that if $A{\perp}\alpha$ is non- empty, then $A{\div}\alpha \in A{\perp}\alpha$.

Suppose that $A{\perp}\alpha$ is non-empty. Then $\nvdash \alpha$, and it follows from *success* that $A{\div}\alpha \nvdash \alpha$. It follows from *inclusion* that $A{\div}\alpha \subseteq A$. To prove that $A{\div}\alpha \in A{\perp}\alpha$ it remains (cf. Definition 1.35) to show that if $A{\div}\alpha \subset B \subseteq A$, then $B \vdash \alpha$. Suppose that $A{\div}\alpha \subset B \subseteq A$. There is then some β such that $\beta \in B$ and $\beta \notin A{\div}\alpha$. It follows from *fullness* that $(A{\div}\alpha) \cup \{\beta\} \vdash \alpha$, and since $(A{\div}\alpha) \cup \{\beta\} \subseteq B$ we can conclude that $B \vdash \alpha$. Thus, the first of the conditions for γ to be a maxichoice selection function is satisfied.

Part 2B: We need to show that if $A{\perp}\alpha$ is empty, then $\gamma(A{\perp}\alpha) = \{A\}$. Suppose that $A{\perp}\alpha$ is empty. Then $\vdash \alpha$. We are going to show that $A{\div}\alpha = A$. It follows by *inclusion* that $A{\div}\alpha \subseteq A$. To prove that $A \subseteq A{\div}\alpha$, suppose to the contrary that $A \nsubseteq A{\div}\alpha$. Let $\beta \in A \backslash (A{\div}\alpha)$. Then it follows from *fullness* that $\alpha \notin \mathrm{Cn}(A{\div}\alpha)$

and $\alpha \in \text{Cn}((A{\div}\alpha \cup \{\beta\})$. This, however is impossible since $\vdash \alpha$ makes $\alpha \notin \text{Cn}(A{\div}\alpha)$ impossible. We can conclude from this contradiction that $A \subseteq A{\div}\alpha$. Since we already have $A{\div}\alpha \subseteq A$, it follows that $A{\div}\alpha = A$. By the definition of γ, $\gamma(A{\perp}\alpha) = \{A\}$, as desired.

Part 3: That $\bigcap\gamma(A{\perp}\alpha) = A{\div}\alpha$ follows directly from the definition of γ. ■

When proving a representation theorem for partial meet contraction in general, the construction used for maxichoice contraction cannot be applied. There is, however, a standard construction (introduced in the classic AGM paper [1]) that has turned out to work very well for most representation theorems for partial meet contraction. Let $\div$ be an operator for A, and let α be a non-tautological sentence. (The limiting case $\vdash \alpha$ must be treated separately.) If $A{\div}\alpha$ is an operator of partial meet contraction, then there is, by the upper bound property, at least one element X of $A{\perp}\alpha$ such that $A{\div}\alpha \subseteq X$. Let $\gamma(A{\perp}\alpha)$ consist of those elements of $A{\perp}\alpha$ that have this property, i.e.:

If $A{\perp}\alpha$ is non-empty, then $\gamma(A{\perp}\alpha) = \{X \in A{\perp}\alpha \mid A{\div}\alpha \subseteq X\}$.

If $\div$ is a partial meet contraction, then $\bigcap\gamma(A{\perp}\alpha) = A{\div}\alpha$ will follow. (Cf. Exercise 86.) Now, let us use this construction to prove a representation theorem.

> The operator $\div$ is an operator of partial meet contraction for a set A if and only if it satisfies the postulates of *success, inclusion, relevance,* and *uniformity.*
> [Theorem 2.2.]

Proof. *Construction-to-postulates:* This part of the proof has already been given in Section 2.14+.

Postulates-to-construction: Let $\div$ be an operation for A that satisfies *success, inclusion, relevance,* and *uniformity*. Let γ be such that:

1. If $A{\perp}\alpha \neq \emptyset$, then $\gamma(A{\perp}\alpha) = \{X \in A{\perp}\alpha \mid A{\div}\alpha \subseteq X\}$.
2. If $A{\perp}\alpha = \emptyset$, then $\gamma(A{\perp}\alpha) = \{A\}$.

We need to show, (1) that γ is a (well-defined) function, (2) that γ is a selection function, and (3) that for all α, $\bigcap\gamma(A{\perp}\alpha) = A{\div}\alpha$.

Part 1: That γ is a function follows from *uniformity* in the same way as in the foregoing proof.

Part 2: For γ to be a selection function, it is (as can be seen from Definition 1.2) sufficient to show that if $A{\perp}\alpha$ is non-empty, then so is $\gamma(A{\perp}\alpha)$. Suppose that $A{\perp}\alpha$ is non-empty. Then $\nvdash \alpha$, and it follows from *success* that $\alpha \notin \text{Cn}(A{\div}\alpha)$. It follows by *inclusion* that $A{\div}\alpha \subseteq A$. By the upper bound property, there is some B such that $A{\div}\alpha \subseteq B \in A{\perp}\alpha$. By the construction of γ, $B \in \gamma(A{\perp}\alpha)$, which proves that $\gamma(A{\perp}\alpha)$ is non- empty.

Part 3: There are two cases, according to whether or not $\vdash \alpha$.

First case, $\vdash \alpha$: It follows that $A\perp\alpha = \emptyset$. Our definition of γ yields $\gamma(A\perp\alpha) = \{A\}$. and thus $\bigcap\gamma(A\perp\alpha) = A$. As was shown in Observation 2.3 (proved in Section 2.12^{+}), it follows from *inclusion* and *relevance* that *failure* is satisfied, so that $A{\div}\alpha = A$. We thus have $\bigcap\gamma(A\perp\alpha) = A = A{\div}\alpha$.

Second case, $\nvdash \alpha$: In this case, $A\perp\alpha$ is non-empty, and we have shown in Part 2 of the present proof that $\gamma(A\perp\alpha)$ is non-empty as well. It follows from our definition of γ that $A{\div}\alpha$ is a subset of every element of $\gamma(A\perp\alpha)$, from which we may conclude that $A{\div}\alpha \subseteq \bigcap\gamma(A\perp\alpha)$.

In order to show that $\bigcap\gamma(A\perp\alpha) \subseteq A{\div}\alpha$, let $\varepsilon \notin A{\div}\alpha$. We are going to show that $\varepsilon \notin \bigcap\gamma(A\perp\alpha)$. This is obvious if $\varepsilon \notin A$. In the remaining case, when $\varepsilon \in A$, we have $\varepsilon \in A$ and $\varepsilon \notin A{\div}\alpha$. It follows from *relevance* that there is some set B such that $A{\div}\alpha \subseteq B \subseteq A$, $B \nvdash \alpha$ and $B \cup \{\varepsilon\} \vdash \alpha$. It follows by the upper bound property from $B \subseteq A$ and $B \nvdash \alpha$ that there is some set D such that $B \subseteq D \in A\perp\alpha$. Clearly, $\varepsilon \notin D$. (It would otherwise follow from $\varepsilon \in D$, $B \subseteq D$, and $B \cup \{\varepsilon\} \vdash \alpha$ that $D \vdash \alpha$, contrary to $D \in A\perp\alpha$.) It follows from $A{\div}\alpha \subseteq B \subseteq D$, by our definition of γ, that $D \in \gamma(A\perp\alpha)$. From this and $\varepsilon \notin D$ we can conclude that $\varepsilon \notin \bigcap\gamma(A\perp\alpha)$. This concludes the proof. ■

The following proof of the representation theorem for unified (global) partial meet contraction is based on the foregoing proof.

> The following three conditions on a global operator $\div$ are equivalent:
>
> 1. [50] It is an operator of partial meet contraction that is based on a unified selection function.
> 2. (Hans Rott) It is an operator of partial meet contraction that is based on a perfectly unified selection function.
> 3. [50] It satisfies *success, inclusion, relevance, uniformity*, and in addition the following:
>   If $\alpha \notin \mathrm{Cn}(\emptyset)$, and each element of Z implies α, then: $A{\div}\alpha = (A \cup Z){\div}\alpha$. (*redundancy*)
>
> [Theorem 2.56.]

Proof. In order to show that (1), (2), and (3) are equivalent, it is sufficient to show that (1) implies (3), that (3) implies (2), and that (2) implies (1). Since all perfectly unified selection functions are unified, it is immediate that (2) implies (1).

(1) *implies* (3): (This is a 'construction-to-postulates' proof.) Let γ be a unified two-place selection function and $\sim_\gamma$ the contraction operator generated by γ. It follows from Theorem 2.2 that *success, inclusion, relevance*, and *uniformity* hold. We are going to show that *redundancy* holds.

Suppose that $\alpha \notin \mathrm{Cn}(\emptyset)$ and that each element of Z implies α. It follows from Observation 1.40 that $(A \cup Z)\perp\alpha = A\perp\alpha \neq \emptyset$. Since γ is unified,

$$\bigcap \gamma_{A\cup Z}((A \cup Z)\perp\alpha) = \bigcap \gamma_A(A\perp\alpha),$$

i.e. $(A \cup Z)\sim_\gamma\alpha = A\sim_\gamma\alpha$. Hence, *redundancy* holds.

(3) *implies* (2): (This is a 'postulates-to-construction' proof.) Let $\div$ be a global contraction operator that satisfies the five postulates listed in the theorem. It follows from Theorem 2.2 that for each subset A of $\mathcal{L}$ there is a one-place selection function γ_A for A such that for all sentences α, $A\div\alpha = \bigcap\gamma_A(A\perp\alpha)$. Let γ be the two-place selection function that coincides with γ_A for each A. We have to show that γ is perfectly unified. Let A_1 and A_2 be subsets of $\mathcal{L}$, and α_1 and α_2 sentences, such that $A_1\perp\alpha_1 = A_2\perp\alpha_2 \neq \emptyset$. We have to show that $\gamma_{A_1}(A_1\perp\alpha_1) = \gamma_{A_2}(A_2\perp\alpha_2)$.

Let $\delta \in A_1\backslash A_2$. We then have $\delta \notin \bigcup(A_2\perp\alpha_2)$, and thus $\delta \notin \bigcup(A_1\perp\alpha_1)$. It follows from this and $\delta \in A_1$ that $\delta \vdash \alpha_1$.

Since every element of $A_1\backslash A_2$ implies α_1, it follows (Observation 1.40) that $A_1\perp\alpha_1 = (A_1 \cap A_2)\perp\alpha_1$. In the same way, $A_2\perp\alpha_2 = (A_1 \cap A_2)\perp\alpha_2$. Thus $(A_1 \cap A_2)\perp\alpha_1 = (A_1 \cap A_2)\perp\alpha_2$.

We now have:

$$\begin{aligned}
&A_1\div\alpha_1 = A_1\sim_\gamma\alpha_1 \\
&= (A_1 \cap A_2)\sim_\gamma\alpha_1 && (\textit{redundancy}) \\
&= \bigcap\gamma_{A_1\cap A_2}((A_1 \cap A_2)\perp\alpha_1) \\
&= \bigcap\gamma_{A_1\cap A_2}((A_1 \cap A_2)\perp\alpha_2) && (\text{since } (A_1 \cap A_2)\perp\alpha_1 = (A_1 \cap A_2)\perp\alpha_2) \\
&= (A_1 \cap A_2)\sim_\gamma\alpha_2 \\
&= A_2\sim_\gamma\alpha_2 && (\textit{redundancy}) \\
&= A_2\div\alpha_2.
\end{aligned}$$

We now have both $A_1\perp\alpha_1 = A_2\perp\alpha_2$ and $A_1\div\alpha_1 = A_2\div\alpha_2$. We can therefore use the construction of γ (cf. the proof of Theorem 2.2) and obtain:

$$\begin{aligned}
&\gamma_{A_1}(A_1\perp\alpha_1) = \{X \in A_1\perp\alpha_1 \mid A_1\div\alpha_1 \subseteq X\} \\
&= \{X \in A_2\perp\alpha_2 \mid A_2\div\alpha_2 \subseteq X\} \\
&= \gamma_{A_2}(A_2\perp\alpha_2).
\end{aligned}$$

This concludes the proof. ■

Essentially the same method that we have used for belief bases can be employed to prove the classic AGM representation theorem for partial meet contraction on logically closed sets:

> The operator $\div$ is an operator of partial meet contraction for a logically closed set A if and only if it satisfies the postulates of *closure, inclusion, vacuity, success, extensionality*, and *recovery*.
> [Theorem 2.7.]

Proof. [1] *Construction-to-postulates:* This part of the proof has already been given in Section 2.14+.

Postulates-to-construction: Let $\div$ be an operation for a logically closed set A that satisfies *closure, inclusion, vacuity, success, extensionality,* and *recovery.* We will again use the standard method for constructing a selection function, i.e. we define γ as follows:

1. If $A\perp\alpha \neq \emptyset$, then $\gamma(A\perp\alpha) = \{X \in A\perp\alpha \mid A\div\alpha \subseteq X\}$.
2. If $A\perp\alpha = \emptyset$, then $\gamma(A\perp\alpha) = \{A\}$.

We need to show, (1) that γ is a (well-defined) function, (2) that γ is a selection function, and (3) that for all α, $\bigcap\gamma(A\perp\alpha) = A\div\alpha$.

Part 1: In order for γ to be a function, it must be the case that for all α_1 and α_2, if $A\perp\alpha_1 = A\perp\alpha_2$, then $\gamma(A\perp\alpha_1) = \gamma(A\perp\alpha_2)$. As can be seen from the definition of γ, to prove this it is sufficient to show that if $A\perp\alpha_1 = A\perp\alpha_2$, then $A\div\alpha_1 = A\div\alpha_2$.

Suppose that $A\perp\alpha_1 = A\perp\alpha_2$. Then, by Observation 1.39, any subset of A implies α_1 if and only if it implies α_2. It follows from *extensionality* and *vacuity* that *uniformity* holds (Observation 2.4). Therefore, $A\div\alpha_1 = A\div\alpha_2$.

Part 2: This part coincides with Part 2 of the proof of Theorem 2.2.

Part 3: There are two cases, according to whether or not $\vdash \alpha$.

First case, $\vdash \alpha$: It follows that $A\perp\alpha = \emptyset$. Our definition of γ yields $\gamma(A\perp\alpha) = \{A\}$, and thus $\bigcap\gamma(A\perp\alpha) = A$. We therefore need to show that $A\div\alpha = A$. It follows from *inclusion* that $A\div\alpha \subseteq A$. It remains to be shown that $A \subseteq A\div\alpha$.

Let $\varepsilon \in A$. By *recovery*, $A \subseteq \text{Cn}((A\div\alpha)\cup\{\alpha\})$, so that $\varepsilon \in \text{Cn}((A\div\alpha)\cup\{\alpha\})$. By the deduction property of Cn, $\alpha\rightarrow\varepsilon \in \text{Cn}(A\div\alpha)$. It follows from $\vdash \alpha$ that $\alpha\rightarrow\varepsilon$ and ε are logically equivalent, and we therefore have $\varepsilon \in \text{Cn}(A\div\alpha)$ and, by *closure*, $\varepsilon \in A\div\alpha$. Since this was shown to follow from $\varepsilon \in A$, we have shown that $A \subseteq A\div\alpha$. This finishes the first case.

Second case, $\nvdash \alpha$: In this case, $A\perp\alpha$ is non- empty, and we have shown in Part 2 of the present proof that $\gamma(A\perp\alpha)$ is non-empty as well. It follows from our definition of γ that $A\div\alpha$ is a subset of every element of $\gamma(A\perp\alpha)$, from which we may conclude that $A\div\alpha \subseteq \bigcap\gamma(A\perp\alpha)$.

In order to show that $\bigcap\gamma(A\perp\alpha) \subseteq A\div\alpha$, let $\varepsilon \notin A\div\alpha$. We are going to show that $\varepsilon \notin \bigcap\gamma(A\perp\alpha)$. This follows directly from the definition of γ if $\varepsilon \notin A$. In the remaining case, when $\varepsilon \in A$, it follows from *recovery* that $\varepsilon \in \text{Cn}((A\div\alpha)\cup\{\alpha\})$. By the deduction property of Cn, $\alpha\rightarrow\varepsilon \in \text{Cn}(A\div\alpha)$, and by *closure*, $\alpha\rightarrow\varepsilon \in A\div\alpha$. It follows by *closure* from this and $\varepsilon \notin A\div\alpha$ that $\alpha\vee\varepsilon \notin A\div\alpha$. (To see this, note that $\alpha\rightarrow\varepsilon$ and $\alpha\vee\varepsilon$ together imply ε.) It follows from the upper bound property that there is a set $X \in A\perp(\alpha\vee\varepsilon)$ such that $A\div\alpha \subseteq X$. By Observation 1.53, since $X \nvdash \alpha$ we have $X \in A\perp\alpha$. It follows from $X \in A\perp(\alpha\vee\varepsilon)$ that $X \nvdash \varepsilon$ and from the construction of γ that $X \in \gamma(A\perp\alpha)$. We can conclude that $\varepsilon \notin \bigcap\gamma(A\perp\alpha)$. This finishes the proof. ■

The proofs of Theorems 2.2 and 2.56 exemplify that often a representation theorem can be supplemented with both an additional specification of the construction and some additional postulate. As a further example of this, the foregoing theorem can be supplemented with (1) the additional specification that the partial meet contraction is a full meet contraction, and (2) the additional postulate of meet identity (namely: If $\alpha, \beta \in A$, then $(A{\div}\alpha) \cap (A{\div}\beta) = A{\div}(\alpha\&\beta)$). The proof of such a supplemented representation theorem can be simplified by reference to the less specified theorem on which it is based:

> The operator $\div$ is an operator of full meet contraction for a logically closed set A if and only if it satisfies the postulates of *closure, inclusion, vacuity, success, extensionality, recovery*, and *meet identity.* [Theorem 2.11.]

Proof. *Construction-to-postulates:* This was shown in Section 2.14+.

Postulates-to-construction: Let A be a logically closed set, and let $\div$ be an operation on A that satisfies *closure, inclusion, vacuity, success, extensionality, recovery* and *meet identity.* It follows from Theorem 2.7 (the foregoing proof) that $\div$ is a partial meet contraction generated by some selection function γ, thus $A{\div}\alpha = \bigcap\gamma(A{\perp}\alpha)$. We need to show that $\div$ is full meet contraction, i.e. that for all α, if $A{\perp}\alpha$ is non-empty, then $A{\div}\alpha = \bigcap(A{\perp}\alpha)$.

If $A{\perp}\alpha$ is non-empty, then $\gamma(A{\perp}\alpha)$ is a non-empty subset of $A{\perp}\alpha$. It follows set-theoretically that $\bigcap(A{\perp}\alpha) \subseteq \bigcap\gamma(A{\perp}\alpha)$. It now remains to be shown that $\bigcap\gamma(A{\perp}\alpha) \subseteq \bigcap(A{\perp}\alpha)$.

If $\alpha \notin A$, then we have $A{\perp}\alpha = \{A\}$, so that $\gamma(A{\perp}\alpha) = \{A\}$, from which $\bigcap\gamma(A{\perp}\alpha) \subseteq \bigcap(A{\perp}\alpha)$ follows directly.

If $\alpha \in A$, then it follows from Observation 2.12 that $\bigcap(A{\perp}\alpha) = A \cap \mathrm{Cn}(\{\neg\alpha\})$, so we have to prove that $\bigcap\gamma(A{\perp}\alpha) \subseteq A \cap \mathrm{Cn}(\{\neg\alpha\})$. Clearly, $\bigcap\gamma(A{\perp}\alpha) \subseteq A$. It remains to be shown that $\bigcap\gamma(A{\perp}\alpha) \subseteq \mathrm{Cn}(\{\neg\alpha\})$. This is what we need *meet identity* for.

Let $\beta \in \bigcap\gamma(A{\perp}\alpha)$. Since α and $(\alpha\vee\beta)\&(\alpha\vee\neg\beta)$ are logically equivalent, it follows from *meet identity* and *extensionality* that $A{\sim_\gamma}(\alpha\vee\beta) \cap A{\sim_\gamma}(\alpha\vee\neg\beta) = A{\sim_\gamma}\alpha$, thus $\beta \in A{\sim_\gamma}(\alpha\vee\beta)$, thus $A{\sim_\gamma}(\alpha\vee\beta) \vdash \alpha\vee\beta$, thus by *success* $\vdash \alpha\vee\beta$, thus $\vdash \neg\alpha\rightarrow\beta$, thus (by the deduction property of Cn) $\beta \in \mathrm{Cn}(\{\neg\alpha\})$. We have shown that $\bigcap\gamma(A{\perp}\alpha) \subseteq \mathrm{Cn}(\{\neg\alpha\})$, and as was noted above this is sufficient to complete the proof. ■

The reader who wants to devise new representation theorems may wonder which is the best, to begin with postulates and search for a construction, or the other way around. There is no general answer to this question. Both strategies have been successfully employed by logicians. Often, both the construction and the postulates have been adjusted in the process of transforming the researcher's first idea into a stringently proved representation theorem.

Exercises

86. [1] Let γ be a selection function for A. Show that if $A\bot\alpha \neq \emptyset$, then

$$A{\sim_\gamma}\alpha = \bigcap\{X \in A\bot\alpha \mid A{\sim_\gamma}\alpha \subseteq X\}.$$

87. [1] Prove the following representation theorem:
The operator $\div$ for a logically closed set A is a maxichoice operator if and only if it satisfies *closure, inclusion, vacuity, success, extensionality, recovery* and:
If $\beta \in A, \delta \in A$, and $\beta \vee \delta \in A \div \alpha$, then either $\beta \in A \div \alpha$ or $\delta \in A \div \alpha$. (*primeness*)

88. (a) Let A be any set, and let $\div$ be any operator for A that satisfies *success, inclusion*, and *uniformity*. Show that there is some operator $\sim_\gamma$ of partial meet contraction for A such that $A\div\alpha \subseteq A{\sim_\gamma}\alpha$ for all sentences α.
(b) Let A be a logically closed set, and let $\div$ be any operator for A that satisfies *success, inclusion, extensionality*, and *vacuity*. Show that there is some operator $\sim_\gamma$ of partial meet contraction for A such that $A\div\alpha \subseteq A{\sim_\gamma}\alpha$ for all sentences α.

16+ MULTIPLE CONTRACTION

In this section, some of the results from the foregoing sections will be generalized to contractions by sets. We will not be concerned with operations of the type $A\div\alpha$, as in the rest of the book, but with operations of the type $A\div B$, where B is a set of sentences. Although B may be a set of any size that the language permits (including the empty set), the most interesting cases are contractions by sets with more than one element, and therefore contraction by sets is commonly called *multiple contraction* [21].

There are at least two plausible interpretations of contraction by a set of sentences [21]. One is to remove *all of the sentences*. This will be called 'package contraction', since the set is removed in one single package. The other interpretation is to remove *at least one of the sentences*. This will be called 'choice contraction' [25]. Package contraction seems to be the most interesting of these operations, both from an intuitive and from a formal point of view.

The simplest way to construct package contraction is to use remainders and selection functions in the same way as for contraction by single sentences:

DEFINITION 2.61 ([25; 42]) *γ is a* package selection function *for A if and only if for all sets B:*

1. *If $A\bot B$ is non-empty, then $\gamma(A\bot B)$ is a non- empty subset of $A\bot B$, and*
2. *If $A\bot B$ is empty, then $\gamma(A\bot B) = \{A\}$.*

An operator $\div$ for A is an operator of partial meet package contraction *if and only if there is some package selection function γ such that $A\div B = \bigcap\gamma(A\bot B)$ for all sets B.*

The difference between a package selection function for A and an (ordinary) single-sentence selection function for A is that the former is defined for a wider domain.

Is partial meet package contraction really different from partial meet contraction by single sentences? The answer is yes, and the reason is that partial meet package contraction cannot in general be easily reduced to contraction by single sentences. It does not hold in general, for instance, that $A \div \{\alpha, \beta\} = A \div \{\alpha \& \beta\}$ or that $A \div \{\alpha, \beta\} = A \div \{\alpha \vee \beta\}$. This can be seen from the following example:

Let the language consist of the two logically independent sentences p and q and their truth-functional combinations. Let $A = Cn(\{p, q\})$. Then, as can easily be verified with the help of Figure 1.1 on p. 33:

$$\begin{aligned} A\bot\{p,q\} &= \{\mathrm{Cn}(\{p\leftrightarrow q\}), \mathrm{Cn}(\{p\vee q\})\} \\ A\bot\{p\&q\} &= \{\mathrm{Cn}(\{p\}), \mathrm{Cn}(\{p\leftrightarrow q\}), \mathrm{Cn}(\{q\})\} \\ A\bot\{p\vee q\} &= \{\mathrm{Cn}(\{p\leftrightarrow q\})\}. \end{aligned}$$

We can now let

$$\begin{aligned} \gamma(A\bot\{p,q\}) &= \{\mathrm{Cn}(\{p\vee q\})\} \\ \gamma(A\bot\{p\&q\}) &= \{\mathrm{Cn}(\{q\})\} \\ \gamma(A\bot\{p\vee q\}) &= \{\mathrm{Cn}(\{p\leftrightarrow q\})\} \end{aligned}$$

so that both $A \div \{p, q\} \neq A \div \{p\&q\}$ and $A \div \{p, q\} \neq A \div \{p \vee q\}$.

Partial meet package contraction can be axiomatically characterized in a way that is very similar to our characterization of partial meet single-sentence contraction (Theorem 2.2):

THEOREM 2.62 ([25]) *An operator $\div$ for a set A is an operator of partial meet package contraction if and only if it satisfies the following conditions:*
If $B \cap \mathrm{Cn}(\emptyset) = \emptyset$ then $B \cap \mathrm{Cn}(A \div B) = \emptyset$ (P-success)
$A \div B \subseteq A$ (P-inclusion)
If $\beta \in A$ and $\beta \notin A \div B$, then there is a set A' such that $A \div B \subseteq A' \subseteq A$ and $B \cap \mathrm{Cn}(A') = \emptyset$ but $B \cap \mathrm{Cn}(A' \cup \{\beta\}) \neq \emptyset$. (P-relevance)
If every subset of A implies some element of B_1 if and only if it implies some element of B_2, then $A \div B_1 = A \div B_2$. (P-uniformity)

A proof of this theorem can be obtained by fairly straight-forward adjustments of the proof of Theorem 2.2. It is left to the reader as an exercise.

The recovery postulate can be generalized to partial meet package contraction:

P-recovery:
$A \subseteq \mathrm{Cn}((A \div B) \cup B)$.

In most contractions of practical interest, the removed set is finite.[2] The more restricted postulate of *finite P-recovery* says that recovery holds in these cases:

[2] *Note added in proof*: Recently, Jun Li at Nankai University (China) has shown that P-recovery does not hold for multiple (package) partial meet contraction in the infinite case. In fact, it does not even hold for multiple (package) maxichoice contraction.

Finite P-recovery:
If B is finite, then $A \subseteq \text{Cn}((A \div B) \cup B)$.

Finite P-recovery holds for partial meet package contraction on belief sets. In fact, it holds for all multiple operations that satisfy P-relevance.

OBSERVATION 2.63 ([25]) *If an operator $\div$ for a logically closed set A satisfies P-relevance, then it satisfies finite P-recovery.*

Proof. Let A be a logically closed set and let $\div$ be an operation for A that satisfies *P-relevance*. Suppose that *finite P-recovery* is not satisfied. There is then some finite set B and some sentence β such that $\beta \in A$ and $\beta \notin \text{Cn}((A \div B) \cup B)$. Hence, by the deduction property, $\&(B) \rightarrow \beta \notin A \div B$. It follows from *P-relevance* that there is some X such that $A \div B \subseteq X \subseteq A$, $\text{Cn}(X) \cap B = \emptyset$ and $\text{Cn}(X \cup \{\&(B) \rightarrow \beta\}) \cap B \neq \emptyset$. It follows from the last of these expressions that $X \vdash (\&(B) \rightarrow \beta) \rightarrow \varepsilon$ for some $\varepsilon \in B$. Since $\varepsilon \in B$ we have $\vdash (\&(B) \rightarrow \varepsilon$, and it follows truth-functionally that $(\&(B) \rightarrow \beta) \rightarrow \varepsilon$ is equivalent to ε, so that $X \vdash \varepsilon$ and thus $\text{Cn}(X) \cap B \neq \emptyset$, contrary to the initial conditions for X. We can conclude from this contradiction that *finite P-recovery* holds. ■

Finite P-recovery also holds for a wider category of package contractions that includes partial meet package contraction. These operations will be called *subremainder contractions*. The following definition serves to introduce them: (Remember that $A \Delta B = \bigcup\{A \perp \beta \mid \beta \in B\}$.)

DEFINITION 2.64 ([25; 42]) Γ *is a* covering function *for A if and only if for all B:*

i. if $B \cap \text{Cn}(\emptyset) = \emptyset$, then $\Gamma(B)$ is a subset of $A \Delta B$ such that $\Gamma(B) \cap (A \perp \beta) \neq \emptyset$ for all $\beta \in B$, and

ii. if $B \cap \text{Cn}(\emptyset) \neq \emptyset$, then $\Gamma(B) = \{A\}$.

The operator $\div$ for A is an operator of subremainder contraction *if and only if there is some covering function Γ for A such that $A \div B = \bigcap \Gamma(B)$ for all B.*

The next observation establishes that partial meet package contractions are a proper special case of subremainder contractions:

OBSERVATION 2.65 ([25; 42]) *1. If the operator $\div$ for A is a partial meet package contraction, then it is a subremainder contraction.*

2. It does not hold in general that if the operator $\div$ for A is a subremainder contraction, then it is a partial meet package contraction.

Proof. *Part 1:* Let $\sim_\gamma$ be a partial meet package contraction for A. For every $X \in A\perp B$, let

$$f(X,B) = \{Y \mid X \subseteq Y \in A\perp\beta \text{ for some } \beta \in B\}$$

Let $\Gamma(B) = \{f(X,B) \mid X \in \gamma(A\perp B)\}$. It follows from Observation 1.47 that $X = \bigcap f(X,B)$ for every $X \in A\perp B$. We therefore have:

$$\bigcap\Gamma(B) = \bigcap\{f(X,B) \mid X \in \gamma(A\perp B)\} = \bigcap\{X \mid X \in \gamma(A\perp B)\} = \bigcap\gamma(A\perp B).$$

Part 2: For this direction of the proof, we are going to construct a counterexample. Let p, q, and r be three logically independent sentences, and let A be a logically closed set such that $\{p,q,r\} \subseteq A$. Then $\{p, r\rightarrow q\}$ is a subset of A that does not imply q, and it follows from the upper bound property that there is a set Z_1 such that

$$\{p, r\rightarrow q\} \subseteq Z_1 \in A\perp q.$$

Similarly, $\{p\vee q, p\rightarrow r, r\rightarrow q\}$ is a subset of A that does not imply r, and it follows from the upper bound property that there is some Z_2 such that

$$\{p\vee q, p\rightarrow r, r\rightarrow q\} \subseteq Z_2 \in A\perp r.$$

Let $\div$ be a subremainder contraction that is generated by a covering function such that $\Gamma(\{q,r\}) = \{Z_1, Z_2\}$. We are going to show that $\div$ is not a partial meet package contraction. Since Z_1 and Z_2 are remainders of A, they are both logically closed (cf. Observation 1.48).

It follows from $p \in Z_1$, since Z_1 is logically closed, that $p\vee q \in Z_1$. We therefore have $\{p\vee q, r\rightarrow q\} \subseteq Z_1 \cap Z_2$. By our construction of $\div$, $A\div\{q,r\} = Z_1 \cap Z_2$. It follows that $\{p\vee q, r\rightarrow q\} \subseteq A\div\{q,r\}$.

Since $p\rightarrow r \in Z_2 \in A\perp r$, we also have $p \notin Z_2$, and thus $p \notin A\div\{q,r\}$.

Now suppose that $\div$ is also a partial meet package contraction. Then, according to Theorem 2.62, it must satisfy *P-relevance*. Since $p \in A$ and $p \notin A\div\{q,r\}$, there must be some set A' such that $A\div\{q,r\} \subseteq A' \subseteq A$, $\{q,r\} \cap \mathrm{Cn}(A') = \emptyset$, and $\{q,r\} \cap \mathrm{Cn}(A' \cup \{p\}) \neq \emptyset$. It follows from the latter expression that either q or r is an element of $\mathrm{Cn}(A' \cup \{p\})$. There are two cases:

Case 1, $q \in \mathrm{Cn}(A' \cup \{p\})$: By the deduction property of Cn, $p\rightarrow q \in \mathrm{Cn}(A')$. Since $\{p\vee q, r\rightarrow q\} \subseteq A\div\{q,r\} \subseteq A'$, we also have $p\vee q \in A'$. Since $p\rightarrow q$ and $p\vee q$ together imply q, we obtain $q \in \mathrm{Cn}(A')$, contrary to $\{q,r\} \cap \mathrm{Cn}(A') = \emptyset$.

Case 2, $r \in \mathrm{Cn}(A' \cup \{p\})$: By the deduction property of Cn, $p\rightarrow r \in \mathrm{Cn}(A')$. Since $\{p\vee q, r\rightarrow q\} \subseteq A\div\{q,r\} \subseteq A'$, we also have $p\vee q \in A'$ and $r\rightarrow q \in A'$. Since $p\vee q$, $p\rightarrow r$, and $r\rightarrow q$ together imply q, we again obtain $q \in \mathrm{Cn}(A')$, contrary to $\{q,r\} \cap \mathrm{Cn}(A') = \emptyset$.

Thus, in both cases, the assumption that $\div$ is a partial meet package contraction leads to contradiction. We may conclude that $\div$ is not a partial meet package contraction. ∎

The final result of this section includes a proof that subremainder contractions on logically closed sets satisfy *finite P-recovery*. It follows directly from this that partial meet package contractions, being special cases of subremainder contractions, satisfy *finite P-recovery*. Indeed, we are going to prove a bit more, namely that *finite P-recovery* together with five other postulates exactly characterizes subremainder contraction by finite sets.

THEOREM 2.66 ([25]) *An operator $\div$ for contraction of a logically closed set A by finite sets is an operator of subremainder contraction if and only if it satisfies the following postulates:*
$A \div B = \mathrm{Cn}(A \div B)$ *(P-closure)*
$A \div B \subseteq A$ *(P-inclusion)*
If $B \cap \mathrm{Cn}(A) = \emptyset$, *then* $A = A \div B$ *(P-vacuity)*
If $B \cap \mathrm{Cn}(\emptyset) = \emptyset$ *then* $B \cap \mathrm{Cn}(A \div B) = \emptyset$ *(P-success)*
If $B \cap \mathrm{Cn}(\emptyset) \neq \emptyset$ *then* $A = A \div B$ *(P-failure)*
If B *is finite, then* $A \subseteq \mathrm{Cn}((A \div B) \cup \{B\})$ *(finite P-recovery)*

Proof. *Construction-to-postulates*: Let $\div$ be a subremainder contraction for a logically closed set A, based on the covering function Γ. The proof that the first five postulates hold is left to the reader as an exercise. Here follows a proof that *finite P-recovery* is satisfied.

If $B \cap \mathrm{Cn}(\emptyset) \neq \emptyset$, then it follows from Definition 2.64 that $\Gamma(B) = \{A\}$, from which *finite P-recovery* follows directly.

For the principal case, $B \cap \mathrm{Cn}(\emptyset) = \emptyset$, let $\alpha \in A$. We are going to show that $\alpha \in \mathrm{Cn}((A \div B) \cup \{B\})$. Let $Z \in \Gamma(B)$. Then there is some $\beta \in B$ such that $Z \in A \perp \beta$.

We are going to prove that $(\&B \rightarrow \alpha) \in Z$. For that purpose, suppose to the contrary that $(\&B \rightarrow \alpha) \notin Z$. From $\alpha \in A$ and the logical closure of A we obtain $(\&B \rightarrow \alpha) \in A$. It follows from this and $(\&B \rightarrow \alpha) \notin Z \in A \perp \beta$ that $\beta \in \mathrm{Cn}(Z \cup \{\&B \rightarrow \alpha\})$. By the deduction property of Cn, $(\&B \rightarrow \alpha) \rightarrow \beta \in \mathrm{Cn}(Z)$. Since β is one of the conjuncts of B, this is equivalent to $((\&B)\&\beta \rightarrow \alpha) \rightarrow \beta \in \mathrm{Cn}(Z)$. As can be shown, e.g. with a truth-table, $((\&B)\&\beta \rightarrow \alpha) \rightarrow \beta$ is logically equivalent to β. We therefore have $\beta \in \mathrm{Cn}(Z)$, contrary to $Z \in A \perp \beta$. From this contradiction we may conclude that $(\&B \rightarrow \alpha) \in Z$.

Since this holds for every $Z \in \Gamma(B)$, we have $(\&B \rightarrow \alpha) \in \bigcap \Gamma(B) = A \div B$. The rest is simple: It follows from $(\&B \rightarrow \alpha) \in A \div B$, by the deduction property of Cn, that $\alpha \in \mathrm{Cn}((A \div B) \cup \{\&B\})$, and thus $\alpha \in \mathrm{Cn}((A \div B) \cup B)$.

Postulates-to-construction: Let $\div$ be an operator that satisfies the postulates given in the theorem. Let Γ be such that for all sets A:

1. if $B \cap \mathrm{Cn}(\emptyset) = \emptyset$, then $\Gamma(B) = \{Z \in A \Delta B \mid A \div B \subseteq Z\}$
2. if $B \cap \mathrm{Cn}(\emptyset) \neq \emptyset$, then $\Gamma(B) = \{A\}$.

It can be seen from the definition that Γ is a (well-defined) function. It remains to be shown (1) that Γ is a covering function for A, and (2) that $A \div B = \bigcap \Gamma(B)$ for all B.

Part 1: As can be seen from Definition 2.64, it is sufficient to show that if $B \cap \mathrm{Cn}(\emptyset) = \emptyset$, then $\Gamma(B) \cap (A \bot \beta) \neq \emptyset$ for all $\beta \in B$.

Let $B \cap \mathrm{Cn}(\emptyset) = \emptyset$ and $\beta \in B$. It follows from *P-success* that $B \cap \mathrm{Cn}(A \div B) = \emptyset$ and consequently $\beta \notin \mathrm{Cn}(A \div B)$. From *P-inclusion* we also have $A \div B \subseteq A$. It follows from the upper bound property that there is some Z such that $A \div B \subseteq Z \in A \bot \beta$. Then $Z \in A \Delta B$, and it follows from our definition of Γ that $Z \in \Gamma(B)$, so that $\Gamma(B) \cap (A \bot \beta) \neq \emptyset$.

Part 2: There are three cases:

Case 1, $B \cap \mathrm{Cn}(\emptyset) \neq \emptyset$. Our definition of Γ yields $\Gamma(B) = \{A\}$, so that $\bigcap \Gamma(B) = A$. It follows from *P-failure* that $A \div B = A$, and we can conclude that $A \div B = A = \bigcap \Gamma(B)$.

Case 2, $B \cap \mathrm{Cn}(A) = \emptyset$: Then $A \Delta B = \{A\}$, and our definition of Γ yields $\Gamma(B) = \{A\}$, so that $\bigcap \Gamma(B) = A$. It follows from *P-vacuity* that $A \div B = A$. We thus have $A \div B = A = \bigcap \Gamma(B)$.

Case 3, $B \cap \mathrm{Cn}(\emptyset) = \emptyset \neq B \cap \mathrm{Cn}(A)$: We are first going to show that $A \div B \subseteq \bigcap \Gamma(B)$. In this case, we have $\Gamma(B) = \{Z \in A \Delta B \mid A \div B \subseteq Z\}$, and it was shown in Part 1 of the proof that $\Gamma(B)$ is non-empty. It follows that $A \div B \subseteq \bigcap \Gamma(B)$.

In order to prove that $\bigcap \Gamma(B) \subseteq A \div B$, let $\alpha \notin A \div B$. Our task is to show that $\alpha \notin \bigcap \Gamma(B)$. Since $\bigcap \Gamma(B)$ is by definition a subset of A, this is obvious if $\alpha \notin A$. For the principal case, we assume that $\alpha \in A$.

It follows from *finite P-recovery* that $\alpha \in \mathrm{Cn}((A \div B) \cup B)$, thus we have $\alpha \in \mathrm{Cn}((A \div B) \cup \{\&B\})$ and, by the deduction property of Cn, $\&B \rightarrow \alpha \in \mathrm{Cn}(A \div B)$. Suppose that $\alpha \vee \beta \in \mathrm{Cn}(A \div B)$ for all $\beta \in B$. Then $\alpha \in \mathrm{Cn}(A \div B)$. ($\alpha$ follows truth-functionally from $\beta_1 \& \ldots \& \beta_n \rightarrow \alpha$ and $\alpha \vee \beta_1, \ldots, \alpha \vee \beta_n$.) From our definition of α we have $\alpha \notin A \div B$, and from *P-closure* it follows that $\alpha \notin \mathrm{Cn}(A \div B)$. We can conclude from this contradiction that there is some $\beta \in B$ such that $\alpha \vee \beta \notin \mathrm{Cn}(A \div B)$.

It follows by the upper bound property from $\alpha \vee \beta \notin \mathrm{Cn}(A \div B)$ and $A \div B \subseteq A$ (that we have from *P-inclusion*) that there is some X such that $A \div B \subseteq X \in A \bot (\alpha \vee \beta)$. By Observation 1.53, $X \in A \bot \beta$, and thus $X \in A \Delta B$. By the definition of Γ, $X \in \Gamma(B)$, and thus $\bigcap \Gamma(B) \subseteq X$. It follows from $X \in A \bot (\alpha \vee \beta)$ that $\alpha \notin \mathrm{Cn}(X)$, and thus from $\bigcap \Gamma(B) \subseteq X$ that $\alpha \notin \bigcap \Gamma(B)$. This concludes the proof. ■

Exercises

89. Prove Theorem 2.62.

90. Which of the following properties are satisfied by partial meet package contraction? Explain why.

    (a) [101] $A\div\{\alpha,\alpha\} = A\div\{\alpha\}$.
    (b) [101] If $\beta \notin \text{Cn}(A)$, then $A\div\{\alpha,\beta\} = A\div\{\alpha\}$.
    (c) $A\div\{\alpha\} = A\div\{\alpha\&\beta,\alpha\}$.
    (d) $A\div\{\alpha,\beta\} = A\div\{\alpha\&\beta,\alpha,\beta\}$.
    (e) $A\div\{\alpha\&\beta\} = A\div\{\alpha,\beta\}$.

91. [25; 42] Prove the part left out in the proof of Theorem 2.66 above, namely that subremainder contraction, as applied to a logically closed set, satisfies *P-closure, P-inclusion, P-vacuity, P-success*, and *P-failure*.

92. (Hans Rott)

    (a) Let A, B, and D be sets of sentences, and let $\beta \in A$. Show that the following two conditions are equivalent:
    (1) There is some X such that $D \subseteq X \subseteq A$, $B \cap \text{Cn}(X) = \emptyset$, and $B \cap \text{Cn}(X \cup \{\beta\}) \neq \emptyset$.
    (2) There is some X such that $D \subseteq X \in A\perp B$ and $\beta \notin X$.
    (b) Show that, excepting the limiting case when $B \cap \text{Cn}(\emptyset) \neq \emptyset$, if *P-success* holds, then *P-relevance* is equivalent to
    $A\div B = \bigcap\{X \in A\perp B \mid A\div B \subseteq X\}$.

93. [25] Let $\angle$ denote *choice remainders*, defined so that $X \in A\angle B$ if and only if (1) $X \subseteq A$, (2) $B \not\subseteq \text{Cn}(X)$, and (3) If $X \subset Y \subseteq A$, then $B \subseteq \text{Cn}(Y)$.
Let *choice selection functions* be defined just as package selection functions (replace $\perp$ by $\angle$ in Definition 2.61), and let $\div$ be a *partial meet choice contraction* if and only if there is some choice selection function γ such that $A\div B = \bigcap\gamma(A\angle B)$ for all B.

    (a) Show that $\div$ is an operation of partial meet choice contraction if and only if it satisfies the following four postulates:
    If $B \not\subseteq \text{Cn}(\emptyset)$, then $B \not\subseteq \text{Cn}(A\div B)$ (*C-success*)
    $A\div B \subseteq A$ (*C-inclusion*)
    If $\alpha \in A$ and $\alpha \notin A\div B$, then there is some A' such that $A\div B \subseteq A' \subseteq A$, $B \not\subseteq \text{Cn}(A')$, and $B \subseteq \text{Cn}(A' \cup \{\alpha\})$ (*C-relevance*)
    If $B_1 \subseteq \text{Cn}(X)$ iff $B_2 \subseteq \text{Cn}(X)$ for all $X \subseteq A$, then $A\div B_1 = A\div B_2$. (*C-uniformity*).
    (b) Let $\div$ be an operation of partial meet choice contraction. Construct an operator $\div'$ of partial meet single-sentence contraction such that: For all finite sets B, $A\div B = A\div'(\&B)$.

17+ COMPLETED SELECTION FUNCTIONS

In several proofs we have made use of the following property of partial meet contraction:

If $\div$ is a partial meet contraction for A, then for all α: if $\alpha \notin \mathrm{Cn}(\emptyset)$, then $A \div \alpha = \bigcap\{X \mid A \div \alpha \subseteq X \in A \perp \alpha\}$.

This relationship can be used to obtain, given an operator of partial meet contraction, a selection function that generates it. (This is what we have done in most proofs of representation theorems.) We can also use it to obtain, given a selection function, another selection function that generates the same partial meet contraction.

DEFINITION 2.67 (AGM [1]) *Let γ be a selection function for a set A. The* completion *of γ is the function $\hat{\gamma}$ such that:*
$\hat{\gamma}(A \perp \alpha) = \{X \mid \bigcap \gamma(A \perp \alpha) \subseteq X \in A \perp \alpha\}$ *if $A \perp \alpha$ is non-empty*
$\hat{\gamma}(A \perp \alpha) = \{A\}$ *if $A \perp \alpha$ is empty.*

A selection function γ is completed *if and only if $\gamma = \hat{\gamma}$.*

OBSERVATION 2.68 (AGM [1]) *Let γ be a selection function for a set A. Then:*

1. *$\hat{\gamma}$ is a selection function for A*
2. *$\gamma(A \perp \alpha) \subseteq \hat{\gamma}(A \perp \alpha)$ for all α*
3. *$\bigcap \gamma(A \perp \alpha) = \bigcap \hat{\gamma}(A \perp \alpha)$ for all α.*

Proof. *Part 1*: This can be seen by checking the two clauses of the definition of a selection function (Definition 1.2).

Part 2: If $A \perp \alpha = \emptyset$, then $\gamma(A \perp \alpha) = \hat{\gamma}(A \perp \alpha) = \{A\}$, from which the desired conclusion follows directly. If $A \perp \alpha \neq \emptyset$, then it holds for every $X \in \gamma(A \perp \alpha)$ that $\bigcap \gamma(A \perp \alpha) \subseteq X$, and thus by the definition of $\hat{\gamma}$ that $X \in \hat{\gamma}(A \perp \alpha)$.

Part 3: There are two cases, according to whether or not $A \perp \alpha = \emptyset$.

Case 1, $A \perp \alpha = \emptyset$. We then have $\gamma(A \perp \alpha) = \hat{\gamma}(A \perp \alpha) = \{A\}$, so that $\bigcap \gamma(A \perp \alpha) = \bigcap \hat{\gamma}(A \perp \alpha)$.

Case 2, $A \perp \alpha \neq \emptyset$. It follows from the definition of $\hat{\gamma}$ that $\bigcap \gamma(A \perp \alpha) \subseteq X$ for every $X \in \hat{\gamma}(A \perp \alpha)$. Thus, $\bigcap \gamma(A \perp \alpha) \subseteq \bigcap \hat{\gamma}(A \perp \alpha)$. Furthermore, by Part 2 of the present proof, $\gamma(A \perp \alpha) \subseteq \hat{\gamma}(A \perp \alpha)$. It follows from this that $\bigcap \hat{\gamma}(A \perp \alpha) \subseteq \bigcap \gamma(A \perp \alpha)$, and we can conclude that $\bigcap \hat{\gamma}(A \perp \alpha) = \bigcap \gamma(A \perp \alpha)$. ■

Observation 2.68 has the following direct consequence:

COROLLARY (AGM [1]) *An operator $\div$ for a set A is a partial meet contraction by a completed selection function if and only if it is a partial meet contraction (by any selection function).*

Completed selection functions are much easier to handle than uncompleted selection functions. This is mostly due to the two properties shown in the following observation.

OBSERVATION 2.69 *Let A be a set and γ a completed selection function for A. Furthermore, let $\alpha \in A \backslash \mathrm{Cn}(\emptyset)$. Then:*

1. (AGM [1]) *For all* X: $X \in \gamma(A\bot\alpha)$ *if and only if* $\bigcap\gamma(A\bot\alpha) \subseteq X \in A\bot\alpha$.
2. (Hans Rott [116]) *If A is logically closed, then for all* X: $X \in \gamma(A\bot\alpha)$ *if and only if* $\bigcap\gamma(A\bot\alpha) \subseteq X \in A\bot\beta$ *for some* $\beta \in A$.

Proof. *Part 1*: For one direction, let $X \in \gamma(A\bot\alpha)$. It follows from the definition of a selection function that $X \in A\bot\alpha$, and from set theory that $\bigcap\gamma(A\bot\alpha) \subseteq X$.

For the other direction, let $\bigcap\gamma(A\bot\alpha) \subseteq X \in A\bot\alpha$. Since γ is completed, it follows from Definition 2.67 that $X \in \gamma(A\bot\alpha)$.

Part 2: For one direction, let $X \in \gamma(A\bot\alpha)$. It follows from Part 1 that $\bigcap\gamma(A\bot\alpha) \subseteq X \in A\bot\beta$ if we let $\beta = \alpha$, and since $\alpha \in A$ we are done.

For the other direction, let $\bigcap\gamma(A\bot\alpha) \subseteq X \in A\bot\beta$ for some $\beta \in A$. Since $\beta \in A$ and A is logically closed, it follows from the recovery property of partial meet contraction that $\beta \in \text{Cn}((\bigcap\gamma(A\bot\alpha)) \cup \{\alpha\})$, thus $\alpha \rightarrow \beta \in \text{Cn}(\bigcap\gamma(A\bot\alpha))$. We have $\bigcap\gamma(A\bot\alpha) \subseteq X$ and consequently $\text{Cn}(\bigcap\gamma(A\bot\alpha)) \subseteq \text{Cn}(X)$. We can conclude that $\alpha \rightarrow \beta \in \text{Cn}(X)$. It follows from $X \vdash \alpha \rightarrow \beta$ and $X \nvdash \beta$ (that we know since $X \in A\bot\beta$) that $X \nvdash \alpha$. We can therefore apply Observation 1.53 to $X \nvdash \alpha$, $\alpha \in A$, and $X \in A\bot\beta$, and obtain $X \in A\bot\alpha$. It follows from Part 1 of the present observation that $X \in \gamma(A\bot\alpha)$. ■

It follows from this observation that if we wish to prove that $X \in \gamma(A\bot\alpha)$, then it is — given that γ is completed — sufficient to prove that $\bigcap\gamma(A\bot\alpha) \subseteq X$ and $X \in A\bot\alpha$. If A is logically closed, then it is sufficient to show that $\bigcap\gamma(A\bot\alpha) \subseteq X$ and that $X \in A\bot\beta$ for some $\beta \in A$.

Not all selection functions are completed [1]. However, if a set A is both finite and logically closed, then all selection functions for A are completed.

OBSERVATION 2.70 (AGM [1]) *Let γ be a selection function for a set A that is both finite and logically closed. Then* $\hat{\gamma} = \gamma$.

Proof. In order to prove $\hat{\gamma} = \gamma$, we need to show that $\hat{\gamma}(A\bot\alpha) = \gamma(A\bot\alpha)$ for all α. Suppose to the contrary that this is not the case. Then there is some α such that $\hat{\gamma}(A\bot\alpha) \neq \gamma(A\bot\alpha)$. Since both $\hat{\gamma}$ and γ are selection functions for A (Observation 2.68), they would coincide if $\vdash \alpha$ (clause (ii) of Definition 1.2), so we may conclude that $\nvdash \alpha$.

By Observation 2.68, $\gamma(A\bot\alpha) \subseteq \hat{\gamma}(A\bot\alpha)$. It therefore follows from $\hat{\gamma}(A\bot\alpha) \neq \gamma(A\bot\alpha)$ that there must be some X such that $X \in \hat{\gamma}(A\bot\alpha)$ and $X \notin (A\bot\alpha)$.

Let $Y \in \gamma(A\bot\alpha)$. Then $X \neq Y$, and since X and Y are both elements of $A\bot\alpha$ it also follows that $X \not\subset Y$. We can conclude from this that $X \not\subseteq Y$. Since Y is logically closed, it follows that $\&X \notin Y$. ($\&X$ is well-defined since A is finite.) It follows from $X \subseteq A$, by the logical closure of A, that $\&X \in A$. We therefore have $\&X \in A$ and $\&X \notin Y \in A\bot\alpha$, from which we may conclude that $\&X \rightarrow \alpha \in Y$. Since this holds for all $Y \in \gamma(A\bot\alpha)$, we may conclude that $\&X \rightarrow \alpha \in \bigcap\gamma(A\bot\alpha)$.

By Observation 2.68, $\bigcap\hat{\gamma}(A\bot\alpha) = \bigcap\gamma(A\bot\alpha)$, so that $\&X\rightarrow\alpha \in \bigcap\hat{\gamma}(A\bot\alpha)$. It follows from $X \in \hat{\gamma}(A\bot\alpha)$ that $\bigcap\hat{\gamma}(A\bot\alpha) \subseteq X$, and thus $\&X\rightarrow\alpha \in X$, from which it follows that $X \vdash \alpha$, contrary to $X \in A\bot\alpha$. This contradiction allows us to conclude that $\hat{\gamma}(A\bot\alpha) \neq \gamma(A\bot\alpha)$ does not hold. ∎

Exercises

94. [1] Show that if γ is a selection function, then $\hat{\gamma} = \hat{\hat{\gamma}}$ (i.e. the completion of any selection function is its own completion).

95. Let A be any set of sentences, and let γ_1 and γ_2 be selection functions for A. Show that if $\gamma_1(A\bot\alpha) \subseteq \gamma_2(A\bot\alpha) \subseteq \hat{\gamma}_1(A\bot\alpha)$, then $\bigcap\gamma_1(A\bot\alpha) = \bigcap\gamma_2(A\bot\alpha)$.

96. Let A be a logically closed set and γ a selection function for A. Let $\alpha, \beta \in A\backslash\text{Cn}(\emptyset)$. Show that if $\gamma(A\bot\alpha) \subseteq \gamma(A\bot\beta)$, then $\hat{\gamma}(A\bot\alpha) \subseteq \hat{\gamma}(A\bot\beta)$.

97. Let A be logically closed, and let γ be a completed selection function for A. Furthermore, let α and β be elements of $A\backslash\text{Cn}(\emptyset)$.

    (a) Show that $A{\sim}_\gamma\alpha \subseteq A{\sim}_\gamma\beta$ if and only if $\gamma(A\bot\beta) \subseteq \gamma(A\bot\alpha)$.
    (b) Show that if $(A{\sim}_\gamma\alpha) \cup (A{\sim}_\gamma\beta) \nvdash \alpha$, then $\gamma(A\bot\alpha) \cap \gamma(A\bot\beta) \neq \emptyset$.

98. [116] Let $\div$ be an operator of partial meet contraction for a logically closed set A. Show that the following two conditions are equivalent:
    (I) If $\beta \in A$ and $\beta \notin A\div(\alpha\&\beta)$, then $A\div(\alpha\&\beta) \subseteq A\div\alpha$.
    (II) $\div$ is based on a selection function γ such that for all $\alpha, \beta \in A\backslash\text{Cn}(\emptyset)$, if $\beta \notin \bigcap\gamma(A\bot\alpha\&\beta)$, then $\gamma(A\bot\alpha) \subseteq \gamma(A\bot(\alpha\&\beta))$.

18+ RELATIONAL SELECTION FUNCTIONS

In Section 2.6 we introduced *relational* selection functions. A selection function for A is relational if and only if there is some relation $\sqsubseteq$ (the *marking-off relation*) such that for all sentences α, if $A\bot\alpha$ is non-empty, then the following *marking-off* identity is satisfied:

$$\gamma(A\bot\alpha) = \{B \in A\bot\alpha \mid C \sqsubseteq B \text{ for all } C \in A\bot\alpha\}.$$

The marking-off identity does not make any explicit requirement on the marking-off relation. However, this permissiveness is illusive. A selection function can be based on a relation $\sqsubseteq$ only if $\sqsubseteq$ is such that it generates, through the marking-off identity, a selection function. In this way, the marking-off identity makes *implicit* requirements on the marking-off relation.

To illustrate this, let $A = \{p, q\}$, and let $\sqsubseteq$ be a relation such that $\{p\} \sqsubseteq \{p\}$ does not hold. Then no selection function can be based on $\sqsubseteq$. Since $A\bot q = \{\{p\}\}$, if γ is a selection function then $\gamma(\{\{p\}\}) = \{\{p\}\}$, but if γ is based on the relation $\sqsubseteq$ just referred to, then $\gamma(\{\{p\}\}) = \emptyset$.

Does it really make a difference to require that the selection function be relational? Can an operator of partial meet contraction be non-relational? The following example shows that it can. Let the language consist of the two atomic sentences p and q and their truth-functional combinations. Furthermore, let:

$$\begin{aligned} A &= \mathrm{Cn}(\{p\&q\}) \\ A_1 &= \mathrm{Cn}(\{p\}) \\ A_2 &= \mathrm{Cn}(\{p\leftrightarrow q\}) \\ A_3 &= \mathrm{Cn}(\{q\}) \end{aligned}$$

It can be shown that:

$$\begin{aligned} A\bot p &= \{A_2, A_3\} \\ A\bot q &= \{A_1, A_2\} \\ A\bot(p\&q) &= \{A_1, A_2, A_3\} \end{aligned}$$

Next, let us suppose that:

$$A\div p = A\div q = A_2$$
$$A\div(p\&q) = A_1$$

This is clearly compatible with $\div$ being a partial meet contraction (and indeed a maxichoice contraction). But can it be a relational partial meet contraction? Suppose that it is. Then it is based on a selection function γ that is in its turn based on a marking-off relation $\sqsubseteq$.

Since $\div$ is based on γ, and $A\div p = A_2$, we have $\bigcap\gamma(A\bot p) = A_2$, i.e. $\bigcap\gamma(\{A_2, A_3\}) = A_2$. By the definition of a selection function, $\gamma(A_2, A_3)$ is either $\{A_2\}$, $\{A_3\}$, or $\{A_2, A_3\}$. Only in the first case is $\bigcap\gamma(\{A_2, A_3\}) = A_2$. We can therefore conclude that $\gamma(\{A_2, A_3\}) = \{A_2\}$. Since γ is based on the marking-off relation $\sqsubseteq$, it follows from this that $A_3 \sqsubseteq A_2$ and $A_2 \sqsubseteq A_2$.

In exactly the same way, it follows from $A\div q = A_2$ and $\bigcap\gamma(A\bot q) = A_2$ that $A_1 \sqsubseteq A_2$ (and $A_2 \sqsubseteq A_2$, which we already know). Summing up this, if $\div$ is based on a relational selection function, then the marking-off relation must satisfy $A_1 \sqsubseteq A_2, A_2 \sqsubseteq A_2$, and $A_3 \sqsubseteq A_2$. It follows from this, and $A\bot(p\&q) = \{A_1, A_2, A_3\}$, that $A_2 \in \gamma(A\bot(p\&q))$. Since $p \notin A_2$, we can then conclude that $p \notin \bigcap\gamma(A\bot(p\&q))$, i.e. that $p \notin A\div(p\&q)$. However, we have defined $A\div(p\&q) = A_1$, and $p \in A_1$. This contradiction shows that $\div$ cannot be relational.

From this example, we may conclude that *not all partial meet contractions are relational*. Since we chose our example to be an operation on a (logically closed) belief set, we can also conclude that *not all partial meet contractions on belief sets are relational*.

The following are two conditions that a selection function (for a logically closed set) must satisfy in order to be relational.

Choice-distributivity: If $\alpha, \beta \in A \backslash \mathrm{Cn}(\emptyset)$, then
$\gamma(A \perp (\alpha \& \beta)) \subseteq \gamma(A \perp \alpha) \cup \gamma(A \perp \beta)$.
Choice-expansion:
If $\alpha, \beta \in \backslash \mathrm{Cn}(\emptyset)$, then $\gamma(A \perp \alpha) \cap \gamma(A \perp \beta) \subseteq \gamma(A \perp (\alpha \& \beta))$.

In order to see the intuitive meaning of these properties, observe that since A is logically closed, we have $A \perp (\alpha \& \beta) = (A \perp \alpha) \cup (A \perp \beta)$. Choice-distributivity says that whatever is best in the union of two sets $((A \perp \alpha) \cup (A \perp \beta))$ must be best in at least one of these two sets ($A \perp \alpha$ or $A \perp \beta$). Choice-expansion says that whatever is best in both of the two sets must also be best in their union.

The intuitive meaning of the two postulates can perhaps best be seen from a non-epistemic example. First, suppose that David Hilbert was one of the best mathematicians among those that have studied either in Königsberg or in Heidelberg. Then he was either one of the best mathematicians among those who have studied in Königsberg or one of the best mathematicians among those who have studied in Heidelberg (choice-distributivity). Next, suppose that David Hilbert was one of the best mathematicians among those who have studied in Königsberg and that he was also one of the best mathematicians among those who have studied in Heidelberg. Then he was one of the best mathematicians among those that have studied mathematics either in Königsberg or in Heidelberg (choice-expansion).

As the following observation shows, choice-distributivity and choice- expansion are not only necessary but also sufficient conditions for γ to be relational.

OBSERVATION 2.71 (Hans Rott [116]) *Let γ be a selection function for a logically closed set A. Then γ is relational if and only if it satisfies choice- distributivity and choice-expansion.*

Proof. *Construction-to-postulates*: Let γ be relational by $\sqsubseteq$ and let $\alpha, \beta \in A \backslash \mathrm{Cn}(\emptyset)$. Since A is logically closed, we have $A \perp (\alpha \& \beta) = (A \perp \alpha) \cup (A \perp \beta)$ by Observation 1.55.

Choice-distributivity: Let $X \in \gamma(A \perp (\alpha \& \beta))$. Then either $X \in A \perp \alpha$ or $X \in A \perp \beta$.

First case, $X \in A \perp \alpha$: Let $Y \in A \perp \alpha$. We are going to show that $Y \sqsubseteq X$. It follows from $A \perp (\alpha \& \beta) = (A \perp \alpha) \cup (A \perp \beta)$ that $Y \in A \perp (\alpha \& \beta)$. Since γ is relational by $\sqsubseteq$, it follows from $Y \in A \perp (\alpha \& \beta)$ and $X \in \gamma(A \perp (\alpha \& \beta))$ that $Y \sqsubseteq X$, as desired. Since this holds for all $Y \in A \perp \alpha$, and we also have $X \in A \perp \alpha$, we can conclude from the marking-off identity that $X \in \gamma(A \perp \alpha)$.

Second case, $X \in A \perp \beta$: It follows in exactly the same way that $X \in \gamma(A \perp \beta)$.

Putting together the two cases, it holds that either $X \in \gamma(A \perp \alpha)$ or $X \in \gamma(A \perp \beta)$, thus $X \in \gamma(A \perp \alpha) \cup \gamma(A \perp \beta)$.

Choice-expansion: Let $X \in \gamma(A \perp \alpha) \cap \gamma(A \perp \beta)$. Let $Y \in A \perp (\alpha \& \beta)$. We are going to show that $Y \sqsubseteq X$.

It follows from $A\perp(\alpha\&\beta) = (A\perp\alpha) \cup (A\perp\beta)$ that Y is either an element of $A\perp\alpha$ or an element of $A\perp\beta$.

First case, $Y \in A\perp\alpha$: It follows from $Y \in A\perp\alpha$ and $X \in \gamma(A\perp\alpha)$, by the marking-off identity, that $Y \sqsubseteq X$.

Second case, $Y \in A\perp\beta$: It follows from $Y \in A\perp\beta$ and $X \in \gamma(A\perp\beta)$, by the marking-off identity, that $Y \sqsubseteq X$.

Thus, in both cases we have $Y \sqsubseteq X$. Since this holds for all $Y \in A\perp(\alpha\&\beta)$, and since we also have $X \in A\perp(\alpha\&\beta)$, we can conclude that $X \in \gamma(A\perp(\alpha\&\beta))$.

Postulates-to-construction: The following construction can be used:

$Z_1 \sqsubseteq Z_2$ if and only if there is some η such that $Z_1 \in (A\perp\eta)$ and $Z_2 \in \gamma(A\perp\eta)$.

(I.e. Z_2 is at least as good as Z_1 if and only if there is some remainder set in which they are both elements, and Z_2 is among the best elements of that remainder set). We need to show that for all α:

$$\gamma(A\perp\alpha) = \{X \in A\perp\alpha \mid Y \sqsubseteq X \text{ for all } Y \in A\perp\alpha\}.$$

For one direction, let $X \in \gamma(A\perp\alpha)$. Then it holds for all $Y \in A\perp\alpha$ that $Y \sqsubseteq X$, as can be seen by substituting α for η in the definition of $\sqsubseteq$. We can conclude that $\gamma(A\perp\alpha) \subseteq \{X \in A\perp\alpha \mid Y \sqsubseteq X \text{ for all } Y \in A\perp\alpha\}$.

For the other direction, let $X \in \{X \in A\perp\alpha \mid Y \sqsubseteq X \text{ for all } Y \in A\perp\alpha\}$. Then, by the definition of $\sqsubseteq$, for all $Y \in A\perp\alpha$ there is some sentence β_Y such that $Y \in A\perp\beta_Y$ and $X \in \gamma(A\perp\beta_Y)$.

It follows from this that $A\perp\alpha \subseteq \bigcup\{A\perp\beta_Y \mid Y \in A\perp\alpha\}$. We can use Observation 1.66 (remainder compactness) to conclude that there is some finite subset B of $\{\beta_Y \mid Y \in A\perp\alpha\}$ such that $A\perp\alpha \subseteq \bigcup\{A\perp\beta \mid \beta \in B\}$. By repeated application of Observation 1.55 we obtain $\bigcup\{A\perp\beta \mid \beta \in B\} = A\perp(\&B)$, so that $A\perp\alpha \subseteq A\perp(\&B)$.

Since $X \in \gamma(A\perp\beta)$ for all $\beta \in B$, we can apply choice-expansion repeatedly and obtain $X \in \gamma(A\perp(\&B))$.

We have $A\perp\alpha \subseteq A\perp(\&B)$. It follows from Observation 1.65 that $(A\perp(\&B))\setminus(A\perp\alpha) = A\perp(\alpha\rightarrow\&B)$. We therefore have:

$$A\perp(\&B) = A\perp\alpha \cup A\perp(\alpha\rightarrow\&B).$$

Applying choice-distributivity to this, we obtain

$$\gamma(A\perp(\&B)) \subseteq \gamma(A\perp\alpha) \cup \gamma(A\perp(\alpha\rightarrow\&B)).$$

It follows that

$$(A\perp\alpha) \cap (\gamma(A\perp(\&B))) \subseteq (A\perp\alpha) \cap (\gamma(A\perp\alpha) \cup \gamma(A\perp(\alpha\rightarrow\&B))).$$

Since $\gamma(A\perp\alpha) \subseteq A\perp\alpha$ and $(A\perp\alpha) \cap (\gamma(A\perp(\alpha\rightarrow\&B))) = \emptyset$ this is equivalent to:

$$(A\perp\alpha) \cap (\gamma(A\perp(\&B))) \subseteq \gamma(A\perp\alpha).$$

We already have $X \in A\bot\alpha$ and $X \in \gamma(A\bot(\&B))$. We can conclude that $X \in \gamma(A\bot\alpha)$. This completes the proof. ■

Conditions such as choice-distributivity and choice-expansion are not acceptable as postulates for contraction, since they refer to the selection function. An acceptable postulate should only mention the operator of contraction that is generated by γ, not γ itself.

It is fairly easy to find a contraction postulate that corresponds to choice distributivity. As the reader may already have guessed, that property is closely related to the postulate of *conjunctive overlap*. This relationship is verified in the following proof:

OBSERVATION 2.72 (Hans Rott [116]) *Let A be a logically closed set and $\div$ an operation on A. Then the following two conditions are equivalent:*

1. *$\div$ satisfies closure, inclusion, vacuity, success, extensionality, recovery, and conjunctive overlap.*
2. *$\div$ is a partial meet contraction that is based on a selection function that satisfies choice-distributivity.*

Proof. *Construction-to-postulates*: Let $\div$ be equal to $\sim_\gamma$, with γ a selection function for A that satisfies choice-distributivity. It follows from Theorem 2.7 that closure, inclusion, vacuity, success, extensionality, and recovery are satisfied. It remains to be shown that conjunctive overlap is satisfied.

Before treating the principal case, we must take care of four limiting cases:

Case 1, $\vdash \alpha$: Then $A{\sim_\gamma}\alpha = A$, and β is logically equivalent to $\alpha\&\beta$, so that $A{\sim_\gamma}\beta = A{\sim_\gamma}(\alpha\&\beta)$. Conjunctive overlap follows directly.

Case 2, $\vdash \beta$: Symmetrical with case 1.

Case 3, $\alpha \notin A$: Since A is logically closed, we then have $\alpha\&\beta \notin A$. It follows that $A{\sim_\gamma}(\alpha\&\beta) = A$, from which conjunctive overlap follows directly.

Case 4, $\beta \notin A$: Symmetrical with case 3.

Case 5, $\alpha, \beta \in A\backslash\mathrm{Cn}(\emptyset)$: It follows in this case from choice-distributivity that $\gamma(A\bot(\alpha\&\beta)) \subseteq \gamma(A\bot\alpha) \cup \gamma(A\bot\beta)$. We can conclude from this by set theory that $\bigcap(\gamma(A\bot\alpha) \cup \gamma(A\bot\beta)) \subseteq \bigcap\gamma(A\bot(\alpha\&\beta))$, i.e. $A{\sim_\gamma}\alpha \cap A{\sim_\gamma}\beta \subseteq A{\sim_\gamma}(\alpha\&\beta)$.

Postulates-to-construction: Let $\div$ be an operator on A that satisfies the seven listed postulates. It was shown in the proof of Theorem 2.7 that the function γ, such that:

1. If $A\bot\alpha \neq \emptyset$, then $\gamma(A\bot\alpha) = \{X \in A\bot\alpha \mid A{\div}\alpha \subseteq X\}$
2. If $A\bot\alpha = \emptyset$, then $\gamma(A\bot\alpha) = \{A\}$.

is a selection function for A and that for all $\alpha, \bigcap\gamma(A\bot\alpha) = A{\div}\alpha$. It remains to be shown that γ satisfies choice-distributivity. Let $\alpha, \beta \in A\backslash\mathrm{Cn}(\emptyset)$ and $X \in \gamma(A\bot(\alpha\&\beta))$. We need to show that $X \in \gamma(A\bot\alpha) \cup \gamma(A\bot\beta)$.

Suppose to the contrary that $X \notin \gamma(A\bot\alpha) \cup \gamma(A\bot\beta)$, i.e. $X \notin \gamma(A\bot\alpha)$ and $X \notin \gamma(A\bot\beta)$. It then follows from the construction of γ that $\bigcap\gamma(A\bot\alpha) \not\subseteq X$ and $\bigcap\gamma(A\bot\beta) \not\subseteq X$. Let $\delta \in \bigcap\gamma(A\bot\alpha)\setminus X$ and $\varepsilon \in \bigcap\gamma(A\bot\beta)\setminus X$. Since $X \in A\bot(\alpha\&\beta)$ it follows from $\delta \in A\setminus X$ and $\varepsilon \in A\setminus X$, by Observation 1.49 (the Corollary) that $\delta\vee\varepsilon \notin X$.

It follows from $X \in \gamma(A\bot(\alpha\&\beta))$ that $\bigcap\gamma(A\bot(\alpha\&\beta)) \subseteq X$, and then from conjunctive overlap that $\bigcap\gamma(A\bot\alpha) \cap \bigcap\gamma(A\bot\beta) \subseteq X$. Since $\delta \in \bigcap\gamma(A\bot\alpha)$ and $\varepsilon \in \bigcap\gamma(A\bot\alpha)$, we can conclude from this that $\delta\vee\varepsilon \in X$, contrary to what we have just shown. This contradiction concludes the proof. ■

From Observations 2.71 and 2.72 we can immediately conclude:

> Let A be a logically closed set and γ a relational selection function for A. Then $\sim_\gamma$ satisfies *conjunctive overlap*.
> [Observation 2.20.]

Choice-expansion has a similar, but perhaps less obvious, connection to the postulate of *weak conjunctive inclusion*. This connection only holds if the selection function is completed.

OBSERVATION 2.73 (Hans Rott [116]) *Let A be a logically closed set and $\div$ an operation on A. Then the following two conditions are equivalent:*

1. *$\div$ satisfies closure, inclusion, vacuity, success, extensionality, recovery, and: $A\sim_\gamma(\alpha\&\beta) \subseteq \mathrm{Cn}(A\sim_\gamma\alpha \cup A\sim_\gamma\beta)$. (weak conjunctive inclusion).*
2. *$\div$ is a partial meet contraction that is based on a completed selection function that satisfies choice-expansion.*

Proof. *Construction-to-postulates*: Let $\div$ be equal to $\sim_\gamma$, with γ a completed selection function for A that satisfies choice-expansion. It follows from Theorem 2.7 that closure, inclusion, vacuity, success, extensionality, and recovery are satisfied. It remains to be shown that weak conjunctive inclusion is satisfied. There are four limiting cases:

Case 1, $\vdash \alpha$: Then $A\sim_\gamma\alpha = A$, so that $\mathrm{Cn}(A\sim_\gamma\alpha \cup A\sim_\gamma\beta) = \mathrm{Cn}(A) = A$. Weak conjunctive inclusion follows directly.

Case 2, $\vdash \beta$: Symmetrical with case 1.

Case 3, $\alpha \notin A$: Since A is logically closed, we then have $A\sim_\gamma\alpha = A$, and we can proceed as in case 1.

Case 4, $\beta \notin A$: Symmetrical with case 3.

Case 5, $\alpha, \beta \in A\setminus\mathrm{Cn}(\emptyset)$: Let $\varepsilon \in A\sim_\gamma(\alpha\&\beta)$. We are going to show that $\varepsilon \in \mathrm{Cn}(A\sim_\gamma\alpha \cup A\sim_\gamma\beta)$. Suppose to the contrary that $\varepsilon \notin \mathrm{Cn}(A\sim_\gamma\alpha \cup A\sim_\gamma\beta)$.

It follows from choice-expansion that $\gamma(A\bot\alpha) \cap \gamma(A\bot\beta) \subseteq \gamma(A\bot(\alpha\&\beta))$, and thus $\bigcap\gamma(A\bot(\alpha\&\beta)) \subseteq \bigcap(\gamma(A\bot\alpha) \cap \gamma(A\bot\beta))$. Since $\varepsilon \in A\sim_\gamma(\alpha\&\beta) = \bigcap\gamma(A\bot(\alpha\&\beta))$, we therefore have $\varepsilon \in \bigcap(\gamma(A\bot\alpha) \cap \gamma(A\bot\beta))$.

It follows from our assumption $\varepsilon \notin \mathrm{Cn}(A\sim_\gamma\alpha \cup A\sim_\gamma\beta)$, by the upper bound property, that there is some X such that $\mathrm{Cn}(A\sim_\gamma\alpha \cup A\sim_\gamma\beta) \subseteq X \in A\perp\varepsilon$. Using Part 2 of Observation 2.69 we can conclude from $A\sim_\gamma\alpha \subseteq X \in A\perp\varepsilon$ that $X \in \gamma(A\perp\alpha)$. (Note that Observation 2.69 requires that γ is completed.) Similarly, it follows from $A\sim_\gamma\beta \subseteq X \in A\perp\varepsilon$ that $X \in \gamma(A\perp\beta)$. Thus $X \in \gamma(A\perp\alpha) \cap \gamma(A\perp\beta)$. Since $\varepsilon \notin X$ we obtain $\varepsilon \notin \bigcap(\gamma(A\perp\alpha) \cap \gamma(A\perp\beta))$, contrary to what was shown in the foregoing paragraph.

We can conclude from this contradiction that if $\varepsilon \in A\sim_\gamma(\alpha\&\beta)$, then $\varepsilon \in \mathrm{Cn}(A\sim_\gamma\alpha \cup A\sim_\gamma\beta)$, so that weak conjunctive inclusion holds.

Postulates-to-construction: Let $\div$ be an operator on A that satisfies the seven listed postulates. It was shown in the proof of Theorem 2.7 that the function γ, such that:

1. If $A\perp\alpha \neq \emptyset$, then $\gamma(A\perp\alpha) = \{X \in A\perp\alpha \mid A\div\alpha \subseteq X\}$
2. If $A\perp\alpha = \emptyset$, then $\gamma(A\perp\alpha) = \{A\}$

is a selection function for A and that for all α, $\bigcap\gamma(A\perp\alpha) = A\div\alpha$. It remains to be shown that γ satisfies choice-expansion. Let $\alpha, \beta \in A\backslash\mathrm{Cn}(\emptyset)$ and $X \in \gamma(A\perp\alpha) \cap \gamma(A\perp\beta)$. We need to show that $X \in \gamma(A\perp(\alpha\&\beta))$.

It follows from $X \in \gamma(A\perp\alpha)$ that $\bigcap\gamma(A\perp\alpha) \subseteq X$ and from $X \in \gamma(A\perp\beta)$ that $\bigcap\gamma(A\perp\beta) \subseteq X$. We therefore have $\bigcap\gamma(A\perp\alpha) \cup \bigcap\gamma(A\perp\beta) \subseteq X$, and (since X is logically closed) thus $\mathrm{Cn}(\bigcap\gamma(A\perp\alpha) \cup \bigcap\gamma(A\perp\beta)) \subseteq X$. It follows from weak conjunctive inclusion that $A\sim_\gamma(\alpha\&\beta) \subseteq X$. Furthermore, it follows from $X \in A\perp\alpha$ that $X \in A\perp(\alpha\&\beta)$ (Observation 1.55), so that we have $A\sim_\gamma(\alpha\&\beta) \subseteq X \in A\perp(\alpha\&\beta)$. According to the construction of γ it follows that $X \in \gamma(A\perp(\alpha\&\beta))$, so that choice-expansion holds. ■

We can now combine the results of this section to obtain the following representation theorem:

THEOREM 2.74 (Hans Rott [116]) *Let A be a logically closed set and $\div$ an operator for A. Then $\div$ is an operator of partial meet contraction with a relational and completed selection function if and only if it satisfies closure, inclusion, vacuity, success, extensionality, recovery, conjunctive overlap, and weak conjunctive inclusion.*

Proof. Directly from Theorem 2.7 and Observations 2.71, 2.72, and 2.73. ■

It was shown in Observation 2.70 that for finite and logically closed sets, all selection functions are completed. Therefore, Theorem 2.74 has the following corollary:

COROLLARY (Hans Rott [116]) *Let A be a finite and logically closed set and $\div$ an operator for A. Then $\div$ is an operator of relational partial meet contraction if and only if it satisfies closure, inclusion, vacuity, success, extensionality, recovery, conjunctive overlap, and weak conjunctive inclusion.*

Exercises

99. Let A be logically closed, and let α and β be elements of $A\backslash\text{Cn}(\emptyset)$. Furthermore, let γ be a selection function for A that is relational by a relation $\sqsubseteq$.
    (a) Show that if $X \in A\bot\alpha$ and $Y \in A\bot\beta$, then there is some Z such that $X \sqsubseteq Z$ and $Y \sqsubseteq Z$.
    (b) Show that $\gamma(A\bot(\alpha\&\beta)) \cap (A\bot\alpha) \subseteq \gamma(A\bot\alpha)$.

100. Let A be a logically closed set, and let γ be a selection function for A that is both relational and maxichoice. Let $\alpha, \beta \in A\backslash\text{Cn}(\emptyset)$.
    (a) Show that if $A\bot\alpha \subseteq A\bot\beta$ and $A{\sim_\gamma}\beta \nvdash \alpha$, then $A{\sim_\gamma}\alpha = A{\sim_\gamma}\beta$.
    (b) Show that if $\vdash \beta\rightarrow\alpha$, then either $\alpha \in A{\sim_\gamma}\beta$ or $A{\sim_\gamma}\alpha = A{\sim_\gamma}\beta$.
    (c) Show that either $A{\sim_\gamma}(\alpha\&\beta) = A{\sim_\gamma}\alpha$ or $A{\sim_\gamma}(\alpha\&\beta) = A{\sim_\gamma}\beta$.

101. [116] Let A be a logically closed set and γ a selection function for A. Show that choice-distributivity is equivalent to the following condition:
If $\alpha, \beta \in A\backslash\text{Cn}(\emptyset)$ and $A\bot\alpha \subseteq A\bot\beta$, then $(A\bot\alpha) \cap \gamma(A\bot\beta) \subseteq \gamma(A\bot\alpha)$ (Sen's property α).

19+ TRANSITIVE AND MAXIMIZING MARKING-OFF RELATIONS

In Section 2.6, we introduced two major requirements on the marking-off relation to make the contraction operation more orderly: transitivity and the maximizing property.

The following example can be used to show that not all relational selection functions are transitively relational. Let the language consist of the two atomic sentences p and q and their truth-functional combinations. Furthermore, let:

$$\begin{aligned} A &= \text{Cn}(\{p\&q\}) \\ A_1 &= \text{Cn}(\{p\}) \\ A_2 &= \text{Cn}(\{p\leftrightarrow q\}) \\ A_3 &= \text{Cn}(\{q\}). \end{aligned}$$

We then have:

$$\begin{aligned} A\bot p &= \{A_2, A_3\} \\ A\bot q &= \{A_1, A_2\} \\ A\bot(p\leftrightarrow q) &= \{A_1, A_3\} \\ A\bot(p\&q) &= \{A_1, A_2, A_3\}. \end{aligned}$$

Let the selection function γ be such that:

$$\begin{aligned} \gamma(\{A_1, A_2\}) &= \{A_1, A_2\} \\ \gamma(\{A_2, A_3\}) &= \{A_2, A_3\} \\ \gamma(\{A_1, A_3\}) &= \{A_1\} \\ \gamma(\{A_1, A_2, A_3\}) &= \{A_1, A_2\}. \end{aligned}$$

This is a relational selection function. According to its marking-off relation, A_2 is at least as much worth retaining as A_1, and A_3 at least as much as A_2, but A_3 is less worth retaining than A_1. This relation is not transitive. The selection function exhibited in the example is relational but not transitively relational.

The following observation provides three useful properties of transitive relations. These are standard results from the logic of binary relations. (Remember that $\sqsubset$ represents the strict part of $\sqsubseteq$, i.e. $X \sqsubset Y \leftrightarrow X \sqsubseteq Y \& \neg(Y \sqsubseteq X)$.)

OBSERVATION 2.75 *Let* $\sqsubseteq$ *be a relation that satisfies transitivity (i.e. the property* $X \sqsubseteq Y \& Y \sqsubseteq Z \rightarrow X \sqsubseteq Z$*). It then also satisfies:*

1. $X \sqsubseteq Y \& Y \sqsubset Z \rightarrow X \sqsubset Z$
2. $X \sqsubset Y \& Y \sqsubseteq Z \rightarrow X \sqsubset Z$
3. $X \sqsubset Y \& Y \sqsubset Z \rightarrow X \sqsubset Z$ *(quasi-transitivity)*

Proof. *Part 1*: Let $X \sqsubseteq Y \& Y \sqsubset Z$. It follows from $Y \sqsubset Z$ that $Y \sqsubseteq Z$, and by transitivity from $X \sqsubseteq Y$ and $Y \sqsubseteq Z$ that $X \sqsubseteq Z$.

Suppose that $Z \sqsubseteq X$. Since $X \sqsubseteq Y$ it would then follow by transitivity that $Z \sqsubseteq Y$, contrary to $Y \sqsubset Z$. We may conclude from this contradiction that $\neg(Z \sqsubseteq X)$. Since we already have $X \sqsubseteq Z$, we may conclude that $X \sqsubset Z$.

Part 2 and *Part 3* are left to the reader as exercises. ■

The *maximizing* property (if $X \subset Y$, then $X \sqsubset Y$), taken alone, is an empty requirement on a selection function:

> Let A be a set and $\sim_\gamma$ an operator of partial meet contraction for that set. Then $\sim_\gamma$ is relational if and only if it is maximizingly relational. [Observation 2.17.]

Proof. Clearly, if $\sim_\gamma$ if maximizingly relational, then it is relational. For the other direction, let $\sim_\gamma$ be relational by the relation $\sqsubseteq$. Define the relation $\sqsubseteq'$ (and its strict part $\sqsubset'$) as follows:

1. If $X \subset Y$, then $X \sqsubset' Y$.
2. If $X \not\subset Y$ and $Y \not\subset X$, then $X \sqsubseteq' Y$ if and only if $X \sqsubseteq Y$.

We need to show that $\sqsubseteq'$ is maximizing and that $\sim_\gamma$ is relational by $\sqsubseteq'$. That it is maximizing follows from clause (1) of the definition. To show that $\sim_\gamma$ is relational by $\sqsubseteq'$, let X and Y be elements of a remainder set $A \perp \alpha$. Then $X \not\subset Y$ and $Y \not\subset X$, and it follows by clause (2) that $X \sqsubseteq' Y$ if and only if $X \sqsubseteq Y$. Since $\sim_\gamma$ is relational by $\sqsubseteq$, it is relational by $\sqsubseteq'$. ■

As we have already seen in Section 2.6, the maximizing property gains importance from its combination with transitivity. Some transitively relational partial meet contractions are not transitively maximizingly relational. Those that are turn out to be much more orderly. The rest of this section will be devoted to showing that transitively maximizingly relational (TMR) partial meet contraction satisfies some of the conjunctive properties introduced in Section 2.5.

For two of the properties, namely conjunctive overlap and conjunctive trisection, a weakened form of the maximizing property will turn out to be sufficient:

If $A \subset B$, then $A \sqsubseteq B$ (*weak maximizing property*)

A selection function is *transitively, weakly maximizingly relational* if and only if it is relational by some marking-off relation that is both transitive and weakly maximizing. Clearly, all transitively maximizingly relational selection functions are also transitively, weakly maximizingly relational, but the converse does not hold.

> Let γ be a transitively, weakly maximizingly relational selection function for A. Then:
> $(A{\sim}_\gamma\alpha) \cap (A{\sim}_\gamma\beta) \subseteq A{\sim}_\gamma(\alpha\&\beta)$ (*conjunctive overlap*)
> [Observation 2.19, Part 1, strengthened.]

Proof. Let $\sqsubseteq$ be the transitive and weakly maximizing relation on which γ is based. There are three cases, two of which are simple limiting cases:

Case 1, $\alpha \in \text{Cn}(\emptyset)$: Then β and $\alpha\&\beta$ are logically equivalent. It follows that $A\bot\beta = A\bot(\alpha\&\beta)$, and consequently $A{\sim}_\gamma\beta = A{\sim}_\gamma(\alpha\&\beta)$, from which the desired result follows.

Case 2, $\beta \in \text{Cn}(\emptyset)$: Symmetrical with case 1.

Case 3, $\alpha \notin \text{Cn}(\emptyset)$ and $\beta \notin \text{Cn}(\emptyset)$: Then $\alpha\&\beta \notin \text{Cn}(\emptyset)$. Suppose that $(A{\sim}_\gamma\alpha) \cap (A{\sim}_\gamma\beta) \subseteq (A{\sim}_\gamma(\alpha\&\beta))$ does not hold. Then there is some ε such that $\varepsilon \in A{\sim}_\gamma\alpha, \varepsilon \in A{\sim}_\gamma\beta$, and $\varepsilon \notin A{\sim}_\gamma(\alpha\&\beta)$. From $\varepsilon \notin A{\sim}_\gamma(\alpha\&\beta)$, i.e. $\varepsilon \notin \bigcap\gamma(A\bot(\alpha\&\beta))$, it follows that there is some $X \in \gamma(A\bot(\alpha\&\beta))$ such that $\varepsilon \notin X$. It follows by Observation 1.55 from $X \in A\bot(\alpha\&\beta)$ that either $X \in A\bot\alpha$ or $X \in A\bot\beta$. Without loss of generality we may assume that $X \in A\bot\alpha$. (This is another way of saying that the two cases are similar and that we will only treat one of them.)

Since $\varepsilon \in A{\sim}_\gamma\alpha, X \notin \gamma(A\bot\alpha)$. Let $Y \in \gamma(A\bot\alpha)$. From $\varepsilon \in A{\sim}_\gamma\alpha$ it follows that $\varepsilon \in Y$. It follows by the marking-off identity from $Y \in \gamma(A\bot\alpha)$ and $X \in A\bot\alpha$ that $X \sqsubseteq Y$. We are going to show that $Y \sqsubseteq X$ does not hold. Suppose to the contrary that it holds. Let $Z \in A\bot\alpha$. Then $Y \in \gamma(A\bot\alpha)$ would yield $Z \sqsubseteq Y$, and by transitivity we would have $Z \sqsubseteq X$. Since this would hold for all $Z \in A\bot\alpha, X \in \gamma(A\bot\alpha)$ would follow, contrary to the conditions. We may conclude that $Y \sqsubseteq X$ does not hold. Since we already have $X \sqsubseteq Y$, we may conclude that $X \sqsubset Y$.

From $Y \in A\bot\alpha$ it follows by the upper bound property that there is some Y' such that $Y \subseteq Y'$ and $Y' \in A\bot(\alpha\&\beta)$. If $Y = Y'$ we have $X \sqsubset Y'$ directly from $X \sqsubset Y$. If $Y \subset Y'$, then the weak maximizing property yields $Y \sqsubseteq Y'$, which with $X \sqsubset Y$ and transitivity yields $X \sqsubset Y'$. (Cf. Observation 2.75.) Thus, in both cases $X \sqsubset Y'$, $X \in \gamma(A\bot(\alpha\&\beta))$ and $Y' \in A\bot(\alpha\&\beta)$. This contradicts the marking-off identity, and the contradiction concludes the proof. ∎

> Let γ be a transitively, weakly maximizingly relational selection function for a logically closed set A. Then:
> If $\alpha \in A{\sim_\gamma}(\alpha\&\beta)$, then $\alpha \in A{\sim_\gamma}(\alpha\&\beta\&\delta)$ (*conjunctive trisection*)
> [Part of Observation 2.19, strengthened.]

Proof. Let $\sqsubseteq$ be the transitive and weakly maximizing relation on which γ is based. There are four cases, three of which are fairly simple limiting cases.

Case 1, $\vdash \alpha$: It follows from the logical closure of $A{\sim_\gamma}(\alpha\&\beta\&\delta)$ that $\alpha \in A{\sim_\gamma}(\alpha\&\beta\&\delta)$.

Case 2, $\vdash \beta$: Then $\alpha\&\beta$ is logically equivalent to α, and consequently we have $A{\sim_\gamma}(\alpha\&\beta) = A{\sim_\gamma}\alpha$. Suppose that $\alpha \in A{\sim_\gamma}(\alpha\&\beta)$, i.e. $\alpha \in A{\sim_\gamma}\alpha$. It follows that $\alpha \in \mathrm{Cn}(\emptyset)$, and we are back in case 1.

Case 3, $\vdash \delta$: Then $\alpha\&\beta\&\delta$ is logically equivalent to $\alpha\&\beta$, and we conclude that $A{\sim_\gamma}(\alpha\&\beta\&\delta) = A{\sim_\gamma}(\alpha\&\beta)$, from which the desired result follows directly.

Case 4, $\nvdash \alpha$ $\nvdash \beta$ and $\nvdash \delta$: Let $\alpha \in A{\sim_\gamma}(\alpha\&\beta) = \bigcap\gamma(A\bot(\alpha\&\beta))$.We are going to show that if $X \in \gamma(A\bot(\alpha\&\beta\&\delta))$, then $\alpha \in X$. Suppose not, i.e. that there is some X such that $\alpha \notin X \in \gamma(A\bot(\alpha\&\beta\&\delta))$. It follows from Observation 1.53 that $X \in A\bot(\alpha\&\beta)$. (Note that Observation 1.53 requires that A is logically closed.)

Suppose that $X \in \gamma(A\bot(\alpha\&\beta))$. Then $\alpha \notin \bigcap\gamma(A\bot(\alpha\&\beta))$, contrary to the conditions. By this contradiction, $X \notin \gamma(A\bot(\alpha\&\beta))$.

Next, let $Y \in \gamma(A\bot(\alpha\&\beta))$. Then $X \sqsubset Y$. Since $Y \nvdash \alpha\&\beta\&\delta$ there is, by the upper bound property, some Y' such that $Y \subseteq Y' \in A\bot(\alpha\&\beta\&\delta)$. If $Y = Y'$, then $X \sqsubset Y'$ follows directly from $X \sqsubset Y$. If $Y \subset Y'$, then the weak maximizing property yields $Y \sqsubseteq Y'$. It follows by transitivity from $X \sqsubset Y$ and $Y \sqsubseteq Y'$ that $X \sqsubset Y'$. (Cf. Observation 2.75.) In both cases, we have $X \sqsubset Y'$, $X \in \gamma(A\bot(\alpha\&\beta\&\delta))$ and $Y' \in A\bot(\alpha\&\beta\&\delta)$. This contradicts the marking-off identity. The contradiction shows that our assumption $\alpha \notin X$ cannot hold. We can conclude that if $X \in \gamma(A\bot(\alpha\&\beta\&\delta))$, then $\alpha \in X$.

From this it follows directly that $\alpha \in \bigcap\gamma(A\bot(\alpha\&\beta\&\delta))$, and the proof is finished. ∎

> Let γ be a transitively, maximizingly relational selection function for a set A that is either (1) logically closed, or (2) finite and disjunctively closed. Then:
> If $\alpha \notin \mathrm{Cn}(A{\sim_\gamma}(\alpha\&\beta))$ then $A{\sim_\gamma}(\alpha\&\beta) \subseteq A{\sim_\gamma}\alpha$. (*conjunctive inclusion*)
> [Part of Observation 2.19.]

Proof. Let $\sqsubseteq$ be the transitive and maximizing relation on which γ is based. There are three cases:

Case 1, $\vdash \alpha$: Then $A{\sim}_\gamma\alpha = A$, from which the desired conclusion follows directly.

Case 2, $\vdash \beta$: Then $\alpha\&\beta$ and α are logically equivalent, so that $A{\sim}_\gamma(\alpha\&\beta) = A{\sim}_\gamma\alpha$, from which the desired conclusion follows directly.

Case 3, $\nvdash \alpha$ and $\nvdash \beta$: Let $\alpha \notin \text{Cn}(A{\sim}_\gamma(\alpha\&\beta))$.

If A is logically closed, then $\alpha \notin A{\sim}_\gamma(\alpha\&\beta)$, and there must be some $X \in \gamma(A\bot(\alpha\&\beta))$, such that $\alpha \notin X$. It follows from Observation 1.53 that $X \in A\bot\alpha$.

If A is finite and disjunctively closed, then it follows by repeated use of Observation 1.34 that $\text{Cn}(A{\sim}_\gamma(\alpha\&\beta)) = \bigcap\{\text{Cn}(X) \mid X \in \gamma(A\bot(\alpha\&\beta))\}$, so that there must be some $X \in \gamma(A\bot(\alpha\&\beta))$ with $\alpha \notin \text{Cn}(X)$. It follows from $X \in A\bot(\alpha\&\beta)$ and $\alpha \notin \text{Cn}(X)$ that $X \in A\bot\alpha$.

Hence, in both cases we have some $X \in \gamma(A\bot(\alpha\&\beta))$ such that $A\bot\alpha$.

Let $Y \in \gamma(A\bot\alpha)$. We are first going to show that $Y \in A\bot(\alpha\&\beta)$. Suppose to the contrary that $Y \notin A\bot(\alpha\&\beta)$. Then, by the upper bound property, there is some Y' such that $Y \subset Y' \in A\bot(\alpha\&\beta)$. By the maximizing property of $\sqsubseteq$, $Y \sqsubset Y'$. From $X \in A\bot\alpha$ and $Y \in \gamma(A\bot\alpha)$ follows $X \sqsubseteq Y$. Thus, by transitivity, $X \sqsubset Y'$. As can be seen from the marking-off identity, $X \sqsubset Y'$ contradicts $X \in \gamma(A\bot(\alpha\&\beta))$ and $Y' \in A\bot(\alpha\&\beta)$. We can conclude from this contradiction that $Y \in A\bot(\alpha\&\beta)$.

Next, we are going to show that $Y \in \gamma(A\bot(\alpha\&\beta))$. This can be done by showing that if $Z \in A\bot(\alpha\&\beta)$, then $Z \sqsubseteq Y$. Let $Z \in A\bot(\alpha\&\beta)$. Since $X \in \gamma(A\bot(\alpha\&\beta))$ it follows from the marking-off identity that $Z \sqsubseteq X$. We have already shown that $X \sqsubseteq Y$, and transitivity yields $Z \sqsubseteq Y$, as desired.

We have proved that if $Y \in \gamma(A\bot\alpha)$, then $Y \in \gamma(A\bot(\alpha\&\beta))$, i.e. $\gamma(A\bot\alpha) \subseteq \gamma(A\bot(\alpha\&\beta))$. It follows by set theory that $\bigcap\gamma(A\bot(\alpha\&\beta)) \subseteq \bigcap\gamma(A\bot\alpha)$, i.e. $A{\sim}_\gamma(\alpha\&\beta) \subseteq A{\sim}_\gamma\alpha$, and we are done. ■

> Let γ be a transitively, maximizingly relational selection function for a set A that is either (1) logically closed, or (2) finite and disjunctively closed. Then:
> Either $A{\sim}_\gamma(\alpha\&\beta) = A{\sim}_\gamma\alpha$, $A{\sim}_\gamma(\alpha\&\beta) = A{\sim}_\gamma\beta$, or $A{\sim}_\gamma(\alpha\&\beta) = A{\sim}_\gamma\alpha \cap A{\sim}_\gamma\beta$ *(conjunctive factoring)*.
> [Part of Observation 2.19.]

Proof. Let $\sqsubseteq$ be the transitive and maximizing relation on which γ is based. It follows from the previous results of this section that conjunctive overlap and conjunctive inclusion are satisfied.

There are three cases, two of which are simple limiting cases.

Case 1, $\vdash \alpha$: Then $\alpha\&\beta$ and β are logically equivalent, and $A{\sim}_\gamma(\alpha\&\beta) = A{\sim}_\gamma\beta$.

Case 2, $\vdash \beta$: Then $\alpha\&\beta$ and α are logically equivalent, and $A\sim_\gamma(\alpha\&\beta) = A\sim_\gamma\alpha$.

Case 3, $\nvdash \alpha$ and $\nvdash \beta$: Then $\nvdash \alpha\&\beta$, from which it follows directly that $\alpha\&\beta \notin \text{Cn}(A\sim_\gamma(\alpha\&\beta))$. At most one of α and β can be an element of $\text{Cn}(A\sim_\gamma(\alpha\&\beta))$. There are three subcases:

Case 3A: $\alpha \notin \text{Cn}(A\sim_\gamma(\alpha\&\beta))$ and $\beta \notin \text{Cn}(A\sim_\gamma(\alpha\&\beta))$: By conjunctive inclusion we then have $A\sim_\gamma(\alpha\&\beta) \subseteq A\sim_\gamma\alpha$ and $A\sim_\gamma(\alpha\&\beta) \subseteq A\sim_\gamma\beta$, from which follows $A\sim_\gamma(\alpha\&\beta) \subseteq (A\sim_\gamma\alpha) \cap (A\sim_\gamma\beta)$. Conjunctive overlap yields $(A\sim_\gamma\alpha)\cap(A\sim_\gamma\beta) \subseteq A\sim_\gamma(\alpha\&\beta)$. We may conclude from this that $A\sim_\gamma(\alpha\&\beta) = (A\sim_\gamma\alpha) \cap (A\sim_\gamma\beta)$, which finishes the proof of this case.

Case 3B: $\alpha \notin \text{Cn}(A\sim_\gamma(\alpha\&\beta))$ and $\beta \in \text{Cn}(A\sim_\gamma(\alpha\&\beta))$. In this part of the proof, let $X \in \gamma(A\perp(\alpha\&\beta))$.

If A is logically closed, then it follows from $\beta \in A\sim_\gamma(\alpha\&\beta)$ that $\beta \in X$, and hence $\alpha \notin X$. We can use Observation 1.53 to obtain $X \in A\perp\alpha$.

If A is finite and disjunctively closed, then it follows by repeated use of Observation 1.34 that $\text{Cn}(A\sim_\gamma(\alpha\&\beta)) = \bigcap\{\text{Cn}(X) \mid X \in \gamma(A\perp(\alpha\&\beta))\}$ and it follows that $\beta \in \text{Cn}(X)$. Hence, $\alpha \notin \text{Cn}(X)$. It follows from $\alpha \notin \text{Cn}(X)$ and $X \in A\perp(\alpha\&\beta)$ that $X \in A\perp\alpha$.

Hence, in both cases, it follows that $X \in A\perp\alpha$.

We are going to show that $X \in \gamma(A\perp\alpha)$. Suppose to the contrary that $X \notin \gamma(A\perp\alpha)$. Let Y be any set such that $Y \in \gamma(A\perp\alpha)$. It then follows by the marking-off identity that $X \sqsubset Y$. It follows from $Y \in A\perp\alpha$ that $Y \nvdash \alpha$ and consequently $Y \nvdash \alpha\&\beta$. According to the upper bound property there is then some Y' such that $Y \subseteq Y' \in A\perp(\alpha\&\beta)$. If $Y = Y'$, then we have $X \sqsubset Y'$ directly from $X \sqsubset Y$. If $Y \subset Y'$, then the maximizing property yields $Y \sqsubset Y'$, and transitivity yields $X \sqsubset Y'$. In both cases we have $X \sqsubset Y'$, $X \in \gamma(A\perp(\alpha\&\beta))$ and $Y' \in A\perp(\alpha\&\beta)$. This is impossible according to the marking-off identity. From this contradiction we may conclude that our assumption that $X \notin \gamma(A\perp\alpha)$ was false. We have shown that that $X \in \gamma(A\perp\alpha)$.

Since this was shown to hold for any $X \in \gamma(A\perp(\alpha\&\beta))$, we have proved that $\gamma(A\perp(\alpha\&\beta)) \subseteq \gamma(A\perp\alpha)$. It follows from this by set theory that $\bigcap\gamma(A\perp\alpha) \subseteq \bigcap\gamma(A\perp(\alpha\&\beta))$, i.e. $A\sim_\gamma\alpha \subseteq A\sim_\gamma(\alpha\&\beta)$. It follows by conjunctive inclusion that $A\sim_\gamma(\alpha\&\beta) \subseteq A\sim_\gamma\alpha$, and we may conclude that $A\sim_\gamma(\alpha\&\beta) = A\sim_\gamma\alpha$, which concludes the proof of this case.

Case 3C: $\alpha \in \text{Cn}(A\sim_\gamma(\alpha\&\beta))$ and $\beta \notin \text{Cn}(A\sim_\gamma(\alpha\&\beta))$. This case is symmetrical with case 3B, and we can in the same way prove that $A\sim_\gamma(\alpha\&\beta) = A\sim_\gamma\beta$. ■

Exercises

102. Prove Parts 2 and 3 of Observation 2.75.

103. Let $\sqsubseteq$ be a transitive and maximizing relation. Show that:

(a) If $X \subset Y \sqsubseteq Z$, then $X \sqsubset Z$.
(b) If $X \sqsubseteq Y \subset Z$, then $X \sqsubset Z$.
(c) If $X \subseteq Y \sqsubset Z$, then $X \sqsubset Z$.
(d) If $X \sqsubset Y \subseteq Z$, then $X \sqsubset Z$.
(e) If $X \subseteq Y \sqsubseteq Z$, then $X \sqsubseteq Z$.
(f) If $X \sqsubseteq Y \subseteq Z$, then $X \sqsubseteq Z$.

104. Let γ be a selection function for A, and $\sqsubseteq$ a transitive relation such that γ is relational by $\sqsubseteq$. Let $X \in \gamma(A\perp\alpha), Y \in A\perp\alpha$, and $X \sqsubseteq Y$. Show that $Y \in \gamma(A\perp\alpha)$.

105. [3] Let A be a set, and let γ be a selection function for A that is both maxichoice and transitively relational. $\sim_\gamma$ is the partial meet contraction generated by γ.

(a) Show that $\sim_\gamma$ satisfies the following property:
If $A{\sim_\gamma}\alpha \in A\perp\beta$ and $A{\sim_\gamma}\beta \in A\perp\alpha$, then $A{\sim_\gamma}\alpha = A{\sim_\gamma}\beta$.

(b) Show that if A is logically closed, then $\sim_\gamma$ satisfies the following property:
If $A{\sim_\gamma}\alpha \nvdash \beta$ and $A{\sim_\gamma}\beta \nvdash \alpha$, then $A{\sim_\gamma}\alpha = A{\sim_\gamma}\beta$.

106. Let γ be a transitively, weakly maximizingly relational selection function for a finite and disjunctively closed set A. Show that $\sim_\gamma$ satisfies the following variant of conjunctive trisection: If $A{\sim_\gamma}(\alpha\&\beta) \vdash \alpha$, then $A{\sim_\gamma}(\alpha\&\beta\&\delta) \vdash \alpha$.

20+ LOGICAL CLOSURE BRINGS IN MORE ORDER

When transitively relational partial meet contraction is applied to a logically closed set, stronger results can be obtained than those reported in the foregoing section, and a more well-ordered pattern emerges. As an example of this, transitivity of the marking-off relation is a sufficient condition for conjunctive inclusion.

OBSERVATION 2.76 (AGM [1]) *Let A be a logically closed set and γ a transitively relational selection function for A. Then $\sim_\gamma$ satisfies:*
If $\alpha \notin \text{Cn}(A{\sim_\gamma}(\alpha\&\beta))$ then $A{\sim_\gamma}(\alpha\&\beta) \subseteq A{\sim_\gamma}\alpha$. (conjunctive inclusion)

Proof. [116] The proof will proceed in two steps. In the first step, transitivity of the marking-off relation will be shown to induce a certain property ('condition T') of the selection function, and in the second step this property is shown to give rise to the property of conjunctive inclusion on the operator of contraction.

Step 1: Let A be a logically closed set and γ a transitively relational selection function for A. We are going to show that the following property is satisfied:

For all $\alpha, \beta \in A\backslash\text{Cn}(\emptyset)$, if $\alpha \notin \bigcap\gamma(A\perp(\alpha\&\beta))$, then $\gamma(A\perp\alpha) \subseteq \gamma(A\perp(\alpha\&\beta))$. (*condition* T)

Suppose that $\alpha \notin \bigcap\gamma(A\bot(\alpha\&\beta))$. Then there is some X such that $\alpha \notin X \in \gamma(A\bot(\alpha\&\beta))$. It follows from Observation 1.53 that $X \in A\bot\alpha$. In order to prove that $\gamma(A\bot\alpha) \subseteq \gamma(A\bot(\alpha\&\beta))$, let $Z \in \gamma(A\bot\alpha)$. It follows from $Z \in A\bot\alpha$ that $Z \in A\bot(\alpha\&\beta)$ (Observation 1.55). Let $V \in A\bot(\alpha\&\beta)$. We need to show that $V \sqsubseteq Z$.

It follows from $X \in A\bot\alpha$ and $Z \in \gamma(A\bot\alpha)$, by the marking-off identity, that $X \sqsubseteq Z$. Similarly, it follows from $V \in A\bot(\alpha\&\beta)$ and $X \in \gamma(A\bot(\alpha\&\beta))$ that $V \sqsubseteq X$. Transitivity yields $V \sqsubseteq Z$. Since this holds for all $V \in A\bot(\alpha\&\beta)$ and we also have $Z \in A\bot(\alpha\&\beta)$, we can conclude that $Z \in \gamma(A\bot(\alpha\&\beta))$. This completes the first step of the proof.

Step 2: This step is quite straight-forward, but we have to take care of the limiting cases.

Case 1, $\vdash \alpha$: Then $A\sim_\gamma\alpha = A$, from which conjunctive inclusion follows directly.

Case 2, $\alpha \notin A$: Then $A\sim_\gamma\alpha = A$, just as in case 1.

Case 3, $\vdash \beta$: Then $\alpha\&\beta$ and α are logically equivalent, so that $A\sim_\gamma(\alpha\&\beta) = A\sim_\gamma\alpha$, from which conjunctive inclusion follows directly.

Case 4, $\beta \notin A$: Then $\alpha\&\beta \notin A$, and $A\sim_\gamma(\alpha\&\beta) = A$. It therefore follows from $\alpha \notin A\sim_\gamma(\alpha\&\beta)$ that $\alpha \notin A$. From this we may conclude that $A\sim_\gamma\alpha = A$.

Case 5, $\alpha, \beta \in A\backslash\mathrm{Cn}(\emptyset)$: Let $\alpha \notin A\sim_\gamma(\alpha\&\beta)$, i.e. $\alpha \notin \bigcap\gamma(A\bot(\alpha\&\beta))$. It follows from condition T that $\gamma(A\bot\alpha) \subseteq \gamma(A\bot(\alpha\&\beta))$, and consequently we have $\bigcap\gamma(A\bot(\alpha\&\beta)) \subseteq \bigcap\gamma(A\bot\alpha)$, i.e. $A\sim_\gamma(\alpha\&\beta) \subseteq A\sim_\gamma\alpha$. ■

We can conclude from Observations 2.20 and 2.76 that transitively relational partial meet contractions on logically closed sets satisfy *conjunctive overlap* and *conjunctive inclusion*. From this it follows, due to Observation 2.15, that *conjunctive trisection* and *conjunctive factoring* are also satisfied.

The following proof shows that *conjunctive overlap* and *conjunctive inclusion* are sufficient conditions for partial meet contraction on belief sets to be transitively relational. Unfortunately, the proof is quite long, but it is entirely based on proof methods that we have already used.

OBSERVATION 2.77 (AGM [1]) *Let A be a logically closed set and $\div$ an operator for A that satisfies closure, inclusion, vacuity, success, extensionality, recovery, conjunctive overlap, and conjunctive inclusion. Then $\div$ is an operator of partial meet contraction with a completed and transitively relational selection function.*

Proof. [1] It follows from Theorem 2.7 that $\div$ is an operator of partial meet contraction, i.e. that there is a selection function γ such that $A\div\alpha = \bigcap\gamma(A\bot\alpha)$ for all α. Let $\sqsubseteq$ be the relation on the domain $A\Delta\mathcal{L} = \{V \mid V \in A\bot\varepsilon \text{ for some } \varepsilon\}$ such that:

$V_1 \sqsubseteq V_2$ iff $V_1, V_2 \in A\Delta\mathcal{L}$ and either

(i) $V_2 = A$ or both of the following:

(iia) there is some $\varepsilon \in A$ such that $A \div \varepsilon \subseteq V_2 \in A \perp \varepsilon$, and

(iib) for all ε, if $V_1, V_2 \in A \perp \varepsilon$ and $A \div \varepsilon \subseteq V_1$, then $A \div \varepsilon \subseteq V_2$.

We are going to show (1) that $\sqsubseteq$ is transitive, and (2) that $\sqsubseteq$ generates the completion $\hat{\gamma}$ of γ via the marking-off identity. Since $\bigcap \hat{\gamma}(A \perp \alpha) = \bigcap \gamma(A \perp \alpha)$ for all α (Observation 2.68), this is sufficient to prove the theorem.

PART 1, TRANSITIVITY: Let $X \sqsubseteq Y \sqsubseteq Z$. We are going to show that $X \sqsubseteq Z$. If $Z = A$, then this follows directly from clause (i) of the definition. For the principal case, we can assume that $Z \neq A$. We have to show that clauses (iia)-(iib) of the definition are satisfied.

That (iia) holds (for Z) follows directly from the definition by $Y \sqsubseteq Z$ and $Z \neq A$.

The remaining task is to show that (iib) holds (for X and Z). Let α be such that $X, Z \in A \perp \alpha$ and $A \div \alpha \subseteq X$. We need to show that $A \div \alpha \subseteq Z$.

The first step is to show that there is some $\beta \in A$ such that $A \div \beta \subseteq Y \in A \perp \beta$. It follows from $Y \sqsubseteq Z$ and $Z \neq A$, by the definition of $\sqsubseteq$, that $Y \neq A$. It follows from $Y \neq A$ and $X \sqsubseteq Y$, again by the definition of $\sqsubseteq$, clause (iia), that there is some $\beta \in A$ such that $A \div \beta \subseteq Y \in A \perp \beta$.

It follows from $Z \neq A$ and $Z \in A \perp \alpha$ that $\alpha \in A$. From $\alpha \in A$ and $\beta \in A$ we can conclude (by Observation 1.55) that $A \perp (\alpha \& \beta) = A \perp \alpha \cup A \perp \beta$. It follows directly that X, Y, and Z are all elements of $A \perp (\alpha \& \beta)$.

It can be seen from conjunctive inclusion that either $A \div (\alpha \& \beta) \subseteq A \div \alpha$ or $A \div (\alpha \& \beta) \subseteq A \div \beta$. (This is the postulate of conjunctive covering that was referred to in Exercise 73.) Next, we are going to show that in both these cases, $A \div (\alpha \& \beta) \subseteq Z$. (As will soon be clear, we can use this to prove that $A \div \alpha \subseteq Z$.)

First case, $A \div (\alpha \& \beta) \subseteq A \div \alpha$: Since $A \div \alpha \subseteq X$ we then have $A \div (\alpha \& \beta) \subseteq X$. We also have $X \sqsubseteq Y$, and since $Y \neq A$, clause (i) of the definition is not applicable, so (iib) must hold. It therefore follows from $X \in A \perp (\alpha \& \beta), Y \in A \perp (\alpha \& \beta)$, and $A \div (\alpha \& \beta) \subseteq X$ that $A \div (\alpha \& \beta) \subseteq Y$. The same argument can be repeated for $Y \sqsubseteq Z$: Since $Z \neq A$, clause (i) is not applicable for Y and Z, so (iib) must hold. We have $Y \in A \perp (\alpha \& \beta)$, $Z \in A \perp (\alpha \& \beta)$, and $A \div (\alpha \& \beta) \subseteq Y$, and from this we can conclude that $A \div (\alpha \& \beta) \subseteq Z$.

Second case, $A \div (\alpha \& \beta) \subseteq A \div \beta$: Since $A \div \beta \subseteq Y$ it follows that $A \div (\alpha \& \beta) \subseteq Y$. We have $Y \sqsubseteq Z$. Since $Z \neq A$, clause (i) is not applicable for Y and Z, so (iib) must hold. We have $Y \in A \perp (\alpha \& \beta)$, $Z \in A \perp (\alpha \& \beta)$, and $A \div (\alpha \& \beta) \subseteq Y$, and from this we can conclude that $A \div (\alpha \& \beta) \subseteq Z$.

Thus, in both cases, $A \div (\alpha \& \beta) \subseteq Z$. Armed with this result, we can now prove that $A \div \alpha \subseteq Z$. Let $\delta \in A \div \alpha$. We have to show that $\delta \in Z$.

Since $A \div \alpha$ is logically closed, it follows from $\delta \in A \div \alpha$ that $\alpha \vee \delta \in A \div \alpha$. Since conjunctive overlap is satisfied, so is partial antitony, and we therefore have $(A \div \alpha) \cap \mathrm{Cn}(\{\alpha\}) \subseteq A \div (\alpha \& \beta)$. (Observation 2.60.) We can therefore conclude from $\alpha\vee\delta \in A\div\alpha$ and $\alpha\vee\delta \in \mathrm{Cn}(\{\alpha\})$ that $\alpha\vee\delta \in A\div(\alpha\&\beta)$. We have just shown that $A\div(\alpha\&\beta) \subseteq Z$. Thus $\alpha\vee\delta \in Z$.

We also have $Z \in A\bot\alpha$, from which it follows (Observation 2.5) that $A \subseteq \mathrm{Cn}(Z \cup \{\alpha\})$. Since $\delta \in A$, we therefore have $\delta \in \mathrm{Cn}(Z \cup \{\alpha\})$ and, by the deduction property of Cn, $\alpha\rightarrow\delta \in \mathrm{Cn}(Z)$. Since $\alpha\vee\delta$ and $\alpha\rightarrow\delta$ together imply δ, it follows from $\alpha\vee\delta \in Z$ and $\alpha\rightarrow\delta \in \mathrm{Cn}(Z)$ that $\delta \in \mathrm{Cn}(Z)$. Z is logically closed, so that $\delta \in Z$. We have shown this to hold for all $\delta \in A\div\alpha$, and by this we have established that $A\div\alpha \subseteq Z$, which is what we needed to show that $\sqsubseteq$ is transitive.

PART 2, $\hat{\gamma}$ IS GENERATED: We need to show that if $A\bot\alpha \neq \emptyset$, then

$$\hat{\gamma}(A\bot\alpha) = \{Y \in A\bot\alpha \mid X \sqsubseteq Y \text{ for all } X \in A\bot\alpha\}.$$

Let $A\bot\alpha \neq \emptyset$.

For one direction of this proof, let $Z \notin \hat{\gamma}(A\bot\alpha)$. We need to show that $Z \notin \{Y \in A\bot\alpha \mid X \sqsubseteq Y \text{ for all } X \in A\bot\alpha\}$.

First case, $\alpha \notin A$: Then $A\bot\alpha = \{A\}$, and consequently $\hat{\gamma}(A\bot\alpha) = \{A\}$. It follows from $Z \notin \hat{\gamma}(A\bot\alpha)$ that $Z \notin A\bot\alpha$, from which $Z \notin \{Y \in A\bot\alpha \mid X \sqsubseteq Y$ for all $X \in A\bot\alpha\}$ follows directly.

Second case, $\alpha \in A$: The desired conclusion follows trivially if $Z \notin A\bot\alpha$, so for the principal case we may assume that $Z \in A\bot\alpha$.

It follows from $Z \in A\bot\alpha$ that $Z \neq A$. Since $A\bot\alpha$ is nonempty, so is $\hat{\gamma}(A\bot\alpha)$ (Definition 2.67). Let $V \in \hat{\gamma}(A\bot\alpha)$. We then have $A\div\alpha = \bigcap\hat{\gamma}(A\bot\alpha) \subseteq V$. On the other hand, since $Z \notin \hat{\gamma}(A\bot\alpha)$, we can conclude by the completion property of $\hat{\gamma}$ that $\bigcap\hat{\gamma}(A\bot\alpha) \not\subseteq Z$. Since $A\div\alpha = \bigcap\hat{\gamma}(A\bot\alpha)$, we now have $Z, V \in A\bot\alpha$, $A\div\alpha \subseteq V$ and $A\div\alpha \not\subseteq Z$. It follows from the definition of $\sqsubseteq$ (clause iib) that $V \not\sqsubseteq Z$. Thus $X \sqsubseteq Z$ does not hold for all $X \in A\bot\alpha$, i.e. $Z \notin \{Y \in A\bot\alpha \mid X \sqsubseteq Y \text{ for all } X \in A\bot\alpha\}$.

For the other direction of this proof, let $Z \in \hat{\gamma}(A\bot\alpha)$. We need to show that $Z \in \{Y \in A\bot\alpha \mid X \sqsubseteq Y \text{ for all } X \in A\bot\alpha\}$. To do this, we have to show that if $X \in A\bot\alpha$, then $X \sqsubseteq Z$. Let $X \in A\bot\alpha$.

First case, $\alpha \notin A$: It follows from $X \in A\bot\alpha$ and $Z \in A\bot\alpha$ that $X = Z = A$. It follows from clause (i) of the definition of $\sqsubseteq$ that $X \sqsubseteq Z$.

Second case, $\alpha \in A$: As can be seen from the definition of $\sqsubseteq$, in order to show that $X \sqsubseteq Z$ we have to show that clause (iib) is satisfied, i.e. that for all β, if $X, Z \in A\bot\beta$ and $A\div\beta \subseteq X$, then $A\div\beta \subseteq Z$. (Clause (iia) is satisfied since $A\div\alpha = \bigcap\hat{\gamma}(A\bot\alpha) \subseteq Z \in A\bot\alpha$.) Let β be such that $X, Z \in A\bot\beta$ and $A\div\beta \subseteq X$. We are going to show that $A\div\beta \subseteq Z$.

The first step in this proof is to show that $A\div(\alpha\&\beta) \subseteq A\div\alpha$. It follows from *conjunctive covering* (that follows from *conjunctive inclusion*, see Exercise 73 and the proof of Observation 2.77) that either $A\div(\alpha\&\beta) \subseteq A\div\alpha$ or $A\div(\alpha\&\beta) \subseteq A\div\beta$. Suppose that $A\div(\alpha\&\beta) \subseteq A\div\beta$. It then follows from $A\div(\alpha\&\beta) \subseteq A\div\beta$

$\subseteq X \in A\bot\alpha$ that $\alpha \notin A\div(\alpha\&\beta)$, and thus by *conjunctive inclusion* that $A\div(\alpha\&\beta) \subseteq A\div\alpha$. Thus, in both cases, $A\div(\alpha\&\beta) \subseteq A\div\alpha$.

In order to prove that $A\div\beta \subseteq Z$, let $\varepsilon \in A\div\beta$. Since $A\div\beta$ is logically closed, it follows that $\beta\vee\varepsilon \in A\div\beta$. It follows from *conjunctive overlap* that *partial antitony* holds, so that $A\div\beta \cap \mathrm{Cn}(\{\beta\}) \subseteq A\div(\alpha\&\beta)$. (Observation 2.60.) Since $\beta\vee\varepsilon \in \mathrm{Cn}(\{\beta\})$, we therefore have $\beta\vee\varepsilon \in A\div(\alpha\&\beta)$. Since $A\div(\alpha\&\beta) \subseteq A\div\alpha \subseteq Z$, we can conclude that $\beta\vee\varepsilon \in Z$.

It follows from $Z \in A\bot\beta$ that $A \subseteq \mathrm{Cn}(Z \cup \{\beta\})$ (Observation 2.5), and since $\varepsilon \in A$ we have $\varepsilon \in \mathrm{Cn}(Z \cup \{\beta\})$. The deductive property of Cn yields $\beta\rightarrow\varepsilon \in \mathrm{Cn}(Z)$. Since $\beta\vee\varepsilon$ and $\beta\rightarrow\varepsilon$ together imply ε, it follows from $\beta\vee\varepsilon \in Z$ and $\beta\rightarrow\varepsilon \in \mathrm{Cn}(Z)$ that $\varepsilon \in \mathrm{Cn}(Z)$, and by the logical closure of Z that $\varepsilon \in Z$. We have shown this to hold for all $\varepsilon \in A\div\beta$. It follows that $A\div\beta \subseteq Z$, and this is all that remained to show that $X \sqsubseteq Z$. With this the proof is finished. ■

The relation $\sqsubseteq$ is intended to capture the intuition that $X \sqsubseteq Y$ if and only if Y is at least as much worth retaining as X It is not unreasonable to require that every remainder should be at least as much worth retaining as itself, i.e. that $\sqsubseteq$ satisfies:

Reflexivity:
$X \sqsubseteq X$

Furthermore, it could be maintained that all pairs of remainders should be comparable by $\sqsubseteq$, i.e. that at least one of X and Y should be at least as much worth retaining as the other:

Connectivity:
$(X \sqsubseteq Y)\vee(Y \sqsubseteq X)$.

A relation is *connected* if and only if it satisfies connectivity. ('Completeness' and 'complete relations' are common synonyms, but in order to avoid confusion with completed selection functions, these terms will not be used here.) All connected relations are also reflexive. (To see this, just substitute Y for X in the above defining formula for connectivity.)

Interestingly enough, it makes no difference if we make the additional requirement that the marking-off relation should be connected:

OBSERVATION 2.78 (AGM [1]) *Let A be a logically closed set and $\div$ an operator for A that satisfies closure, inclusion, vacuity, success, extensionality, recovery, conjunctive overlap, and conjunctive inclusion. Then $\div$ is an operator of partial meet contraction with a completed and transitively connectedly relational selection function.*

Proof. [1] This proof continues the proof of Observation 2.77. It consists of two steps. In the first step, we are going to consider the set of remainders that are selected by γ out of at least one remainder set. This is the set

$$\mathcal{U}_\gamma = \{X \mid X \in \gamma(A\bot\alpha) \text{ for some } \alpha\}.$$

We are going to show that $\sqsubseteq$ is connected over this set. In the next step, we are going to construct, based on $\sqsubseteq$, a new marking-off relation $\sqsubseteq'$ that has all the desired properties.

FIRST STEP: Let X and Y be elements of $\mathcal{U}_\gamma$, such that $Y \not\sqsubseteq X$. We are going to show that $X \sqsubseteq Y$.

If $Y = A$, then $X \sqsubseteq Y$ follows directly. In the principal case, we can assume that $Y \neq A$ and $X \neq A$ (which follows from $Y \not\sqsubseteq X$).

In order to show that $X \sqsubseteq Y$, we must show that conditions (iia)-(iib) of the definition of $\sqsubseteq$ (in the proof of Observation 2.77) are satisfied. It follows from $Y \in \mathcal{U}_\gamma$ that there is some α such that $A{\div}\alpha = \bigcap\gamma(A\bot\alpha) \subseteq Y \in A\bot\alpha$, so that (iia) is satisfied.

It follows from $Y \not\sqsubseteq X$, by the definition of $\sqsubseteq$, that there is some δ such that $X, Y \in A\bot\delta$, $A{\div}\delta \subseteq Y$, and $A{\div}\delta \not\subseteq X$. Since γ is completed, it follows from $\bigcap\gamma(A\bot\delta) = A{\div}\delta \subseteq Y$ that $Y \in \gamma(A\bot\delta)$. It follows from $X \in A\bot\delta$ and $Y \in \gamma(A\bot\delta)$, by the marking-off identity, that $X \sqsubseteq Y$. This concludes the first step of the proof.

SECOND STEP: We are going to introduce a relation $\sqsubseteq'$ with the domain $A\Delta\mathcal{L} = \{X \mid X \in A\bot\alpha \text{ for some } \alpha\}$. It is defined as follows:

(I) If $X, Y \in \mathcal{U}_\gamma$, then $X \sqsubseteq' Y$ if and only if $X \sqsubseteq Y$.
(II) If $X \in \mathcal{U}_\gamma$ and $Y \notin \mathcal{U}_\gamma$, then $X \not\sqsubseteq' Y$.
(III) If $X \notin \mathcal{U}_\gamma$, then $X \sqsubseteq' Y$.

We need to show (1) that $\sqsubseteq'$ is connected, (2) that $\sqsubseteq'$ is transitive, and (3) that $\sqsubseteq'$ generates the same selection function for A as $\sqsubseteq$.

(1) follows directly from the definition of $\sqsubseteq'$ and the result of step 1.

For (2), suppose that $X \sqsubseteq' Y \sqsubseteq' Z$. We have to show that $X \sqsubseteq' Z$. There are two cases:

First case, $X \notin \mathcal{U}_\gamma$: Then $X \sqsubseteq' Z$ follows from clause (III) of the definition of $\sqsubseteq'$.

Second case, $X \in \mathcal{U}_\gamma$. Then it follows from $X \sqsubseteq' Y$ and clause (II) that $Y \in \mathcal{U}_\gamma$, and from clause (I) that $X \sqsubseteq Y$. Similarly, it follows from $Y \sqsubseteq' Z$ and $Y \in \mathcal{U}_\gamma$, by clause (II), that $Z \in \mathcal{U}_\gamma$. By clause (I) we obtain $Y \sqsubseteq Z$. It follows from $X \sqsubseteq Y$ and $Y \sqsubseteq Z$, by the transitivity of $\sqsubseteq$, that $X \sqsubseteq Z$, from which it follows by clause (I) that $X \sqsubseteq' Z$.

For (3), we are going to show that it makes no difference if we use $\sqsubseteq$ or $\sqsubseteq'$ in the marking-off relation, i.e. that for all α:

$$\{Y \in A\bot\alpha \mid X \sqsubseteq' Y \text{ for all } X \in A\bot\alpha\} =$$
$$\{Y \in A\bot\alpha \mid X \sqsubseteq Y \text{ for all } X \in A\bot\alpha\}.$$

Left-to-right: Let Y be an element of $A\bot\alpha$ such that $X \sqsubseteq' Y$ for all $X \in A\bot\alpha$. If $Y = A$, then $X \sqsubseteq Y$ follows immediately from the definition of $\sqsubseteq$, and we are done. For the principal case, let $Y \neq A$.

Suppose that $Y \notin \mathcal{U}_\gamma$. It then follows by clause (II) of the definition that $X \notin \mathcal{U}_\gamma$ for all $X \in A\perp\alpha$, so that (by the definition of $\mathcal{U}_\gamma$) $\gamma(A\perp\alpha)$ is empty, which is impossible since $A\perp\alpha$ is nonempty (we have assumed that $Y \in A\perp\alpha$). We may conclude that $Y \in \mathcal{U}_\gamma$. Let $X \in A\perp\alpha$. We need to show that $X \sqsubseteq Y$.

Case 1, $X \in \mathcal{U}_\gamma$: Then $X \sqsubseteq Y$ follows by clause (I) of the definition.

Case 2, $X \notin \mathcal{U}_\gamma$: Then it follows by the definition of $\mathcal{U}_\gamma$ that $X \notin \gamma(A\perp\alpha)$. Let $Z \in \gamma(A\perp\alpha)$. Since $\sqsubseteq$ satisfies the marking-off relation for γ (as shown in the proof of Observation 2.77), we have $X \sqsubseteq Z$. By our condition for Y, it follows from $Z \in A\perp\alpha$ that $Z \sqsubseteq' Y$. Since $Z \in \mathcal{U}_\gamma$, it follows by clause (I) of the definition that $Z \sqsubseteq Y$. It follows from $X \sqsubseteq Z$ and $Z \sqsubseteq Y$ by the transitivity of $\sqsubseteq$ that $X \sqsubseteq Y$.

Right-to-left: Let Y be an element of $A\perp\alpha$ such that $X \sqsubseteq Y$ for all $X \in A\perp\alpha$. Then, since $\sqsubseteq$ is a marking-off relation for γ (as shown in the proof of Observation 2.77), we have $Y \in \gamma(A\perp\alpha)$ and consequently $Y \in \mathcal{U}_\gamma$. Let $X \in A\perp\alpha$. We need to show that $X \sqsubseteq' Y$.

Case 1, $X \in \mathcal{U}_\gamma$: Then $X \sqsubseteq' Y$ follows by clause (I) of the definition.

Case 2, $X \notin \mathcal{U}_\gamma$: Then $X \sqsubseteq' Y$ follows by clause (III) of the definition.

This finishes the proof. ■

The maximizing property has as little effect on transitively relational partial meet contraction on belief sets as has connectivity. This is quite easy to prove, since if $X \in A\perp\alpha$ and $Y \in A\perp\beta$ for some $\alpha, \beta \in A$, then $X \not\subset Y$.

OBSERVATION 2.79 ([49]) *Let A be a logically closed set and $\div$ an operator for A that satisfies closure, inclusion, vacuity, success, extensionality, recovery, conjunctive overlap, and conjunctive inclusion. Then $\div$ is an operator of partial meet contraction with a completed and transitively, connectively, maximizingly relational selection function.*

Proof. Let $\sqsubseteq'$ be the relation introduced in Observation 2.78. We are going to show that $\sqsubseteq'$ is maximizing. Let $X, Y \in A\Delta\mathcal{L} = \{X \mid X \in A\perp\alpha \text{ for some } \alpha\}$. We are going to show that if $X \subset Y$, then $X \sqsubset' Y$. Let $X \subset Y$.

Suppose that $Y \neq A$. It follows from $X \subset Y$ that $X \neq A$. However, it follows by Observation 1.53 from $X \neq A \neq Y$ that $X \not\subset Y$. We can conclude from this contradiction that $Y = A$.

We thus have $X \subset Y = A$. It follows from this and $X \in A\Delta\mathcal{L}$ that there is some $\alpha \in A$ such that $X \in A\perp\alpha$.

Case 1, $X \notin \mathcal{U}_\gamma$: $X \sqsubseteq' Y$ follows by clause (III) of the definition of $\sqsubseteq'$, and $Y \not\sqsubseteq X$ by clause (II). We can conclude that $X \sqsubset' Y$.

Case 2, $X \in \mathcal{U}_\gamma$: Since $Y \in \mathcal{U}_\gamma$, clause (I) of the same definition says that $X \sqsubseteq' Y$ holds if and only if $X \sqsubseteq Y$. It follows from $Y = A$ that $X \sqsubseteq Y$, thus $X \sqsubseteq' Y$. Furthermore, clause (I) says that $Y \sqsubseteq' X$ holds if and only if $Y \sqsubseteq X$.

It follows from $Y = A$ and $X \neq A$ that $Y \not\sqsubseteq X$, thus $Y \not\sqsubseteq' X$. We can conclude that $X \sqsubset' Y$. This concludes the proof. ■

Combining the results of this section, we arrive at the following strengthened version of the AGM representation theorem for transitively relational partial meet contraction:

THEOREM 2.80 *Let A be a logically closed set and $\div$ an operator for A. Then the following three conditions are equivalent:*

1. *$\div$ satisfies closure, inclusion, vacuity, success, extensionality, recovery, conjunctive overlap, and conjunctive inclusion.*
2. *$\div$ is a partial meet contraction that is relational by a transitive marking-off relation (transitively relational)*
3. *$\div$ is a partial meet contraction that is relational by a transitive, maximizing, and connected marking-off relation that generates a completed selection function.*

[This includes Observation 2.18 and Theorem 2.21.]

Exercises

107. [49] Let A be a finite (but not necessarily logically closed) set and γ a relational selection function for A. Show:
    (a) γ is relational by some reflexive marking-off relation. (Hint: Use Observation 1.70.)
    (b) If γ is transitively relational, then it is relational by some transitive and reflexive marking-off relation.
108. [115] Instead of the marking-off identity used throughout this book, namely:
    $\gamma(A\perp\alpha) = \{X \in A\perp\alpha \mid Y \sqsubseteq X \text{ for all } Y \in A\perp\alpha\}$ ($\sqsubseteq$-identity)
    it is possible to use the following:
    $\gamma(A\perp\alpha) = \{X \in A\perp\alpha \mid X < Y \text{ for no } Y \in A\perp\alpha\}$ ($<$-identity)
    (a) Show that γ is relational by some $\sqsubseteq$-identity if and only if it is relational by some $<$-identity.
    (b) Show that γ is relational by some $\sqsubseteq$-identity with a connective relation $\sqsubseteq$ if and only if it is relational by some $<$-identity with a relation $<$ that satisfies:
    $X < Y \rightarrow \neg(Y < X)$ *(asymmetry)*
    (c) Find a property (P) such that γ is relational by some $\sqsubseteq$-identity with a relation $\sqsubseteq$ that satisfies
    $X \sqsubseteq Z \rightarrow X \sqsubseteq Y \vee Y \sqsubseteq Z$ *(virtual connectivity)*
    if and only if it is relational by some $<$-identity that satisfies P.
109. [48] Show that Observation 2.18 does not hold for package selection functions as defined in Section 2.16$^+$. (Hint: Let $A = \text{Cn}(\{p,q\})$, and consider $A\perp\{p\}$ and $A\perp\{p, p\leftrightarrow q\}$.)

110. [48] Let $\sqsubseteq$ be a relation on the A-closed subsets of A, such that some relational partial meet package contraction for A is based on $\sqsubseteq$ (cf. Definition 2.61). Show that:
   (a) $\sqsubseteq$ is reflexive (Hint: Use Observation 1.67.)
   (b) For all A-closed subsets A_1 and A_2 of A, either $A_1 \subset A_2, A_2 \subset A_1, A_1 \sqsubseteq A_2$ or $A_2 \sqsubseteq A_1$. (Hint: Use Observation 1.68.)
   (c) There is a connective relation $\sqsubseteq'$ on the A-closed subsets of A, such that $\sqsubseteq'$ generates the same partial meet contraction as $\sqsubseteq$.

21+ SATURATABILITY AND LEVI-CONTRACTIONS

Before proving the theorems and observations on Levi-contractions from Section 2.7, we are going to prove some properties of saturatable sets.

> Let A be logically closed, and let $\alpha \in A$. Then it holds for all $X \in A\bot\alpha$ that X is α-saturatable.
> [Observation 2.23.]

Proof. According to Definition 2.22, we need to show (i) that X is logically closed and (ii) that $\text{Cn}(X \cup \{\neg\alpha\}) \in \mathcal{L}\bot\bot$. It follows from Observation 1.48 that (i) is satisfied. In order to prove (ii) it is sufficient to show that $\text{Cn}(X \cup \{\neg\alpha\})$ is consistent and that for all β, either $\beta \in \text{Cn}(X \cup \{\neg\alpha\})$ or $\neg\beta \in \text{Cn}(X \cup \{\neg\alpha\})$.

In order to show that $\text{Cn}(X \cup \{\neg\alpha\})$ is consistent, suppose to the contrary that it is inconsistent. Then it implies α, i.e. $\alpha \in \text{Cn}(X \cup \{\neg\alpha\})$. By deduction, it follows that $\neg\alpha \rightarrow \alpha \in \text{Cn}(X)$, or equivalently $\alpha \in \text{Cn}(X)$, contrary to $X \in A\bot\alpha$. We can conclude from this contradiction that $\text{Cn}(X \cup \{\neg\alpha\})$ is consistent.

Next, let β be any sentence. It follows from Observation 1.51 that either $\alpha \vee \beta \in X$ or $\alpha \vee \neg\beta \in X$. Since $\alpha \vee \beta$ is equivalent to $\neg\alpha \rightarrow \beta$ and $\alpha \vee \neg\beta$ is equivalent to $\neg\alpha \rightarrow \neg\beta$, we can use deduction to conclude that either $\beta \in \text{Cn}(X \cup \{\neg\alpha\})$ or $\neg\beta \in \text{Cn}(X \cup \{\neg\alpha\})$. ■

Next, we are going to verify two properties of saturatable sets that are analogous to properties that we have already shown to hold for remainders. The following observation is an analogue of Observation 1.45:

OBSERVATION 2.81 ([60]) *Let A be a logically closed set. Then it holds for all sentences α and β that $S(A, \alpha\&\beta) \subseteq S(A, \alpha) \cup S(A, \beta)$*

Proof. Let $X \in S(A, \alpha\&\beta)$. According to Definition 2.24, $\text{Cn}(X \cup \{\neg\alpha \vee \neg\beta\})$ is maximally consistent. Since it is maximally consistent and contains $\neg\alpha \vee \neg\beta$ it contains either $\neg\alpha$ or $\neg\beta$. (Cf. Observation 1.57.)

Case 1: $\neg\alpha \in \text{Cn}(X \cup \{\neg\alpha \vee \neg\beta\})$. Then $\text{Cn}(X \cup \{\neg\alpha\}) = \text{Cn}(X \cup \{\neg\alpha \vee \neg\beta\})$, so that $\text{Cn}(X \cup \{\neg\alpha\})$ is maximally consistent. Since we already know that $X = \text{Cn}(X) \subseteq A$, we can conclude that $X \in S(A, \alpha)$.

Case 2: $\neg\beta \in \mathrm{Cn}(X \cup \{\neg\alpha\vee\neg\beta\})$. It follows in the same way that $X \in S(A,\beta)$. ■

It follows from Observation 1.55 that if $Y \in A\perp\alpha$ and A is logically closed, then $Y \in A\perp(\alpha\&\beta)$. This is a useful result, that has been referred to repeatedly in the foregoing sections. The corresponding property does not hold for saturatable subsets of A, i.e. it may very well be the case that $Y \in S(A,\alpha)$ and $Y \notin S(A,\alpha\&\beta)$. However, the following weaker property can serve a similar function in some proofs.

OBSERVATION 2.82 ([60]) *Let α, β, and δ be elements of the logically closed set A. If $\delta \notin Y \in S(A,\alpha)$, then there is some Z such that $Y \subseteq Z \in S(A,\alpha\&\beta)$ and $\delta \notin Z$.*

Proof. Let $\delta \notin Y \in S(A,\alpha)$. There are two cases:

Case 1: Either $\alpha\vee\delta \notin Y$ or $\beta\rightarrow\delta \notin Y$:

Let $Z = \mathrm{Cn}(Y \cup \{\alpha\rightarrow\beta\})$. Since $\mathrm{Cn}(\{\alpha\rightarrow\beta, \neg\alpha\vee\neg\beta\}) = \mathrm{Cn}(\{\neg\alpha\})$, it follows that $\mathrm{Cn}(Z \cup \{\neg\alpha\vee\neg\beta\}) = \mathrm{Cn}(Y \cup \{\neg\alpha\})$. Since $Y \in S(A,\alpha)$, we have $\mathrm{Cn}(Y \cup \{\neg\alpha\}) \in \mathcal{L}\perp\perp$, and thus $\mathrm{Cn}(Z \cup \{\neg\alpha\vee\neg\beta\}) \in \mathcal{L}\perp\perp$.

Suppose that $\delta \in Z$. Then $Y \vdash (\alpha\rightarrow\beta)\rightarrow\delta$, from which follows $Y \vdash \beta\rightarrow\delta$. Furthermore, from $\delta \in Z$ and $Z \subseteq \mathrm{Cn}(Y \cup \{\neg\alpha\})$, we obtain $Y \cup \{\neg\alpha\} \vdash \delta$, and thus $Y \vdash \alpha\vee\delta$. Since Y is logically closed, both $\beta\rightarrow\delta$ and $\alpha\vee\delta$ are elements of Y, contrary to the condition. We may conclude that $\delta \notin Z$.

Case 2: $\{\alpha\vee\delta, \beta\rightarrow\delta\} \subseteq Y$:

Let $Y' = \mathrm{Cn}(Y \cup \{\alpha, \delta\rightarrow\beta\})$. We are going to show that $Y' \nvdash \alpha\&\beta$. Suppose to the contrary that $Y' \vdash \alpha\&\beta$. Then $Y' \cup \{\neg\alpha\vee\neg\beta\}$ is inconsistent, i.e. $Y \cup \{\alpha, \delta\rightarrow\beta, \neg\alpha\vee\neg\beta\} \vdash \perp$. However, since $\{\alpha\vee\delta, \beta\rightarrow\delta\} \subseteq Y$, we have $\mathrm{Cn}(Y \cup \{\alpha, \delta\rightarrow\beta, \neg\alpha\vee\neg\beta\}) \subseteq \mathrm{Cn}(Y \cup \{\neg\delta\})$, so that $\mathrm{Cn}(Y \cup \{\neg\delta\}) \vdash \perp$, contrary to $\delta \notin Y$. We can conclude from this contradiction that $Y' \nvdash \alpha\&\beta$.

Since $Y' \subseteq A$, it follows from the upper bound property that there is some Z such that $Y' \subseteq Z \in A\perp(\alpha\&\beta)$. It follows from $Z \in A\perp(\alpha\&\beta)$ that $Z \in S(A,\alpha\&\beta)$. It remains to be shown that $\delta \notin Z$. Suppose to the contrary that $\delta \in Z$. Since $\{\alpha, \delta\rightarrow\beta\} \subseteq Z$ we then have $\alpha\&\beta \in Z$, contrary to $Z \in A\perp(\alpha\&\beta)$. We can conclude from this contradiction that $\delta \notin Z$. ■

The proof of the representation theorem is quite similar to that of the representation theorem for partial meet contraction that we proved in Section 2.15+, but the postulates-to-contractions part is somewhat more complex in this case.

> Let A be a logically closed set. Then the operator $\div$ is a Levi-contraction for A if and only if it satisfies *closure*, *inclusion*, *success*, *vacuity*, *extensionality*, and *failure*.
> [Theorem 2.26.]

Proof. *Construction-to-postulates*: Let $\div$ be an operator of Levi-contraction for A. We are going to show that $\div$ satisfies the properties given in the theorem.

Closure: Directly from Definition 2.24, since the elements of $S(A,\alpha)$ are logically closed.

Inclusion: Directly from Definition 2.24.

Success: It follows from Definition 2.24 that if $\nvdash \alpha$, then $\alpha \notin X$ for all $X \in S(A,\alpha)$.

Extensionality: Let $\vdash \alpha \leftrightarrow \beta$. To prove extensionality it suffices to show that $\bigcap\gamma(S(A,\alpha)) = \bigcap\gamma(S(A,\beta))$. We are going to prove that $S(A,\alpha) = S(A,\beta)$. From this the desired result follows, since γ is a function.

To prove that $S(A,\alpha) \subseteq S(A,\beta)$, let $X \in S(A,\alpha)$. It follows from $\vdash \alpha \leftrightarrow \beta$ that $\text{Cn}(X \cup \{\neg\alpha\}) = \text{Cn}(X \cup \{\neg\beta\})$. Thus, $\text{Cn}(X \cup \{\neg\beta\}) \in \mathcal{L}\bot^{\bot}$. Since X is a logically closed subset of A, it follows that $X \in S(A,\beta)$. It follows in the same way that $S(A,\beta) \subseteq S(A,\alpha)$.

Vacuity: Directly from Definition 2.25, clause (2).

Failure: If $\vdash \alpha$, then $S(A,\alpha) = \emptyset$. Thus $\gamma(S(A,\alpha)) = \{A\}$ and $\bigcap\gamma(S(A,\alpha)) = A$.

Postulates-to-construction: Let $\div$ be an operation that satisfies the listed postulates. To show that $\div$ is a Levi-contraction operator we need to find a selection function γ such that $A \div \alpha = \bigcap\gamma(S(A,\alpha))$ if $\alpha \in A$. (The case when $\alpha \notin A$ follows trivially since *vacuity* holds.) Let γ be such that:

(i) $\gamma(S(A,\alpha)) = \{A\}$ if $S(A,\alpha) = \emptyset$.
(ii) $\gamma(S(A,\alpha)) = \{X \in S(A,\alpha) \mid A \div \alpha \subseteq X\}$ otherwise.

We have to prove that (1) γ is a well-defined function, (2) γ is a selection function, and (3) $\bigcap\gamma(S(A,\alpha)) = A \div \alpha$ for all $\alpha \in A$.

Part 1: To prove that γ is well-defined, we have to show that if $S(A,\alpha) = S(A,\beta)$, then $\gamma(S(A,\alpha)) = \gamma(S(A,\beta))$.

Let $S(A,\alpha) = S(A,\beta)$. We are first going to show that if $B \subseteq A$ then $B \vdash \alpha$ iff $B \vdash \beta$. Suppose not. We can then, without loss of generality, asume that there is some $B \subseteq A$ such that $B \vdash \beta$ but $B \nvdash \alpha$. Then it follows from the upper bound property that there exists a set B' such that $B \subseteq B' \in A \bot \alpha$ and thus $B' \in S(A,\alpha)$. But $B' \notin S(A,\beta)$ since $B' \vdash \beta$. We can conclude from this contradiction that if $B \subseteq A$ then $B \vdash \alpha$ iff $B \vdash \beta$.

Since $\div$ satisfies *extensionality* and *vacuity*, it follows from Observation 2.4 that it satisfies *uniformity*, and thus $A \div \alpha = A \div \beta$. According to the definition of γ, we have $\gamma(S(A,\alpha)) = \gamma(S(A,\beta))$.

Part 2: In order to show that γ is a selection function we have to prove that if $S(A,\alpha) \neq \emptyset$, then $\gamma(S(A,\alpha)) \neq \emptyset$. Let $S(A,\alpha) \neq \emptyset$. Then $\nvdash \alpha$. *Success* implies that $A \div \alpha \nvdash \alpha$. By *inclusion* $A \div \alpha \subseteq A$. Thus there exists an X such that $A \div \alpha \subseteq X \in A \bot \alpha \subseteq S(A,\alpha)$. It follows from the definition of γ that $X \in \gamma(S(A,\alpha))$, and thus $\gamma(S(A,\alpha)) \neq \emptyset$.

Part 3: Finally, we must prove that, for all $\alpha \in A, \bigcap\gamma(S(A,\alpha)) = A\div\alpha$. There are two cases.

Case 1, $S(A,\alpha) = \emptyset$: Then $\vdash \alpha$ and it follows from *failure* that $A\div\alpha = A$. Furthermore $\bigcap\gamma(S(A,\alpha)) = A$ by clause (i) in the definition of γ. Thus the desired result holds in this case.

Case 2, $S(A,\alpha) \neq \emptyset$: $A\div\alpha \subseteq \bigcap\gamma(S(A,\alpha))$ holds since $A\div\alpha \subseteq X$ for every $X \in \gamma(S(A,\alpha))$. For the other direction we are going to show that if $\beta \notin A\div\alpha$, then $\beta \notin \bigcap\gamma(S(A,\alpha))$. This holds if $\beta \notin A$, since $\bigcap\gamma(S(A,\alpha)) \subseteq A$.

Let $\beta \in A\backslash(A\div\alpha)$. It suffices to show that there exists an X such that:

1. $\beta \notin X$,
2. $A\div\alpha \subseteq X \subseteq A$,
3. $X = \mathrm{Cn}(X)$, and
4. $\mathrm{Cn}(X \cup \{\neg\alpha\}) \in \mathcal{L}\perp^{\perp}$.

Subcase 2A, $A\div\alpha \nvdash \alpha\vee\beta$: According to the upper bound property, there is some set X such that $A\div\alpha \subseteq X \in A\perp(\alpha\vee\beta)$. It follows directly that (1), (2), and (3) are satisfied. It remains to show that (4) is satisfied. It follows from Observation 1.53 that $X \in A\perp\alpha$. According to Observation 2.23, $\mathrm{Cn}(X \cup \{\neg\alpha\}) \in \mathcal{L}\perp^{\perp}$.

Subcase 2B, $A\div\alpha \vdash \alpha\vee\beta$: According to the upper bound property, there is some set X such that $A\div\alpha \subseteq X \in A\perp\{\alpha,\beta\}$. It follows directly that (1), (2), and (3) are satisfied. It remains to be shown that (4) is satisfied. Let $\delta \notin \mathrm{Cn}(X \cup \{\neg\alpha\})$. We are going to show that $\neg\delta \in \mathrm{Cn}(X \cup \{\neg\alpha\})$.

It follows from $\delta \notin \mathrm{Cn}(X\cup\{\neg\alpha\})$, by the deduction property of Cn, that $\alpha\vee\delta \notin \mathrm{Cn}(X)$ and consequently $\alpha\vee\delta \notin X$. Since $\alpha \in A$, and A is logically closed, we have $\alpha\vee\delta \in A$. It follows from $\alpha\vee\delta \in A\backslash X$ and $X \in A\perp\{\alpha,\beta\}$ that either $X \cup \{\alpha\vee\delta\} \vdash \alpha$ or $X \cup \{\alpha\vee\delta\} \vdash \beta$.

Suppose that $X \cup \{\alpha\vee\delta\} \vdash \beta$. It then follows that $X \vdash \alpha\rightarrow\beta$. This, however, is incompatible with $X \vdash \alpha\vee\beta$ and $X \nvdash \beta$, that both follow from our definition of X. We can conclude that $X \cup \{\alpha\vee\delta\} \nvdash \beta$, and consequently $X \cup \{\alpha\vee\delta\} \vdash \alpha$. It follows from $X\cup\{\alpha\vee\delta\} \vdash \alpha$ that $X \vdash \delta\rightarrow\alpha$, and thus $X \vdash \neg\alpha\rightarrow\neg\delta$, from which we can conclude that $\neg\delta \in \mathrm{Cn}(X \cup \{\neg\alpha\})$, as desired. Just as in the first subcase it follows that $\mathrm{Cn}(X \cup \{\neg\alpha\}) \in \mathcal{L}\perp^{\perp}$. ■

The rest of this section will be devoted to value-based Levi-contractions. The following simple observation will be useful in the proofs:

OBSERVATION 2.83 ([60]) *Let γ be a selection function that is based on a weakly monotonic measure (cf. Definition 2.27). If $Z \in \gamma(S(A,\alpha))$ and $Z \subseteq Z' \in A\perp\alpha$, then $Z' \in \gamma(S(A,\alpha))$.*

Proof. Let $Z \in \gamma(S(A,\alpha))$ and $Z \subseteq Z' \in A\perp\alpha$. It follows from the weak monotonicity of the measure V that $V(Z) \leq V(Z')$. It follows from $Z \in \gamma(S(A,\alpha))$

and $Z' \in S(A,\alpha)$ that $V(Z') \leq V(Z)$. Thus, $V(Z') = V(Z)$. We can conclude that $Z' \in \gamma(S(A,\alpha))$. ■

We can now prove that value-based Levi-contraction satisfies *conjunctive overlap* and *conjunctive inclusion.*

Let A be a logically closed set and $\div$ a value-based Levi-contraction on A. Then $\div$ satisfies *conjunctive overlap.*
[Part of Observation 2.28.]

Proof. Let γ be the selection function on which $\div$ is based, and let V be the measure on which γ is based. We are going to show that $(A\div\alpha)\cap(A\div\beta) \subseteq A\div(\alpha\&\beta)$. There are five cases.

Case 1, $\alpha \in \text{Cn}(\emptyset)$: $A\div\alpha = \bigcap\gamma(\emptyset) = \bigcap\{A\} = A$, so that $A\div\alpha \cap A\div\beta = A\div\beta$. Since $\alpha \in \text{Cn}(\emptyset)$, β and $\alpha\&\beta$ are logically equivalent. Since *extensionality* is satisfied (Theorem 2.26), $A\div(\alpha\&\beta) = A\div\beta$. It follows directly from this that $(A\div\alpha)\cap(A\div\beta) \subseteq A\div(\alpha\&\beta)$.

Case 2, $\beta \in \text{Cn}(\emptyset)$: This case is symmetrical to Case 1.

Case 3, $\alpha \notin A$: Then $A\div\alpha = A$. Furthermore, $\alpha \notin A$ entails $\alpha\&\beta \notin A$, so that $A\div(\alpha\&\beta) = A$. It follows directly from this that $(A\div\alpha)\cap(A\div\beta) \subseteq A\div(\alpha\&\beta)$.

Case 4, $\beta \notin A$: This case is symmetrical to Case 3.

Case 5. $\alpha, \beta \in A\backslash\text{Cn}(\emptyset)$:

Let $\varepsilon \in (A\div\alpha)\cap(A\div\beta)$. We have to prove that $\varepsilon \in A\div(\alpha\&\beta)$. It follows from $\varepsilon \in (A\div\alpha)\cap(A\div\beta)$ that if $X \in \gamma(S(A,\alpha))$ or $X \in \gamma(S(A,\beta))$, then $\varepsilon \in X$.

Now let $Y \in \gamma(S(A,\alpha\&\beta))$. It follows from Observation 2.81 that either $Y \in S(A,\alpha)$ or $Y \in S(A,\beta)$. Without loss of generality, we may assume that $Y \in S(A,\alpha)$. According to the upper bound property there is then some Y' such that $Y \subseteq Y' \in A\bot\alpha$. By Observation 1.55, $Y' \in A\bot(\alpha\&\beta)$. We can use Observation 2.83 to conclude that $Y' \in \gamma(S(A,\alpha\&\beta))$.

We are going to prove that $Y \in \gamma(S(A,\alpha))$. To do this, it is sufficient to show that if $Z \in S(A,\alpha)$, then $V(Z) \leq V(Y)$. Suppose to the contrary that $Z \in S(A,\alpha)$ and $V(Y) < V(Z)$. It follows by the upper bound property from $Z \in S(A,\alpha)$ that there is some Z' such that $Z \subseteq Z' \in A\bot\alpha$. According to Observation 1.55, $Z' \in A\bot(\alpha\&\beta)$. By weak monotonicity, $V(Z) \leq V(Z')$. We therefore have $V(Y') = V(Y) < V(Z) \leq V(Z')$, so that $V(Y') < V(Z')$. This, however, cannot hold since $Y' \in \gamma(S(A,\alpha\&\beta))$ and $Z' \in S(A,\alpha\&\beta)$. We can conclude from this contradiction that if $Z \in S(A,\alpha)$, then $V(Z) \leq V(Y)$, and consequently that $Y \in \gamma(S(A,\alpha))$. It follows from $Y \in \gamma(S(A,\alpha))$ that $\varepsilon \in Y$. Since this holds for all $Y \in \gamma(S(A,\alpha\&\beta))$, we can conclude that $\varepsilon \in \bigcap\gamma S(A,\alpha\&\beta)) = A\div(\alpha\&\beta)$. ■

Let A be a logically closed set and $\div$ a value-based Levi-contraction on A. Then $\div$ satisfies *conjunctive inclusion.*
[Part of Observation 2.28.]

Proof. Let $\alpha \notin \text{Cn}(A\div(\alpha\&\beta))$. We are going to show that $A\div(\alpha\&\beta) \subseteq A\div\alpha$. There are five cases.

Case 1, $\alpha \notin A$: Then, by the definition of $\div$, $A\div\alpha = A$. Also $\alpha\&\beta \notin A$, and consequently $A\div(\alpha\&\beta) = A$. Hence $A\div(\alpha\&\beta) \subseteq A\div\alpha$ as desired.

Case 2, $\beta \notin A$: Then, $\alpha\&\beta \notin A$, so that $A\div(\alpha\&\beta) = A$. Since by hypothesis $\alpha \notin A\div(\alpha\&\beta)$, it follows that $\alpha \notin A$. By the same reasoning as in case 1, we may conclude that $A\div(\alpha\&\beta) \subseteq A\div\alpha$.

Case 3, $\alpha \in \text{Cn}(\emptyset)$: Then $\alpha \in A\div(\alpha\&\beta)$ so that the postulate holds vacuously.

Case 4, $\beta \in \text{Cn}(\emptyset)$: Then $\alpha\&\beta$ is equivalent with α, and since *extensionality* is satisfied (Theorem 2.26), $A\div(\alpha\&\beta) = A\div\alpha$.

Case 5, $\alpha, \beta \in A\backslash\text{Cn}(\emptyset)$: Since $\alpha \notin A\div(\alpha\&\beta)$ there is some Z such that $\alpha \notin Z \in \gamma(S(A, \alpha\&\beta))$.

We have $\text{Cn}(Z \cup \{\neg\alpha\vee\neg\beta\}) \in \mathcal{L}\bot^{\bot}$, and thus either α or $\neg\alpha$ is an element of $\text{Cn}(Z\cup\{\neg\alpha\vee\neg\beta\})$. Suppose that $\alpha \in \text{Cn}(Z\cup\{\neg\alpha\vee\neg\beta\})$. Then $Z \vdash \neg\alpha\vee\neg\beta\rightarrow\alpha$, or equivalently $Z \vdash \alpha$, contrary to the conditions. It follows from this that $\neg\alpha \in \text{Cn}(Z \cup \{\neg\alpha\vee\neg\beta\})$ or equivalently $\alpha\rightarrow\beta \in Z$.

Since $\alpha\rightarrow\beta \in Z$ we have $\text{Cn}(Z \cup \{\neg\alpha\vee\neg\beta\}) = \text{Cn}(Z \cup \{\neg\alpha\})$, and thus $Z \in S(A, \alpha)$.

Now let X be any element of $S(A, \alpha)$. There is then, according to the upper bound property, some X' such that $X \subseteq X' \in A\bot\alpha$. Since, by Observation 1.55, $A\bot\alpha \subseteq A\bot(\alpha\&\beta)$, we also have $X' \in A\bot(\alpha\&\beta)$, and thus $X' \in S(A, \alpha\&\beta)$.

It follows by weak monotonicity from $X \subseteq X'$ that $V(X) \leq V(X')$. It follows from $X' \in S(A, \alpha\&\beta)$ and $Z \in \gamma(S(A, \alpha\&\beta))$ that $V(X') \leq V(Z)$. Thus $V(X) \leq V(Z)$. Since this holds for all $X \in S(A, \alpha)$, we can conclude that $Z \in \gamma(S(A, \alpha))$.

We are now ready to show that $A\div(\alpha\&\beta) \subseteq A\div\alpha$, i.e. that $\bigcap\gamma(S(A, \alpha\&\beta)) \subseteq \bigcap\gamma(S(A, \alpha))$. Let $\delta \notin \bigcap\gamma(S(A, \alpha))$. Then there is some $Y \in \gamma(S(A, \alpha))$ such that $\delta \notin Y$. It follows from Observation 2.82 that there is some W such that $Y \subseteq W \in S(A, \alpha\&\beta)$ and $\delta \notin W$.

It follows from $Z, Y \in \gamma(S(A, \alpha))$ that $V(Z) = V(Y)$ and from $Y \subseteq W$, by weak monotonicity, that $V(Y) \leq V(W)$. Thus, $V(Z) \leq V(W)$.

It follows from $V(Z) \leq V(W)$, $Z \in \gamma(S(A, \alpha\&\beta))$ and $W \in S(A, \alpha\&\beta)$ that $W \in \gamma(S(A, \alpha\&\beta))$. Since $\delta \notin W$, we can conclude that $\delta \notin \bigcap\gamma(S(A, \alpha\&\beta))$, as desired. ■

Exercises

111. Let A be logically closed. Show that $S(A, \alpha)$ is empty if and only if $A\bot\alpha$ is empty.

112. Let A be logically closed, and let $\alpha \in A$ and $\beta \in A$. Show that if $S(A, \alpha) = S(A, \beta)$, then $A\bot\alpha = A\bot\beta$.

113. An operator $\div$ for a logically closed set A is an operator of *maxichoice Levi-contraction* if and only if it is a Levi-contraction operator based on a selection function γ

such that for all α, $\gamma(S(A,\alpha))$ has at most one element. Show that if $\div$ is an operator of maxichoice partial meet contraction for A, then it is a maxichoice Levi-contraction operator for A. (Hint: The foregoing exercise may be helpful.)

114. (David Makinson) Let A be a logically closed set and let $\alpha \in A$. Show that the following three conditions on the set Y are equivalent:

   (a) $Y \in S(A,\alpha)$,
   (b) $Y = \mathrm{Cn}(Y) \subseteq A$ and $Y \nvdash \alpha$ and it holds for all $Z \in A\bot\alpha$ that if $Y \subseteq Z$ then $Z \cap \mathrm{Cn}(\{\alpha\}) \subseteq Y$, and
   (c) $Y = \mathrm{Cn}(Y)$ and there is some Z such that $Z \cap \mathrm{Cn}(\{\alpha\}) \subseteq Y \subseteq Z \in A\bot\alpha$.

115. Let A be a logically closed set, and let $\div$ be the Levi-contraction based on a selection function γ such that $S(A,\alpha) \subseteq \gamma(S(A,\alpha))$ for all α (full meet Levi contraction). Let $\sim$ be full meet AGM contraction. Furthermore, let $\alpha \in A\backslash\mathrm{Cn}(\emptyset)$.

   (a) (David Makinson) Show that $A\div\alpha = (A\sim\alpha) \cap \mathrm{Cn}(\{\alpha\})$.
   (b) [60] Show that $A\div\alpha = \mathrm{Cn}(\emptyset)$.

22$^+$ KERNELS AND INCISIONS

In order to investigate the formal properties of kernel and safe contraction, we need some basic results on kernels and kernel sets. As was said in Section 2.8, the *kernel set* $A\perp\!\!\!\perp\alpha$ is the set such that $X \in A\perp\!\!\!\perp\alpha$ if and only if:

1. $X \subseteq A$
2. $X \vdash \alpha$
3. If $Y \subset X$, then $Y \nvdash \alpha$.

The elements of $A\perp\!\!\!\perp\alpha$ are the *α-kernels* of A.

Before proceeding, the reader is advised to rehearse the definitions of incision functions and kernel contractions. (See p. 89.)

It was shown in Observation 1.39 that $A\bot\alpha = A\bot\beta$ holds if and only if it holds for all subsets B of A that $B \vdash \alpha$ iff $B \vdash \beta$. A corresponding property can be shown to hold for kernel sets:

OBSERVATION 2.84 ([52]) *The following three conditions are equivalent:*

1. $A\bot\alpha = A\bot\beta$
2. $A\perp\!\!\!\perp\alpha = A\perp\!\!\!\perp\beta$
3. For all subsets B of A: $B \vdash \alpha$ iff $B \vdash \beta$.

Proof. It was shown in Observation 1.39 that (1) and (3) are equivalent. To complete the proof, it is sufficient to show that (2) implies (3) and that (3) implies (2).

(2) *implies* (3): Suppose that (3) does not hold. Without loss of generality, we may then assume that there is some subset B of A such that $B \vdash \alpha$ and $B \nvdash \beta$. By

compactness, there is some finite subset B' of A such that $B' \vdash \alpha$. There is then some element B'' of $A \perp\!\!\!\perp \alpha$ such that $B'' \subseteq B'$. Since $B'' \subseteq B$ and $B \not\vdash \beta$, we have $B'' \not\vdash \beta$, so that $B'' \notin A \perp\!\!\!\perp \beta$. It follows from $B'' \in A \perp\!\!\!\perp \alpha$ and $B'' \notin A \perp\!\!\!\perp \beta$ that (2) does not hold.

(3) *implies* (2): Suppose that (2) does not hold, i.e. that $A \perp\!\!\!\perp \alpha \neq A \perp\!\!\!\perp \beta$. Without loss of generality we may assume that there is some $X \in A \perp\!\!\!\perp \alpha$ such that $X \notin A \perp\!\!\!\perp \beta$. There are two cases:

First case, $X \not\vdash \beta$: Then we have $X \vdash \alpha$ and $X \not\vdash \beta$, showing that (3) is violated.

Second case, $X \vdash \beta$: Then it follows from $X \notin A \perp\!\!\!\perp \beta$ that there is some X' such that $X' \subset X$ and $X' \vdash \beta$. It follows from $X' \subset X \in A \perp\!\!\!\perp \alpha$ that $X' \not\vdash \alpha$. We than have $X' \vdash \beta$ and $X' \not\vdash \alpha$, which is sufficient to show that (3) does not hold. ∎

The *α-core* of A is the set of sentences in A that can be added to or subtracted from any subset of A without affecting whether or not it implies α. In Observation 2.10 it was shown that the α-core is equal to $\bigcap(A \perp \alpha)$, i.e. to the outcome of full meet contraction of A by α. It can also be defined in terms of kernels:

OBSERVATION 2.85 ([52]) $\bigcap(A \perp \alpha) = A \backslash (\bigcup(A \perp\!\!\!\perp \alpha)) = \{\beta \in A \mid \textit{For all } B \subseteq A : B \vdash \alpha \textit{ iff } B \cup \{\beta\} \vdash \alpha\}$.

Proof. We will use the abbreviation $c(A, \alpha)$ for $\{\beta \in A \mid \text{For all } B \subseteq A : B \vdash \alpha \text{ iff } B \cup \{\beta\} \vdash \alpha\}$ (the α-core of A). It was shown in Observation 2.10 that $\bigcap(A \perp \alpha) = c(A, \alpha)$. It remains to be proved that $A \backslash (\bigcup(A \perp\!\!\!\perp \alpha)) = c(A, \alpha)$.

$c(A, \alpha) \subseteq A \backslash (\bigcup(A \perp\!\!\!\perp \alpha))$: Let $\beta \notin A \backslash (\bigcup(A \perp\!\!\!\perp \alpha))$. If $\beta \notin A$, then $\beta \notin c(A, \alpha)$ follows from $c(A, \alpha) \subseteq A$. If $\beta \in A$, then $\beta \in \bigcup(A \perp\!\!\!\perp \alpha)$. Let B be a set such that $\beta \notin B$ and $B \cup \{\beta\} \in A \perp\!\!\!\perp \alpha$. Then $B \subseteq A$, $B \not\vdash \alpha$ and $B \cup \{\beta\} \vdash \alpha$, so that $\beta \notin c(A, \alpha)$.

$A \backslash (\bigcup(A \perp\!\!\!\perp \alpha)) \subseteq c(A, \alpha)$: Let $\beta \notin c(A, \alpha)$. If $\beta \notin A$, then $\beta \notin A \backslash (\bigcup(A \perp\!\!\!\perp \alpha))$ follows directly. If $\beta \in A$, then there is some B such that $B \subseteq A$, $B \not\vdash \alpha$ and $B \cup \{\beta\} \vdash \alpha$. By compactness, there is some finite subset B' of B such that $B' \cup \{\beta\} \vdash \alpha$. Since $B \not\vdash \alpha$ there is then some subset B'' of B' such that $B'' \cup \{\beta\} \in A \perp\!\!\!\perp \alpha$. It follows that $\beta \in \bigcup(A \perp\!\!\!\perp \alpha)$, and thus $\beta \notin A \backslash (\bigcup(A \perp\!\!\!\perp \alpha))$. ∎

Another useful connection between kernel sets and remainder sets is the following. (Note that for simplicity of exposition, we treat logically equivalent sentences as identical.)

OBSERVATION 2.86 ([52]) *$A \perp \alpha$ has exactly one element if and only if all elements of $A \perp\!\!\!\perp \alpha$ have exactly one element.*

Proof. For one direction, suppose that $A \perp \alpha$ has an element X with at least two non-identical elements, β_1 and β_2. Then $X \backslash \{\beta_1\} \not\vdash \alpha$ and $X \backslash \{\beta_2\} \not\vdash \alpha$. It follows by the upper bound property that there is a set Y_1 such that $X\backslash\{\beta_1\} \subseteq Y_1 \in A\bot\alpha$ and a set Y_2 such that $X\backslash\{\beta_2\} \subseteq Y_2 \in A\bot\alpha$. It follows that $\beta_1 \notin Y_1$. Since $\beta_1 \in Y_2, Y_1 \neq Y_2$, so that $A\bot\alpha$ has at least two elements.

For the other direction, suppose that $A\bot\alpha$ has at least two distinct elements. Let $Y_1 \neq Y_2$ and $\{Y_1, Y_2\} \subseteq A\bot\alpha$. It follows from $\{Y_1, Y_2\} \subseteq A\bot\alpha$ that $Y_1 \not\subseteq Y_2$. We can therefore conclude that $Y_2\backslash Y_1$ is non-empty. Let $\varepsilon \in Y_2\backslash Y_1$.

It follows from $\varepsilon \in Y_2$ that $\varepsilon \nvdash \alpha$ and from $\varepsilon \in A\backslash Y_1$ and $Y_1 \in A\bot\alpha$ that $Y_1 \cup \{\varepsilon\} \vdash \alpha$. It follows by compactness that there is some finite subset Y_1' of Y_1 such that $Y_1' \cup \{\varepsilon\} \vdash \alpha$. From this follows that there is some $Z \subseteq Y_1'$ such that $\varepsilon \notin Z$ and $Z \cup \{\varepsilon\} \in A\perp\!\!\!\perp\alpha$. Since $\varepsilon \nvdash \alpha$, Z is non-empty. It follows that not every element of $A\perp\!\!\!\perp\alpha$ has exactly one element. ■

Observation 2.86 connects kernel contraction to partial meet contraction in their extreme 'no-choice' cases. If $A\bot\alpha$ has only one element, $A\bot\alpha = \{B\}$, then $\gamma(A\bot\alpha) = \{B\}$ and consequently $A\sim_\gamma\alpha = B$ for all selection functions γ and partial meet contractions $\sim_\gamma$. Similarly, if every element of $A\perp\!\!\!\perp\alpha$ has exactly one element, then it follows from the definition of an incision function that $\sigma(A\perp\!\!\!\perp\alpha) = \bigcup(A\perp\!\!\!\perp\alpha)$ and consequently $A \approx_\sigma \alpha = A\backslash(\bigcup(A\perp\!\!\!\perp\alpha))$. These are the cases in which selection functions and incision functions have no real choice. The observation shows that the no-choice cases coincide for the two types of contractions.

Let us now go straight ahead and prove the general representation theorem for kernel contraction. The proof is quite similar to that of the corresponding representation theorem for partial meet contraction (Theorem 2.2, see Section 2.15$^+$). The major new feature is the construction used in the postulates-to-construction part: the very natural construction $\sigma(A\perp\!\!\!\perp\alpha) = A\backslash(A\div\alpha)$ turns out to work well in this proof (and in several proofs to follow).

The operator $\div$ for A is a kernel contraction if and only if it satisfies:

1. If $\nvdash \alpha$, then $A\div\alpha \nvdash \alpha$. (*success*)
2. $A\div\alpha \subseteq A$ (*inclusion*)
3. If $\beta \in A$ and $\beta \notin A\div\alpha$, then there is some subset B of A such that $B \nvdash \alpha$ and $B \cup \{\beta\} \vdash \alpha$. (*core-retainment*)
4. If it holds for all subsets B of A that $B \vdash \alpha$ if and only if $B \vdash \beta$, then $A\div\alpha = A\div\beta$. (*uniformity*)

[Theorem 2.32.]

Proof. *Construction-to-postulates*: Let $\approx_\sigma$ be a kernel contraction for A. We need to show that it satisfies the four conditions of the theorem.

For *success*, suppose to the contrary that $\nvdash \alpha$ and $A\approx_\sigma\alpha \vdash \alpha$. By compactness, there is a finite subset Z of $A \approx_\sigma \alpha$ such that $Z \vdash \alpha$. There is then an α-kernel Z' such that $Z' \subseteq Z$. Since $Z \subseteq A\approx_\sigma\alpha \subseteq A$, Z' is also an α-kernel of A. We then have $Z' \in A \perp\!\!\!\perp \alpha$ and $Z' \subseteq A \approx_\sigma \alpha$. However, it follows from $\nvdash \alpha$ that $Z' \neq \emptyset$. By clause (ii) of Definition 2.30, there is some $\varepsilon \in Z'$ such that $\varepsilon \in \sigma(A \perp\!\!\!\perp \alpha)$. It follows that $\varepsilon \notin A \backslash \sigma(A \perp\!\!\!\perp \alpha) = A \approx_\sigma \alpha$, contrary to $\varepsilon \in Z' \subseteq A \approx_\sigma \alpha$.

Inclusion follows directly from the definition of kernel contraction.

For *core-retainment*, suppose that $\beta \in A$ and $\beta \notin A \approx_\sigma \alpha$. Then $\beta \in \sigma(A \perp\!\!\!\perp \alpha)$. By Definition 2.30, $\sigma(A \perp\!\!\!\perp \alpha) \subseteq \bigcup(A \perp\!\!\!\perp \alpha)$, so that there is some set D such that $\beta \in D \in A \perp\!\!\!\perp \alpha$. Let $B = D \backslash \{\beta\}$. Then $B \nvdash \alpha$ and $B \cup \{\beta\} \vdash \alpha$, which shows that *core-retainment* is satisfied.

For *uniformity*, suppose that it holds for all subsets B of A that $B \vdash \alpha$ if and only if $B \vdash \beta$. By Observation 2.84, $A \perp\!\!\!\perp \alpha = A \perp\!\!\!\perp \beta$. It follows from this that $\sigma(A \perp\!\!\!\perp \alpha) = \sigma(A \perp\!\!\!\perp \beta)$, and by the definition of $\approx_\sigma$ that $A \approx_\sigma \alpha = A \approx_\sigma \beta$, so that *uniformity* is satisfied.

Postulates-to-construction: Let $\div$ and A be such that the four conditions of the theorem are satisfied. We are going to show that $\div$ is a kernel contraction. For that purpose, let σ be such that for all α:

$$\sigma(A \perp\!\!\!\perp \alpha) = A \backslash (A \div \alpha).$$

We need to verify that σ is an incision function for A. To be that, it must (1) be a function and (2) satisfy conditions (i) and (ii) of Definition 2.30. Furthermore, we need to verify (3) that $\approx_\sigma$, as applied to A, coincides with $\div$.

Proof that σ is a function: Let α and β be two sentences such that $A \perp\!\!\!\perp \alpha = A \perp\!\!\!\perp \beta$. We need to show that $\sigma(A \perp\!\!\!\perp \alpha) = \sigma(A \perp\!\!\!\perp \beta)$. It follows from $A \perp\!\!\!\perp \alpha = A \perp\!\!\!\perp \beta$, by Observation 2.84, that every subset of A implies α if and only if it implies β. Thus, by *uniformity*, $A \div \alpha = A \div \beta$. It follows from the definition of σ that $\sigma(A \perp\!\!\!\perp \alpha) = \sigma(A \perp\!\!\!\perp \beta)$.

Proof that (i) is satisfied: We are going to show that $\sigma(A \perp\!\!\!\perp \alpha) \subseteq \bigcup(A \perp\!\!\!\perp \alpha)$. Let $\beta \in \sigma(A \perp\!\!\!\perp \alpha)$. It follows by *core-retainment* that there is some $B \subseteq A$ such that $B \nvdash \alpha$ and $B \cup \{\beta\} \vdash \alpha$. By compactness, there is some finite subset B' of B such that $B' \cup \{\beta\} \vdash \alpha$. Since $B \nvdash \alpha$ we have $B' \nvdash \alpha$. It follows from $B' \nvdash \alpha$ and $B' \cup \{\beta\} \vdash \alpha$ that there is some α-kernel B'' that contains β. It follows from $\beta \in B'' \in A \perp\!\!\!\perp \alpha$ that $\beta \in \bigcup(A \perp\!\!\!\perp \alpha)$.

Proof that (ii) is satisfied: Suppose that $\emptyset \neq X \in A \perp\!\!\!\perp \alpha$. It follows from this that $\nvdash \alpha$. By *success*, $A \div \alpha \nvdash \alpha$. Since $X \vdash \alpha$ we may conclude that $X \nsubseteq A \div \alpha$, i.e. that there is some ε such that $\varepsilon \in X$ and $\varepsilon \notin A \div \alpha$. Since $X \subseteq A$ it follows that $\varepsilon \in A \backslash (A \div \alpha)$, i.e. $\varepsilon \in \sigma(A \perp\!\!\!\perp \alpha)$. Thus, $\varepsilon \in X \cap \sigma(A \perp\!\!\!\perp \alpha)$, which is sufficient to show that (ii) is satisfied.

Proof that $\approx_\sigma$ coincides with $\div$: It follows from *inclusion* ($A \div \alpha \subseteq A$) and our definition $\sigma(A \perp\!\!\!\perp \alpha) = A \backslash (A \div \alpha)$ that $A \div \alpha = A \backslash \sigma(A \perp\!\!\!\perp \alpha)$. This finishes the proof. ■

The foregoing proof can be used as a basis for the proof of the representation theorem for finitely global kernel contraction.

The finitely global operator $\div$ is an operator of finitely global kernel contraction if and only if it satisfies *success*, *inclusion*, *core-retainment*, *uniformity*, and:

If $(A\div\alpha)+\beta \neq (A+\beta)\div\alpha$, then there is some δ such that $A\div\delta \nvdash \alpha$ and $(A\div\delta)+\beta \vdash \alpha$. (*permutation*)

where $+$ denotes non-closing expansion. $(A+\beta = A \cup \{\beta\})$.

[Theorem 2.58.]

Proof. *Construction to postulates*: Let σ be a finitely global incision function. It follows from Theorem 2.32 that *success*, *inclusion*, *core-retainment*, and *uniformity* are satisfied. It remains to be shown that *permutation* holds.

If $\vdash \alpha$, then $A\approx_\sigma\alpha = A$ and $(A+\beta)\approx_\sigma\alpha = A+\beta$, from which permutation follows directly. For the principal case, when $\nvdash \alpha$, suppose that $(A\approx_\sigma\alpha)+\beta \neq (A+\beta)\approx_\sigma\alpha$. The cases when $\beta \in A$ and $\beta \notin A$ will be treated separately.

Case 1, $\beta \in A$: Since $A+\beta = A$ it follows from $(A\approx_\sigma\alpha)+\beta \neq (A+\beta) \approx_\sigma \alpha$ that $\beta \notin A \approx_\sigma \alpha$, thus $\beta \in \sigma(A\perp\!\!\!\perp\alpha)$. Let X be such that $\beta \notin X$ and $X \cup \{\beta\} \in A\perp\!\!\!\perp\alpha$. By the upper bound property there is some Y such that $X \subseteq Y \in A\perp\alpha$. Since A is finite, it follows from Observation 1.70 that there is some δ such that $\{Y\} = A\perp\delta$. According to Observation 2.86 every element of $A\perp\!\!\!\perp\delta$ is a singleton, so that $\sigma(A\perp\!\!\!\perp\delta) = \bigcup(A\perp\!\!\!\perp\delta)$ and $A\approx_\sigma\delta = A\setminus\bigcup(A\perp\!\!\!\perp\delta)$. According to Observation 2.85, $A\setminus\bigcup(A\perp\!\!\!\perp\delta) = \bigcap(A\perp\delta)$, so that $A \approx_\sigma \delta = Y$. We then have $A \approx_\sigma \delta \nvdash \alpha$ but, since $X \subseteq Y$, $(A\approx_\sigma\delta)+\beta \vdash \alpha$.

Case 2, $\beta \notin A$: We are first going to show that $A\perp\!\!\!\perp\alpha \neq (A\cup\{\beta\})\perp\!\!\!\perp\alpha$. Suppose to the contrary that $A\perp\!\!\!\perp\alpha = (A\cup\{\beta\})\perp\!\!\!\perp\alpha$. Then it holds for all $X \subseteq A$ that $X \vdash \alpha$ iff $X \cup \{\beta\} \vdash \alpha$. It follows that $(A\approx_\sigma\alpha)+\beta = (A\setminus\sigma(A\perp\!\!\!\perp\alpha)) \cup \{\beta\} = (A \cup \{\beta\})\setminus\sigma(A\perp\!\!\!\perp\alpha) = (A \cup \{\beta\})\setminus\sigma((A \cup \{\beta\})\perp\!\!\!\perp\alpha) = (A+\beta)\approx_\sigma\alpha$, contrary to our assumptions. We may conclude from this contradiction that $A\perp\!\!\!\perp\alpha \neq (A\cup\{\beta\})\perp\!\!\!\perp\alpha$.

It follows that there is some $X \subseteq A$ such that $X \nvdash \alpha$ and $X \cup \{\beta\} \vdash \alpha$. By the upper bound property, there is some Y such that $X \subseteq Y \in A\perp\alpha$. It follows in the same way as in case 1 that $Y = A\approx_\sigma\delta$ for some δ. We then have $A\approx_\sigma\delta \nvdash \alpha$ and $(A\approx_\sigma\delta)+\beta \vdash \alpha$, thus concluding this part of the proof.

Postulates-to-construction: Let $\div$ be a finitely global operation that satisfies *success*, *inclusion*, *core-retainment*, *uniformity*, and *permutation*. It follows from our proof of Theorem 2.32 that for every finite set A the incision function σ_A such that $\sigma_A(A\perp\!\!\!\perp\alpha) = A\setminus(A\div\alpha)$ for all α is an incision function, and $A\div\alpha = A\approx_{\sigma_A}\alpha$. It remains to be shown that these incisions functions all coincide, i.e. that if $A\perp\!\!\!\perp\alpha = B\perp\!\!\!\perp\beta$, then $\sigma_A(A\perp\!\!\!\perp\alpha) = \sigma_B(B\perp\!\!\!\perp\beta)$.

Let $A\perp\!\!\!\perp\alpha = B\perp\!\!\!\perp\beta$, and let $W = \bigcup(A\perp\!\!\!\perp\alpha) = \bigcup(B\perp\!\!\!\perp\beta)$. Then $W\perp\!\!\!\perp\alpha = A\perp\!\!\!\perp\alpha = B\perp\!\!\!\perp\beta = W\perp\!\!\!\perp\beta$. By the functionality of σ_W, that was shown in the proof of Theorem 2.32, we have $\sigma_W(W\perp\!\!\!\perp\alpha) = \sigma_W(W\perp\!\!\!\perp\beta)$. In order to show that $\sigma_A(A\perp\!\!\!\perp\alpha) = \sigma_B(B\perp\!\!\!\perp\beta)$ it is therefore sufficient to show that $\sigma_A(A\perp\!\!\!\perp\alpha) =$

$\sigma_W(W \perp\!\!\!\perp \alpha)$ and $\sigma_B(B \perp\!\!\!\perp \beta) = \sigma_W(W \perp\!\!\!\perp \beta)$. For symmetry reasons, we only have to prove the first of these identities.

By our definition, $\sigma_A(A \perp\!\!\!\perp \alpha) = A \backslash (A \div \alpha)$, and $\sigma_W(W \perp\!\!\!\perp \alpha) = W \backslash (W \div \alpha)$. What we need to show, therefore, is that $A \backslash (A \div \alpha) = W \backslash (W \div \alpha)$.

Since A is finite, there is a finite series of sets $W, Z_1, \ldots Z_n, A$ in which each set is obtained by addition of one element to its predecessor. We also have for each $Z_k : W \perp\!\!\!\perp \alpha = Z_k \perp\!\!\!\perp \alpha = A \perp\!\!\!\perp \alpha$. Therefore, it is sufficient to show that for all finite sets Y: if $Y \perp\!\!\!\perp \alpha = (Y \cup \{\varepsilon\}) \perp\!\!\!\perp \alpha$, then $Y \backslash (Y \div \alpha) = (Y \cup \{\varepsilon\}) \backslash ((Y \cup \{\varepsilon\}) \div \alpha)$.

In order to show this, let $Y \perp\!\!\!\perp \alpha = (Y \cup \{\varepsilon\}) \perp\!\!\!\perp \alpha$. Excluding a trivial case, we may assume that $\varepsilon \notin Y$. Suppose that for some δ, $Y \div \delta \nvdash \alpha$ and $(Y \div \delta) \cup \{\varepsilon\} \vdash \alpha$. By *inclusion*, there is then some X such that $Y \div \delta \subseteq X \in Y \perp \alpha$. Then $X \subseteq Y$, $X \nvdash \alpha$ and $X \cup \{\varepsilon\} \vdash \alpha$. By compactness, there is a finite subset X' of X such that $X' \nvdash \alpha$ and $X' \cup \{\varepsilon\} \vdash \alpha$. It follows that there is a subset X'' of X' such that $X'' \cup \{\varepsilon\} \in (Y \cup \{\varepsilon\}) \perp\!\!\!\perp \alpha$, contrary to our assumption that $Y \perp\!\!\!\perp \alpha = (Y \cup \{\varepsilon\}) \perp\!\!\!\perp \alpha$. We can conclude from this contradiction that there is no δ such that $Y \div \delta \nvdash \alpha$ and $(Y \div \delta) \cup \{\varepsilon\} \vdash \alpha$. By *permutation*, $(Y \div \alpha) + \varepsilon = (Y + \varepsilon) \div \alpha$. It follows that $(Y + \varepsilon) \backslash ((Y \div \alpha) + \varepsilon) = (Y + \varepsilon) \backslash ((Y + \varepsilon) \div \alpha)$. Since $(Y + \varepsilon) \backslash ((Y \div \alpha) + \varepsilon) = Y \backslash (Y \div \alpha)$ it follows that $Y \backslash (Y \div \alpha) = (Y \cup \{\varepsilon\}) \backslash ((Y \cup \{\varepsilon\}) \div \alpha)$, which completes the proof. ■

We have defined a kernel contraction for A to be *smooth* if it is based on an incision function σ such that for all subsets B of A: If $B \vdash \beta$ and $\beta \in \sigma(A \perp\!\!\!\perp \alpha)$, then $B \cap \sigma(A \perp\!\!\!\perp \alpha) \neq \emptyset$. The addition of this condition is exactly what is needed to ensure that $\approx_\sigma$ satisfies the postulate of relative closure, $A \cap \mathrm{Cn}(A \div \alpha) \subseteq A \div \alpha$.

> The operator $\div$ for a set A is a smooth kernel contraction if and only if it satisfies *success*, *inclusion*, *core-retainment*, *uniformity*, and *relative closure*.
> [Theorem 2.34.]

Proof. *Construction-to-postulates*: Let $\approx_\sigma$ be a smooth kernel contraction. It follows from Theorem 2.32 that *success*, *inclusion*, *core-retainment*, and *uniformity* are satisfied. To see that *relative closure* is satisfied, suppose that $\beta \notin A \approx_\sigma \alpha$. We need to show that $\beta \notin A \cap \mathrm{Cn}(A \approx_\sigma \alpha)$.

Case 1, $\beta \notin A$: Then $\beta \notin A \cap \mathrm{Cn}(A \approx_\sigma \alpha)$ follows directly.

Case 2, $\beta \in A$: It then follows from $\beta \notin A \approx_\sigma \alpha$ that $\beta \in \sigma(A \perp\!\!\!\perp \alpha)$. Suppose that $\beta \in \mathrm{Cn}(A \approx_\sigma \alpha)$, i.e. $A \backslash \sigma(A \perp\!\!\!\perp \alpha) \vdash \beta$. Letting $B = A \backslash \sigma(A \perp\!\!\!\perp \alpha)$, we then have $B \subseteq A$, $B \vdash \beta$, $\beta \in \sigma(A \perp\!\!\!\perp \alpha)$ and $B \cap \sigma(A \perp\!\!\!\perp \alpha) = \emptyset$, contrary to the smoothness of σ. It follows from this contradiction that $\beta \notin \mathrm{Cn}(A \approx_\sigma \alpha)$, so that $\beta \notin A \cap \mathrm{Cn}(A \approx_\sigma \alpha)$, as required.

Postulates-to-construction: Let $\div$ be an operator that satisfies the five postulates listed in the theorem. Let σ be such that for all α :

$$\sigma(A \perp\!\!\!\perp \alpha) = A \backslash (A \div \alpha).$$

This is the same construction that was used in the proof of Theorem 2.32. It follows in the same way that σ is an incision function for A and that $\approx_\sigma$, as applied to A, coincides with $\div$. It remains to be shown that σ is smooth.

For that purpose, let B be a subset of A such that $B \vdash \beta$ and $\beta \in \sigma(A \perp\!\!\!\perp \alpha)$. We need to show that $B \cap \sigma(A \perp\!\!\!\perp \alpha) \neq \emptyset$.

Suppose that $A \div \alpha \vdash \beta$. It can be concluded from $\beta \in \sigma(A \perp\!\!\!\perp \alpha)$ and $\sigma(A \perp\!\!\!\perp \alpha) = A \backslash (A \div \alpha)$ that $\beta \in A$. By *relative closure*, it follows from $A \div \alpha \vdash \beta$ and $\beta \in A$ that $\beta \in A \div \alpha$. This contradicts $\beta \in \sigma(A \perp\!\!\!\perp \alpha) = A \backslash (A \div \alpha)$, and we may conclude that $A \div \alpha \nvdash \beta$.

Since we have assumed that $B \vdash \beta$ we can conclude from $A \div \alpha \nvdash \beta$ that $B \nsubseteq A \div \alpha$. Thus, there is some sentence δ such that $\delta \in B$ and $\delta \notin A \div \alpha$. It follows that $\delta \in A \backslash (A \div \alpha)$, i.e. $\delta \in \sigma(A \perp\!\!\!\perp \alpha)$. We therefore have $\delta \in B \cap \sigma(A \perp\!\!\!\perp \alpha)$, so that $B \cap \sigma(A \perp\!\!\!\perp \alpha) \neq \emptyset$ as desired. ■

We have also introduced an alternative method to obtain relative closure, namely to perform contraction by any incision function, and afterwards 'saturate' the result by closing it relative to A. For every kernel contraction $\approx_\sigma$ there is a saturated kernel contraction $\hat{\approx}_\sigma$ such that for all α, $A \hat{\approx}_\sigma \alpha = A \cap \text{Cn}(A \approx_\sigma \alpha)$. It is easy to show that saturated kernel contraction satisfies relative closure:

$$\begin{aligned}
&A \cap \text{Cn}(A \hat{\approx}_\sigma \alpha) = A \cap \text{Cn}(A \cap \text{Cn}(A \approx_\sigma \alpha)) \\
&\subseteq A \cap \text{Cn}(\text{Cn}(A \approx_\sigma \alpha)) \\
&= A \cap \text{Cn}(A \approx_\sigma \alpha) \\
&= A \hat{\approx}_\sigma \alpha.
\end{aligned}$$

The two ways to obtain relative closure (smoothness and saturation) are equivalent in their effects on the resulting contraction. The proof of this is very similar in structure to proofs of representation theorems.

> An operator $\div$ for a set A is a saturated kernel contraction if and only if it is a smooth kernel contraction.
> [Theorem 2.36.]

Proof. *Smoothness-to-saturation*: Let $\approx_\sigma$ be a smooth kernel contraction. It follows from Theorem 2.34 that it satisfies *relative closure*, i.e. that for all α :

$$A \cap \text{Cn}(A \approx_\sigma \alpha) \subseteq A \approx_\sigma \alpha.$$

By the same theorem, $\approx_\sigma$ satisfies *inclusion*. We may conclude that $A \approx_\sigma \alpha = A \cap \text{Cn}(A \approx_\sigma \alpha)$, so that $\approx_\sigma$ is itself a saturated kernel contraction.

Saturation-to-smoothness: Let $\hat{\approx}_\sigma$ be a saturated kernel contraction. Let σ' be such that for all α :

$$\sigma'(A \perp\!\!\!\perp \alpha) = A \backslash (A \hat{\approx}_\sigma \alpha).$$

(Note that this is the same construction that we have used in the proofs of representation theorems.) We need to show that σ' is a smooth incision function, i.e. (1) that it is a function, (2) that it satisfies conditions (i)–(ii) of Definition 2.30, and (3) that it is smooth. Furthermore, we have to show (4) that $\approx_{\sigma'}$ and $\hat{\approx}_\sigma$ coincide, as applied to A.

Part 1: Let α and β be two sentences such that $A \perp\!\!\!\perp \alpha = A \perp\!\!\!\perp \beta$. We need to show that $\sigma'(A \perp\!\!\!\perp \alpha) = \sigma'(A \perp\!\!\!\perp \beta)$.

It follows from $A \perp\!\!\!\perp \alpha = A \perp\!\!\!\perp \beta$, by Observation 2.84, that any subset of A implies α if and only if it implies β. By Theorem 2.32, $\approx_\sigma$ satisfies uniformity, so that $A \approx_\sigma \alpha = A \approx_\sigma \beta$. It follows from the definition of $\hat{\approx}_\sigma$ that $A \hat{\approx}_\sigma \alpha = A \hat{\approx}_\sigma \beta$. Hence it follows from the definition of σ' that $\sigma'(A \perp\!\!\!\perp \alpha) = \sigma'(A \perp\!\!\!\perp \beta)$.

Part 2:i: In order to show that $\sigma'(A \perp\!\!\!\perp \alpha) \subseteq \bigcup(A \perp\!\!\!\perp \alpha)$, let $\beta \notin \bigcup(A \perp\!\!\!\perp \alpha)$. We need to show that $\beta \notin \sigma'(A \perp\!\!\!\perp \alpha)$. Since $\sigma'(A \perp\!\!\!\perp \alpha)$ is by definition a subset of A, this holds trivially if $\beta \notin A$.

In the remaining case, $\beta \in A \backslash \bigcup(A \perp\!\!\!\perp \alpha)$. Since σ is an incision function, we have $\sigma(A \perp\!\!\!\perp \alpha) \subseteq \bigcup(A \perp\!\!\!\perp \alpha)$ and consequently $A \backslash \bigcup(A \perp\!\!\!\perp \alpha) \subseteq A \backslash \sigma(A \perp\!\!\!\perp \alpha)$, so that $\beta \in A \backslash \sigma(A \perp\!\!\!\perp \alpha)$. It follows that $\beta \in A \cap \mathrm{Cn}(A \backslash \sigma(A \perp\!\!\!\perp \alpha))$, i.e. $\beta \in A \hat{\approx}_\sigma \alpha$. Since $\sigma'(A \perp\!\!\!\perp \alpha) = A \backslash (A \hat{\approx}_\sigma \alpha)$, we may conclude that $\beta \notin \sigma'(A \perp\!\!\!\perp \alpha)$.

Part 2:ii: Suppose that $\emptyset \neq X \in A \perp\!\!\!\perp \alpha$. We need to show that $X \cap \sigma'(A \perp\!\!\!\perp \alpha) \neq \emptyset$.

We are first going to show that $X \not\subseteq A \hat{\approx}_\sigma \alpha$. Suppose to the contrary that $X \subseteq A \hat{\approx}_\sigma \alpha$. Then $A \hat{\approx}_\sigma \alpha \vdash \alpha$, from which it follows by Definition 2.35 that $A \approx_\sigma \alpha \vdash \alpha$. Since it follows from $\emptyset \neq X \in A \perp\!\!\!\perp \alpha$ that $\not\vdash \alpha$, $A \approx_\sigma \alpha \vdash \alpha$ contradicts the success postulate for kernel contraction that was shown to hold in Theorem 2.32. We may conclude from this contradiction that $X \not\subseteq A \hat{\approx}_\sigma \alpha$. It follows from $X \in A \perp\!\!\!\perp \alpha$ that $X \subseteq A$. From $X \subseteq A$ and $X \not\subseteq A \hat{\approx}_\sigma \alpha$ we obtain $X \cap (A \backslash (A \hat{\approx}_\sigma \alpha)) \neq \emptyset$, i.e. $X \cap \sigma'(A \perp\!\!\!\perp \alpha) \neq \emptyset$, as desired.

Part 3: Let B be a subset of A such that $B \vdash \beta$ and $\beta \in \sigma'(A \perp\!\!\!\perp \alpha)$. It follows by the definition of σ' from $\beta \in \sigma'(A \perp\!\!\!\perp \alpha)$ that $\beta \in A$ and that $\beta \notin A \hat{\approx}_\sigma \alpha = A \cap \mathrm{Cn}(A \backslash \sigma(A \perp\!\!\!\perp \alpha))$, thus $\beta \notin \mathrm{Cn}(A \backslash \sigma(A \perp\!\!\!\perp \alpha))$. Since $B \vdash \beta$, it follows that $B \not\subseteq \mathrm{Cn}(A \backslash \sigma(A \perp\!\!\!\perp \alpha))$. There is then some $\delta \in B$ such that $\delta \notin \mathrm{Cn}(A \backslash \sigma(A \perp\!\!\!\perp \alpha))$. It follows from the definition of $\hat{\approx}_\sigma$ that $\delta \notin A \hat{\approx}_\sigma \alpha$ and from the definition of σ' that $\delta \in \sigma'(A \perp\!\!\!\perp \alpha)$, so that $B \cap \sigma'(A \perp\!\!\!\perp \alpha) \neq \emptyset$ as desired.

Part 4: It follows from the definition of $\hat{\approx}_\sigma$ that $A \hat{\approx}_\sigma \alpha \subseteq A$. From this it follows that $A \hat{\approx}_\sigma \alpha = A \backslash (A \backslash (A \hat{\approx}_\sigma \alpha)) = A \backslash \sigma'(A \perp\!\!\!\perp \alpha) = A \approx_{\sigma'} \alpha$. ■

For logically closed sets, smooth kernel contraction coincides with partial meet contraction.

> Let A be a logically closed set. Then $\div$ is a smooth kernel contraction for A if and only if it is a partial meet contraction for A.
> [Theorem 2.37.]

Proof. *Kernel-to-partial-meet*: Let $\div$ be a smooth kernel contraction. According to Theorem 2.34 it satisfies *inclusion* and *success*. It follows from Theorem 2.34 and Observation 2.3 that it satisfies *vacuity*, *closure*, and *extensionality*. It follows from Theorem 2.34 and Observation 2.9 that is satisfies *recovery*. We can use Theorem 2.7 to conclude that $\div$ is a partial meet contraction.

Partial-meet-to-kernel: Let $\div$ be a partial meet contraction. According to Theorem 2.2, it satisfies *success*, *inclusion*, and *uniformity*. According to Theorem 2.2 and Observation 2.3, it satisfies *relative closure* and *core-retainment*. We can use Theorem 2.34 to conclude that $\div$ is a smooth kernel contracion. ■

Exercises

116. Let p and q be logically independent sentences, and let $A = \{p, q, p \vee q\}$. Identify the following kernel sets:
    (a) $A \perp\!\!\!\perp p$
    (b) $A \perp\!\!\!\perp (p \vee q)$
    (c) $A \perp\!\!\!\perp (p \& q)$
    (d) $A \perp\!\!\!\perp (p \rightarrow q)$
    (e) $A \perp\!\!\!\perp (p \vee \neg p)$
    (f) $A \perp\!\!\!\perp (p \& \neg p)$

117. Let p and q be logically independent sentences, and let $A = \{p, q\}$. Identify the following kernel sets:
    (a) $(\mathrm{Cn}(A)) \perp\!\!\!\perp p$
    (b) $(\mathrm{Cn}(A)) \perp\!\!\!\perp (p \vee q)$
    (c) $(\mathrm{Cn}(A)) \perp\!\!\!\perp (p \vee \neg p)$
    (d) $(\mathrm{Cn}(A)) \perp\!\!\!\perp (p \& \neg p)$

118. Prove the following properties of kernel sets: ($\wp(B)$, the *power set* of B, is the set of subsets of B, i.e. $X \in \wp(B)$ iff $X \subseteq B$.)
    (a) If $A \subseteq B$, then $A \perp\!\!\!\perp \alpha \subseteq B \perp\!\!\!\perp \alpha$
    (b) $(B \perp\!\!\!\perp \alpha) \cap \wp(A) \subseteq A \perp\!\!\!\perp \alpha$
    (c) If $A \subseteq B$, then $A \perp\!\!\!\perp \alpha = (B \perp\!\!\!\perp \alpha) \cap \wp(A)$
    (d) $X \in A \perp\!\!\!\perp \alpha$ if and only if $X \subseteq A$ and $X \in X \perp\!\!\!\perp \alpha$.
    (e) If $\delta \in X \in A \perp\!\!\!\perp \alpha$, then $X \setminus \{\delta\} \nvdash \delta$.
    (f) $(A \perp\!\!\!\perp \alpha) \cap (A \perp\!\!\!\perp \beta) \subseteq A \perp\!\!\!\perp (\alpha \& \beta)$
    (g) If $X \subseteq Y$, $X \in A \perp\!\!\!\perp \alpha$, and $Y \in A \perp\!\!\!\perp \beta$, then $Y \in A \perp\!\!\!\perp (\alpha \& \beta)$

119. Let $Y \in A \perp\!\!\!\perp (\delta \vee \alpha)$ and $Z = \{\delta \vee \psi \mid \psi \in Y\}$. Show that $Z \in A \perp\!\!\!\perp (\delta \vee \alpha)$.

120. Let σ be an incision function for A. Show that $\approx_\sigma$ is a maxichoice contraction if and only if σ satisfies the following condition:
    If $\beta \in \sigma(A \perp\!\!\!\perp \alpha)$, then there is some $X \in A \perp\!\!\!\perp \alpha$ such that $X \cap \sigma(A \perp\!\!\!\perp \alpha) = \{\beta\}$. (*unicity*)

121. [52] Let A be a finite set of sentences and $\approx_\sigma$ an operator of kernel contraction for A. Show that the following two properties hold:

    (a) If $A\approx_\sigma\delta \vdash \alpha$ iff $A\approx_\sigma\delta \vdash \beta$ for all δ, then $A\approx_\sigma\alpha = A\approx_\sigma\beta$. (*symmetry*)

    (b) If $A\approx_\sigma\beta \not\subseteq A\approx_\sigma\alpha$, then there is some sentence δ such that $A\approx_\sigma\delta \nvdash \alpha$ and $(A\approx_\sigma\beta) \cup (A\approx_\sigma\delta) \vdash \alpha$. (*weak conservativity*)

23+ PROPERTIES OF SAFE CONTRACTION

The purpose of this section is to prove the properties of safe contraction that were introduced in Section 2.9. To begin with, the following are properties of a relation $\prec$ that we will have use for in this section:

1. It is *not* the case that $\alpha_1 \prec \alpha_2 \prec \ldots \prec \alpha_n \prec \alpha_1$. (*acyclicity*)
2. If $\alpha\leftrightarrow\alpha' \in \mathrm{Cn}(\emptyset)$ and $\beta\leftrightarrow\beta' \in \mathrm{Cn}(\emptyset)$, then $\alpha \prec \beta$ holds if and only if $\alpha' \prec \beta'$. (*intersubstitutivity*)
3. If $\alpha \prec \beta$ and $\beta \vdash \delta$, then $\alpha \prec \delta$. (*continuing-up*)
4. If $\alpha \vdash \beta$ and $\beta \prec \delta$, then $\alpha \prec \delta$. (*continuing-down*)
5. If $\alpha \prec \beta$ then either $\alpha \prec \delta$ or $\delta \prec \beta$. (*virtual connectivity*)

If $\prec$ satisfies (1)–(2), then it is a *hierarchy*. If it satisfies (1)–(4), then it is a *regular hierarchy*.

In the presence of (1) and (5), (3) and (4) are equivalent:

> If a relation satisfies acyclicity and virtual connectivity, then it satisfies continuing-up if and only if it satisfies continuing-down.
> [Observation 2.46.]

Proof. For one direction, let $\prec$ be a relation that satisfies acyclicity, virtual connectivity, and continuing-up. Let α, β, and δ be sentences such that $\alpha \vdash \beta$ and $\beta \prec \delta$. It follows by virtual connectivity from $\beta \prec \delta$ that either $\beta \prec \alpha$ or $\alpha \prec \delta$. In the former case, we have $\beta \prec \alpha$ and $\alpha \vdash \beta$, and continuing-up yields $\beta \prec \beta$, which violates acyclicity. We can conclude from this that $\alpha \prec \delta$, and consequently that continuing-down is satisfied.

For the other direction, let $\prec$ be a relation that satisfies acyclicity, virtual connectivity, and continuing-down. Let α, β, and δ be sentences such that $\alpha \prec \beta$ and $\beta \vdash \delta$. It follows by virtual connectivity from $\alpha \prec \beta$ that either $\alpha \prec \delta$ or $\delta \prec \beta$. In the latter case, we have $\beta \vdash \delta$ and $\delta \prec \beta$, and continuing-down yields $\beta \prec \beta$, which violates acyclicity. We can conclude from this that $\alpha \prec \delta$, and consequently that continuing-up is satisfied. ■

In many proofs for safe contraction we can make use of the results already obtained for the more general category of kernel contractions. The following observation provides us with the essential reason why safe contraction is indeed a variant of kernel contraction.

Let $\prec$ be a relation on A that satisfies *acyclicity*. Then the function s that is based on $\prec$ in the manner of Definition 2.40 is a kernel selection function.
[Observation 2.42.]

Proof. Let s be the function such that for all $X \in A\perp\!\!\!\perp\alpha, \beta \in s(X)$ if and only if $\beta \in X$ and there is no $\delta \in X$ such that $\delta \prec \beta$. It follows directly that $s(X) \subseteq X$. In order to verify that s is a kernel selection function it remains to be shown that if $X \neq \emptyset$, then $s(X) \neq \emptyset$. Let $\emptyset \neq X \in A\perp\!\!\!\perp\alpha$. It follows from compactness that X is finite.

Suppose that $s(X)$ is empty. Then for every element β of X, there is some element β' such that $\beta' \prec \beta$. We can therefore define a function f such that for all elements β of X, $f(\beta)$ is an element of X such that $f(\beta) \prec \beta$.

Let β be any element of X. By repeated application of f we obtain the chain:

$$\ldots f(f(f(f(\beta)))) \prec f(f(f(\beta))) \prec f(f(\beta)) \prec f(\beta) \prec \beta.$$

This chain can be continued indefinitely to the left. Since all its elements are included in the finite set X, it must contain a cycle, so that $\prec$ is not acyclic, contrary to the conditions. This contradiction concludes the proof. ■

The following is a useful property of incision functions that are generated from hierarchies.

OBSERVATION 2.87 (Alchourrón and Makinson [4]) *Let σ be the incision function that is based on a hierarchy $\prec$ over a set A. Then it holds for all sentences α and β that:*
$\sigma(A\perp\!\!\!\perp(\alpha\&\beta)) \subseteq \sigma(A\perp\!\!\!\perp\alpha) \cup \sigma(A\perp\!\!\!\perp\beta)$.

Proof. Let s be the kernel selection function that is based on $\prec$, and let σ be the cumulation of s. Furthermore, let $\delta \in \sigma(A\perp\!\!\!\perp(\alpha\&\beta))$. Then there is some $X \in A\perp\!\!\!\perp(\alpha\&\beta)$ such that $\delta \in s(X)$.

It follows from $\delta \in X \in A\perp\!\!\!\perp(\alpha\&\beta)$ that either $X\backslash\{\delta\} \nvdash \alpha$ or $X\backslash\{\delta\} \nvdash \beta$.

Case 1, $X\backslash\{\delta\} \nvdash \alpha$: Since $X\backslash\{\delta\} \vdash \delta\rightarrow\alpha$, there is a finite subset X' of $X\backslash\{\delta\}$ such that $X' \in A\perp\!\!\!\perp(\delta\rightarrow\alpha)$. Then $X' \cup \{\delta\} \in A\perp\!\!\!\perp\alpha$.

Since s is based on $\prec$, and $\delta \in s(X)$, there is no $\varepsilon \in X$ such that $\varepsilon \prec \delta$. Since $X' \cup \{\delta\} \subseteq X$, there is no $\varepsilon \in X' \cup \{\delta\}$ such that $\varepsilon \prec \delta$. Thus $\delta \in s(X' \cup \{\delta\}) \subseteq \sigma(A\perp\!\!\!\perp\alpha)$.

Case 2, $X\backslash\{\delta\} \nvdash \beta$: Then $\delta \in \sigma(A\perp\!\!\!\perp\beta)$ follows in the same way. ■

In order to establish the additional properties that follow from the continuing-up postulate we will have use for the following technical observation:

OBSERVATION 2.88 (Alchourrón and Makinson [4]) *Let σ be the incision function that is based on a hierarchy $\prec$ over a set A. If $\prec$ satisfies continuing-up, then for all $\alpha, \beta, \delta \in A$:*
If $\beta \vdash \delta$ and $\delta \in \sigma(A \perp\!\!\!\perp \alpha)$, then $\beta \in \sigma(A \perp\!\!\!\perp \alpha)$.

Proof. Case 1, $\delta \in \mathrm{Cn}(\emptyset)$: Then $\delta \notin X$ for all $X \in A \perp\!\!\!\perp \alpha$, and thus $\delta \notin \sigma(A \perp\!\!\!\perp \alpha)$, so that the condition given in the observation is vacuously true.

Case 2, $\delta \notin \mathrm{Cn}(\emptyset)$: Let $\beta \vdash \delta$ and $\delta \in \sigma(A \perp\!\!\!\perp \alpha)$. Then there is some $X \in A \perp\!\!\!\perp \alpha$ such that $\delta \in s(X)$. Since s is based on $\prec$, there is no $\varepsilon \in X$ such that $\varepsilon \prec \delta$.

Let $X' = X \backslash \{\delta\}$. Then $X' \nvdash \alpha$ and $X' \cup \{\beta\} \vdash \alpha$. It follows that there is some $X'' \subseteq X'$ such that $X'' \cup \{\beta\} \in A \perp\!\!\!\perp \alpha$.

We are now going to show that if $\varepsilon \in X'' \cup \{\beta\}$, then $\varepsilon \prec \beta$ does not hold. If $\varepsilon \in \{\beta\}$, i.e. $\varepsilon = \beta$, then this follows from the acyclicity of $\prec$. In the remaining case, when $\varepsilon \in X''$, suppose to the contrary that $\varepsilon \prec \beta$. It follows from the continuing-up condition, since $\beta \vdash \delta$, that $\varepsilon \prec \delta$, contrary to the conditions. We can conclude from this contradiction that $\varepsilon \prec \beta$ does not hold for any $\varepsilon \in X'' \cup \{\beta\}$. Thus, $\beta \in s(X'' \cup \{\beta\}) \subseteq \sigma(A \perp\!\!\!\perp \alpha)$. ■

Armed with Observations 2.87 and 2.88, we can now prove that the continuing-up property induces the postulate of conjunctive overlap on disjunctively closed sets:

> Let $\prec$ be a hierarchy over the disjunctively closed set A, and let $\div$ be the safe contraction that is based on $\prec$. If $\prec$ satisfies *continuing-up*, then $\div$ satisfies *conjunctive overlap*.
> [Observation 2.45, Part 1, strengthened.]

Proof. Let $\delta \in (A \div \alpha) \cap (A \div \beta)$, i.e. $\delta \in \mathrm{Cn}(A \backslash \sigma(A \perp\!\!\!\perp \alpha)) \cap \mathrm{Cn}(A \backslash \sigma(A \perp\!\!\!\perp \beta))$. It follows by compactness that there is a finite subset S_1 of $A \backslash \sigma(A \perp\!\!\!\perp \alpha)$ and a finite subset S_2 of $A \backslash \sigma(A \perp\!\!\!\perp \beta)$ such that $S_1 \vdash \delta$ and $S_2 \vdash \delta$. Let S be the set of disjunctions of one element each from S_1 and S_2, i.e. $S = \{\kappa \vee \lambda \mid (\kappa \in S_1) \& (\lambda \in S_2)\}$. It follows by truth-functional logic that $S \vdash \delta$.

Let $\kappa \in S_1$ and $\lambda \in S_2$. Suppose that $\kappa \vee \lambda \in \sigma(A \perp\!\!\!\perp \alpha)$. Since $\prec$ satisfies *continuing-up*, it then follows by Observation 2.88 from $\kappa \vdash \kappa \vee \lambda$ and $\kappa \vee \lambda \in \sigma(A \perp\!\!\!\perp \alpha)$ that $\kappa \in \sigma(A \perp\!\!\!\perp \alpha)$, contrary to $\kappa \in S_1 \subseteq A \backslash \sigma(A \perp\!\!\!\perp \alpha)$. We can conclude from this contradiction that $\kappa \vee \lambda \notin \sigma(A \perp\!\!\!\perp \alpha)$. Since A is closed under disjunction, $\kappa \vee \lambda \in A$, and thus $\kappa \vee \lambda \in A \backslash \sigma(A \perp\!\!\!\perp \alpha)$. This holds for all elements $\kappa \vee \lambda$ of S, and we can conclude that $S \subseteq A \backslash \sigma(A \perp\!\!\!\perp \alpha)$.

It can be proved in the same way that $S \subseteq A \backslash \sigma(A \perp\!\!\!\perp \beta)$. We can conclude from this that $S \subseteq (A \backslash \sigma(A \perp\!\!\!\perp \alpha)) \cap (A \backslash \sigma(A \perp\!\!\!\perp \beta))$. It follows by set theory from Observation 2.87 that $(A \backslash \sigma(A \perp\!\!\!\perp \alpha)) \cap (A \backslash \sigma(A \perp\!\!\!\perp \beta)) \subseteq A \backslash \sigma(A \perp\!\!\!\perp (\alpha \& \beta))$ and thus $S \subseteq A \backslash \sigma(A \perp\!\!\!\perp (\alpha \& \beta))$. Since $S \vdash \delta$, we can conclude that $\delta \in \mathrm{Cn}(A \backslash \sigma(A \perp\!\!\!\perp (\alpha \& \beta)))$, i.e. $\delta \in A \div (\alpha \& \beta)$, as desired. ■

Although the *continuing-down* condition is similar to the condition of continuing-up, they seem to require quite different proof methods. For our treatment of the *continuing-down* condition, we will have use for the following notation:

DEFINITION 2.89 $A \Vdash\!\!\alpha = \{X \subseteq A \mid X \vdash \alpha\}$. $A \Vdash\!\!\alpha$ *is called an* implicator set, *and its elements are the* α-implicators *of* A.

It should be obvious that $A \perp\!\!\!\perp \alpha \subseteq A \Vdash\!\!\alpha$. Furthermore, if s is the kernel selection function that is based on a hierarchy $\prec$ for A, and σ the corresponding incision function, then:

$$\sigma(A \perp\!\!\!\perp \alpha) = \bigcup\{s(X) \mid X \in A \perp\!\!\!\perp \alpha\} \subseteq \bigcup\{s(X) \mid X \in A \Vdash\!\!\alpha\}.$$

To simplify the notation, we can write $\sigma(A \Vdash\!\!\alpha)$ for $\bigcup\{s(X) \mid X \in A \Vdash\!\!\alpha\}$, and we then have $\sigma(A \perp\!\!\!\perp \alpha) \subseteq \sigma(A \Vdash\!\!\alpha)$. (The formal definitions of s and σ will have to be modified, but the modifications are obvious.) The converse of $\sigma(A \perp\!\!\!\perp \alpha) \subseteq \sigma(A \Vdash\!\!\alpha)$ does not hold, i.e. $\sigma(A \Vdash\!\!\alpha)$ is not in general a subset of $\sigma(A \perp\!\!\!\perp \alpha)$. However, we can come fairly close to the converse inclusion if continuing-down is satisfied:

OBSERVATION 2.90 (Alchourrón and Makinson [4]) *Let* $\prec$ *be a hierarchy for the logically closed set A, and let it satisfy* continuing-down. *Furthermore, let* σ *be the cumulation of the kernel selection function s that is based on* $\prec$. *Then:*
If $\delta \in \sigma(A \Vdash\!\!\alpha)$ *and* $\delta \notin \mathrm{Cn}(\{\neg\alpha\})$, *then* $\delta \in \sigma(A \perp\!\!\!\perp \alpha)$.

Proof. Suppose that $\delta \in \sigma(A \Vdash\!\!\alpha)$ and $\delta \notin \mathrm{Cn}(\{\neg\alpha\})$. There is then some X such that $X \in A \Vdash\!\!\alpha$ and $\delta \in s(X)$. We are going to construct an element of $A \perp\!\!\!\perp \alpha$, from which s selects δ, so that $\delta \in \sigma(A \perp\!\!\!\perp \alpha)$.

The construction: Since $\delta \in X$ and $X \vdash \alpha$, we have $X \backslash \{\delta\} \vdash \delta \rightarrow \alpha$. Let $Y \in (X \backslash \{\delta\}) \perp\!\!\!\perp (\delta \rightarrow \alpha)$, i.e. let Y be a minimal subset of $X \backslash \{\delta\}$ that implies $\delta \rightarrow \alpha$. It follows from compactness that Y is finite. Let $Z = \{\delta \rightarrow \psi \mid \psi \in Y\}$. We are going to show that $Z \cup \{\delta\} \in A \perp\!\!\!\perp \alpha$ and $\delta \in s(Z \cup \{\delta\}) \subseteq \sigma(A \perp\!\!\!\perp \alpha)$. Before doing that, we need to prove two properties of Z.

Properties of Z: We are going to show (1) that $Z \in A \perp\!\!\!\perp (\delta \rightarrow \alpha)$ and (2) that $Z \nvdash \alpha$.

(1) In order to show that $Z \in A \perp\!\!\!\perp (\delta \rightarrow \alpha)$, we are first going to show that $Z \vdash \delta \rightarrow \alpha$. Let $Y = \{\psi_1, \dots \psi_n\}$. Then $Z = \{\delta \rightarrow \psi_1, \dots \delta \rightarrow \psi_n\}$, and thus $Z \vdash \delta \rightarrow (\psi_1 \& \dots \& \psi_n)$. It follows by sentential logic from this and $(\psi_1 \& \dots \& \psi_n) \vdash \delta \rightarrow \alpha$ that $Z \vdash \delta \rightarrow \alpha$.

Next, suppose that $Z \notin A \perp\!\!\!\perp (\delta \rightarrow \alpha)$. Then there is some proper subset Z' of Z such that $Z' \vdash \delta \rightarrow \alpha$. It follows from the construction of Z that there is some proper subset Y' of Y such that $Z' = \{\delta \rightarrow \psi \mid \psi \in Y'\}$. Since Z' is logically equivalent with $\delta \rightarrow \& Y'$, we then have $(\delta \rightarrow \& Y') \vdash \delta \rightarrow \alpha$. From this it follows truth-functionally that $\&Y' \vdash \delta \rightarrow \alpha$, so that $Y' \vdash \delta \rightarrow \alpha$, contrary to $Y' \subset Y$ and $Y \in A \perp (\delta \rightarrow \alpha)$. We can conclude from this contradiction that $Z \in A \perp (\delta \rightarrow \alpha)$.

(2) Next, we are going to show that $Z \nvdash \alpha$. Suppose to the contrary that $Z \vdash \alpha$. Since Z is equivalent with $\delta \rightarrow \&Y'$, we then have $\delta \rightarrow \&Y' \vdash \alpha$, and consequently $\vdash (\delta \rightarrow \&Y') \rightarrow \alpha$, from which follows truth-functionally that $\vdash \neg\alpha \rightarrow \delta$, contrary to our condition $\delta \notin \text{Cn}(\{\neg\alpha\})$. We may conclude that $Z \nvdash \alpha$.

Verification of the construction: We are going to show that $\delta \in \sigma(A \perp \alpha)$. Since σ is the cumulation of s, this can be done by showing (1) that $Z \cup \{\delta\} \in A \perp \alpha$ and (2) that $\delta \in s(Z \cup \{\delta\})$.

(1) It follows from $Z \in A \perp (\delta \rightarrow \alpha)$ that $Z \cup \{\delta\} \vdash \alpha$. In order to show that $Z \cup \{\delta\} \in A \perp \alpha$, suppose to the contrary that there is some proper subset of $Z \cup \{\delta\}$ that implies α. Since $Z \nvdash \alpha$, there must then be some proper subset Z' of Z such that $Z' \cup \{\delta\} \vdash \alpha$. Then $Z' \vdash \delta \rightarrow \alpha$, but this cannot hold since $Z' \subset Z$ and $Z \in A \perp (\delta \rightarrow \alpha)$. We can conclude from this contradiction that $Z \cup \{\delta\} \in A \perp \alpha$.

(2) It remains to be shown that that $\delta \in s(Z \cup \{\delta\})$. Let $\varepsilon \in Z \cup \{\delta\}$. If $\varepsilon \in \{\delta\}$, i.e. $\varepsilon = \delta$, then it follows from the acyclicity of $\prec$ that $\varepsilon \prec \delta$ does not hold. If $\varepsilon \in Z$ then $\varepsilon = \delta \rightarrow \psi$ and consequently $\psi \vdash \varepsilon$ for some $\psi \in Y \subseteq X$. Suppose that $\varepsilon \prec \delta$. Then it follows from the continuing-down property that $\psi \prec \delta$, contrary to $\delta \in s(X)$. We can conclude from this contradiction that $\varepsilon \prec \delta$ does not hold for any element ε of $Z \cup \{\delta\}$, and consequently $\delta \in s(Z \cup \{\delta\})$. ■

Observation 2.90 can be used to prove that the continuing-down property guarantees that *conjunctive overlap* is satisfied. Note that although the continuing-up and continuing-down properties both have this effect (on logically closed sets), the proofs are based on different principles.

> Let $\prec$ be a hierarchy over the logically closed set A, and let $\div$ be the safe contraction that is based on $\prec$. If $\prec$ satisfies *continuing-down*, then $\div$ satisfies *conjunctive overlap*.
> [Observation 2.45, Part 2.]

Proof. *First step*: We are first going to show that if $\delta \in A \backslash \sigma(A \perp \alpha)$, then $\delta \in \text{Cn}(\{\neg\alpha\}) \cup (A \backslash \sigma(A \perp (\alpha \& \beta)))$.

Let $\delta \in A \backslash \sigma(A \perp \alpha)$ and $\delta \notin \text{Cn}(\{\neg\alpha\})$. We can use Observation 2.90 to conclude that $\delta \in A \backslash \sigma(A \Perp \alpha)$.

Since every element of $A \perp (\alpha \& \beta)$ implies α we have $A \perp (\alpha \& \beta) \subseteq A \Perp \alpha$. Since σ is cumulative, it follows from this that $\sigma(A \perp (\alpha \& \beta)) \subseteq \sigma(A \Perp \alpha)$ and consequently $A \backslash \sigma(A \Perp \alpha) \subseteq A \backslash \sigma(A \perp (\alpha \& \beta))$. Thus, $\delta \in A \backslash \sigma(A \perp (\alpha \& \beta))$.

Second step: Let $\delta \in (A \div \alpha) \cap (A \div \beta)$.

It follows from $\delta \in (A \div \alpha)$, i.e. $\delta \in \text{Cn}(A \backslash \sigma(A \perp \alpha))$, by the first step of this proof that $\delta \in \text{Cn}(\text{Cn}(\{\neg\alpha\}) \cup A \backslash \sigma(A \perp (\alpha \& \beta)))$, or equivalently, $\alpha \vee \delta \in \text{Cn}(A \backslash \sigma(A \perp (\alpha \& \beta)))$, i.e. $\alpha \vee \delta \in A \div (\alpha \& \beta)$. In the same way it follows from

$\delta \in (A{\div}\beta)$ that $\beta \vee \delta \in A{\div}(\alpha\&\beta)$. Since $\div$ is a partial meet contraction (Theorem 2.37), it satisfies *recovery*, and we therefore also have $\alpha\&\beta \rightarrow \delta \in A{\div}(\alpha\&\beta)$. Since $\alpha \vee \delta$, $\beta \vee \delta$, and $\alpha\&\beta \rightarrow \delta$ together imply δ, we can finally conclude that $\delta \in A{\div}(\alpha\&\beta)$. ■

Observation 2.90 is again put to use in the following proof that regular and virtually connected hierarchies give rise to safe contractions that satisfy *conjunctive inclusion*.

OBSERVATION 2.91 (Alchourrón and Makinson [4]) *Let A be a logically closed set and $\div$ a safe contraction on A that is based on a regular and virtually connected hierarchy $\prec$. Then $\div$ satisfies conjunctive inclusion.*

Proof. Let $\alpha \notin \mathrm{Cn}(A{\div}(\alpha\&\beta))$. We are going to show that $A{\div}(\alpha\&\beta) \subseteq A{\div}\alpha$.

First step: To begin with, we are going to show that $\sigma(A \perp\!\!\!\perp \alpha) \subseteq \sigma(A \perp\!\!\!\perp (\alpha\&\beta))$. Let $\delta \in \sigma(A \perp\!\!\!\perp \alpha)$. Then there is some $X \in A \perp\!\!\!\perp \alpha$ such that $\delta \in s(X)$.

Since $\alpha \notin A{\div}(\alpha\&\beta)$ we have $A \setminus \sigma(A \perp (\alpha\&\beta)) \nvdash \alpha$. Since $\sigma(A \perp (\alpha\&\beta)) \subseteq \sigma(A \perp\!\!\!\perp (\alpha\&\beta))$ we also have $A \setminus \sigma(A \perp\!\!\!\perp (\alpha\&\beta)) \subseteq A \setminus \sigma(A \perp (\alpha\&\beta))$, and consequently $A \setminus \sigma(A \perp\!\!\!\perp (\alpha\&\beta)) \nvdash \alpha$. It follows that $X \nsubseteq A \setminus \sigma(A \perp\!\!\!\perp (\alpha\&\beta))$. Let $\xi \in X \cap \sigma(A \perp\!\!\!\perp (\alpha\&\beta))$. Then there is some $Y \in A \perp\!\!\!\perp (\alpha\&\beta)$ such that $\xi \in s(Y)$.

Clearly, $X \cup Y \in A \perp\!\!\!\perp \alpha$. We are now going to show that $\delta \in s(X \cup Y)$. Suppose to the contrary that there is some $\varepsilon \in X \cup Y$ such that $\varepsilon \prec \delta$. Since $\delta \in s(X)$, ε cannot be an element of X so it must be an element of Y. Since $\prec$ is virtually connected, it follows from $\varepsilon \prec \delta$ that either $\varepsilon \prec \xi$ or $\xi \prec \delta$. However, $\varepsilon \prec \xi$ is not possible since $\varepsilon \in Y$ and $\xi \in s(Y)$. Similarly, $\xi \prec \delta$ is impossible since $\xi \in X$ and $\delta \in s(X)$. We can conclude from this that $\delta \in s(X \cup Y)$, and thus $\delta \in \sigma(A \perp\!\!\!\perp (\alpha\&\beta))$, as desired.

Second step: We are going to show that $A \setminus \sigma(A \perp (\alpha\&\beta)) \subseteq \mathrm{Cn}(A \setminus \sigma(A \perp \alpha))$. Let $\delta \in A \setminus \sigma(A \perp (\alpha\&\beta))$.

We know from Observation 2.90 that if $\delta \notin \mathrm{Cn}(\{\neg(\alpha\&\beta)\})$, then it holds that if $\delta \in \sigma(A \perp\!\!\!\perp (\alpha\&\beta))$ then $\delta \in \sigma(A \perp (\alpha\&\beta))$. It follows from this that if $\delta \notin \sigma(A \perp (\alpha\&\beta))$, then either $\delta \notin \sigma(A \perp\!\!\!\perp (\alpha\&\beta))$ or $\delta \in \mathrm{Cn}(\{\neg(\alpha\&\beta)\})$. We already know from $\delta \in A \setminus \sigma(A \perp (\alpha\&\beta))$ that $\delta \notin \sigma(A \perp (\alpha\&\beta))$, so that either $\delta \notin \sigma(A \perp\!\!\!\perp (\alpha\&\beta))$ or $\delta \in \mathrm{Cn}(\{\neg(\alpha\&\beta)\})$.

Case 1, $\delta \notin \sigma(A \perp\!\!\!\perp (\alpha\&\beta))$: It follows from the first step of the present proof that $\delta \notin \sigma(A \perp\!\!\!\perp \alpha)$. Since σ is cumulative and $A \perp \alpha \subseteq A \perp\!\!\!\perp \alpha$, we also have $\sigma(A \perp \alpha) \subseteq \sigma(A \perp\!\!\!\perp \alpha)$ and thus $\delta \notin \sigma(A \perp \alpha)$. Since $\delta \in A$, it follows that $\delta \in A \setminus \sigma(A \perp \alpha)$ and thus $\delta \in \mathrm{Cn}(A \setminus \sigma(A \perp \alpha))$, as desired.

Case 2, $\delta \in \mathrm{Cn}(\{\neg(\alpha\&\beta)\})$: Then $\delta \in \mathrm{Cn}(\{\neg\alpha\})$, thus $\neg\alpha \rightarrow \delta \in \mathrm{Cn}(\emptyset)$. Since $\div$ is a partial meet contraction (Theorem 2.37), we have by *recovery*: $\alpha \rightarrow \delta \in A{\div}\alpha = \mathrm{Cn}(A \setminus \sigma(A \perp \alpha))$. Since $\neg\alpha \rightarrow \delta$ and $\alpha \rightarrow \delta$ together imply δ, we can conclude that $\delta \in \mathrm{Cn}(A \setminus \sigma(A \perp \alpha))$, in this case as well.

We have proved that $A\backslash\sigma(A\perp(\alpha\&\beta)) \subseteq \mathrm{Cn}(A\backslash\sigma(A\perp\alpha))$. It follows directly that $\mathrm{Cn}(A\backslash\sigma(A\perp(\alpha\&\beta))) \subseteq \mathrm{Cn}(A\backslash\sigma(A\perp\alpha))$, i.e. $A\div(\alpha\&\beta) \subseteq A\div\alpha$. ■

We have now proved all the results reported in Section 2.9, with the exception of the following:

> Let A be a logically closed set and $\div$ an operation on A. Then $\div$ is a safe contraction, based on a regular and virtually connected hierarchy, if and only if it satisfies both the basic and the supplementary Gärdenfors postulates (i.e. *closure*, *inclusion*, *vacuity*, *success*, *extensionality*, *recovery*, *conjunctive overlap*, and *conjunctive inclusion*). [Theorem 2.47.]

We have already proved the construction-to-postulates part of this theorem: If a safe contraction is based on a regular and virtually connected hierarchy, then it satisfies the six basic Gärdenfors postulates (Theorem 2.37), conjunctive overlap (Observation 2.45) and conjunctive inclusion (Observation 2.91). The postulates-to-construction part of this theorem seems to be more difficult. The only published full proof (by Hans Rott) is quite complex, and the reader who wishes to study it is referred to Rott's paper [114]. A few words should be said, however, about the very interesting construction that is used in that proof.

Let $\div$ be an operation on A that satisfies the postulates listed in the theorem. It turns out that the following relation

$$\beta \prec \delta \text{ if and only if } \beta \notin A\div(\beta\&\delta) \text{ and } \delta \in A\div(\beta\&\delta)$$

is a regular and virtually connected hierarchy, and that the safe contraction that it generates coincides with $\div$. This result also reveals a close relation between safe contraction and epistemic entrenchment. Let $\leq$ be the entrenchment ordering defined from $\div$ through the $(C\leq)$ identity introduced in Section 2.10. Then $\prec$ is the strict counterpart of $\leq$, i.e. $(\beta \prec \delta)\leftrightarrow(\beta \leq \delta\&\neg(\delta \leq \beta))$. Thus, if we define $\leq$ from $\div$ according to $(C\leq)$, we can regain $\div$ from $\leq$ in two different ways: (1) by using $\leq$ as an entrenchment ordering in Gärdenfors's entrenchment-based contraction, and (2) by using its strict part $\prec$ as a hierarchy to generate a safe contraction.

Exercises

122. Show that all hierarchies that satisfy transitivity and strict dominance (If $\mathrm{Cn}(\{\beta\}) \subset \mathrm{Cn}(\{\alpha\})$ then $\alpha \prec \beta$) also satisfy:
    (a) continuing-up
    (b) continuing-down
123. [4] Show that if a hierarchy satisfies virtual connectivity, then it satisfies transitivity.
124. [2; 4] Let $\prec$ be a hierarchy over a logically closed set A. Let s be the kernel selection function that is based on $\prec$, and let $\sigma(A \perp\!\!\!\perp \alpha) = \bigcup\{s(X) \mid X \in A \perp\!\!\!\perp \alpha\}$. Let $A\div\alpha = \mathrm{Cn}(A\backslash\sigma(A \perp\!\!\!\perp \alpha))$. (In other words, replace $\perp$ by $\perp\!\!\!\perp$ in the definition of safe contraction.).

(a) Show that $\div$ satisfies the basic Gärdenfors postulates except *recovery*.

(b) Show that if $A \neq \mathrm{Cn}(\emptyset)$, then $\div$ does not satisfy *failure*.

(c) Show that $\div$ does not satisfy *recovery*.

125. [4] Let A be a set of sentences and let σ be an incision function that is based on a hierarchy over A. Show that
$\sigma(A {\perp\!\!\!\perp} \alpha) \cap \mathrm{Cn}(\{\neg\alpha\}) = \emptyset$.

126. [4] Let A be a logically closed set and $\prec$ a hierarchy over A that satisfies continuing-down. Let s be the selection function that is based on $\prec$, and let σ be the cumulation of s. Show that:
$A \backslash \sigma(A {\perp\!\!\!\perp} \alpha) = (A \backslash \sigma(A \mathbin{\dot{\perp\!\!\!\perp}} \alpha)) \cup (A \cap \mathrm{Cn}(\{\neg\alpha\}))$.

127. [4] Let A be a logically closed set and let $\prec$ be the empty hierarchy, i.e. the hierarchy such that there are no sentences α and β such that $\alpha \prec \beta$. Let $\div$ be the safe contraction that is based on $\prec$. Show that $A \div \alpha = \bigcap(A \perp \alpha)$, i.e. that $\div$ coincides with full meet contraction. (Hint: use Observation 2.85.)

24⁺ THE LOGIC OF ENTRENCHMENT

The purpose of this section is to prove the formal results on entrenchment referred to in Section 2.10, and in particular the representation theorem (Theorem 2.50) that connects entrenchment-based contraction to other constructions of contraction operators. For ready reference, the standard set of entrenchment postulates is as follows:

If $\alpha \leq \beta$ and $\beta \leq \delta$, then $\alpha \leq \delta$ (*transitivity*)
If $\alpha \vdash \beta$, then $\alpha \leq \beta$ (*dominance*)
Either $\alpha \leq \alpha \& \beta$ or $\beta \leq \alpha \& \beta$ (*conjunctiveness*)
If the belief set A is consistent, then $\alpha \notin A$ if and only if $\alpha \leq \beta$ for all β. (*minimality*)
If $\beta \leq \alpha$ for all β, then $\vdash \alpha$ (*maximality*)

Note that the transitivity of $\leq$ has immediate consequences for the properties of the corresponding strict relation $<$, as can be seen from Observation 2.75.

The following definitions are used to connect entrenchment with contraction:

$(C\leq)$ $\alpha \leq \beta$ if and only if $\alpha \notin A \div (\alpha \& \beta)$ or $\vdash \alpha \& \beta$.
$(G\div)$ $\beta \in A \div \alpha$ if and only if $\beta \in A$ and either $\alpha < (\alpha \vee \beta)$ or $\vdash \alpha$.
$(R\div)$ $\beta \in A \div \alpha$ if and only if $\beta \in A$ and either $\alpha < \beta$ or $\vdash \alpha$.

The next four observations provide us with some consequences of the standard entrenchment postulates, that can be proved with elementary logical methods. (Some further such consequences are introduced below in the exercises.)

OBSERVATION 2.92 ([40]) *Let $\leq$ be a relation that satisfies transitivity and dominance. Then it also satisfies:*
If $\alpha \leftrightarrow \alpha' \in \mathrm{Cn}(\emptyset)$ and $\beta \leftrightarrow \beta' \in \mathrm{Cn}(\emptyset)$, then $\alpha \leq \beta$ if and only if $\alpha' \leq \beta'$. (intersubstitutivity)

Proof. Let $\alpha \leftrightarrow \alpha' \in \mathrm{Cn}(\emptyset)$ and $\beta \leftrightarrow \beta' \in \mathrm{Cn}(\emptyset)$.

First, let $\alpha \leq \beta$. It follows by *dominance* that $\alpha' \leq \alpha$ and $\beta \leq \beta'$. We can use *transitivity* to obtain $\alpha' \leq \beta'$ from $\alpha' \leq \alpha, \alpha \leq \beta$, and $\beta \leq \beta'$.

For the other direction, let $\alpha' \leq \beta'$. It follows by *dominance* that $\alpha \leq \alpha'$ and $\beta' \leq \beta$. We can use *transitivity* to obtain $\alpha \leq \beta$ from $\alpha \leq \alpha', \alpha' \leq \beta'$, and $\beta' \leq \beta$. ■

> If the relation $\leq$ (of epistemic entrenchment) satisfies *transitivity*, *dominance*, and *conjunctiveness*, then it satisfies:
> Either $\alpha \leq \beta$ or $\beta \leq \alpha$ (*connectivity*)
> [Observation 2.48.]

Proof. It follows from *conjunctiveness* that either $\alpha \leq \alpha \& \beta$ or $\beta \leq \alpha \& \beta$.

If $\alpha \leq \alpha \& \beta$, we use *dominance* to obtain $\alpha \& \beta \leq \beta$ and *transitivity* to obtain $\alpha \leq \beta$. If $\beta \leq \alpha \& \beta$, we use *dominance* to obtain $\alpha \& \beta \leq \alpha$ and *transitivity* to obtain $\beta \leq \alpha$. ■

OBSERVATION 2.93 (Gärdenfors and Makinson [38]) *Let $\leq$ be a relation that satisfies transitivity, dominance, and conjunctiveness. Then it also satisfies:*

1. *If $\alpha \& \beta \leq \delta$, then either $\alpha \leq \delta$ or $\beta \leq \delta$.*
2. *If $\delta < \alpha$ and $\delta < \beta$, then $\delta < \alpha \& \beta$ (conjunction up* [40]*)*

Proof. *Part 1*: Let $\alpha \& \beta \leq \delta$. It follows from *conjunctiveness* that either $\alpha \leq \alpha \& \beta$ or $\beta \leq \alpha \& \beta$. In the first case, we can conclude by *transitivity* that $\alpha \leq \delta$, and in the second case in the same way that $\beta \leq \delta$.

Part 2: Let $\delta < \alpha$ and $\delta < \beta$. Then neither $\alpha \leq \delta$ nor $\beta \leq \delta$, and it follows from Part 1 that $\neg(\alpha \& \beta \leq \delta)$. *Connectivity* (Observation 2.48) yields $\delta < \alpha \& \beta$. ■

> If the belief set A is consistent and $\leq$ satisfies *transitivity*, *connectivity*, and *minimality*, then:
>
> 1. if $\alpha \notin A$ and $\beta \in A$, then $\alpha < \beta$
> 2. if $\alpha \notin A$ and $\beta \notin A$, then $\alpha \equiv \beta$
>
> [Observation 2.49.]

Proof. *Part 1*: It follows from $\beta \in A$, by *minimality*, that there is some ε such that $\neg(\beta \leq \varepsilon)$. By *connectivity*, $\varepsilon < \beta$. Suppose that $\beta \leq \alpha$. Then *transitivity* and Observation 2.75 yield $\varepsilon < \alpha$, contrary to *minimality* and $\alpha \notin A$. We can conclude that $\neg(\beta \leq \alpha)$, and by *connectivity* $\alpha < \beta$.

Part 2: Suppose that $\alpha \notin A$ and $\beta \notin A$. It follows from *minimality* and $\alpha \notin A$ that $\alpha \leq \beta$, and likewise from *minimality* and $\beta \notin A$ that $\beta \leq \alpha$. Thus, $\alpha \equiv \beta$. ■

Our major task in this section is to prove the representation theorem for Gärdenfors's entrenchment-based contraction. For one direction, we are going to take a standard entrenchment ordering for given, and show that the operator defined from it according to $(G\div)$ satisfies $(C \leq)$ and the eight Gärdenfors postulates. For the other direction, a contraction operator that satisfies the postulates will be taken for given. A relation is defined according to $(C \leq)$, and shown to satisfy $(G\div)$ and the standard entrenchment postulates. Thus, there is a lot to be proved, and the proof is a long one. However, most parts of it are fairly elementary.

> Let $\leq$ be a standard entrenchment ordering on the consistent belief set A. Furthermore, let $\div$ be the Gärdenfors entrenchment-based contraction on A that is based on $\leq$. Then $\div$ satisfies the six basic and two supplementary Gärdenfors postulates, as well as $(C \leq)$.
> [Theorem 2.50, Part 1.]

Proof. [38] Let A be a logically closed set and $\leq$ an entrenchment ordering for A. Let $\div$ be the Gärdenfors's entrenchment-based contraction derived from $\leq$ according to $(G\div)$.

Inclusion: Follows directly from $(G\div)$.

Closure: If $\vdash \alpha$, then it follows from $(G\div)$ that $A\div\alpha = A$, so that $A\div\alpha$ is logically closed. For the principal case, let $\nvdash \alpha$.

Let $\delta \in \mathrm{Cn}(A\div\alpha)$. According to $(G\div)$, in order to show that $\delta \in A\div\alpha$, we need to show that (1) $\delta \in A$ and (2) $\alpha < \alpha\vee\delta$.

First case, $A\div\alpha \neq \emptyset$: Since $\delta \in \mathrm{Cn}(A\div\alpha)$, by compactness, there is some finite subset $\{\beta_1, \ldots \beta_n\}$ of $A\div\alpha$ that implies δ.

(1): Since $\{\beta_1, \ldots \beta_n\} \subseteq A\div\alpha$ and (as we have already noted) *inclusion* holds for $\div$, we have $\{\beta_1, \ldots \beta_n\} \subseteq A$. Since δ follows from $\{\beta_1, \ldots \beta_n\}$ and A is logically closed, it follows that $\delta \in A$.

(2): It follows from $(G\div)$ that $\alpha < \alpha\vee\beta_k$ for each β_k. (Note that the existence of such β_k requires that $A\div\alpha$ is non-empty, which is why we need to treat the fictitious case $A\div\alpha = \emptyset$ separately.) It follows from Observation 2.93 that $\alpha < ((\alpha\vee\beta_1)\&\ldots\&(\alpha\vee\beta_n))$. Thus, by *intersubstitutivity* (Observation 2.92), $\alpha < \alpha\vee(\beta_1\&\ldots\&\beta_n)$. Since $\beta_1\&\ldots\&\beta_n \vdash \delta$ we also have $\alpha\vee(\beta_1\&\ldots\&\beta_n) \vdash \alpha\vee\delta$ and thus by *dominance* $\alpha\vee(\beta_1\&\ldots\&\beta_n) \leq \alpha\vee\delta$. We can now use *transitivity* (and Observation 2.75) to obtain $\alpha < \alpha\vee\delta$. This completes the proof that *closure* holds in this case.

Second case, $A \div \alpha = \emptyset$: (1) It follows from $\delta \in \text{Cn}(A \div \alpha)$ and $A \div \alpha = \emptyset$ that δ is a tautology. Since A is logically closed and δ a tautology, we may conclude that $\delta \in A$.

(2) Since δ is a tautology, so is $\alpha \vee \delta$, and it follows from *dominance* that $\varepsilon \leq \alpha \vee \delta$ for all ε. But since $\nvdash \alpha$, it follows from *maximality* that $\neg(\varepsilon \leq \alpha)$ for some ε. Due to *connectivity* (Observation 2.48) we then have $\alpha < \varepsilon$. We can apply *transitivity* (and Observation 2.75) to $\alpha < \varepsilon \leq \alpha \vee \delta$ and obtain $\alpha < \alpha \vee \delta$. and the proof of this case is finished.

Vacuity: Let $\alpha \notin A$. It follows from *inclusion* that $A \div \alpha \subseteq A$. In order to prove $A \subseteq A \div \alpha$, let $\beta \in A$. We need to show that $\beta \in A \div \alpha$.

It follows from $\beta \in A$ by *minimality* that $\neg(\beta \leq \varepsilon)$ for some ε, and thus from *connectivity* (Observation 2.48) that $\varepsilon < \beta$. *Dominance* yields $\beta \leq \alpha \vee \beta$. Since $\alpha \notin A$ it follows from *minimality* that $\alpha \leq \varepsilon$. We can now apply *transitivity* and Observation 2.75 to $\alpha \leq \varepsilon, \varepsilon < \beta$, and $\beta \leq \alpha \vee \beta$, and obtain $\alpha < \alpha \vee \beta$.

It follows by $(G\div)$ from $\beta \in A$ and $\alpha < \alpha \vee \beta$ that $\beta \in A \div \alpha$.

Success: Let $\nvdash \alpha$. We need to show that $\alpha \notin A \div \alpha$. It follows by *dominance* from $\alpha \vee \alpha \vdash \alpha$ that $\alpha \vee \alpha \leq \alpha$ and thus $\neg(\alpha < \alpha \vee \alpha)$. It follows from this and $\nvdash \alpha$, by $(G\div)$, that $\alpha \notin A \div \alpha$.

Extensionality: Let $\alpha \leftrightarrow \beta \in \text{Cn}(\emptyset)$. We are first going to show that $A \div \alpha \subseteq A \div \beta$.

Let $\delta \in A \div \alpha$. Then, by $(G\div)$, $\delta \in A$ and either $\alpha < \alpha \vee \delta$ or $\vdash \alpha$. It follows from $\alpha \leftrightarrow \beta \in \text{Cn}(\emptyset)$ that $(\alpha \vee \delta) \leftrightarrow (\beta \vee \delta) \in \text{Cn}(\emptyset)$. Thus, according to the *intersubstitutivity* of $\leq$ (Observation 2.92), $\alpha < \alpha \vee \delta$ holds if and only if $\beta < \beta \vee \delta$.

We have shown that $\delta \in A$ and that either $\beta < \beta \vee \delta$ or $\vdash \alpha$. Clearly, $\vdash \alpha$ holds if and only if $\vdash \beta$. Again using $(G\div)$, we can conclude that $\delta \in A \div \beta$.

Thus, $A \div \alpha \subseteq A \div \beta$. We can prove $A \div \beta \subseteq A \div \alpha$ in the same way, and conclude that $A \div \alpha = A \div \beta$.

Recovery: Let $\beta \in A$. We are going to show that $\alpha \rightarrow \beta \in A \div \alpha$, from which *recovery* follows immediately.

Since A is logically closed, it follows from $\beta \in A$ that $\alpha \rightarrow \beta \in A$.

Case 1, $\vdash \alpha$: Using $(G\div)$, we can conclude from $\alpha \rightarrow \beta \in A$ and $\vdash \alpha$ that $\alpha \rightarrow \beta \in A \div \alpha$.

Case 2, $\nvdash \alpha$: It follows from *maximality* that $\neg(\varepsilon \leq \alpha)$ for some ε, and from *connectivity* (Observation 2.48) that $\alpha < \varepsilon$. Since $\alpha \vee (\alpha \rightarrow \beta)$ is a tautology, *dominance* yields $\varepsilon \leq \alpha \vee (\alpha \rightarrow \beta)$. We can use *transitivity* and Observation 2.75 to obtain $\alpha < (\alpha \vee (\alpha \rightarrow \beta))$. It follows from this and $\alpha \rightarrow \beta \in A$, by $(G\div)$, that $\alpha \rightarrow \beta \in A \div \alpha$.

Conjunctive overlap: Let $\delta \in (A \div \alpha) \cap (A \div \beta)$. There are three cases:

Case 1, $\vdash \alpha$: Then $\beta \leftrightarrow (\alpha \& \beta) \in \text{Cn}(\emptyset)$. It follows from *extensionality*, that we have already proved, that $A \div (\alpha \& \beta) = A \div \beta$, and thus $\delta \in A \div (\alpha \& \beta)$, as desired.

Case 2, $\vdash \beta$: This proof is similar to that of case 1.

Case 3, $\nvdash \alpha$ and $\nvdash \beta$: It follows from *dominance* that $\alpha\&\beta \leq \alpha$. Furthermore, it follows from $\delta \in A \div \alpha$ that $\alpha < \alpha \vee \delta$. We can conclude, using *transitivity* and Observation 2.75, that $\alpha\&\beta < \alpha \vee \delta$. Similarly, it follows from *dominance* that $\alpha\&\beta \leq \beta$ and from $\delta \in A \div \beta$ that $\beta < \beta \vee \delta$, and thus $\alpha\&\beta < \beta \vee \delta$.

Using Observation 2.93, we can conclude from $\alpha\&\beta < \alpha \vee \delta$ and $\alpha\&\beta < \beta \vee \delta$ that $\alpha\&\beta < ((\alpha \vee \delta)\&(\beta \vee \delta))$. *Intersubstitutivity* (Observation 2.92) yields $\alpha\&\beta < ((\alpha\&\beta)\vee\delta)$.

It follows by $(G\div)$ from $\delta \in A \div \alpha$ that $\delta \in A$. We can conclude from $\delta \in A$ and $\alpha\&\beta < ((\alpha\&\beta)\vee\delta)$ that $\delta \in A \div (\alpha\&\beta)$.

Conjunctive inclusion: For this part of the proof, let $\alpha \notin \mathrm{Cn}(A \div (\alpha\&\beta))$. We have to show that $A \div (\alpha\&\beta) \subseteq A \div \alpha$. Clearly, $\nvdash \alpha$. There are two cases:

Case 1, $\alpha \notin A$: Then we have $\alpha\&\beta \notin A$, and it follows by *vacuity* that $A \div \alpha = A \div (\alpha\&\beta) = A$. (We can, of course, freely use the properties of $\div$ that we have already proved.)

Case 2, $\alpha \in A$: It follows from $\nvdash \alpha$ that $\nvdash \alpha\&\beta$.

Let $\delta \notin A \div \alpha$. We are going to show that $\delta \notin A \div (\alpha\&\beta)$. This follows by *inclusion* if $\delta \notin A$, so for the principal case let $\delta \in A$.

It follows by *dominance* that $(\alpha\&\beta)\vee\delta \leq \alpha \vee \delta$.

It follows by $(G\div)$ from $\delta \notin A \div \alpha$ and $\delta \in A$ that $\neg(\alpha < \alpha\vee\delta)$. By *connectivity* (Observation 2.48), $\alpha\vee\delta \leq \alpha$.

Since $\alpha \notin A \div (\alpha\&\beta)$ and $\alpha \in A$, $(G\div)$ yields $\neg(\alpha\&\beta < (\alpha\&\beta)\vee\alpha)$, so that by *connectivity* $(\alpha\&\beta)\vee\alpha \leq \alpha\&\beta$. By *intersubstitutivity* (Observation 2.92), $\alpha \leq \alpha\&\beta$.

We can now apply *transitivity* to $(\alpha\&\beta)\vee\delta \leq \alpha\vee\delta$, $\alpha\vee\delta \leq \alpha$, and $\alpha \leq \alpha\&\beta$, and obtain $(\alpha\&\beta)\vee\delta \leq \alpha\&\beta$, and thus $\neg(\alpha\&\beta < (\alpha\&\beta)\vee\delta)$. $(G\div)$ yields $\delta \notin A \div (\alpha\&\beta)$, as desired.

Condition $(C \leq)$: For one direction, let $\alpha \leq \beta$. We need to show that if $\alpha \in A \div (\alpha\&\beta)$, then $\vdash \alpha\&\beta$.

Let $\alpha \in A \div (\alpha\&\beta)$. It follows from $(G\div)$ that $\alpha \in A$ and that either $\vdash \alpha\&\beta$ or $(\alpha\&\beta) < (\alpha\&\beta)\vee\alpha$.

It follows from *conjunctiveness* that either $\alpha \leq \alpha\&\beta$ or $\beta \leq \alpha\&\beta$. In the latter case, *transitivity* and $\alpha \leq \beta$ yield $\alpha \leq \alpha\&\beta$. Thus, $\alpha \leq \alpha\&\beta$ holds in both cases. It follows from *intersubstitutivity* (Observation 2.92) that $(\alpha\&\beta)\vee\alpha \leq \alpha\&\beta$, hence $\neg(\alpha\&\beta < (\alpha\&\beta)\vee\alpha)$.

Since we already know that either $\vdash \alpha\&\beta$ or $\alpha\&\beta < (\alpha\&\beta)\vee\alpha$, we can conclude that $\vdash \alpha\&\beta$, as desired.

For the other direction we need to show that if $\alpha \notin A \div (\alpha\&\beta)$ or $\vdash \alpha\&\beta$, then $\alpha \leq \beta$. There are two cases.

Case 1, $\vdash \alpha\&\beta$: Then $\vdash \alpha$ and $\vdash \beta$. Since A is logically closed, we have $\beta \in A$. It follows from $(G\div)$ that $\alpha \leq \beta$.

Case 2, $\nvdash \alpha\&\beta$: It follows from $\alpha \notin A\div(\alpha\&\beta)$ and $\nvdash \alpha\&\beta$, according to $(G\div)$, that either $\alpha \notin A$ or $\neg(\alpha\&\beta < (\alpha\&\beta)\vee\alpha)$. If $\alpha \notin A$, then $\alpha \leq \beta$ follows from *minimality*. If $\neg(\alpha\&\beta < (\alpha\&\beta)\vee\alpha)$, then by *connectivity* $(\alpha\&\beta)\vee\alpha \leq \alpha\&\beta$. We can use *dominance* to obtain $\alpha \leq (\alpha\&\beta)\vee\alpha$ and $\alpha\&\beta \leq \beta$. Applying *transitivity* to these three expressions, we obtain $\alpha \leq \beta$. This concludes the proof. ■

> Let $\div$ be an operation on the consistent belief set A that satisfies the six basic and two supplementary Gärdenfors postulates. Furthermore, let $\leq$ be the relation that is derived from $\div$ through $(C \leq)$. Then $\leq$ satisfies the standard entrenchment postulates, and it also satisfies $(G\div)$. [Theorem 2.50, Part 2.]

Proof. [38] We need to show that the ordering defined by $(C \leq)$ satisfies the five standard entrenchment postulates, and in addition $(G\div)$.

Transitivity: Let $\alpha \leq \beta$ and $\beta \leq \delta$. There are four (potential) cases:

Case 1 $\vdash \alpha\&\beta$ and $\vdash \beta\&\delta$: Then $\vdash \alpha\&\delta$, and $(C \leq)$ yields $\alpha \leq \delta$.

Case 2, $\vdash \alpha\&\beta$ and $\beta \notin A\div(\beta\&\delta)$: This is an impossible case, since $\vdash \alpha\&\beta$ yields $\vdash \beta$, and $A\div(\beta\&\delta)$ is (by *closure*) logically closed.

Case 3, $\alpha \notin A\div(\alpha\&\beta)$ and $\vdash \beta\&\delta$: It follows from $\vdash \beta\&\delta$ that $\vdash \beta$ and $\vdash \delta$. Thus, $\alpha\&\beta$ and $\alpha\&\delta$ are logically equivalent. It follows by *extensionality* that $\alpha \notin A\div(\alpha\&\delta)$, and thus $\alpha \leq \delta$.

Case 4, $\alpha \notin A\div(\alpha\&\beta)$ and $\beta \notin A\div(\beta\&\delta)$: We are first going to show that $\alpha\&\beta \notin A\div(\alpha\&\beta\&\delta)$. If $\delta \in A\div(\alpha\&\beta\&\delta)$, then this follows by *success*. If $\delta \notin A\div(\alpha\&\beta\&\delta)$, then we also have $\beta\&\delta \notin A\div(\alpha\&\beta\&\delta)$. *Conjunctive inclusion* yields $A\div(\alpha\&\beta\&\delta) \subseteq A\div(\beta\&\delta)$. Since $\beta \notin A\div(\beta\&\delta)$, we can conclude that $\beta \notin A\div(\alpha\&\beta\&\delta)$, and thus $\alpha\&\beta \notin A\div(\alpha\&\beta\&\delta)$ in this case as well.

It follows directly from *conjunctive inclusion* and $\alpha\&\beta \notin A\div(\alpha\&\beta\&\delta)$ that $A\div(\alpha\&\beta\&\delta) \subseteq A\div(\alpha\&\beta)$. Since $\alpha \notin A\div(\alpha\&\beta)$, we can conclude from this that $\alpha \notin A\div(\alpha\&\beta\&\delta)$. *Conjunctive trisection* holds according to Observation 2.15, and it yields $\alpha \notin A\div(\alpha\&\delta)$. Thus, $\alpha \leq \delta$.

Dominance: Let $\alpha \vdash \beta$. If $\vdash \alpha$, then $\vdash \alpha\&\beta$ and thus $\alpha \leq \beta$. If $\nvdash \alpha$, then we can make use of the fact that α and $\alpha\&\beta$ are equivalent, so that *extensionality* yields $A\div\alpha = A\div(\alpha\&\beta)$. It follows from $\nvdash \alpha$ by *success* that $\alpha \notin A\div\alpha$, i.e. that $\alpha \notin A\div(\alpha\&\beta)$, and consequently $\alpha \leq \beta$.

Conjunctiveness: If $\vdash \alpha\&\beta$, then $\vdash \alpha\&(\alpha\&\beta)$, and $(C \leq)$ yields $\alpha \leq (\alpha\&\beta)$. If $\nvdash \alpha\&\beta$, then by *success* $\alpha\&\beta \notin A\div(\alpha\&\beta)$, so that (by *closure*) either $\alpha \notin A\div(\alpha\&\beta)$ or $\beta \notin A\div(\alpha\&\beta)$. In the first case, *extensionality* can be used to obtain $\alpha \notin A\div(\alpha\&(\alpha\&\beta))$, and $(C \leq)$ yields $\alpha \leq \alpha\&\beta$. In the second case, $\beta \leq \alpha\&\beta$ follows in the same way.

Minimality: For one direction, let $\alpha \notin A$. Then by *inclusion*, $\alpha \notin A\div(\alpha\&\beta)$ for all β, and thus by $(C \leq)$, $\alpha \leq \beta$ for all β.

For the other direction suppose that $\alpha \leq \beta$ for all β. Let $\beta \notin A$. Then, since A is logically closed, $\nvdash \beta$ and thus $\nvdash \alpha\&\beta$. It follows by $(C \leq)$ from $\alpha \leq \beta$ and $\nvdash \alpha\&\beta$ that $\alpha \notin A\div(\alpha\&\beta)$. Since $\beta \notin A$ and consequently $\alpha\&\beta \notin A$, we know from *vacuity* that $A\div(\alpha\&\beta) = A$, and thus $\alpha \notin A$.

Maximality: Suppose that $\beta \leq \alpha$ for all β. Let β be any logical truth, i.e., let $\vdash \beta$. It follows from *closure* that $\beta \in A\div(\alpha\&\beta)$. From this and $\beta \leq \alpha$ follows, by $(C \leq)$, that $\vdash \alpha\&\beta$, and thus $\vdash \alpha$.

Condition $(G\div)$: For one direction, let $\beta \in A\div\alpha$. It follows from *inclusion* that $\beta \in A$. It remains to be shown that if $\nvdash \alpha$, then $\alpha < \alpha\vee\beta$.

Let $\nvdash \alpha$. We can conclude by *closure* from $\beta \in A\div\alpha$ that $\alpha\vee\beta \in A\div\alpha$, and *extensionality* yields $\alpha\vee\beta \in A\div((\alpha\vee\beta)\&\alpha)$. Clearly, $\nvdash (\alpha\vee\beta)\&\alpha$, and we can conclude from $(C \leq)$ that $\neg(\alpha\vee\beta \leq \alpha)$. Due to the connectivity of $\leq$, that follows from the postulates already proven (Observation 2.48), we can conclude that $\alpha < \alpha\vee\beta$.

For the other direction, let $\beta \in A$. We need to show that (1) if $\vdash \alpha$ then $\beta \in A\div\alpha$, and (2) if $\alpha < (\alpha\vee\beta)$, then $\beta \in A\div\alpha$.

(1) If follows from Theorems 2.7 and 2.2 and Observation 2.3 that *failure* holds. Thus, we may conclude from $\vdash \alpha$ that $A\div\alpha = A$, so that $\beta \in A\div\alpha$ follows from $\beta \in A$.

(2) Since the case $\vdash \alpha$ was treated in (1), we may assume that $\nvdash \alpha$, or equivalently $\nvdash (\alpha\&(\alpha\vee\beta))$. It follows from $\alpha < (\alpha\vee\beta)$ that $\neg((\alpha\vee\beta) \leq \alpha)$. $(C \leq)$ yields $\alpha\vee\beta \in A\div(\alpha\&(\alpha\vee\beta))$. *Extensionality* yields $\alpha\vee\beta \in A\div\alpha$.

Suppose that $\beta \notin A\div\alpha$. Then *recovery* yields $\alpha\rightarrow\beta \in A\div\alpha$, which with $\alpha\vee\beta \in A\div\alpha$ yields $\beta \in A\div\alpha$. We may conclude that $\beta \in A\div\alpha$. ■

Next, we are going to prove some properties of Rott's entrenchment-based contraction. First, let us verify that it satisfies the basic and supplementary contraction postulates, with the notable exception of *recovery*. This proof is quite similar to that of the first part of Theorem 2.50, and much of it is therefore left to the reader as an exercise.

> Let $\leq$ be a standard entrenchment ordering on a belief set A, and $\div_R$ Rott's entrenchment-based contraction on A, based on $\leq$. Then $\div_R$ satisfies *closure*, *inclusion*, *vacuity*, *success*, *extensionality*, *conjunctive overlap*, and *conjunctive inclusion*.
> [Observation 2.51, Part 1.]

Proof. Let $\div$ be Rott's entrenchment-based contraction, derived from $\leq$ according to $(R\div)$.

Inclusion: Follows directly from $(R\div)$.

Closure: Let $\delta \in \text{Cn}(A\div\alpha)$. Then, by compactness, there is some finite subset $\{\beta_1, \ldots, \beta_n\}$ of $A\div\alpha$ that implies δ. We need to show that (1) $\delta \in A$ and (2) $\alpha < \delta$ unless $\vdash \alpha$.

(1): Since $\{\beta_1, \ldots \beta_n\} \subseteq A \div \alpha$ and (as we already know) *inclusion* holds for $\div$, we have $\{\beta_1, \ldots \beta_n\} \subseteq A$. Since δ follows from $\{\beta_1, \ldots \beta_n\}$ and A is logically closed, it follows that $\delta \in A$.

(2): If $\nvdash \alpha$, then it follows from $(R\div)$ that $\alpha < \beta_k$ for each β_k, and from Observation 2.93 that $\alpha < (\beta_1 \& \ldots \& \beta_n)$. Since $\beta_1 \& \ldots \& \beta_n \vdash \delta$, *dominance* yields $\beta_1 \& \ldots \& \beta_n \leq \delta$. We can use *transitivity* (and Observation 2.75) to obtain $\alpha < \delta$. This completes the proof that *closure* holds.

Vacuity: Let $\alpha \notin A$ and $\beta \in A$. We need to show that $\beta \in A \div \alpha$.

It follows from $\beta \in A$ by *minimality* that $\neg(\beta \leq \varepsilon)$ for some ε, and thus by *connectivity* (Observation 2.48) that $\varepsilon < \beta$. Since $\alpha \notin A$ it follows by *minimality* that $\alpha \leq \varepsilon$. We can now apply *transitivity* and Observation 2.75 to $\alpha \leq \varepsilon$ and $\varepsilon < \beta$, to obtain $\alpha < \beta$.

It follows by $(R\div)$ from $\beta \in A$ and $\alpha < \beta$ that $\beta \in A \div \alpha$.

The rest of this proof is left to the reader as an exercise. ■

Next, let us prove that $\div_R$ does not satisfy *recovery*. As usual, the non-satisfaction of a postulate is proved by a counter-example.

> Let $\leq$ be a standard entrenchment ordering on a belief set A, and $\div_R$ Rott's entrenchment-based contraction on A, based on $\leq$. It does not hold in general that $\div_R$ satisfies *recovery*.
> [Observation 2.51, Part 2.]

Proof. Let $\mathcal{L}$ consist of the logically independent sentences p and q and their truth-functional combinations. Let $A = \text{Cn}(\{p, q\})$. Let v be a function such that for any sentence $\alpha \in \mathcal{L}$:

$$v(\alpha) = 1 \text{ if } \alpha \in \text{Cn}(\emptyset)$$
$$v(\alpha) = 1/2 \text{ if } \alpha \in A \backslash \text{Cn}(\emptyset)$$
$$v(\alpha) = 0 \text{ if } \alpha \notin A$$

Let $\leq$ be defined so that $\alpha \leq \beta$ if and only if $v(\beta) - v(\alpha)$ is non-negative.

It follows directly that $\leq$ satisfies *transitivity*.

Next, we are going to show that $\leq$ satisfies *dominance*. Let $\alpha \vdash \beta$. (1) If $\alpha \notin A$, then $v(\beta) - v(\alpha)$ is non-negative for any β. (2) If $\alpha \in A \backslash \text{Cn}(\emptyset)$, then $v(\alpha) = 1/2$. It follows from $\alpha \vdash \beta$, since A is logically closed, that $\beta \in A$, so that $v(\beta)$ is either 1/2 or 1. In both cases, $v(\beta) - v(\alpha)$ is non-negative. (3) Finally, if $\alpha \in \text{Cn}(\emptyset)$, then $\alpha \vdash \beta$ yields $\beta \in \text{Cn}(\emptyset)$ so that $v(\beta) - v(\alpha) = 0$.

For *conjunctiveness*, it is again useful to consider three cases separately. (1) If $\alpha \& \beta \notin A$, then since A is closed either $\alpha \notin A$ or $\beta \notin A$, from which the desired conclusion follows directly. (2) If $\alpha \& \beta \in A \backslash \text{Cn}(\emptyset)$, then $\alpha \in A$ and $\beta \in A$, but either $\alpha \notin \text{Cn}(\emptyset)$ or $\beta \notin \text{Cn}(\emptyset)$. Thus either $\alpha \in A \backslash \text{Cn}(\emptyset)$ or $\beta \in A \backslash \text{Cn}(\emptyset)$, and we are done. (3) If $\alpha\&\beta \in \text{Cn}(\emptyset)$, then $v(\alpha\&\beta) = 1$, and thus both $v(\alpha\&\beta)-v(\alpha)$ and $v(\alpha\&\beta) - v(\beta)$ are non-negative.

Minimality and *maximality* follow directly from our definitions of v and $\leq$, and we can conclude that $\leq$ satisfies the five standard postulates of entrenchment.

Let $\div_R$ be Rott's entrenchment-based contraction, based on $\leq$. Then it holds for all sentences β that $\beta \in A\div_R p$ if and only if $p < \beta$, i.e. if and only if $\beta \in \text{Cn}(\emptyset)$. It follows that $A\div_R p = \text{Cn}(\emptyset)$. It follows that $\text{Cn}((A\div_R p) \cup \{p\}) = \text{Cn}(\{p\})$. Thus, $q \in A$ and $q \notin \text{Cn}((A\div_R p) \cup \{p\})$, and *recovery* is violated. ■

Next, let us prove that $\div_R$ but not $\div_G$ satisfies *expulsiveness*. (If $\nvdash \alpha$ and $\nvdash \beta$, then either $\alpha \notin A\div\beta$ or $\beta \notin A\div\alpha$.)

> Let $\leq$ be a standard entrenchment ordering for the belief set A, and let $\div_R$ and $\div_G$ be Rott's and Gärdenfors's entrenchment-based contractions, based on $\leq$. Then:
>
> 1. $\div_R$ satisfies *expulsiveness*, but
> 2. $\div_G$ does not in general satisfy *expulsiveness*.
>
> [Observation 2.52.]

Proof. *Part 1.* We are first going to show that $\div_R$ satisfies the following condition:

If $\nvdash \alpha$, then $\beta \in A\div\alpha$ if and only if $\beta \in A\div(\alpha\&\beta)$ (*condition* X)

Let $\nvdash \alpha$. For one direction let $\beta \in A\div_R\alpha$. By $(R\div)$, $\alpha < \beta$. By *dominance*, $\alpha\&\beta \leq \alpha$. By *transitivity* and Observation 2.75, $\alpha\&\beta < \beta$. $(R\div)$ yields $\beta \in A\div_R(\alpha\&\beta)$.

For the other direction, let $\beta \in A\div_R(\alpha\&\beta)$. By $(R\div)$, $\alpha\&\beta < \beta$. By *conjunctiveness*, either $\alpha \leq \alpha\&\beta$ or $\beta \leq \alpha\&\beta$. The latter case is impossible, since $\alpha\&\beta < \beta$. Thus $\alpha \leq \alpha\&\beta$. By *transitivity* and Observation 2.75, $\alpha < \beta$, and by $(R\div)$, $\beta \in A\div_R\alpha$. This concludes the proof of condition (X).

We can now prove *expulsiveness*. Let $\nvdash \alpha$ and $\nvdash \beta$. Then $\nvdash \alpha\&\beta$. It follows from *success* and *closure* that either $\alpha \notin A\div_R(\alpha\&\beta)$ or $\beta \notin A\div_R(\alpha\&\beta)$. In the former case, it follows from condition (X) that $\alpha \notin A\div_R\beta$. In the latter case, it follows in the same way that $\beta \notin A\div_R\alpha$. This finishes Part 1 of the proof.

Part 2. Suppose that A contains the two logically independent sentences p and q. We are going to show that $p\rightarrow q \in A\div_G p$ and $p \in A\div_G(p\rightarrow q)$.

It follows from Theorem 2.50 that $\div_G$ satisfies *closure* and *recovery*. By *recovery*, $p\rightarrow q \in \text{Cn}((A\div_G p) \cup \{p\})$. The deduction property yields $p\rightarrow(p\rightarrow q) \in \text{Cn}(A\div_G p)$, which is equivalent to $p\rightarrow q \in \text{Cn}(A\div_G p)$. By *closure*, $p\rightarrow q \in A\div_G p$.

It also follows from *recovery* that $p \in \text{Cn}((A\div_G(p\rightarrow q)) \cup \{p\rightarrow q\})$. The deduction property yields $(p\rightarrow q)\rightarrow p \in \text{Cn}(A\div_G(p\rightarrow q))$, which is equivalent to $p \in \text{Cn}(A\div_G(p\rightarrow q))$. By *closure*, $p \in A\div_G(p\rightarrow q)$. ■

Note that the proof of Part 2 depends on only two properties of $\div_G$, namely recovery and closure. Recovery and expulsiveness are not compatible, given closure.

Our final task in this section is to prove the following observation, that strongly suggests that a plausible operator of contraction should be positioned somewhere between $\div_R$ and $\div_G$.

> Let $\div$ be an operator for the belief set A. Let $\leq$ be the relation defined from $\div$ via $(C\leq)$. Furthermore, let $\div_G$ and $\div_R$ be Gärdenfors's and Rott's (entrenchment-based) contractions, based on $\leq$. Then:
>
> 1. If $\div$ satisfies *inclusion, closure, success*, and *extensionality*, then $A\div\alpha \subseteq A\div_G\alpha$ for all α.
> 2. If $\div$ satisfies *closure, failure*, and *conjunctive inclusion*, then $A\div_R\alpha \subseteq A\div\alpha$ for all α.
>
> [Observation 2.53.]

Proof. *Part 1*: Case 1, $\vdash\alpha$: Let $\beta \in A\div\alpha$. It follows from *inclusion* that $\beta \in A$, and thus from $(G\div)$ that $\beta \in A\div_G\alpha$.

Case 2, $\nvdash\alpha$: Let $\beta \in A\div\alpha$. It follows from *inclusion* that $\beta \in A$. It also follows by *closure* from $\beta \in A\div\alpha$ that $\alpha\vee\beta \in A\div\alpha$, and then from *extensionality* that $\alpha\vee\beta \in A\div(\alpha\&(\alpha\vee\beta))$. It follows from *success* that $\alpha \notin A\div\alpha$, and *extensionality* yields $\alpha \notin A\div(\alpha\&(\alpha\vee\beta))$. We can conclude from $\alpha \notin A\div(\alpha\&(\alpha\vee\beta))$ and $\alpha\vee\beta \in A\div(\alpha\&(\alpha\vee\beta))$ that $\alpha < \alpha\vee\beta$. (Cf. Exercise 135.)

Thus, $\beta \in A$ and $\alpha < \alpha\vee\beta$. It follows from $(G\div)$ that $\beta \in A\div_G\alpha$.

Part 2: Case 1, $\vdash\alpha$: Let $\beta \in A\div_R\alpha$. It follows from $(R\div)$ that $\beta \in A$ and from *failure* that $A = A\div\alpha$. Thus, $\beta \in A\div\alpha$.

Case 2, $\nvdash\alpha$: Let $\beta \in A\div_R\alpha$. It follows from $(R\div)$ that $\alpha < \beta$. Since *closure* is satisfied, we may conclude that $\alpha \notin A\div(\alpha\&\beta)$ and $\beta \in A\div(\alpha\&\beta)$. (Cf. Exercise 135.) It follows from $\alpha \notin A\div(\alpha\&\beta)$, again due to *closure*, that $\alpha \notin \mathrm{Cn}(A\div(\alpha\&\beta))$, and then from *conjunctive inclusion* that $A\div(\alpha\&\beta) \subseteq A\div\alpha$. From this and $\beta \in A\div(\alpha\&\beta)$ we can conclude that $\beta \in A\div\alpha$, as desired. ■

Exercises

128. Let $\leq$ be a relation that satisfies *transitivity, dominance*, and *conjunctiveness*. Show that it also satisfies the following properties:

    (a) $\alpha \leq \alpha$ (*reflexivity*)
    (b) If $\alpha\leftrightarrow\beta \in \mathrm{Cn}(\emptyset)$, then $\alpha \leq \beta$.
    (c) $\alpha \leq \beta$ if and only if $\alpha \leq \alpha\&\beta$.
    (d) [19] If $\alpha \leq \beta$, then $\alpha\&\delta \leq \beta$.
    (e) If $\alpha \leq \beta$, then $\alpha\&\delta \leq \beta\vee\varepsilon$.
    (f) [38] If $\delta \leq \alpha$ and $\delta \leq \beta$, then $\delta \leq (\alpha\&\beta)$

(g) [19] If $\alpha \leq \beta$ then $\alpha\&\delta \leq \beta\&\delta$.

129. Let $\leq$ be a relation that satisfies *transitivity*, *dominance*, and *conjunctiveness*. Show that the corresponding strict relation $<$ satisfies the following properties:

(a) [35] If $\alpha < \beta$ then $\alpha\&\beta < \beta$.
(b) [19] If $\alpha < \beta$, then $\alpha\&\delta < \beta$.
(c) [19] If $\alpha < \beta$, then $\alpha < \beta\vee\delta$.
(d) If $\alpha < \beta$, then $\alpha\&\delta < \beta\vee\varepsilon$.
(e) [35] If $\alpha\&\beta < \beta$ then $\alpha < \beta$.
(f) If $\alpha < \beta$ and $\beta\&\delta \vdash \alpha$, then $\delta < \beta$.
(g) [19] If $\beta\&\delta < \alpha$, then either $\beta < \alpha$ or $\delta < \alpha$.
(h) [40] If $\alpha\&\delta < \beta\&\delta$, then $\alpha < \beta$.
(i) [40] If $\alpha < \beta$ and $\delta < \varepsilon$, then $\alpha\&\delta < \beta\&\varepsilon$.
(j) $\neg\alpha < \alpha\rightarrow\beta$ if and only if $\alpha\rightarrow\neg\beta < \alpha\rightarrow\beta$.

130. Let $\leq$ be a standard entrenchment ordering for a set A. Show that if $\vdash \alpha$ and $\alpha \leq \beta$, then $\vdash \beta$.

131. [35] Let $\leq$ be a relation that satisfies *connectivity* and the following condition:
If $\delta \leq \alpha$ and $\delta \leq \beta$ then $\delta \leq \alpha\&\beta$.
Show that $\leq$ satisfies *conjunctiveness*.

132. [114] Let $\leq$ be a relation that satisfies *transitivity*, *dominance*, and *conjunctiveness*. Show that the corresponding strict relation $<$ is a regular and virtually connected hierarchy, i.e., that it:

(a) is a hierarchy
(b) satisfies *continuing-up* (If $\alpha < \beta$ and $\beta \vdash \delta$, then $\alpha < \delta$)
(c) satisfies *continuing-down* (If $\alpha \vdash \beta$ and $\beta < \delta$, then $\alpha < \delta$)
(d) satisfies *virtual connectivity* (If $\alpha < \beta$ then $\alpha < \delta$ or $\delta < \beta$)

133. [115] Hans Rott has proposed the following five postulates for 'generalized epistemic entrenchment':

(EE1) $\neg(\top < \top)$ (*non-triviality*)
(EE2↑) If $\alpha < \beta$ and $\beta \vdash \delta$, then $\alpha < \delta$ (*continuing-up*)
(EE2↓) If $\alpha \vdash \beta$ and $\beta < \delta$, then $\alpha < \delta$ (*continuing-down*)
(EE3↑) If $\alpha < \beta$ and $\alpha < \delta$ then $\alpha < \beta\&\delta$ (*conjunction up*)
(EE3↓) If $\alpha\&\beta < \beta$ then $\alpha < \beta$ (*conjunction down*)

(a) Show that if a relation $\leq$ satisfies *transitivity*, *dominance*, and *conjunctiveness*, then its strict part $<$ satisfies EE1, EE2↑, EE2↓, EE3↑, and EE3↓.
(b) Let $<$ be a relation that satisfies EE1, EE2↑, EE2↓, EE3↑, and EE3↓. Let $\leq$ be the relation such that for all sentences α, β:
$\alpha \leq \beta$ if and only if $\neg(\beta < \alpha)$.
Show that $\leq$ satisfies *dominance* and *conjunctiveness*.

(c) Show that EE2↑ and EE3↑, taken together, are equivalent to the following postulate:
(EE↑) If $\alpha < \beta$ for every β in a non-empty set B, and $B \vdash \delta$, then $\alpha < \delta$. (*closure-up*)

(d) [111] Show that EE2↓ and EE3↓, taken together, are equivalent to the following postulate:
(EE↓) If $\{\alpha, \delta\} \vdash \beta$ and $\beta < \delta$, then $\alpha < \delta$ (*closure-down*)

134. [113] Let $\leq$ be an entrenchment ordering for a consistent belief set A, such that $\leq$ satisfies the five standard postulates. Show that A can be recovered from $\leq$ through the following identity:
$A = \{\delta \mid \beta < \delta \text{ for some } \beta\}$

135. Show that if $\div$ satisfies *closure*, then the following condition follows from $(C \leq)$:
$(C <)$ $\alpha < \beta$ iff $\alpha \notin A\div(\alpha\&\beta)$ and $\beta \in A\div(\alpha\&\beta)$.

136. Complete the proof of Observation 2.51 by showing that $\div_R$ satisfies *success*, *extensionality*, *conjunctive overlap*, and *conjunctive inclusion*.

137. [38] Let E be a function such that if $\div$ is an operator on the consistent belief set A, then $E(\div)$ is the relation $\leq$ defined from $\div$ according to $(C \leq)$. Furthermore, let C be a function such that for any relation $\leq$ on the same set A, $C(\leq)$ is the operator $\div$ defined from $\leq$ according to $(G\div)$.

(a) Show that if $\div$ is an operator that satisfies Gärdenfors's six basic and two supplementary postulates, then $C(E(\div)) = \div$.

(b) Show that if $\leq$ is a standard entrenchment ordering, then $E(C(\leq)) = \leq$.

138. [15] Let N be a *necessity measure*, i.e. a function from $\mathcal{L}$ to the set of real numbers between 0 and 1, such that:
(N1) $N(\top) = 1$ and $N(\bot) = 0$.
(N2) $N(\alpha\&\beta) = min(N(\alpha), N(\beta))$
(N3) If $\alpha\leftrightarrow\beta \in \text{Cn}(\emptyset)$, then $N(\alpha) = N(\beta)$
where, for two real numbers x and y, $min(x, y) = x$ if $x \leq y$ and $min(x, y) = y$ if $y \leq x$.

(a) Show that for all sentences α, $min(N(\alpha), N(\neg\alpha)) = 0$.

(b) Show that for all sentences α and β, $N(\alpha\vee\beta) \geq max(N(\alpha), N(\beta))$, where for two real numbers x and y, $max(x, y) = x$ if $x \geq y$ and $max(x, y) = y$ if $y \geq x$.

(c) Show that if $\alpha \vdash \beta$, then $N(\alpha) \leq N(\beta)$.

(d) Show that $\{\alpha \mid N(\alpha) > 0\}$ is logically closed.

(e) Let $\leq$ be a relation such that for all sentences α and β : $\alpha \leq \beta$ if and only if $N(\alpha) \leq N(\beta)$. Show that $\leq$ satisfies four out of the five postulates required of a standard entrenchment ordering for the set $\{\alpha \mid N(\alpha) > 0\}$, namely *transitivity*, *dominance*, *conjunctiveness*, and *minimality*.

CHAPTER 3

TAKING ON BELIEFS

In Section 2.1 we found that contraction in its pure form is rare, if it does at all occur. Revision, on the other hand, is far from rare. Most examples of belief change that readily come to mind are examples of belief revision.

Sections 3.1–3.3 are devoted to revision of belief bases, and Sections 3.4–3.10 to revision of belief sets. Section 3.11 introduces some connections between belief revision and non-monotonic reasoning. Section 3.12 treats non-prioritized belief change, i.e. belief change in which the new information is not always accepted.

1 PROPERTIES OF BASE REVISION

The simplest way to introduce a new sentence into a belief base is to add it set-theoretically. For convenience, we will use $+$ to denote this operation of *(non-closing) expansion*, i.e.:

$$A + \alpha = A \cup \{\alpha\}.$$

In cases when the new belief does not contradict the original belief base, expansion is a suitable way of incorporating the new belief.

> **Example**
> I did not know if parking was allowed in this street. Then I saw the 'No Parking' sign.

In this case, the resulting new belief state can be represented by the set $A + \alpha$ that consists of the old belief base plus the new belief α. ('Parking is prohibited in this street'.)

Expansion is not in general suitable if the new belief contradicts the old belief base.

> **Example**
> I thought parking was allowed in this street. Then I saw the 'No Parking' sign.

In this case, the original belief base contained the sentence $\neg\alpha$. ('Parking is not prohibited in this street'.) The outcome of expansion by α is a belief base that contains both α and $\neg\alpha$. Such inconsistent belief bases should be avoided. In this example, $\neg\alpha$ should be replaced by α.

This is why we need the more complex operation of revision. Just like expansion, revision should result in a new belief base in which the new belief has been included. Let $*$ denote revision. Then:

Success: [31]
$\alpha \in A * \alpha$

Contrary to expansion, however, revision should avoid inconsistencies. As a preliminary formulation, we might require that:

$A * \alpha$ is consistent.

However, if α is inconsistent, then $A * \alpha$ can only be consistent if $\alpha \notin A * \alpha$, i.e. if success is violated. The success postulate and the consistency postulate in the above formulation cannot both hold if α is inconsistent. There are two ways out of this dilemma. Either we restrict success to hold only if α is consistent, or we restrict the consistency postulate to hold only if α is consistent. The conventional solution is to give priority to the success postulate, and thus restrict the consistency postulate as follows:

Consistency: [1]
$A * \alpha$ is consistent if α is consistent.

According to the consistency postulate, 'one should not end up believing *everything* on accommodating a new belief unless the new belief is contradictory (in which case success makes this unavoidable)' [91].

The revised belief base $A * \alpha$ should consist of (1) α, and (2) those elements of A that have not been excluded in order to give way to α. It follows from this that $A * \alpha$ should be a subset of $A \cup \{\alpha\}$:

Inclusion:
$A * \alpha \subseteq A \cup \{\alpha\}$

None of the three postulates that we have now introduced — success, consistency, and inclusion — serves to prevent unnecessarily large losses from the original belief base A. Indeed, an operation such that:

$A * \alpha = \{\alpha\}$ for all α

is compatible with the three postulates. We need to ensure that nothing is lost from A unless its exclusion serves to make room for α. For this purpose we can use a postulate that is very similar to the one that we used for contraction:

Relevance: [50]
If $\beta \in A$ and $\beta \notin A * \alpha$, then there is some A' such that $A * \alpha \subseteq A' \subseteq A \cup \{\alpha\}$, A' is consistent but $A' \cup \{\beta\}$ is inconsistent.

Relevance expresses the intuition that nothing is removed from the original belief base unless its removal in some way contributes to making the new belief base consistent. In the limiting case when the sentence α by which we revise is inconsistent, there is no point in removing anything from the original belief base, since we cannot make the outcome consistent anyhow. Therefore, the whole original belief base should be retained in that case:

> *Inconsistent expansion:*
> If $\neg\alpha \in \mathrm{Cn}(\emptyset)$ then $A * \alpha = A \cup \{\alpha\}$.

(Note that $\neg\alpha \in \mathrm{Cn}(\emptyset)$ holds if and only if α is inconsistent.) As we should expect, inconsistent expansion follows from relevance and the other basic postulates:

OBSERVATION 3.1 *If an operator $*$ for A satisfies success, inclusion, and relevance, then it satisfies inconsistent expansion.*
[Proof: p. 244.]

Revision operators are primarily intended to be applied when the new information contradicts the old belief base. However, it is convenient at least from a formal point of view to have these operators defined for all sentences α. We therefore need to determine what it means to revise a belief base by a sentence that it is not contradicted by.

> **Example**
> I had no idea how much it rains in Lima. When I was told that most years it does not rain at all, I revised my belief state to include this new information.

In this case, no previous beliefs had to be removed in order to accommodate the new belief without violating the consistency postulate. In such (non-belief-contravening) revision, the outcome should be the same as after expansion:

> *Vacuity:* [31]
> If $\neg\alpha \notin \mathrm{Cn}(A)$, then $A * \alpha = A \cup \{\alpha\}$.

Just like inconsistent expansion, vacuity can be shown to follow from relevance and the other basic postulates:

OBSERVATION 3.2 *If an operator $*$ for A satisfies success, inclusion, and relevance, then it satisfies vacuity.*
[Proof: p. 244.]

Since we are modelling belief revision in an entirely logical framework, the choice which elements of A to retain should depend on their logical relations to the new information. Therefore, if two sentences α and β are inconsistent with the same subsets of A, they should push out the same elements from A:

Uniformity: [50]
If for all $A' \subseteq A$, $A' \cup \{\alpha\}$ is inconsistent if and only if $A' \cup \{\beta\}$ is inconsistent, then $A \cap (A * \alpha) = A \cap (A * \beta)$.

A very special case of revision is ***redundant revision***, in which a belief base A is revised by a sentence α that is already an element of A. (If A is inconsistent and α a consistent element of A, then $A * \alpha$ will, if consistency and inclusion are satisfied, be a consistent subset of A that contains α.) Uniformity can be weakened by only being required to hold for redundant revision:

Weak uniformity: [50]
If α and β are elements of A and it holds for all $A' \subseteq A$ that $A' \cup \{\alpha\}$ is inconsistent if and only if $A' \cup \{\beta\}$ is inconsistent, then $A \cap (A * \alpha) = A \cap (A * \beta)$.

If the inclusion postulate is satisfied, then the concluding formula of this definition can be replaced by $A * \alpha = A * \beta$.

The operators of revision and expansion are closely related. Expansion performs one of the two major tasks of a revision operator: it adds the new belief to the belief base. (The other task is to keep the belief base consistent.) We can therefore expect that the successive performance of expansion by α and revision by α should have the same effect as that of only performing the revision. Since expansion can take place either before or after revision, this requirement can be divided into two postulates:

Pre-expansion: [50]
$A + \alpha * \alpha = A * \alpha$

Post-expansion:
$A * \alpha + \alpha = A * \alpha$

Pre-expansion will turn out to be a useful postulate. Post-expansion is of less interest, since it can be shown to be equivalent with *success*:

OBSERVATION 3.3 *An operator $*$ satisfies post-expansion if and only if it satisfies success.*
[Proof: p. 244.]

If A contains some element β that logically implies $\neg\alpha$, then β will have to go when A is revised by α. It would seem reasonable to require that such a sentence should not influence which of the other elements of A are retained. This requirement is closely related to the redundancy property of contraction operators, and it will also be given the same name:

Redundancy: [50]
If α is consistent, and $\beta \vdash \neg\alpha$ for each $\beta \in B$, then $A * \alpha = (A \cup B) * \alpha$.

The reader may have found it confusing that the same names — such as 'success', 'inclusion', etc. — are used both for properties of contraction and for (related but different) properties of revision. However, most of these names are already well-established in both uses, and it would not be easy to find short and adequate, non-duplicated names to replace them. Whenever necessary, the more precise terms 'contraction-success', 'revision-success', etc. will be used.

2 INTERNAL AND EXTERNAL REVISION

The two major tasks of a revision operator are (1) to add a new belief α to the belief base, and (2) to ensure that the resulting belief base is consistent (unless α is inconsistent). The first task can be accomplished by expansion by α. The second task can be accomplished by contraction by its negation $\neg\alpha$. (If a belief base does not imply $\neg\alpha$, then it is consistent, and α can be consistently added to it.)

An operator of revision can therefore be constructed out of two suboperations: expansion by α and contraction by $\neg\alpha$. The traditional arrangement of the two operations is to first contract, and then expand:

1. Contract by $\neg\alpha$
2. Expand by α

More succinctly, this composition of suboperations is expressed by the *Levi identity* [3; 30; 70]:

$$A * \alpha = (A \div \neg\alpha) + \alpha.$$

We will mostly assume that the contraction operator $\div$ referred to in the Levi identity is an operator of partial meet contraction, i.e. that it is identical to $\sim_\gamma$ for some selection function γ for A. The following notation will be used:

DEFINITION 3.4 *Let γ be a selection function for the belief base A. Then the operator $\mp_\gamma$ of* internal partial meet revision *for A is defined as follows:*

$$A \mp_\gamma \alpha = (A \sim_\gamma \neg\alpha) \cup \{\alpha\}.$$

Note that $\mp_\gamma$ stands in the same relation to $*$ as $\sim_\gamma$ to $\div$. We use $*(\div)$ to denote operators of revision (contraction) in general, and $\mp_\gamma(\sim_\gamma)$ to denote the operator that is generated by a particular selection function γ.

The Levi identity is not the only possible account of how one performs the two suboperations of adding a new belief and deleting its negation. Alternatively, the two suboperations may take place in reverse order [50]:

1. Expand by α
2. Contract by $\neg\alpha$

More compactly, this is expressed by the *reversed Levi identity* [50]:

$$A * \alpha = (A + \alpha) \div \neg\alpha.$$

If $\div$ is partial meet contraction, then this composite operation $*$ is *external partial meet revision*, defined as follows:

DEFINITION 3.5 *Let γ be a two-place selection function. Then the global operator $\pm_\gamma$ of* external partial meet revision *is defined as follows:*

$$A \pm_\gamma \alpha = (A \cup \{\alpha\}) \sim_\gamma \neg\alpha.$$

The names 'internal' and 'external' indicate that in internal revision, the suboperation of contraction takes place inside the original belief base, whereas in external revision it takes place outside of the original set. The symbols $\pm$ and $\mp$ should be read top-down: in external revision ($\pm$) expansion ($+$) takes place first, and is followed by contraction ($-$).

In internal revision, when one and the same belief base (A) is revised by two different sentences α and β, the suboperation of contraction will be applied to the same set (namely A, in the contractions $A \div \neg\alpha$ and $A \div \neg\beta$). Therefore, in order to perform internal revisions on a set A, we only need a *local* operator of partial meet contraction. In external revision, however, the suboperation of contraction will be applied to different belief bases ($A \cup \{\alpha\}$ and $A \cup \{\beta\}$, respectively). Therefore, in external revision, we need a *global* contraction operator.

Another important difference between the two types of revision is that consistency is preserved in every step of internal revision, whereas in external revision the intermediate belief state will often be inconsistent. In typical cases, external revision has an *intermediate inconsistent state* in which both α and $\neg\alpha$ are believed, whereas internal revision has an *intermediate non-committed state* in which neither α nor $\neg\alpha$ is believed.

Which of the two operations is the more plausible? Our intuitions about this seem to be different in different cases:

> **Example**
> Anthony and Beatrice are a married couple. I used to think that they were both Roman Catholics. Then I heard Beatrice say: 'In our marriage, it was never a problem that we belong to different denominations'. When I heard this, I gave up my belief that Beatrice is a Roman Catholic, but I retained my belief that Anthony is so (since I have seen him enter the local Catholic Church several times).
>
> *Account in terms of internal revision*: Before accepting what Beatrice said, I reconsidered my beliefs about each of them, and found that I should rather give up the idea that Beatrice is a Roman Catholic. After

I had given up that belief, I accepted the new information that Anthony and Beatrice belong to different denominations.

Account in terms of external revision: I immediately accepted what Beatrice said. Realizing that this was inconsistent with my previous beliefs, I afterwards adjusted them in order to make them consistent with the new information. I did this by giving up my belief that Beatrice is a Roman Catholic.

Example
I previously believed that moles are rodents. Then I read in a book that they belong to the class of insectivores (the class that also contains hedgehogs and shrews). I accepted this, and consequently gave up my old belief that moles are rodents.

Account in terms of internal revision: Before accepting what the book said, I gave up my belief that moles are rodents, in order to make room for the new belief that they are insectivores. After I had done this, I acquired the new belief that moles are insectivores.

Account in terms of external revision: I first accepted what the book said. Then I found that this was inconsistent with my previous belief that moles are rodents, so I gave up that belief.

In these two cases, the 'external' account seems to be the most plausible one. More generally: when it is obvious that the new information must be accepted, but less obvious which previous belief(s) it should push out, external revision seems to be closest to the actual psychological process.

The following examples are of a different nature:

Example
I was very surprised when Peter said that professor Inglefield's father is a carpenter. I had always thought of her as a person with an aristocratic background. However, after some hesitation, I accepted what he told me.

Example
When Joseph Black learned of the results of Lavoisier's new experiments, he gave up his previous belief in the phlogiston theory of combustion, and accepted Lavoisier's oxygen theory.

In both of these cases, there seems to have been a phase in which neither the new belief nor its negation was accepted. Internal revision is closer than external revision to this kind of process.

In many cases, it is difficult to determine if internal or external revision is the most adequate model.

Example

I believed that John was dead. Then I met him in the street.

In this case, it is not obvious that one of the two suboperations of giving up the belief that John was dead and acquiring the belief that John is alive took place before the other. Intuitively, the two operations seem to be simultaneous— a feature that is not easy to capture in logical representation.

How important is the distinction between internal and external revision? If we could show that all operators of internal partial meet revision are also external partial meet revisions (and/or vice versa), then the distinction would have been of relatively little interest. To the contrary, however, neither external nor internal revision can be subsumed under the other. The following is an example of an external partial meet revision that is not also an internal partial meet revision.

Example [50]

A man has died in a remote place in which only two other persons, Adam and Bob, were present. Initially, the public prosecutor believes that neither Adam nor Bob has killed him. Thus her belief base contains $\neg\kappa_A$ (Adam has not killed the deceased) and $\neg\kappa_B$ (Bob has not killed the deceased). For simplicity, we may assume that her belief base is $\{\neg\kappa_A, \neg\kappa_B\}$.

Case 1: The prosecutor receives a police report saying (1) that the deceased has been murdered, and that either Adam or Bob must have done it (i.e. $\kappa_A \vee \kappa_B$) and (2) that Adam has previously been convicted of murder several times (π_A). After receiving the report, she revises her belief base by $(\kappa_A \vee \kappa_B)\&\pi_A$. Her new belief base, after this revision, is $\{\neg\kappa_B, (\kappa_A \vee \kappa_B)\&\pi_A\}$.

Case 2 differs from case 1 only in that it is Bob who has previously been convicted of murder (π_B). Thus, the new information consists of $(\kappa_A \vee \kappa_B)\&\pi_B$. The new belief base is $\{\neg\kappa_A, (\kappa_A \vee \kappa_B)\&\pi_B\}$.

This example can be represented as an external partial meet revision. However, it cannot be represented as an internal partial meet revision. To see this, let us perform the first of the two suboperations of internal revision, namely contraction. In the first case, the contractive suboperation is

$$\{\neg\kappa_A, \neg\kappa_B\} \div \neg((\kappa_A \vee \kappa_B)\&\pi_A),$$

and in the second case it is

$$\{\neg\kappa_A, \neg\kappa_B\} \div \neg((\kappa_A \vee \kappa_B)\&\pi_B).$$

Since

$$\begin{aligned}&\{\neg\kappa_A, \neg\kappa_B\} \perp (\neg((\kappa_A \vee \kappa_B)\&\pi_A)) = \\ &\{\neg\kappa_A, \neg\kappa_B\} \perp (\neg((\kappa_A \vee \kappa_B)\&\pi_B)) = \\ &\{\{\neg\kappa_A\}, \{\neg\kappa_B\}\},\end{aligned}$$

and $\div$ is a partial meet contraction, it follows that

$$\{\neg\kappa_A, \neg\kappa_B\}\div\neg((\kappa_A\vee\kappa_B)\&\pi_A) = \{\neg\kappa_A, \neg\kappa_B\}\div\neg((\kappa_A\vee\kappa_B)\&\pi_B).$$

From this it follows that the pattern indicated in the example, in which $\neg\kappa_B$ is retained in the first case but not in the second, is impossible. (The second suboperation, expansion by $(\kappa_A\vee\kappa_B)\&\pi_A$ or $(\kappa_A\vee\kappa_B)\&\pi_B$, can of course not add or delete $\neg\kappa_B$.) The example shows that external partial meet revision cannot in general be reduced to internal revision.

The following is a pattern of change that can be modelled as internal revision but not as external revision:

Example
I believe that Brian is a Catholic priest (α). I also believe that if Brian is married, then he is not a Catholic priest ($\beta\rightarrow\neg\alpha$).
Case 1: I find out that Brian is married (β), and revise my belief base in order to incorporate this new information. After that, I do not any longer believe that he is a Catholic priest.
Case 2: Upon being told that Brian is married (β), I add this new information to my belief base (by expansion), thus inadvertently making it inconsistent. Very soon afterwards, I discover the inconsistency, and remove it through contraction by $\neg\beta$. After that, I still believe that Brian is a Catholic priest (but I have lost the belief that if he is married, he is not a Catholic priest).

This example can be modelled as internal revision. In the first case, the revision $A\mp_\gamma\beta$ takes place, and we have $\alpha \notin A\mp_\gamma\beta$. In the second case, we have $\alpha \in (A+\beta)\sim_\gamma\neg\beta$. To see how this is possible, let $A = \{\alpha, \beta\rightarrow\neg\alpha\}$. We then have

$$A\perp\neg\beta = \{\{\alpha\}, \{\beta\rightarrow\neg\alpha\}\}$$
$$(A+\beta)\perp\neg\beta = \{\{\alpha,\beta\}, \{\beta\rightarrow\neg\alpha, \beta\}\}.$$

It may very well be the case that

$$\gamma(A\perp\neg\beta) = \{\{\beta\rightarrow\neg\alpha\}\}$$
$$\gamma((A+\beta)\perp\neg\beta) = \{\{\alpha,\beta\}\}.$$

If this is so, then

$$A\mp_\gamma\beta = (\bigcap\gamma(A\perp\neg\beta)) \cup \{\beta\} = \{\beta\rightarrow\neg\alpha, \beta\}$$
$$(A+\beta)\sim_\gamma\neg\beta = \bigcap\gamma((A+\beta)\perp\neg\beta) = \{\alpha,\beta\}.$$

However, external revision cannot be used to model this example, since it holds for all operators $\pm_\gamma$ of external revision that $A\pm_\gamma\beta = (A+\beta)\sim_\gamma\neg\beta$.

We can conclude from the last two examples that internal and external partial meet revision represent different ways of changing one's mind, neither of which can, in general, be reduced to the other.

The differences between the two types of revision can also be seen from the following two axiomatic characterizations:

THEOREM 3.6 ([50]) *The operator $*$ is an operator of internal partial meet revision for a belief base A if and only if it satisfies consistency, inclusion, relevance, success, and uniformity.*
[Proof: p. 240.]

THEOREM 3.7 ([50]) *The operator $*$ is an operator of external partial meet revision if and only if it satisfies consistency, inclusion, relevance, success, weak uniformity, and pre-expansion.*
[Proof: p. 249.]

Four postulates are mentioned in both theorems, namely consistency, inclusion, relevance, and success. Weak uniformity, that is used to characterize external revision, holds for internal revision as well. (It follows from uniformity.) The characteristic postulates are therefore uniformity for internal revision and pre-expansion for external revision.

OBSERVATION 3.8 ([50]) *(1) Uniformity does not hold in general for external partial meet revision.*

(2) Pre-expansion does not hold in general for internal partial meet revision.
[Proof: pp. 252 and 239.]

The postulate of redundancy can be used, both for internal and external revision, to ensure that the selection function is unified:

THEOREM 3.9 ([50]) *The operator $*$ is an operator of unified internal partial meet revision (internal partial meet revision with a unified selection function) for a belief base A if and only if it satisfies consistency, inclusion, relevance, success, uniformity, and redundancy.*
[Proof: p. 242.]

THEOREM 3.10 ([50]) *The operator $*$ is an operator of unified external partial meet revision if and only if it satisfies consistency, inclusion, relevance, success, weak uniformity, pre-expansion, and redundancy.*
[Proof: p. 252.]

We have defined revision in terms of contraction (and of the simple set-theoretical operation of expansion). Conversely, contraction can be defined in terms of internal partial meet revision:

OBSERVATION 3.11 *Let A be any set and γ a selection function for A.*
Then $A \sim_\gamma \alpha = A \cap (A \mp_\gamma \neg\alpha)$ (the Harper identity)
[Proof: p. 239.]

The Harper identity (sometimes called the 'Gärdenfors identity' [82]) can be seen as the inverse form of the Levi identity. The Levi identity takes us from an operator of partial meet contraction to the corresponding operator of internal partial meet revision. The Harper identity takes us from an operator of internal partial meet revision to the corresponding operator of partial meet contraction. Together, the two identities make contraction and (internal) revision interchangeable.

For external partial meet revision, no such 'way back' from revision to contraction seems to be available. From the point of view of logical analysis, the Harper identity is an advantage of internal over external revision.

3 LIMITING CASES OF BASE REVISION

The limiting *maxichoice* and *full meet* cases of internal and external revision are defined just as for contraction: If the selection function is maxichoice, then it gives rise to an internal (external) maxichoice revision operator. If the selection function is that of full meet, then we have internal (external) full meet revision.

The following postulate:

> *Tenacity:* [35]
> For all $\beta \in A$, either $\beta \in A * \alpha$ or $\neg\beta \in \mathrm{Cn}(A * \alpha)$

can be used to characterize the maxichoice variants of both internal and external partial meet revision.

THEOREM 3.12

1. [50] *An operator of internal partial meet revision is maxichoice if and only if it satisfies tenacity.*
2. *An operator of external partial meet revision is maxichoice if and only if it satisfies tenacity.*

[Proof: pp. 250 and 257.]

The following example shows that tenacity is not on all occasions a realistic property of belief revision.

> **Example**
> I thought that John's mother was alive. Then a friend told me that she had met John's daughter, 'who was very sad since her grandmother is dead'. Hearing this, I revised my belief state to include the new belief that either John's mother or his mother-in-law is dead.

After this revision, I did not any longer believe that John's mother was alive. Neither did I believe that she was dead. I was in a state of suspense, not knowing whether or not she was dead.

Let β denote that John's mother is alive. In order to account for this example, we need a belief base A such that $\beta \in A$, but neither β nor $\neg\beta$ is implied by the revised belief base. Hence, tenacity does not hold in this case.

The other limiting case, full meet revision, can be characterized by the following postulate:

Inertness:
If $\beta \in A * \alpha$, then it holds for all sets B that if $\alpha \in B \subseteq A \cup \{\alpha\}$, then B is consistent if and only if $B \cup \{\beta\}$ is consistent.

According to inertness, all elements of $A*\alpha$ are inert in the sense of not influencing whether or not a subset of A is consistent with α.

Just like tenacity, inertness can be applied to both internal and external partial meet revision. Furthermore, it turns out that full meet internal revision and full meet external revision coincide. (Internal and and external maxichoice revision do not coincide.)

THEOREM 3.13 *Let A be a set and $*$ an operator for A. Then the following three statements are equivalent:*

1. *$*$ satisfies inclusion, relevance, success, uniformity, and inertness.*
2. *$*$ is an operator of internal full meet revision ($\mp$)*
3. *$*$ is an operator of external full meet revision ($\pm$)*

[Proof: pp. 247 and 256.]

The following example shows that inertness is not plausible as a general property of rational belief revision:

Example
Helen has two daughters, Alice who is 21 and Beatrice who is 15. Until recently, I believed that both daughters were unmarried. Then I heard Helen say that one of her two daughters is married. After that, I believe that Alice is married, but I still believe that Beatrice is unmarried.

Let α denote that Alice is married and β that Beatrice is married. We can assume that both $\neg\alpha$ and $\neg\beta$ were elements of the original belief base A. After revision by $\alpha\vee\beta$, $\neg\beta$ was retained but $\neg\alpha$ was discarded. This pattern is incompatible with inertness. Let $B = \{\alpha\vee\beta, \neg\alpha\}$. Then $\neg\beta \in A * (\alpha\vee\beta)$ and also $\alpha\vee\beta \in B \subseteq A\cup\{\alpha\vee\beta\}$, but B is consistent and $B\cup\{\neg\beta\}$ inconsistent, contrary to inertness.

In summary, both limiting cases have implausible properties.

4 REVISING BELIEF SETS

Revision of (logically closed) belief sets can be based on the same two suboperations as revision of belief bases: In order to revise A by α, we contract by $\neg\alpha$ and expand by α. Contraction is defined in the same way for belief sets as for belief bases. Expansion, on the other hand, is defined differently, and this difference has important consequences for belief set revision.

Whereas belief bases are expanded by non-closing expansion, $A+\alpha = A\cup\{\alpha\}$, belief sets are expanded by *closing expansion*, $A+\alpha = \text{Cn}(A\cup\{\alpha\})$. The reason for this is, of course, that expansion of a belief set should preserve logical closure. We want the outcome of expanding a belief set to be a new belief set.

The definitions of internal and external partial meet revision can be transferred to belief sets as follows:

$A\mp_\gamma\alpha = (A\sim_\gamma\neg\alpha) + \alpha$ (*internal partial meet revision*)
$A\pm_\gamma\alpha = (A+\alpha) \sim_\gamma \neg\alpha$ (*external partial meet revision*)

External partial meet revision on belief sets has implausible properties. If $\neg\alpha \in A$, then $A+\alpha = \text{Cn}(A\cup\{\alpha\})$ is inconsistent and logically closed, i.e. $\text{Cn}(A\cup\{\alpha\}) = \mathcal{L}$. (The only logically closed inconsistent set is the whole language itself.)

Let A_1 and A_2 be two belief sets that both contain $\neg\alpha$. We then have:

$A_1\pm_\gamma\alpha = (A_1+\alpha)\sim_\gamma\neg\alpha = \mathcal{L}\sim_\gamma\neg\alpha$ and
$A_2\pm_\gamma\alpha = (A_2+\alpha)\sim_\gamma\neg\alpha = \mathcal{L}\sim_\gamma\neg\alpha$,

so that $A_1\pm_\gamma\alpha = A_2\pm_\gamma\alpha$. In other words, all belief sets that contain $\neg\alpha$ yield the same result when revised by α. This is an absurd pattern, as can be seen from the following example:

Example
George and Hubert differed a lot in what they knew and believed. However, they both believed that Tycho Brahe, the 16th century Danish astronomer, used a telescope. One day, they both revised their belief sets to include the new belief that Tycho Brahe did not use a telescope. After this, their belief sets turned out identical, i.e. George believed everything that Hubert believed, and vice versa.

The information inherent in the previous belief set is completely lost in belief-contravening external partial meet revision. Therefore, it does not make sense to apply external partial meet revision to belief sets.

Internal partial meet revision, on the other hand, is a plausible way to revise belief sets. Historically, this was the original form of partial meet revision. It was introduced as part of the AGM model of belief change [1]. In what follows, by partial meet revision of a belief set will always be meant internal partial meet revision.

Partial meet revision on belief sets has been axiomatically characterized as follows:

THEOREM 3.14 ((AGM [1; 35]) *Let A be a logically closed set. The operator* $*$ *is an operator of partial meet revision for A if and only if it satisfies:*
$A * \alpha$ *is a belief set (closure)*
$\alpha \in A * \alpha$ *(success)*
$A * \alpha \subseteq A + \alpha$ *(inclusion)*
If $\neg\alpha \notin A$, *then* $A * \alpha = A + \alpha$. *(vacuity)*
$A * \alpha$ *is consistent if* α *is consistent. (consistency)*
If $(\alpha \leftrightarrow \beta) \in \mathrm{Cn}(\emptyset)$, *then* $A * \alpha = A * \beta$. *(extensionality)*
[Proof: p. 279.]

The six postulates of this theorem are commonly called the *basic Gärdenfors postulates for revision.* Two of them, namely *success* and *consistency,* coincide with postulates for belief bases that were introduced in Section 3.1. (But historically, they were first proposed for belief sets.) Another two, namely *inclusion* and *vacuity,* almost coincide: The same formulas can be used for both belief bases and belief sets, but '+' must be interpreted as non-closing expansion in the former case and as closing expansion in the latter.

The Harper identity, that was introduced above for belief bases, holds for belief sets as well. It, too, was first proposed as a property of operations on belief sets [30].

OBSERVATION 3.15 (AGM [1]) *Let A be a (logically closed) belief set and* γ *a selection function for A . Then* $A \sim_\gamma \alpha = A \cap (A \mp_\gamma \neg\alpha)$. *(the Harper identity)*
[Proof: p. 280.]

Through the Levi and Harper identities, revision and contraction operators are interdefinable. To express this more precisely, it is convenient to introduce functions that take us from contractions to revisions and vice versa. This can be done as follows:

DEFINITION 3.16 (Makinson [83]) *Let A be a belief set. Then* $\mathbb{R}$ *is the function such that for every operator* $\div$ *for A:*
$\mathbb{R}(\div)$ *is the operator for A such that for all* α: $A(\mathbb{R}(\div))\alpha = \mathrm{Cn}((A \div \neg\alpha) \cup \{\alpha\})$
Furthermore, $\mathbb{C}$ *is the function such that for every operator* $*$ *for A:*
$\mathbb{C}(*)$ *is the operator for A such that for all* α: $A(\mathbb{C}(*))\alpha = A \cap (A * \neg\alpha)$

The definition can also be expressed as follows: For every operator $\div$ of contraction, $\mathbb{R}(\div)$ is the operator generated from $\div$ through the Levi identity. Thus, if $\mathbb{R}(\div) = *$, then $A * \alpha = \mathrm{Cn}((A \div \neg\alpha) \cup \{\alpha\})$ for all α. Correspondingly, for every revision operator $*$, $\mathbb{C}(*)$ is the operator generated from $*$ by the Harper identity. Thus, if $\mathbb{C}(*) = \div$, then $A \div \alpha = A \cap (A * \neg\alpha)$ for all α.

It follows from the definition of partial meet revision that if $\div$ is an operator of partial meet contraction, then $\mathbb{R}(\div)$ is an operator of partial meet revision. Furthermore, it follows from Observation 3.15 that if $*$ is an operator of partial meet revision, then $\mathbb{C}(*)$ is an operator of partial meet contraction. From this we can conclude that for any operator $\div$ of partial meet contraction, $\mathbb{C}(\mathbb{R}(\div))$ is an operator of partial meet contraction. It can also be shown that $\mathbb{C}(\mathbb{R}(\div))$ is identical to $\div$. Furthermore, if $*$ is a partial meet revision, then $\mathbb{R}(\mathbb{C}(*))$ can be shown to be identical to $*$.

OBSERVATION 3.17 (Makinson [83])
1. If $\div$ is a partial meet contraction, then $\mathbb{C}(\mathbb{R}(\div)) = \div$.
2. If $*$ is a partial meet revision, then $\mathbb{R}(\mathbb{C}(*)) = *$.
[Proof: p. 279.]

5 HAVE WE DONE ALL THIS IN VAIN?

The following is a direct consequence of the definitions introduced in the foregoing section:

> If $\div$ is a partial meet contraction, then $\mathbb{R}(\div)$ is a partial meet revision.

As we saw in Section 2.3, an operator $\div$ is a partial meet contraction if and only if it satisfies the six basic Gärdenfors postulates. The following is therefore an equivalent formulation:

> If $\div$ satisfies the contraction-postulates *closure*, *inclusion*, *vacuity*, *success*, *extensionality*, and *recovery*, then $\mathbb{R}(\div)$ is a partial meet revision.

This result can be strengthened in an interesting and perhaps surprising way: For $\mathbb{R}(\div)$ to be a partial meet revision, it is not necessary for $\div$ to be a partial meet contraction. It is sufficient that it is a withdrawal, i.e. that it satisfies the first five of the basic postulates (excluding recovery):

OBSERVATION 3.18 (Makinson [83]) *Let A be a belief set and let $\div$ be a withdrawal for A (i.e. it satisfies the contraction-postulates closure, inclusion, vacuity, success, and extensionality). Then $\mathbb{R}(\div)$ is a partial meet revision.*
[Proof: p. 280.]

It follows from Observations 3.15 and 3.18 that if $\div$ is a withdrawal, then $\mathbb{C}(\mathbb{R}(\div))$ is a partial meet contraction. Furthermore, since $\mathbb{R}(\div)$ is a partial meet revision, it follows from Part 2 of Observation 3.17 that $\mathbb{R}(\mathbb{C}(\mathbb{R}(\div))) = \mathbb{R}(\div)$. This is another way of saying that $\mathbb{C}(\mathbb{R}(\div))$ and $\div$ give rise to the same operator of partial meet revision.

We can call two contraction operators *revision-equivalent* if they give rise to the same revision, i.e.:

DEFINITION 3.19 (Makinson [83]) *Two contraction operators* $\div$ *and* $\div'$ *are* revision-equivalent *if and only if* $\mathbb{R}(\div) = \mathbb{R}(\div')$.

We have shown that:

OBSERVATION 3.20 (Makinson [83]) *Let A be a belief set and let* $\div$ *be a withdrawal for A. Then* $\mathbb{C}(\mathbb{R}(\div))$

1. *is an operator of partial meet contraction for A, and*
2. *is revision-equivalent with* $\div$.

[Proof: see above.]

In Section 2.1, we found that (pure) contraction is rare. The major use of contraction is as a suboperation of revision. In Chapter 2, we developed quite elaborate constructions of partial meet contraction. At first hand, Observation 3.20 gives the impression that all this was done to no avail, at least from the point of view of belief revision. If the purpose of contraction operators is to use them as suboperators in revision, then we do not seem to need partial meet contraction. According to Observation 3.20 we can instead employ withdrawals, that are arguably much simpler from a formal point of view. Have our studies of contraction been futile? Have we done all this in vain?

Fortunately, the answer is no. Observation 3.20 shows that in saying that an operator of revision is based on some operator of partial meet contraction (with no further specification), we say neither more nor less than if we had said that it is based on some operator of withdrawal. However, if we further specify the type of partial meet contraction, then this will have effects on the resulting operator of revision. In the next two sections, we will study revision operators that are based on more specified types of partial meet contraction (maxichoice, transitively relational, etc.) Such revision operators have properties not shared by withdrawal-based revision in general.

6 LIMITING CASES OF BELIEF SET REVISION

Full meet revision ($\mp$) of a belief set represents an extremely cautious pattern of belief change:

OBSERVATION 3.21 (Alchourrón and Makinson [3]) *Let A be a logically closed set, and let* $\mp = \mathbb{R}(\sim)$, *i.e. let* $\mp$ *be full meet revision for A. Then:*

1. *If* $\neg\alpha \in A$, *then* $A \mp \alpha = \mathrm{Cn}(\{\alpha\})$.
2. *If* $\neg\alpha \notin A$, *then* $A \mp \alpha = \mathrm{Cn}(A \cup \{\alpha\})$.

[Proof: p. 286.]

If an agent performs full meet revision after receiving some new information that contradicts her previous beliefs, then she gives up all previous beliefs and replaces them by the new information and its logical consequences. It is not easy to find a single case in which such a model of belief revision is compatible with sanity.

Maxichoice revision of belief sets does not fare much better, as can be seen from the following observation. (A similar result for belief bases was reported in Theorem 3.12.)

OBSERVATION 3.22 (Alchourrón and Makinson [3]) *Let A be a logically closed set and* $\mp_\gamma$ *an operator of maxichoice revision for A. Then it holds for all sentences* α *and* β *that:*
If $\neg\alpha \in A$, *then either* $\beta \in A \mp_\gamma \alpha$ *or* $\neg\beta \in A \mp_\gamma \alpha$.
[Proof: p. 287.]

In other words, every belief-contravening maxichoice revision transforms the belief set into a consistent set that contains the negation of every sentence that it does not contain. After maxichoice revision, the agent has an opinion on everything.

> **Example**
> Mary was a normal person until she once changed her mind on a trivial issue. After that she became an intolerable *Besserwisser*, who behaved as if she knew everything. It was impossible to find a question that she did not answer confidently, one way or the other.

Hence, full meet revision and maxichoice revision have equally absurd but very different effects on belief sets.

7 REVISING BY CONJUNCTIONS AND DISJUNCTIONS

In our search for additional plausible properties of belief set revision, it is natural to investigate revisions by conjunctions, just as we studied contractions by conjunctions in Section 2.5.

The postulate of inclusion ($A * \alpha \subseteq A + \alpha$) says that revision by a sentence always yields a subset of the outcome of expansion by the same sentence. This postulate can be strengthened with respect to revision by a conjunction $\alpha \& \beta$. Not only should $A * (\alpha \& \beta)$ be a subset of $A + (\alpha \& \beta)$. It should also be a subset of $(A * \alpha) + \beta$, i.e. to first revise by one sentence and then expand by another should not lead to a smaller set than to revise in one step by both of them.

Superexpansion: [29; 31]
$A * (\alpha \& \beta) \subseteq (A * \alpha) + \beta$

According to superexpansion, if we exclude one of the conjuncts from the revision, and instead expand by it afterwards, then we obtain a *super*set of what we would have otherwise obtained. This postulate has also been called 'conjunctive inclusion' [23] and 'conjunction 1' [40].

The converse relationship,

$$(A * \alpha) + \beta \subseteq A * (\alpha \& \beta)$$

cannot hold in general, since if $\neg\beta \in \mathrm{Cn}(A * \alpha)$ then $(A * \alpha) + \beta$ is inconsistent, whereas $A * (\alpha \& \beta)$ is consistent if $\alpha \& \beta$ is consistent. If we exclude this case, however, then it can reasonably be required that $(A * \alpha) + \beta \subseteq A * (\alpha \& \beta)$:

Subexpansion: [31]
If $\neg\beta \notin \mathrm{Cn}(A * \alpha)$, then $(A * \alpha) + \beta \subseteq A * (\alpha \& \beta)$.

According to subexpansion, if we exclude one of the conjuncts from the revision, and instead expand by it afterwards, then if the outcome is consistent it is a *sub*set of what we would have obtained through revision in one step by both conjuncts, Subexpansion has also been called 'conjunctive vacuity' [23], 'conjunction 2' [40], and 'rational monotony' [40].

Together, superexpansion and subexpansion imply that $A*(\alpha\&\beta)$ is identical to $(A*\alpha)+\beta$, unless β contradicts $A*\alpha$. The following example serves to illustrate this principle:

Example (Peter Gärdenfors [35])
I revise my present belief state by accepting the belief α that J. S. Bach did not compose the Toccata and Fugue in D minor for organ. After that I add to the new state of belief the belief β that the composer of the Toccata and Fugue also wrote a duet for flute and lute (which Bach never did). Since β is consistent with $A * \alpha$, it can be accommodated by simple expansion. The net result of the two changes, $(A * \alpha) + \beta$, should be the same as revising A by the composite belief $\alpha \& \beta$ that someone, not identical with J. S. Bach, wrote both the Toccata and Fugue and a duet for flute and lute, $A * (\alpha \& \beta)$.

Further insights into the logic of revision can be gained by investigating revision by disjunctions, and in particular by comparing $A*(\alpha \vee \beta)$ to $A*\alpha$ and $A*\beta$. One fairly reasonable principle is that if an element of A is retained after revision by α, and it is also retained after revision by β, then it is retained after revision by $\alpha \vee \beta$. The disjunctive sentence $\alpha \vee \beta$ has no force to push out what is not pushed out by either α or β. Similarly, if revision by α leads to the acceptance of some new belief δ, and revision by β also leads to the acceptance of δ, then revision by $\alpha \vee \beta$ should lead to the acceptance of δ. Somewhat more generally:

Disjunctive overlap: [35]
$(A * \alpha) \cap (A * \beta) \subseteq A * (\alpha \vee \beta)$.

The following example illustrates disjunctive overlap:

Example
I believe that Mary has no child ($\neg\delta$). I also believe that John, her husband, has no child.
Case 1: I overhear a conversation between John and an old friend of his, in which he uses the phrase 'My son'. I revise my beliefs to incorporate the new belief that John has a son (α). After doing this, I still believe that Mary has no child ($\neg\delta$).
Case 2: The phrase that I hear John use is 'My daughter'. I revise my beliefs to incorporate the new belief that John has a daughter (β). After doing this, I still believe that Mary has no child ($\neg\delta$).
Case 3: The phrase that I hear instead is 'My child'. I revise my beliefs to incorporate the new belief that John has either a son or a daughter ($\alpha \vee \beta$). Do I still believe that Mary has no child ($\neg\delta$)?

The most natural answer to this question is 'yes', which corroborates the postulate of disjunctive overlap. For further corroboration of the postulate, change the descriptions of cases 1 and 2 so that 'Mary has a child' (δ) is accepted both as a consequence of revision by α (case 1) and as a result of revision by β (case 2). We can then expect δ to be accepted after revision by $\alpha \vee \beta$ as well, again in conformity with disjunctive overlap.

Disjunctive overlap is similar in structure to the postulate of conjunctive overlap for belief contraction. What about the corresponding property

$$(A * \alpha) \cap (A * \beta) \subseteq A * (\alpha \& \beta)$$

of 'conjunctive overlap' for revision? The following example shows that this is not a reasonable postulate:

Example
I believe that John is a monogamous person (δ). I do not know if he has a girlfriend.
Case 1: I am told that he has a relationship with Annabel (α). After revising my beliefs to include this new information, I still believe that he is a monogamous person (δ).
Case 2: I am told that he has a relationship with Belinda (β). After revising my beliefs to include this new information, I still believe that he is a monogamous person (δ).
Case 3: I am told that he has relationships both with Annabel and with Belinda ($\alpha \& \beta$). After revising my beliefs to include this new information, I do not any longer believe him to be monogamous (δ).

Expansion has the neat property $A + (\alpha \vee \beta) \subseteq A + \alpha$. The following example shows that the corresponding property for revision, $A * (\alpha \vee \beta) \subseteq A * \alpha$, does not hold in general:

> **Example**
> Four-year-old Jane comes into the playground with a doll in one hand and in the other a black object that I first believe to be a water-pistol.
>
> *Case 1*: When she comes near, I see that the black object is either a real pistol (α) or a well-made full-sized replica of a pistol (β). I revise my beliefs to include $\alpha \vee \beta$. After that, I believe that it is a full-sized replica of a pistol (β). I also believe that it is not a real pistol ($\neg\alpha$).
>
> *Case 2*: When she comes near, I can see that it is a real pistol. I revise my set of beliefs to include the new information (α), and after that I believe that the object is a real pistol (α).

The general principle illustrated in this example is that sometimes revision by $\alpha \vee \beta$ results in a belief state that contains β and $\neg\alpha$. Such a belief set implies $\alpha \vee \beta$, so that *success* is satisfied. However, if α is consistent, then it follows from *success* and *consistency* that $\neg\alpha \notin A * \alpha$. We can conclude from $\neg\alpha \in A * (\alpha \vee \beta)$ and $\neg\alpha \notin A * \alpha$ that $A * (\alpha \vee \beta) \not\subseteq A * \alpha$.

This argument shows that $A * (\alpha \vee \beta) \subseteq A * \alpha$ does not hold if $\neg\alpha \in A * (\alpha \vee \beta)$. However, it says nothing against $A * (\alpha \vee \beta) \subseteq A * \alpha$ in the remaining case when $\neg\alpha \notin A * (\alpha \vee \beta)$. In that case, the postulate is quite plausible:

> *Disjunctive inclusion:* [35]
> If $\neg\alpha \notin \mathrm{Cn}(A * (\alpha \vee \beta))$, then $A * (\alpha \vee \beta) \subseteq A * \alpha$.

The following example illustrates the postulate of disjunctive inclusion:

> **Example**
> There are two species of eagle in Sweden, the white-tailed eagle and the golden eagle. My friend Peter has been on vacations in Sweden.
>
> *Case 1*: He says: 'I saw an eagle in Sweden'. I then revise my belief set to include $\alpha \vee \beta$, where α denotes that he has seen a white-tailed eagle and β that he has seen a golden eagle.
>
> *Case 2*: He says: 'I saw a white-tailed eagle in Sweden'. I then revise my belief set to include α.

We can expect that the resulting belief set in case 1, $A * (\alpha \vee \beta)$, should be a subset of the resulting belief set in case 2, $A * \alpha$ — unless I concluded in case 1 that the eagle he saw could not have been a white-tailed eagle. (This conclusion might be justified if I know which parts of Sweden he visited.) This is the exception provided for by the condition 'If $\neg\alpha \notin \mathrm{Cn}(A * (\alpha \vee \beta)) \dots$' of the postulate.

There are three ways to revise your beliefs by a disjunction $\alpha\vee\beta$: either you accept α, or you accept β, or you remain in suspense between them. We can use the same example of eagle-watching to illustrate this. The first way to revise by $\alpha\vee\beta$ results in a belief set that includes α. Then we should expect that $A * (\alpha\vee\beta) = A * \alpha$. If the information that my friend has seen an eagle leads me to believe that he has seen a white-tailed eagle, then it should not have made any difference if I had instead received the information that he has seen a white-tailed eagle. Similarly, in the second case, we should expect that $A * (\alpha\vee\beta) = A * \beta$.

In the third case, the information that my friend has seen an eagle results in a belief state that keeps me in suspense with respect to the choice between α and β. I then believe what I would also believe both if I were led to believe that he saw a white-tailed eagle and if I were led to believe that he saw a golden eagle. In other words, we should expect that $A * (\alpha\vee\beta) = (A * \alpha) \cap (A * \beta)$ in this case.

Summarizing the three cases, we arrive at the following postulate for belief revision:

> *Disjunctive factoring:* [1]
> Either $A * (\alpha\vee\beta) = A * \alpha$, $A * (\alpha\vee\beta) = A * \beta$, or $A * (\alpha\vee\beta) = (A * \alpha) \cap (A * \beta)$.

Given the basic Gärdenfors postulates for belief revision, the five new postulates that we have introduced in this section are closely interconnected:

OBSERVATION 3.23 *Let A be a logically closed set and $\mp_\gamma$ a partial meet revision for A. Then:*

1. (Peter Gärdenfors [35]) $\mp_\gamma$ *satisfies superexpansion if and only if it satisfies disjunctive overlap.*
2. (Hans Rott [35]) $\mp_\gamma$ *satisfies subexpansion if and only if it satisfies disjunctive inclusion.*
3. (Hans Rott [35]) $\mp_\gamma$ *satisfies disjunctive factoring if and only if it satisfies both disjunctive overlap and disjunctive inclusion.*

[Proof: pp. 270, 271 and 272.]

This observation allows us to restrict our attention to only two of the five postulates. Traditionally, *superexpansion* and *subexpansion* are singled out as the two major additional postulates. They are the *supplementary Gärdenfors postulates* for belief revision.

The supplementary postulates for revision are closely related to those for contraction:

OBSERVATION 3.24 (AGM [1]) *Let A be a logically closed set and γ a selection function for A (so that $\sim_\gamma$ is a partial meet contraction and $\mp_\gamma$ a partial meet revision for A). Then:*

1. $\mp_\gamma$ *satisfies superexpansion if and only if* $\sim_\gamma$ *satisfies conjunctive overlap.*
2. $\mp_\gamma$ *satisfies subexpansion if and only if* $\sim_\gamma$ *satisfies conjunctive inclusion.*

[Proof: pp. 282 and 284.]

Combining this with Theorems 2.21 and 3.14, we obtain the following representation theorem:

THEOREM 3.25 (AGM [1]) *Let A be a logically closed set and* * *an operation for A . Then* * *is a transitively relational partial meet revision if and only if it satisfies closure, success, inclusion, vacuity, consistency, extensionality, superexpansion, and subexpansion.*
[Proof: p. 285.]

8   POSSIBLE WORLD MODELS

For every set A of sentences, we can form the set $A\bot^\bot$, where $\bot$ represents a logically false sentence (such as $p\&\neg p$). $A\bot^\bot$ is the set of *maximal consistent subsets* of A. If A is consistent, then $A\bot^\bot = \{A\}$, but if A is inconsistent then $A\bot^\bot$ consists of all those proper subsets of A that are consistent but cannot be enlarged within A without becoming inconsistent.

The largest set from which we can form maximal consistent subsets is the logical language itself, i.e., the set of all expressions. It is denoted by $\mathcal{L}$, and consequently $\mathcal{L}\bot^\bot$ is the set of maximal consistent subsets of the language, or in short: the set of *maximal consistent sets*.

For an example, let $\mathcal{L}$ consist only of the sentences p and q, and their truth-functional combinations (i.e. the sentences that can be formed from p and q with $\neg$, $\vee$, and other truth-functional operators). Then it can be shown that

$$\mathcal{L}\bot^\bot = \{\text{Cn}(\{p, q\}), \text{Cn}(\{\neg p, q\}), \text{Cn}(\{p, \neg q\}), \text{Cn}(\{\neg p, \neg q\})\}.$$

In general, a set X is an element of $\mathcal{L}\bot^\bot$ if and only if:

  (i) X is a set of sentences,
  (ii) X is consistent, and
  (iii) it holds for every set X' of sentences that if $X \subset X'$, then X' is inconsistent.

This definition is only a direct application of our general definition of remainders (Definition 1.35). Maximal consistent sets have many useful logical properties. One of them is that if W is a maximal consistent set, then W contains the negation of every sentence that it does not contain. Since W never contains both a sentence and its negation (that would lead to inconsistency), $\alpha \notin W$ holds if and only if $\neg\alpha \in W$.

In philosophical logic, a maximal consistent set is commonly interpreted as a representation, in the language used, of a possible state of the world. For shortness, maximal consistent sets are called *possible worlds*. Sets of possible worlds are also called *propositions*.

Sets of possible worlds can be used as an alternative representation of belief states. A belief state can be represented by the proposition (set of possible worlds) that contains exactly those possible worlds that are compatible with the agent's beliefs. In this way, propositions can represent belief states, just as belief sets and belief bases can do the same.

There is a close connection between propositions and belief sets. To see this, let the belief set A and the proposition (set of possible worlds) $\mathcal{W}$ represent one and the same belief state. Then a possible world W should be an element of $\mathcal{W}$ if and only if it is compatible with the beliefs that the agent has in A, i.e. if and only if it does not contradict A. Thus:

$W \in \mathcal{W}$ if and only if there is no sentence $\alpha \in A$ such that $\neg\alpha \in W$.

Since W is maximal consistent, $\neg\alpha \in W$ is equivalent to $\alpha \notin W$, and we can restate the condition as follows:

$W \in \mathcal{W}$ if and only if there is no $\alpha \in A$ such that $\alpha \notin W$.

By set theory, this is equivalent to the following:

$W \in \mathcal{W}$ if and only if $A \subseteq W$.

It follows that if the belief set A and the proposition $\mathcal{W}$ represent the same belief state, then $\mathcal{W}$ consists of exactly those possible worlds that contain A. This set of possible worlds will be denoted by $[A]$.

DEFINITION 3.26 *Let A be a belief set. Then:*

$$[A] = \{W \in \mathcal{L}\bot^{\bot} \mid A \subseteq W\}.$$

For any sentence α, $[\alpha]$ *is an abbreviation of* $[\text{Cn}(\{\alpha\})]$.

Hence, a proposition $\mathcal{W}$ represents the same belief state as a belief set A if and only if $\mathcal{W} = [A]$. For every belief set A there is a set $[A]$ of possible worlds (a proposition) that represents the same belief state as A. If A is the inconsistent belief set, then $[A] = \emptyset$. Otherwise, $[A]$ is a non-empty subset of $\mathcal{L}\bot^{\bot}$.

OBSERVATION 3.27
1. Let A be a belief set. Then $\bigcap[A] = A$.
2. Let $\mathcal{W}$ *be a set of possible worlds. Then* $\bigcap \mathcal{W}$ *is a belief set.*
[Proof: p. 287.]

Propositions provide us with a more intuitively clear picture of some aspects of belief change. It is convenient to represent $\mathcal{L}\perp^{\perp}$ (the set of possible worlds) as a geometrical surface. In Figure 3.1, think of every point on the rectangle's surface as representing a possible world. The circle marked $[A\ ]$ represents those possible worlds in which all sentences in A are true, i.e. the set $[A\ ]$ of possible worlds. The area marked $[\alpha]$ represents those possible worlds in which the sentence α is true.

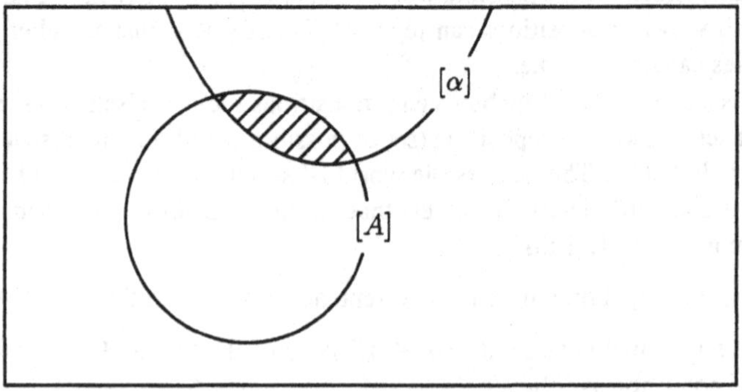

Figure 3.1. Revision of A by α.

In Figure 3.1, $[A]$ and $[\alpha]$ have a non-empty intersection, which means that A is compatible with α. The revision of A by α is therefore not belief-contravening. Its outcome is obtained by giving up those elements of $[A\ ]$ that are incompatible with α. In other words, the result of revising $[A\ ]$ by $[\alpha]$ should be equal to $[A] \cap [\alpha]$.

If $[A\ ]$ and $[\alpha]$ do not intersect, then the outcome of the revision must be sought outside of $[A\ ]$. In the revised belief state, α should be held to be true, i.e. the outcome of the revision should be a subset of $[\alpha]$, as in Figure 3.2.

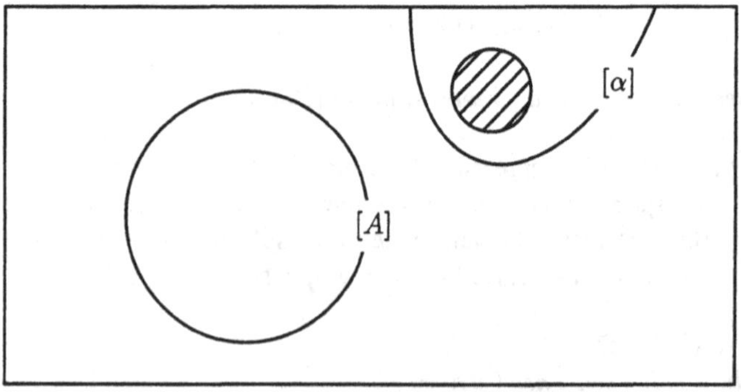

Figure 3.2. Revision of A by α (the belief-contravening case).

In the limiting case when α is logically false, it follows from Definition 3.26 that $[\alpha]$ is empty. The resulting belief state should nevertheless be a subset of $[\alpha]$, i.e. the outcome will in this case be the empty set of possible worlds (that corresponds to the inconsistent belief set).

We can summarize this as follows:

The outcome of revising $[A]$ by $[\alpha]$ is a subset of $[\alpha]$ that is

1. non-empty if $[\alpha]$ is non-empty, and
2. equal to $[A] \cap [\alpha]$ if $[A] \cap [\alpha]$ is non-empty.

This simple rule for revision can be shown to *correspond exactly to partial meet revision.*

The above rule for revision is highly unspecified. It allows us, if $[A] \cap [\alpha] = \emptyset$, to choose any non-empty subset of $[\alpha]$ as the outcome of the revision. We do not want the revised belief state to differ more from the original belief state $[A]$ than what is motivated by $[\alpha]$. This can be achieved by requiring that the outcome of revising $[A]$ by $[\alpha]$ consists of those elements of $[\alpha]$ that are as close as possible to $[A]$. For that purpose, we can think of $[A]$ as surrounded by a system of concentric spheres [41]. Each sphere represents a degree of closeness or similarity to $[A]$. The spheres around a set of possible worlds have also been called its 'fallbacks' [79].

The outcome of revising $[A]$ by $[\alpha]$ should be the intersection of $[\alpha]$ with the narrowest sphere ('fallback') around $[A]$ that has a non-empty intersection with $[\alpha]$, as in Figure 3.3. This construction was invented by Adam Grove, who also proved that such sphere-based revision *corresponds exactly to transitively relational partial meet revision* [41].

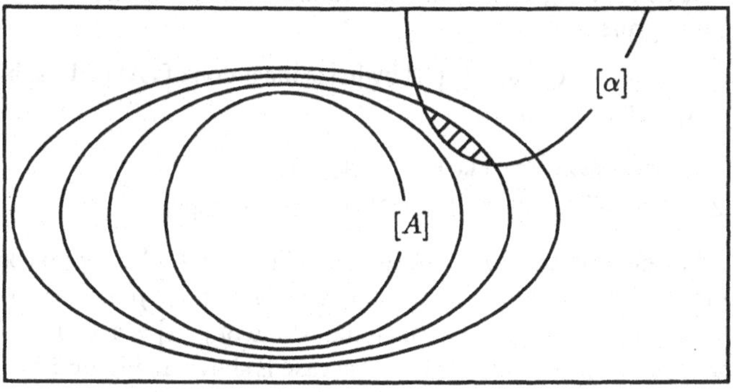

Figure 3.3. Sphere-based revision of A by α.

In order to account for *iterated* revision, the spheres model has to be generalized so that there is a system of spheres (fallbacks) around every set of possible worlds.

Hence, in Figure 3.3, there must be a system of spheres around the outcome of revising $[A]$ by $[\alpha]$. These spheres are needed to perform further revisions.

Wlodek Rabinowicz has proposed that such a generalized spheres model can be based on a four-place similarity model between possible worlds [105]. For any four elements W_1, W_2, W_3, and W_4 of $\mathcal{L}\perp^{\perp}$, let $sim(W_1, W_2, W_3, W_4)$ denote that W_1 is at least as close to W_2 as W_3 is to W_4. Then a system of spheres around each $[A]$ can be defined as follows:

1. For any set X of worlds, let $\leq_X$ (the similarity ordering of worlds with respect to X) be the relation such that $W \leq_X V$ holds if and only if: For every $V' \in X$ there is some $W' \in X$ such that $sim(W', W, V', V)$
2. A set Y is a sphere around $[A]$ if and only if (i) $Y \neq \emptyset$ if $[A] \neq \emptyset$, and (ii) for every $W \in \mathcal{L}\perp^{\perp}$ and every $V \in Y$, if $W \leq_{[A]} V$, then $W \in Y$ (closure downwards of Y with respect to $\leq_{[A]}$).

In this way, a global revision operator can be obtained that coincides, for each belief state, with a sphere-based revision operator as defined above. Further properties of this construction remain to be investigated.

Possible world models can also be used for contraction. In contraction, a restriction on what worlds are possible (compatible with the agent's beliefs) is removed. Thus, the set of possibilities is enlarged. We should therefore expect the contraction of $[A]$ by $[\alpha]$ to be a superset of $[A]$. Furthermore, the new possibilities should be worlds in which α does not hold, i.e., they should be worlds in which $\neg\alpha$ holds. The result of contracting by α should be that $\neg\alpha$ is held to be possible.

In the limiting case when $[A]$ and $[\neg\alpha]$ have a non-empty intersection, no enlargement of $[A]$ is necessary to make $\neg\alpha$ possible, and the original belief state will therefore be unchanged. In summary, contraction can be performed according to the following rule:

> The outcome of contracting $[A]$ by $[\alpha]$ is the union of $[A]$ and a subset of $[\neg\alpha]$ that is
>
> 1. non-empty if $[\neg\alpha]$ is non-empty, and
> 2. equal to $[A] \cap [\neg\alpha]$ if $[A] \cap [\neg\alpha]$ is non-empty.

Belief-contravening contraction is illustrated in Figure 3.4. Contraction performed according to this rule can be shown to *correspond exactly to partial meet contraction*. Furthermore, the special case when the whole of $[\neg\alpha]$ is added to $[A]$ *corresponds exactly to full meet contraction*. That case is shown in Figure 3.5. The other extreme case, when only one element of $[\neg\alpha]$ (a 'point' on the surface) is added to $[A]$ corresponds exactly to maxichoice contraction. Thus, in maxichoice contraction by α we add only one possible way in which α can be false ($\neg\alpha$ can be true).

Spheres around the original set of possible worlds can also be used for contraction. In sphere-based contraction of $[A]$ by $[\alpha]$, those elements of $[\neg\alpha]$ are added

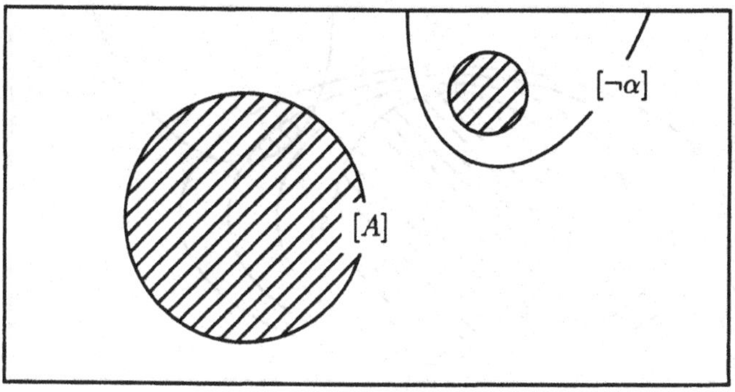

Figure 3.4. Contraction of A by α.

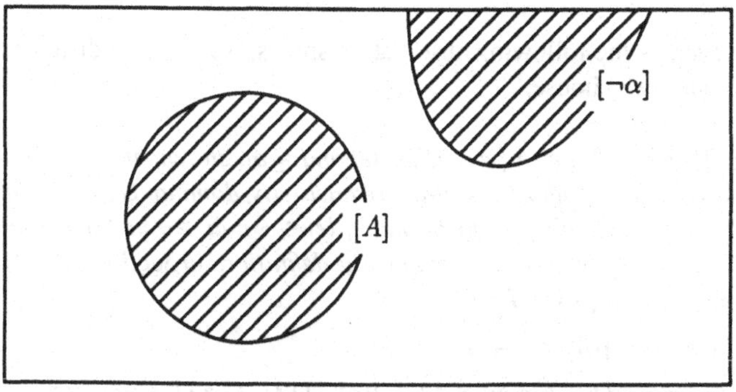

Figure 3.5. Full meet contraction of A by α.

that belong to the closest sphere around $[A]$ that has a non-empty intersection with $[\neg\alpha]$. The procedure is shown in Figure 3.6. Sphere-based contraction *corresponds exactly to transitively relational partial meet contraction.*

In this section, the connections between partial meet operations and operations on propositions (sets of possible worlds) have been given in a rather loose, intuitive way. The reader who prefers exact mathematical statements of these connections is referred to Sections 3.23⁺–3.24⁺.

9 ENTRENCHMENT-BASED REVISION

The Levi identity can be used to derive operators of revision from entrenchment-based contraction operators. Since there are two types of entrenchment-based contraction, constructed by Gärdenfors and Rott, respectively, there are two ways to do

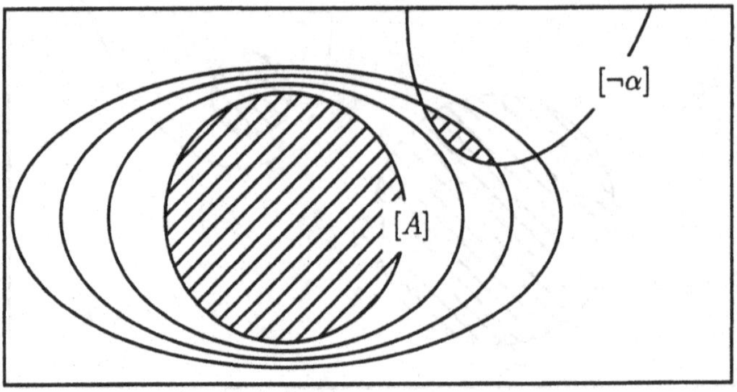

Figure 3.6. Sphere-based contraction of A by α.

this. However, as the following observation shows, it makes no difference which of the two ways we choose.

OBSERVATION 3.28 *Let A be a belief set and $\leq$ an entrenchment ordering on A that satisfies the five standard postulates (transitivity, dominance, conjunctiveness, minimality, and maximality). Furthermore, let $\div_G$ and $\div_R$ be the entrenchment-based contraction operators according to the definitions in Section 2.10. Let $\mp_G = \mathbb{R}(\div_G)$ and $\mp_R = \mathbb{R}(\div_R)$. Then:*

1. (Hans Rott [110]) $\mp_G = \mp_R$
2. (Lindström and Rabinowicz [79], Rott [113]) *For all sentences α and β: $\beta \in A \mp_G \alpha$ if and only if either $(\alpha \rightarrow \neg\beta) < (\alpha \rightarrow \beta)$ or $\vdash \neg\alpha$.*

[Proof: p. 303.]

Thus, the two entrenchment-based contraction operators are revision-equivalent. Part (2) of the observation provides us with a plausible way to define entrenchment-based revision directly from an entrenchment ordering, without reference to a contraction operator. To see why this definition works, consider the case of a belief-contravening revision, i.e. let us revise the consistent belief set A by a sentence α such that $\neg\alpha \in A$. For each sentence β, both $\alpha \rightarrow \beta$ and $\alpha \rightarrow \neg\beta$ are logical consequences of $\neg\alpha$, and therefore they are both elements of A.

Since we want the revision-operator $*$ to satisfy *success*, $\alpha \in A * \alpha$. Therefore, on pain of inconsistency, $\alpha \rightarrow \beta$ and $\alpha \rightarrow \neg\beta$ cannot both be elements of $A * \alpha$. At most one of them can be retained. If one of them is more entrenched than the other, then the most entrenched one should be retained. If they are equally entrenched, then we have no means of adjudicating between them, and they will both have to go.

There is one exception to this. If α is inconsistent, i.e., $\vdash \neg\alpha$, then $A * \alpha$ is (due to *success* and *closure*) identical to $\mathcal{L}$, i.e., to the (inconsistent) set of all sentences. This is why a special clause is needed to ensure that if $\vdash \neg\alpha$, then $\beta \in A * \alpha$ for all sentences β.

Example

Let α denote that my friend Bob has consumed alcohol today. Furthermore, let β denote that Bob is drunk and let δ denote that the Duke of Monaco is drunk.

I believe that Bob has not consumed alcohol today ($\neg\alpha$). As a logical consequence of this, I also believe that (1) if Bob has consumed alcohol today, then he is drunk ($\alpha\rightarrow\beta$) and (2) if Bob has consumed alcohol today, then he is not drunk ($\alpha\rightarrow\neg\beta$). The former of these beliefs is more entrenched than the other. When I am told that Bob has been seen drinking whisky in the afternoon, I revise my beliefs to include α. I cannot then retain both my belief in $\alpha\rightarrow\beta$ and my belief in $\alpha\rightarrow\neg\beta$. Since the former is more entrenched, it is the one that I retain, and as a consequence of this, I acquire, with α, a belief in β.

As a consequence of my belief in $\neg\alpha$, *I* also believe both $\alpha\rightarrow\delta$ and $\alpha\rightarrow\neg\delta$. However, since these two beliefs have equal (indeed, equally low) entrenchment, neither is retained. Therefore, the new belief state after revision by α contains neither δ nor $\neg\delta$. I still have no idea whether or not the Duke of Monaco is drunk.

In Section 2.10 we saw that operations of contraction that are based on transitively relational selection functions are interchangeable, from a formal point of view, with operations that are based on standard entrenchment orderings. We should therefore expect entrenchment to be expressible in sphere models, and indeed it is.

Remember that $\alpha < \beta$, α is less entrenched than β, indicates that the epistemic agent is more willing to give up α than to give up β. To give up α means, in possible world modelling, to accept as possible some world in which $\neg\alpha$ is true. Therefore, $\alpha < \beta$ can be interpreted as saying that the epistemic agent is more willing to accept as possible some world in which $\neg\alpha$ holds than some world in which $\neg\beta$ holds. In a sphere model, this means that the closest sphere containing some $\neg\alpha$-world is closer than the closest sphere containing some $\neg\beta$-world. Figure 3.7 illustrates a case in which $\alpha < \beta$ holds. It can be shown that the relation defined in this way satisfies the five standard entrenchment postulates *transitivity, dominance, conjunctiveness, minimality*, and *maximality*. Furthermore, the contraction operator that is based on this relation via Gärdenfors's definition ($G\div$) coincides with the contraction operator that is based directly on the spheres, as explained in Section 3.8. (A more precise formulation of this coincidence can be found in Section 3.25^{+}.)

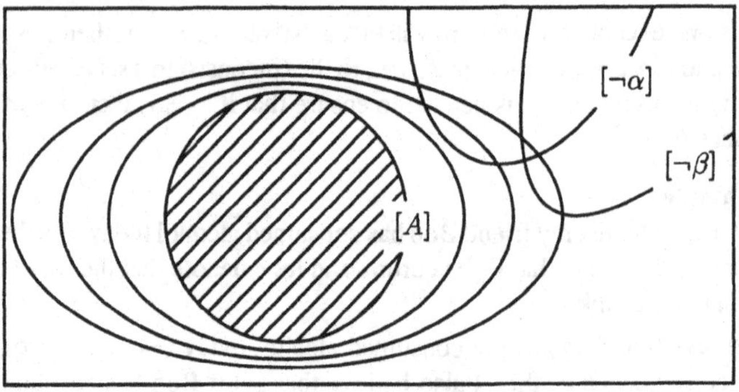

Figure 3.7. α is less entrenched than β.

A very nice mental picture of the relationship between entrenchment and the spheres model has been proposed by Abhaya Nayak:

> Instead of looking at a belief state as a system of spheres, represent it as a graduated, flat-bottom cup. Each point on the surface of the cup will represent a possible world, the bottom of the cup representing $[A]$. The agent is taken to be incapable of distinguishing between any two worlds that lie between two consecutive graduating lines. Now every proposition can be represented as some part of this cup. The degree of epistemic entrenchment assigned to any sentence α in this belief state will then be reflected by the amount of liquid the corresponding cup-part $[\alpha]$ can hold. For instance, if $\alpha \notin A$, then the bottom $[A]$ is not included in the cup-part $[\alpha]$, which means that $[\alpha]$ is a part of the cup in question with a hole in its bottom (maybe it is completely bottomless). Thus it cannot hold any liquid at all, whereby $[\alpha]$ will have minimum epistemic entrenchment. At the other extreme, if $\vdash \alpha$ then α will represent the whole cup, whereby it can hold the whole cupful of liquid. Accordingly it is maximally entrenched. [93]

10 UPDATES

In 1985, Arthur Keller and Marianne Winslett observed that there are two types of reasons why we add new information to the belief set [68]. One is that the world has changed, and the other that we have received new information about the world. The first type, *change-recording incorporation* of new information, is often called *updating*. The term *revision* can then be reserved for the second type, *knowledge-adding incorporation* of new information.

Examples

1. Previously, Brian had no pet, but yesterday he bought a poodle. I have therefore incorporated the new belief that Brian has a poodle into my set of beliefs.
2. Previously, I believed that Brian had no pet, but yesterday I learnt that I have been mistaken and that he owns a poodle. I have therefore incorporated the new belief that Brian has a poodle into my set of beliefs.

The first of these examples is a case of updating, and the second a case of (knowledge-adding) revision.

The following example has often been used to show that the logical properties of revision do not hold for updates:

> **Example** (Marianne Winslett [127])
> In the beginning, all we know about a certain table is that there is either a book on the table (α) or a magazine on the table (β), but not both. A robot is instructed to put a book on the table. We change our beliefs to incorporate α into the belief set.

The original belief set can be represented by $\mathrm{Cn}(\{(\alpha\&\neg\beta)\vee(\neg\alpha\&\beta)\})$, which is equivalent with $\mathrm{Cn}(\{\neg\alpha\leftrightarrow\beta\})$. The new belief α is therefore compatible with the original belief set. If we *revise* the belief set to include α, in the AGM fashion, then the new belief set will be $\mathrm{Cn}(\{\neg\alpha\leftrightarrow\beta, \alpha\})$, which is equivalent with $\mathrm{Cn}(\{\alpha, \neg\beta\})$. This result is strange, since we do not seem to have any good reason to conclude that there is no magazine on the table ($\neg\beta$). In other words, the postulate of vacuity does not seem to hold for updates. Non-belief-contravening updates can lead to losses of previous beliefs.

On the other hand, the following somewhat related postulate has been proposed for updates [67]:

> *Idempotence:*
> If $\alpha \in A$, then $A * \alpha = A$.

In our example, if the robot follows the instruction to put the book on the table, but the book is already there, then we assume that nothing has been changed, and the belief set remains unchanged.

It follows from *idempotence* that if A is inconsistent, then so is $A*\alpha$ for every α. This is a property that partial meet revision does not have. If we *revise* an inconsistent belief set by a consistent sentence, then the outcome is a consistent belief set. To the contrary, a good case can be made that once the belief set is inconsistent, it cannot be made consistent again *through updating*. 'We can never repair an inconsistent theory using update, because update specifies a change in the world. If there is no set of worlds that fits our current description, we have no way of recording the change in the real world.' [67]

It has also been proposed that the following postulate should hold for updates [67]:

Monotonicity:
If $A \subseteq B$, then $A * \alpha \subseteq B * \alpha$

The following example shows, however, that monotonicity does not hold in general for updating:

Example
The door to the bathroom is closed. A switch on the outside is connected to a lamp inside the bathroom.

Case 1: I have no information about the present state of the light bulb. I turn the switch to the 'on' position. After that, I believe that the lamp is shining.

Case 2: I know that the light bulb is broken. I turn the switch to the 'on' position. After that, I do not believe that the lamp is shining.

Let A denote the belief set in case 1, B the belief set in case 2, α the sentence that the switch is on, and β the sentence that the bathroom is lit. We then have $A \subseteq B, \beta \in A * \alpha$, and $\beta \notin B * \alpha$, so that monotonicity does not hold. Yet this is clearly an example of updating.

One of the most promising approaches to updating is to assign time indices to the sentences, as proposed by Katsuno and Mendelzon [67]. Then the belief set will not consist of sentences α but of pairs $\langle \alpha, t_1 \rangle$ of a sentence α and a point in time t_1 signifying, of course, that α holds at t_1. To illustrate this approach, let us return to the book-and-magazine example. Let t_1 denote some point in time just before the book was moved, and t_2 the moment when the robot has moved the book. The original belief set contained the pair $\langle \neg\alpha \leftrightarrow \beta, t_1 \rangle$. Updating by α can be represented by the incorporation of $\langle \alpha, t_2 \rangle$ into the belief set, and revision by α by the incorporation of $\langle \alpha, t_1 \rangle$. It follows quite naturally that $\langle \neg\beta, t_1 \rangle$ is implied by the revised belief set but not by the updated belief set.

A formal development of this account of updates would have to include background beliefs about the *persistence* of various facts. If α denotes that there is a book on the table, then we tend to conclude from $\langle \alpha, t_1 \rangle$ that $\langle \alpha, t_2 \rangle$ for a point in time t_2 five minutes later than t_1, unless there are reasons to believe otherwise. The same would, presumably, not hold, if we instead let α denote that there is a housefly on the table. The logical properties of time-indexed sentences remain to be investigated.

11 NON-MONOTONIC REASONING

The consequence operator Cn and its corresponding relation $\vdash$ represent *deductive* reasoning, i.e. reasoning according to the laws of logic. If $\alpha \in \mathrm{Cn}(A)$, then α is an absolutely certain conclusion, given the premise A. However, most of the conclusions that we draw (outside of logic and mathematics) are less certain than that. We typically draw more conclusions from information that we receive than what logic alone allows us to do.

Example
When Mr. Jones' fingerprints were found on the pistol with which his wife was shot, the police officer concluded that Mr. Jones had shot his wife.

This is a clear case of non-deductive reasoning. Most of the inferences of everyday life are non-deductive (and so are most inferences in science).

Studies of non-deductive reasoning is a rapidly growing field of research, and just like belief dynamics it has been much stimulated by developments in computer science. Computer scientists want computers to draw conclusions in an intelligent way, much the same way as a human being does, and for that purpose precise models of non-deductive reasoning are required. Since the early 1980's, a large number of different models for non-deductive reasoning have been proposed. Many if not most of them have been developed with a view to computer applications.

One of the best ways to study models of reasoning systematically is to focus on the *inference relation* that such a model gives rise to [27]. That relation is denoted by the symbol $\mid\!\sim$. $A \mid\!\sim \alpha$ means that A is a good enough reason to believe that α or that α is a plausible consequence of A [69].

We can also define an operation C that stands in the same relation to $\mid\!\sim$ as Cn to $\vdash$, i.e., $\mathrm{C}(A)$ is the set of inferences from A according to $\mid\!\sim$, or somewhat more precisely:

$$\mathrm{C}(A) = \{\beta \mid A \mid\!\sim \beta\}.$$

Non-deductive inference operations (C) differ from logical inference operations (Cn) in several ways. One of the most essential differences concerns the property of *monotony*. Any consequence operator Cn satisfies the following condition:

If $A \subseteq B$ then $\mathrm{Cn}(A) \subseteq \mathrm{Cn}(B)$ (*monotony*)

In other words, if the set of premises (A) is enlarged, then this never leads to the loss of any conclusion. The corresponding property does not hold in general for non-deductive inferences, as can be seen from the following extension of the above example:

Example
Let α denote that Mr. Jones' fingerprints have been found on the pistol

with which his wife was shot. Let β denote that rubber gloves that have been moulded to leave Mr. Jones' fingerprints have been found in the home of Mrs. Jones' lover. Let δ denote that Mr. Jones killed his wife.

From α, the police officer draws the conclusion that δ. (I.e. $\alpha \mid\!\sim \delta$, or equivalently: $\delta \in \mathrm{C}(\{\alpha\})$.)

From α and β, the police officer does not infer that δ. (Thus, $\{\alpha, \beta\} \not\mid\!\sim \delta$, or equivalently: $\delta \notin \mathrm{C}(\{\alpha, \beta\})$.

In this case, $\mathrm{C}(\{\alpha\}) \not\subseteq \mathrm{C}(\{\alpha, \beta\})$, so that monotony does not hold. Failure of monotony is such a characteristic property of non-deductive reasoning that this field of study is most commonly called *non-monotonic reasoning* (although 'non-deductive reasoning' or 'defeasible reasoning' [85] are perhaps more precise terms).

There is a close connection between non-monotonic reasoning and belief revision. Let A be a belief set and $*$ an operator of revision for A. Then $\beta \in A * \alpha$ means that from the new information α we infer that β, given the set A of background beliefs. This is just another way of saying that $\alpha \mid\!\sim \beta$, where $\mid\!\sim$ denotes inferences according to A. If we want to be more precise, we can write $\alpha \mid\!\sim_A \beta$, but the subscript can be omitted if the set of background beliefs is fixed.

This connection can also be expressed as a *translation procedure* between non-monotonic reasoning and belief revision [88]. Let A be a fixed and consistent belief set that represents the background beliefs. We can then translate between the two frameworks according to the following rule:

Translation rule 1 [88]
$\alpha \mid\!\sim \beta$ if and only if $\beta \in A * \alpha$

This translation rule does not provide directly for translations of expressions such as $B \mid\!\sim \beta$, where B is a set containing more than one sentence. However if B is finite, then we can for most purposes use the conjunction of all its elements ($\&B$) to represent it, and assume that $B \mid\!\sim \beta$ holds if and only if $\beta \in A * (\&B)$.

Translation rule 2, for a finite set B [88]
$B \mid\!\sim \beta$ if and only if $\beta \in A * (\&B)$.

Still, this does not cover expressions of the form $B \mid\!\sim \beta$ if B is infinite. The reason for this is that ordinary logic does not allow us to form the conjunction of an infinite set of sentences. Arguably, the case when B is infinite is of little practical interest. If we wish to cover it, then the best option is probably to enlarge our account of belief revision to (multiple) revision by infinite sets, and let $B \mid\!\sim \beta$ hold if and only if $\beta \in A * B$.

Several of the postulates for belief revision contain expressions such as $\alpha \in A$. To translate such expressions, we can make use of the fact that if A is consistent, then $A = A * \top$ for any tautology $\top$. According to translation rule 1, we can translate $\beta \in A * \top$ into $\top \mid\!\sim \beta$. If A is consistent, then $\beta \in A$ can also be translated into $\top \mid\!\sim \beta$. In analogy with the usage for $\vdash$, we can use $\mid\!\sim \beta$ as an abbreviation for $\top \mid\!\sim \beta$.

Translation rule 3, provided that A is consistent [88]
$\mid\!\sim \beta$ if and only if $\beta \in A$.

The following example [88] shows that the inference operator that derives from belief revision according to these three rules is typically non-monotonic: Let p and q be two logically independent sentences, and let A be the belief set $\text{Cn}(\{\neg p \vee \neg q\})$. Furthermore, let $*$ be an operator for A that satisfies the basic Gärdenfors postulates success, consistency, and vacuity. It follows from vacuity that $\neg p \vee \neg q \in A * p$, and then from the translation procedure that $\neg p \vee \neg q \in \text{C}(\{p\})$. However, it follows from success that $p \& q \in A * (p \& q)$ and thus from consistency that $\neg p \vee \neg q \notin A * (p \& q)$. The translation procedure yields $\neg p \vee \neg q \notin \text{C}(\{p, q\})$. We therefore have $\text{C}(\{p\}) \not\subseteq \text{C}(\{p, q\})$, so that monotony does not hold.

In the remainder of this section, we are going to apply the translation rules to some belief revision postulates in order to see what they look like after translation from $*$ language into $\mid\!\sim$ language.

Let us begin with the simple *success* postulate, $\alpha \in A * \alpha$. It translates directly into the following postulate for inference relations:

$\alpha \mid\!\sim \alpha$ ('reflexivity' [69; 88]).

Reflexivity is a basic requirement on inference, just as success is a basic requirement on belief revision. It 'holds of all non-monotonic inference relations currently in the literature and indeed... should hold of any relation that deserves the name of "inference relation" ' [88]. Reflexivity follows from the following property:

$\text{Cn}(B) \subseteq \text{C}(B)$ for all B ('supraclassicality' [86])

that has a central rôle in many discussions on non-monotonic logic. Supraclassicality expresses the intuition that (logical) deduction is so compelling that it must be included in any reasonable account of rational inference.

The *closure* postulate of belief revision, $A * \alpha = \text{Cn}(A * \alpha)$, corresponds to the following postulate for inference operations:

$\text{C}(\{\alpha\}) = \text{Cn}(\text{C}(\{\alpha\}))$ ('left absorption' [86], 'closure' [76])

According to left absorption, whatever can be concluded by applying first non-monotonic inference and then deductive logic can also be obtained by using non-monotonic inference only. This property should be expected if C includes deductive inference [86].

The revision postulate of *extensionality* (If $\alpha \leftrightarrow \beta \in \text{Cn}(\emptyset)$ then $A * \alpha = A * \beta$) is easy to translate if we note that $\alpha \leftrightarrow \beta \in \text{Cn}(\emptyset)$ is equivalent to $\text{Cn}(\{\alpha\}) = \text{Cn}(\{\beta\})$. Extensionality corresponds to the following postulate for inference operations:

If $\mathrm{Cn}(\{\alpha\}) = \mathrm{Cn}(\{\beta\})$ then $\mathrm{C}(\{\alpha\}) = \mathrm{C}(\{\beta\})$ ('left logical equivalence' [69; 86], 'congruence' [76])

The revision postulate of *consistency*, namely

If α is consistent, then $A * \alpha$ is consistent

can be translated into the following:

If $\alpha \nvdash \bot$ then $\alpha \not\mid\!\sim \bot$ ('consistency preservation' [76; 86; 88])

According to consistency preservation, non-monotonic inference never leads us into contradiction unless the premises are deductively inconsistent. The reasoning agent shuns inconsistencies. She never makes an inference that leads to inconsistency unless the inference is deductive, and therefore unavoidable.

Disjunctive overlap, i.e., $(A * \alpha) \cap (A * \beta) \subseteq A * (\alpha \vee \beta)$ corresponds to the principle

If $\alpha \mid\!\sim \delta$ and $\beta \mid\!\sim \delta$, then $\alpha \vee \beta \mid\!\sim \delta$ ('unit distribution' [88])

and thus to the sensible principle that whatever can be inferred from each of two sentences also follows from their disjunction.

Superexpansion, $A * (\alpha \& \beta) \subseteq A * \alpha + \beta$, can be translated as follows:

If $\alpha \& \beta \mid\!\sim \delta$, then $\alpha \mid\!\sim \beta \rightarrow \delta$ ('conditionalization' [88])

(Note on the translation: Due the the deduction property of Cn, a sentence δ is an element of $A * \alpha + \beta = \mathrm{Cn}((A * \alpha) \cup \{\beta\})$ if and only if $\beta \rightarrow \delta \in A * \alpha$.)

Conditionalization is an often discussed property of non-monotonic inference. It essentially corresponds to one direction of the deduction property:

$\delta \in \mathrm{C}(X \cup \{\beta\})$ if and only if $\beta \rightarrow \delta \in \mathrm{C}(X)$

(To see this, substitute $\{\alpha\}$ for X. We assume that the inferences from $\{\alpha, \beta\}$ are the same as those from $\{\alpha \& \beta\}$.)

The revision postulate of *inclusion*, $A * \beta \subseteq A + \beta$, corresponds to the following property of inference:

If $\beta \mid\!\sim \delta$, then $\mid\!\sim \beta \rightarrow \delta$ ('weak conditionalization ' [88]).

Weak conditionalization follows from conditionalization. (To see this, let α be a tautology.)

Finally let us translate the following principle of inference into a revision postulate:

If $\alpha \mid\!\sim \beta$ and $\alpha \& \beta \mid\!\sim \delta$ then $\alpha \mid\!\sim \delta$ ('cut' [69]).

Cut is an important inferential principle. It says that once inferred, a conclusion 'may be called upon in conjunction with the original information, and anything obtained with their combined use will be implied by the original information' [86]. The importance of this inferential principle lends interest to its translation

$$\text{If } \beta \in A * \alpha, \text{ then } A * (\alpha \& \beta) \subseteq A * \alpha$$

that can be shown to hold for relational partial meet revision [40].

Translations between belief revision and non-monotonic inference contribute to our understanding of both fields of research. The interconnections between the two fields have been the subject of several studies [39; 76; 85; 88], but much remains to be explored.

12 NON-PRIORITIZED BELIEF CHANGE

By belief revision is meant an operation that receives new information and accepts it. Any conflict between old and new information is resolved by giving up some of the old information. Revision satisfies unrestricted 'primacy of new information' [11]. In practice, however, new information is often rejected if it contradicts more entrenched previous beliefs. The new information may be less reliable than conflicting old information [9].

> It follows from the postulates for revision that the system is totally trusting at each stage about the input information; it is willing to give up whatever elements of the background theory must be abandoned to render it consistent with the new information. Once this information has been incorporated, however, it is at once as susceptible to revision as anything else in the current theory.
>
> Such a rule of revision seems to place an inordinate value on novelty, and its behaviour towards what it learns seems capricious [10].

By *non-prioritized belief change* is meant a process in which new information is received, and weighed against old information, with no special priority assigned to the new information due to its novelty. (This is also called 'autonomous belief revision' since it allows for an autonomous agent who decides herself whether or not to accept an input [28].)

In non-prioritized belief change, a belief-contravening epistemic input is accepted if it has more epistemic value than the original beliefs that contradict it. In that case, enough of the previous sentences are deleted to make the resulting set consistent. Otherwise, the input itself is rejected. The formal operation consists of two suboperations:

1. Expand by α.
2. Restore consistency by giving up either α or some original belief(s).

Since the first step (expansion by α) may result in an inconsistent belief state, this process cannot be modelled in a belief set approach. As we saw in Section 1.6, all inconsistent belief sets are identical. In a belief base model, however, this difficulty does not arise. We will therefore discuss non-prioritized belief change in the framework of belief bases.[1]

The first suboperation is simply (non-closing) expansion. The second suboperation, that makes a belief base consistent, will be called *consolidation*. As a formal account of consolidation we can use *partial meet consolidation*, denoted $\sim_\gamma \perp$. The partial meet consolidation $A\sim_\gamma\perp$ of a set A is the intersection of its 'most preferred' maximal consistent subsets. The maximal consistent subsets of A are the elements of $A\bot\perp$ (where $\perp$ denotes logical contradiction), and we therefore have:

$$A\sim_\gamma\perp = \bigcap\gamma(A\bot\perp)$$

We can now rewrite the two suboperations as follows:

1. Expand by α.
2. Contract by $\perp$.

This sequence of operations is reminiscent of external revision. The difference is that in external revision, the second suboperation is contraction by $\neg\alpha$ rather than by $\perp$. There are close formal connections between external partial meet revision and the composite operation of expansion-consolidation.

OBSERVATION 3.29 ([43]) *Let $\pm_\gamma$ be the operator of external partial meet revision and $\sim_\gamma\perp$ the consolidation operator that are generated by one and the same (two-place) selection function γ. Furthermore, let A be a set of sentences and α a sentence. Then:*

1. *If γ is relational and $\alpha \in A+\alpha\sim_\gamma\perp$, then $A\pm_\gamma\alpha \subseteq A+\alpha\sim_\gamma\perp$.*
2. *If γ is transitively relational and $\alpha \in A+\alpha\sim_\gamma\perp$, then $A\pm_\gamma\alpha = A+\alpha\sim_\gamma\perp$.*

[Proof: p. 254.]

For transitively relational selection functions, external revision may be seen as a special case of expansion-consolidation in which the new epistemic input is accepted.[2]

The expansion-consolidation account of belief change can accommodate an important feature of human belief that has no room in a model based on contractions and revisions: the *stubbornness* of human belief.

Examples

1. Alice is a fundamentalist. Nothing whatever can bring her to believe that anything in the Bible is wrong.

[1] *Note added in proof:* Some new approaches to non-prioritized revision of belief sets are reported in a forthcoming special issue of *Theoria*.

[2] *Note added in proof:* Additional results on expansion-consolidation (also called semi-revision) are provided in a recent paper, 'Semi-revision', in the *Journal of Applied Non-Classical Logic*, vol. 7, no. 2, pp. 151–175, 1997.

2. Bernard is an atheist. Nothing could bring him to believe that God exists.
3. Cynthia is convinced that at the bottom of his heart, John loves her. Nothing can make her give up this conviction.

In an account of belief change based on revisions and contractions, stubbornness such as in these examples cannot be adequately accounted for. Alice's fundamentalism is lost if her belief set is revised by any sentence $\neg\alpha$ such that α is implied by the biblical text. Bernard becomes a theist if he revises his belief set by 'God exists', and Cynthia can easily contract the sentence 'John loves me' from her belief set.

In a framework with no other operations than expansion and consolidation, these examples can be much better accounted for. To take just one example, Alice's doxastic behaviour can be represented by an operator of consolidation that rejects all new information that contradicts the Bible. Thus, if α is a sentence implied by the Bible, then $\neg\alpha \notin (A+\neg\alpha)\sim_\gamma\perp$.

For a more developed discussion of what beliefs an agent can or cannot acquire, we need a formal language that contains modal expressions, i.e. expressions that represent necessity and possibility. However, we are not going to introduce these expressions into the *object language* ($\mathcal{L}$) that belief bases (and belief sets) are made of. Instead, we are going to introduce them into the *metalanguage* that we use when talking about beliefs.

Let B stand for '(the agent) believes'. $B\alpha$ is true if and only if α is implied by the agent's belief base. Furthermore, let L stand for 'necessarily' and M for 'possibly'. Our modal language will consist of:

1. all expressions of the form $B\alpha$, where $\alpha \in \mathcal{L}$, and
2. all expressions formed by prefixing a string of L's, M's, and $\neg$'s to $B\alpha$, where $\alpha \in \mathcal{L}$.

$B\alpha, \neg B(\alpha\leftrightarrow\delta), LB(\alpha\rightarrow\beta), \neg MB\beta, \neg LM\neg B\alpha$, and $LML\neg LMB(\alpha\vee\delta\vee\neg\varepsilon)$ are examples of expressions in the modal metalanguage. (These expressions give rise to a *modal logic*, i.e. a logic of necessity and possibility; see Section 3.18$^+$.) The meaning of such expressions can be exemplified as follows:

$B\alpha$	The agent believes that α.
$\neg B\alpha$	The agent does not believe that α.
$LB\alpha$	The agent necessarily believes that α, i.e. she believes that α, and no epistemic input can change this.
$M\neg B\alpha$	It is possible for the agent to to arrive at some state of belief in which α is not believed.
$MLB\alpha$	It is possible for the agent to arrive at some state in which she believes that α and will always continue to do so.

$LMLB\alpha$ It is and will always be possible for the agent to arrive at some state in which she believes that α and will always continue to do so.

Examples

1. Doris is not a believer, but she has religious leanings. She does not believe that God exists ($\neg B\alpha$), but it is possible for her to become a believer ($MB\alpha$), and it is even possible for her to become a believer that henceforth cannot lose her faith ($MLB\alpha$).
2. Ellen, on the other hand, is a believer ($B\alpha$). However, it may very well happen that she loses her faith so definitely that she can never become a believer in God again ($ML\neg B\alpha$).
3. Florence is an inveterate doubter. Nothing can bring her to a state of firm (irreversible) belief ($\neg MLB\alpha$), and neither can she be brought to a state of firm disbelief ($\neg MLB\neg\alpha$).

By allowing the agent not to accept all new information, the model of non-prioritized belief change that has been introduced in this section brings us closer to some properties of actual belief change. Nevertheless it has serious limitations. One of these is that every piece of new information that is logically consistent with the original belief set has to be accepted. (If $A+\alpha$ is consistent, then $A+\alpha\sim_\gamma\perp = A+\alpha$.) In actual life, we often reject new information even if it is *logically* compatible with our previous beliefs. One of the reasons for this is that we prefer to have a belief system that is as coherent as possible, i.e., such that its different parts support each other. We tend to accept new information that increases the coherence of our belief system, rather than information that makes it less coherent [28]. Models of belief change that take this into account are currently being developed by Erik Olsson [102]. His basic idea is to replace consolidation as defined in this section by 'coherence consolidation', an operation that deletes enough elements of an incoherent belief base to make it coherent.

CHAPTER 3+

THE LOGIC OF REVISION

This chapter contains proofs of the theorems and observations of Chapter 3. In addition, it contains some results on multiple revision (Section 3.17+), a modal account of belief change (Section 3.18+), and a formalized theory for operations on sets of possible worlds (Sections 3.24+–3.25+). Sections 3.13+–3.18+ are devoted to revision of belief bases, and Sections 3.19+–3.25+ to revision of belief sets.

13+ INTERNAL REVISION

Internal partial meet revision ($\mp_\gamma$) on belief bases is directly based on partial meet contraction through the Levi identity. Most of its properties can therefore be obtained from the properties of partial meet contraction. The following property of partial meet contraction is useful in studies of revision:

OBSERVATION 3.30 *If* $\neg\alpha \in A$, *then* $\neg\alpha \in A{\sim_\gamma}\alpha$. *(negation-retainment)*

Proof. Suppose to the contrary that $\neg\alpha \in A$ and $\neg\alpha \notin A{\sim_\gamma}\alpha$. Then there is some $X \in \gamma(A\perp\alpha)$ such that $\neg\alpha \notin X$. It follows that $X \cup \{\neg\alpha\} \vdash \alpha$. The deduction property yields $X \vdash \neg\alpha \rightarrow \alpha$, or equivalently $X \vdash \alpha$, contrary to $X \in A\perp\alpha$. This contradiction concludes the proof. ■

The following proof of the Harper identity shows why this observation is useful:

> Let A be any set and γ a selection function for A.
> Then $A{\sim_\gamma}\alpha = A \cap (A\mp_\gamma\neg\alpha)$. (*the Harper identity*)
> [Observation 3.11.]

Proof. By definition, $A\mp_\gamma\neg\alpha = (A{\sim_\gamma}\alpha) \cup \{\neg\alpha\}$. From this and $A{\sim_\gamma}\alpha \subseteq A$ we obtain $A{\sim_\gamma}\alpha \subseteq A \cap (A\mp_\gamma\neg\alpha)$ by set theory.

For the other direction, let $\beta \in A \cap (A\mp_\gamma\neg\alpha)$, i.e. $\beta \in A \cap ((A{\sim_\gamma}\alpha) \cup \{\neg\alpha\})$. Then either $\beta \in A \cap (A{\sim_\gamma}\alpha)$ or $\beta \in A \cap \{\neg\alpha\}$. In the first case $\beta \in A{\sim_\gamma}\alpha$ follows directly. In the second case, it follows from $\beta \in A \cap \{\neg\alpha\}$ that β is identical to $\neg\alpha$ and that $\neg\alpha \in A$. It follows from Observation 3.30 that $\neg\alpha \in A{\sim_\gamma}\alpha$. Since β is identical to $\neg\alpha$, it follows that $\beta \in A{\sim_\gamma}\alpha$ holds in this case as well. ■

The representation theorems for internal partial meet revision can be proved in much the same way as those for partial meet contraction. The only major new difficulty is to find the construction to be used in the postulates-to-construction part. It turns out that the Harper identity can help us here. In Section 2.15$^+$, when constructing a selection function for a given operator $\div$ of partial meet contraction, we used, for the principal case, the construction:

$$\gamma(A\perp\alpha) = \{X \in A\perp\alpha \mid A\div\alpha \subseteq X\}.$$

Now it is our task to construct a selection function that generates a given operator of internal partial meet revision. To do this, we can insert the Harper identity $A\div\alpha = A \cap (A * \neg\alpha)$ into the same definition, and obtain:

$$\gamma(A\perp\alpha) = \{X \in A\perp\alpha \mid A \cap (A * \neg\alpha) \subseteq X\}.$$

This construction will be used in the following proof:

> The operator $*$ is an operator of internal partial meet revision for a belief base A if and only if it satisfies the following postulates:
> $A * \alpha$ is consistent if α is consistent. (*consistency*)
> $A * \alpha \subseteq A \cup \{\alpha\}$ (*inclusion*)
> If $\beta \in A$ and $\beta \notin A * \alpha$, then there is some A' such that $A * \alpha \subseteq A' \subseteq A \cup \{\alpha\}$, A' is consistent but $A' \cup \{\beta\}$ is inconsistent. (*relevance*)
> $\alpha \in A * \alpha$ (*success*)
> If for all $A' \subseteq A$, $A' \cup \{\alpha\}$ is inconsistent if and only if $A' \cup \{\beta\}$ is inconsistent, then $A \cap (A * \alpha) = A \cap (A * \beta)$. (*uniformity*)
> [Theorem 3.6.]

Proof. *Construction-to-postulates*: The proof that *consistency, inclusion, success,* and *uniformity* are satisfied by internal partial meet revision is left to the reader as an exercise. That *relevance* is satisfied can be shown as follows:

Let $\mp_\gamma$ be an operator of internal partial meet revision. There are two cases, depending on whether or not α is consistent.

If α is inconsistent, then $\neg\alpha \in \text{Cn}(\emptyset)$, and $A\perp\neg\alpha$ is empty so that $\gamma(A\perp\neg\alpha) = \{A\}$ and consequently $A\mp_\gamma\alpha = \bigcap\gamma(A\perp\neg\alpha) \cup \{\alpha\} = A \cup \{\alpha\}$. Thus, there can be no β such that $\beta \in A$ and $\beta \notin A\mp_\gamma\alpha$, and *relevance* is vacuously satisfied.

If α is consistent, let $\beta \in A\backslash(A\mp_\gamma\alpha)$. Then $\beta \notin A\sim_\gamma\neg\alpha$, so that there must be some X such that $\beta \notin X \in \gamma(A\perp\neg\alpha)$. It follows that $\neg\alpha \notin \text{Cn}(X)$ and $\neg\alpha \in \text{Cn}(X \cup \{\beta\})$. It follows from this that $X \cup \{\alpha\}$ is consistent and $(X \cup \{\alpha\}) \cup \{\beta\}$ is inconsistent. We can also conclude from the definition of internal partial meet revision that $A\mp_\gamma\alpha \subseteq X \cup \{\alpha\} \subseteq A \cup \{\alpha\}$. From this we may conclude that *relevance* is satified.

Postulates-to-construction: Let $*$ be an operator for A that satisfies the listed postulates. Let γ be defined as follows:

1. If $A\perp\alpha$ is empty, then $\gamma(A\perp\alpha) = \{A\}$.
2. If $A\perp\alpha$ is non-empty, then $\gamma(A\perp\alpha) = \{X \in A\perp\alpha \mid A \cap (A * \neg\alpha) \subseteq X\}$

We have to prove (I) that γ is a (one-place) selection function and (II) that $A\mp_\gamma\alpha = A * \alpha$ for all α.

Part I: For γ to be a selection function, it must be a function. This is unproblematic in clause (1) of the definition. For clause (2), let α_1 and α_2 be two sets such that $A\perp\alpha_1 = A\perp\alpha_2$. It follows from Observation 1.39 that for all subsets A' of A, $\alpha_1 \in \mathrm{Cn}(A')$ if and only if $\alpha_2 \in \mathrm{Cn}(A')$, thus $A' \cup \{\neg\alpha_1\}$ is inconsistent if and only if $A' \cup \{\neg\alpha_2\}$ is inconsistent. It follows from *uniformity* that $A \cap (A * \neg\alpha_1) = A \cap (A * \neg\alpha_2)$. This is sufficient to show that γ is indeed a function.

To prove that γ is a one-place selection function, it now remains to be shown that if $A\perp\alpha$ is non-empty, then $\gamma(A\perp\alpha)$ is also non-empty. Suppose that $A\perp\alpha$ is non-empty. Then α is not a tautology, and consequently $\neg\alpha$ is consistent. By *consistency*, $A * \neg\alpha$ is also consistent. By *success*, $\neg\alpha \in A * \neg\alpha$. Thus $A * \neg\alpha$ does not imply α, so that $A \cap (A * \neg\alpha)$ does not imply α. It follows from the upper bound property that there is some X such that $A \cap (A * \neg\alpha) \subseteq X \in A\perp\alpha$. Then, by the definition of γ, $\gamma(A\perp\alpha)$ is non-empty.

Part II: The proof that $A\mp_\gamma\alpha = A * \alpha$ will be divided into two cases, according to whether or not α is inconsistent.

Case 1, α is inconsistent: By *relevance*, if $\varepsilon \in A\backslash(A * \alpha)$, then there is some A' such that $A * \alpha \subseteq A' \subseteq A \cup \{\alpha\}$, A' is consistent but $A' \cup \{\varepsilon\}$ is inconsistent. This, however, is impossible since it follows from *success* that $\alpha \in A * \alpha$ and thus $\alpha \in A'$, so that A' is inconsistent. Thus $A\backslash(A * \alpha)$ is empty, i.e. $A \subseteq A * \alpha$.

By *success* and *inclusion* we may then conclude that $A * \alpha = A \cup \{\alpha\}$. Since $A\mp_\gamma\alpha = A \cup \{\alpha\}$ when α is inconsistent, it follows that $A\mp_\gamma\alpha = A * \alpha$.

Case 2, α is consistent: To prove that $A * \alpha \subseteq A\mp_\gamma\alpha$: It follows from our definition of γ that $A \cap (A * \alpha) \subseteq \bigcap\gamma(A\perp\neg\alpha)$. By this and *inclusion* follows that $A * \alpha \subseteq (\bigcap\gamma(A\perp\neg\alpha)) \cup \{\alpha\} = A\mp_\gamma\alpha$.

To prove that $A\mp_\gamma\alpha \subseteq A * \alpha$: Since $A\mp_\gamma\alpha = (\bigcap\gamma(A\perp\neg\alpha)) \cup \{\alpha\}$ and, by *success*, $\alpha \in A * \alpha$, it now only remains to be shown that $\bigcap\gamma(A\perp\neg\alpha) \subseteq A * \alpha$. We will do this by showing that if $\varepsilon \notin A * \alpha$, then $\varepsilon \notin \bigcap\gamma(A\perp\neg\alpha)$. Since this is trivial when $\varepsilon \notin A$, we may assume that $\varepsilon \in A\backslash(A * \alpha)$.

It follows by *relevance* from $\varepsilon \in A\backslash(A * \alpha)$ that there is some set Y such that $A * \alpha \subseteq Y \subseteq A \cup \{\alpha\}$, Y is consistent but $Y \cup \{\varepsilon\}$ is inconsistent. By *success*, $\alpha \in A * \alpha$ and thus $\alpha \in Y$. Let $Z = Y \cap A$. Then $Y = Z \cup \{\alpha\}$. Since Y is consistent, we have $\neg\alpha \notin \mathrm{Cn}(Z)$, and since $Y \cup \{\varepsilon\}$ is inconsistent, we have $\neg\alpha \in \mathrm{Cn}(Z \cup \{\varepsilon\})$.

It follows by the upper bound property from $Z \subseteq A$ and $\neg\alpha \notin \mathrm{Cn}(Z)$ that there is a set Z' such that $Z \subseteq Z' \in A\perp\neg\alpha$. Since $\neg\alpha \in \mathrm{Cn}(Z \cup \{\varepsilon\})$, we also have $\varepsilon \notin Z'$. From $A * \alpha \subseteq Y$ and $Y \cap A \subseteq Z'$ follows $A \cap (A * \alpha) \subseteq Z'$ so that, by the definition of γ, $Z' \in \gamma(A\bot\neg\alpha)$. Since $\varepsilon \notin Z'$ we then have $\varepsilon \notin \bigcap\gamma(A\bot\neg\alpha)$, which is what we needed to complete the proof. ■

The following additional postulate:

Redundancy:
If α is consistent, and $\beta \vdash \neg\alpha$ for each $\beta \in B$, then $A{*}\alpha = (A{\cup}B){*}\alpha$.

is sufficient to ensure that a global operator of internal partial meet revision is based on a unified selection function. In order to prove this, we need to to modify the construction that was used in the foregoing proof. According to *redundancy*, if those elements of A_1 that do not imply $\neg\alpha$ are the same as those elements of A_2 that do not imply $\neg\alpha$, then $A_1 * \alpha = A_2 * \alpha$. Since $\bigcup(A_1\bot\neg\alpha)$ is the set of elements of A_1 that do not imply $\neg\alpha$, and similarly for A_2, we can also express this as follows:

If $\bigcup(A_1\bot\neg\alpha) = \bigcup(A_2\bot\neg\alpha)$,
then $A_1 * \alpha = A_2 * \alpha = (\bigcup(A_1\bot\neg\alpha)) * \alpha$

This property is used in the postulates-to-construction part of the following theorem:

The operator $*$ is an operator of unified internal partial meet revision (internal partial meet revision with a unified selection function) for a belief base A if and only if it satisfies *consistency*, *inclusion*, *relevance*, *success*, *uniformity*, and *redundancy*.
[Theorem 3.9.]

Proof. *Construction-to-postulates*: Let γ be a unified two-place selection function and $\mp_\gamma$ the operator of internal partial meet revision generated by γ. It follows from Theorem 3.6 that *consistency*, *inclusion*, *relevance*, *success*, and *uniformity* hold. In order to show that *redundancy* holds, suppose that α is consistent, and that $\beta \vdash \neg\alpha$ for each $\beta \in B$. Then, by Observation 1.40, $(A \cup B)\bot\neg\alpha = A\bot\neg\alpha \neq \emptyset$. Then, since γ is unified, $\gamma_{A\cup B}((A \cup B)\bot\neg\alpha) = \gamma_A(A\bot\neg\alpha)$, from which follows $A\mp_\gamma\alpha = (A \cup B)\mp_\gamma\alpha$.

Postulates-to-construction: Let $*$ be an operator that satisfies the postulates listed in the theorem. Let γ be a two-place function such that for each set A, $\gamma(A, \ ) = \gamma_A(\ )$ has the following properties:

1. If $A\bot\alpha$ is empty, then $\gamma_A(A\bot\alpha) = \{A\}$.
2. If $A\bot\alpha$ is non-empty, then
$\gamma_A(A\bot\alpha) = \{X \in A\bot\alpha \mid (\bigcup(A\bot\alpha)) \cap ((\bigcup(A\bot\alpha)) * \neg\alpha) \subseteq X\}$.

We are going to show (I) that γ is a two-place selection function, i.e., that for all sets A, γ_A is a one-place selection function, (II) that γ is unified, and (III) that $A\mp_\gamma\alpha = A * \alpha$ for all A and α.

Part I: For γ_A to be a one-place selection function, it must be a function. This is unproblematic in clause (1) of the definition. For clause (2), let α_1 and α_2 be two sentences such that $A\bot\alpha_1 = A\bot\alpha_2$. Let $A'' = \bigcup(A\bot\alpha_1) = \bigcup(A\bot\alpha_2)$. It follows from Observation 1.39 that every subset X of A implies α_1 if and only if it implies α_2, and thus $X\cup\{\neg\alpha_1\}$ is consistent if and only if $X\cup\{\neg\alpha_2\}$ is consistent. Since $A'' \subseteq A$ this also holds for every subset X of A'', and we may conclude from *uniformity* that $A''\cap(A''*\neg\alpha_1) = A''\cap(A''*\neg\alpha_2)$. We therefore have

$$\begin{aligned}&(\bigcup(A\bot\alpha_1))\cap((\bigcup(A\bot\alpha_1))*\neg\alpha_1)\\ &= A''\cap(A''*\neg\alpha_1)\\ &= A''\cap(A''*\neg\alpha_2)\\ &= (\bigcup(A\bot\alpha_2))\cap((\bigcup(A\bot\alpha_2))*\neg\alpha_2)\end{aligned}$$

It follows from our definition of γ that γ is indeed a function.

To prove that γ_A is a one-place selection function, it now remains to be shown that if $A\bot\alpha$ is non-empty, then so is $\gamma_A(A\bot\alpha)$. Suppose that $A\bot\alpha \neq \emptyset$. Then α is not a tautology, and consequently $\neg\alpha$ is not inconsistent, and by *consistency*, $(\bigcup(A\bot\alpha))*\neg\alpha$ is consistent. By *success*, $\neg\alpha \in (\bigcup(A\bot\alpha))*\neg\alpha$. From this we may conclude that $(\bigcup(A\bot\alpha))*\neg\alpha$ does not imply α, and neither does its subset $(\bigcup(A\bot\alpha))\cap((\bigcup(A\bot\alpha))*\neg\alpha)$. It follows that there is some X such that

$$(\bigcup(A\bot\alpha))\cap((\bigcup(A\bot\alpha))*\neg\alpha) \subseteq X \in (\bigcup(A\bot\alpha))\bot\alpha = A\bot\alpha.$$

Then, by the definition, $\gamma_A(A\bot\alpha)$ is non-empty.

Part II: Let $A_1\bot\alpha_1 = A_2\bot\alpha_2 \neq \emptyset$. Let $A'' = \bigcup(A_1\bot\alpha_1) = \bigcup(A_2\bot\alpha_2)$.

Since every element of $A_1\backslash A''$ implies α_1, we can apply *redundancy* and obtain $A''*\neg\alpha_1 = A_1*\neg\alpha_1$. Similarly, $A''*\neg\alpha_2 = A_2*\neg\alpha_2$.

It follows from Observation 1.40 that $A''\bot\alpha_1 = A''\bot\alpha_2$, and then from Observation 1.39 that every subset of A'' implies α_1 (is inconsistent with $\neg\alpha_1$) if and only if it implies α_2 (is inconsistent with $\neg\alpha_2$). It follows from *uniformity* that $A''\cap(A''*\neg\alpha_1) = A''\cap(A''*\neg\alpha_2)$. We therefore have

$$\begin{aligned}&(\bigcup(A_1\bot\alpha_1))\cap((\bigcup(A_1\bot\alpha_1))*\neg\alpha_1) = A''\cap(A''*\neg\alpha_1)\\ &= A''\cap(A''*\neg\alpha_2) = (\bigcup(A_2\bot\alpha_2))\cap((\bigcup(A_2\bot\alpha_2))*\neg\alpha_2)\end{aligned}$$

It follows from our definition of γ that γ is unified.

Part III: The proof that $A\mp_\gamma\alpha = A*\alpha$ will be divided into two cases, according to whether or not α is inconsistent.

Case 1, α is inconsistent: This part of the proof coincides with the corresponding part of the proof of Theorem 3.6.

Case 2, α is consistent: According to *redundancy*, $A*\alpha = (\bigcup(A\bot\neg\alpha))*\alpha$. Furthermore, by *consistency* and *success*, $\neg\alpha \notin \mathrm{Cn}(A*\alpha)$. Since every element of $A\backslash\bigcup(A\bot\neg\alpha)$ implies $\neg\alpha$, it follows that $A\cap(A*\alpha) \subseteq \bigcup(A\bot\neg\alpha)$, so that:

$$A\cap(A*\alpha) = (\bigcup(A\bot\neg\alpha))\cap((\bigcup(A\bot\neg\alpha))*\alpha).$$

The definition of $\gamma_A(A\bot\neg\alpha)$ can then be simplified to:

$$\gamma_A(A\bot\neg\alpha) = \{X \in A\bot\neg\alpha \mid A \cap (A * \alpha) \subseteq X\}.$$

The rest of the proof follows exactly as the proof of the corresponding case of Theorem 3.6. ■

In addition to the postulates given in the above theorems, internal partial meet revision satisfies the postulates of *vacuity*, *inconsistent expansion*, and *post-expansion*. This can be proved by showing that these properties follow from the postulates that have already been shown to hold for internal partial meet revision. These proofs are quite simple, and only use methods that we know from Chapter 2^+:

> If an operator $*$ for A satisfies *success*, *inclusion*, and *relevance*, then it satisfies:
> If $\neg\alpha \notin \text{Cn}(A)$, then $A * \alpha = A \cup \{\alpha\}$. (*vacuity*).
> [Observation 3.2.]

Proof. Let the operator $*$ for A satisfy *success*, *inclusion*, and *relevance*. Furthermore let $\neg\alpha \notin \text{Cn}(A)$.

We are first going to show that $A \subseteq A * \alpha$. Suppose not. Then there is some β such that $\beta \in A$ and $\beta \notin A * \alpha$. It follows from *relevance* that there is some A' such that $A' \subseteq A \cup \{\alpha\}$ and $A' \cup \{\beta\}$ is inconsistent. Since $\beta \in A$ we then have $A' \cup \{\beta\} \subseteq A \cup \{\alpha\}$. It follows from $\neg\alpha \notin \text{Cn}(A)$ that $A \cup \{\alpha\}$ is consistent, and then so is its subset $A' \cup \{\beta\}$. We can conclude from this contradiction that $A \subseteq A * \alpha$.

It follows from *success* that $\alpha \in A * \alpha$. Thus, $A \cup \{\alpha\} \subseteq A * \alpha$. It follows from *inclusion* that $A * \alpha \subseteq A \cup \{\alpha\}$. Hence $A * \alpha = A \cup \{\alpha\}$, as required. ■

> If an operator $*$ for A satisfies *success*, *inclusion*, and *relevance*, then it satisfies:
> If $\neg\alpha \in \text{Cn}(\emptyset)$ then $A * \alpha = A \cup \{\alpha\}$ (*inconsistent expansion*).
> [Observation 3.1.]

Proof. Let the operator $*$ for A satisfy *success*, *inclusion*, and *relevance*. Furthermore let $\neg\alpha \in \text{Cn}(\emptyset)$. Then α is inconsistent.

We are first going to show that $A \subseteq A * \alpha$. Suppose not. Then there is some β such that $\beta \in A$ and $\beta \notin A * \alpha$. It follows from *relevance* that there is some A' such that $A * \alpha \subseteq A'$ and A' is consistent. This, however, is impossible since it follows by *success* from the inconsistency of α that $A * \alpha$ is inconsistent. We may conclude that $A \subseteq A * \alpha$.

It follows from *success* that $\alpha \in A * \alpha$. Thus, $A \cup \{\alpha\} \subseteq A * \alpha$. It follows from *inclusion* that $A * \alpha \subseteq A \cup \{\alpha\}$. Hence $A * \alpha = A \cup \{\alpha\}$, as required. ■

An operator $*$ satisfies *post-expansion* ($A*\alpha+\alpha = A*\alpha$) if and only if it satisfies *success* ($\alpha \in A * \alpha$).
[Observation 3.3.]

Proof. It follows from set theory that $A*\alpha+\alpha = A*\alpha$, i.e. $(A*\alpha)\cup\{\alpha\} = A*\alpha$, holds if and only if $\alpha \in A * \alpha$. ■

For pre-expansion we have a negative result, that is therefore proved by a counter-example:

Pre-expansion ($A+\alpha*\alpha = A*\alpha$) does not hold in general for internal partial meet revision.
[Observation 3.8, Part 2.]

Proof. Let $A = \{p\rightarrow r, p\rightarrow\neg r\}$. Let the (two-place) selection function γ be unified and such that:

$$\gamma(\{p\rightarrow r, p\rightarrow\neg r\}\bot\neg p) = \{p\rightarrow r\}$$
$$\gamma(\{p\rightarrow r, p\rightarrow\neg r, p\}\bot\neg p) = \{p\rightarrow\neg r, p\}$$

We then have $A\mp_\gamma p = \{p\rightarrow r, p\}$ and $(A + p)\mp_\gamma p = \{p\rightarrow\neg r, p\}$, so that pre-expansion does not hold. ■

Exercises

139. Let p and q be logically independent sentences, and let $A = \{p, p\rightarrow q, q\}$. Let γ be a selection function for A such that for all sentences α, if $A\bot\alpha$ is non-empty, then $\gamma(A\bot\alpha)$ consists of those elements of $A\bot\alpha$ that have the highest number of elements. Perform the following operations:

    (a) $A\mp_\gamma\neg q$

    (b) $A\mp_\gamma(\neg p\vee\neg q)$

    (c) $A\mp_\gamma(\neg p\&\neg q)$

    (d) $A\mp_\gamma(q\rightarrow p)$

140. Let p, q, and r be logically independent sentences, and let $A = \{\neg p, q\}$. Let $\mp_\gamma$ be any operator of internal partial meet revision for A. Show that $A \cap (A\mp_\gamma p) = A \cap (A\mp_\gamma(p\&r))$.

141. Let $\mp_\gamma$ be an operator of internal partial meet revision. Complete the proof of Theorem 3.6 by showing that it satisfies

    (a) *consistency*,

    (b) *inclusion*,

    (c) *success*, and

    (d) *uniformity*.

142. Does the following postulate:
If $\alpha \in A$ then $A * \alpha = A$ (*idempotence*)
hold for internal partial meet revision?

143. Show that if a global operator $*$ for belief bases satisfies the revision-postulates *success* and *consistency*, then it does not satisfy:
$A * \alpha * \beta = A * \beta * \alpha$ (*commutativity*)

14+ LIMITING CASES OF INTERNAL REVISION

In this section, the axiomatic characterizations of internal full meet revision and internal maxichoice revision on belief bases will be proved. The characteristic postulate for *full meet* revision is inertness:

Inertness:
If $\beta \in A * \alpha$, then it holds for all sets B that if $\alpha \in B \subseteq A \cup \{\alpha\}$, then B is consistent if and only if $B \cup \{\beta\}$ is consistent.

An axiomatic characterization of internal full meet contraction can be obtained by adding inertness to the five characteristic postulates of internal partial meet contraction (namely consistency, inclusion, relevance, success, and uniformity). However, although this is a correct characterization it is uneconomical, since one of its six axioms, namely consistency, can be dispensed with:

OBSERVATION 3.31 *If an operator $*$ for A satisfies success, inclusion, and inertness, then it satisfies consistency.*

Proof. Let $*$ be an operator for A that satisfies the three listed postulates. Suppose to the contrary that it does not satisfy *consistency*. Then there is some α such that α is consistent and $A * \alpha$ is inconsistent.

Let $B \in (A * \alpha)\perp\neg\alpha$. By *success*, $\alpha \in A * \alpha$. Suppose that $\alpha \notin B$. Then $B \cup \{\alpha\} \vdash \neg\alpha$, i.e. (by the deduction property) $B \vdash \alpha\rightarrow\neg\alpha$, or equivalently $B \vdash \neg\alpha$, which contradicts $B \in (A * \alpha)\perp\neg\alpha$. We can conclude that $\alpha \in B$.

By *inclusion*, $A * \alpha \subseteq A \cup \{\alpha\}$, and consequently $B \subseteq A \cup \{\alpha\}$. Now let $\beta \in (A * \alpha)\setminus B$. (That $(A * \alpha)\setminus B$ is non-empty follows from $B \subseteq A * \alpha$, $B \nvdash \perp$ and $A * \alpha \vdash \perp$.) Since $B \in (A * \alpha)\perp\neg\alpha$, we then have $B \cup \{\beta\} \vdash \neg\alpha$, and since $\alpha \in B$, $B \cup \{\beta\}$ is inconsistent.

We have shown that $\alpha \in B \subseteq A \cup \{\alpha\}$, that$B$ is consistent and that $B \cup \{\beta\}$ is inconsistent. This contradicts *inertness*. We can conclude from this contradiction that *consistency* holds. ∎

It follows from this observation that if we add *inertness* to the postulates of Theorem 3.6, then consistency becomes redundant and need not be mentioned. We can now prove the following axiomatic characterization of internal full meet revision:

The operator $*$ for the belief base A is the operator of internal full meet revision if and only if it satisfies *inclusion, relevance, success, uniformity*, and *inertness*.
[Part of Theorem 3.13.]

Proof. *Construction-to-postulates*: Let $\mp$ be the operator of internal full meet revision for A. It follows from Theorem 3.6 that *inclusion, relevance, success*, and *uniformity* hold. It remains to be shown that *inertness* holds. We are going to prove inertness in its converse form. Let β and B be such that $\alpha \in B \subseteq A \cup \{\alpha\}$, $B \nvdash \bot$ and $B \cup \{\beta\} \vdash \bot$. We need to show that $\beta \notin A \mp \alpha$. Since this is trivial unless $\beta \in A \cup \{\alpha\}$, we can assume that $\beta \in A \cup \{\alpha\}$. It then follows from $\alpha \in B$ and $B \neq B \cup \{\beta\}$ that β is not identical to α, and thus $\beta \in A \setminus \{\alpha\}$.

Let $B' = B\setminus\{\alpha\}$. Then $B = B' \cup \{\alpha\}$. We have $B \nvdash \bot$, i.e. $B' \cup \{\alpha\} \nvdash \bot$, and it follows by the deduction property that $B' \nvdash \alpha \rightarrow \bot$, or equivalently $B' \nvdash \neg\alpha$. Similarly, it follows from $B \cup \{\beta\} \vdash \bot$, i.e. $B' \cup \{\alpha, \beta\} \vdash \bot$, that $B' \cup \{\beta\} \vdash \alpha \rightarrow \bot$, or equivalently $B' \cup \{\beta\} \vdash \neg\alpha$.

Since $B' \subseteq A$ it follows from $B' \nvdash \neg\alpha$, by the upper bound property, that there is some B'' such that $B' \subseteq B'' \in A \bot \neg\alpha$. Since $B' \cup \{\beta\} \vdash \neg\alpha$, we have $\beta \notin B''$, and thus $\beta \notin \bigcap(A \bot \neg\alpha)$. We have already shown that β is not identical to α, and we can conclude that $\beta \notin \bigcap(A \bot \neg\alpha) \cup \{\alpha\}$, i.e. $\beta \notin A \mp \alpha$, as desired. This completes the proof that *inertness* holds.

Postulates-to-construction: Let $*$ be an operator for A that satisfies the postulates listed in the theorem. It follows from Observation 3.31 that *consistency* holds, and thus from Theorem 3.6 that $*$ is an operator of internal partial meet revision, i.e. that it coincides with $\mp_\gamma$ for some selection function γ for A. We need to show that $\mp_\gamma$ coincides with the operator $\mp$ of internal full meet contraction for A.

It holds for all α that $\bigcap(A \bot \neg\alpha) \subseteq \bigcap\gamma(A \bot \neg\alpha)$ and thus $\bigcap(A \bot \neg\alpha) \cup \{\alpha\} \subseteq \bigcap\gamma(A \bot \neg\alpha) \cup \{\alpha\}$, i.e. $A \mp \alpha \subseteq A \mp_\gamma \alpha$.

For the other direction, suppose to the contrary that $A \mp_\gamma \alpha \nsubseteq A \mp \alpha$. Then there is some ε such that $\varepsilon \in A \mp_\gamma \alpha$ and $\varepsilon \notin A \mp \alpha$. It follows from $\varepsilon \notin A \mp \alpha$ that $\varepsilon \notin \bigcap(A \bot \neg\alpha)$, so that there must be some $X \in A \bot \neg\alpha$ with $\varepsilon \notin X$. Let $B = X \cup \{\alpha\}$. Since $X \nvdash \neg\alpha$, B is consistent. Since $\varepsilon \in A \mp_\gamma \alpha$ and $\varepsilon \notin A \mp \alpha$, we have $\varepsilon \in A$. From this and $\varepsilon \notin X \in A \bot \neg\alpha$ we can conclude that $X \cup \{\varepsilon\} \vdash \neg\alpha$ and consequently that $B \cup \{\varepsilon\} = X \cup \{\alpha, \varepsilon\}$ is inconsistent.

In summary, $\varepsilon \in A \mp_\gamma \alpha, \alpha \in B \subseteq A \cup \{\alpha\}$, B is consistent and $B \cup \{\varepsilon\}$ is inconsistent. This contradicts *inertness*, and we can conclude that $A \mp_\gamma \alpha \subseteq A \mp \alpha$. This finishes the proof that $\mp_\gamma$ (and thus $*$) coincides with $\mp$. ■

Next, let us turn to the other limiting case: internal *maxichoice* revision. The characteristic postulate for maxichoice revision is tenacity:

Tenacity: [35]
For all $\beta \in A$, either $\beta \in A * \alpha$ or $\neg\beta \in \mathrm{Cn}(A * \alpha)$

An axiomatic characterization of internal maxichoice revision can be obtained by just adding tenacity to the five characteristic postulates of internal partial meet revision (namely consistency, inclusion, relevance, success, and uniformity). However, in order to obtain a somewhat more economical characterization we can replace relevance by the weaker postulate of *inconsistent expansion*. (If $\neg\alpha \in \text{Cn}(\emptyset)$, then $A * \alpha = A \cup \{\alpha\}$.) In the presence of tenacity and two other basic postulates, relevance will nevertheless be satisfied:

OBSERVATION 3.32 *If an operator $*$ for a belief base A satisfies inclusion, consistency, inconsistent expansion, and tenacity, then it satisfies relevance.*

Proof. Let $*$ be an operation for A that satisfies *inclusion*, *consistency*, *inconsistent expansion*, and *tenacity*.

Case 1, α is consistent: In order to show that *relevance* is satisfied, let $\beta \in A$ and $\beta \notin A*\alpha$. We need to show that there is some A' such that $A*\alpha \subseteq A' \subseteq A \cup \{\alpha\}$, A' is consistent and $A' \cup \{\beta\}$ is inconsistent.

Let $A' = A * \alpha$. It follows from *inclusion* that $A * \alpha \subseteq A \cup \{\alpha\}$, and from *consistency* that $A * \alpha$ is consistent. Furthermore, it follows from *tenacity*, $\beta \in A$, and $\beta \notin A * \alpha$ that $\neg\beta \in \text{Cn}(A * \alpha)$. We can conclude that $(A * \alpha) \cup \{\beta\}$ is inconsistent.

Case 2, α is inconsistent: It follows from *inconsistent expansion* that $A \subseteq A*\alpha$, so that *relevance* holds vacuously. ■

We are now ready for the representation theorem for internal maxichoice revision. Its proof can be based largely on Theorem 3.6:

THEOREM 3.33 *Let A be a belief base and $*$ an operator for A. Then $*$ is an operator of internal maxichoice revision if and only if it satisfies consistency, inclusion, inconsistent expansion, success, uniformity, and tenacity.*

Proof. *Construction-to-postulates*: Let $\mp_\gamma$ be an operator of internal maxichoice revision. It follows from Theorem 3.6 that *consistency*, *inclusion*, *success*, and *uniformity* are satisfied and from Observation 3.1 that *inconsistent expansion* is satisfied. It remains to be shown that *tenacity* holds.

Let $\beta \in A$ and $\beta \notin A\mp_\gamma\alpha$. We need to show that $\neg\beta \in \text{Cn}(A\mp_\gamma\alpha)$. Since $\mp_\gamma$ is maxichoice, there is some X such that $X \in A\perp\neg\alpha$ and $A\mp_\gamma\alpha = X\cup\{\alpha\}$. Then $\beta \in A\backslash X$. From this and $X \in A\perp\neg\alpha$ we can conclude that $X \cup \{\beta\} \vdash \neg\alpha$. We can use the deduction property to obtain $X \vdash \beta\rightarrow\neg\alpha$, or equivalently $X \vdash \alpha\rightarrow\neg\beta$. Again using the deduction property, we obtain $X \cup \{\alpha\} \vdash \neg\beta$, i.e. $A\mp_\gamma\alpha \vdash \neg\beta$, as desired.

Postulates-to-construction: Let $*$ be an operation for A that satisfies the postulates listed in the theorem. It follows from Observation 3.32 that *relevance* is satisfied, and thus from Theorem 3.6 that $*$ is an operator of internal partial meet revision, i.e. that it is identical to $\mp_\gamma$ for some selection function γ for A. It remains to be shown that γ is maxichoice.

Suppose to the contrary that γ is not maxichoice. Then there is some α such that $\not\vdash \alpha$ and $A{\sim_\gamma}\alpha \notin A\bot\alpha$. Since $\sim_\gamma$ satisfies *contraction-inclusion* and *contraction-success*, we can conclude that there is some sentence $\beta \in A\backslash(A{\sim_\gamma}\alpha)$ such that $(A{\sim_\gamma}\alpha) \cup \{\beta\} \not\vdash \alpha$. By the deduction property, $A{\sim_\gamma}\alpha \not\vdash \beta\rightarrow\alpha$, or equivalently $A{\sim_\gamma}\alpha \not\vdash \neg\alpha\rightarrow\neg\beta$. One more application of the deduction property yields $(A{\sim_\gamma}\alpha)\cup\{\neg\alpha\} \not\vdash \neg\beta$, i.e. $\neg\beta \notin \mathrm{Cn}(A\mp_\gamma\neg\alpha)$. It follows by *tenacity* from $\beta \in A$ and $\neg\beta \notin \mathrm{Cn}(A\mp_\gamma\neg\alpha)$ that $\beta \in A\mp_\gamma\neg\alpha$. Since $\beta \notin A{\sim_\gamma}\alpha$, this means that β is identical to $\neg\alpha$. Since $\beta \in A\backslash(A{\sim_\gamma}\alpha)$ we then have $\neg\alpha \in A\backslash(A{\sim_\gamma}\alpha)$, i.e. $\neg\alpha \in A$ and $\neg\alpha \notin \bigcap\gamma(A\bot\alpha)$, contrary to Observation 3.30. This contradiction concludes the proof. ■

It follows directly from Theorems 3.6 and 3.33 and Observation 3.32 that:

> An operator of internal partial meet revision is maxichoice if and only if it satisfies *tenacity*.
> [Theorem 3.12, Part 1.]

Exercises

144. Let $\mp$ be internal full meet revision. Perform the following operations:
    (a) $\{p, q\}\mp\neg p$
    (b) $\{p, q\}\mp(\neg p\vee\neg q)$
    (c) $\{p, q, p\rightarrow q\}\mp(p\&\neg q)$
    (d) $\{p\rightarrow q, q\rightarrow p\}\mp(p\leftrightarrow\neg q)$.
145. Let p and q be logically independent sentences, and let $*$ be an operator for $\{p, q\}$. Show that if $*$ is internal full meet revision, then it is not internal maxichoice revision.
146. Let $\mp$ be internal full meet revision. Show that $A\mp\alpha \subseteq A\mp_\gamma\alpha$ for all operators $\mp_\gamma$ of internal partial meet revision.
147. Show that internal full meet revision satisfies pre-expansion ($(A+\alpha)\mp\alpha = A\mp\alpha$). (Hint: use Observation 1.41.)
148. [50] Show that if the language contains at least two logically independent sentences, then no global operator $*$ of internal partial meet revision satisfies:
    For all $\varepsilon \in \mathrm{Cn}(A)$, either $\varepsilon \in \mathrm{Cn}(A * \alpha)$ or $\neg\varepsilon \in \mathrm{Cn}(A * \alpha)$. (*extreme tenacity*).

15+ EXTERNAL REVISION

In the treatment of external revision we will have use for the following observation, that was proved in Section 1.12+ :

1. If $X \in A\bot\beta$ then $X \cup \{\neg\beta\} \in (A \cup \{\neg\beta\})\bot\beta$.

2. If $\neg\beta \notin A$, then $X \in A\perp\beta$ if and only if $\neg\beta \notin X$ and $X \cup \{\neg\beta\} \in (A \cup \{\neg\beta\})\perp\beta$.

[Observation 1.41.]

The following representation theorem for external partial meet revision can be proved in much the same way as the corresponding theorem for internal revision:

The operator $*$ is an operator of external partial meet revision if and only if it satisfies:

$A * \alpha$ is consistent if α is consistent. (*consistency*)

$A * \alpha \subseteq A \cup \{\alpha\}$. (*inclusion*)

If $\beta \in A$ and $\beta \notin A * \alpha$, then there is some A' such that $A * \alpha \subseteq A' \subseteq A \cup \{\alpha\}$, A' is consistent but $A' \cup \{\beta\}$ is inconsistent. (*relevance*)

$\alpha \in A * \alpha$. (*success*)

If α and β are elements of A and it holds for all $A' \subseteq A$ that $A' \cup \{\alpha\}$ is inconsistent if and only if $A' \cup \{\beta\}$ is inconsistent, then $A \cap (A * \alpha) = A \cap (A * \beta)$. (*weak uniformity*)

$A + \alpha * \alpha = A * \alpha$. (*pre-expansion*).

[Theorem 3.7.]

Proof. *Construction-to-postulates*: Let $\pm_\gamma$ be an operator of external partial meet revision. The proofs that *consistency*, *inclusion*, *success*, and *pre-expansion* are satisfied are left to the reader as an exercise.

Relevance: Let $\varepsilon \in A \setminus (A \pm_\gamma \alpha)$. Then there is some $Z \in \gamma((A \cup \{\alpha\})\perp\neg\alpha)$ such that $\varepsilon \notin Z$, thus $Z \cup \{\varepsilon\} \vdash \neg\alpha$. We have $A \pm_\gamma \alpha = \bigcap \gamma((A \cup \{\alpha\})\perp\neg\alpha) \subseteq Z$. Furthermore, it follows from *success* that $\alpha \in Z$. In summary, $A \pm_\gamma \alpha \subseteq Z \subseteq A \cup \{\alpha\}$, Z is consistent and $Z \cup \{\varepsilon\}$ is inconsistent. This is sufficient to establish that relevance holds.

Weak uniformity: Let α and β be elements of A such that, for all subsets A' of A, $A' \cup \{\alpha\}$ is inconsistent iff $A' \cup \{\beta\}$ is inconsistent. Then every subset of A implies $\neg\alpha$ if and only if it implies $\neg\beta$, and it follows from Observation 1.39 that $A\perp\neg\alpha = A\perp\neg\beta$. Since $A = A \cup \{\alpha\} = A \cup \{\beta\}$, it follows that

$$\begin{aligned}
&A \pm_\gamma \alpha \\
&= \gamma_{A \cup \{\alpha\}}((A \cup \{\alpha\})\perp\neg\alpha) \\
&= \gamma_A(A\perp\neg\alpha) \\
&= \gamma_A(A\perp\neg\beta) \\
&= \gamma_{A \cup \{\beta\}}((A \cup \{\beta\})\perp\neg\beta) \\
&= A \pm_\gamma \beta.
\end{aligned}$$

Postulates-to-construction: Let $*$ be an operator that satisfies the postulates listed in the theorem. Let γ be a two-place function such that for each set $A, \gamma(A,\ ) = \gamma_A(\ )$ has the following properties:

1. If $A\perp\beta$ is empty, then $\gamma_A(A\perp\beta) = \{A\}$.
2. If $A\perp\beta$ is non-empty and there is some sentence $\alpha \in A$ such that $A\perp\beta = A\perp\neg\alpha$, then $\gamma_A(A\perp\beta) = \{X \in A\perp\beta \mid A * \alpha \subseteq X\}$
3. Otherwise $\gamma_A(A\perp\beta) = A\perp\beta$.

(Comment: Clause (2) represents the principal case. Its construction is derived from the definition of external partial meet revision. Clause (3) will never be appealed to, since it represents the contractions that are not used in external partial meet revision. Its construction is arbitrary in the sense that it can be chosen in any way that satisfies the restriction that γ_A is a selection function for A.)

We have to prove (I) that γ is a two-place selection function, i.e. that for each A, γ_A is a one-place selection function for A, and (II) that $A\pm_\gamma\alpha = A * \alpha$ for all sentences α.

Part I: For γ_A to be a selection function, it must be a function. This is obvious in clauses (1) and (3) of the definition. To prove it in clause (2), let α_1 and α_2 be elements of A such that $A\perp\neg\alpha_1 = A\perp\neg\alpha_2 \neq \emptyset$. We have to prove that $\gamma_A(A\perp\neg\alpha_1) = \gamma_A(A\perp\neg\alpha_2)$.

Let A' be a subset of A. Then it follows by Observation 1.39 from $A\perp\neg\alpha_1 = A\perp\neg\alpha_2$ that A' implies $\neg\alpha_1$ if and only if it implies $\neg\alpha_2$, thus $A' \cup \{\alpha_1\}$ is inconsistent if and only if $A' \cup \{\alpha_2\}$ is inconsistent. By *weak uniformity*, $A \cap (A * \alpha_1) = A \cap (A * \alpha_2)$. Since α_1 and α_2 are elements of A, it follows from *inclusion* that $A * \alpha_1 \subseteq A$ and $A * \alpha_2 \subseteq A$. We can conclude that $A * \alpha_1 = A * \alpha_2$, from which the desired result follows directly by the definition of γ_A.

To show that γ_A is a one-place selection function it now remains to show that $\gamma_A(A\perp\beta)$ is non-empty for all sentences β. This is obvious in clauses (1) and (3) of the definition. To show that it holds in clause (2), let α be a sentence such that $\alpha \in A$ and $A\perp\neg\alpha \neq \emptyset$. We need to show that there is some $X \in A\perp\neg\alpha$ such that $A * \alpha \subseteq X$.

Since $A\perp\neg\alpha$ is non-empty we have $\neg\alpha \notin \text{Cn}(\emptyset)$, from which it follows that α is consistent. By *consistency*, $A * \alpha$ is consistent. It then follows from *success* that $\neg\alpha \notin \text{Cn}(A*\alpha)$. Furthermore, it follows from *inclusion* and $\alpha \in A$ that $A*\alpha \subseteq A$. By the upper bound property, there is some X such that $A * \alpha \subseteq X \in A\perp\neg\alpha$.

Part II: The proof that $A\pm_\gamma\alpha = A * \alpha$ for all α will be divided into two cases according to whether or not α is consistent.

Case 1, α is inconsistent: By *relevance*, if $\varepsilon \in A\backslash(A * \alpha)$, then there is some A' such that $A * \alpha \subseteq A' \subseteq A \cup \{\alpha\}$, A' is consistent but $A' \cup \{\varepsilon\}$ is inconsistent. This, however, is impossible since it follows from *success* that $\alpha \in A'$ so that A' is inconsistent. Thus $A\backslash(A * \alpha)$ is empty, i.e. $A \subseteq A * \alpha$. By *success* and *inclusion* we may then conclude that $A * \alpha = A \cup \{\alpha\}$.

We can also conclude from the first clause of the definition of γ that if α is inconsistent, then $A\pm_\gamma\alpha = A \cup \{\alpha\}$. We have thus shown that $A\pm_\gamma\alpha = A * \alpha$.

Case 2, α is consistent: Then, it follows from the definition of external partial meet revision and clause (2) of the definition of γ in this proof that:

$$\begin{aligned}&A\pm_\gamma\alpha = \\ &= \bigcap \gamma_{A\cup\{\alpha\}}((A\cup\{\alpha\})\perp\neg\alpha) \\ &= \bigcap\{X \in (A\cup\{\alpha\})\perp\neg\alpha \mid (A\cup\{\alpha\}) * \alpha \subseteq X\}.\end{aligned}$$

It follows directly from this that $(A\cup\{\alpha\})*\alpha \subseteq A\pm_\gamma\alpha$, and thus by *pre-expansion* that $A * \alpha \subseteq A\pm_\gamma\alpha$.

In order to prove that $A\pm_\gamma\alpha \subseteq A * \alpha$, let $\varepsilon \notin A * \alpha$. We are going to show that $\varepsilon \notin A\pm_\gamma\alpha$. Since this is trivial if $\varepsilon \notin A \cup \{\alpha\}$, we will assume that $\varepsilon \in A \cup \{\alpha\}$.

From $\varepsilon \notin A * \alpha$ it follows, by *pre-expansion*, that $\varepsilon \notin (A \cup \{\alpha\}) * \alpha$. From $\varepsilon \in A \cup \{\alpha\}$ and $\varepsilon \notin (A \cup \{\alpha\}) * \alpha$ it follows by *relevance* that there is some Z such that $(A \cup \{\alpha\}) * \alpha \subseteq Z \subseteq A \cup \{\alpha\}$, Z is consistent and $Z \cup \{\varepsilon\}$ is inconsistent. By *success*, $\alpha \in Z$, so that $\neg\alpha \notin \mathrm{Cn}(Z)$. It follows from the upper bound property that there is some $Z' \in (A \cup \{\alpha\})\perp\neg\alpha$ with $Z \subseteq Z'$. It follows from $Z \subseteq Z'$ that $(A \cup \{\alpha\}) * \alpha \subseteq Z'$. By clause (2) of the definition of γ, we have $Z' \in \gamma_{A\cup\{\alpha\}}((A \cup \{\alpha\})\perp\neg\alpha)$. Since $\varepsilon \notin Z'$, it follows that $\varepsilon \notin A\pm_\gamma\alpha$. This completes the proof. ■

In this theorem, only weak uniformity (uniformity restricted to redundant revision) is referred to. The full uniformity postulate, that was used in the axiomatic characterization of internal partial meet revision, does not hold in general for its external counterpart:

> *Uniformity* does not hold in general for external partial meet revision. [Observation 3.8, Part 1.]

Proof. Let $A = \{p\rightarrow r, p\rightarrow\neg r\}$. It follows that:

$$\begin{aligned}&(A\cup\{p\})\perp\neg p = \{\{p\rightarrow r, p\}, \{p\rightarrow\neg r, p\}\} \\ &(A\cup\{p\&q\})\perp\neg(p\&q) = \{\{p\rightarrow r, p\&q\}, \{p\rightarrow\neg r, p\&q\}\}\end{aligned}$$

Let the (two-place) selection function γ be such that:

$$\begin{aligned}&\gamma((A\cup\{p\})\perp\neg p) = \{\{p\rightarrow r, p\}\} \\ &\gamma((A\cup\{p\&q\})\perp\neg(p\&q)) = \{\{p\rightarrow\neg r, p\&q\}\}\end{aligned}$$

We then have:

$$\begin{aligned}&A\pm_\gamma p = \{p\rightarrow r, p\} \\ &A\pm_\gamma(p\&q) = \{p\rightarrow\neg r, p\&q\}\end{aligned}$$

It can easily be verified that for each subset A' of A, $A'\cup\{p\}$ is inconsistent if and only if $A'\cup\{p\&q\}$ is inconsistent. However, $A\cap(A\pm_\gamma p) \neq A\cap(A\pm_\gamma(p\&q))$, so that *uniformity* does not hold. ■

In Section 3.13+ we saw that that redundancy is a characteristic postulate for unified internal partial meet revision. It is also a characteristic postulate for unified external partial meet revision.

> The operator $*$ is an operator of unified external partial meet revision if and only if it satisfies *consistency, inclusion, relevance, success, weak uniformity, pre-expansion*, and *redundancy*.
> [Theorem 3.10.]

Proof. *Construction-to-postulates*: For one direction of the proof, let γ be a unified two-place selection function and $\pm_\gamma$ the operator of external partial meet revision generated by γ. In addition to what was shown in Theorem 3.7, we have to show that *redundancy* holds.

Suppose that γ is unified, that α is consistent, and that $\beta \vdash \neg\alpha$ for each $\beta \in B$. It follows from Observation 1.40 that

$$(A \cup B \cup \{\alpha\})\perp\neg\alpha = (A \cup \{\alpha\})\perp\neg\alpha$$

and thus, since γ is unified:

$$\begin{aligned}&(A \cup B)\pm_\gamma\alpha\\ &= \bigcap\gamma_{A\cup B\cup\{\alpha\}}((A \cup B \cup \{\alpha\})\perp\neg\alpha)\\ &= \bigcap\gamma_{A\cup\{\alpha\}}((A \cup \{\alpha\})\perp\neg\alpha)\\ &= A\pm_\gamma\alpha.\end{aligned}$$

Postulates-to-construction: Let $*$ be an operator that satisfies the postulates listed in the theorem. Let γ be a two-place function such that for each $A, \gamma(A, \ ) = \gamma_A(\ )$ has the following properties:

1. If $A\perp\beta$ is empty, then $\gamma_A(A\perp\beta) = \{A\}$.
2. If $A\perp\beta$ is non-empty and there is a set A' and a sentence $\alpha \in A'$ such that $A\perp\beta = A'\perp\neg\alpha$, then:
   $\gamma_A(A\perp\beta) = \{X \in A\perp\beta \mid A' * \alpha \subseteq X\}$
3. Otherwise $\gamma_A(A\perp\beta) = A\perp\beta$.

(Comment: Compare this construction to the one used in the proof of Theorem 3.7. The second clause has been adjusted. The third clause is arbitrary in the same sense as in Theorem 3.7.)

We have to prove (I) that γ is a two-place selection function, i.e. that for each A, γ_A is a one-place selection function for A, (II) that γ is unified, and (III) that $A\pm_\gamma\alpha = A * \alpha$ for all sentences α.

Part I: For γ_A to be a selection function, it must be a function. This is obvious in clauses (1) and (3) of the definition. To prove it in clause (2), let A_1 and A_2 be sets and α_1 and α_2 sentences such that $\alpha_1 \in A_1, \alpha_2 \in A_2$ and $A_1\perp\neg\alpha_1 = A_2\perp\neg\alpha_2 \neq \emptyset$. We have to prove that $\gamma_{A_1}(A_1\perp\neg\alpha_1) = \gamma_{A_2}(A_2\perp\neg\alpha_2)$.

Let $W = \bigcup(A_1 \perp \neg\alpha_1)$. It follows from Observation 1.40 that $W \perp \neg\alpha_1 = A_1 \perp \neg\alpha_1$. Furthermore, since $A_1 \perp \neg\alpha_1 = A_2 \perp \neg\alpha_2$, we have $W = \bigcup(A_2 \perp \neg\alpha_2)$ and thus, again according to Observation 1.40, $W \perp \neg\alpha_2 = A_2 \perp \neg\alpha_2$. We can conclude that $W \perp \neg\alpha_1 = W \perp \neg\alpha_2$. It follows from Observation 3.30 that $\alpha_1 \in W$ and $\alpha_2 \in W$.

It follows from $W \perp \neg\alpha_1 = W \perp \neg\alpha_2$, by Observation 1.39, that every subset of W implies $\neg\alpha_1$ if and only if it implies $\neg\alpha_2$. Thus, it is consistent with α_1 if and only if it is consistent with α_2. It follows from *weak uniformity* that $W \cap (W * \alpha_1) = W \cap (W * \alpha_2)$. Since $\alpha_1 \in W$ we can conclude from *inclusion* that $W * \alpha_1 \subseteq W$, and in the same way it follows from $\alpha_2 \in W$ that $W * \alpha_2 \subseteq W$. We can conclude that $W * \alpha_1 = W * \alpha_2$.

Each element of $A_1 \backslash (\bigcup(A_1 \perp \neg\alpha_1))$, i.e. of $A_1 \backslash W$, implies $\neg\alpha_1$. Therefore, it follows from *redundancy* that $A_1 * \alpha_1 = W * \alpha_1$. In the same way it follows that $A_2 * \alpha_2 = W * \alpha_2$. Since we already know that $W * \alpha_1 = W * \alpha_2$, we can conclude that $A_1 * \alpha_1 = A_2 * \alpha_2$. By clause (2) of the definition, it follows that $\gamma_{A_1}(A_1 \perp \neg\alpha_1) = \gamma_{A_2}(A_2 \perp \neg\alpha_2)$. This concludes the proof that γ is a function.

To show that γ_A is a one-place selection function it now remains to show that $\gamma_A(A \perp \beta)$ is non-empty if $A \perp \beta$ is so. This can be done in the same way as in the proof of Theorem 3.7.

Part II: The proof that γ is unified is trivial in clauses (1) and (3). For clause (2), let A_1, A_2, α_1, and α_2 be such that $\neg\alpha_1 \in A_1, \neg\alpha_2 \in A_2$, and $A_1 \perp \alpha_1 = A_2 \perp \alpha_2 \neq \emptyset$. Let $W = \bigcup(A_1 \perp \alpha_1) = \bigcup(A_2 \perp \alpha_2)$. We then have $W \perp \alpha_1 = A_1 \perp \alpha_1$ and $W \perp \alpha_2 = A_2 \perp \alpha_2$. Furthermore, it follows from *redundancy* that $W * \neg\alpha_1 = A_1 * \neg\alpha_1$ and $W * \neg\alpha_2 = A_2 * \neg\alpha_2$. It follows from *weak uniformity* and $W \perp \alpha_1 = W \perp \alpha_2$ that $W \cap (W * \neg\alpha_1) = W \cap (W * \neg\alpha_2)$. Since both $\neg\alpha_1$ and $\neg\alpha_2$ are elements of W, it follows by *inclusion* that $W * \neg\alpha_1 = W * \neg\alpha_2$. We therefore have $A_1 * \neg\alpha_1 = A_2 * \neg\alpha_2$, and it follows from the definition of γ that $\gamma_{A_1}(A_1 \perp \alpha_1) = \gamma_{A_2}(A_2 \perp \alpha_2)$.

Part III follows in the same way as Part II of the proof of Theorem 3.7. ■

In Section 3.12 it was pointed out that there is a close connection between external partial meet revision ($A \pm_\gamma \alpha = A + \alpha \sim_\gamma \neg\alpha$) and the composite operation of expansion and partial meet consolidation ($A + \alpha \sim_\gamma \perp$). This connection can be proved as follows:

> Let $\pm_\gamma$ be the operator of external partial meet revision and $\sim_\gamma \perp$ the consolidation operator that are generated by one and the same (two-place) selection function γ. Furthermore, let A be a set of sentences and α a sentence. Then:
>
> 1. If γ is relational and $\alpha \in A + \alpha \sim_\gamma \perp$, then $A \pm_\gamma \alpha \subseteq A + \alpha \sim_\gamma \perp$.
> 2. If γ is transitively relational and $\alpha \in A + \alpha \sim_\gamma \perp$, then $A \pm_\gamma \alpha = A + \alpha \sim_\gamma \perp$.

[Observation 3.29.]

Proof. *Part 1*: Let γ be a two-place selection function that is based on the marking-off relation $\sqsubseteq$ (cf. Definition 2.55). Suppose that $\alpha \in A+\alpha\sim_{\gamma}\perp$. We are going to show that $\gamma((A\cup\{\alpha\})\perp\perp) \subseteq \gamma((A\cup\{\alpha\})\perp\neg\alpha)$. Let $X \in \gamma((A\cup\{\alpha\})\perp\perp)$. It follows from $\alpha \in A+\alpha\sim_{\gamma}\perp = \bigcap\gamma((A\cup\{\alpha\})\perp\perp$ that $\alpha \in X$. We can conclude that $X \in (A\cup\{\alpha\})\perp\neg\alpha$. (Cf. Exercise 33.) Next, let $Y \in (A\cup\{\alpha\})\perp\neg\alpha$. Then $Y \in (A\cup\{\alpha\})\perp\perp$. (Again, cf. Exercise 33.) It follows from $X \in \gamma((A\cup\{\alpha\})\perp\perp)$ and $Y \in (A\cup\{\alpha\})\perp\perp$ that $Y \sqsubseteq X$. Since this holds for all $Y \in (A\cup\{\alpha\})\perp\neg\alpha$, and $X \in (A\cup\{\alpha\})\perp\neg\alpha$, we may conclude that $X \in \gamma((A\cup\{\alpha\})\perp\neg\alpha)$.

We have proved that $\gamma((A\cup\{\alpha\})\perp\perp) \subseteq \gamma((A\cup\{\alpha\})\perp\neg\alpha)$. It follows that $\bigcap\gamma((A\cup\{\alpha\})\perp\neg\alpha) \subseteq \bigcap\gamma((A\cup\{\alpha\})\perp\perp)$, i.e. $A\pm_{\gamma}\alpha \subseteq A+\alpha\sim_{\gamma}\perp$.

Part 2: Suppose, in addition to our assumptions for Part 1, that $\sqsubseteq$ is transitive. We are going to show that $\gamma((A\cup\{\alpha\})\perp\neg\alpha) \subseteq \gamma((A\cup\{\alpha\})\perp\perp)$. Let $X \in \gamma((A\cup\{\alpha\})\perp\neg\alpha)$. Then $X \in (A\cup\{\alpha\})\perp\perp$. (Cf. Exercise 33.) Next, let $Y \in \gamma((A\cup\{\alpha\})\perp\perp)$. It follows from $\alpha \in A+\alpha\sim_{\gamma}\perp = \bigcap\gamma((A\cup\{\alpha\})\perp\perp$ that $\alpha \in Y$. Then $Y \in (A\cup\{\alpha\})\perp\neg\alpha$. (Again, cf. Exercise 33.) From this in combination with $X \in \gamma((A\cup\{\alpha\})\perp\neg\alpha)$ it follows that $Y \sqsubseteq X$.

Let $Z \in (A\cup\{\alpha\})\perp\perp$. It follows from $Y \in \gamma((A\cup\{\alpha\})\perp\perp)$ that $Z \sqsubseteq Y$. Since we already know that $Y \sqsubseteq X$, we can use the transitivity of $\sqsubseteq$ to conclude that $Z \sqsubseteq X$. Since this holds for all $Z \in (A\cup\{\alpha\})\perp\perp$, and $X \in (A\cup\{\alpha\})\perp\perp$, $X \in \gamma((A\cup\{\alpha\})\perp\perp)$.

We have proved that $\gamma((A\cup\{\alpha\})\perp\neg\alpha) \subseteq \gamma((A\cup\{\alpha\})\perp\perp)$. Since we know from Part 1 that $\gamma((A\cup\{\alpha\})\perp\perp) \subseteq \gamma((A\cup\{\alpha\})\perp\neg\alpha)$, we can conclude that $\gamma((A\cup\{\alpha\})\perp\neg\alpha) = \gamma((A\cup\{\alpha\})\perp\perp)$, and thus we have $\bigcap\gamma((A\cup\{\alpha\})\perp\neg\alpha) = \bigcap\gamma((A\cup\{\alpha\})\perp\perp)$, i.e. $A\pm_{\gamma}\alpha = A+\alpha\sim_{\gamma}\perp$. ■

Exercises

149. Let γ be a (unified) global selection function such that if $A\perp\alpha$ is non-empty, then $\gamma(A\perp\alpha)$ consists of those elements of $A\perp\alpha$ that have the highest number of elements. Perform the following operations:

    (a) $\{p, q\rightarrow p\}\pm_{\gamma}\neg p$
    (b) $\{p, q\rightarrow r, \neg q\rightarrow r\}\pm_{\gamma}(\neg p\vee\neg r)$
    (c) $\{p, q, q\&r\}\pm_{\gamma}(p\&q)$
    (d) $\{p, q, q\&r\}\pm_{\gamma}\neg(p\&q)$.

150. Complete the proof of Theorem 3.7 by showing that external partial meet revision satisfies *consistency*, *inclusion*, *success*, and *pre-expansion*.

151. [50] Let γ be a two-place selection function. Show that it holds for all sentences α and sets A of sentences that if $\alpha \in A$ then $A\pm_{\gamma}\alpha = A\mp_{\gamma}\alpha$. (Redundant external revision coincides with redundant internal revision.)

152. Let γ be a two-place selection function, and let A be a set and α a sentence such that $A\bot\neg\alpha$ has exactly one element. Show that $A\pm_\gamma\alpha = A\mp_\gamma\alpha$. (External and internal revision coincide in the no-choice cases.)

16+ LIMITING CASES OF EXTERNAL REVISION

This section is devoted to the limiting cases of external partial meet revision. One of them, namely external full meet revision ($\pm$), turns out to coincide with the corresponding limiting case of internal revision, internal full meet revision ($\mp$).

It holds for all sets A and sentences α that
$A\pm\alpha = A\mp\alpha$,
[Part of Theorem 3.13.]

Proof. *For one direction*, let $\varepsilon \notin A\mp\alpha$. We are going to show that $\varepsilon \notin A\pm\alpha$. Since both $A\pm\alpha$ and $A\mp\alpha$ are subsets of $A\cup\{\alpha\}$, and both contain α, this is trivial unless $\varepsilon \in A$. We will therefore assume that $\varepsilon \in A\backslash(A\mp\alpha)$.

It follows from $\varepsilon \in A\backslash(A\mp\alpha)$ that $\varepsilon \in A\backslash(A \sim \neg\alpha)$. Therefore, there must be some set X such that $\varepsilon \notin X \in A\bot\neg\alpha$. It follows from $X \in A\bot\neg\alpha$, by Observation 1.41, that $X \cup \{\alpha\} \in (A \cup \{\alpha\})\bot\neg\alpha$. Since $\varepsilon \notin X$ and ε is not identical to α (which we know since $\varepsilon \notin A\mp\alpha$ and $\alpha \in A\mp\alpha$) we have $\varepsilon \notin X \cup \{\alpha\} \in (A \cup \{\alpha\})\bot\neg\alpha$, and thus $\varepsilon \notin \bigcap((A \cup \{\alpha\})\bot\neg\alpha)$, i.e. $\varepsilon \notin A\pm\alpha$.

For the other direction, let $\varepsilon \notin A\pm\alpha$. We are going to show that $\varepsilon \notin A\mp\alpha$. It follows from $\varepsilon \notin A\pm\alpha = \bigcap((A \cup \{\alpha\})\bot\neg\alpha)$ that there must be some X such that $\varepsilon \notin X \in (A \cup \{\alpha\})\bot\neg\alpha$. There are two cases.

First case, $\alpha \in A$: Then $A \cup \{\alpha\} = A$, and we have $\varepsilon \notin X \in A\bot\neg\alpha$, so that $\varepsilon \notin A \sim \neg\alpha$.

Second case, $\alpha \notin A$: Then it follows from $X \in (A \cup \{\alpha\})\bot\neg\alpha$ that $X\backslash\{\alpha\} \in A\bot\neg\alpha$ (Observation 1.41), so that $\varepsilon \notin X\backslash\{\alpha\} \in A\bot\neg\alpha$, and consequently $\varepsilon \notin A \sim \neg\alpha$.

Both cases: Since ε is not identical to α (which we know from $\varepsilon \notin A\pm\alpha$ and $\alpha \in A\pm\alpha$), we then have $\varepsilon \notin (A \sim \neg\alpha) \cup \{\alpha\}$, i.e. $\varepsilon \notin A\mp\alpha$. This completes the proof. ■

The other limiting case, external maxichoice revision, does not coincide with its internal counterpart (internal maxichoice revision). However, the two are closely related in the sense that the same characteristic postulate, tenacity, can be used for both of them.

THEOREM 3.34 *Let A be a belief base and $*$ an operator for A. Then $*$ is an operator of external maxichoice revision if and only if it satisfies consistency, inclusion, success, weak uniformity, inconsistent expansion, pre-expansion, and:*
For all $\beta \in A$, either $\beta \in A * \alpha$ or $\neg\beta \in \mathrm{Cn}(A * \alpha)$ (tenacity)

Proof. *Construction-to-postulates*: Let $\pm_\gamma$ be an operator of external maxichoice revision. It follows from Theorem 3.7 and Observation 3.1 that the listed properties except *tenacity* are satisfied. In order to show that *tenacity* holds, let $\beta \in A$ and $\beta \notin A\pm_\gamma\alpha$. We need to show that $\neg\beta \in \text{Cn}(A\pm_\gamma\alpha)$.

It can be concluded from $\beta \in A$ and $\beta \notin A\pm_\gamma\alpha$ that $\beta \in A \cup \{\alpha\}$ and also that $\beta \notin (A \cup \{\alpha\})\sim_\gamma\neg\alpha$. Since $\sim_\gamma$ is maxichoice, $(A \cup \{\alpha\})\sim_\gamma\neg\alpha \in (A \cup \{\alpha\})\bot\neg\alpha$. Thus, $((A \cup \{\alpha\})\sim_\gamma\neg\alpha) \cup \{\beta\} \vdash \neg\alpha$. By the deduction property, $((A \cup \{\alpha\})\sim_\gamma\neg\alpha) \vdash \beta\rightarrow\neg\alpha$, or equivalently $((A \cup \{\alpha\})\sim_\gamma\neg\alpha) \vdash \alpha\rightarrow\neg\beta$.

It follows from Observation 3.30 that $\alpha \in (A \cup \{\alpha\})\sim_\gamma\neg\alpha$. We can conclude from this and $(A \cup \{\alpha\})\sim_\gamma\neg\alpha \vdash \alpha\rightarrow\neg\beta$ that $\neg\beta \in \text{Cn}((A \cup \{\alpha\})\sim_\gamma\neg\alpha)$, i.e. $\neg\beta \in \text{Cn}(A\pm_\gamma\alpha)$, as desired.

Postulates-to-construction: Let $*$ be an operation for A that satisfies the postulates listed in the theorem. It follows from Observation 3.32 that *relevance* holds, and thus from Theorem 3.7 that $*$ is an operator of external partial meet revision. It is therefore identical to $\pm_\gamma$ for some two-place selection function γ. It remains to be shown that it is identical to $\pm_{\gamma'}$ for some maxichoice selection function γ'.

Let γ'' be any two-place maxichoice selection function, and let γ' be a two-place selection function such that:

(I) If $\neg\delta$ is logically equivalent with an element of A, then $A\sim_{\gamma'}\delta = A\sim_\gamma\delta$.
(II) Otherwise, $A\sim_{\gamma'}\delta = A\sim_{\gamma''}\delta$:

(Comment: Clause (I) covers all cases that we need for the construction. Clause (II) has been added to ensure that γ' is defined for all arguments.)

We need to show (1) that γ' is maxichoice and (2) that $\pm_{\gamma'}$ coincides with $\pm_\gamma$.

Part 1: Since the maxichoice property follows directly when clause (II) is applicable, it remains to show that it holds in clause (I). Due to *contraction-extensionality*, it is sufficient to show that if $\neg\delta \in A$, then $A\sim_\gamma\delta \in A\bot\delta$ if $A\bot\delta$ is non-empty.

Let $\neg\delta \in A$. Then $A \cup \{\neg\delta\} = A$, so that $A\pm_\gamma\neg\delta = A\sim_\gamma\delta$. Let $\beta \in A\backslash(A\sim_\gamma\delta)$. Then $\beta \in A\backslash(A\pm_\gamma\neg\delta)$, and it follows directly from *tenacity* that $\neg\beta \in \text{Cn}(A\pm_\gamma\neg\delta)$, and consequently $\neg\beta \in \text{Cn}(A\sim_\gamma\delta)$. Hence $(A\sim_\gamma\delta) \cup \{\beta\}$ is inconsistent, and thus it implies δ. Since this holds for every $\beta \in A\backslash(A\sim_\gamma\delta)$, we can conclude that $A\sim_\gamma\delta \in A\bot\delta$, as desired.

Part 2: For any set A and sentence β, $A\pm_\gamma\beta = (A \cup \{\beta\})\sim_\gamma\neg\beta$. By clause (I) of the definition of γ', $(A \cup \{\beta\})\sim_{\gamma'}\neg\beta = (A \cup \{\beta\})\sim_\gamma\neg\beta$, and thus $A\pm_{\gamma'}\beta = A\pm_\gamma\beta$. ■

It follows from Theorems 3.7 and 3.34 and Observation 3.32 that:

> An operator of external partial meet revision is maxichoice if and only if it satisfies *tenacity*.
> [Theorem 3.12, Part 2.]

Exercises

153. Show that *uniformity* does not hold for external maxichoice revision.

154. [50] Let γ be a two-place selection function. Show that even if γ is maxichoice and transitively, maximizingly relational, it does not hold for all α that $A\pm_\gamma\alpha \subseteq A\mp_\gamma\alpha$ or $A\mp_\gamma\alpha \subseteq A\pm_\gamma\alpha$.

17+ MULTIPLE REVISION

In this section we are going to generalize the revision operators to revision by sets of sentences (multiple revision). Revision of a belief base by a single sentence α consists of two suboperations: (non-closing) expansion by α and contraction by $\neg\alpha$. It is not difficult to generalize (non-closing) expansion to the multiple case: to expand A by B we just form their union $A \cup B$. It is less obvious how to generalize contraction by $\neg\alpha$ to an operation that removes a set B. Contrary to single sentences, sets of sentences do not have negations. We need to find, for each set B that we wish to contract by, some set that stands (for our present purposes) in the same relation to it as the negation of a sentence to that sentence itself.

To do this, let us first have a closer look at the reason why we contract by $\neg\alpha$ when we revise by α. The reason is that we wish to obtain a subset of the original set to which we can add α without making the outcome inconsistent. Let $X = A\cap(A*\alpha)$, i.e. let X be the part of the original set that is retained after the revision. We want X to be consistent with α, i.e.:

$$X \cup \{\alpha\} \nvdash \bot.$$

By the deduction property, this is equivalent to $X \nvdash \alpha\rightarrow\bot$ and thus to

$$X \nvdash \neg\alpha.$$

In other words, what we want to achieve by deleting elements from A is that the resulting set X does not imply $\neg\alpha$. This is why we contract by $\neg\alpha$ when we revise by α.

Let us now apply the same kind of reasoning to revision of A by a set B. The reason why we are willing to give up elements of A in this process is that we want the resulting subset X of A to be consistent with$B$, i.e.:

$$X \cup B \nvdash \bot.$$

By the compactness property of Cn, this is equivalent to:

$$X \cup B' \nvdash \bot \text{ for all finite subsets } B' \text{ of } B.$$

This is equivalent to:

$$X \cup (\&B') \nvdash \bot \text{ for all finite subsets } B' \text{ of } B,$$

and by the deduction property to

$$X \nvdash (\&B') \rightarrow \bot \text{ for all finite subsets } B' \text{ of } B,$$

or equivalently:

$$X \nvdash \neg(\&B') \text{ for all finite subsets } B' \text{ of } B.$$

In order to achieve this, we should contract A by the set containing all sentences that have the form $\neg(\&B')$ for some finite subset B' of B. This set can therefore, for our present purposes, be regarded as the negation of the set B. In an alternative formulation:

DEFINITION 3.35 ([43]) *For any set B of sentences, $\neg B$ (the negation of B) is the set such that $\beta \in \neg B$ if and only if β is either*

1. $\bot$
2. *a negation of some sentence in B, or*
3. *a (finite) disjunction of sentences that are negations of elements of B.*

Clause (1) is in a sense redundant, since by convention, the disjunction of an empty set is equal to $\bot$.

As an example, $\neg\{\alpha, \neg\beta\} = \{\bot, \neg\alpha, \beta, \neg\alpha \vee \beta\}$.

For finite sets, this definition can be simplified. Instead of contracting by the set $\neg B$ we can, if B is finite, contract by a single sentence, namely the disjunction of all negations of elements of B.

DEFINITION 3.36 ([45]) *Let B be a finite set of sentences. Then $n(B)$ (the sentential negation of B) is defined as follows:*

1. $n(\emptyset) = \bot$,
2. *If B is a singleton, $B = \{\beta\}$, then $n(B) = \neg\beta$.*
3. *If $B = \{\beta_1, \ldots \beta_m\}$ for some $m > 1$, then $n(B) = \neg\beta_1 \vee \neg\beta_2 \ldots \vee \neg\beta_m$.*

OBSERVATION 3.37 ([43]) *Let $\div$ be an operator of multiple partial meet contraction. It then holds for all sets A and all finite sets B that $A \div \neg B = A \div n(B)$.*

Proof. A subset of A logically implies $n(B)$ if and only if it implies some element of $\neg B$. It follows from Observation 1.39 that $A \bot \neg B = A \bot n(B)$. Thus, for every selection function γ, $\gamma(A \bot \neg B) = \gamma(A \bot n(B))$, so that $A \sim_\gamma \neg B = A \sim_\gamma n(B)$. ■

Now that we know how to negate sets, we can define multiple partial meet revision, of both the internal and the external variant:

DEFINITION 3.38 *Let γ be a (two-place) multiple selection function. Then for all belief bases A:*
$A \mp_\gamma B = (A {\sim_\gamma} \neg B) \cup B$ *(multiple internal partial meet revision)*
$A \pm_\gamma B = (A \cup B) {\sim_\gamma} \neg B$ *(multiple external partial meet revision)*
Furthermore, if A is a belief set, then
$A \mp_\gamma B = \mathrm{Cn}((A {\sim_\gamma} \neg B) \cup B)$ *(multiple partial meet revision of a belief set)*

If B is finite, then $\neg B$ can be replaced by $n(B)$ throughout Definition 3.38.

Several of the major formal results for internal and external revision of belief bases can be generalized to multiple revision [45; 50]. Due to Observation 3.37, the generalization is straight-forward for revision by finite sets.

Exercises

155. Spell out the following:
   (a) $\neg\{\alpha\}$
   (b) $n(\{\alpha\})$
   (c) $\neg\{\alpha, \beta, \delta\}$
   (d) $n(\{\alpha, \beta, \delta\})$

156. For each of the following equations, either provide a solution or prove that it has no solution.
   (a) $\neg X = \{\perp, p, q, p \vee q\}$
   (b) $\neg X = \{\perp, p \vee q\}$
   (c) $\neg X = \{\perp, p, q\}$

157. Show that if $B \cap \neg B \neq \emptyset$, then $B \vdash \perp$.

158. Show that $\neg B \cap \mathrm{Cn}(\emptyset) = \emptyset$ if and only if $B \nvdash \perp$.

159. (a) Show that if $X \in A \perp \neg B$, then $A \cap B \subseteq X$.
   (b) Show that if $B \subseteq A$ and $X \in A \perp \neg B$, then $B \subseteq X$.

160. [43] Show that $X \in (A \cup B) \perp \neg B$ iff $B \subseteq X \in (A \cup B) \perp \perp$.

161. [50] Let γ be a multiple two-place selection function and $\pm_\gamma$ and $\mp_\gamma$ the operators of external and internal partial meet revision, respectively, that are based on γ.
   (a) Show that if $B \subseteq A$, then $A \pm_\gamma B = A \mp_\gamma B$.
   (b) Show that if B is inconsistent, then $A \mp_\gamma B = A \cup B$.

162. [50] Show if $*$ is an operator of multiple internal partial meet revision for the belief base A, then it satisfies:
   (a) $A * B$ is consistent if B is consistent. (*P-consistency*)
   (b) If $\varepsilon \in A \backslash (A * B)$, then there is some A' such that $A * B \subseteq A' \subseteq A \cup B$, A' is consistent and $A' \cup \{\varepsilon\}$ is inconsistent (*P-relevance*).

18+ MODALITIES OF BELIEF CHANGE

It was mentioned in Section 3.12 that the account of non-prioritized belief change in terms of consolidation and expansion can be used to develop a modal model of belief change, i.e., a model of necessary and possible belief changes. For that purpose, we will make use of the modal metalanguage of belief that was introduced in Section 3.12. The formal definition is as follows:

DEFINITION 3.39 ([43]) *The* restricted modal belief language $\mathcal{L}_M$ *based on* $\mathcal{L}$ *consists of exactly the expressions given by the following two rules:*

1. *If* $\alpha \in \mathcal{L}$, *then* $B\alpha \in \mathcal{L}_M$
2. *If* $\alpha \in \mathcal{L}_M$, *then* $\neg\alpha$, $L\alpha$, *and* $M\alpha$ *are elements of* $\mathcal{L}_M$.

This language is called restricted for two reasons. First, $\mathcal{L}_M$ does not allow for iterations of the belief operator (B). Sentences such as $BB\alpha$ (the agent believes himself to believe that α) are not included. Secondly, $\mathcal{L}_M$ is not closed under truth-functional operations other than negation. In other words, expressions such as $L(MB\alpha \vee MB\neg\alpha)$ are not part of the language. These restrictions have no other motivation than that they simplify the formal treatment.

Let A_1 and A_2 be belief bases. Then A_2 is *directly accessible* from A_1 if and only if A_2 can be reached from A_1 through a single expansion, followed by consolidation. In other words, A_2 is *directly accessible* from A_1 if and only if there is some sentence α such that $A_2 = A_1 + \alpha{\sim_\gamma}\bot$. Clearly, if A_2 is directly accessible from A_1, then A_2 is a possible belief base, from the starting-point of A_1. However, there are also other belief bases that can be reached from A_1, namely all those that can be reached through a series of expansions and consolidations. These are the *accessible* belief bases:

DEFINITION 3.40 ([43]) *Let* A_1 *and* A_2 *be belief bases. Then* A_2 *is* accessible *from* A_1 *(by a given two-place selection function* γ*) if and only if there is a finite series of sentences* $\alpha_1, \ldots \alpha_n$ *such that*

$$A_2 = A_1 + \alpha_1{\sim_\gamma}\bot \ldots + \alpha_n{\sim_\gamma}\bot.$$

A_1RA_2 *denotes that* A_2 *is* accessible *from* A_1. R *is the* accessibility relation.

Note that ARA holds if and only if A is consistent. (If A is consistent, then $A = A+\bot{\sim_\gamma}\bot$.) An inconsistent set is not accessible from any set, not even from itself.

It follows from the definition that the accessibility relation satisfies *transitivity*, i.e. if ARB and BRC, then ARC.

The accessibility relation R can be used to evaluate sentences in the modal language. This will be done in the same way as in Kripke–Kanger models in modal logic: A sentence α can possibly be believed if and only if there is some accessible belief base in which it is believed. It is necessarily believed if and only if it is believed in all accessible belief bases. To express this formally, we can assign to every belief base a *display set* that contains all the sentences in $\mathcal{L}_M$ that are validated in our model, with this particular belief base as the epistemic starting-point.

DEFINITION 3.41 ([43]) *Given a two-place selection function γ, to each belief base A is assigned a* display set $m(A)$ *that contains exactly the sentences given by the following rules:*

1. *If $B\alpha \in \mathcal{L}_M$, then $B\alpha \in m(A)$ if and only if $\alpha \in \mathrm{Cn}(A)$.*
2. *If $L\alpha \in \mathcal{L}_M$, then $L\alpha \in m(A)$ if and only if $\alpha \in A'$ for all A' such that ARA'.*
3. *If $M\alpha \in \mathcal{L}_M$, then $M\alpha \in m(A)$ if and only if $\alpha \in A'$ for some A' such that ARA'.*
4. *If $\alpha \in \mathcal{L}_M$, then $\neg\alpha \in m(A)$ if and only if $\alpha \notin m(A)$.*

Note that this definition applies also to iterated modal operators. E.g., $MLB\alpha \in m(A)$ holds if and only if there is some belief base A' such that ARA' and $LB\alpha \in A'$.

We are now ready for the full modal model:

DEFINITION 3.42 ([43]) *A quadruple $\langle \mathcal{L}, \mathrm{Cn}, A_0, \gamma\rangle$ of a language, a consequence operator, a consistent belief base, and a two-place selection function constitutes a modal* interpretation of piecemeal belief change *(PBC), such that for each sentence $\alpha \in \mathcal{L}_M$, α is* true *in this interpretation if and only if $\alpha \in m(A_0)$, where m is defined according to Definition 3.41 (with reference to R, see Definition 3.40).*

*A sentence $\alpha \in \mathcal{L}_M$ is PBC-*valid *if and only if it is true in all PBC interpretations.*

Since logical implication cannot be expressed in the restricted language, relations of consequence will have to be introduced metalinguistically:

DEFINITION 3.43 ([43]) *Let α and β be two elements of $\mathcal{L}_M$. Then $\alpha \vDash \beta$ (β is a* PBC-consequence *of α) holds if and only if β is true in all PBC interpretations in which α is true. Furthermore, $\alpha \mathrel{=\!\mid\!\vDash} \beta$ (α is* PBC-equivalent *to β) holds if and only if both $\alpha \vDash \beta$ and $\beta \vDash \alpha$.*

Every sentence in $\mathcal{L}_M$ consists of two parts, the modal and the non-modal part. The modal part is a string of modal symbols and negation symbols, ending in B. The non-modal part is the affixed sentence in $\mathcal{L}$. In the sentence $L\neg MB(\alpha\rightarrow\beta)$, for example, $L\neg MB$ is the modal part and $(\alpha\rightarrow\beta)$ the non-modal part. Two sentences have the same *modality* if their modal parts are identical. Thus, $L\neg MB(\alpha\rightarrow\beta)$ and $L\neg MB\delta$ have the same modality.

Since there is no limit to the length of the modal part of a sentence in $\mathcal{L}_M$, there is in principle an infinite number of modalities. The diversity is not, however, as large as it first seems. The reason for this is that some modalities are interchangeable. For instance, it holds for all sentences α that $LLB\alpha$ is true in an interpretation if and only if $LB\alpha$ is true in that same interpretation. In formal notation: $LLB\alpha \dashv\models LB\alpha$. Among exchangeable modalities, the shortest is commonly preferred, and the longer modalities are said to be *reducible* to the shorter ones. In the rest of this section, we are going to explore the reducibility of modalities in PBC models.

The following observation contains some results that are useful for the reduction of modalities:

OBSERVATION 3.44 ([43]) *Let* $\alpha \in \mathcal{L}_M$. *Then:*

1. $L\alpha \dashv\models \neg M \neg \alpha$.
2. $L\alpha \models \alpha$
3. $\alpha \models M\alpha$
4. $L\alpha \models LL\alpha$

Proof. *Part 1*: For one direction, suppose that $L\alpha$ holds in a PBC interpretation with A_0 as its original belief base. To prove that $\neg M \neg \alpha$ holds in the same interpretation, suppose to the contrary that this is not the case. Then, by clause (4) of Definition 3.41, $M\neg\alpha$ holds so that, by clause (3), there is some A' with $A_0 R A'$ and $\neg\alpha \in m(A')$. By clause (2), from $L\alpha \in m(A_0)$ and $A_0 R A'$ follows $\alpha \in m(A')$. According to the definition of R, A' is consistent. From this contradiction we may conclude that $\neg M \neg \alpha$ holds in this PBC interpretation. Thus, in general: $L\alpha \models \neg M \neg \alpha$.

For the other direction, suppose that $\neg M \neg \alpha$ is true in a PBC interpretation. To prove that $L\alpha$ holds in the same interpretation, suppose to the contrary that this is not the case. Then, by clause (2) of Definition 3.41, there is some A' such that $A_0 R A'$ and $\alpha \notin m(A')$. By clause (4), $\neg\alpha \in m(A')$. Thus, by clause (3), $M\neg\alpha \in m(A_0)$, thus by clause (4) $\neg M \neg \alpha \notin m(A_0)$, so that $\neg M \neg \alpha$ is not true, contrary to the conditions. Thus $L\alpha$ holds in every interpretation in which $\neg M \neg \alpha$ holds, i.e. $\neg M \neg \alpha \models L\alpha$.

Part 2: Suppose that $L\alpha$ is true in an interpretation with A_0 as the original belief base. Since A_0 is consistent, $A_0 R A_0$, and it follows by clause (2) of Definition 3.41 that $\alpha \in m(A_0)$. Thus, α is true in the interpretation.

Part 3: Suppose that α is true in an interpretation with A_0 as the original belief set. Since A_0 is consistent, $A_0 R A_0$, and it follows by clause (3) of Definition 3.41 that $M\alpha \in m(A_0)$. Thus, $M\alpha$ is true in the interpretation.

Part 4: Suppose to the contrary that $L\alpha \in m(A_0)$ and $LL\alpha \notin m(A_0)$ in some PBC interpretation. It follows from clause (2) of Definition 3.41 that there is some

A_1 such that A_0RA_1 and $L\alpha \notin m(A_1)$. It follows from $L\alpha \notin m(A_1)$, with one more application of clause (2), that there is some A_2 such that A_1RA_2 and $\alpha \notin m(A_2)$. It follows from A_0RA_1 and A_1RA_2 that A_0RA_2. We can conclude from $\alpha \notin m(A_2)$ and A_0RA_2 that $L\alpha \notin m(A_0)$, contrary to the conditions. This contradiction concludes the proof. ■

The properties proved in the above observation are all standard conditions in modal logic. Clause (1) says that something holds necessarily if and only if it is not possible that it does not hold. According to clause (2), the necessary is true, and according to clause (3) the true is possible. Clause (4) is the most contestable of the four conditions. It stipulates that whatever is necessary, is necessarily necessary. In the present interpretation, this is a plausible condition. If I will always, whatever happens, believe that α, then it will always be the case that I will always believe that α. (I.e. if $LB\alpha$, then $LLB\alpha$.)

This observation provides us with some tools to reduce epistemic modalities. Two further such tools, in the form of derivation rules, are introduced in the following observation:

OBSERVATION 3.45 ([43]) *Let* $\alpha, \beta \in \mathcal{L}_M$.

(DR1) If $\alpha \vDash \beta$ *then* $L\alpha \vDash L\beta$.

(DR2) If $\alpha \vDash \beta$ *then* $M\alpha \vDash M\beta$.

Proof. Let A_0 be the original belief base.

Part 1: Suppose that $\alpha \vDash \beta$ and that $L\alpha \in m(A_0)$. Then $\alpha \in m(A')$ for all A' such that A_0RA'. Since $\alpha \vDash \beta$ it follows that $\beta \in m(A')$ for all A' such that A_0RA', thus $L\beta \in m(A_0)$.

Part 2: Suppose that $\alpha \vDash \beta$ and that $M\alpha \in m(A_0)$. Then there is some A' such that A_0RA' and $\alpha \in m(A')$. It follows from $\alpha \vDash \beta$ that $\beta \in m(A')$, and thus $M\beta \in m(A_0)$. ■

We can now derive the following reduction rules:

OBSERVATION 3.46 ([43])

(RR1) $LL\alpha \dashv\vDash L\alpha$,

(RR2) $MM\alpha \dashv\vDash M\alpha$,

(RR3) $LMLM\alpha \dashv\vDash LM\alpha$, *and*

(RR4) $MLML\alpha \dashv\vDash ML\alpha$

Proof. 1. It follows from Part 2 of Observation 3.44 that $L\alpha \vDash \alpha$. Applying (DR1), we obtain $LL\alpha \vDash L\alpha$. In combination with Part 4 of Observation 3.44, this yields $LL\alpha \dashv\vDash L\alpha$.

2. Apply Part 1 of Observation 3.44 to (RR1).

3. From Part 2 of Observation 3.44 follows $LM\alpha \vDash M\alpha$, thus by (DR2) $MLM\alpha \vDash MM\alpha$, and then by (DR1), $LMLM\alpha \vDash LMM\alpha$. We have $MM\alpha \vDash M\alpha$ from (RR2), and it follows from (DR1) that $LMM\alpha \vDash LM\alpha$. We may conclude that $LMLM\alpha \vDash LM\alpha$.

Part 3 of Observation 3.44 yields $LM\alpha \vDash MLM\alpha$, thus by (DR1) $LLM\alpha \vDash LMLM\alpha$. From Part 4 of Observation 3.44 follows $LM\alpha \vDash LLM\alpha$, so that $LM\alpha \vDash LMLM\alpha$ follows. From $LMLM\alpha \vDash LM\alpha$ and $LM\alpha \vDash LMLM\alpha$ follows $LMLM\alpha \dashv\vDash LM\alpha$.

4. Apply Part 1 of Observation 3.44 to (RR3). ■

These are all the reduction rules that we need to reduce PBC modalities. In the theorem that we are heading for, we are also going to show that these reduction rules can perform all the reductions that are possible. Therefore, we will need a set of *negative results* on reductions that are not possible. They are given in the following observation: ($LMLB\alpha \nvDash B\alpha$ means, of course, that $LMLB\alpha \vDash B\alpha$ does not hold.)

OBSERVATION 3.47 ([43])

(n1) $LMLB\alpha \nvDash B\alpha$

(n2) $MLB\alpha \nvDash LMB\alpha$

(n3) $MLB\alpha \nvDash B\alpha$

(n4) $LMB\alpha \nvDash MLB\alpha$

(n5) $LMB\alpha \nvDash B\alpha$

(n6) $MLMB\alpha \nvDash MLB\alpha$

(n7) $MLMB\alpha \nvDash LMB\alpha$

(n8) $MLMB\alpha \nvDash B\alpha$

(n9) $B\alpha \nvDash MLMB\alpha$

(n10) $MB\alpha \nvDash B\alpha$

(n11) $MB\alpha \nvDash MLMB\alpha$

Proof. Let p and q be two logically independent elements of $\mathcal{L}$.

Proof of (n1), (n3), (n5), (n8), and (n10): Let $A_0 = \emptyset$ and $A_1 = \{p\}$, and let γ be such that:

1. If $p \in A$ then $\gamma(A\bot^{\bot}) = \{X \in A\bot^{\bot} \mid p \in A\}$.
2. Otherwise, $\gamma(A\bot^{\bot}) = A\bot^{\bot}$.

We have $p \notin \mathrm{Cn}(A_0)$, so that $Bp \notin m(A_0)$. We also have A_0RA_1 and $p \in \mathrm{Cn}(A_1)$, so that $MBp \in m(A_0)$. This proves (n10).

It follows from the construction of γ that $LBp \in m(A_1)$. Since A_0RA_1 it follows that $MLBp \in m(A_0)$. This proves (n3).

Let A_k be any set such that $A_0 R A_k$. Let $A_m = A_k + p\sim_\gamma\perp$. Then $A_k R A_m$ and $p \in m(A_m)$, so that $MBp \in m(A_k)$. Since this holds for all A_k with $A_0 R A_k$ it follows that $LMBp \in m(A_0)$. This proves (n5).

It also follows from $Bp \in m(A_m)$, by the construction of γ, that $LBp \in m(A_m)$. $A_k R A_m$ yields $MLBp \in m(A_k)$. Since this holds for all A_k with $A_0 R A_k$, we have $LMLBp \in m(A_0)$, which proves (n1).

Since $A_0 R A_0$, it follows from $LMBp \in m(A_0)$ that $MLMBp \in m(A_0)$. This proves (n8).

Proof of (n2) and (n7): Let $A_0 = \emptyset$. Let γ be such that:

1. If $\{p, q\} \subseteq A$ and $\{\neg p, \neg q\} \not\subseteq A$, then:
   $\gamma(A\perp\perp) = \{X \in A\perp\perp \mid \{p, q\} \subseteq X\}$.
2. If $\{\neg p, \neg q\} \subseteq A$ and $\{p, q\} \not\subseteq A$, then:
   $\gamma(A\perp\perp) = \{X \in A\perp\perp \mid \{\neg p, \neg q\} \subseteq X\}$.
3. Otherwise: $\gamma(A\perp\perp) = A\perp\perp$.

Let $A_1 = A_0 + \neg p\sim_\gamma\perp$ and $A_2 = A_1 + \neg q\sim_\gamma\perp$. Then $A_2 = \{\neg p, \neg q\}$, and $MBp \notin m(A_2)$ so that $LMBp \notin m(A_0)$.

Let $A_3 = A_0 + p\sim_\gamma\perp$ and $A_4 = A_3 + q\sim_\gamma\perp$. Then $LBp \in m(A_4)$, so that $MLBp \in m(A_0)$ which proves (n2). We also have $LMBp \in m(A_4)$ and thus $MLMBp \in m(A_0)$, which proves (n7).

Proof of (n4) and (n6): Let the language be denumerably infinite, and let γ be such that:

1. If $p \in A$ and A is an inconsistent set with an odd number of elements, then
   $\gamma(A\perp\perp) = \{X \in A\perp\perp \mid p \in A\}$.
2. If $p \in A$ and A is an inconsistent set with an even number of elements, then
   $\gamma(A\perp\perp) = \{X \in A\perp\perp \mid p \notin A\}$.
3. Otherwise, $\gamma(A\perp\perp) = A\perp\perp$.

Let A_k be any set such that $A_0 R A_k$. We can construct a set A_m such that $A_k R A_m$ and $Bp \notin m(A_m)$. (The exact construction will depend on the number of elements in A_k.) Thus, $LBp \notin m(A_k)$. Since this holds for all A_k with $A_0 R A_k$, we have $MLBp \notin m(A_0)$.

In a similar way, for any set A_k such that $A_0 R A_k$ we can construct a set A_n such that $A_k R A_n$ and $Bp \in m(A_n)$. (The exact construction will, again, depend on the number of elements in A_k.) Thus $MBp \in m(A_k)$ for all A_k such that $A_0 R A_k$, thus $LMBp \in m(A_0)$, which proves (n4). It follows from $LMBp \in m(A_0)$ that $MLMBp \in m(A_0)$, which proves (n6).

Proof of (n9) and (n11): Let $A_0 = \{p\}$ and let γ be such that

1. If $\neg p \in A$ then $\gamma(A\perp\perp) = \{X \in A\perp\perp \mid \neg p \in A\}$.
2. Otherwise, $\gamma(A\perp\perp) = A\perp\perp$.

Let A_0RA_k and let $A_m = A_k + \neg p \sim_\gamma \bot$. Then it holds for all A_n that if A_mRA_n, then $Bp \notin m(A_n)$. It follows that $MBp \notin m(A_m)$ and $LMBp \notin m(A_k)$. Since this holds for all A_k such that A_0RA_k, we have $MLMBp \notin m(A_0)$. However, it is clear that $Bp \in m(A_0)$, which proves (n9), and that $MBp \in m(A_0)$, which proves (n11). ■

We are now ready for the theorem:

THEOREM 3.48 ([43]) *The irreducible modalities of PBC models are those shown in Figure 3.8, and their negations. Their relations of consequence are exhaustively as indicated by the arrows.*

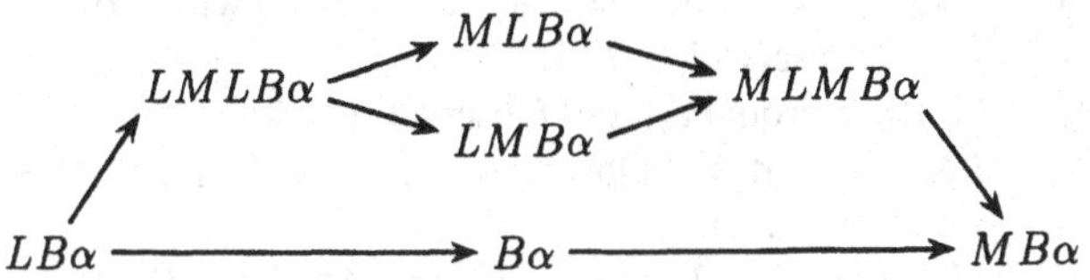

Figure 3.8.

Proof. The proof consists of three parts. In Part I, it is shown that all expressions i $\mathcal{L}_M$ can be reduced to (i.e., are interchangeable with) one of the fourteen forms stated in the theorem. In Part II, it is shown that the relations of PBC-consequence indicated in the diagram hold. In Part III, finally, it is shown that no other relations of PBC-consequence hold between the fourteen modalities. From this it also follows that the modalities cannot be further reduced.

Part I: The reduction takes place in two steps.

First step: In this step, we are going to show that each expression in $\mathcal{L}_M$ is equivalent to an expression of either the form $\Pi B\alpha$ or the form $\neg\Pi B\alpha$, where Π is a (possibly empty) sequence of L's and M's.

We can show this by proving that any negation sign not furthest to the left can either be deleted or be moved one step to the left. If a negation sign is not furthest to the left, it is preceded by an instance of either L, M, or $\neg$. Thus, the formula is of one of the three forms $\Pi_1 L\neg\Pi_2 B\alpha$, $\Pi_1 M\neg\Pi_2 B\alpha$, or $\Pi_1\neg\neg\Pi_2 B\alpha$, where Π_1 is a non-empty and Π_2 a possibly empty sequence of L, M, and $\neg$.

It follows from Part (4) of Definition 3.41 that for all display sets $m(A)$, $\neg\neg\Pi_2 B\alpha \in m(A)$ if and only if $\Pi_2 B\alpha \in m(A)$. Thus, $\Pi_1\neg\neg\Pi_2 B\alpha$ can be reduced to $\Pi_1\Pi_2 B\alpha$.

It holds for all sets A that $L\neg\Pi_2 B\alpha \in m(A)$ if and only if $\neg\Pi_2 B\alpha \in m(A')$ for all A' such that ARA', thus if and only if $\Pi_2 B\alpha \notin m(A')$ for all A' such that

ARA', thus if and only if $\Pi_2 B\alpha \in m(A')$ for no A' such that ARA', thus if and only if $M\Pi_2 B\alpha \notin m(A)$, thus if and only if $\neg M\Pi_2 B\alpha \in m(A)$. We can therefore replace $\Pi_1 L\neg\Pi_2 B\alpha$ by $\Pi_1\neg M\Pi_2 B\alpha$ without affecting the evaluation of the formula.

In the same way it follows that $\Pi_1 M\neg\Pi_2 B\alpha$ can be replaced by $\Pi_1\neg L\Pi_2 B\alpha$.

Second step: We now have a formula either of of the form $\Pi B\alpha$ or $\neg\Pi B\alpha$, with Π a sequence of L's and M's. We can use (RR1) and (RR2) to delete repetitions of L and M in Π (i.e. LL is replaced by L and MM by M). If the resulting formula contains four or more instances of the letters L and M, then it can be further reduced with (RR3) and (RR4) until it contains at most three such instances. After this reduction, it has one of the fourteen forms listed in the theorem.

Part II: $LB\alpha \vDash LMLB\alpha$: Part 3 of Observation 3.44 yields $LB\alpha \vDash MLB\alpha$. (DR1) yields $LLB\alpha \vDash LMLB\alpha$. This can be combined with $LB\alpha \vDash LLB\alpha$ that follows from Part 4 of Observation 3.44.

$LMLB\alpha \vDash MLB\alpha$: From Part 2 of Observation 3.44.

$LMLB\alpha \vDash LMB\alpha$: Part 2 of Observation 3.44 yields $LB\alpha \vDash B\alpha$. Apply to this first (DR2) and then (DR1).

$MLB\alpha \vDash MLMB\alpha$: Part 3 of Observation 3.44 yields $B\alpha \vDash MB\alpha$. Apply to this first (DR1) and then (DR2).

$LMB\alpha \vDash MLMB\alpha$: From Part 3 of Observation 3.44.

$MLMB\alpha \vDash MB\alpha$: Part 2 of Observation 3.44 yields $LMB\alpha \vDash MB\alpha$ and (DR2) yields $MLMB\alpha \vDash MMB\alpha$. This can be combined with $MMB\alpha \vDash MB\alpha$, that follows from (RR2).

$LB\alpha \vDash B\alpha$: Part 2 of Observation 3.44.

$B\alpha \vDash MB\alpha$: Part 3 of Observation 3.44.

Part III: First suppose that a positive modality $\Pi_1 B\alpha$ implies a negative modality $\neg\Pi_2 B\alpha$. Since $LB\alpha \vDash \Pi_1 B\alpha$ for all positive modalities Π_1, and $\neg\Pi_2 B\alpha \vDash \neg LB\alpha$ for all negative modalities $\neg\Pi_2$, it follows that $LB\alpha \vDash \neg LB\alpha$, which is clearly not the case.

Next, suppose that a negative modality $\neg\Pi_1 B\alpha$ implies a positive modality Π_2 $B\alpha$. Then in the same way $\neg MB\alpha \vDash MB\alpha$, which is not either the case.

It follows that any implication between modalities, in addition to the ones listed in the theorem, must hold between two positive modalities or between two negative modalities. Since $\neg\Pi_1 B\alpha \vDash \neg\Pi_2 B\alpha$ holds iff $\Pi_2 B\alpha \vDash \Pi_1 B\alpha$, only the positive modalities need to be treated. Thus it is sufficient to investigate if any of $LMLB\alpha, MLB\alpha, LMB\alpha, MLMB\alpha, B\alpha$ or $MB\alpha$ implies some modality not indicated in the diagram.

1. If $LMLB\alpha$ implies some additional modality, then $LMLB\alpha \vDash B\alpha$. By (n1), this is not the case.
2. If $MLB\alpha$ implies some additional modality, then either $MLB\alpha \vDash LMB\alpha$ or$MLB\alpha \vDash B\alpha$. (Note that, as can be seen from the diagram, a sentence

that implies either $LB\alpha$ or $LMLB\alpha$ also implies $LM\alpha$.) By (n2) and (n3), this is not the case.

3. If $LMB\alpha$ implies some additional modality, then either $LMB\alpha \vDash MLB\alpha$ or $LMB\alpha \vDash B\alpha$. By (n4) and (n5), this is not the case.
4. If $MLMB\alpha$ implies some additional modality, then either $MLMB\alpha \vDash MLB\alpha, MLMB\alpha \vDash LMB\alpha$, or $MLMB\alpha \vDash B\alpha$. By (n6), (n7), and (n8), this is not the case.
5. If $B\alpha$ implies some additional modality, then $B\alpha \vDash MLMB\alpha$. By (n9), this is not the case.
6. If $MB\alpha$ implies some modality other than itself, then either $MB\alpha \vDash B\alpha$ or $MB\alpha \vDash MLMB\alpha$. By (n10) and (n11), this is not the case.

This concludes the proof of the theorem. ■

The modalities of PBC models are the same as those of the modal system S4.

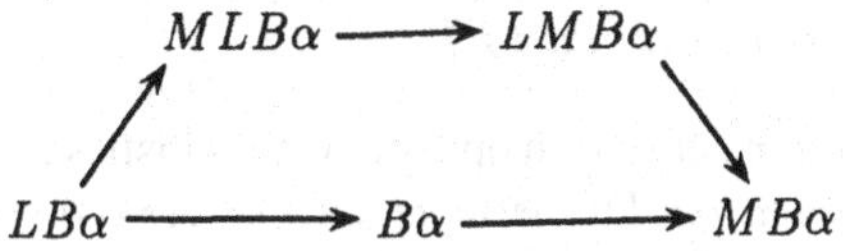

Figure 3.9.

Exercises

163. [43] Models of *batchwise belief change* (BBC) differ from those of piecemeal belief change (PBC) only in that expansion by sets rather than by sentences is used in the definition of accessibility. Thus, Definition 3.40 is adjusted so that A_2 is *accessible* from A_1 (A_1RA_2) if and only if there is a finite series of sets $D_1, \dots D_n$ such that $A_2 = A_1 + D_1 \sim_\gamma \bot \dots + D_n \sim_\gamma \bot$. The rest of the definitions coincide with those of PBC. Show that in BBC:

   (a) $ML\alpha \vDash LM\alpha$
   (b) $LL\alpha \mathrel{=}\!\!\mid\!\vDash L\alpha$
   (c) $MM\alpha \mathrel{=}\!\!\mid\!\vDash M\alpha$
   (d) $MLM\alpha \mathrel{=}\!\!\mid\!\vDash LM\alpha$
   (e) $LML\alpha \mathrel{=}\!\!\mid\!\vDash ML\alpha$
   (f) Show that all modalities can be reduced to the following five and their negations: $B\alpha, LB\alpha, MB\alpha, MLB\alpha$, and $LMB\alpha$.
   (g) Prove the logical relations that are indicated by the arrows in Figure 3.9.

19⁺ PROPERTIES OF BELIEF SET REVISION

In the rest of this chapter, we are going to study various aspects of revision of belief *sets*. This section is devoted to the interrelations between some major postulates for belief set revision. In particular, we will be concerned with the postulates for revision by conjunctions and by disjunctions that were introduced in Section 3.7. There are close connections between the way a revision operator treats disjunctions and the way it treats conjunctions. To begin with, we are going to show that the following two conditions

$$A * (\alpha \& \beta) \subseteq (A * \alpha) + \beta \qquad \textit{(superexpansion)}$$
$$(A * \alpha) \cap (A * \beta) \subseteq A * (\alpha \vee \beta) \qquad \textit{(disjunctive overlap)}$$

are equivalent in the presence of three of the basic postulates.

OBSERVATION 3.49 (Peter Gärdenfors [35]) *Let A be a logically closed set and $*$ an operation for A that satisfies extensionality, closure, and success. Then $*$ satisfies disjunctive overlap if and only if it satisfies superexpansion.*
[This proves Observation 3.23, Part 1.]

Proof. *For one direction*, let $*$ be an operation that satisfies *extensionality, closure, success*, and *superexpansion*. Furthermore, let $\varepsilon \in (A*\alpha)\cap(A*\beta)$. We are going to show that $\varepsilon \in A*(\alpha\vee\beta)$.

It follows from $\varepsilon \in A*\alpha$ by *extensionality* that $\varepsilon \in A*((\alpha\vee\beta)\&\alpha)$. By *superexpansion*, $\varepsilon \in (A*(\alpha\vee\beta)+\alpha) = \text{Cn}((A*(\alpha\vee\beta))\cup\{\alpha\})$. It follows from the deduction property that $\alpha\rightarrow\varepsilon \in \text{Cn}(A*(\alpha\vee\beta))$.

It follows in the same way from $\varepsilon \in A*\beta$ that $\beta\rightarrow\varepsilon \in \text{Cn}(A*(\alpha\vee\beta))$. Since $\alpha\rightarrow\varepsilon$ and $\beta\rightarrow\varepsilon$ together imply $\alpha\vee\beta\rightarrow\varepsilon$, we have $\alpha\vee\beta\rightarrow\varepsilon \in \text{Cn}(A*(\alpha\vee\beta))$. It follows from *success* that $\alpha\vee\beta \in \text{Cn}(A*(\alpha\vee\beta))$, and we can therefore conclude that $\varepsilon \in \text{Cn}(A*(\alpha\vee\beta))$. By *closure*, $\varepsilon \in A*(\alpha\vee\beta)$.

For the other direction, let $*$ be an operation that satisfies *extensionality, closure, success*, and *disjunctive overlap*. Furthermore, let $\varepsilon \in A*(\alpha\&\beta)$. We are going to show that $\varepsilon \in (A*\alpha)+\beta$.

It follows by *closure* from $\varepsilon \in A*(\alpha\&\beta)$ that $\beta\rightarrow\varepsilon \in A*(\alpha\&\beta)$. Furthermore, it follows by *success* that $\neg\beta \in A*(\alpha\&\neg\beta)$, and by *closure* (since $\neg\beta$ implies $\beta\rightarrow\varepsilon$) that $\beta\rightarrow\varepsilon \in A*(\alpha\&\neg\beta)$.

By *disjunctive overlap*, $\beta\rightarrow\varepsilon \in A*(\alpha\&\beta)$ and $\beta\rightarrow\varepsilon \in A*(\alpha\&\neg\beta)$ yield $\beta\rightarrow\varepsilon \in A*((\alpha\&\beta)\vee(\alpha\&\neg\beta))$. Since $(\alpha\&\beta)\vee(\alpha\&\neg\beta)$ is logically equivalent to α, it follows by *extensionality* that $\beta\rightarrow\varepsilon \in A*\alpha$. It follows by the deduction property that $\varepsilon \in \text{Cn}((A*\alpha)\cup\beta)$, i.e. $\varepsilon \in (A*\alpha)+\beta$. ■

Similarly, the following two properties are equivalent, given the same three basic postulates:

If $A * \alpha \nvdash \neg\beta$, then $(A * \alpha) + \beta \subseteq A * (\alpha\&\beta)$. (*subexpansion*)
If $A * (\alpha\vee\beta) \nvdash \neg\alpha$, then $A * (\alpha\vee\beta) \subseteq A * \alpha$. (*disjunctive inclusion*)

(Observations 3.50 and 3.51 were first proved by Hans Rott in a letter to Peter Gärdenfors. They were published by Gärdenfors, who of course referred to Rott as the originator.)

OBSERVATION 3.50 (Hans Rott [35]) *Let A be a logically closed set and* $*$ *an operation for A that satisfies extensionality, closure, and success. Then* $*$ *satisfies disjunctive inclusion if and only if it satisfies subexpansion.*
[This proves Observation 3.23, Part 2.]

Proof. *For one direction,* let $*$ be an operation that satisfies *extensionality* and *subexpansion.* (*Closure* and *success* are not needed for this direction of the proof.) In order to show that *disjunctive inclusion* holds, let $A * (\alpha\vee\beta) \nvdash \neg\alpha$. We are going to show that $A * (\alpha\vee\beta) \subseteq A * \alpha$.

Clearly, $A * (\alpha\vee\beta) \subseteq (A * (\alpha\vee\beta)) + \alpha$. Since $A * (\alpha\vee\beta) \nvdash \neg\alpha$, it follows from *subexpansion* that $(A * (\alpha\vee\beta)) + \alpha \subseteq A * ((\alpha\vee\beta)\&\alpha)$. Since $(\alpha\vee\beta)\&\alpha$ is equivalent with α, *extensionality* yields $A * ((\alpha\vee\beta)\&\alpha) = A * \alpha$. We have proved that $A * (\alpha\vee\beta) \subseteq A * \alpha$.

For the other direction, let $*$ be an operation that satisfies *extensionality, closure, success,* and *disjunctive inclusion.* In order to show that *subexpansion* holds, let $A * \alpha \nvdash \neg\beta$. We are going to show that $(A * \alpha) + \beta \subseteq A * (\alpha\&\beta)$.

We are first going to show that $A * \alpha \nvdash \neg(\alpha\&\beta)$. Suppose to the contrary that $A * \alpha \vdash \neg(\alpha\&\beta)$. Since it follows from *success* that $\alpha \in A * \alpha$, and since α and $\neg(\alpha\&\beta)$ together imply $\neg\beta$, we then have $A * \alpha \vdash \neg\beta$, contrary to our assumption. This contradiction is sufficient to prove that $A * \alpha \nvdash \neg(\alpha\&\beta)$.

Since α is logically equivalent with $(\alpha\&\beta)\vee(\alpha\&\neg\beta)$, it follows by *extensionality* from $A * \alpha \nvdash \neg(\alpha\&\beta)$ that $A * ((\alpha\&\beta)\vee(\alpha\&\neg\beta)) \nvdash \neg(\alpha\&\beta)$. It follows from this, by *disjunctive inclusion*, that $A * ((\alpha\&\beta)\vee(\alpha\&\neg\beta)) \subseteq A * (\alpha\&\beta)$. One more application of *extensionality* yields $A * \alpha \subseteq A * (\alpha\&\beta)$.

It follows set-theoretically from $A * \alpha \subseteq A * (\alpha\&\beta)$ that $(A * \alpha) \cup \{\beta\} \subseteq (A * (\alpha\&\beta)) \cup \{\beta\}$, and thus $\mathrm{Cn}((A * \alpha) \cup \{\beta\}) \subseteq \mathrm{Cn}((A * (\alpha\&\beta)) \cup \{\beta\})$. By the definition of expansion, $\mathrm{Cn}((A * \alpha) \cup \{\beta\}) = (A * \alpha) + \beta$. By *success*, $\beta \in A * (\alpha\&\beta)$ so that $\mathrm{Cn}((A * (\alpha\&\beta)) \cup \{\beta\}) = \mathrm{Cn}(A * (\alpha\&\beta))$, and by *closure*, $\mathrm{Cn}(A * (\alpha\&\beta)) = A * (\alpha\&\beta)$. We have proved that $(A * \alpha) + \beta \subseteq A * (\alpha\&\beta)$.
■

It is often convenient in proofs to switch back and forth between the conjunction-related postulates (superexpansion, subexpansion) and their disjunction-related counterparts (disjunctive overlap, disjunctive inclusion). The following proof is an example of this.

Either $A * (\alpha\vee\beta) = A * \alpha, A * (\alpha\vee\beta) = A * \beta$, or $A * (\alpha\vee\beta) = (A * \alpha) \cap (A * \beta)$.
(disjunctive factoring)

OBSERVATION 3.51 (Hans Rott [35]) *Let A be a logically closed set and $*$ an operation for A that satisfies extensionality, closure, success, and consistency. Then $*$ satisfies disjunctive factoring if and only if it satisfies both disjunctive overlap and disjunctive inclusion.*
[This proves Observation 3.23, Part 3.]

Proof. *For one direction*, let $*$ be an operator that satisfies *extensionality, closure, success, consistency, disjunctive overlap*, and *disjunctive inclusion*. It follows from Observations 3.49 and 3.50 that *superexpansion* and *subexpansion* are satisfied.

Case 1, $\alpha\vee\beta$ is inconsistent: Then so is α. It follows by *success* that $A * \alpha$ and $A * (\alpha\vee\beta)$ are inconsistent, and by *closure* that $A * \alpha = A * (\alpha\vee\beta) = \mathcal{L}$.

Case 2, $\alpha\vee\beta$ is consistent. There are three subcases:

Case 2a, $\neg\beta \in A * (\alpha\vee\beta)$: By *success*, $\alpha\vee\beta \in A * (\alpha\vee\beta)$. Since $\neg\beta$ and $\alpha\vee\beta$ together imply α, it follows that $\alpha \in \text{Cn}(A * (\alpha\vee\beta))$, and thus by *closure* that $\alpha \in A * (\alpha\vee\beta)$ and $A * (\alpha\vee\beta) = (A * (\alpha\vee\beta)) + \alpha$.

It follows by *superexpansion* that $A * ((\alpha\vee\beta)\&\alpha) \subseteq (A * (\alpha\vee\beta)) + \alpha$. By *extensionality*, $A * ((\alpha\vee\beta)\&\alpha) = A * \alpha$. Thus $A * \alpha \subseteq A * (\alpha\vee\beta)$.

Next, suppose that $A * (\alpha\vee\beta) \vdash \neg\alpha$. Since $\alpha \in A * (\alpha\vee\beta)$, $A * (\alpha\vee\beta)$ is then inconsistent. Since $\alpha\vee\beta$ is consistent, this contradicts the postulate of *consistency*. We can conclude that $A * (\alpha\vee\beta) \nvdash \neg\alpha$.

It follows by *subexpansion* from $A * (\alpha\vee\beta) \nvdash \neg\alpha$ that $(A * (\alpha\vee\beta)) + \alpha \subseteq A * ((\alpha\vee\beta)\&\alpha)$. As we have already shown, $(A * (\alpha\vee\beta)) + \alpha = A * (\alpha\vee\beta)$. By *extensionality*, $A * ((\alpha\vee\beta)\&\alpha) = A * \alpha$. We can conclude that $A * (\alpha\vee\beta) \subseteq A * \alpha$. Since we already know that $A * \alpha \subseteq A * (\alpha\vee\beta)$, we may conclude that $A * (\alpha\vee\beta) = A * \alpha$.

Case 2b, $\neg\alpha \in A * (\alpha\vee\beta)$: Then $A * (\alpha\vee\beta) = A * \beta$ follows in the same way as in the foregoing case.

Case 2c, $\neg\beta \notin A * (\alpha\vee\beta)$ and $\neg\alpha \notin A * (\alpha\vee\beta)$. It follows by *closure* that $A * (\alpha\vee\beta) \nvdash \neg\beta$ and $A * (\alpha\vee\beta) \nvdash \neg\alpha$.

It follows from $A*(\alpha\vee\beta) \nvdash \neg\beta$ by *disjunctive inclusion* that $A*(\alpha\vee\beta) \subseteq A*\beta$ and from $A*(\alpha\vee\beta) \nvdash \neg\alpha$ that $A*(\alpha\vee\beta) \subseteq A*\alpha$. From this follows $A*(\alpha\vee\beta) \subseteq (A * \alpha) \cap (A * \beta)$. It follows from *disjunctive overlap* that $(A * \alpha) \cap (A * \beta) \subseteq A * (\alpha\vee\beta)$. We can conclude that $A * (\alpha\vee\beta) = (A * \alpha) \cap (A * \beta)$.

For the other direction, suppose that *extensionality, closure, success*, and *disjunctive factoring* are satisfied. *Disjunctive overlap* follows directly by set theory. It remains to be shown that *disjunctive inclusion* is satisfied. According to Observation 3.50, this can be done by showing that *subexpansion* holds. Let $A*\alpha \nvdash \neg\beta$.

It follows from *extensionality* that $A * \alpha = A * ((\alpha \& \beta) \vee (\alpha \& \neg\beta))$, and thus by *disjunctive factoring* that $A * \alpha$ coincides with either $A * (\alpha\&\beta)$, $A * (\alpha\&\neg\beta)$, or $A * (\alpha\&\beta) \cap A * (\alpha\&\neg\beta)$. These three cases will be treated separately.

Case 1, $A * \alpha = A * (\alpha\&\beta)$: Then $(A * \alpha) + \beta = A * (\alpha\&\beta) + \beta$. It follows by *success* that $\beta \in A * (\alpha\&\beta)$, so that $A * (\alpha\&\beta) + \beta = A * (\alpha\&\beta)$. We have proved that $(A * \alpha) + \beta = A * (\alpha\&\beta)$, which is sufficient to show that *subexpansion* holds.

Case 2, $A * \alpha = A * (\alpha\&\neg\beta)$: It follows by *success* that $\neg\beta \in A * \alpha$, and thus *subexpansion* holds vacuously.

Case 3, $A * \alpha = A * (\alpha\&\beta) \cap A * (\alpha\&\neg\beta)$. Let $\delta \in (A * \alpha) + \beta$. We are going to show that $\delta \in A * (\alpha\&\beta)$. This can be done as follows:

$\delta \in (A * \alpha) + \beta$
$\beta \rightarrow \delta \in A * \alpha$
$\beta \rightarrow \delta \in A * (\alpha\&\beta) \cap A * (\alpha\&\neg\beta)$
$\beta \rightarrow \delta \in A * (\alpha\&\beta)$
$A * (\alpha\&\beta) \cup \{\beta\} \vdash \delta$ (deduction property)
$A * (\alpha\&\beta) \vdash \delta$ (since $\beta \in A * (\alpha\&\beta)$)
$\delta \in A * (\alpha\&\beta)$ (*closure*)

This is sufficient to show that *subexpansion* holds in this case as well. ■

The following postulate is a weakened form of superexpansion:

Cut: [88]
If $\beta \in A * \alpha$, then $A * (\alpha\&\beta) \subseteq A * \alpha$

A similar postulate, namely the following:

Cautious monotony: [88]
If $\beta \in A * \alpha$, then $A * \alpha \subseteq A * (\alpha\&\beta)$

can be seen, in the context of the basic postulates, as a weakened version of subexpansion:

OBSERVATION 3.52 (Makinson and Gärdenfors [88]) *Let A be a logically closed set and $*$ an operation for A. If $*$ satisfies consistency, closure, success, and subexpansion then it satisfies cautious monotony.*

Proof. Let $\beta \in A * \alpha$. If α is inconsistent, then so is $\alpha\&\beta$, and it follows by *success* and *closure* that $A * (\alpha\&\beta) = \mathcal{L}$, so that $A * \alpha \subseteq A * (\alpha\&\beta)$.

If α is consistent, then it follows by *consistency* from $\beta \in A * \alpha$ that $\neg\beta \notin \mathrm{Cn}(A * \alpha)$. We can then use *subexpansion* to obtain $(A * \alpha) + \beta \subseteq A * (\alpha\&\beta)$ and consequently $A * \alpha \subseteq A * (\alpha\&\beta)$. ■

The combined effect of *cut* and *cautious monotony* is the same as that of the following elegant identity criterion:

Reciprocity: [31]
$A * \alpha = A * \beta$ if and only if $\beta \in A * \alpha$ and $\alpha \in A * \beta$.

OBSERVATION 3.53 (Gärdenfors and Rott [40]) *Let A be a logically closed set and $*$ an operation for A that satisfies closure and success. Then it satisfies reciprocity if and only if it satisfies both cut and cautious monotony.*

Proof. *For one direction*, suppose that *reciprocity* is satisfied. Furthermore, suppose that $\beta \in A * \alpha$.

It follows from *success* that $\alpha \in A * \alpha$. We can use *closure* to conclude from $\alpha \in A * \alpha$ and $\beta \in A * \alpha$ that $\alpha\&\beta \in A * \alpha$.

It follows from *success* that $\alpha \in \text{Cn}(A * (\alpha\&\beta))$, and from *closure* that $\alpha \in A * (\alpha\&\beta)$. We now have both $\alpha\&\beta \in A * \alpha$ and $\alpha \in A * (\alpha\&\beta)$, and we can conclude by *reciprocity* that $A * \alpha = A * (\alpha\&\beta)$.

We have shown that if $\beta \in A*\alpha$, then $A*\alpha = A*(\alpha\&\beta)$ from which it follows that both *cut* and *cautious monotony* hold.

For the other direction, suppose that *cut* and *cautious monotony* are satisfied, and suppose that $\alpha \in A * \beta$ and $\beta \in A * \alpha$. It follows from $\alpha \in A * \beta$ by *cut* and *cautious monotony* that $A * \beta = A * (\alpha\&\beta)$. Similarly, it follows from $\beta \in A * \alpha$ that $A * \alpha = A * (\alpha\&\beta)$. This is sufficient to show that $A * \alpha = A * \beta$. The other direction of *reciprocity* follows directly from *success*. ■

Exercises

164. Let A be a logically closed set and $*$ an operator for A. Show that if $*$ satisfies *success* and *closure*, then it satisfies the following property:
If $\alpha \vdash \beta$, then $\beta \in A * \alpha$.

165. If the following condition:
If $\neg\alpha \notin \text{Cn}(A)$ and $\beta \in A$, then $\beta \in A * \alpha$ (*preservation* [33])
replaces one of the basic Gärdenfors postulates for revision, then a logically equivalent set of postulates is obtained.

    (a) Which is the postulate that can be replaced?

    (b) Prove the logical equivalence of the two sets of postulates.

166. [35] Let A be a logically closed set and $*$ an operator for A. Show that if $*$ satisfies *success*, *closure*, and *reciprocity*, then it satisifies *extensionality*.

167. [40] Let A be a logically closed set and $*$ an operator for A. Show that if $*$ satisfies *success*, *consistency*, and *disjunctive inclusion*, then it satisfies the following postulate:
$A * (\alpha \vee \beta) \subseteq \text{Cn}((A * \alpha) \cup (A * \beta))$ (*weak disjunctive inclusion*)

168. [35] Let A be a logically closed set and $*$ an operator for A.

(a) Show that if $*$ satisfies *success* and *closure*, then it satisfies the following postulate:
If $A * \alpha = A * \beta$, then $\alpha \leftrightarrow \beta \in A * \alpha$.

(b) Show that if $*$ satisfies *inclusion*, *success*, and *closure*, then it satisfies the following postulate:
If $A * \alpha = A * \beta$, then $\alpha \leftrightarrow \beta \in A$.

169. [35] Let A be a logically closed set and $*$ an operator for A. Show that if $*$ satisfies *inclusion*, *success*, and *closure*, then it satisfies:
$A * \alpha = (A \cap (A * \alpha)) + \alpha$.

170. (a) Let $A_0 = \mathrm{Cn}(\emptyset)$ and let $*$ be an operator for A_0 that satisfies *success*, *inclusion*, and *closure*. Show that $\alpha \vdash \beta$ iff $A_0 * \beta \subseteq A_0 * \alpha$.

(b) [35] Let A be a logically closed set and $*$ an operator for A that satisfies *inclusion*, *success*, and *consistency*. Show that it does *not* in general hold that if $\alpha \vdash \beta$, then $A * \beta \subseteq A * \alpha$.

171. Let A be a logically closed set, and $*$ a global operation that satisfies *success*, *consistency*, *vacuity*, and *closure*. Show that $A * \alpha = (A * \alpha) * \alpha$.

172. Let $\mathcal{L}$ contain at least two logically independent sentences, and let $*$ be a global revision operator for belief sets.

(a) Show that if $*$ satisfies *success* and *consistency*, then it does not satisfy:
$A * \alpha * \beta = A * \beta * \alpha$ (*commutativity*)

(b) Show that if $*$ satisfies *vacuity* and *consistency*, then it does not satisfy:
If $A_1 \subseteq A_2$, then $A_1 * \alpha \subseteq A_2 * \alpha$. (*monotonicity*)

(c) [20] Show that if $*$ satisfies *vacuity* and *consistency*, then it does not satisfy:
$(A_1 \cap A_2) * \alpha = (A_1 * \alpha) \cap (A_2 * \alpha)$.

(d) [20] Show that if $*$ satisfies *vacuity*, *success*, and *closure*, then it does not satisfy:
If $\alpha \vdash \neg\beta$, then $A * \beta * \alpha = A * \alpha$.

20+ THE BASIC CONNECTION WITH CONTRACTION

The connections between revision and contraction through the Levi and Harper identities provide efficient means for proving the various representation theorems for partial meet revision. These proofs are therefore much simpler than most of the proofs of representation theorems in Chapter 2+.

The functions $\mathbb{R}$ and $\mathbb{C}$ from Definition 3.16 are useful tools in these proofs. For any operator $\div$, $\mathbb{R}(\div)$ is the operator generated from $\div$ through the Levi identity. Thus, if $\mathbb{R}(\div) = *$, then $A * \alpha = \mathrm{Cn}((A \div \neg\alpha) \cup \{\alpha\})$ for all α. We typically apply $\mathbb{R}$ to operators of contraction (but the definition of $\mathbb{R}$ is not restricted to contraction operators).

Similarly, $\mathbb{C}(*)$ is the operator generated from $*$ by the Harper identity. Thus, if $\mathbb{C}(*) = \div$, then $A\div\alpha = A \cap (A * \neg\alpha)$ for all α. The function $\mathbb{C}$ is intended for (but not formally restricted to) cases when $*$ is a revision operator.

One of the basic results on $\mathbb{R}$ and the Levi identity is that if $\div$ satisfies four of the six basic Gärdenfors postulates for contraction, then $\mathbb{R}(\div)$ satisfies all the six basic Gärdenfors postulates for revision. (See pp. 111 and 212 for lists of the basic postulates. The two missing—or rather redundant—contraction postulates in this observation are closure and recovery.)

OBSERVATION 3.54 (AGM [1; 83]) *Let A be a logically closed set and $\div$ an operator for A that satisfies the contraction-postulates inclusion, vacuity, success, and extensionality. Then $\mathbb{R}(\div)$ is an operator for A that satisfies the revision-postulates closure, success, inclusion, vacuity, consistency, and extensionality.*

Proof. Let $\div$ be an operator that satisfies the four listed contraction-postulates, and let $* = \mathbb{R}(\div)$. Then it holds for all α that $A * \alpha = \mathrm{Cn}((A\div\neg\alpha) \cup \{\alpha\})$.

Revision-closure: Directly from $A * \alpha = \mathrm{Cn}((A\div\neg\alpha) \cup \{\alpha\})$.

Revision-success: Directly from $A * \alpha = \mathrm{Cn}((A\div\neg\alpha) \cup \{\alpha\})$.

Revision-inclusion: It follows from *contraction-inclusion* that $A\div\neg\alpha \subseteq A$. We can conclude from this that $\mathrm{Cn}((A\div\neg\alpha) \cup \{\alpha\}) \subseteq \mathrm{Cn}(A \cup \{\alpha\})$, i.e. $A * \alpha \subseteq \mathrm{Cn}(A \cup \{\alpha\})$.

Revision-vacuity: Suppose that $\neg\alpha \notin A$. Then it follows from *contraction-vacuity* that $A\div\neg\alpha = A$. We therefore have $A * \alpha = \mathrm{Cn}((A\div\neg\alpha) \cup \{\alpha\}) = \mathrm{Cn}(A \cup \{\alpha\})$.

Revision-consistency: Let α be a consistent sentence. Then $\neg\alpha$ is not a tautology, and it follows by *contraction-success* that $\neg\alpha \notin \mathrm{Cn}(A\div\neg\alpha)$, or equivalently $\alpha\rightarrow\neg\alpha \notin \mathrm{Cn}(A\div\neg\alpha)$, By deduction, $\neg\alpha \notin \mathrm{Cn}((A\div\neg\alpha) \cup \{\alpha\}) = A * \alpha$. It follows from this that $A * \alpha$ is consistent.

Revision-extensionality: Let $\alpha\leftrightarrow\beta \in \mathrm{Cn}(\emptyset)$. It follows that $\neg\alpha\leftrightarrow\neg\beta \in \mathrm{Cn}(\emptyset)$, and we can conclude from *contraction-extensionality* that $A\div\neg\alpha = A\div\neg\beta$. We can conclude that $\mathrm{Cn}((A\div\neg\alpha)\cup\{\alpha\}) = \mathrm{Cn}((A\div\neg\beta)\cup\{\beta\})$, i.e. $A*\alpha = A*\beta$. ■

The corresponding result on $\mathbb{C}$ shows that if we apply the Harper identity to a revision-operator that satisfies five of the six basic Gärdenfors postulates for revision, then we obtain a contraction operator that satisfies all the six basic postulates for contraction. Here, the missing or redundant revision-postulate is inclusion.

OBSERVATION 3.55 (AGM [1; 83]) *Let A be a logically closed set and $*$ an operator for A that satisfies the revision-postulates closure, success, vacuity, consistency, and extensionality. Then $\mathbb{C}(*)$ is an operator for A that satisfies the contraction-postulates closure, inclusion, vacuity, success, extensionality, and recovery.*

Proof. Let $*$ be an operator for A that satisfies the five listed revision-postulates, and let $\div = \mathbb{C}(*)$. Then $A\div\alpha = A \cap (A * \neg\alpha)$ for all α.

Contraction-closure: We have assumed that A is logically closed, and it follows from *revision-closure* that $A * \neg\alpha$ is logically closed. Since the intersection of two logically closed sets is logically closed, $A \cap (A * \neg\alpha) = A\div\alpha$ is logically closed.

Contraction-inclusion: Directly from $A\div\alpha = A \cap (A * \neg\alpha)$.

Contraction-vacuity: Let $\alpha \notin \text{Cn}(A)$. It then follows from *revision-vacuity* that $A*\neg\alpha = \text{Cn}(A\cup\{\neg\alpha\})$, and thus $A = A\cap\text{Cn}(A\cup\{\neg\alpha\}) = A\cap(A*\neg\alpha) = A\div\alpha$.

Contraction-success: Let $\alpha \notin \text{Cn}(\emptyset)$. Then $\neg\alpha$ is consistent, and it follows from *revision-consistency* that $A * \neg\alpha$ is consistent, and from *revision-success* that $\neg\alpha \in A * \neg\alpha$. It follows that $\alpha \notin \text{Cn}(A * \neg\alpha)$, and thus $\alpha \notin A * \neg\alpha$, from which we can conclude that $\alpha \notin A \cap (A * \neg\alpha)$.

Contraction-extensionality: Let $\alpha\leftrightarrow\beta \in \text{Cn}(\emptyset)$. Then $\neg\alpha\leftrightarrow\neg\beta \in \text{Cn}(\emptyset)$, and it follows by *revision-extensionality* that $A * \neg\alpha = A * \neg\beta$, from which we may conclude that $A \cap (A * \neg\alpha) = A \cap (A * \neg\beta)$.

Recovery: If $\alpha \notin A$, then it follows from *contraction-vacuity*, that we have just proved, that $A\div\alpha = A$, and $A \subseteq \text{Cn}((A\div\alpha) \cup \{\alpha\})$ follows directly.

For the principal case, let $\alpha \in A$. We then have:

$\varepsilon \in \text{Cn}((A\div\alpha) \cup \{\alpha\})$
iff $\varepsilon \in \text{Cn}((A \cap (A * \neg\alpha)) \cup \{\alpha\})$ (definition of $\div$)
iff $\alpha\rightarrow\varepsilon \in \text{Cn}(A \cap (A * \neg\alpha))$
iff $\alpha\rightarrow\varepsilon \in \text{Cn}(\text{Cn}(A) \cap \text{Cn}(A * \neg\alpha))$ (*revision-closure* and $A = \text{Cn}(A)$)
iff $\alpha\rightarrow\varepsilon \in \text{Cn}(A) \cap \text{Cn}(A * \neg\alpha)$
iff $\alpha\rightarrow\varepsilon \in \text{Cn}(A)$ and $\alpha\rightarrow\varepsilon \in \text{Cn}(A * \neg\alpha)$
iff $\varepsilon \in \text{Cn}(A \cup \{\alpha\})$ and $\varepsilon \in \text{Cn}((A * \neg\alpha) \cup \{\alpha\})$
iff $\varepsilon \in \text{Cn}(A \cup \{\alpha\})$ and $\varepsilon \in \mathcal{L}$ (*revision-success*)
iff $\varepsilon \in \text{Cn}(A \cup \{\alpha\})$

Thus, $\text{Cn}((A\div\alpha) \cup \{\alpha\}) = \text{Cn}(A \cup \{\alpha\})$. It follows that $A \subseteq \text{Cn}(A \cup \{\alpha\}) = \text{Cn}((A\div\alpha) \cup \{\alpha\})$. ■

These two observations make it possible to obtain an operator of revision from an operator of contraction, and vice versa. If $\div$ satisfies the basic contraction postulates, then so does $\mathbb{C}(\mathbb{R}(\div))$. Similarly, if $*$ satisfies the basic revision postulates, then so does $\mathbb{R}(\mathbb{C}(*))$. However, this is not quite sufficient to allow free switches back and forth between contraction and revision operators. For that purpose, it should also be the case that $\mathbb{C}(\mathbb{R}(\div)) = \div$ and $\mathbb{R}(\mathbb{C}(*)) = *$. These two properties can indeed be shown to follow from the basic Gärdenfors postulates.

OBSERVATION 3.56 (David Makinson [83]) *Let A be a logically closed set and $\div$ an operator for A that satisfies the contraction-postulates closure, inclusion, vacuity, extensionality, and recovery. Then* $\mathbb{C}(\mathbb{R}(\div)) = \div$.

Proof. [35] Let $\mathbb{R}(\div) = *$ and $\mathbb{C}(\mathbb{R}(\div)) = \div'$. Then:

$$\begin{aligned} A\div'\alpha &= A \cap (A * \neg\alpha) \\ &= A \cap (\mathrm{Cn}((A\div\neg\neg\alpha) \cup \{\neg\alpha\})) \\ &= A \cap (\mathrm{Cn}((A\div\alpha) \cup \{\neg\alpha\})). \end{aligned}$$

(Note that *contraction-extensionality* was used in the last step.) We have to show that $A \cap (\mathrm{Cn}((A\div\alpha) \cup \{\neg\alpha\})) = A\div\alpha$. There are two cases, according to whether or not $\alpha \in A$.

Case 1, $\alpha \notin A$: It follows from *contraction-vacuity* that $A\div\alpha = A$, and thus $A\div'\alpha = A \cap (\mathrm{Cn}((A\div\alpha) \cup \{\neg\alpha\})) = A \cap (\mathrm{Cn}(A) \cup \{\neg\alpha\}) = A = A\div\alpha$.

Case 2, $\alpha \in A$: It follows from *recovery* that $A \subseteq \mathrm{Cn}((A\div\alpha) \cup \{\alpha\})$. Furthermore, it follows from *contraction-inclusion* that $A\div\alpha \subseteq A$. Since A is logically closed, we can conclude that $A = \mathrm{Cn}((A\div\alpha) \cup \{\alpha\})$. We therefore have $A \cap (\mathrm{Cn}((A\div\alpha) \cup \{\neg\alpha\})) = (\mathrm{Cn}((A\div\alpha) \cup \{\alpha\})) \cap (\mathrm{Cn}((A\div\alpha) \cup \{\neg\alpha\}))$, and consequently:

$\varepsilon \in A\div'\alpha$
iff $\varepsilon \in A \cap (\mathrm{Cn}((A\div\alpha) \cup \{\neg\alpha\}))$
iff $\varepsilon \in (\mathrm{Cn}((A\div\alpha) \cup \{\alpha\})) \cap (\mathrm{Cn}((A\div\alpha) \cup \{\neg\alpha\}))$ (*recovery*)
iff $\varepsilon \in \mathrm{Cn}((A\div\alpha) \cup \{\alpha\})$ and $\varepsilon \in \mathrm{Cn}((A\div\alpha) \cup \{\neg\alpha\})$
iff $\alpha\rightarrow\varepsilon \in \mathrm{Cn}(A\div\alpha)$ and $\neg\alpha\rightarrow\varepsilon \in \mathrm{Cn}(A\div\alpha)$
iff $(\alpha\rightarrow\varepsilon)\&(\neg\alpha\rightarrow\varepsilon) \in \mathrm{Cn}(A\div\alpha)$
iff $\varepsilon \in \mathrm{Cn}(A\div\alpha)$
iff $\varepsilon \in A\div\alpha$ (*contraction-closure*)

so that $A\div'\alpha = A\div\alpha$, as desired. ■

OBSERVATION 3.57 (David Makinson [83]) *Let A be a logically closed set and $*$ an operator for A that satisfies the revision-postulates closure, success, inclusion, and extensionality. Then $\mathbb{R}(\mathbb{C}(*)) = *$.*

Proof. Let $\mathbb{C}(*) = \div$ and $\mathbb{R}(\mathbb{C}(*)) = *'$. We then have:

$$\begin{aligned} A *' \alpha &= \mathrm{Cn}((A\div\neg\alpha) \cup \{\alpha\}) \\ &= \mathrm{Cn}((A \cap (A * \alpha)) \cup \{\alpha\}). \end{aligned}$$

(*Revision-extensionality* was used in the last step.) Our task is to show that $\mathrm{Cn}((A \cap (A * \alpha)) \cup \{\alpha\}) = A * \alpha$.

We can use *revision-inclusion* to obtain $A*\alpha \subseteq \mathrm{Cn}(A \cup \{\alpha\})$ and then set theory to obtain $A*\alpha = (A*\alpha) \cap \mathrm{Cn}(A \cup \{\alpha\})$. By *revision-success* and *revision-closure*, $A * \alpha = \mathrm{Cn}((A * \alpha) \cup \{\alpha\})$. We therefore have

$$A * \alpha = \mathrm{Cn}((A * \alpha) \cup \{\alpha\}) \cap \mathrm{Cn}(A \cup \{\alpha\}),$$

and we can proceed as follows:

$\varepsilon \in A * \alpha$
iff $\varepsilon \in \mathrm{Cn}((A * \alpha) \cup \{\alpha\}) \cap \mathrm{Cn}(A \cup \{\alpha\})$
iff $\varepsilon \in \mathrm{Cn}((A * \alpha) \cup \{\alpha\})$ and $\varepsilon \in \mathrm{Cn}(A \cup \{\alpha\})$
iff $\alpha \to \varepsilon \in \mathrm{Cn}(A * \alpha)$ and $\alpha \to \varepsilon \in \mathrm{Cn}(A)$ (deduction property)
iff $\alpha \to \varepsilon \in A * \alpha$ and $\alpha \to \varepsilon \in A$ (*revision-closure*, logical closure of A)
iff $\alpha \to \varepsilon \in A \cap (A * \alpha)$
iff $\alpha \to \varepsilon \in \mathrm{Cn}(A \cap (A * \alpha))$
iff $\varepsilon \in \mathrm{Cn}((A \cap (A * \alpha)) \cup \{\alpha\})$
iff $\varepsilon \in A *' \alpha$

We therefore have $A * \alpha = A *' \alpha$, as desired. ■

Note that whereas only four out of the six basic contraction postulates are needed for Observation 3.54, and only five for Observation 3.56, all six of them are required for both observations to hold. Similarly, neither Observation 3.55 nor Observation 3.57 depends on all the six basic revision postulates, but all of them are needed to obtain both observations. In summary, we need the full set of six contraction postulates and six revision postulates to obtain full interchangeability between operators of revision and operators of contraction.

We can now prove the major results of Sections 3.4 and 3.5:

> Let A be a logically closed set. The operator $*$ is an operator of partial meet revision for A if and only if it satisfies: *closure*, *success*, *inclusion*, *vacuity*, *consistency*, and *extensionality*.
> [Theorem 3.14.]

Proof. For one direction, let $*$ be an operator of partial meet revision. Then $* = \mathbb{R}(\div)$ for some partial meet contraction $\div$. It follows from Theorem 2.7 that $\div$ satisfies the contraction-postulates *inclusion*, *vacuity*, *success*, and *extensionality*, and we can conclude from Observation 3.54 that $\mathbb{R}(\div)$ satisfies the listed revision-postulates (namely the six basic Gärdenfors postulates).

For the other direction, suppose that $*$ satisfies the listed postulates. It follows from Observation 3.55 that $\mathbb{C}(*)$ is an operator of partial meet contraction. Then $\mathbb{R}(\mathbb{C}(*))$ is by definition an operator of partial meet revision. According to Observation 3.57, $\mathbb{R}(\mathbb{C}(*)) = *$, and we are done. ■

> 1. If $\div$ is a partial meet contraction, then $\mathbb{C}(\mathbb{R}(\div)) = \div$.
> 2. If $*$ is a partial meet revision, then $\mathbb{R}(\mathbb{C}(*)) = *$.
>
> [Observation 3.17.]

Proof. Directly from Observations 3.56 and 3.57, using the axiomatic characterizations of partial meet contraction and revision (Theorems 2.7 and 3.14). ■

> Let A be a (logically closed) belief set and γ a selection function for A. Then $A{\sim}_\gamma\alpha = A \cap (A\mp_\gamma\neg\alpha)$. (*the Harper identity*).
> [Observation 3.15.]

Proof. Directly from Observation 3.56, using the axiomatic characterization of partial meet contraction (Theorem 2.7). ■

> Let A be a belief set and let $\div$ be a withdrawal for A (i.e. it satisfies the contraction-postulates *closure, inclusion, vacuity, success,* and *extensionality*). Then $\mathbb{R}(\div)$ is a partial meet revision.
> [Observation 3.18.]

Proof. It follows from Observation 3.54 that $\mathbb{R}(\div)$ satisfies the six basic Gärdenfors postulates, and then from Theorem 3.14 that it is a partial meet revision. ■

Exercises

173. Let A be a logically closed set and $\div$ an operator for A that satisfies the contraction-postulates *closure* and *extensionality*. Let $\mathbb{R}(\div) = *$. Show that $\div$ and $*$ satisfy the following condition:
 If $\beta\rightarrow\alpha \in A\div\alpha$, then $\neg\beta \in A * \neg\alpha$.

174. [99] Let A be a logically closed set and $*$ an operator for A that satisfies *revision-success*. Let $\mathbb{C}(*) = \div$. Show that if A is inconsistent then $\neg\alpha \in A\div\alpha$.

175. [83] Let $\div$ be a withdrawal on the logically closed set A. (I.e. it satisfies the contraction-postulates *closure, inclusion, vacuity, success,* and *extensionality*.) Furthermore, let $\div' = \mathbb{C}(\mathbb{R}(\div))$.
 (a) Show that $\div$ and $\div'$ are revision-equivalent, i.e. that $\mathbb{R}(\div) = \mathbb{R}(\div')$.
 (b) Show that $A\div\alpha \subseteq A\div'\alpha$ for all α.
 (c) Is it necessary for $A\div\alpha \subseteq A\div'\alpha$ that $\div$ satisfies all the five postulates for withdrawals? If not, which can be dispensed with?
 (d) Let $\div''$ be a withdrawal on A. Show that if $\div$ and $\div''$ are revision-equivalent, then $A\div''\alpha \subseteq A\div'\alpha$ for all α (so that $\div' = \mathbb{C}(\mathbb{R}(\div))$ is maximal among those withdrawals that are revision-equivalent with $\div$).

21⁺ SUPPLEMENTARY CONNECTIONS WITH CONTRACTION

The connection between partial meet contraction and partial meet revision can be elegantly extended to the supplementary postulates. Given the basic postulates, each of the supplementary postulates for revision that was introduced in Section

3.7 can be shown to correspond exactly to one of the supplementary postulates for contraction from Section 2.5, and vice versa. The proofs are based on the Levi and Harper identities and De Morgan's laws in sentential logic. According to one of these laws, $\neg(\alpha\vee\beta)$ is equivalent to $\neg\alpha\&\neg\beta$. Therefore, contraction by the negation of a disjunction (which is required by the Levi identity in revision by a disjunction) can be reformulated as contraction by a conjunction. Similarly, $\neg(\alpha\&\beta)$ is equivalent to $\neg\alpha\vee\neg\beta$. Therefore, revision by the negation of a conjunction (as required by the Harper identity in contraction by a conjunction) can be reformulated as revision by a disjunction.

OBSERVATION 3.58 (Hans Rott [115]) *Let A be a logically closed set and γ a selection function for A. Then the following two conditions are equivalent:*

1. $\sim_\gamma$ *satisfies* conjunctive overlap ($(A\sim_\gamma\alpha)\cap(A\sim_\gamma\beta)\subseteq A\sim_\gamma(\alpha\&\beta)$)
2. $\mp_\gamma$ *satisfies* disjunctive overlap ($(A\mp_\gamma\alpha)\cap(A\mp_\gamma\beta)\subseteq A\mp_\gamma(\alpha\vee\beta)$)

Proof. *(1) to (2)*: Case 1, $\neg\alpha\notin A$: Then $\neg(\alpha\vee\beta)\notin A$, and thus $A\mp_\gamma(\alpha\vee\beta) = \mathrm{Cn}(A\cup\{\alpha\vee\beta\})$. Given this, *disjunctive overlap* can be proved as follows:

$\varepsilon\in(A\mp_\gamma\alpha)\cap(A\mp_\gamma\beta)$
$\varepsilon\in A\mp_\gamma\alpha$ and $\varepsilon\in A\mp_\gamma\beta$
$\varepsilon\in\mathrm{Cn}(A\cup\{\alpha\})$ and $\varepsilon\in\mathrm{Cn}(A\cup\{\beta\})$ (*revision-inclusion*)
$\alpha\rightarrow\varepsilon\in\mathrm{Cn}(A)$ and $\beta\rightarrow\varepsilon\in\mathrm{Cn}(A)$ (deduction property)
$\alpha\vee\beta\rightarrow\varepsilon\in\mathrm{Cn}(A)$ (truth-functional logic)
$\varepsilon\in\mathrm{Cn}(A\cup\{\alpha\vee\beta\})$ (deduction property)
$\varepsilon\in A\mp_\gamma(\alpha\vee\beta)$ (see above)

Case 2, $\neg\beta\notin A$: Symmetrical with case 1.

Case 3, $\neg\alpha\in A$ and $\neg\beta\in A$: Let (1) be satisfied, and let $\varepsilon\in(A\mp_\gamma\alpha)\cap(A\mp_\gamma\beta)$. We then have:

$\varepsilon\in(A\mp_\gamma\alpha)\cap(A\mp_\gamma\beta)$
$\varepsilon\in\mathrm{Cn}((A\sim_\gamma\neg\alpha)\cup\{\alpha\})\cap\mathrm{Cn}((A\sim_\gamma\neg\beta)\cup\{\beta\})$ (Levi identity)
$\varepsilon\in\mathrm{Cn}((A\sim_\gamma\neg\alpha)\cup\{\alpha\})$ and $\varepsilon\in\mathrm{Cn}((A\sim_\gamma\neg\beta)\cup\{\beta\})$
$\alpha\rightarrow\varepsilon\in\mathrm{Cn}(A\sim_\gamma\neg\alpha)$ and $\beta\rightarrow\varepsilon\in\mathrm{Cn}(A\sim_\gamma\neg\beta)$ (deduction property)

It follows from *recovery* that $\neg\alpha\rightarrow\neg\beta\in\mathrm{Cn}(A\sim_\gamma\neg\alpha)$, or equivalently $\beta\rightarrow\alpha\in\mathrm{Cn}(A\sim_\gamma\neg\alpha)$. It follows from this and $\alpha\rightarrow\varepsilon\in\mathrm{Cn}(A\sim_\gamma\neg\alpha)$ that $\alpha\vee\beta\rightarrow\varepsilon\in\mathrm{Cn}(A\sim_\gamma\neg\alpha)$. In the same way it follows that $\alpha\vee\beta\rightarrow\varepsilon\in\mathrm{Cn}(A\sim_\gamma\neg\beta)$. We can continue:

$\alpha\vee\beta\rightarrow\varepsilon \in \mathrm{Cn}(A\sim_\gamma\neg\alpha)$ and $\alpha\vee\beta\rightarrow\varepsilon \in \mathrm{Cn}(A\sim_\gamma\neg\beta)$
$\alpha\vee\beta\rightarrow\varepsilon \in A\sim_\gamma\neg\alpha$ and $\alpha\vee\beta\rightarrow\varepsilon \in A\sim_\gamma\neg\beta$ (*contraction-closure*)
$\alpha\vee\beta\rightarrow\varepsilon \in (A\sim_\gamma\neg\alpha)\cap(A\sim_\gamma\neg\beta)$
$\alpha\vee\beta\rightarrow\varepsilon \in (A\sim_\gamma(\neg\alpha\&\neg\beta))$ (*conjunctive overlap*)
$\varepsilon \in \mathrm{Cn}((A\sim_\gamma(\neg\alpha\&\neg\beta))\cup\{\alpha\vee\beta\})$ (deduction property)
$\varepsilon \in \mathrm{Cn}((A\sim_\gamma\neg(\alpha\vee\beta))\cup\{\alpha\vee\beta\})$
(De Morgan, *contraction-extensionality*)
$\varepsilon \in A\mp_\gamma(\alpha\vee\beta)$ (Levi identity)

(2) to (1): Let (2) is satisfied, and let $\varepsilon \in (A\sim_\gamma\alpha)\cap(A\sim_\gamma\beta)$. We then have:

$\varepsilon \in (A\sim_\gamma\alpha)\cap(A\sim_\gamma\beta)$
$\varepsilon \in (A\cap(A\mp_\gamma\neg\alpha))\cap(A\cap(A\mp_\gamma\neg\beta))$ (Harper identity)
$\varepsilon \in A\cap((A\mp_\gamma\neg\alpha)\cap(A\mp_\gamma\neg\beta))$
$\varepsilon \in A\cap(A\mp_\gamma(\neg\alpha\vee\neg\beta))$ (*disjunctive overlap*)
$\varepsilon \in A\cap(A\mp_\gamma\neg(\alpha\&\beta))$ (De Morgan, *revision-extensionality*)
$\varepsilon \in A\sim_\gamma(\alpha\&\beta)$ (Harper identity) ■

Given the equivalence (in the presence of the basic postulates) of the revision postulates disjunctive overlap and superexpansion, the following result is now immediate:

Let A be a logically closed set and γ a selection function for A. Then the following two conditions are equivalent:

1. $\sim_\gamma$ satisfies *conjunctive overlap* $((A\sim_\gamma\alpha)\cap(A\sim_\gamma\beta)\subseteq A\sim_\gamma(\alpha\&\beta))$
2. $\mp_\gamma$ satisfies *superexpansion* $(A\mp_\gamma(\alpha\&\beta)\subseteq(A\mp_\gamma\alpha)+\beta)$

[Observation 3.24, Part 1.]

Proof. Directly from Observations 3.49 and 3.58. ■

A similar relationship holds for the other supplementary Gärdenfors postulates, namely conjunctive inclusion (for contraction) and disjunctive inclusion or subexpansion (for revision). The proof is similar:

OBSERVATION 3.59 *Let A be a logically closed set and γ a selection function for A. Then the following two conditions are equivalent:*

1. *$\sim_\gamma$ satisfies conjunctive inclusion*
(If $A\sim_\gamma(\alpha\&\beta)\nvdash\alpha$, then $A\sim_\gamma(\alpha\&\beta)\subseteq A\sim_\gamma\alpha$)
2. *$\mp_\gamma$ satisfies disjunctive inclusion*
(If $A\mp_\gamma(\alpha\vee\beta)\nvdash\neg\alpha$, then $A\mp_\gamma(\alpha\vee\beta)\subseteq A\mp_\gamma\alpha$)

Proof. *(1) to (2)*: Let (1) be satisfied, and let $A \mp_\gamma (\alpha \vee \beta) \nvdash \neg\alpha$. We have to show that if $\varepsilon \in A \mp_\gamma (\alpha \vee \beta)$, then $\varepsilon \in A \mp_\gamma \alpha$. We first need to show that *conjunctive inclusion* can be applied to the expression $\neg\alpha \& \neg\beta$ that we obtain from $\alpha \vee \beta$ through De Morgan's laws.

$A \mp_\gamma (\alpha \vee \beta) \nvdash \neg\alpha$
$\neg\alpha \notin \text{Cn}((A \sim_\gamma \neg(\alpha \vee \beta)) \cup \{\alpha \vee \beta\})$ (Levi identity)
$\alpha \vee \beta \rightarrow \neg\alpha \notin \text{Cn}(A \sim_\gamma \neg(\alpha \vee \beta))$ (deduction property)
$\neg\alpha \notin \text{Cn}(A \sim_\gamma \neg(\alpha \vee \beta))$ (sentential logic, $\neg\alpha$ implies $\alpha \vee \beta \rightarrow \neg\alpha$)
$\neg\alpha \notin \text{Cn}(A \sim_\gamma (\neg\alpha \& \neg\beta))$ (De Morgan, *conjunction-extensionality*)
$A \sim_\gamma (\neg\alpha \& \neg\beta) \subseteq A \sim_\gamma \neg\alpha$ (*conjunctive inclusion*)

Using this result, we obtain the following:

$\varepsilon \in A \mp_\gamma (\alpha \vee \beta)$
$\varepsilon \in \text{Cn}((A \sim_\gamma \neg(\alpha \vee \beta)) \cup \{\alpha \vee \beta\})$ (Levi identity)
$\varepsilon \in \text{Cn}((A \sim_\gamma (\neg\alpha \& \neg\beta)) \cup \{\alpha \vee \beta\})$ (De Morgan, *contraction-extensionality*)
$\varepsilon \in \text{Cn}((A \sim_\gamma \neg\alpha) \cup \{\alpha \vee \beta\})$ (*conjunctive inclusion*, see above)
$\varepsilon \in \text{Cn}((A \sim_\gamma \neg\alpha) \cup \{\alpha\})$ (property of Cn)
$\varepsilon \in A \mp_\gamma \alpha$ (Levi identity)

(2) to (1): Let (2) be satisfied, and let $A \sim_\gamma (\alpha \& \beta) \nvdash \alpha$. We have to show that if $\varepsilon \in A \sim_\gamma (\alpha \& \beta)$, then $\varepsilon \in A \sim_\gamma \alpha$. If $\alpha \notin A$, then $\alpha \& \beta \notin A$, so that $A \sim_\gamma \alpha = A \sim_\gamma (\alpha \& \beta) = A$, and we are done.

In the principal case, when $\alpha \in A$, we first need to show that *disjunctive inclusion* can be applied to $\neg\alpha \vee \neg\beta$, the negation of $\alpha \& \beta$:

$A \sim_\gamma (\alpha \& \beta) \nvdash \alpha$
$\alpha \notin A \sim_\gamma (\alpha \& \beta)$
$\alpha \notin A \cap (A \mp_\gamma \neg(\alpha \& \beta))$ (Harper identity)
$\alpha \notin A \cap (A \mp_\gamma (\neg\alpha \vee \neg\beta))$ (De Morgan, *revision-extensionality*)
$\alpha \notin A \mp_\gamma (\neg\alpha \vee \neg\beta)$ (since $\alpha \in A$ holds by assumption)
$A \mp_\gamma (\neg\alpha \vee \neg\beta) \subseteq A \mp_\gamma \neg\alpha$ (*disjunctive inclusion*)

We can now obtain:

$\varepsilon \in A \sim_\gamma (\alpha \& \beta)$
$\varepsilon \in A \cap (A \mp_\gamma \neg(\alpha \& \beta))$ (Harper identity)
$\varepsilon \in A \cap (A \mp_\gamma (\neg\alpha \vee \neg\beta))$ (De Morgan, *revision-extensionality*)
$\varepsilon \in A \cap (A \mp_\gamma \neg\alpha)$ (*disjunctive inclusion*, see above)
$\varepsilon \in A \sim_\gamma \alpha$ (Harper identity) ■

Since *disjunctive inclusion* is interchangeable with *subexpansion* (if the basic postulates are satisfied), the following equivalence follows directly:

Let A be a logically closed set and γ a selection function for A. Then the following two conditions are equivalent:

1. $\sim_\gamma$ satisfies *conjunctive inclusion*
2. $\mp_\gamma$ satisfies *subexpansion*

[Observation 3.24, Part 2.]

Proof. Directly from Observations 3.50 and 3.59. ■

We have shown that (given the basic postulates) each of the two supplementary Gärdenfors postulates for contraction has an equivalent counterpart in one of the supplementary postulates for revision, and vice versa. Similar equivalences can be shown for several weakened forms of these postulates.

OBSERVATION 3.60 (Hans Rott [115]) *Let A be a logically closed set and γ a selection function for A. Then the following two conditions are equivalent:*

1. *$\sim_\gamma$ satisfies: If $\beta \in A{\sim_\gamma}(\alpha\&\beta)$, then $A{\sim_\gamma}\alpha \subseteq A{\sim_\gamma}(\alpha\&\beta)$*
2. *$\mp_\gamma$ satisfies: If $\beta \in A{\mp_\gamma}\alpha$, then $A{\mp_\gamma}(\alpha\&\beta) \subseteq A{\mp_\gamma}\alpha$ (cut)*

Proof. *(1) to (2):* Let (1) be satisfied, and let $\beta \in A{\mp_\gamma}\alpha$. We need to show that $A{\mp_\gamma}(\alpha\&\beta) \subseteq A{\mp_\gamma}\alpha$.

$\beta \in A{\mp_\gamma}\alpha$
$\beta \in \mathrm{Cn}((A{\sim_\gamma}\neg\alpha) \cup \{\alpha\})$ (Levi identity)
$\alpha\rightarrow\beta \in \mathrm{Cn}(A{\sim_\gamma}\neg\alpha)$ (deduction property)
$\alpha\rightarrow\beta \in A{\sim_\gamma}\neg\alpha$ (*contraction-closure*)
$\alpha\rightarrow\beta \in A{\sim_\gamma}((\neg\alpha\vee\neg\beta)\&(\alpha\rightarrow\beta))$ (*contraction-extensionality*)
$A{\sim_\gamma}(\neg\alpha\vee\neg\beta) \subseteq A{\sim_\gamma}((\neg\alpha\vee\neg\beta)\&(\alpha\rightarrow\beta))$ (from (1))
$A{\sim_\gamma}(\neg(\alpha\&\beta)) \subseteq A{\sim_\gamma}\neg\alpha$ (*contraction-extensionality*)
$\mathrm{Cn}((A{\sim_\gamma}(\neg(\alpha\&\beta))) \cup \{\alpha\&\beta\}) \subseteq \mathrm{Cn}((A{\sim_\gamma}\neg\alpha) \cup \{\alpha\&\beta\})$ (property of Cn)
$A{\mp_\gamma}(\alpha\&\beta) \subseteq \mathrm{Cn}((A{\sim_\gamma}\neg\alpha) \cup \{\alpha\&\beta\})$ (Levi identity)
$A{\mp_\gamma}(\alpha\&\beta) \subseteq \mathrm{Cn}(\mathrm{Cn}((A{\sim_\gamma}\neg\alpha) \cup \{\alpha\}) \cup \{\beta\})$ (property of Cn)
$A{\mp_\gamma}(\alpha\&\beta) \subseteq \mathrm{Cn}((A{\mp_\gamma}\alpha) \cup \{\beta\})$ (Levi identity)
$A{\mp_\gamma}(\alpha\&\beta) \subseteq A{\mp_\gamma}\alpha$ (*revision-closure* and $\beta \in A{\mp_\gamma}\alpha$)

(2) to (1): Let *cut* hold, i.e. let (2) be satisfied, and let $\beta \in A{\sim_\gamma}(\alpha\&\beta)$. We need to show that $A{\sim_\gamma}\alpha \subseteq A{\sim_\gamma}(\alpha\&\beta)$.

$\beta \in A{\sim_\gamma}(\alpha\&\beta)$
$\beta \in A \cap (A{\mp_\gamma}\neg(\alpha\&\beta))$ (Harper identity)
$\beta \in A{\mp_\gamma}\neg(\alpha\&\beta)$
$\alpha\rightarrow\beta \in A{\mp_\gamma}\neg(\alpha\&\beta)$ (*revision-closure*)
$A{\mp_\gamma}(\neg(\alpha\&\beta)\&(\alpha\rightarrow\beta)) \subseteq A{\mp_\gamma}\neg(\alpha\&\beta)$ (*cut*)
$A{\mp_\gamma}\neg\alpha \subseteq A{\mp_\gamma}\neg(\alpha\&\beta)$ (*revision-extensionality*)
$A \cap (A{\mp_\gamma}\neg\alpha) \subseteq A \cap (A{\mp_\gamma}\neg(\alpha\&\beta))$ (set theory)
$A{\sim_\gamma}\alpha \subseteq A{\sim_\gamma}(\alpha\&\beta)$ (Harper identity) ■

OBSERVATION 3.61 (Gärdenfors and Rott [40]) *Let A be a logically closed set and γ a selection function for A. Then the following two conditions are equivalent:*

1. *$\sim_\gamma$ satisfies weak conjunctive inclusion,*
   $A{\sim_\gamma}(\alpha\&\beta) \subseteq \mathrm{Cn}((A{\sim_\gamma}\alpha)\cup(A{\sim_\gamma}\beta))$
2. *$\mp_\gamma$ satisfies weak disjunctive inclusion,*
   $A{\mp_\gamma}(\alpha\vee\beta) \subseteq \mathrm{Cn}((A{\mp_\gamma}\alpha)\cup(A{\mp_\gamma}\beta))$

Proof. *(1) to (2)*: Let (1) hold. We then have:

$\varepsilon \in A{\mp_\gamma}(\alpha\vee\beta)$
$\varepsilon \in \mathrm{Cn}((A{\sim_\gamma}\neg(\alpha\vee\beta))\cup\{\alpha\vee\beta\})$ (Levi identity)
$\varepsilon \in \mathrm{Cn}((A{\sim_\gamma}(\neg\alpha\&\neg\beta))\cup\{\alpha\vee\beta\})$ (De Morgan, *contraction-extensionality*)
$\varepsilon \in \mathrm{Cn}((\mathrm{Cn}((A{\sim_\gamma}\neg\alpha)\cup(A{\sim_\gamma}\neg\beta)))\cup\{\alpha\vee\beta\})$ (from (1))
$\varepsilon \in \mathrm{Cn}(\mathrm{Cn}((A{\sim_\gamma}\neg\alpha)\cup\{\alpha\})\cup\mathrm{Cn}((A{\sim_\gamma}\neg\beta)\cup\{\beta\}))$ (properties of Cn)
$\varepsilon \in \mathrm{Cn}((A{\mp_\gamma}\alpha)\cup(A{\mp_\gamma}\beta))$

(2) to (1): Let (2) hold. We then have:

$\varepsilon \in A{\sim_\gamma}(\alpha\&\beta)$
$\varepsilon \in A\cap(A{\mp_\gamma}\neg(\alpha\&\beta))$ (Harper identity)
$\varepsilon \in A\cap(A{\mp_\gamma}(\neg\alpha\vee\neg\beta))$ (*revision-extensionality*)
$\varepsilon \in A$ and $\varepsilon \in \mathrm{Cn}((A{\mp_\gamma}\neg\alpha)\cup(A{\mp_\gamma}\neg\beta))$ (from (2))

It follows from this, by compactness, that there is a finite set $D_1 \subseteq A{\mp_\gamma}\neg\alpha$ and a finite set $D_2 \subseteq A{\mp}\gamma\neg\beta$ such that $D_1 \cup D_2 \vdash \varepsilon$ and consequently $(\&D_1)\&(\&D_2) \vdash \varepsilon$. From this result we can conclude that $((\&D_1)\&(\&D_2))\vee\varepsilon \vdash \varepsilon$, or equivalently $((\&D_1)\vee\varepsilon)\&((\&D_2)\vee\varepsilon) \vdash \varepsilon$. Since $((\&D_1)\vee\varepsilon) \in A\cap(A{\mp_\gamma}\neg\alpha)$ and $((\&D_2)\vee\varepsilon) \in A\cap(A{\mp_\gamma}\neg\beta)$, we can therefore conclude that

$\varepsilon \in \mathrm{Cn}((A\cap(A{\mp_\gamma}\neg\alpha))\cup(A\cap(A{\mp_\gamma}\neg\beta)))$
$\varepsilon \in \mathrm{Cn}((A{\sim_\gamma}\alpha)\cup(A{\sim_\gamma}\beta))$ ■

The representation theorem for transitively relational partial meet revision is now quite easy to prove:

> Let A be a logically closed set and $*$ an operation for A. Then $*$ is a transitively relational partial meet revision if and only if it satisfies *closure, success, inclusion, vacuity, consistency, extensionality, superexpansion*, and *subexpansion*.
> [Theorem 3.25.]

Proof. *Construction-to-postulates*: Let $\mp_\gamma$ be a transitively relational partial meet revision. It follows from Theorem 3.14 that it satisfies the six basic postulates: *closure, success, inclusion, vacuity, consistency*, and *extensionality*. It follows from

Theorem 2.21 that the corresponding contraction operator $\sim_\gamma$ satisfies *conjunctive overlap* and *conjunctive inclusion.* We can use Observation 3.24 to conclude that $\mp_\gamma$ satisfies *superexpansion* and *subexpansion.*

Postulates-to-construction: Let $*$ be an operator that satisfies the eight listed postulates. It follows from Theorem 3.14 that it is a partial meet revision. Let $\sim_\gamma$ be the partial meet contraction that is based on the same selection function. Then it follows from Observation 3.24 that $\sim_\gamma$ satisfies *conjunctive overlap* and *conjunctive inclusion.* We can use Theorem 2.21 to conclude that γ (and thus $*$) is transitively relational. ■

Exercises

176. [115] Let A be a logically closed set and γ a selection function for A. Show that the following two conditions are equivalent:

    (a) If $\beta \in A\sim_\gamma(\alpha\&\beta)$, then $A\sim_\gamma(\alpha\&\beta) \subseteq A\sim_\gamma\alpha$.
    (b) If $\beta \in A\mp_\gamma\alpha$, then $A\mp_\gamma\alpha \subseteq A\mp_\gamma(\alpha\&\beta)$ (*cautious monotony*)

177. [35] Let A be a logically closed set and γ a selection function for A. Show that the following two conditions are equivalent:

    (a) $A\mp_\gamma\alpha = A\mp_\gamma\beta$ if and only if $\beta \in A\mp_\gamma\alpha$ and $\alpha \in A\mp_\gamma\beta$. (*reciprocity*)
    (b) If $\beta\rightarrow\alpha \in A\sim_\gamma\alpha$ and $\alpha\rightarrow\beta \in A\sim_\gamma\beta$, then $A\sim_\gamma\alpha = A\sim_\gamma\beta$.

22+ THE TRIVIAL LIMITING CASES

The following may be seen as a triviality result since it shows that full meet revision on a belief set is a trivial and implausible operation. To prove it, we can combine the Levi identity with an observation on full meet contraction from Section 2.4.

Let A be a logically closed set, and let $\mp = \mathbb{R}(\sim)$, i.e. let $\mp$ be full meet revision for A. Then:

1. If $\neg\alpha \in A$, then $A\mp\alpha = \text{Cn}(\{\alpha\})$.
2. If $\neg\alpha \notin A$, then $A\mp\alpha = \text{Cn}(A \cup \{\alpha\})$

[Observation 3.21.]

Proof. For (1), we make use of Observation 2.12, according to which it follows from $\neg\alpha \in A$ that $A \sim \neg\alpha = A \cap \text{Cn}(\{\alpha\})$. We then have:

$$A\mp\alpha = \text{Cn}((A \sim \neg\alpha) \cup \{\alpha\}) \text{ (Levi identity)}$$
$$= \text{Cn}((A \cap \text{Cn}(\{\alpha\})) \cup \{\alpha\}) \text{ (Observation 2.12)}$$
$$= \text{Cn}(\{\alpha\}) \text{ (properties of Cn)}$$

(2) follows from *vacuity*, that holds for all partial meet contractions and therefore also for full meet contraction. ■

The following result for maxichoice revision has also been prepared for in Section 2.4:

> Let A be a logically closed set and $\mp_\gamma$ an operator of maxichoice revision for A. Then it holds for all sentences α and β that:
> If $\neg\alpha \in A$, then either $\beta \in A\mp_\gamma\alpha$ or $\neg\beta \in A\mp_\gamma\alpha$.
> [Observation 3.22.]

Proof. Let $\neg\alpha \in A$. Then:

$\alpha\rightarrow\beta \in A\sim_\gamma\neg\alpha$ or $\alpha\rightarrow\neg\beta \in A\sim_\gamma\neg\alpha$ (Observation 2.14)
$\beta \in \mathrm{Cn}((A\sim_\gamma\neg\alpha)\cup\{\alpha\})$ or $\neg\beta \in \mathrm{Cn}((A\sim_\gamma\neg\alpha)\cup\{\alpha\})$ (deduction)
$\beta \in A\mp_\gamma\alpha$ or $\neg\beta \in A\mp_\gamma\alpha$ (Levi identity) ■

It follows from this that if γ is maxichoice and $\neg\alpha \in A$, then $A\mp_\gamma\alpha \in \mathcal{L}\perp^\perp$.

Exercises

178. Let A be a logically closed set. Let $\sim$ be full meet contraction, and let $\div_m$ be the minimal (smallest possible) withdrawal of A, namely the operation $\div_m$ such that:
If $\alpha \in A$, then $A\div_m\alpha = \mathrm{Cn}(\emptyset)$.
If $\alpha \notin A$, then $A\div_m\alpha = A$.
Show that $\mathbb{R}(\div_m) = \mathbb{R}(\sim)$.

179. Let A be logically closed and γ a selection function that is both maxichoice and transitively relational. Show that:
Either $A * (\alpha\vee\beta) = A * \alpha$ or $A * (\alpha\vee\beta) = A * \beta$.

23+ POSSIBLE WORLDS AND PROPOSITIONAL CHANGE

In Section 3.8, an alternative representation of belief states as propositions (sets of possible worlds) was introduced. Several close connections were indicated that hold between operators on propositions and operators on belief sets. All this was done in a somewhat informal manner. In order to prove these connections, we need to reformulate them in a more rigorous fashion.

To begin with, we need to prove the basic observation, given in Section 3.8, that allows us to freely refer to propositions instead of belief sets. Remember that for any set $A, [A] = \{X \mid A \subseteq X \in \mathcal{L}\perp^\perp\}$ is the set of maximal consistent sets (possible worlds) that contain A. The limiting case of empty sets of possible worlds is taken care of by postulation:

POSTULATE 3.62 $\bigcap\emptyset = \mathcal{L}$.

This is the observation to be proved:

1. Let A be a belief set. Then $\bigcap[A] = A$.

2. (2) Let $\mathcal{W}$ be a set of possible worlds. Then $\bigcap \mathcal{W}$ is a belief set.

[Observation 3.27.]

Proof. *Part 1*: It follows directly from the definition of $[A]$ that A is a subset of every element of $[A]$, and thus $A \subseteq \bigcap[A]$.

For the other direction, let $\delta \notin A$. It follows that $A \cup \{\neg\delta\} \nvdash \bot$, and thus there is, by the upper bound property, some X such that $A \cup \{\neg\delta\} \subseteq X \in \mathcal{L}\bot\bot$, and consequently $\delta \notin X \in [A]$ so that $\delta \notin \bigcap[A]$.

Part 2: Case 1, $\mathcal{W} \neq \emptyset$: Since each element of $\mathcal{W}$ is logically closed, so is the intersection $\bigcap \mathcal{W}$, and thus $\bigcap \mathcal{W}$ is a belief set.

Case 2, $\mathcal{W} = \emptyset$: $\bigcap \mathcal{W} = \mathcal{L}$ according to Postulate 3.62, and $\mathcal{L}$ is a belief set. ■

Every sentence α in the language is represented by the proposition $[\alpha]$. ($[\alpha]$ is an abbreviation of $[\text{Cn}(\{\alpha\})]$.) However, it is important to note that if $\mathcal{L}$ is infinite, then there are propositions that do not represent any sentence. To see this, let $\mathcal{L}$ consist of the infinite list $p_0, p_1, p_2 \ldots$ of logically independent (atomic) sentences and their truth-functional combinations. Let $W \in \mathcal{L}\bot\bot$. Then $\{W\}$ is a proposition. Suppose that $\{W\} = [\alpha]$ for some sentence α. We then have:

$$\begin{aligned} W &= \textstyle\bigcap\{W\} \text{ (set theory)}\\ &= \textstyle\bigcap[\alpha] \text{ (by assumption)}\\ &= \textstyle\bigcap[\text{Cn}(\{\alpha\})] \text{ (definition of [ ])}\\ &= \text{Cn}(\{\alpha\}) \text{ (Observation 3.27)} \end{aligned}$$

Since $W \in \mathcal{L}\bot\bot$, it holds for every atomic sentence p_n that either $W \vdash p_n$ or $W \vdash \neg p_n$, and thus either $\alpha \vdash p_n$ or $\alpha \vdash \neg p_n$. This shows that α cannot be a finite truth-functional combination of atomic sentences, contrary to the assumption that $\alpha \in \mathcal{L}$. We can conclude from this that the proposition $\{W\}$ does not represent any sentence. Thus, whereas every proposition represents a belief set (Part 2 of Observation 3.27), there are propositions that do not represent a sentence.

Many authors use another terminology for essentially the same concepts [65; 66]. If $W \in \mathcal{L}\bot\bot$, then for all sentences α either $\alpha \in W$ or $\neg\alpha \in W$. If $\alpha \in W$, then α is true in the possible world W, and if $\neg\alpha \in W$ then α is false in W. We can therefore replace W by a function that assigns to each sentence α either truth (denoted T) or falsehood (denoted F). Instead of talking about possible worlds (or maximal consistent sets) we can talk about functions from $\mathcal{L}$ to the set $\{\mathsf{T}, \mathsf{F}\}$. Such functions are called *interpretations*. Let I be an interpretation. Then I is a *model* of a sentence α if and only if $I(\alpha) = \mathsf{T}$. Furthermore, I is a model of a set A of sentences if and only if $I(\alpha) = \mathsf{T}$ for all $\alpha \in A$. Let $Mod(\alpha)$ and $Mod(A)$ denote the set of models of α and A, respectively.

The function $t(I) = \{\alpha \mid I(\alpha) = \mathrm{T}\}$ can be used to translate between the two terminologies. They are connected as follows:

$$t(I) \in \mathcal{L}\bot^{\bot}$$
$$[\alpha] = \{t(X) \mid X \in Mod(\alpha)\}$$
$$[A] = \{t(X) \mid X \in Mod(A)\}$$

It is a matter of taste whether you choose to think in terms of interpretations and models or in terms of maximal consistent sets (possible worlds) [66]. Here, the latter terminology will be used, but the reader who so wishes should not find it difficult to translate the rest of this chapter into the language of interpretations and models.

Before introducing revision and contraction of propositions, let us consider the simpler operation of expansion. Since $A + \alpha$ is characterized by containing both A and α, the outcome of expanding $[A]$ with $[\alpha]$ should be the set of possible worlds that are contained in both $[A]$and $[\alpha]$. More precisely:

DEFINITION 3.63 *The (global) operator* $\oplus$ *of* propositional expansion *for* $\mathcal{W}$ *is the operator such that for all propositions* $\mathcal{W}$ *and sentences* α :

$$\mathcal{W} \oplus [\alpha] = \mathcal{W} \cap [\alpha].$$

Thus, propositional expansion coincides with set-theoretical intersection. The following observation confirms that this simple (or shall we say trivial) operation on propositions corresponds to (closing) expansion as we have defined it on belief sets.

OBSERVATION 3.64 (Adam Grove [41]) *Let* $\mathcal{W}$ *be a proposition and* α *a sentence. Then:*

$$\bigcap(\mathcal{W} \oplus [\alpha]) = (\bigcap \mathcal{W}) + \alpha.$$

where $\oplus$ *is propositional expansion and* $+$ *is closing expansion.*

Proof. The crucial step in the derivation makes use of the observation that if $X \in \mathcal{L}\bot^{\bot}$, then $\alpha \rightarrow \beta \in X$ if and only it is the case that if $\alpha \in X$, then $\beta \in X$. (Observation 1.57.) We have:

$\beta \in \bigcap(\mathcal{W} \oplus [\alpha])$
iff $\beta \in \bigcap(\mathcal{W} \cap [\alpha])$ (Definition 3.63)
iff $\beta \in X$ for all X such that $X \in \mathcal{W}$ and $X \in [\alpha]$
iff $\beta \in X$ for all X such that $X \in \mathcal{W}$ and $\mathrm{Cn}(\{\alpha\}) \subseteq X$ (Definition 3.26)
iff $\beta \in X$ for all X such that $X \in \mathcal{W}$ and $\alpha \in X$
iff $\alpha \rightarrow \beta \in X$ for all $X \in \mathcal{W}$ (Observation 1.57)
iff $\alpha \rightarrow \beta \in \bigcap \mathcal{W}$
iff $\beta \in \mathrm{Cn}((\bigcap \mathcal{W}) \cup \{\alpha\})$ (deduction property)
iff $\beta \in (\bigcap \mathcal{W}) + \alpha$ (Definition 1.5) ■

Next, let us give a more precise statement of the recipe for revision given in Section 3.8. As can be seen e.g. in Figures 3.1 and 3.2, when revising $[A]$ by $[\alpha]$ we choose a subset of $[\alpha]$ that is non-empty if possible and equal to $[A] \cap [\alpha]$ if possible. For this purpose, we need to introduce propositional selection functions.

DEFINITION 3.65 *Let $\mathcal{W}$ be a proposition. A* propositional selection function f *for $\mathcal{W}$ is a function from sentence-representing propositions to propositions, such that for all sentences α :*

(I) $f([\alpha]) \subseteq [\alpha]$,

(II) if $[\alpha] \neq \emptyset$, then $f([\alpha]) \neq \emptyset$, and

(III) if $\mathcal{W} \cap [\alpha] \neq \emptyset$, then $f([\alpha]) = \mathcal{W} \cap [\alpha]$.

DEFINITION 3.66 *Let $\mathcal{W}$ be a proposition. An operator $\circledast$ is a* propositional revision operator *for $\mathcal{W}$ if and only if there is a propositional selection function f for $\mathcal{W}$ such that for all sentences α :*

$$\mathcal{W} \circledast [\alpha] = f([\alpha]).$$

Definitions 3.65 and 3.66 express in a formal way the procedure shown in Figures 3.1 and 3.2. The following observation shows that this procedure corresponds exactly to partial meet revision:

OBSERVATION 3.67 (Adam Grove [41]) *Let A be a logically closed set. Then:*

1. *If $*$ is an operator of partial meet revision for A, then there is a propositional revision operator $\circledast$ for $[A]$ such that $A * \alpha = \bigcap([A] \circledast [\alpha])$ for all sentences α.*
2. *If $\circledast$ is a propositional revision operator for $[A]$, then the operator $*$ for A such that $A * \alpha = \bigcap([A] \circledast [\alpha])$ for all sentences α is an operator of partial meet revision.*

Proof. *Part 1*: Let $*$ be an operator of partial meet revision for A. Furthermore, let f and $\circledast$ be so defined that for all α :

$$f([\alpha]) = \{W \mid A * \alpha \subseteq W \in \mathcal{L}\perp^{\perp}\} \text{ and}$$
$$[A] \circledast [\alpha] = f([\alpha]).$$

We need to show (A) that f is a (well-defined) function, (B) that f is a propositional selection function for $[A]$, and (C) that $A * \alpha = \bigcap([A] \circledast [\alpha])$ for all α.

Part 1A: For f to be a function, it must be the case that if $[\alpha] = [\beta]$, then $f([\alpha]) = f([\beta])$. Let $[\alpha] = [\beta]$, i.e. $[\text{Cn}(\{\alpha\})] = [\text{Cn}(\{\beta\})]$. It follows that $\bigcap[\text{Cn}(\{\alpha\})] = \bigcap[\text{Cn}(\{\beta\})]$, and by Observation 3.27 that $\text{Cn}(\{\alpha\}) = \text{Cn}(\{\beta\})$. Thus, $\alpha \leftrightarrow \beta \in \text{Cn}(\emptyset)$. Since partial meet revision satisfies *extensionality*, $A * \alpha = A * \beta$. It follows from the definition of f that $f([\alpha]) = f([\beta])$.

Part 1B: We are going to show that f satisfies the three conditions of Definition 3.65:

Condition I: Since $*$ satisfies *success*, it follows from our definition of f that if $W \in f([\alpha])$ then $\alpha \in W \in \mathcal{L}\perp^{\perp}$, and thus $W \in [\alpha]$.

Condition II: Let $[\alpha] \neq \emptyset$. Then α is consistent, and by *consistency* so is $A*\alpha$. It follows from the upper bound property that there is at least one W such that $A*\alpha \subseteq W \in \mathcal{L}\perp^{\perp}$, and thus $W \in f([\alpha])$.

Condition III: Suppose that $[A] \cap [\alpha] \neq \emptyset$, i.e. that there is a $W \in \mathcal{L}\perp^{\perp}$ such that $A \subseteq W$ and $\alpha \in W$. It follows that $A \cup \{\alpha\}$ is consistent, and we can conclude from *vacuity* that $A * \alpha = \text{Cn}(A \cup \{\alpha\})$. We therefore have:

$$\begin{aligned}
&f([\alpha]) = \{W \mid \text{Cn}(A \cup \{\alpha\}) \subseteq W \in \mathcal{L}\perp^{\perp}\}\\
&= \{W \mid (\text{Cn}(A) \subseteq W)\&(\alpha \in W)\&(W \in \mathcal{L}\perp^{\perp})\}\\
&= \{W \mid \text{Cn}(A) \subseteq W \in \mathcal{L}\perp^{\perp}\} \cap \{W \mid \alpha \in W \in \mathcal{L}\perp^{\perp})\}\\
&= [A] \cap [\alpha].
\end{aligned}$$

Part 1C: This follows from our definitions:

$$\begin{aligned}
&\bigcap([A]\circledast[\alpha]) = \bigcap f([\alpha]) \text{ (definition of } \circledast \text{ above)}\\
&= \bigcap\{W \mid A * \alpha \subseteq W \in \mathcal{L}\perp^{\perp}\} \text{ (definition of } f \text{ above)}\\
&= \bigcap[A * \alpha] \text{ (Definition 3.26)}\\
&= A * \alpha \text{ (Observation 3.27)}
\end{aligned}$$

Part 2: We are going to show that $*$ satisfies the six characteristic postulates for partial meet revision according to Theorem 3.14. Let f be the propositional selection function on which $\circledast$ is based. Then $A * \alpha = \bigcap([A]\circledast[\alpha]) = \bigcap f([\alpha])$.

Closure: Each element of $[\alpha]$ is logically closed, and since $f([\alpha]) \subseteq [\alpha]$, we can conclude that $\bigcap f([\alpha])$ is also logically closed.

Success: We have $f([\alpha]) \subseteq [\alpha]$, thus $\bigcap([\alpha]) \subseteq \bigcap f([\alpha])$, thus $\alpha \in \bigcap f([\alpha])$.

Inclusion: Let $X \in [\text{Cn}(A \cup \{\alpha\})]$. Then $X \in [A] \cap [\alpha]$, and it follows from clause (III) of Definition 3.65 that $f([\alpha]) = [A] \cap [\alpha]$, thus $f([\alpha]) = [\text{Cn}(A \cup \{\alpha\})]$ (cf. Exercise 180c), thus $X \in f([\alpha])$. We can conclude that $[\text{Cn}(A \cup \{\alpha\})] \subseteq f([\alpha])$ and consequently $\bigcap f([\alpha]) \subseteq \bigcap[\text{Cn}(A \cup \{\alpha\})]$. Thus: $A*\alpha = \bigcap f([\alpha]) \subseteq \bigcap[\text{Cn}(A \cup \{\alpha\})] = \text{Cn}(A \cup \{\alpha\}) = A + \alpha$.

Vacuity: Suppose that $\neg\alpha \notin A$. Then $A \cup \{\alpha\}$ is consistent, and consequently $[A] \cap [\alpha]$ is non-empty. According to clause (III) of Definition 3.65 we have $f([\alpha]) = [A] \cap [\alpha]$, thus $f([\alpha]) = [\text{Cn}(A \cup \{\alpha\})]$, and it follows that $A * \alpha = \bigcap f([\alpha]) = \bigcap[\text{Cn}(A \cup \{\alpha\})] = \text{Cn}(A \cup \{\alpha\}) = A + \alpha$.

Consistency: If α is consistent, then $[\alpha]$ is non-empty, thus by clause (II) $f([\alpha])$ is non-empty and thus $\bigcap f([\alpha])$ is consistent.

Extensionality: If $\alpha \leftrightarrow \beta \in \text{Cn}(\emptyset)$, then $[\alpha] = [\beta]$ and hence $A*\alpha = \bigcap f([\alpha]) = \bigcap f([\beta]) = A * \beta$. ■

The following definition is a formalization of the procedure for contraction illustrated Figure 3.4.

DEFINITION 3.68 *Let $\mathcal{W}$ be a proposition. An operator $\ominus$ is a* propositional contraction operator *for $\mathcal{W}$ if and only if there is a propositional selection function f for $\mathcal{W}$ such that for all α :*

$$\mathcal{W} \ominus [\alpha] = \mathcal{W} \cup f([\neg\alpha]).$$

Note the similarity between this definition and the Harper identity. For belief sets, contraction is the simpler type of operation, from which revision is defined. For propositions, revision is the simpler of the two operations, and contraction is defined in terms of revision.

The propositional contraction operators on $[A]$ coincide exactly with the partial meet contractions on A. Instead of proving this from scratch, we can apply the Levi and Harper identities to the results already obtained for revision.

OBSERVATION 3.69 (Adam Grove [41]) *Let A be a belief set. Then:*

1. *If $\div$ is an operator of partial meet contraction for A, then there is a propositional contraction operator $\ominus$ for $[A]$ such that $A \div \alpha = \bigcap([A] \ominus [\alpha])$ for all sentences α.*
2. *If $\ominus$ is a propositional contraction operator for $[A]$, then the operator $\div$ for A such that $A \div \alpha = \bigcap([A] \ominus [\alpha])$ for all sentences α is an operator of partial meet contraction.*

Proof. *Part 1*: Let $*$ be the partial meet revision that is obtained from $\div$ through the Levi identity. It follows from Observation 3.67 that there is a propositional revision operator $\circledast$ for $[A]$ such that $A * \alpha = \bigcap([A] \circledast [\alpha])$ for all α. Let f be the propositional selection function on which $\circledast$ is based, and let $\ominus$ be the propositional contraction operator that is based on f. We then have $A * \alpha = \bigcap f([\alpha])$ for all α, and:

$$\begin{aligned}
A \div \alpha &= A \cap (A * \neg\alpha) \text{ (Harper identity)}\\
&= A \cap (\bigcap f([\neg\alpha])) \text{ (see above)}\\
&= (\bigcap [A]) \cap (\bigcap f([\neg\alpha])) \text{ (Observation 3.27)}\\
&= \bigcap([A] \cup f([\neg\alpha]))\\
&= \bigcap([A] \ominus [\alpha])).
\end{aligned}$$

Part 2: Let f be the propositional selection function on which $\ominus$ is based. Then the operator $\circledast$ such that $[A] \circledast [\alpha] = f([\alpha])$ for all α is a propositional revision operator, and according to Observation 3.67 there is some partial meet revision $*$

such that $A * \alpha = \bigcap([A] \circledast [\alpha]) = \bigcap f([\alpha])$ for all α. We have:

$$\begin{aligned} A \div \alpha &= \bigcap([A] \ominus [\alpha]) \\ &= \bigcap([A] \cup f([\neg\alpha])) \quad \text{(Definition 3.68)} \\ &= (\bigcap[A]) \cap (\bigcap f([\neg\alpha])) \\ &= A \cap (\bigcap f([\neg\alpha])) \quad \text{(Observation 3.27)} \\ &= A \cap f([\neg\alpha]) \\ &= A \cap (A * \neg\alpha) \end{aligned}$$

It follows from the Harper identity (Observation 3.15) that $A \div \alpha$ is a partial meet contraction. ■

The propositional counterparts of maxichoice contraction and full meet contraction are quite simple. A partial meet contraction $\div$ is maxichoice if and only if it holds for all non-tautological α that $[A \div \alpha] = [A] \cup \{W\}$ for some $W \in [\neg\alpha]$. It is full meet if and only if $[A \div \alpha] = [A] \cup [\neg\alpha]$ whenever the contraction is belief-contravening. The proof for maxichoice contraction makes use of Grove's bijection (Observation 1.64).

OBSERVATION 3.70 (Adam Grove [41]) *Let A be logically closed, $\div$ an operator of partial meet contraction for A and $\ominus$ a propositional contraction operator for $[A]$ such that $A \div \alpha = \bigcap([A] \ominus [\alpha])$ for all α. Let f be the propositional selection function on which $\ominus$ is based. Then $\div$ is maxichoice if and only if it holds for all α that $f([\alpha])$ has at most one element.*

Proof. $\div$ is an operator of maxichoice contraction if and only if $A \div \alpha \in A \bot \alpha$ for all non-tautological α, i.e. by Observation 1.64, if and only if $[A \div \alpha] = [A] \cup \{W\}$ for some $W \in [\neg\alpha]$. ■

OBSERVATION 3.71 (Adam Grove [41]) *Let A be logically closed, $\sim$ the operator of full meet contraction for A and $\ominus$ the propositional contraction operator for $[A]$ that is based on a propositional selection function such that $f([\alpha]) = [\alpha]$ whenever $[A] \cap [\alpha] = \emptyset$. Then $A \sim \alpha = \cap([A] \ominus [\alpha])$ for all α.*

Proof. *Case 1*, $\alpha \notin A$: Then $[A] \cap [\neg\alpha] \neq \emptyset$, and clause (III) of Definition 3.65 yields $f([\neg\alpha]) = [A] \cap [\neg\alpha]$. Hence $\bigcap([A] \ominus [\alpha]) = \bigcap([A] \cup f([\neg\alpha])) = \bigcap([A]) = A$. Since $\alpha \notin A$, $A \sim \alpha = A$, and this case is finished.

Case 2, $\alpha \in A$: Then $[A] \cap [\neg\alpha] = \emptyset$, and it follows from the condition given in the observation that $f([\neg\alpha]) = [\neg\alpha]$. Thus, $[A] \ominus [\alpha] = [A] \cup f([\neg\alpha]) = [A] \cup [\neg\alpha]$. It also follows from $\alpha \in A$ by Observation 2.12 that $A \sim \alpha = A \cap \mathrm{Cn}(\{\neg\alpha\}) = (\bigcap[A]) \cap (\bigcap[\neg\alpha]) = \bigcap([A] \cup [\neg\alpha])$. This finishes the proof of the second case. ■

Exercises

180. Let A and B be logically closed sets and α and β sentences. Show the following:

   (a) If $W \in \mathcal{L}\bot\!\!\bot$, then $W \in [\alpha]$ if and only if $W \notin [\neg\alpha]$.
   (b) $A \subseteq B$ if and only if $[B] \subseteq [A]$.
   (c) $[\mathrm{Cn}(A \cup B)] = [A] \cap [B]$
   (d) $[A] \cup [B] \subseteq [A \cap B]$
   (e) $[\alpha] \subseteq [\beta]$ if and only if $\vdash \alpha \rightarrow \beta$.
   (f) $[\alpha \& \beta] = [\alpha] \cap [\beta]$
   (g) $[\alpha \vee \beta] = [\alpha] \cup [\beta]$
   (h) $[\alpha \rightarrow \beta] = [\neg\alpha] \cup [\beta]$
   (i) $[\alpha \rightarrow \beta] \cap [\beta \rightarrow \alpha] = [\alpha \& \beta] \cup [\neg\alpha \& \neg\beta]$

181. Let A be a finite set and (as in Section 3.17$^+$) let $n(A)$ be the disjunction of the negations of elements of A, so that if $A = \{\alpha_1, \ldots \alpha_n\}$, then $n(A) = \neg\alpha_1 \vee \ldots \vee \neg\alpha_n$. Show that $W \in [\mathrm{Cn}(A)]$ if and only if $W \notin [n(A)]$.

182. What are, in formal language, the counterparts for propositional revision and contraction of:

   (a) the Levi identity
   (b) the Harper identity

183. What is the propositional counterpart of

   (a) maxichoice revision?
   (b) full meet revision?

24$^+$ SPHERE-BASED MODELS

The most interesting connection between operations on belief sets and on propositions makes use of (concentric) spheres around a proposition. This construction was developed by Adam Grove [41], who generalized the systems of spheres for conditional logic that were introduced by David Lewis in the early 1970s [75]. Whereas the innermost sphere in Lewis's system is a single possible world (representing the actual world), the innermost sphere in Grove's system is a proposition (that represents the present belief state).

DEFINITION 3.72 (Adam Grove [41]) *Let $\mathcal{W}$ be a proposition. A set $\mathfrak{S}$ of subsets of $\mathcal{L}\bot\!\!\bot$ is a* system of spheres centered on $\mathcal{W}$ *if and only if:*

1. *If $S_1, S_2 \in \mathfrak{S}$, then either $S_1 \subseteq S_2$ or $S_2 \subseteq S_1$.*
2. *$\mathcal{W} \in \mathfrak{S}$, and $\mathcal{W} \subseteq S$ for all $S \in \mathfrak{S}$.*
3. *$\mathcal{L}\bot\!\!\bot \in \mathfrak{S}$.*

4. *For all sentences* α *and spheres* $S \in \mathfrak{S}$, *if* $[\alpha] \cap S \neq \emptyset$, *then there is some* $S' \in \mathfrak{S}$ *such that* $[\alpha] \cap S' \neq \emptyset$ *and that* $[\alpha] \cap S'' = \emptyset$ *for all* $S'' \in \mathfrak{S}$ *such that* $S'' \subset S'$.

(1) says that spheres are concentric (totally ordered by set inclusion). (2) says that $\mathcal{W}$ itself is the minimal sphere. When applying this definition, we will assume that $\mathcal{W} = [A]$ for some belief set A. It then follows from the combination of (1) and (2) that a possible world is as close as possible to $[A]$ if and only if it is an element of $[A]$. (3) says that the set of all possible worlds ($\mathcal{L}\perp^{\perp}$, the rectangle in the diagrams) is itself the maximal sphere, i.e. the sphere that represents the lowest degree of similarity with $\mathcal{W}$. Thus, all possible worlds have at least some degree of similarity with $\mathcal{W}$ (namely at least the lowest degree).

It follows from (3) that for any sentence α, if α is consistent, then $[\alpha]$ intersects with a some sphere (i.e. there is some $S \in \mathfrak{S}$ such that $[\alpha] \cap S \neq \emptyset$). We can therefore read (4) as follows: If a sentence α is consistent, then there is a smallest sphere that intersects with $[\alpha]$. This condition is trivially true if the number of spheres is finite. If there are an infinite number of spheres, however, it need not hold. This can be shown with the following variation of an example from Lewis [75]:

Let the language contain all sentences l_x where x is a non-negative real number. Let $\vdash l_x \rightarrow l_y$ hold if and only if $x \geq y$. For each non-negative real number x, let $S_x = [\mathrm{Cn}(\{l_x\})]$. Let $A = \mathrm{Cn}(\{l_0\}), \mathcal{W} = [A]$, and $\alpha = \neg l_0$. In order to verify that (4) is not satisfied, let S_x be any sphere such that $S_x \cap [\neg l_0] \neq \emptyset$. Then $x > 0$, and it follows from $x > x/2 > 0$ that $S_{x/2} \subset S_x$ and also that $S_{x/2} \cap [\neg l_0] \neq \emptyset$. To make this example concrete, for each x let l_x denote that the Eiffel Tower is at least x meters higher than the Empire State Building. This system of spheres represents the eccentric (but logically handy) behaviour of a person who believes that the Eiffel Tower is not higher than the Empire State Building, and who measures the similarity of a possible world to his present belief state in terms of how much higher the Empire State Building is than the Eiffel Tower in that world.

It should be clear from this example that (4) is not a redundant condition if $\mathfrak{S}$ is infinite. The need for (4) can be seen from the informal description in Section 3.8 of how the sphere system is used for belief revision. When revising by α, we search for the minimal sphere that intersects with $[\alpha]$, so for revision to be well-defined there must be such a minimal intersecting sphere.

Sphere-based propositional revision and contraction can be defined in terms of propositional selection functions that are based on a system of spheres:

DEFINITION 3.73 (Adam Grove [41]) *A propositional selection function f for a proposition* $\mathcal{W}$ *is* sphere-based *if and only if it there is a system* $\mathfrak{S}$ *of spheres around* $\mathcal{W}$ *such that for all* α: *if* $[\alpha]$ *is non-empty, then* $f([\alpha])$ *is the intersection of* $[\alpha]$ *with the smallest (inclusion-minimal) element of* $\mathfrak{S}$ *that has a non-empty intersection with* $[\alpha]$.

Let $\circledast$ *be a propositional revision operator for* $[A]$. *Then it is an operator of* sphere-based revision *if and only if it is based on a sphere-based propositional selection function.*

Let $\ominus$ *be a propositional contraction operator for* $[A]$. *Then it is an operator of* sphere-based contraction *if and only if it is based on a sphere-based propositional selection function.*

Note that clause 2 of Definition 3.72 ($\mathcal{W}$ is the smallest element of $\mathfrak{S}$) is necessary for this definition to be compatible with clause III of Definition 3.65 (if $\mathcal{W} \cap [\alpha] \neq \emptyset$, then $f([\alpha]) = \mathcal{W} \cap [\alpha]$).

The following theorem connects sphere-based revision to partial meet revision:

THEOREM 3.74 (Adam Grove [41]) *Let* A *be logically closed.*

1. *Let* $*$ *be an operator of transitively relational partial meet revision for* A. *Then there is a sphere-based revision operator* $\circledast$ *for* $[A]$ *such that* $A * \alpha = \bigcap([A]\circledast[\alpha])$ *for all sentences* α.
2. *Let* $\circledast$ *be a sphere-based revision operator for* $[A]$. *Let* $*$ *be the operator for* A *such that* $A * \alpha = \bigcap([A]\circledast[\alpha])$ *for all* α. *Then* $*$ *is an operator of transitively relational partial meet revision for* A.

Proof. PART 1: *The construction*: We are going to use the following construction: $\mathfrak{S}$ is the set of subsets of $\mathcal{L}\bot\bot$ such that $S \in \mathfrak{S}$ if and only if either

1. $S = \mathcal{L}\bot\bot$,
2. $S = [A]$, or
3. $S \subseteq \{W \mid W \in [A * \alpha]$ for some $\alpha \in \mathcal{L}\}$ and $[A * \alpha] \subseteq S$ for all α such that $S \cap [\alpha] \neq \emptyset$.

There are two facts that we have to prove about $\mathfrak{S}$: that $\mathfrak{S}$ is a system of spheres, and that the revision operator that is based on $\mathfrak{S}$ coincides with $*$ as stated in the theorem.

Comment: Clauses (i) and (ii) ensure that the minimal and maximal spheres are included. (Clause (ii) is redundant if A is consistent, since it then follows from (iii) by letting α be a tautology.)

Clause (iii) is somewhat less transparent. First of all, the requirement $S \subseteq \{W \mid W \in [A * \alpha]$ for some $\alpha \in \mathcal{L}\}$ ensures that worlds that cannot be reached through revision of A have the lowest degree of closeness to $[A]$, i.e. they are elements of no other sphere than the maximal sphere $\mathcal{L}\bot\bot$. The condition that $[A * \alpha] \subseteq S$ for all α such that $S \cap [\alpha] \neq \emptyset$ can perhaps best be understood from Figure 3.10. The condition $S \cap [\alpha] \neq \emptyset$ is satisfied by S_2, S_3, and S_4 in the diagram. Since S_2 is the minimal of these, if the theorem is correct then S_2 should contain $[A * \alpha]$. It should follow from this that S_3 and S_4 also cointain $[A * \alpha]$.

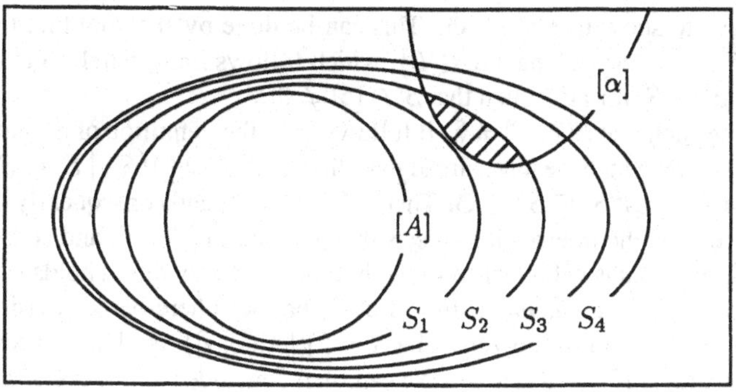

Figure 3.10.

Verification that $\mathfrak{S}$ *is a system of spheres*: We have to verify the four conditions of Definition 3.72.

First condition ($S_1 \subseteq S_2$ or $S_2 \subseteq S_1$): Suppose to the contrary that $S_1 \not\subseteq S_2 \not\subseteq S_1$. There is then some $W_1 \in S_1 \backslash S_2$. Then $W_1 \in [A * \alpha_1]$ for some sentence α_1, and by *success*, $\alpha_1 \in A * \alpha_1$ and thus $[A * \alpha_1] \subseteq [\alpha_1]$, so that $S_1 \cap [\alpha_1] \neq \emptyset$, and thus, by the construction of $\mathfrak{S}$, $[A * \alpha_1] \subseteq S_1$. On the other hand, it follows from $W_1 \notin S_2$ that $S_2 \cap [\alpha_1] = \emptyset$. (Since $S_2 \cap [\alpha_1] \neq \emptyset$ would imply $[A * \alpha_1] \subseteq S_2$ and thus $W_1 \in S_2$.) Thus, $S_2 \subseteq [\neg\alpha_1]$.

In the same way we can verify that there is some $W_2 \in S_2 \backslash S_1$, and consequently some α_2 such that $[A * \alpha_2] \subseteq S_2$ and $S_1 \subseteq [\neg\alpha_2]$.

Since $[\alpha_1] \subseteq [\alpha_1 \vee \alpha_2]$, we can conclude from $S_1 \cap [\alpha_1] \neq \emptyset$ that $S_1 \cap [\alpha_1 \vee \alpha_2] \neq \emptyset$ and thus $[A*(\alpha_1 \vee \alpha_2)] \subseteq S_1$. In the same way it follows that $[A*(\alpha_1 \vee \alpha_2)] \subseteq S_2$. Since $S_1 \subseteq [\neg\alpha_2]$ and $S_2 \subseteq [\neg\alpha_1]$, we therefore have $[A*(\alpha_1 \vee \alpha_2)] \subseteq S_1 \cap S_2 \subseteq [\neg\alpha_1] \cap [\neg\alpha_2] = [\neg\alpha_1 \& \neg\alpha_2]$, and thus $\bigcap[\neg\alpha_1 \& \neg\alpha_2] \subseteq \bigcap[A * (\alpha_1 \vee \alpha_2)]$, i.e. $\neg\alpha_1 \& \neg\alpha_2 \in A * (\alpha_1 \vee \alpha_2)$.

It follows from $W_1 \in [A * \alpha_1]$ that α_1 is consistent and from $W_2 \in [A * \alpha_2]$ that α_2 is consistent. Thus $\alpha_1 \vee \alpha_2$ is consistent, and it follows from *success* and *consistency* that $\neg\alpha_1 \& \neg\alpha_2 \notin A * (\alpha_1 \vee \alpha_2)$. This contradiction concludes this part of the proof.

Second condition: It follows directly from the definition of $\mathfrak{S}$ that $[A] \in \mathfrak{S}$. We also have to show that $[A] \subseteq S$ for all $S \in \mathfrak{S}$. In clauses (i) and (ii) of the definition of $\mathfrak{S}$, this follows directly. In clause (iii), note that for all $S \in \mathfrak{S}$, $S \cap [\top] \neq \emptyset$ so that $[A * \top] \subseteq S$ which is, by *vacuity*, equivalent to $[A] \subseteq S$.

Third condition: Directly from the definition of $\mathfrak{S}$.

Fourth condition: Let $[\alpha] \cap S \neq \emptyset$. We need to show that there is some minimal sphere S' such that $[\alpha] \cap S' \neq \emptyset$. Let S' be the intersection of all S such that $[\alpha] \cap S \neq \emptyset$.

We have to show that $S' \in \mathfrak{S}$. This can be done by showing first that $S' \subseteq \{W \mid W \in [A * \alpha]$ for some $\alpha \in \mathcal{L}\}$, which follows immediately, and secondly that $[A * \beta] \subseteq S'$ for all β such that $S' \cap [\beta] \neq \emptyset$.

Let β be such that $S' \cap [\beta] \neq \emptyset$. It follows from the definition of S' and the first condition on $\mathfrak{S}$, which we have already verified, that $S' = \bigcap\{S'' \mid S' \subseteq S'' \in \mathfrak{S}\}$. Let S'' be such that $S' \subseteq S'' \in \mathfrak{S}$. Then $S'' \cap [\beta] \neq \emptyset$, and consequently $[A * \beta] \subseteq S''$. Hence S' is the intersection of sets that all contain $[A * \beta]$, and consequently $[A * \beta] \subseteq S'$. This is sufficient to show that the fourth condition holds.

Verification of coincidence with $*$: Let $\circledast$ be the sphere-based revision that is based on $\mathfrak{S}$. We need to show that $A * \alpha = \bigcap([A]\circledast[\alpha])$ for all sentences α.

This is simple if $\neg\alpha \in \text{Cn}(\emptyset)$. We can then conclude from *success* that $A * \alpha$ is inconsistent, and from *closure* that $A * \alpha = \mathcal{L}$. Furthermore, since $[\alpha] = \emptyset$, it follows that $[A]\circledast[\alpha] = \emptyset$ and thus $\bigcap([A]\circledast[\alpha]) = \mathcal{L}$.

Now let us turn to the principal case, when $\neg\alpha \notin \text{Cn}(\emptyset)$. We are going to use the following set:

$$S = \bigcup\{[A * \beta] \mid [\alpha] \subseteq [\beta]\}.$$

We need to show (1) that $S \in \mathfrak{S}$, (2) that S is the minimal sphere that intersects with $[\alpha]$, and (3) that $S \cap [\alpha] = [A * \alpha]$. Since it follows from (1) and (2) that $[A]\circledast[\alpha] = S \cap [\alpha]$, and $A * \alpha = \bigcap[A * \alpha]$, this is sufficient to prove that $A * \alpha = \bigcap([A]\circledast[\alpha])$.

(1) We are first going to show that $S \in \mathfrak{S}$. This can be done by verifying that if $[\delta] \cap S \neq \emptyset$, then $[A*\delta] \subseteq S$. Let $[\delta] \cap S \neq \emptyset$. It follows from our definition of S that $[\delta] \cap [A * \beta] \neq \emptyset$ for some β such that $[\alpha] \subseteq [\beta]$. We then have $[\alpha] \subseteq [\beta] \subseteq [\beta \vee \delta]$, and the definition of S yields $[A * (\beta \vee \delta)] \subseteq S$.

Suppose that $\neg\delta \in A*(\beta\vee\delta)$. It follows from *success* and *consistency* that $\neg\delta \notin A * \delta$. We can therefore use *disjunctive factoring* (Observation 3.51) to conclude that $A * (\beta\vee\delta) = A * \beta$. Since $\neg\delta \in A * (\beta\vee\delta)$ we then have $\neg\delta \in A * \beta$. This contradicts our assumption that $[\delta] \cap [A * \beta] \neq \emptyset$, and we can conclude from this contradiction that $\neg\delta \notin A * (\beta\vee\delta)$.

Subexpansion and $\neg\delta \notin A * (\beta\vee\delta)$ yield $A * (\beta\vee\delta) + \delta \subseteq A * ((\beta\vee\delta)\&\delta)$. It can be concluded from *extensionality* that $A * (\beta\vee\delta) + \delta \subseteq A * \delta$ and thus $A * (\beta\vee\delta) \subseteq A * \delta$. It follows from this that $[A * \delta] \subseteq [A * (\beta\vee\delta)]$, and since we already know that $[A * (\beta\vee\delta)] \subseteq S$, we can conclude that $[A * \delta] \subseteq S$, which is what we needed to show that S is a sphere.

(2) It follows from the definition of S (by letting $\beta = \alpha$) that $[A * \alpha] \subseteq S$. By *success*, $[A * \alpha] \subseteq [\alpha]$, so that $S \cap [\alpha] \neq \emptyset$. In order to show that S is the minimal sphere with this property, let $S' \subset S$. There is then, by the definition of S, some β such that $[\alpha] \subseteq [\beta]$ and $[A*\beta] \not\subseteq S'$. It follows from $[A*\beta] \not\subseteq S'$, by the definition of $\mathfrak{S}$, that $S' \cap [\beta] = \emptyset$. Since $[\alpha] \subseteq [\beta]$ it follows that $S' \cap [\alpha] = \emptyset$.

(3) Our next task is to show that $[A*\alpha] = S \cap [\alpha]$. It follows from the definition of S (by letting $\beta = \alpha$) that $[A*\alpha] \subseteq S$, and it follows from *success* that $[A*\alpha] \subseteq$

$[\alpha]$, so that $[A * \alpha] \subseteq S \cap [\alpha]$. It remains to be shown that $S \cap [\alpha] \subseteq [A * \alpha]$. It follows by set theory from the definition of S that

$$S \cap [\alpha] = \bigcup\{[\alpha] \cap [A * \beta] \mid [\alpha] \subseteq [\beta]\}$$

so we can complete our task by showing that if $W \in [\alpha] \cap [A * \beta]$ and $[\alpha] \subseteq [\beta]$, then $W \in [A * \alpha]$.

Let $W \in [\alpha] \cap [A * \beta]$ and $[\alpha] \subseteq [\beta]$. We then have $[\alpha] \cap [A * \beta] \neq \emptyset$, and consequently $\neg\alpha \notin A * \beta$. It follows from *superexpansion* and *subexpansion* that $A * \beta + \alpha = A * (\alpha\&\beta)$. It follows from $[\alpha] \subseteq [\beta]$ that $\vdash \alpha \rightarrow \beta$, and thus $\alpha\&\beta$ is equivalent with α, so that *extensionality* yields $A * (\alpha\&\beta) = A * \alpha$. We therefore have $A * \beta + \alpha = A * \alpha$, from which follows $[A * \beta + \alpha] = [A * \alpha]$, and (by Observation 3.64) $[A * \beta] \cap [\alpha] = [A * \alpha]$. We can therefore conclude from $W \in [\alpha] \cap [A * \beta]$ that $W \in [A * \alpha]$. This finishes this part of the proof.

PART 2: It follows from Observation 3.67 that $*$ is an operator of partial meet revision. To show that it is transitively relational it is, according to Theorem 3.25, sufficient to show that it satisfies superexpansion and subexpansion.

Superexpansion: Let S_α be the minimal sphere that intersects with $[\alpha]$ and $S_{\alpha\&\beta}$ the minimal sphere that intersects with $[\alpha\&\beta]$. Since $[\alpha\&\beta] \subseteq [\alpha]$, $S_{\alpha\&\beta}$ intersects with $[\alpha]$, and due to the minimality of S_α we can conclude that $S_\alpha \subseteq S_{\alpha\&\beta}$. Given this, we have:

$[\alpha] \cap [\beta] \cap S_\alpha \subseteq [\alpha] \cap [\beta] \cap S_{\alpha\&\beta}$
$[\alpha] \cap S_\alpha \cap [\beta] \subseteq [\alpha\&\beta] \cap S_{\alpha\&\beta}$ (cf. Exercise 180f)
$([A] \circledast [\alpha]) \cap [\beta] \subseteq ([A] \circledast [\alpha\&\beta])$ (Definition 3.73)
$([A] \circledast [\alpha]) \oplus [\beta] \subseteq ([A] \circledast [\alpha\&\beta])$ (Definition 3.63)
$\bigcap([A] \circledast [\alpha\&\beta]) \subseteq \bigcap(([A] \circledast [\alpha]) \oplus [\beta])$
$\bigcap([A] \circledast [\alpha\&\beta]) \subseteq \bigcap([A] \circledast [\alpha]) + \beta$ (Observation 3.64)
$A * (\alpha\&\beta) \subseteq (A * \alpha) + \beta$

Subexpansion: Let $A * \alpha \nvdash \neg\beta$. Then:

$(A * \alpha) + \beta$ is consistent
$\bigcap[A * \alpha] + \beta$ is consistent (Observation 3.27)
$\bigcap([A * \alpha] \oplus [\beta])$ is consistent (Observation 3.64)
$[A * \alpha] \oplus [\beta] \neq \emptyset$
$[A * \alpha] \cap [\beta] \neq \emptyset$ (Definition 3.63)
$[\alpha] \cap S_\alpha \cap [\beta] \neq \emptyset$ (Definitions 3.66 and 3.73)
$[\alpha\&\beta] \cap S_\alpha \neq \emptyset$ (cf. Exercise 180f)
$[\alpha\&\beta] \cap S_{\alpha\&\beta} \subseteq [\alpha\&\beta] \cap S_\alpha$ (definition of $S_{\alpha\&\beta}$)
$[\alpha\&\beta] \cap S_{\alpha\&\beta} \subseteq [\alpha] \cap S_\alpha \cap [\beta]$ (cf. Exercise 180f)

The rest of the proof of *subexpansion* is almost identical to the derivation of *superexpansion*. (Just exchange the left-hand and right-hand parts of the expressions.)

■

Exercises

184. Let $\mathfrak{S}$ be a system of spheres. Let S_α be the minimal sphere that intersects with $[\alpha]$ and S_β the minimal sphere that intersects with $[\beta]$.
    (a) Show that if $[\beta] \cap S_\alpha \neq \emptyset$, then $S_\beta \subseteq S_\alpha$.
    (b) Show that if $\vdash \alpha \rightarrow \beta$, then $S_\beta \subseteq S_\alpha$.
    (c) Show that if $[\alpha] \cap S_\beta \neq \emptyset$ and $[\beta] \cap S_\alpha \neq \emptyset$ then $S_\alpha = S_\beta$.

25+ SPHERE-BASED AND ENTRENCHMENT-BASED REVISION

Sphere systems provide us with a neat interpretation of epistemic entrenchment. For any sentence δ, let S_δ be the minimal sphere that intersects with $[\delta]$. We can then define a relation $\leq$ such that $\alpha \leq \beta$ whenever $S_{\neg\alpha} \subseteq S_{\neg\beta}$.

S_δ is undefined in the limiting case when no sphere, not even the maximal sphere $\mathcal{L}\bot\!\!\!\!\bot$, intersects with $[\delta]$. This is the case when δ is inconsistent, i.e., $\neg\delta$ is a tautology. In order to cover this case we have to add the extra clause that $\alpha \leq \beta$ holds if $[\neg\beta]$ intersects with no sphere.

The relation $\leq$ defined in this way satisfies the standard entrenchment postulates. To prove this, we only need the properties of spheres that we are already acquainted with.

OBSERVATION 3.75 (Adam Grove [35; 41]) *Given a system $\mathfrak{S}$ of spheres, for any sentence δ, let S_δ be the minimal sphere that intersects with $[\delta]$. Furthermore, let $\leq$ be the relation such that $\alpha \leq \beta$ if and only if either $S_{\neg\alpha} \subseteq S_{\neg\beta}$ or $[\neg\beta]$ intersects with no element of $\mathfrak{S}$.*
Then $\leq$ satisfies the standard entrenchment postulates transitivity, dominance, conjunctiveness, minimality, and maximality.

Proof. *Transitivity*: Let $\alpha \leq \beta$ and $\beta \leq \delta$. There are four (potential) cases:

Case 1, $S_{\neg\alpha} \subseteq S_{\neg\beta}$ and $S_{\neg\beta} \subseteq S_{\neg\delta}$: It follows that $S_{\neg\alpha} \subseteq S_{\neg\delta}$, so that $\alpha \leq \delta$.

Case 2, $S_{\neg\alpha} \subseteq S_{\neg\beta}$ and $[\neg\delta]$ intersects with no element of $\mathfrak{S}$: It follows directly that $\alpha \leq \delta$.

Case 3, $[\neg\beta]$ intersects with no element of $\mathfrak{S}$, and $S_{\neg\beta} \subseteq S_{\neg\delta}$: This is impossible.

Case 4, Neither $[\neg\beta]$ nor $[\neg\delta]$intersects with any element of $\mathfrak{S}$: It follows directly that $\alpha \leq \delta$.

Dominance: Let $\alpha \vdash \beta$. Then $\neg\beta \vdash \neg\alpha$. There are two cases:

Case 1, $[\neg\beta]$ intersects with some element of $\mathfrak{S}$: Then so does $[\neg\alpha]$, and it follows (cf. Exercise 184b) that $S_{\neg\alpha} \subseteq S_{\neg\beta}$, i.e. $\alpha \leq \beta$.

Case 2, $[\neg\beta]$ does not intersect with any element of $\mathfrak{S}$: It follows directly that $\alpha \leq \beta$.

Conjunctiveness: Again there are two cases.

Case 1, $\alpha\&\beta$ intersects with some element of $\mathfrak{S}$: We have $S_{\neg(\alpha\&\beta)} = S_{\neg\alpha\vee\neg\beta}$. Since $S_{\neg\alpha\vee\neg\beta}$ contains some world in which $\neg\alpha\vee\neg\beta$ holds, it follows from Observation 1.57 that it either contains some world in which $\neg\alpha$ holds or some world in which $\neg\beta$ holds. In the former case, we have $S_{\neg\alpha} = S_{\neg\alpha\vee\neg\beta} = S_{\neg(\alpha\&\beta)}$ and thus $\alpha \leq \alpha\&\beta$. In the latter case, $\beta \leq \alpha\&\beta$ follows in the same way.

Case 2, $\alpha\&\beta$ intersects with no element of $\mathfrak{S}$: Then both $\alpha \leq \alpha\&\beta$ and $\beta \leq \alpha\&\beta$ follow directly.

Minimality:

$\alpha \notin A$
iff $[A] \not\subseteq [\alpha]$
iff $[A] \cap [\neg\alpha] \neq \emptyset$
iff $S_{\neg\alpha} \subseteq [A]$ (since $[A]$ is a sphere)
iff $S_{\neg\alpha} \subseteq S_{\neg\beta}$ for all β (since $[A]$ is the minimal sphere)
iff $\alpha \leq \beta$ for all β

Maximality: $\beta \leq \alpha$ for all β holds if and only if $[\neg\alpha]$ intersects with no sphere, if and only if $\neg\alpha$ is inconsistent, if and only if $\vdash \alpha$. ■

Next, let us verify that the entrenchment ordering thus defined gives rise to an operator of contraction that coincides with the sphere-based contraction that we can obtain from the same system of spheres.

OBSERVATION 3.76 (Adam Grove [35; 41]) *Given a system $\mathfrak{S}$ of spheres for the belief set A, let $\leq$ be the relation defined in Observation 3.75. Let $\div_G$ be Gärdenfors's entrenchment-based contraction on A, based on $\leq$. Furthermore, let $\ominus$ be the sphere-based contraction operator that is based on $\mathfrak{S}$. Then for all sentences α: $A\div_G\alpha = \bigcap([A]\ominus[\alpha])$.*

Proof. *Case 1*, $\vdash \alpha$: Then $[A]\ominus[\alpha] = [A]$, and thus $\bigcap([A]\ominus[\alpha]) = \bigcap[A] = A$. Furthermore, it follows from $(G\div)$ (Section 2.10) that $A\div_G\alpha = A$. Thus, $\bigcap([A]\ominus[\alpha]) = A\div_G\alpha$.

Case 2, $\not\vdash \alpha$: Then :

$$\begin{aligned}
&\bigcap([A]\ominus[\alpha]) = \bigcap([A] \cup ([\neg\alpha] \cap S_{\neg\alpha}))\\
&= \bigcap[A] \cap \bigcap([\neg\alpha] \cap S_{\neg\alpha})\\
&= A \cap \{\beta \mid \text{If } W \in ([\neg\alpha] \cap S_{\neg\alpha}), \text{ then } \beta \in W\}\\
&= A \cap \{\beta \mid \text{If } \neg\alpha \in W \text{ and } W \in S_{\neg\alpha}, \text{ then } \beta \in W\}\\
&= A \cap \{\beta \mid \text{If } \neg\alpha \in W \text{ and } W \in S_{\neg\alpha}, \text{ then } \neg\beta \notin W\}\\
&= A \cap \{\beta \mid \text{If } \neg\alpha \in W \text{ and } W \in S_{\neg\alpha}, \text{ then } \neg\alpha\&\neg\beta \notin W\}\\
&= A \cap \{\beta \mid S_{\neg\alpha} \subset S_{\neg\alpha\&\neg\beta}\}\\
&= A \cap \{\beta \mid S_{\neg\alpha} \subset S_{\neg(\alpha\vee\beta)}\}\\
&= A \cap \{\beta \mid \alpha < \alpha\vee\beta\}\\
&= \{\beta \mid \beta \in A \text{ and } \alpha < \alpha\vee\beta\}\\
&= A\div_G\alpha.
\end{aligned}$$

■

Rott's entrenchment-based contraction can also be exactly characterized in terms of spheres:

OBSERVATION 3.77 *Given a system $\mathfrak{S}$ of spheres for the belief set A, let $\leq$ be the relation defined in Observation 3.75. Let $\div_R$ be Rott's entrenchment-based contraction on A, based on $\leq$. Then for all sentences α:*
$A \div_R \alpha = \bigcap S_{\neg\alpha}$ *unless* $\neg\alpha$ *intersects with no sphere, in which case* $A \div_R \alpha = A$.

Proof. *Case 1*, $\neg\alpha$ intersects with no sphere: Then $\vdash \alpha$. It follows from $(R\div)$ (Section 2.10) that $A \div_R \alpha = A$.

Case 2, $\neg\alpha$ intersects with some sphere:

$\bigcap S_{\neg\alpha} = \{\beta \mid \text{If } W \in S_{\neg\alpha}, \text{ then } \beta \in W\}$
$= \{\beta \mid \text{If } W \in S_{\neg\alpha}, \text{ then } W \in [\beta]\}$
$= \{\beta \mid S_{\neg\alpha} \subseteq [\beta]\}$
$= \{\beta \mid [A] \subseteq [\beta] \text{ and } S_{\neg\alpha} \subseteq [\beta]\}$ ($[A]$ is the minimal sphere, hence $[A] \subseteq S_{\neg\alpha}$)
$= \{\beta \mid \beta \in A \text{ and } S_{\neg\alpha} \subset S_{\neg\beta}\}$
$= \{\beta \mid \beta \in A \text{ and } \alpha < \beta\}$
$= A \div_R \alpha.$ ■

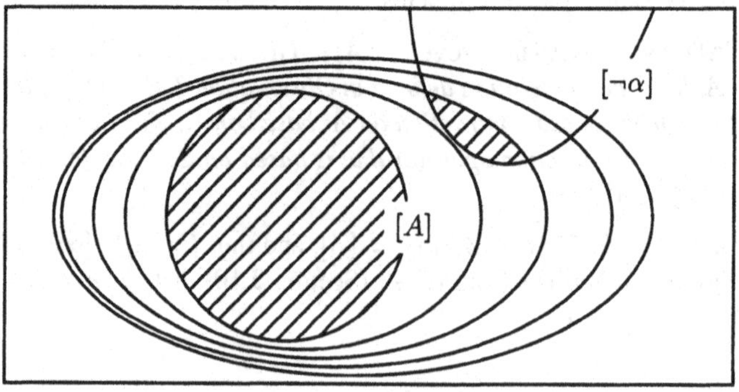

Figure 3.11. Gärdenfors's entrenchment-based contraction of A by α.

The relation between $\div_G$ and $\div_R$ is illustrated in Figures 3.11 and 3.12. It can be seen from the diagrams (and it also follows directly from Observations 3.76 and 3.77) that for all α, $A \div_R \alpha \subseteq A \div_G \alpha$. The diagrams also provide a plausible background for the proposal by Lindström and Rabinowicz that was mentioned in Section 2.10, namely that a realistic entrenchment-based contraction should be positioned somewhere between $\div_R$ and $\div_G$. [79]

The following observation can be used to base revision directly on an entrenchment ordering, without referring to a contraction operator:

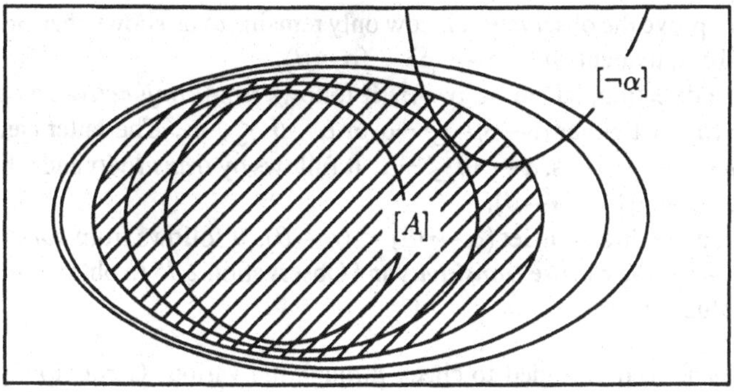

Figure 3.12. Rott's entrenchment-based contraction of A by α.

Let A be a belief set and $\leq$ a standard entrenchment ordering on A. (Thus, it satisfies *transitivity*, *dominance*, *conjunctiveness*, *minimality*, and *maximality*). Furthermore, let $\div_G$ and $\div_R$ be the entrenchment-based contraction operators according to the definitions in Section 2.10. Let $\mp_G = \mathbb{R}(\div_G)$ and $\mp_R = \mathbb{R}(\div_R)$. Then:

1. $\mp_G = \mp_R$
2. For all sentences α and β,
   $\beta \in A{\mp_G}\alpha$ if and only if either $(\alpha{\rightarrow}\neg\beta) < (\alpha{\rightarrow}\beta)$ or $\vdash \neg\alpha$.

[Observation 3.28.]

Proof. *Part 1*:

$\beta \in A{\mp_G}\alpha$
iff $\beta \in \text{Cn}((A{\div_G}\neg\alpha) \cup \{\alpha\})$ (Levi identity)
iff $\alpha{\rightarrow}\beta \in A{\div_G}\neg\alpha$ (deduction property, *closure*)
iff $\alpha{\rightarrow}\beta \in A$ and either $\neg\alpha < (\neg\alpha \vee (\alpha{\rightarrow}\beta))$ or $\vdash \neg\alpha$ (definition of $\div_G$)
iff $\alpha{\rightarrow}\beta \in A$ and either $\neg\alpha < (\alpha{\rightarrow}\beta)$ or $\vdash \neg\alpha$ (intersubstitutivity, Observation 2.92)
iff $\alpha{\rightarrow}\beta \in A{\div_R}\neg\alpha$ (definition of $\div_R$)
iff $\beta \in \text{Cn}((A{\div_R}\neg\alpha) \cup \{\alpha\})$ (deduction property, *closure*)
iff $\beta \in A{\mp_R}\alpha$ (Levi identity)

Part 2: We know from Part (1) that:

$$\beta \in A{\mp_G}\alpha \text{ iff } \alpha{\rightarrow}\beta \in A \text{ and either } \neg\alpha < (\alpha{\rightarrow}\beta) \text{ or } \vdash \neg\alpha.$$

It follows from $\neg\alpha < (\alpha{\rightarrow}\beta)$ by *minimality* that $\alpha{\rightarrow}\beta \in A$. Furthermore, since A is logically closed, $\alpha{\rightarrow}\beta \in A$ follows from $\vdash \neg\alpha$ as well. Thus:

$$\beta \in A{\mp_G}\alpha \text{ iff } \neg\alpha < \alpha{\rightarrow}\beta \text{ or } \vdash \neg\alpha.$$

In order to prove the observation it now only remains to be shown that $\neg\alpha < \alpha\rightarrow\beta$ is logically equivalent with $(\alpha\rightarrow\neg\beta) < (\alpha\rightarrow\beta)$.

For one direction, let $\neg\alpha < \alpha\rightarrow\beta$. It follows from *conjunctiveness* and *intersubstitutivity* that either $\alpha\rightarrow\neg\beta \leq \neg\alpha$ or $\alpha\rightarrow\beta \leq \neg\alpha$. The latter cannot hold, since $\neg\alpha < \alpha\rightarrow\beta$. Thus, $\alpha\rightarrow\neg\beta \leq \neg\alpha$. It follows by *transitivity* and Observation 2.75 that $(\alpha\rightarrow\neg\beta) < (\alpha\rightarrow\beta)$.

For the other direction, let $(\alpha\rightarrow\neg\beta) < (\alpha\rightarrow\beta)$. It follows from *dominance* that $\neg\alpha \leq \alpha\rightarrow\neg\beta$. We can use *transitivity* and Observation 2.75 to obtain $\neg\alpha < \alpha\rightarrow\beta$. This concludes the proof. ■

The reader is recommended to check through the various Gärdenfors postulates for contraction and revision, construct the appropriate diagrams, and verify that the postulates are satisfied in a spheres setting. In particular, note how straightforwardly *recovery* follows: $([A]\ominus[\alpha]) \oplus [\alpha] = ([A]\ominus[\alpha]) \cap [\alpha] = [A]$.

Exercise

185. Let A be a logically closed set and let $\leq$ be a standard entrenchment ordering on A. Let $\div_G$ and $\div_R$ be Gärdenfors's and Rott's entrenchment-based contraction operators, based on $\leq$. Let $\div$ be any operation such that for all α, $A\div_R\alpha \subseteq A\div\alpha \subseteq A\div_G\alpha$. Let $* = \mathbb{R}(\div)$. Show that for all α:
$\beta \in A * \alpha$ if and only if either $(\alpha\rightarrow\neg\beta) < (\alpha\rightarrow\beta)$ or $\vdash \neg\alpha$.

CHAPTER 4

HIDDEN STRUCTURES OF BELIEF

In Section 1.9, we discussed the influential proposal by Allen Newell that the behaviour of an intelligent system should be specifiable on the *knowledge level* [100]. On the knowledge level, the behaviour of the system is described entirely in terms of the contents of the knowledge (beliefs), and this description should be independent of the symbolic representation. Belief sets, and operations applied to belief sets, comply with this proposal. Belief bases, however, belong to the symbolic level.

On the other hand, belief bases have other advantages. Operations on belief bases are much more easily accessible to modelling on actual computers than are operations on belief sets. Furthermore, as we saw in Section 1.7, some features of belief change seem to be much more difficult to represent with operations that are applied to belief sets than with operations that are applied to belief bases.

At the conclusion of Section 1.9, we found ourselves facing a dilemma: Either we perform operations of change on belief bases. We then have computational tractability, but no exact characterization of what is happening on the knowledge level. Or else we perform operations of change on belief sets. We can then have an exact characterization of what happens on the knowledge level — this is what the AGM representation theorems do — but we lose in computational tractability and in expressive power.

This dilemma can be solved. It is possible to exactly characterize the operations on a belief set that can be generated by assigning to it a (finite) belief base and operators of contraction and revision that are applied to that belief base. Such *knowledge-level analysis of belief base operations* is the subject of this chapter.

1 BASE-GENERATED CONTRACTION

As has been pointed out by, among others, Bernhard Nebel [98] and André Fuhrmann [24], an operator of contraction on a belief base gives rise to an operator of contraction on its corresponding belief set. Let B be a belief base, and let $\mathbf{K}$ be the corresponding belief set, i.e. let $\mathbf{K} = \mathrm{Cn}(B)$. Furthermore, let $-$ be an operator of contraction on B. The way we have defined contraction (Definition 2.1) this means that (1) success is satisfied, i.e. for all non-tautological sentences α, $\alpha \notin \text{Cn}(B\text{–}\alpha)$, and (2) inclusion is satisfied, so that for all sentences α, $B\text{–}\alpha \subseteq B$.

Now let us define an operator $\div$ on $\mathbf{K}$ as follows:

$$\text{For all } \alpha, \mathbf{K}\div\alpha = \text{Cn}(B - \alpha).$$

It can easily be verified that $\div$ is an operator of contraction on $\mathbf{K}$. In other words, it satisfies success ($\alpha \notin \text{Cn}(\mathbf{K}\div\alpha)$ if α is non-tautological) and inclusion ($\mathbf{K}\div\alpha \subseteq \mathbf{K}$ for all α). In this way, every operator of belief base contraction generates an operator of belief set contraction.

The operator $\div$ on the closure $\text{Cn}(B)$ of B will be called the *closure* of the operator $-$ on B. More generally:

DEFINITION 4.1 *Let* $\circ$ *be an operator for a set* B. *The* closure *of* $\circ$ *is the operator* $\circ'$ *for* $\text{Cn}(B)$ *such that for all sentences* α*:*
$(\text{Cn}(B)) \circ' \alpha = \text{Cn}(B \circ \alpha)$

For simplicity, closures of various types of operations will be referred to as *base-generated* versions of those operations. (The operations that are applied directly to the belief set will be referred to as the *direct* versions.) Thus, the closure of an operator of partial meet contraction will be called a 'base-generated partial meet contraction'. The full definition is as follows:

DEFINITION 4.2 ([51]) *An operator* $\div$ *for a belief set* $\mathbf{K}$ *is a* base-generated partial meet contraction *if and only if there is a belief base* B *for* $\mathbf{K}$ *and an operator* $\sim_\gamma$ *of partial meet contraction for* B *such that for all sentences* α*:*$\mathbf{K}\div\alpha = \text{Cn}(B\sim_\gamma\alpha)$.

Other types of base-generated contraction are defined in the same way. As an example, $\div$ is an operator of base-generated full meet contraction for $\mathbf{K}$ if and only if there is some belief base B for $\mathbf{K}$ such that $\mathbf{K}\div\alpha = \text{Cn}(B \sim \alpha)$ for all α. Note that whereas every belief set $\mathbf{K}$ has exactly one operator of (direct) full meet contraction, it may have many operators of base-generated full meet contraction (generated from various belief bases for $\mathbf{K}$).

When studying the properties of base-generated contraction, it may be instructive to think of the belief set $\mathbf{K}$ and the derived operator $\div$ as *overt structures*, that can, at least ideally, be accessed by observing the behaviour of the epistemic agent. Let us again consider the black box of Sections 1.2–1.4. By asking questions of the type 'Do you believe that . . . ?', we can discover the contents of $\mathbf{K}$. By first giving instructions to contract ('Do not believe that. . . .!') and afterwards asking the same type of questions, we can draw conclusions about the operator $\div$ for $\mathbf{K}$.

In contrast, the base B of $\mathbf{K}$ and the operator $-$ for B are *hidden structures* [57]. They are inside the black box , and cannot be reached by observations of the agent's epistemic behaviour. All that we can conclude from such observations is that the agent behaves *as if* changes on her belief set were generated from a belief base and an operation (of a certain type) on that belief base.

In particular, we do not have to make the strong (and not very plausible) assumption that the epistemic agent herself knows which of her beliefs are basic. A human may behave *as if* her belief changes are base-generated, and yet be as unaware of her belief base as she is of her synapses. Similarly, a computer program may be built on belief base (database) operations, and yet the distinction between basic and non-basic beliefs may not be manifest in the behaviour of the program.

2 CLOSURE-INVARIANT PROPERTIES

We have seen that if an operator for a belief base satisfies the postulate of success, then so does the closure of this operator. We can say that the success postulate is *closure-invariant*. More generally:

DEFINITION 4.3 *A property P of operators is* closure-invariant *if and only if: If P holds for an operator, then it holds for the closure of that operator.*

Success and inclusion, the defining properties of contraction, are closure-invariant. The same applies to several of the other basic postulates for contraction.

OBSERVATION 4.4 *The following contraction-postulates are closure-invariant:*

1. *Inclusion:* $A \div \alpha \subseteq A$
2. *Vacuity: If* $\alpha \notin \mathrm{Cn}(A)$, *then* $A \div \alpha = A$.
3. *Success: If* $\alpha \notin \mathrm{Cn}(\emptyset)$, *then* $\alpha \notin \mathrm{Cn}(A \div \alpha)$
4. *Extensionality: If* $\alpha \leftrightarrow \beta \in \mathrm{Cn}(\emptyset)$, *then* $A \div \alpha = A \div \beta$.
5. *Failure: If* $\alpha \in \mathrm{Cn}(\emptyset)$, *then* $A \div \alpha = A$.

[Proof: p. 323.]

Since all the five postulates mentioned in the observation are satisfied by partial meet contraction (as applied to a belief base), it follows that they are also satisfied by base-generated partial meet contraction. The first four of these postulates coincide with four of the five postulates for a withdrawal in Makinson's sense. The fifth postulate for withdrawals, closure ($A \div \alpha = \mathrm{Cn}(A \div \alpha)$) is satisfied by all base-generated contractions. Hence, *all base-generated partial meet contractions are withdrawals.* However, they do not satisfy recovery, the sixth of the basic Gärdenfors postulates. This negative result holds not only for partial meet contraction, but for a wider category of base-generated contraction operators:

THEOREM 4.5 *Let $\mathcal{L}$ (the language) consist of an infinite number of logically independent (atomic) sentences and their truth-functional combinations. Let* **K** *be a*

belief set such that $\mathbf{K} \neq \mathrm{Cn}(\emptyset)$. *Furthermore, let the operation* $\div$ *on* $\mathbf{K}$ *be generated by a contraction operator* $-$ *on a finite base for* $\mathbf{K}$. *Then* $\div$ *does not satisfy recovery.*
[Proof: p. 334.]

In Section 2.3, we found that recovery was difficult to avoid for operations applied directly to a belief set. Here, we have found it impossible to attain recovery with operations generated from base contractions.

3 NEW BASIC POSTULATES

In order to fully characterize the properties of base-generated contraction, we will need several new postulates. In this section, the intuitive motivations of the most important of these postulates will be given.

We have finite minds, and other belief-carrying systems such as computers and animals are finite as well. A realistic representation of a belief state should reflect the finiteness of actual belief systems. This was pointed out in a 1988 paper by two members of the AGM trio, Peter Gärdenfors and David Makinson. They wrote:

> "In all applications, the knowledge sets [belief sets] will be *finite* in the sense that the consequence relation $\vdash$ partitions the elements of $\mathbf{K}$ into a finite number of equivalence classes." [38]

The property referred to here can also be expressed as follows:

> *Strong finitude*:
> If A is an infinite set such that $\mathrm{Cn}(\{\alpha\}) \neq \mathrm{Cn}(\{\beta\})$ for all $\alpha, \beta \in A$, then $\mathrm{Cn}(A) \not\subseteq \mathbf{K}$.

The following example brings out the force of strong finitude:

> **Example**
> For every positive integer n, let π_n denote that the Roman Catholic Church has at present at least one and at most n popes. I believe in every sentence in the infinite sequence $\pi_1, \pi_2, \pi_3, \ldots$

The 'infiniteness' of this example should be admissible even for a finite mind. Surely a finite mind, such as that of a human being, should be capable of holding all elements of this infinite set of beliefs. Then, however, its belief set will violate strong finitude, since no two sentences in the sequence $\pi_1, \pi_2, \pi_3, \ldots$ are logically equivalent. The finiteness of actual belief systems seems to be weaker than what is expressed by this postulate.

There are at least two weaker finiteness properties that are much more plausible. The first of these is the condition that belief sets have finite representations:

Finite representability: [51; 57]
For every sentence α, there is some finite set A such that $\mathbf{K}\div\alpha = \mathrm{Cn}(A)$.

Finite representability need not be violated in our example. π_1 implies all sentences in the series $\pi_2, \pi_3, \ldots$ Therefore, for the infinite sequence $\pi_1, \pi_2, \pi_3, \ldots$ to be included in **K** (or $\mathbf{K}\div\alpha$) it is sufficient that π_1 is included in the finite representation (base) of **K** (respectively $\mathbf{K}\div\alpha$).

The second of the two finiteness properties states that although there may be infinitely many sentences by which the belief set can be contracted, there are only a finite number of belief sets that can be obtained through contraction.

Finite number of contractions: [51; 57]
$\{\mathbf{K}' \mid \mathbf{K}' = \mathbf{K}\div\alpha \text{ for some } \alpha\}$ is finite.

This postulate need not either be violated in our example. With reasonable background beliefs about the Roman Catholic Church, π_2, π_3, etc. are believed only as a consequence of belief in π_1. They all stand or fall with π_1, so that if one of them is lost, then the rest of them will be lost as well. Thus, e.g. $\mathbf{K}\div\pi_8 = \mathbf{K}\div\pi_9$.

These two finiteness properties can be combined into the following:

Finitude: [51]
There is a finite set A such that for every sentence α, $\mathbf{K}\div\alpha = \mathrm{Cn}(A')$ for some $A' \subseteq A$.

OBSERVATION 4.6 ([51; 57]) *A contraction operator $\div$ for* **K** *satisfies finitude if and only if it satisfies both finite representability and finite number of contractions. [Proof: Exercise 189.]*

Finitude is acceptable as a general requirement on rational belief change.

For the next postulate, we are going to have a closer look at the phenomenon that some beliefs stand or fall together:

Example [51]
I believe that either Paris or Oslo is the capital of France (α). I also believe that either Paris or Stockholm is the capital of France (β). Both these beliefs are entirely based on my belief that Paris is the capital of France. Therefore, a contraction by any sentence δ removes α if and only if it removes β (namely if and only if it removes the common justification of these two beliefs). There is no contraction by which I can retract α without retracting β or vice versa.

This pattern can be generalized. If two beliefs stand or fall together, then this must be because their justifications are the same, so that you cannot remove the justifications of one without removing those of the other. Contraction should be a process in which the belief state is changed so that the belief to be contracted is no longer justified. Therefore it can reasonably be expected that two beliefs that stand or fall together produce the same contraction-outcome. This assumption is expressed in the following postulate:

> *Symmetry*: [51]
> If it holds for all δ that $\mathbf{K}\div\delta \vdash \alpha$ if and only if $\mathbf{K}\div\delta \vdash \beta$, then $\mathbf{K}\div\alpha = \mathbf{K}\div\beta$.

As we saw in Section 4.2, we cannot expect base-generated contraction to satisfy recovery. However, we need some postulate that prevents unmotivated deletions from the original belief set. The following is a first approximation:

1. If $\varepsilon \in \mathbf{K}$ and $\varepsilon \notin \mathbf{K}\div\alpha$, then ε contributes to the fact that $\mathbf{K}$ but not $\mathbf{K}\div\alpha$ implies α.

In order to translate (1) into formal language, we need to interpret what it means to 'contribute to the fact that $\mathbf{K}$ but not $\mathbf{K}\div\alpha$ implies α'. The following seems to be the most natural interpretation:

2. If $\varepsilon \in \mathbf{K}$ and $\varepsilon \notin \mathbf{K}\div\alpha$, then there is a set A such that $\mathbf{K}\div\alpha \subseteq A \subseteq \mathbf{K}$, $\alpha \notin \mathrm{Cn}(A)$ and $\alpha \in \mathrm{Cn}(A \cup \{\varepsilon\})$.

This is nothing else than the postulate of relevance (cf. Section 2.2). Unfortunately, it fails for our purposes. Let $\div$ be generated from a withdrawal $-$ on a base B for $\mathbf{K}$, and suppose that (2) is satisfied. Since $-$ is a withdrawal, so is $\div$ (Observation 4.4). It follows from Observation 2.6 that $\div$ satisfies recovery. However, it follows from Theorem 4.5 that this cannot hold except in trivial cases. We must conclude that (2) is too strong for our purposes.

The following example helps us to see why the application of relevance to belief sets goes wrong.

> **Example**
> Let α denote that John's wife is faithful and β that the Earth rotates around the Sun. When he finds a reason to suspect that she is having a love affair, he contracts his belief set by α. Presumably, his belief in β will remain after this contraction.

It can be shown that in this case relevance allows for the loss, not only of β, but even of $\alpha \vee \beta$, as a consequence of contraction by α. All that (2) demands in order to allow $\alpha \vee \beta \notin \mathbf{K}\div\alpha$ is the existence of some A such that $\mathbf{K}\div\alpha \subseteq A \subseteq \mathbf{K}$ and $\alpha \notin \mathrm{Cn}(A)$ and $\alpha \in \mathrm{Cn}(A \cup \{\alpha \vee \beta\})$.

Let $\mathbf{K}\div\alpha = \mathrm{Cn}(\emptyset)$ and $A = \mathbf{K}\div\alpha \cup \{\beta \rightarrow \alpha\}$. Then $\alpha \notin \mathrm{Cn}(A)$ and $\alpha \in \mathrm{Cn}(A \cup \{\alpha \vee \beta\})$. The existence of this subset A of $\mathbf{K}$ is therefore sufficient to guarantee that $\alpha \vee \beta \notin \mathbf{K}\div\alpha$ is compatible with relevance.

The intuitive interpretation of the example gives an indication of where the problem lies: It does not seem reasonable for John to give up both α and β but retain belief in $\beta \rightarrow \alpha$, that he only believed in as a consequence of his belief in α. Although $\mathbf{K} \div \alpha \cup \{\beta \rightarrow \alpha\}$ is a subset of the original belief set, it is not itself a reasonable set of beliefs (and the same applies to its logical closure). In order to exclude constructions of this type we should require of A in (2) that it be a reasonable belief set (from the perspective of K). This leads us to the following condition:

3. If $\varepsilon \in \mathbf{K}$ and $\varepsilon \notin \mathbf{K} \div \alpha$, then there is a reasonable belief set $\mathbf{K}'$ such that $\mathbf{K} \div \alpha \subseteq \mathbf{K}' \subseteq \mathbf{K}$, $\alpha \notin \mathrm{Cn}(\mathbf{K}')$, and $\alpha \in \mathrm{Cn}(\mathbf{K}' \cup \{\varepsilon\})$.

The next step is to determine which subsets of **K** are reasonable belief sets. It does not seem possible to do this in terms of the truth-functional relationships of the elements of **K**. The only other means that we have at our disposal is the operator of contraction. The following definition employs that operator in what seems to be the most intuitively reasonable way:

(A) A subset $\mathbf{K}'$ of **K** is a reasonable belief set from the viewpoint of **K** if and only if there is some series of contractions of **K** that results in $\mathbf{K}'$, i.e.: $\mathbf{K}' = \mathbf{K} \div \alpha_1 \div \alpha_2 \ldots \div \alpha_n$.

Since iterated contractions are often difficult to handle in a formal context, it is worth investigating whether our purposes can be served by the following approximation of (A):

(B) A subset $\mathbf{K}'$ of **K** is a reasonable belief set from the viewpoint of **K** if and only if there is some sentence α such that $\mathbf{K}' = \mathbf{K} \div \alpha$.

If (B) is applied to (3), then we obtain the following:

4. If $\varepsilon \in \mathbf{K}$ and $\varepsilon \notin \mathbf{K} \div \alpha$, then there is a sentence δ such that $\mathbf{K} \div \alpha \subseteq \mathbf{K} \div \delta \subseteq \mathbf{K}$ and $\alpha \notin \mathrm{Cn}(\mathbf{K} \div \delta)$ and $\alpha \in \mathrm{Cn}(\mathbf{K} \div \delta \cup \{\varepsilon\})$.

Provided that inclusion is satisfied, (4) is equivalent to the following:

5. If $\varepsilon \in \mathbf{K}$ and $\varepsilon \notin \mathbf{K} \div \alpha$, then there is a sentence δ such that $\mathbf{K} \div \alpha \subseteq \mathbf{K} \div \delta \nvdash \alpha$ and $\mathbf{K} \div \delta \cup \{\varepsilon\} \vdash \alpha$.

However, we are not quite finished. In (1), and consequently in (2)–(5), it was assumed that *all* elements ε of **K** are worth retaining, in the sense that if $\varepsilon \notin \mathbf{K} \div \alpha$, then ε contributes to the fact that **K** but not $\mathbf{K} \div \alpha$ implies α. This is not a realistic feature. We have already seen several examples of beliefs that are not worth retaining for their own sake. The following is one more such example:

Example

Let δ denote that John Stuart Mill wrote *On Liberty* and ε that he wrote the *Communist Manifesto*. Since I believe in δ, *I* also believe in $\delta \vee \varepsilon$, i.e. I believe that he wrote either *On Liberty* or the *Communist Manifesto*. However, $\delta \vee \varepsilon$ is a merely derivative belief. I believe in it only as a consequence of my belief in δ, and if my belief in δ is lost then so is my belief in $\delta \vee \varepsilon$. In contrast, δ is self-sustained, in the sense of being worth retaining for its own sake.

We need to restrict (5) to hold, not for every sentence ε in **K** but for every sentence ε in **K** that represents a self-sustained part of **K**:

6. If ε is a self-sustained belief in **K** and $\varepsilon \notin \mathbf{K}\div\alpha$, then there is a sentence δ such that $\mathbf{K}\div\alpha \subseteq \mathbf{K}\div\delta \nvdash \alpha$ and $\mathbf{K}\div\delta \cup \{\varepsilon\} \vdash \alpha$.

Our next task is to explicate in formal terms what it means for beliefs to be self-sustained, or capable of standing on their own. For a part of **K** to be self-sustained, it should be in principle possible to peel off all other beliefs in **K**, and retain only this part. In other words:

(C) ε is a self-sustained belief in **K** if and only if there are sentences $\beta_1, \beta_2, \ldots \beta_n$ such that $\text{Cn}(\{\varepsilon\}) = \mathbf{K}\div\beta_1\div\beta_2\div\ldots\div\beta_n$.

(C) has the same disadvantages as (A). The problems with iterated contraction can be avoided if we focus on those self-sustained parts of **K** that can be reached through only one contraction:

(D) ε is a self-sustained belief in **K** if there is a sentence β such that $\text{Cn}(\{\varepsilon\}) = \mathbf{K}\div\beta$.

By applying (D) to (6) we obtain:

7. If there are ε and β such that $\text{Cn}(\{\varepsilon\}) = \mathbf{K}\div\beta$, and $\varepsilon \in \mathbf{K}$ and $\varepsilon \notin \mathbf{K}\div\alpha$, then there is a sentence δ such that $\mathbf{K}\div\alpha \subseteq \mathbf{K}\div\delta \nvdash \alpha$ and $\mathbf{K}\div\delta \cup \{\varepsilon\} \vdash \alpha$.

Under the assumption that closure holds, $\varepsilon \notin \mathbf{K}\div\alpha$ in (7) can be replaced by $\mathbf{K}\div\beta \nsubseteq \mathbf{K}\div\alpha$. Since **K** is logically closed, $\varepsilon \in \mathbf{K}$ can be replaced by $\mathbf{K}\div\beta \subseteq \mathbf{K}$. Under the assumption that inclusion holds, this is a redundant condition. We can therefore transform (7) to the following:

8. If there are ε and β such that $\text{Cn}(\{\varepsilon\}) = \mathbf{K}\div\beta$, and $\mathbf{K}\div\beta \nsubseteq \mathbf{K}\div\alpha$, then there is a sentence δ such that $\mathbf{K}\div\alpha \subseteq \mathbf{K}\div\delta \nvdash \alpha$ and $\mathbf{K}\div\delta \cup \mathbf{K}\div\beta \vdash \alpha$.

If finite representability holds, then (8) is equivalent to the following:

9. If $\mathbf{K}\div\beta \nsubseteq \mathbf{K}\div\alpha$, then there is some δ such that $\mathbf{K}\div\alpha \subseteq \mathbf{K}\div\delta \nvdash \alpha$ and $\mathbf{K}\div\delta \cup \mathbf{K}\div\beta \vdash \alpha$. (*conservativity*)

Admittedly, the argument that led up to the postulate of conservativity was somewhat roundabout, as a result of compromises aiming at making the underlying intuitions accessible to formal treatment. Nevertheless, conservativity as formulated in (9) is an acceptable first approximation. Only if it does not turn out satisfactorily should we resort to more complex formalizations of the basic intuition that unmotivated losses should be avoided.

One more aspect needs attention: In (1), we required of an excluded sentence ε that it 'contributes to the fact that **K** but not $\mathbf{K}\div\alpha$ implies α'. With equally good reasons, we may content ourselves with the weaker condition that ε 'contributes to the fact that **K** implies α'. The starting-point for our derivation will then be:

1′. If $\varepsilon \in \mathbf{K}$ and $\varepsilon \notin \mathbf{K}\div\alpha$, then ε contributes to the fact that $\mathbf{K}$ implies α.

The same chain of arguments can be applied to (1′) as to (1), leading us to the following postulate:

9′. If $\mathbf{K}\div\beta \not\subseteq \mathbf{K}\div\alpha$, then there is some δ such that $\mathbf{K}\div\delta \nvdash \alpha$ and $\mathbf{K}\div\delta \cup \mathbf{K}\div\beta \vdash \alpha$. (*weak conservativity*)

The relationship between conservativity and weak conservativity is similar to that between relevance and core-retainment (cf. Section 2.2).

4 REPRESENTATION THEOREMS

The postulates finitude, symmetry, and weak conservativity are sufficient to characterize those withdrawals on a belief set that are base-generated kernel contractions:

THEOREM 4.7 ([52]) *An operator $\div$ on a consistent belief set* $\mathbf{K}$ *is generated by an operator of kernel contraction for a finite base for* $\mathbf{K}$ *if and only if $\div$ satisfies closure, inclusion, vacuity, success, extensionality, finitude, symmetry, and weak conservativity.*
[Proof: p. 341.]

By strengthening weak conservativity to conservativity, we obtain a characterization of base-generated partial meet contraction:

THEOREM 4.8 ([51]) *An operator $\div$ on a consistent belief set* $\mathbf{K}$ *is generated by an operator of partial meet contraction for a finite base for* $\mathbf{K}$ *if and only if $\div$ satisfies closure, inclusion, vacuity, success, extensionality, finitude, symmetry, and conservativity.*
[Proof: p. 337.]

These theorems show that base-generated contractions can, just like direct contractions on a belief set, be exactly characterized in terms of the behaviour of the belief set under contraction; i.e. they can be characterized on the knowledge level. Due to the simplicity and plausibility of kernel and partial meet contraction, these theorems also provide support for the liberties taken, for the sake of simplicity, in the construction of the postulates of conservativity and weak conservativity.

An obvious way to strengthen conservativity is to require that if a self-sustained unit of belief $\mathbf{K}\div\beta$ is lost in contraction by α, then α will be implied if $\mathbf{K}\div\beta$ is added to $\mathbf{K}\div\alpha$ (and not merely if it is added to some $\mathbf{K}\div\delta$ such that $\mathbf{K}\div\alpha \subseteq \mathbf{K}\div\delta \nvdash \alpha$):

Strong conservativity:
If $\mathbf{K}\div\beta \not\subseteq \mathbf{K}\div\alpha$ then $\mathbf{K}\div\alpha \nvdash \alpha$ and $\mathbf{K}\div\beta \cup \mathbf{K}\div\alpha \vdash \alpha$.

If we replace conservativity by strong conservativity in Theorem 4.8, then we obtain a characterization of base-generated maxichoice contraction:

THEOREM 4.9 ([51]) *An operator $\div$ on a consistent belief set* $\mathbf{K}$ *is generated by an operator of maxichoice contraction for a finite base for* $\mathbf{K}$ *if and only if $\div$ satisfies closure, inclusion, vacuity, success, extensionality, finitude, symmetry, and strong conservativity.*
[Proof: p. 339.]

Strong conservativity is much less plausible than conservativity, as can be seen from the following example:

> **Example** [51]
> Let α_1 denote that Albert Schweitzer was a German and α_2 that he was a Missionary. I believe that Albert Schweitzer was a German Missionary ($\alpha_1\&\alpha_2$). If I have to contract my belief set by $\alpha_1\&\alpha_2$, then the contracted belief set will contain neither α_1 nor α_2. Admittedly it would be logically sufficient to withdraw one of them. However, they are both equally entrenched, so that I do not know which to choose in preference over the other. Therefore, both will have to go. On the other hand, if I have to contract my belief set by α_1, then I have no reason to let go of α_2. Similarly, α_1 will be retained in contraction by α_2.

In this case, we can expect that $\alpha_1 \notin \mathbf{K}\div(\alpha_1\&\alpha_2), \alpha_2 \notin \mathbf{K}\div(\alpha_1\&\alpha_2), \alpha_1 \in \mathbf{K}\div\alpha_2, \alpha_2 \in \mathbf{K}\div\alpha_1, \mathbf{K}\div(\alpha_1\&\alpha_2) \subseteq \mathbf{K}\div\alpha_1$, and $\mathbf{K}\div(\alpha_1\&\alpha_2) \subseteq \mathbf{K}\div\alpha_2$. However, this is incompatible with strong conservativity. Since $\mathbf{K}\div\alpha_1 \not\subseteq \mathbf{K}\div(\alpha_1\&\alpha_2)$, this postulate requires that $\mathbf{K}\div\alpha_1 \cup \mathbf{K}\div(\alpha_1\&\alpha_2) \vdash \alpha_1\&\alpha_2$. This cannot hold, since it follows from $\mathbf{K}\div(\alpha_1\&\alpha_2) \subseteq \mathbf{K}\div\alpha_1$ that $\mathbf{K}\div\alpha_1 \cup \mathbf{K}\div(\alpha_1\&\alpha_2) = \mathbf{K}\div\alpha_1$, and $\mathbf{K}\div\alpha_1 \not\vdash \alpha_1$.

More generally, strong conservativity is implausible since it precludes the removal of two or more sentences (in this case α_1 and α_2), when it would have been logically sufficient to remove only one of them. Such epistemic behaviour is rational enough when the beliefs in question are equally entrenched, or have equal epistemic utility.

Since strong conservativity is implausible, so is base-generated maxichoice contraction. This result is of some interest, since maxichoice contraction on belief bases has sometimes been acclaimed as a plausible operation. [83]

At the other extreme, an agent may be always indifferent between different ways to remove one and the same sentence. Such an agent is indecisive in the sense of being unable to make a choice among alternative ways to remove a belief, if these are on an equal footing from a logical point of view. Formally, this is close to a reversal of conservativity: If a (self-sustained) unit of belief conflicts with some way to remove α from $\mathbf{K}$, then it is not a part of $\mathbf{K}\div\alpha$.

Indecisiveness:
If there is some δ such that $\mathbf{K}\div\delta \nvdash \alpha$ and $(\mathbf{K}\div\beta)\cup(\mathbf{K}\div\delta) \vdash \alpha$, then $\mathbf{K}\div\beta \not\subseteq \mathbf{K}\div\alpha$.

Indecisiveness is a characteristic postulate for base-generated full meet contraction:

THEOREM 4.10 ([51]) *An operator $\div$ on a consistent belief set* **K** *is generated by full meet contraction on a finite base for* **K** *if and only if $\div$ satisfies closure, inclusion, vacuity, success, extensionality, finitude, conservativity, and indecisiveness.* *[Proof: p. 340.]*

Counter-examples to indecisiveness, and thus to base-generated full meet contraction, are not difficult to find.

Example
Bob, who is an art student, believes that Benvenuto Cellini was Spanish (β) and that he was a painter (δ).
Case 1: Bob says that Cellini was a Spanish painter ($\beta\&\delta$), but he is told that this is wrong. Since Bob is more convinced that Cellini was a painter than that he was Spanish, when contracting by $\beta\&\delta$ he retains δ and gives up β, i.e. $\delta \in \mathbf{K}\div(\beta\&\delta)$.
Case 2: If forced to give up his belief that Cellini was a painter, Bob still believes that he was Spanish, i.e. $\beta \in \mathbf{K}\div\delta$.
Case 3: If forced to give up his belief that Cellini was Spanish, Bob still believes that he was a painter, i.e. $\delta \in \mathbf{K}\div\beta$.

We can reasonably expect in this case that $\mathbf{K}\div\beta \subseteq \mathbf{K}\div(\beta\&\delta)$ (and indeed also that $\mathbf{K}\div\beta = \mathbf{K}\div(\beta\&\delta)$, but that is not needed for the argument). Now let α denote $\beta\&\delta$. Since $\mathbf{K}\div\delta$ does not imply δ we then have $\mathbf{K}\div\delta \nvdash \alpha$. Since $\beta \in \mathbf{K}\div\delta$ and $\delta \in \mathbf{K}\div\beta$, we have $(\mathbf{K}\div\delta)\cup(\mathbf{K}\div\beta) \vdash \alpha$. Yet it holds that $\mathbf{K}\div\beta \subseteq \mathbf{K}\div\alpha$, and thus indecisiveness is violated. (And by the way, Benvenuti Cellini, 1500–1571, was a Florentine goldsmith and sculptor.)

5 DISJUNCTIVELY CLOSED BASES

In Section 1.8, we saw that in some contexts, disjunctively closed bases may be useful for modelling belief change. The justification for disjunctive closure is that (1) the belief base should consist of those beliefs that are worth retaining for their own sake, and (2) a disjunction of two independently justified beliefs may be worth retaining even if neither of the (independently justified) disjuncts can be retained. Thus, if you have to give up either α or β and cannot choose between them so that both must be abandoned, it may be sensible to retain belief in $\alpha\vee\beta$. (See the example on p. 23.)

In order to get a clearer view of what disjunctive closure does, we need to find an axiomatic characterization of those contractions of a given belief set that can be generated by some partial meet contraction on some disjunctively closed base for that belief set. In order to specify the characteristic postulate, we will have use for the following terminology [51]:

$\mathbf{K}\div\beta$ is:

1. an *α-removal* if and only if $\alpha \notin \mathbf{K}\div\beta$.
2. a *preservative α-removal* if and only if it is an α-removal such that $\mathbf{K}\div\alpha \subseteq \mathbf{K}\div\beta$.
3. a *strictly preservative α-removal* if and only if it is an α-removal such that $\mathbf{K}\div\alpha \subset \mathbf{K}\div\beta$.
4. a *maximally preservative α-removal* if and only if it is a preservative α-removal and there is no α-removal $\mathbf{K}\div\delta$ such that $\mathbf{K}\div\beta \subset \mathbf{K}\div\delta$.

Thus, to perform an α-removal is to perform some contraction that removes α. To perform a preservative α-removal is to perform a contraction that removes α, and does this at least as information-economically as the contraction by α. To perform a maximally preservative α-removal is to make the belief set not imply α, making use of information that is sufficiently specified to allow one to remove a part of α so small that no smaller part of it can be removed alone.

We can use the above Albert Schweitzer example to exemplify the terminology:

Example [51]
I believe that Albert Schweitzer was a German (α_1) and that he was a Missionary (α_2). These two beliefs are equally entrenched. Let α denote $\alpha_1\&\alpha_2$.

1. If I have to contract my belief set by α, then the contracted belief set will contain neither α_1 nor α_2. On the other hand, if I have to contract my belief set by α_1, then I have no reason to let go of α_2. To contract by α_1 is, given the structure of my belief state, a more specified way to remove α. Thus, $\mathbf{K}\div\alpha \subset \mathbf{K}\div\alpha_1$. We can conclude that $\mathbf{K}\div\alpha_1$ is a *strictly preservative α-removal.*
2. Let δ denote that Albert Schweitzer was a Swede, and let us consider the contraction of $\mathbf{K}$ by $\alpha_1\vee\delta$, 'Albert Schweitzer was a German or a Swede'. Since I believe in $\alpha_1\vee\delta$ only as a consequence of my belief in α_1, I can only retract $\alpha_1\vee\delta$ by retracting α_1. Therefore, $\mathbf{K}\div(\alpha_1\vee\delta)$ is not a proper superset of $\mathbf{K}\div\alpha_1$, i.e. it is not a more conservative α-withdrawal than $\mathbf{K}\div\alpha_1$. Indeed, the way my beliefs are structured, α_1 cannot be further subdivided in the way that α was subdivided into α_1 and α_2.

There is no part of α_1 that stands on its own and can be retracted from $\mathbf{K}$ without the rest of α_1 being lost as well. In this sense, no α-removal can be more conservative than $\mathbf{K}\div\alpha_1$. Thus, $\mathbf{K}\div\alpha_1$ is a *maximally preservative* α*-removal.*

It follows from the definition of maximally preservative removals that for every sentence α, $\mathbf{K}\div\alpha$ is a subset of every maximally preservative α-removal. It can also be maintained that, conversely, if $\beta \notin \mathbf{K}\div\alpha$, then there should be some maximally preservative α-removal that does not include β.Thus, no element β of $\mathbf{K}$ should be excluded from $\mathbf{K}\div\alpha$ unless there is some maximally information-economical way to remove α that leads to the exclusion of β. This amounts to the following postulate:

Meet maximality:
If α is not logically true, then $\mathbf{K}\div\alpha$ is the intersection of the maximally preservative α-removals by $\div$.

Meet maximality can be used as a characteristic axiom for those operations on a belief set that are generated by partial meet contraction on a finite and disjunctively closed base:

THEOREM 4.11 ([49]) *An operator* $\div$ *on a consistent belief set* $\mathbf{K}$ *is generated by partial meet contraction of a finite, disjunctively closed base for* $\mathbf{K}$ *if and only if* $\div$ *satisfies closure, inclusion, vacuity, success, extensionality, finitude, symmetry, conservativity, and meet maximality.*
[Proof: p. 345.]

One of the major advantages of disjunctively closed bases is that they allow for a neat characterization of base-generated transitively maximizingly relational (TMR) partial meet contraction, that makes use of postulates that we already know from Chapter 2. When TMR partial meet contractions are applied *directly* to the belief set, conjunctive overlap and conjunctive inclusion can be used as characteristic postulates, and furthermore, conjunctive trisection can be shown to hold (though it is not needed for the characterization; see Sections 2.5–2.6). These three postulates can also be used as characteristic postulates for base-generated TMR partial meet contraction from a finite and disjunctively closed base:

THEOREM 4.12 ([49]) *An operator* $\div$ *on a consistent belief set* $\mathbf{K}$ *is generated by a TMR partial meet contraction on some finite, disjunctively closed base for* $\mathbf{K}$ *if and only if* $\div$ *satisfies closure, inclusion, vacuity, success, extensionality, finitude, symmetry, conservativity, conjunctive overlap, conjunctive inclusion, and conjunctive trisection.*
[Proof: p. 347.]

This theorem provides a way to obtain Gärdenfors's supplementary postulates without the more controversial postulate of recovery. This result depends on the assumption that the base is disjunctively closed.

OBSERVATION 4.13 ([49]) *Let the operator $\div$ on the belief set* **K** *be generated by some TMR partial meet contraction of a finite base for* **K**. *Then $\div$ does not in general satisfy conjunctive overlap.*
[Proof: p. 348.]

6 PSEUDO-CONTRACTIONS

In Section 4.2, we noted that the two defining postulates for contraction, the success and inclusion postulates, are closure-invariant. Therefore, if an operator $-$ for a belief base B satisfies these two postulates, then the closure of $-$ satisfies the same two postulates.

However, for $-$ to generate a contraction on the closure **K** of B, it is not necessary (although it is sufficient) for $-$ to be a contraction on B. Although it must satisfy success, it need not necessarily satisfy inclusion ($B-\alpha \subseteq B$). The following weaker property is sufficient:

Logical inclusion [42]
$\mathrm{Cn}(B-\alpha) \subseteq \mathrm{Cn}(B)$.

An operation that satisfies success and logical inclusion will be called a *pseudo-contraction* [49]. (Note that all contractions are also pseudo-contractions.) An operator for B generates a contraction on Cn (B) if and only if it is a pseudo-contraction on B.

OBSERVATION 4.14 ([49]) *An operator is a pseudo-contraction if and only if its closure is a contraction.*
[Proof: p. 324.]

A particularly interesting type of pseudo-contraction has been proposed by Bernhard Nebel [98]. He constructed operators for belief set contraction that are base-generated and yet satisfy recovery. As can be seen from Theorem 4.5, this is not possible if we use a *contraction* of a finite base to generate a contraction of the belief set. It is, however, possible if we instead use a *pseudo-contraction* of a base for the same purpose.

DEFINITION 4.15 ([98]) *Let B be a finite base and γ a selection function for B.* Nebel's pseudo-contraction *by γ is the operation such that:*
$B\tilde{-}_{\gamma}\alpha = B$ *if* $\alpha \in \mathrm{Cn}(\emptyset)$, *and*
$B\tilde{-}_{\gamma}\alpha = \bigcap\gamma(B\perp\alpha) \cup \{\alpha\rightarrow\&B\}$ *otherwise.*

OBSERVATION 4.16 (Bernhard Nebel [98]) *Let $\div$ be an operation for a belief set* **K** *that is generated by a Nebel's pseudo-contraction on a finite base for* **K**. *Then $\div$ satisfies closure, inclusion, vacuity, success, extensionality, and recovery.*
[Proof: p. 334.]

The postulates listed in this observation coincide with the characteristic postulates for (direct) partial meet contraction of a belief set, according to Theorem 2.7. Therefore, Nebel's pseudo-contraction mimics the effects of a direct partial meet contraction on the belief set. Its major advantage is its computational tractability.

If **K** does not have a finite representation, then the following variant of Nebel's operation can be used, with the same effect (but of course without the advantage of finite representability):

$$\bigcap \gamma(B \perp \alpha) \cup \{\alpha \rightarrow \beta \mid \beta \in B\}.$$

If you subscribe to all of Gärdenfors's basic postulates, including recovery, and in addition opt for finite representations and computational tractability, then Nebel's pseudo-contraction should serve you. If, to the contrary, you find the recovery postulate to be counter-intuitive, then the constructions referred to in Sections 4.1–4.5 should be of more interest to you.

7 BASE-GENERATED REVISION

Operators of revision on a belief set can be base-generated in the same sense as operators of contraction. Several of the basic revision-postulates can be shown to be closure-invariant, i.e. if an operator on a base satisfies the postulate, then so does its closure (the operator on the corresponding belief set that it generates).

OBSERVATION 4.17 *The following revision-postulates are closure-invariant:*

1. *Success:* $\alpha \in A * \alpha$
2. *Consistency:* $A * \alpha$ *is consistent if* α *is consistent.*

Furthermore, under the assumption that $+$ is interpreted as non-closing expansion when applied to a belief base and as closing expansion when applied to a belief set, the following revision-postulates are also closure-invariant:

3. *Inclusion:* $A * \alpha \subseteq A + \alpha$
4. *Inconsistent expansion: If* $\neg\alpha \in \mathrm{Cn}(\emptyset)$ *then* $A * \alpha = A + \alpha$.
5. *Vacuity: If* $\neg\alpha \notin \mathrm{Cn}(A)$, *then* $A * \alpha = A + \alpha$.
6. *Superexpansion:* $A * (\alpha \& \beta) \subseteq (A * \alpha) + \beta$.
7. *Subexpansion: If* $\neg\beta \notin \mathrm{Cn}(A * \alpha)$, *then* $(A * \alpha) + \beta \subseteq A * (\alpha \& \beta)$.

[Proof: p. 349.]

Base-generated internal partial meet revision and direct (internal) partial meet revision can be shown to coincide in the following sense:

OBSERVATION 4.18 ([49]) *The following two statements about an operation* $*$ *on a belief set* $\mathbf{K}$ *are equivalent:*

1. *There is some selection function* γ *for* $\mathbf{K}$ *such that for all* α*:*
$$\mathbf{K} * \alpha = \mathbf{K} \mp_{\gamma} \alpha.$$
2. *There is some base* B *for* $\mathbf{K}$ *and some selection function* γ *for* B *such that for all* α*:*
$$\mathbf{K} * \alpha = \mathrm{Cn}(B \mp_{\gamma} \alpha).$$

[Proof: p. 352.]

This coincidence of base-generated and direct revision comes to an end if further requirements are imposed on the revision operators. In particular, this will happen if the operators are required to be transitively maximizingly relational (TMR). The following two statements about an operation $*$ on a logically closed set $\mathbf{K}$ are *not* equivalent:

3. There is some TMR selection function γ for $\mathbf{K}$ such that for all α : $\mathbf{K} * \alpha = \mathbf{K} \mp_{\gamma} \alpha$.
4. There is some base B for $\mathbf{K}$ and some TMR selection function γ for B such that for all α : $\mathbf{K} * \alpha = \mathrm{Cn}(B \mp_{\gamma} \alpha)$

To show that (4) does not imply (3) we can make use of the previously proven fact that the operation $*$ referred to in (3) satisfies disjunctive overlap. (Observation 3.23 and Theorem 3.25.) The operator $*$ of (4) does not, in general, satisfy this postulate:

OBSERVATION 4.19 ([49]) *Let* γ *be a TMR selection function on a finite base* B *for* $\mathbf{K}$*, and let* $*$ *be the closure of* $\mp_{\gamma}$*, i.e.* $\mathbf{K} * \alpha = \mathrm{Cn}(B \mp_{\gamma} \alpha)$ *for all* α*. Then disjunctive overlap is not, in general, satisfied by* $*$*.*
[Proof: p. 353.]

However, if the belief base is also required to be finite and disjunctively closed, then an equivalence similar to that of Observation 4.18 can be obtained.

OBSERVATION 4.20 ([49]) *Let* $\mathcal{L}$ *be finite. Then the following two statements about an operation* $*$ *on a belief set* $\mathbf{K}$ *are equivalent:*

3. *There is some TMR selection function* γ *for* $\mathbf{K}$ *such that for all* α*:*
$$\mathbf{K} * \alpha = \mathbf{K} \mp_{\gamma} \alpha.$$

5. *There is some finite and disjunctively closed base B for* $\mathbf{K}$ *and some TMR selection function* γ *for B such that for all* α*:*

$$\mathbf{K} * \alpha = \mathrm{Cn}(B \mp_{\gamma} \alpha).$$

[Proof: p. 353.]

It follows that the operations referred to in (5) can be axiomatically characterized with the postulates used for (direct) TMR revision on a belief set (Theorem 3.25), namely: closure, success, inclusion, vacuity, consistency, extensionality, superexpansion, and subexpansion.

Thus, disjunctively closed bases make it possible to satisfy Gärdenfors's supplementary postulates for revision as well as for contraction, without having to accept the postulate of recovery.

CHAPTER 4+

THE LOGIC OF BASE-GENERATED OPERATIONS

The notion of closure-invariance is useful for proving the properties of base-generated operations. It is the major tool with which such properties will be established in Sections 4.8+–4.10+. In the proofs of representation theorems (Sections 4.11+–4.13+), some results on remainder equations from Section 1.15+ will turn out to be very useful. In Sections 4.14+–4.15+, results on base-generated revision are proved.

8+ THE USES OF CLOSURE-INVARIANCE

In many cases, the simplest way to show that a base-generated operator has a certain property is to prove (1) that the underlying operation on the base has this property, and (2) that the property is closure-invariant. Thus, in order to show that base-generated partial meet contraction satisfies success, we prove (1) that partial meet contraction satisfies success, and (2) that success is closure-invariant, so that it holds as well for the corresponding operator on the belief set.

It is mostly quite easy to show that a postulate is closure-invariant. We just have to bear in mind the following two facts:

1. If B is a base for $\mathbf{K}$, then $\text{Cn}(B) = \text{Cn}(\mathbf{K}) = \mathbf{K}$, and
2. If the operation $\div$ on $\mathbf{K}$ is the closure of the operation $-$ on B, then it holds for all α that $\text{Cn}(B - \alpha) = \text{Cn}(\mathbf{K}{\div}\alpha) = \mathbf{K}{\div}\alpha$.

The contraction-postulates *inclusion*, *vacuity*, *success*, *extensionality*, and *failure* are closure-invariant.
[Observation 4.4.]

Proof. Here, the proof will only be given for *vacuity*. The rest of the proofs are similar, and are left to the reader as an exercise.

Let *vacuity* hold for the operator $-$ on B. Let $\mathbf{K} = \text{Cn}(B)$ and let $\div$ be the closure of $-$. In order to show that *vacuity* holds for $\mathbf{K}$, we must show that if $\alpha \notin \text{Cn}(\mathbf{K})$, then $\mathbf{K}{\div}\alpha = \mathbf{K}$.

Since $\text{Cn}(B) = \text{Cn}(\mathbf{K})$, it follows from $\alpha \notin \text{Cn}(\mathbf{K})$ that $\alpha \notin \text{Cn}(B)$, and thus by the *vacuity* of $-$ that $B - \alpha = B$ and consequently $\text{Cn}(B - \alpha) = \text{Cn}(B)$. Since $\mathbf{K}{\div}\alpha = \text{Cn}(B - \alpha)$ and $\mathbf{K} = \text{Cn}(B)$, it follows directly that $\mathbf{K}{\div}\alpha = \mathbf{K}$. ■

The same method can be used to show that pseudo-contractions are the operations that have contractions as closures.

> An operator is a pseudo-contraction if and only if its closure is a contraction.
> [Observation 4.14.]

Proof. Let $\mathbf{K} = \text{Cn}(B)$ and let $\div$ be the closure of the operator $-$ on B.

One direction: Let $-$ be a pseudo-contraction, i.e. let it satisfy *success* and *logical inclusion*. Since *success* is closure-invariant (Observation 4.4), $\div$ satisfies *success*. Since $-$ satisfies *logical inclusion*, we have $\text{Cn}(B - \alpha) \subseteq \text{Cn}(B)$, or equivalently $\mathbf{K}\div\alpha \subseteq \mathbf{K}$, so that $\div$ satisfies *inclusion*. This is sufficient to show that $\div$ is a contraction.

The other direction: Let $\div$ be a contraction. In order to show that $-$ satisfies *success*, we need to prove that if $\alpha \notin \text{Cn}(\emptyset)$, then $\alpha \notin \text{Cn}(B - \alpha)$. Since $\div$ is a contraction it satisfies *success*, and therefore it follows from $\alpha \notin \text{Cn}(\emptyset)$ that $\alpha \notin \text{Cn}(\mathbf{K}\div\alpha)$, or equivalently $\alpha \notin \text{Cn}(B - \alpha)$.

Since $\div$ is a contraction it also satisfies *inclusion*. It follows that for all α:$\mathbf{K}\div\alpha \subseteq \mathbf{K}$, or equivalently $\text{Cn}(B - \alpha) \subseteq \text{Cn}(B)$, so that $-$ satisfies *logical inclusion*. ■

For one direction of our representation theorems, we need to show that symmetry is satisfied by base-generated kernel contraction (and thus also by its special case base-generated partial meet contraction). For this purpose, we are going to show (1) that symmetry is satisfied by kernel contraction on a finite base, and (2) that symmetry is closure-invariant. Combining these two results, we will be able to conclude that symmetry holds for base-generated kernel contraction, if the base is finite.

The same method will be used to show that base-generated kernel contraction satisfies weak conservativity, that base-generated partial meet contraction satisfies conservativity, and that base-generated maxichoice contraction satisfies strong conservativity. Let us begin with the easiest part of these two-step proofs, namely closure-invariance:

OBSERVATION 4.21 *The following postulates are closure-invariant:*

1. *If it holds for all δ that $A\div\delta \vdash \alpha$ if and only if $A\div\delta \vdash \beta$, then $A\div\alpha = A\div\beta$. (symmetry)*
2. *If $A\div\beta \not\subseteq A\div\alpha$, then there is some δ such that $A\div\delta \nvdash \alpha$ and $A\div\delta \cup A\div\beta \vdash \alpha$. (weak conservativity)*
3. *If $A\div\beta \not\subseteq A\div\alpha$, then there is some δ such that $A\div\alpha \subseteq A\div\delta \nvdash \alpha$ and $A\div\delta \cup A\div\beta \vdash \alpha$. (conservativity)*
4. *If $A\div\beta \not\subseteq A\div\alpha$ then $A\div\alpha \nvdash \alpha$ and $A\div\beta \cup A\div\alpha \vdash \alpha$. (strong conservativity)*

Proof. Let $\mathbf{K} = \mathrm{Cn}(B)$ and let $\div$ be the closure of the operator $-$ on B.

Part 1: Let $-$ satisfy *symmetry*. In order to show that $\div$ satisfies *symmetry*, suppose that it holds for all δ that $\mathbf{K}\div\delta \vdash \alpha$ if and only if $\mathbf{K}\div\delta \vdash \beta$. We have to show that $\mathbf{K}\div\alpha = \mathbf{K}\div\beta$.

Since $\mathbf{K}\div\delta = \mathrm{Cn}(B-\delta)$ for all δ, $\mathbf{K}\div\delta$ implies α if and only if $B-\delta$ implies α, and similarly for β. We can therefore conclude that for all δ, $B-\delta \vdash \alpha$ if and only if $B-\delta \vdash \beta$. Since $-$ satisfies *symmetry*, we have $B-\alpha = B-\beta$, and consequently $\mathrm{Cn}(B-\alpha) = \mathrm{Cn}(B-\beta)$, i.e. $\mathbf{K}\div\alpha = \mathbf{K}\div\beta$.

Part 2: Suppose that $-$ satisfies *weak conservativity*. In order to show that $\div$ satisfies *weak conservativity*, let $\mathbf{K}\div\beta \not\subseteq \mathbf{K}\div\alpha$. We need to show that there is some δ such that $\mathbf{K}\div\delta \nvdash \alpha$ and $\mathbf{K}\div\delta \cup \mathbf{K}\div\beta \vdash \alpha$.

To begin with, let us suppose that $B-\beta \subseteq B-\alpha$. It follows that $\mathrm{Cn}(B-\beta) \subseteq \mathrm{Cn}(B-\alpha)$, i.e. $\mathbf{K}\div\beta \subseteq \mathbf{K}\div\alpha$, contrary to our assumption. We can conclude from this contradiction that $B-\beta \not\subseteq B-\alpha$.

Since $-$ satisfies *weak conservativity*, it follows from $B-\beta \not\subseteq B-\alpha$ that there is some δ such that $B-\delta \nvdash \alpha$ and $B-\delta \cup B-\beta \vdash \alpha$. Thus, $\mathbf{K}\div\delta \nvdash \alpha$ and $\mathbf{K}\div\delta \cup \mathbf{K}\div\beta \vdash \alpha$.

Parts 3-4 are left to the reader as an exercise. ■

The second part of our two-step proofs is to show that these properties hold for the respective types of base contraction (symmetry for kernel contraction on a finite base, etc.). The simplest of these proofs is the one for strong conservativity:

OBSERVATION 4.22 *Let $\sim_\gamma$ be an operator of maxichoice contraction for a set A. Then $\sim_\gamma$ satisfies strong conservativity.*

Proof. Let $A{\sim_\gamma}\beta \not\subseteq A{\sim_\gamma}\alpha$. Since $A{\sim_\gamma}\beta \subseteq A$ it follows that $A{\sim_\gamma}\alpha \neq A$, so that $\nvdash \alpha$ and consequently $A{\sim_\gamma}\alpha \nvdash \alpha$.

It also follows from $A{\sim_\gamma}\beta \not\subseteq A{\sim_\gamma}\alpha$ that there is some ε such that $\varepsilon \in A{\sim_\gamma}\beta$ and $\varepsilon \notin A{\sim_\gamma}\alpha$. Since $\sim_\gamma$ is maxichoice, we have $\varepsilon \notin A{\sim_\gamma}\alpha \in A\bot\alpha$. It follows from $\varepsilon \in A{\sim_\gamma}\beta$ that $\varepsilon \in A$, and from $\varepsilon \in A\backslash(A{\sim_\gamma}\alpha)$ that $A{\sim_\gamma}\alpha \cup \{\varepsilon\} \vdash \alpha$ and consequently $A{\sim_\gamma}\beta \cup A{\sim_\gamma}\alpha \vdash \alpha$. ■

We can conclude from this observation, in conjunction with Part 4 of Observation 4.21, that base-generated maxichoice contraction satisfies strong conservativity. (Note that for this result the base does not have to be finite.)

Next, we are going to show that partial meet contraction on a finite base satisfies conservativity. For that purpose, we will use a result from Section 1.15+ (Observation 1.70) that will have a central rôle in the rest of this chapter: If A is finite and $X \in A\bot\alpha$, then there is some δ such that $\{X\} = A\bot\delta$. It then follows that for every selection function γ, $\gamma(A\bot\delta) = \{X\}$, and thus $\bigcap\gamma(A\bot\delta) = X$, so that $A{\sim_\gamma}\delta = X$ for every partial meet contraction $\sim_\gamma$. Note that this argument only goes through if A is finite, since otherwise Observation 1.70 cannot be used. This is one of the major reasons why most of the theorems of this chapter refer to operations generated from a *finite* base.

OBSERVATION 4.23 *Let A be a finite set of sentences and $\sim_\gamma$ an operator of partial meet contraction for A. Then $\sim_\gamma$ satisfies conservativity.*

Proof. Let $A{\sim_\gamma}\beta \not\subseteq A{\sim_\gamma}\alpha$. It follows that $A{\sim_\gamma}\alpha \neq A$, so that $\nvdash \alpha$. It also follows that there is some ε such that $\varepsilon \in \bigcap\gamma(A\bot\beta)$ and $\varepsilon \notin \bigcap\gamma(A\bot\alpha)$. Let X be such that $\varepsilon \notin X \in \gamma(A\bot\alpha)$. According to Observation 1.70, there is some δ such that $\{X\} = A\bot\delta$. Then $A{\sim_\gamma}\delta = \bigcap\gamma(A\bot\delta) = X$. It follows from $A{\sim_\gamma}\delta \in \gamma(A\bot\alpha)$ that $A{\sim_\gamma}\alpha \subseteq A{\sim_\gamma}\delta$ and that $A{\sim_\gamma}\delta \nvdash \alpha$. Furthermore, it follows from $\varepsilon \in A{\sim_\gamma}\beta$ that $\varepsilon \in A$, and thus from $\varepsilon \notin A{\sim_\gamma}\delta$ that $A{\sim_\gamma}\delta \cup \{\varepsilon\} \vdash \alpha$ and consequently $A{\sim_\gamma}\delta \cup A{\sim_\gamma}\beta \vdash \alpha$. ■

We can now conclude, from Observations 4.21 and 4.23, that base-generated partial meet contraction from a finite base satisfies conservativity.

The same method can be applied to kernel contraction. In this case, the step from $\{X\} = A\bot\delta$ to $A{\approx_\sigma}\alpha = X$ is less obvious, but it can be taken in the following manner:

OBSERVATION 4.24 ([52]) *Let A be a finite set of sentences and $\approx_\sigma$ an operator of kernel contraction for A. If $\{X\} = A\bot\delta$, then $A{\approx_\sigma}\alpha = X$.*

Proof. Let $\{X\} = A\bot\delta$. It follows from Observation 2.86 that every element of $A\perp\!\!\!\perp\delta$ has exactly one element. It follows from the definition of an incision function (Definition 2.30) that $\sigma(A\perp\!\!\!\perp\delta) = \bigcup(A\perp\!\!\!\perp\delta)$, and thus $A{\approx_\sigma}\alpha = A\setminus\bigcup(A\perp\!\!\!\perp\delta)$. It follows from Observation 2.85 that $\bigcap(A\bot\delta) = A\setminus\bigcup(A\perp\!\!\!\perp\delta)$, and thus $A{\approx_\sigma}\alpha = \bigcap(A\bot\delta) = X$. ■

This observation is used in the proof that kernel contraction on finite sets satisfies symmetry.

OBSERVATION 4.25 ([52]) *Let A be a finite set of sentences and $\approx_\sigma$ an operator of kernel contraction for A. Then $\approx_\sigma$ satisfies symmetry.*

Proof. We are going to assume that $A{\approx_\sigma}\alpha \neq A{\approx_\sigma}\beta$, and show that there is some δ for which it does not hold that $A{\approx_\sigma}\delta \vdash \alpha$ if and only if $A{\approx_\sigma}\delta \vdash \beta$.

It follows from $A{\approx_\sigma}\alpha \neq A{\approx_\sigma}\beta$ by the definition of kernel contraction (Definition 2.31) that $A\perp\!\!\!\perp\alpha \neq A\perp\!\!\!\perp\beta$. According to Observation 2.84, $A\bot\alpha \neq A\bot\beta$. Without loss of generality we may assume that there is some $X \in A\bot\alpha$ such that $X \notin A\bot\beta$. There are two cases:

Case 1, $X \vdash \beta$: According to Observation 1.70, there is some δ such that $\{X\} = A\perp\delta$. Observation 4.24 yields $A\approx_\sigma\delta = X$, so that $A\approx_\sigma\delta \nvdash \alpha$ and $A\approx_\sigma\delta \vdash \beta$, as desired.

Case 2, $X \nvdash \beta$. Then, since A is finite, there is some X' such that $X \subset X' \in A\perp\beta$. It follows from Observation 1.70 that there is some δ such that $\{X'\} = A\perp\delta$, and from Observation 4.24 that $A\approx_\sigma\delta = X'$. It follows that $A\approx_\sigma\delta \vdash \alpha$ and $A\approx_\sigma\delta \nvdash \beta$. ■

We can now conclude from Observations 4.21 and 4.25 that symmetry holds for base-generated kernel contraction from finite bases. Since partial meet contraction is a special case of kernel contraction, it also follows that symmetry holds for base-generated partial meet contraction from finite bases.

Next, let us show that weak conservativity holds for kernel contraction on a finite base. This proof is quite similar to the foregoing one:

OBSERVATION 4.26 ([52]) *Let A be a finite set of sentences and $\approx_\sigma$ an operator of kernel contraction for A. Then $\approx_\sigma$ satisfies weak conservativity.*

Proof. Let $A\approx_\sigma\beta \nsubseteq A\approx_\sigma\alpha$. It follows that $A\approx_\sigma\alpha \neq A$, so that $\nvdash \alpha$. It also follows that there is some ε such that $\varepsilon \in \sigma(A\perp\!\!\!\perp\alpha)$ and $\varepsilon \notin \sigma(A\perp\!\!\!\perp\beta)$. It follows from Definition 2.30 that $\varepsilon \in \bigcup(A\perp\!\!\!\perp\alpha)$, and from Observation 2.85 that $\varepsilon \notin \bigcap(A\perp\alpha)$. Let X be such that $\varepsilon \notin X \in A\perp\alpha$. We can use Observation 1.70 to conclude that there is some δ such that $\{X\} = A\perp\delta$, and Observation 4.24 to conclude that $A\approx_\sigma\delta = X$.

It follows from $\varepsilon \notin X \in A\perp\alpha$ that $X \cup \{\varepsilon\} \vdash \alpha$. Since $\varepsilon \in A\approx_\sigma\beta$, it follows that $X \cup A\approx_\sigma\beta \vdash \alpha$. Hence $A\approx_\sigma\delta \nvdash \alpha$ and $(A\approx_\sigma\beta) \cup (A\approx_\sigma\delta) \vdash \alpha$, as desired. ■

It follows from this, and Part (2) of Observation 4.21, that base-generated kernel contraction from a finite base satisfies weak conservativity.

One of Gärdenfors's supplementary postulates for contraction is closure-invariant.

OBSERVATION 4.27 *The following postulate is closure-invariant:*
If $\alpha \notin \mathrm{Cn}(A\div(\alpha\&\beta))$, then $A\div(\alpha\&\beta) \subseteq A\div\alpha$. (conjunctive inclusion)

Proof. Let $\mathbf{K} = \mathrm{Cn}(B)$ and let $\div$ be the closure of the operator $-$ on B. Suppose that $-$ satisfies conjunctive inclusion. In order to show that $\div$ satisfies the same postulate, let $\alpha \notin \mathrm{Cn}(\mathbf{K}\div(\alpha\&\beta))$. This is equivalent with $\alpha \notin \mathrm{Cn}(B - (\alpha\&\beta))$. Since $-$ satisfies *conjunctive inclusion* it follows that $B-(\alpha\&\beta) \subseteq B-\alpha$, and consequently $\mathrm{Cn}(B - (\alpha\&\beta)) \subseteq \mathrm{Cn}(B - \alpha)$, which is equivalent with $\mathbf{K}\div(\alpha\&\beta) \subseteq \mathbf{K}\div\alpha$. ■

Since TMR partial meet contraction on a finite and disjunctively closed set satisfies conjunctive inclusion (Observation 2.19), it follows that the closure of such an operation satisfies the same postulate.

The following postulate:

Conjunctive trisection:
If $\alpha \in A \div (\alpha \& \beta)$, then $\alpha \in A \div (\alpha \& \beta \& \delta)$.

is not closure-invariant. We can instead use a closely related postulate:

Strong conjunctive trisection:
If $A \div (\alpha \& \beta) \vdash \alpha$, then $A \div (\alpha \& \beta \& \delta) \vdash \alpha$.

Note that the difference between conjunctive trisection and strong conjunctive trisection vanishes for a logically closed set, if the contraction operator satisfies the closure postulate. In other words, if a contraction operator for a belief set satisfies closure, then it satisfies strong conjunctive trisection if and only if it satisfies conjunctive trisection.

Contrary to conjunctive trisection, its strong variant is closure-invariant:

OBSERVATION 4.28

1. *Strong conjunctive trisection is closure-invariant.*
2. *If an operation satisfies strong conjunctive trisection and closure, then the closure of that operation satisfies conjunctive trisection.*

Proof. Let $\mathbf{K} = \mathrm{Cn}(B)$ and let $\div$ be the closure of the operator $-$ on B.

Part 1: Let $-$ satisfy *strong conjunctive trisection*. In order to show that $\div$ satisfies the same postulate, suppose that $\mathbf{K} \div (\alpha \& \beta) \vdash \alpha$. Then, equivalently, $B - (\alpha \& \beta) \vdash \alpha$. Since $-$ satisfies *strong conjunctive trisection* we can conclude that $B - (\alpha \& \beta \& \delta) \vdash \alpha$, or equivalently, $\mathbf{K} \div (\alpha \& \beta \& \delta) \vdash \alpha$.

Part 2: Let $\alpha \in \mathbf{K} \div (\alpha \& \beta)$. Then $\mathbf{K} \div (\alpha \& \beta) \vdash \alpha$, and it follows from Part 1 that $\mathbf{K} \div (\alpha \& \beta \& \delta) \vdash \alpha$. It follows from *closure* that $\alpha \in \mathbf{K} \div (\alpha \& \beta \& \delta)$. ■

Strong conjunctive trisection holds for TMR partial meet contractions on finite and disjunctively closed sets:

OBSERVATION 4.29 *Let γ be a transitively, weakly maximizingly relational selection function for a finite and disjunctively closed set A. Then:*
If $A \sim_\gamma (\alpha \& \beta) \vdash \alpha$, then $A \sim_\gamma (\alpha \& \beta \& \delta) \vdash \alpha$. (strong conjunctive trisection)

Proof. Let $\sqsubseteq$ be the transitive and weakly maximizing relation on which γ is based. There are four cases, three of which are fairly simple limiting cases.

Case 1, $\vdash \alpha$: It follows directly that $A \sim_\gamma (\alpha \& \beta \& \delta) \vdash \alpha$.

Case 2, $\vdash \beta$: Then $\alpha \& \beta$ is logically equivalent with α, and consequently (by *extensionality*) $A \sim_\gamma (\alpha \& \beta) = A \sim_\gamma \alpha$. Suppose that $A \sim_\gamma (\alpha \& \beta) \vdash \alpha$, i.e. $A \sim_\gamma \alpha \vdash$

α. It then follows from the *success* postulate of partial meet contraction that $\alpha \in \mathrm{Cn}(\emptyset)$, and we are back in case 1.

Case 3, $\vdash \delta$: Then $\alpha\&\beta\&\delta$ is logically equivalent with $\alpha\&\beta$, so that *extensionality* yields $A{\sim_\gamma}(\alpha\&\beta\&\delta) = A{\sim_\gamma}(\alpha\&\beta)$, from which the desired result follows directly.

Case 4, $\nvdash \alpha, \nvdash \beta$, and $\nvdash \delta$: Let $\bigcap\gamma(A\bot(\alpha\&\beta)) \vdash \alpha$. We are going to show that if $X \in \gamma(A\bot(\alpha\&\beta\&\delta))$, then $X \vdash \alpha$. Suppose not, i.e. that there is some X such that $X \in \gamma(A\bot(\alpha\&\beta\&\delta))$ and $\alpha \notin \mathrm{Cn}(X)$. It follows that $X \in A\bot(\alpha\&\beta)$.

Suppose that $X \in \gamma(A\bot(\alpha\&\beta))$. Then $\bigcap\gamma(A\bot(\alpha\&\beta)) \nvdash \alpha$, contrary to the conditions. By this contradiction, $X \notin \gamma(A\bot(\alpha\&\beta))$.

Next, let $Y \in \gamma(A\bot(\alpha\&\beta))$. Then $X \sqsubset Y$. Since $Y \nvdash \alpha\&\beta\&\delta$ there is, by the upper bound property, some Y' such that $Y \subseteq Y' \in A\bot(\alpha\&\beta\&\delta)$. If $Y = Y'$, then $X \sqsubset Y'$ follows directly from $X \sqsubset Y$. If $Y \subset Y'$, then the weak maximizing property yields $Y \sqsubseteq Y'$. It follows by transitivity from $X \sqsubset Y$ and $Y \sqsubseteq Y'$ that $X \sqsubset Y'$. (Cf. Observation 2.75.) In both cases, we have $X \sqsubset Y', X \in \gamma(A\bot(\alpha\&\beta\&\delta))$ and $Y' \in A\bot(\alpha\&\beta\&\delta)$. This contradicts the marking-off identity. The contradiction shows that our assumption $\alpha \notin \mathrm{Cn}(X)$ cannot hold. We can conclude that if $X \in \gamma(A\bot(\alpha\&\beta\&\delta))$, then $X \vdash \alpha$. Since A is finite and disjunctively closed, it follows by repeated application of Observation 1.34 that $\bigcap\gamma(A\bot(\alpha\&\beta\&\delta)) \vdash \alpha$. With this, the proof is finished. ■

Exercises

186. Complete the proof of Observation 4.4 by showing that *inclusion, success, extensionality,* and *failure* are closure-invariant.

187. Complete the proof of Observation 4.21 by showing that *conservativity* and *strong conservativity* are closure-invariant.

188. Show that the following postulates are closure-invariant:
    (a) Either $A{\div}(\alpha\&\beta) \subseteq A{\div}\alpha$ or $A{\div}(\alpha\&\beta) \subseteq A{\div}\beta$. (*conjunctive covering*)
    (b) If $\beta \in \mathrm{Cn}(A{\div}(\alpha\&\beta))$, then $A{\div}(\alpha\&\beta) \subseteq A{\div}\alpha$.
    (c) $A{\div}(\alpha\&\beta) \subseteq \mathrm{Cn}((A{\div}\alpha) \cup (A{\div}\beta))$. (*weak conjunctive inclusion*)

189. Prove Observation 4.6, namely: A contraction operator $\div$ for $\mathbf{K}$ satisfies *finitude* if and only if it satisfies both *finite representability* and *finite number of contractions*.

190. (a) Show that the following postulate is closure-invariant:
    If $\vdash \alpha{\rightarrow}\beta$ and $A{\div}\alpha \nvdash \beta$, then $A{\div}\beta = A{\div}\alpha$. (*hyperregularity* [51])
    (b) Show that TMR maxichoice contraction satisfies *hyperregularity*.

191. (Hans Rott) Let $\mathbf{K}$ be a logically closed set that contains two sentences α and β such that $\alpha{\leftrightarrow}\beta \notin \mathrm{Cn}(\emptyset)$. Show that no operator $\div$ for $\mathbf{K}$ can satisfy *success, recovery,* and:
    For all δ, $\mathbf{K}{\div}\delta \vdash \alpha$ if and only if $\mathbf{K}{\div}\delta \vdash \beta$.
    (This is the antecedent of the *symmetry* postulate.)

9+ RESTRICTED CLOSURE-INVARIANCE

In this section, we are going to study some postulates that only satisfy weaker versions of closure-invariance. Our first example is indecisiveness, a characteristic postulate for base-generated full meet contraction. This postulate is not closure-invariant. Instead we can prove the weaker result that if an operator satisfies the three postulates inclusion, relative closure, and indecisiveness, then its closure satisfies indecisiveness. Since we already know that full meet contraction satisfies inclusion and relative closure (see Section 2.2), this restricted version of closure-invariance will serve our purposes. For handy reference, the three postulates follow:

If there is some δ such that $A{\div}\delta \nvdash \alpha$ and $(A{\div}\beta) \cup (A{\div}\delta) \vdash \alpha$, then $A{\div}\beta \not\subseteq A{\div}\alpha$. (*indecisiveness*)
$A \cap \text{Cn}(A{\div}\alpha) \subseteq A{\div}\alpha$. (*relative closure*)
$A{\div}\alpha \subseteq A$ (*inclusion*)

OBSERVATION 4.30 *Let* $\mathbf{K} = \text{Cn}(B)$ *and let* $\div$ *be the closure of the operator* $-$ *on B. If* $-$ *satisfies inclusion, relative closure, and indecisiveness, then* $\div$ *satisfies indecisiveness.*

Proof. Let $-$ satisfy the given postulates, and let δ be such that $\mathbf{K}{\div}\delta \nvdash \alpha$ and $(\mathbf{K}{\div}\beta) \cup (\mathbf{K}{\div}\delta) \vdash \alpha$. We need to show that $\mathbf{K}{\div}\beta \not\subseteq \mathbf{K}{\div}\alpha$.

It follows from $\mathbf{K}{\div}\delta \nvdash \alpha$ that $B{-}\delta \nvdash \alpha$. It also follows from $(\mathbf{K}{\div}\beta){\cup}(\mathbf{K}{\div}\delta) \vdash \alpha$ that $(B - \beta) \cup (B - \delta) \vdash \alpha$. Since $-$ satisfies *indecisiveness*, we can conclude that $B - \beta \not\subseteq B - \alpha$.

It follows from *inclusion* that $B - \alpha \subseteq B$, and thus $B - \alpha \subseteq B \cap (\mathbf{K}{\div}\alpha)$. It follows from *relative closure* that $B \cap (\mathbf{K}{\div}\alpha) \subseteq B - \alpha$. We can conclude that $B \cap (\mathbf{K}{\div}\alpha) = B - \alpha$. In the same way it follows that $B \cap (\mathbf{K}{\div}\beta) = B - \beta$.

Now suppose that $\mathbf{K}{\div}\beta \subseteq \mathbf{K}{\div}\alpha$. We then have $B \cap (\mathbf{K}{\div}\beta) \subseteq B \cap (\mathbf{K}{\div}\alpha)$, i.e. $B - \beta \subseteq B - \alpha$, contrary to what was just shown. We can conclude from this contradiction that $\mathbf{K}{\div}\beta \not\subseteq \mathbf{K}{\div}\alpha$. ■

Observe that in the above proof, inclusion and relative closure are needed for the step from $B - \beta \not\subseteq B - \alpha$ to $\mathbf{K}{\div}\beta \not\subseteq \mathbf{K}{\div}\alpha$.

In order to show that base-generated full meet contraction satisfies indecisiveness, it now remains to show that full meet contraction (on a base) satisfies that property. In this case, we do not need the finiteness requirement. Indecisiveness holds for full meet contraction of both finite and infinite sets.

OBSERVATION 4.31 *Let* $\sim$ *be the operator of full meet contraction for the set A. Then* $\sim$ *satisfies indecisiveness.*

Proof. Let α, β, and δ be such that $A \sim \delta \nvdash \alpha$ and $(A \sim \beta) \cup (A \sim \delta) \vdash \alpha$.

It follows from $A \sim \delta \nvdash \alpha$, by the upper bound property, that there is some X such that $A \sim \delta \subseteq X \in A\bot\alpha$. It follows from the definition of full meet contraction that $A \sim \alpha \subseteq X$.

Suppose that $A \sim \beta \subseteq A \sim \alpha$. Then $A \sim \beta \subseteq X$. Since we also have $A \sim \delta \subseteq X$, it follows from $(A \sim \beta) \cup (A \sim \delta) \vdash \alpha$ that $X \vdash \alpha$, contrary to $X \in A\bot\alpha$. We can conclude from this contradiction that $A \sim \beta \not\subseteq A \sim \alpha$. ■

The following postulate is not either closure-invariant:

Conjunctive overlap:
$(A \div \alpha) \cap (A \div \beta) \subseteq A \div (\alpha \& \beta)$

It can be treated in essentially the same way as indecisiveness, but in this case one more condition must be added: that the base is finite and disjunctively closed.

OBSERVATION 4.32 *Let B be finite and disjunctively closed, and let $-$ be an operator for B. Furthermore, let the operator $\div$ for* $\mathbf{K} = \mathrm{Cn}(B)$ *be the closure of $-$. Then:*
If $-$ satisfies inclusion, relative closure, and conjunctive overlap, then $\div$ satisfies conjunctive overlap.

Proof. In order to show that $\div$ satisfies *conjunctive overlap*, let $\delta \in (\mathbf{K} \div \alpha) \cap (\mathbf{K} \div \beta)$, i.e. $\delta \in \mathrm{Cn}(B - \alpha) \cap \mathrm{Cn}(B - \beta)$. We are going to show that $\delta \in \mathbf{K} \div (\alpha \& \beta)$.

Since *inclusion* and *relative closure* are satisfied, $B - \alpha$ and $B - \beta$ are B-closed subsets of B. Thus by Observation 1.34, we can conclude from $\delta \in \mathrm{Cn}(B - \alpha) \cap \mathrm{Cn}(B - \beta)$ that $\delta \in \mathrm{Cn}((B - \alpha) \cap (B - \beta))$. Since $-$ satisfies *conjunctive overlap* we also have $(B - \alpha) \cap (B - \beta) \subseteq B - (\alpha \& \beta)$, and thus $\delta \in \mathrm{Cn}(B - (\alpha \& \beta))$, or equivalently $\delta \in \mathbf{K} \div (\alpha \& \beta)$. ■

Note that in the above proof, the finiteness and disjunctive closure of the base are necessary to allow us to use Observation 1.34, that we need to distribute Cn over intersection.

We know from Observation 2.19 that a TMR partial meet contraction on any belief base B satisfies conjunctive overlap. We can now conclude from Observation 4.32 that if B is finite and disjunctively closed, then the closure of that operation satisfies the same postulate.

Meet maximality (Section 4.5) can be treated in the same way as conjunctive overlap. Again, closure-invariance holds in a restricted form that requires (1) that the base is finite and disjunctively closed, and (2) that the operator satisfies inclusion and relative closure.

OBSERVATION 4.33 *Let B be finite and disjunctively closed, and let $-$ be an operator for B that satisfies inclusion, relative closure, and meet maximality. Then the closure of $-$ satisfies meet maximality.*

Proof. Let $\mathbf{K} = \mathrm{Cn}(B)$. Let $\div$ be the closure of $-$, and let $\alpha \notin \mathrm{Cn}(\emptyset)$. We need to show that $\mathbf{K}\div\alpha$ is the intersection of the maximally preservative α-removals by $\div$. Since every maximally preservative α-removal is, by definition, a superset of $\mathbf{K}\div\alpha$, it remains to show that if $\varepsilon \notin \mathbf{K}\div\alpha$, then there is a maximally preservative α-removal $\mathbf{K}\div\delta$ such that $\varepsilon \notin \mathbf{K}\div\delta$. Let $\varepsilon \notin \mathbf{K}\div\alpha$.

We then have $\varepsilon \notin \mathrm{Cn}(B - \alpha)$. Since $-$ satisfies *meet maximality*, $B - \alpha$ is the intersection of the maximally preservative α-removals by $-$. Suppose that each of these implies ε. Since B is finite and disjunctively closed it then follows from Observation 1.34 that $\varepsilon \in \mathrm{Cn}(B - \alpha)$. We can conclude from this contradiction that there is some $B - \delta$ that is a maximally preservative α-removal by $-$ and such that $\varepsilon \notin \mathrm{Cn}(B - \delta)$.

We are going to prove that $\mathbf{K}\div\delta$ is a maximally preservative α-removal by $\div$. Since $B-\delta$ is an α-removal, it does not imply α, and then neither does $\mathbf{K}\div\delta$. Thus, $\mathbf{K}\div\delta$ is an α-removal. Since $B - \delta$ is a preservative α-removal, $B - \alpha \subseteq B - \delta$, and thus $\mathbf{K}\div\alpha \subseteq \mathbf{K}\div\delta$, so that $\mathbf{K}\div\delta$ is a preservative α-removal.

Finally, suppose that $\mathbf{K}\div\delta$ is not maximally preservative. Then there is some $\mathbf{K}\div\phi$ such that $\mathbf{K}\div\delta \subset \mathbf{K}\div\phi \nvdash \alpha$. It follows from $\mathbf{K}\div\delta \subseteq \mathbf{K}\div\phi$ that $B - \delta \subseteq \mathrm{Cn}(B - \phi)$. By *inclusion*, $B - \delta \subseteq B$. Thus $B - \delta \subseteq B \cap \mathrm{Cn}(B - \phi)$, and we can use *relative closure* to conclude that $B - \delta \subseteq B - \phi$. Clearly, $B - \phi \subseteq B - \delta$ cannot hold, since we would then have $B - \delta = B - \phi$ and consequently $\mathbf{K}\div\delta = \mathbf{K}\div\phi$, contrary to $\mathbf{K}\div\delta \subset \mathbf{K}\div\phi$. We can conclude that $B - \delta \subset B - \phi$.

It follows from $\mathbf{K}\div\phi \nvdash \alpha$ that $B-\phi \nvdash \alpha$. We thus have $B-\delta \subset B-\phi \nvdash \alpha$, which cannot be true since $B - \delta$ is a maximally preservative α-removal by $-$. We can conclude from this contradiction that $\mathbf{K}\div\delta$ is a maximally preservative α-removal by $\div$.

It only remains to conclude from $\varepsilon \notin \mathrm{Cn}(B - \delta)$ that $\varepsilon \notin \mathbf{K}\div\delta$, and we are finished. ■

OBSERVATION 4.34 *Let A be a finite set and $\sim_\gamma$ an operator of partial meet contraction for A. Then A satisfies meet maximality.*

Proof. It follows from the definition of maximally preservative removals that for every non-tautological sentence α, $A{\sim_\gamma}\alpha$ is a subset of each maximally preservative α-removal, and thus a subset of their intersection. It remains to be shown that this intersection is a subset of $A{\sim_\gamma}\alpha$.

We are going to show that the set of maximally preservative α-removals coincides with $\hat{\gamma}(A\perp\alpha)$ (where $\hat{\gamma}$ is the completion of γ, see Section 2.17$^+$). For one direction, let $X \in \hat{\gamma}(A\perp\alpha)$. It follows from Observation 1.70 that $\{X\} = A\perp\delta$ for some δ, and thus that $X = A{\sim_\gamma}\delta$. Since $\bigcap\gamma(A\perp\alpha) = \bigcap\hat{\gamma}(A\perp\alpha)$ we then have $\bigcap\gamma(A\perp\alpha) \subseteq A{\sim_\gamma}\delta \in A\perp\alpha$. It follows from $A{\sim_\gamma}\delta \in A\perp\alpha$ that there is no ε such that $A{\sim_\gamma}\delta \subset A{\sim_\gamma}\varepsilon \nvdash \alpha$. We can conclude that $X = A{\sim_\gamma}\delta$ is a maximally preservative α-removal.

For the other direction, let $A\sim_\gamma\delta$ be a maximally preservative α-removal. Suppose that $A\sim_\gamma\delta \notin \hat{\gamma}(A\bot\alpha)$. Since $A\sim_\gamma\alpha \subseteq A\sim_\gamma\delta \nvdash \alpha$, there must then be some X such that $A\sim_\gamma\delta \subset X \in \hat{\gamma}(A\bot\alpha)$. It follows from Observation 1.70 that $\{X\} = A\bot\phi$ for some ϕ, and thus that $X = A\sim_\gamma\phi$. We then have $A\sim_\gamma\delta \subset A\sim_\gamma\phi \nvdash \alpha$, contrary to the assumption that $A\sim_\gamma\delta$ is a maximally preservative α-removal. We can conclude from this contradiction that $A\sim_\gamma\delta \in \hat{\gamma}(A\bot\alpha)$.

We have proved that the set of maximally preservative α-removals coincides with $\hat{\gamma}(A\bot\alpha)$. We know from Observation 2.68 that $A\sim_\gamma\alpha = \bigcap\hat{\gamma}(A\bot\alpha)$, which concludes the proof. ■

It follows from Observations 4.33 and 4.34 that meet maximality holds for base-generated partial meet contraction if it is generated from a finite and disjunctively closed base.

Exercises

192. Let $-$ be an operator on a finite and disjunctively closed set B. Let $\mathrm{K} = \mathrm{Cn}(B)$, and let $\div$ be the closure of $-$. Show that if $-$ satisfies *inclusion*, *relative closure*, and the following postulate:
$B - (\alpha\&\beta) = (B - \alpha) \cap (B - \beta)$ (*meet identity*)
then $\div$ also satisfies meet identity.

193. Let $-$ be an operator on a finite and disjunctively closed set B. Let $\mathrm{K} = \mathrm{Cn}(B)$, and let $\div$ be the closure of $-$. Show that if $-$ satisfies *inclusion*, *relative closure*, and the following postulate:
Either $A\div(\alpha\&\beta) = A\div\alpha$, $A\div(\alpha\&\beta) = A\div\beta$, or $A\div(\alpha\&\beta) = (A\div\alpha)\cap(A\div\beta)$. (*conjunctive factoring*)
then $\div$ also satisfies *conjunctive factoring*.

194. Let $\mathrm{K} = \mathrm{Cn}(B)$ and let $\div$ be the closure of the operator $-$ on B. Show that if $-$ satisfies *inclusion* and *relative closure*, then it holds that:

    (a) $\mathrm{K}\div\alpha \subseteq \mathrm{K}\div\beta$ if and only if $B - \alpha \subseteq B - \beta$.
    (b) $\mathrm{K}\div\alpha = \mathrm{K}\div\beta$ if and only if $B - \alpha = B - \beta$.
    (c) $\mathrm{K}\div\alpha \subset \mathrm{K}\div\beta$ if and only if $B - \alpha \subset B - \beta$.

195. Let B be a disjunctively closed set. Let $-$ be an operator on B that satisfies *inclusion* and *relative closure*. Let $\mathrm{K} = \mathrm{Cn}(B)$, and let $\div$ be the closure of $-$. Show that if $(B - \alpha_1) \cap \ldots \cap (B - \alpha_n) \subseteq (B - \beta)$, then $(\mathrm{K}\div\alpha_1) \cap \ldots \cap (\mathrm{K}\div\alpha_n) \subseteq \mathrm{K}\div\beta$.

10+ RECOVERY AND NEBEL'S PSEUDO-CONTRACTION

The postulate of recovery, $A \subseteq \mathrm{Cn}((A\div\alpha)\cup\{\alpha\})$, is closure-invariant. However, we will not have use for this property, since recovery does not hold for the operations on belief bases that we use to derive operations on belief sets. The following proof shows that under reasonably general conditions, recovery does not hold for operations that are generated from contractions on bases.

> Let $\mathcal{L}$ (the language) consist of an infinite number of logically independent (atomic) sentences and their truth-functional combinations. Let $\mathbf{K}$ be a belief set such that $\mathbf{K} \neq \text{Cn}(\emptyset)$. Furthermore, let the operator $\div$ on $\mathbf{K}$ be generated by a contraction operator $-$ on a finite base for $\mathbf{K}$. Then $\div$ does not satisfy *recovery*.
> [Theorem 4.5.]

Proof. Suppose to the contrary that $\div$ satisfies *recovery*.

Since $\text{Cn}(B) = \mathbf{K}$, it follows from $\mathbf{K} \neq \text{Cn}(\emptyset)$ that B contains at least one non-tautological sentence. Let $\beta \in B \backslash \text{Cn}(\emptyset)$.

Since B is finite, and each of its elements is a truth-functional combination of a finite number of atomic sentences, it follows from the infiniteness of the set of atomic sentences that there is some atomic sentence q that does not appear in any element of B.

Since $-$ is a contraction operator, it satisfies *inclusion* and *success*. It follows from *inclusion* that $B - (\beta \vee q) \subseteq B$. Furthermore, since β is non-tautological, and q does not appear in β, $\beta \vee q$ is non-tautological. Thus, by *success*, we have $\beta \vee q \notin \text{Cn}(B - (\beta \vee q))$, and consequently $\beta \notin \text{Cn}(B - (\beta \vee q))$.

We have assumed that $\div$ satisfies *recovery*. Then $\beta \in \text{Cn}((\mathbf{K} \div (\beta \vee q)) \cup \{\beta \vee q\})$. By the deduction property, $\mathbf{K} \div (\beta \vee q) \vdash \beta \vee q \rightarrow \beta$, or equivalently $B - (\beta \vee q) \vdash \beta \vee q \rightarrow \beta$. It follows from this that $B - (\beta \vee q) \vdash \neg q \vee \beta$.

Since q does not appear in any element of B, it does not either appear in any element of its subset $B - (\beta \vee q)$. Therefore, $B - (\beta \vee q) \vdash \neg q \vee \beta$ holds if and only if $B - (\beta \vee q) \vdash \beta$ holds. Since we have just shown that $\beta \notin \text{Cn}(B - (\beta \vee q))$, a contradiction has been derived from the assumption that $\div$ satisfies *recovery*. ■

In order to obtain recovery with a base-generated operation, we must resort to pseudo-contractions on the base. Recovery can be achieved with Nebel's pseudo-contraction, i.e. the operation such that:

$$B \tilde{-}_\gamma \alpha = B \text{ if } \alpha \in \text{Cn}(\emptyset)$$
$$B \tilde{-}_\gamma \alpha = \bigcap \gamma(B \perp \alpha) \cup \{\alpha \rightarrow \& B\} \text{ otherwise.}$$

> Let $\div$ be an operation for a belief set $\mathbf{K}$ that is generated by a Nebel's pseudo-contraction on a finite base B for $\mathbf{K}$. Then $\div$ satisfies *closure, inclusion, vacuity, success, extensionality*, and *recovery*.
> [Observation 4.16.]

Proof. *Closure*: Directly from $\mathbf{K} \div \alpha = \text{Cn}(B - \alpha)$.

Inclusion: Since B is a subset of $\mathbf{K}$, so is $\bigcap\gamma(B\perp\alpha)$. We also have $\alpha\rightarrow\&B \in \mathrm{Cn}(B) = \mathbf{K}$.

Vacuity: Suppose that $\alpha \notin \mathrm{Cn}(\mathbf{K})$. Then $\alpha \notin \mathrm{Cn}(B)$, and thus $\gamma(B\perp\alpha) = \{B\}$. Since $\alpha\rightarrow\&B \in \mathrm{Cn}(B)$ we therefore have $\mathrm{Cn}(B\tilde{\sim}_\gamma\alpha) = \mathrm{Cn}(B) = \mathbf{K}$.

Success: Let $\alpha \notin \mathrm{Cn}(\emptyset)$. Then $\bigcap\gamma(B\perp\alpha) \nvdash \alpha$. Suppose that $\alpha \in \mathrm{Cn}(B\tilde{\sim}_\gamma\alpha)$. We then have $\bigcap\gamma(B\perp\alpha) \cup \{\alpha\rightarrow\&B\} \vdash \alpha$, and thus by the deduction property $\bigcap\gamma(B\perp\alpha) \vdash (\alpha\rightarrow\&B)\rightarrow\alpha$, which implies $\bigcap\gamma(B\perp\alpha) \vdash \alpha$, contrary to what was just established. We can conclude from this contradiction that *success* holds.

Extensionality: If $\alpha\leftrightarrow\beta \in \mathrm{Cn}(\emptyset)$, then $B\perp\alpha = B\perp\beta$, so that $\bigcap\gamma(B\perp\alpha) = \bigcap\gamma(B\perp\beta)$. Furthermore, $\alpha\rightarrow\&B$ and $\beta\rightarrow\&B$ are equivalent, and consequently $\mathrm{Cn}(\bigcap\gamma(B\perp\alpha) \cup \{\alpha\rightarrow\&B\}) = \mathrm{Cn}(\bigcap\gamma(B\perp\beta) \cup \{\beta\rightarrow\&B\})$.

Recovery: It follows from $\alpha\rightarrow\&B \in B\tilde{\sim}_\gamma\alpha$ that $\&B \in \mathrm{Cn}((B\tilde{\sim}_\gamma\alpha) \cup \{\alpha\})$. Since $\mathrm{Cn}(\{\&B\}) = \mathrm{Cn}(B) = \mathbf{K}$ and $\mathrm{Cn}(B\tilde{\sim}_\gamma\alpha) = \mathbf{K}\div\alpha$ this yields $\mathbf{K} \subseteq \mathrm{Cn}((\mathbf{K}\div\alpha) \cup \{\alpha\})$. ■

Exercises

196. [98] Show that for any selection function γ, and any sentence α:
$\mathrm{Cn}((B\sim_\gamma\neg\alpha) \cup \{\alpha\}) = \mathrm{Cn}((B\tilde{\sim}_\gamma\neg\alpha) \cup \{\alpha\})$.

197. Let $\sim$ be full meet contraction. Let $-$ be an operator on a set B. Let $\mathbf{K} = \mathrm{Cn}(B)$ and let $\div$ be the closure of $-$. Show that $\div$ satisfies *recovery* if and only if it holds for all sentences α that $\mathbf{K} \sim \alpha \subseteq \mathrm{Cn}(B - \alpha)$. (Hint: Use Observation 2.12 and show that $\varepsilon \in \mathbf{K} \cap \mathrm{Cn}(\{\neg\alpha\})$ if and only if ε is equivalent to $\alpha\rightarrow\beta$ for some $\beta \in \mathbf{K}$.)

11+ PROVING THE REPRESENTATION THEOREMS

In order to prove the representation theorems of Sections 4.4–4.5, we need to find a construction to be used in the postulates-to-construction part of the proof. When proving the representation theorems of Chapters 2 and 3, we had to construct an operator. Here, we need to construct both a base and an operator.

The following simple construction:

$$B = \{\&\mathbf{K}' \mid \mathbf{K}' = \mathbf{K}\div\alpha \text{ for some } \alpha\}$$

has turned out to be very useful in these proofs. It may be called the *standard base* for theorems on base-generated contraction (from finite bases). The following observation confirms that, in the presence of some of the basic postulates, the standard base is actually a base for the belief set $\mathbf{K}$.

OBSERVATION 4.35 ([51]) *Let $\div$ be an operator on the consistent belief set* $\mathbf{K}$ *that satisfies inclusion, vacuity, and finitude, and let*

$$B = \{\&\mathbf{K}' \mid \mathbf{K}' = \mathbf{K}\div\alpha \textit{ for some } \alpha\}.$$

Then $\text{Cn}(B) = \mathbf{K}$.

Proof. Let ξ be any sentence not in $\mathbf{K}$. It follows from *vacuity* that $\mathbf{K}{\div}\xi = \mathbf{K}$ and from *finitude* that $\&(\mathbf{K}{\div}\xi) = \&\mathbf{K}$ is well-defined. We therefore have $\&\mathbf{K} \in B$, and consequently $\text{Cn}(\{\&\mathbf{K}\}) \subseteq \text{Cn}(B)$, i.e. $\mathbf{K} \subseteq \text{Cn}(B)$.

It follows from *inclusion* that $B \subseteq \mathbf{K}$, and thus $\text{Cn}(B) \subseteq \mathbf{K}$. We can conclude that $\text{Cn}(B) = \mathbf{K}$. ∎

The next two observations introduce two useful properties of the standard base, that will be referred to repeatedly in the proofs of representation theorems.

OBSERVATION 4.36 ([51]) *Let* $\div$ *be an operator for a consistent belief set* $\mathbf{K}$ *that satisfies closure and finitude, and let* $B = \{\&\mathbf{K}' \mid \mathbf{K}' = \mathbf{K}{\div}\alpha$ *for some* $\alpha\}$. *Then for all* α: $\text{Cn}(B \cap (\mathbf{K}{\div}\alpha)) = \mathbf{K}{\div}\alpha$.

Proof. It follows from *finitude* that $\&(\mathbf{K}{\div}\alpha)$ is well-defined for all α, and from the construction of B that $\&(\mathbf{K}{\div}\alpha) \in B$. Since $\&(\mathbf{K}{\div}\alpha)$ follows logically from $\mathbf{K}{\div}\alpha$, it follows from *closure* that $\&(\mathbf{K}{\div}\alpha) \in \mathbf{K}{\div}\alpha$. Consequently, $\&(\mathbf{K}{\div}\alpha) \in B \cap (\mathbf{K}{\div}\alpha)$, so that $\text{Cn}(\{\&(\mathbf{K}{\div}\alpha)\}) \subseteq \text{Cn}(B \cap (\mathbf{K}{\div}\alpha))$. We also have $\mathbf{K}{\div}\alpha \subseteq \text{Cn}(\{\&(\mathbf{K}{\div}\alpha)\})$, so that $\mathbf{K}{\div}\alpha \subseteq \text{Cn}(B \cap (\mathbf{K}{\div}\alpha))$.

By set theory, $B \cap (\mathbf{K}{\div}\alpha) \subseteq \mathbf{K}{\div}\alpha$, and thus $\text{Cn}(B \cap (\mathbf{K}{\div}\alpha)) \subseteq \text{Cn}(\mathbf{K}{\div}\alpha)$. It follows from *closure* that $\text{Cn}(B \cap (\mathbf{K}{\div}\alpha)) \subseteq \mathbf{K}{\div}\alpha$. ∎

OBSERVATION 4.37 ([51]) *Let* $\div$ *be an operator for a consistent belief set* $\mathbf{K}$ *that satisfies closure, success, finitude, and weak conservativity, and furthermore let* $B = \{\&\mathbf{K}' \mid \mathbf{K}' = \mathbf{K}{\div}\alpha$ *for some* $\alpha\}$. *Then for all* δ:
If $\{X\} = B\perp\delta$, *then* $X = B \cap (\mathbf{K}{\div}\delta)$.

Proof. It follows from *finitude* that $\&(\mathbf{K}{\div}\alpha)$ is well-defined for all sentences α.

Let $\{X\} = B\perp\delta$. It follows from *success* that $\mathbf{K}{\div}\delta \nvdash \delta$, and thus $B \cap (\mathbf{K}{\div}\delta) \nvdash \delta$. Thus $B \cap (\mathbf{K}{\div}\delta)$ is a subset of some element of $B\perp\delta$, namely its only element X. We have shown that $B \cap (\mathbf{K}{\div}\delta) \subseteq X$.

For the other direction, suppose to the contrary that $X \nsubseteq B \cap (\mathbf{K}{\div}\delta)$. Since X is a subset of B, there is then, according to the construction of B, some ϕ such that $\&(\mathbf{K}{\div}\phi) \in X$ and $\&(\mathbf{K}{\div}\phi) \notin B \cap (\mathbf{K}{\div}\delta)$.

Suppose that $\mathbf{K}{\div}\phi \subseteq \mathbf{K}{\div}\delta$. Since by *closure*, $\&(\mathbf{K}{\div}\phi) \in \mathbf{K}{\div}\phi$, we then have $\&(\mathbf{K}{\div}\phi) \in \mathbf{K}{\div}\delta$. Since $\&(\mathbf{K}{\div}\phi) \in B$, it follows directly that $\&(\mathbf{K}{\div}\phi) \in B \cap (\mathbf{K}{\div}\delta)$, contrary to what was just shown. We can conclude from this contradiction that $\mathbf{K}{\div}\phi \nsubseteq \mathbf{K}{\div}\delta$.

It follows from *weak conservativity* that there is some ψ such that $\mathbf{K}{\div}\psi \nvdash \delta$ and $(\mathbf{K}{\div}\phi) \cup (\mathbf{K}{\div}\psi) \vdash \delta$.

However, it follows from $\mathbf{K}{\div}\psi \nvdash \delta$ that $B \cap (\mathbf{K}{\div}\psi) \nvdash \delta$ and thus from $\{X\} = B\perp\delta$ that $B \cap (\mathbf{K}{\div}\psi) \subseteq X$. Furthermore, since $\&(\mathbf{K}{\div}\phi) \in X$ we have $\mathbf{K}{\div}\phi =$

$\text{Cn}(\&(\mathbf{K}\div\phi)) \subseteq \text{Cn}(X)$ and thus $B \cap (\mathbf{K}\div\phi) \subseteq B \cap \text{Cn}(X)$. Since X is a B-closed subset of B (Observation 1.36), it follows that $B \cap (\mathbf{K}\div\phi) \subseteq X$. Thus both $B \cap (\mathbf{K}\div\psi)$ and $B \cap (\mathbf{K}\div\phi)$ are subsets of X .

Since $X \nvdash \delta$ it follows from this that $(B \cap (\mathbf{K}\div\psi)) \cup (B \cap (\mathbf{K}\div\phi)) \nvdash \delta$, and consequently $\text{Cn}(B \cap (\mathbf{K}\div\psi)) \cup \text{Cn}(B \cap (\mathbf{K}\div\phi)) \nvdash \delta$. According to Observation 4.36, $\text{Cn}(B \cap (\mathbf{K}\div\psi)) = \mathbf{K}\div\psi$ and $\text{Cn}(B \cap (\mathbf{K}\div\phi)) = \mathbf{K}\div\phi$. We have shown that $(\mathbf{K}\div\phi) \cup (\mathbf{K}\div\psi) \nvdash \delta$, contrary to what we showed to follow from *weak conservativity*. We may conclude from this contradiction that $X = B \cap (\mathbf{K}\div\delta)$. ■

To see why this last observation is useful, note that if $\{X\} = B\bot\delta$, then it holds for all selection functions γ that $\gamma(B\bot\delta) = \{X\}$, so that $B{\sim_\gamma}\delta = X$. We therefore have $B{\sim_\gamma}\delta = B \cap (\mathbf{K}\div\delta)$. This is an important link between an operator on the base and an operator on the belief set.

We are now ready to prove our first representation theorem for base-generated contraction, namely that for base-generated partial meet contraction:

> An operator $\div$ on a consistent belief set $\mathbf{K}$ is generated by an operator of partial meet contraction for a finite base for $\mathbf{K}$ if and only if $\div$ satisfies *closure, inclusion, vacuity, success, extensionality, finitude, symmetry*, and *conservativity*.
> [Theorem 4.8.]

Proof. *Construction-to-postulates*: Let $\div$ be an operator on $\mathbf{K}$ that is generated by an operator $\sim_\gamma$ of partial meet contraction on a finite belief base B for $\mathbf{K}$. It follows from Observation 4.4 that *inclusion, vacuity, success*, and *extensionality* are satisfied by $\div$, and clearly so is *closure*. We can conclude from the finiteness of B that *finitude* is satisfied. It was shown in Section 4.8+ that *symmetry* and *conservativity* are satisfied (Observations 4.21, 4.23, and 4.25).

Postulates-to-construction: Let $B = \{\&\mathbf{K}' \mid \mathbf{K}' = \mathbf{K}\div\alpha \text{ for some } \alpha\}$. Let the function γ be is defined as follows:

1. If $B\bot\alpha \neq \emptyset$, then $\gamma(B\bot\alpha) = \{X \in B\bot\alpha \mid \mathbf{K}\div\alpha \subseteq \text{Cn}(X)\}$, and
2. If $B\bot\alpha = \emptyset$, then $\gamma(B\bot\alpha) = \{B\}$.

We need to show (1) that B is a finite base for $\mathbf{K}$, (2) that γ is a function, (3) that γ is a selection function for B, and (4) that for all α:$\mathbf{K}\div\alpha = \text{Cn}(\bigcap\gamma(B\bot\alpha))$.

Part 1: It follows from Observation 4.35 that $\text{Cn}(B) = \mathbf{K}$. By *finitude*, B is finite.

Part 2: In order to show that γ is a function over the given domain, let $B\bot\alpha = B\bot\beta$. We have to show that $\gamma(B\bot\alpha) = \gamma(B\bot\beta)$.

It follows by Observation 1.39 from $B\bot\alpha = B\bot\beta$ that every subset of B implies α if and only if it implies β. Applying this to the subset $B \cap (\mathbf{K}\div\delta)$ of B, we obtain for all δ:

$$\alpha \in \text{Cn}(B \cap (\mathbf{K}\div\delta)) \text{ if and only if } \beta \in \text{Cn}(B \cap (\mathbf{K}\div\delta)).$$

It follows from Observation 4.36 that $\text{Cn}(B \cap (\mathbf{K}\div\delta)) = \mathbf{K}\div\delta$, and thus for all δ:

$$\mathbf{K}\div\delta \vdash \alpha \text{ iff } \mathbf{K}\div\delta \vdash \beta.$$

It follows from this and *symmetry* that $\mathbf{K}\div\alpha = \mathbf{K}\div\beta$. It can be seen from the definition of γ that if $B\bot\alpha = B\bot\beta$ and $\mathbf{K}\div\alpha = \mathbf{K}\div\beta$, then $\gamma(B\bot\alpha) = \gamma(B\bot\beta)$.

Part 3: In order to prove that γ is a selection function for B, it remains to be shown that if $B\bot\alpha$ is non-empty, then so is $\gamma(B\bot\alpha)$.

If $B\bot\alpha$ is non-empty, then α is not a logical truth. By *success*, $\mathbf{K}\div\alpha \nvdash \alpha$. Thus $B\cap(\mathbf{K}\div\alpha) \nvdash \alpha$, and we can use the upper bound property to conclude that there is some X with $B \cap (\mathbf{K}\div\alpha) \subseteq X \in B\bot\alpha$. According to Observation 4.36, we have $\text{Cn}(B\cap(\mathbf{K}\div\alpha)) = \mathbf{K}\div\alpha$. It follows that $\mathbf{K}\div\alpha \subseteq \text{Cn}(X)$. Then by the definition of γ, $\gamma(B\bot\alpha)$ is non-empty.

Part 4: There are two cases, according to whether or not α is a logical theorem.

Case 1, α is a logical theorem: Let $\beta \notin \mathbf{K}$. It follows from *vacuity* that $\mathbf{K}\div\beta = \mathbf{K}$. By *conservativity*, if $\mathbf{K}\div\beta \nsubseteq \mathbf{K}\div\alpha$, then there is some δ such that $\mathbf{K}\div\delta \nvdash \alpha$. By *closure*, this is impossible. Thus $\mathbf{K}\div\beta \subseteq \mathbf{K}\div\alpha$, i.e. $\mathbf{K} \subseteq \mathbf{K}\div\alpha$. It follows from *inclusion* that $\mathbf{K}\div\alpha \subseteq \mathbf{K}$, and we can conclude that $\mathbf{K} = \mathbf{K}\div\alpha$.

Since α is a logical theorem, $B\bot\alpha$ is empty, and it follows from the above definition of γ that $\gamma(B\bot\alpha) = \{B\}$. Using part 1 of the present proof, we obtain $\text{Cn}(\bigcap\gamma(B\bot\alpha)) = \text{Cn}(B) = \mathbf{K} = \mathbf{K}\div\alpha$.

Case 2, α is not a logical theorem: Then $B\bot\alpha$ is non-empty. It follows from part 3 of the present proof that $\gamma(B\bot\alpha)$ is non-empty.

Let $X \in \gamma(B\bot\alpha)$. Then it follows from the definition of γ that $\mathbf{K}\div\alpha \subseteq \text{Cn}(X)$. It follows from *closure* that $\&(\mathbf{K}\div\alpha) \in \mathbf{K}\div\alpha$, and thus $\&(\mathbf{K}\div\alpha) \in \text{Cn}(X)$. According to the construction of B, we also have $\&(\mathbf{K}\div\alpha) \in B$. Thus, $\&(\mathbf{K}\div\alpha) \in B\cap\text{Cn}(X)$, and since X is a B-closed subset of B (Observation 1.36), $\&(\mathbf{K}\div\alpha) \in X$. Since this holds for all $X \in \gamma(B\bot\alpha)$, we have $\&(\mathbf{K}\div\alpha) \in \bigcap\gamma(B\bot\alpha)$. Since $\text{Cn}(\{\&(\mathbf{K}\div\alpha)\}) = \mathbf{K}\div\alpha$, it follows that $\mathbf{K}\div\alpha \subseteq \text{Cn}(\bigcap\gamma(B\bot\alpha))$.

For the other direction, we are first going to show that $\bigcap\gamma(B\bot\alpha) \subseteq B\cap(\mathbf{K}\div\alpha)$. This we will do by assuming that $\varepsilon \notin B \cap (\mathbf{K}\div\alpha)$, and proving $\varepsilon \notin \cap\gamma(B\bot\alpha)$.

Let $\varepsilon \notin B\cap(\mathbf{K}\div\alpha)$. If there is no β such that $\varepsilon = \&(\mathbf{K}\div\beta)$, then $\varepsilon \notin B$ so that $\varepsilon \notin \bigcap\gamma(B\bot\alpha)$. We can therefore assume that $\varepsilon = \&(\mathbf{K}\div\beta)$ for some β. Thus, $\&(\mathbf{K}\div\beta) \notin B\cap(\mathbf{K}\div\alpha)$.

Suppose that $\mathbf{K}\div\beta \subseteq \mathbf{K}\div\alpha$. It then follows from *closure* that $\&(\mathbf{K}\div\beta) \in \mathbf{K}\div\beta$ and thus $\&(\mathbf{K}\div\beta) \in \mathbf{K}\div\alpha$. Since $\&(\mathbf{K}\div\beta) \in B$, we then have $\&(\mathbf{K}\div\beta) \in B\cap(\mathbf{K}\div\alpha)$, contrary to what was just shown. We can conclude that $\mathbf{K}\div\beta \nsubseteq \mathbf{K}\div\alpha$.

From this it follows, by *conservativity*, that there is some δ such that:

$$\mathbf{K}\div\alpha \subseteq \mathbf{K}\div\delta \nvdash \alpha \text{ and } (\mathbf{K}\div\beta) \cup (\mathbf{K}\div\delta) \vdash \alpha.$$

According to Observation 4.36, we have $\mathbf{K}\div\alpha = \text{Cn}(B\cap(\mathbf{K}\div\alpha))$ and furthermore $\mathbf{K}\div\delta = \text{Cn}(B \cap (\mathbf{K}\div\delta))$. Since we also have $\text{Cn}(\{\&(\mathbf{K}\div\delta)\}) = \mathbf{K}\div\delta$, we can conclude that:

$$B \cap (\mathbf{K} \div \alpha) \subseteq B \cap (\mathbf{K} \div \delta) \nvdash \alpha \text{ and } \{\&(\mathbf{K} \div \beta)\} \cup (B \cap (\mathbf{K} \div \delta)) \vdash \alpha.$$

It follows by the upper bound property from $B \cap (\mathbf{K} \div \delta) \nvdash \alpha$ that there is some Y such that $B \cap (\mathbf{K} \div \delta) \subseteq Y \in B \perp \alpha$. Since $B \cap (\mathbf{K} \div \alpha) \subseteq B \cap (\mathbf{K} \div \delta)$ we have $B \cap (\mathbf{K} \div \alpha) \subseteq Y$, and from $\{\&(\mathbf{K} \div \beta)\} \cup (B \cap (\mathbf{K} \div \delta)) \vdash \alpha$ we can conclude that $\&(\mathbf{K} \div \beta) \notin Y$.

Since $\text{Cn}(B \cap (\mathbf{K} \div \alpha)) = \mathbf{K} \div \alpha$, it follows from $B \cap (\mathbf{K} \div \alpha) \subseteq Y$ that $\mathbf{K} \div \alpha \subseteq \text{Cn}(Y)$. Thus, according to the definition of γ, $Y \in \gamma(B \perp \alpha)$. Since $\&(\mathbf{K} \div \beta) \notin Y$, we have $\&(\mathbf{K} \div \beta) \notin \bigcap \gamma(B \perp \alpha)$, i.e. $\varepsilon \notin \bigcap \gamma(B \perp \alpha)$.

This concludes our proof that if $\varepsilon \notin B \cap (\mathbf{K} \div \alpha)$, then $\varepsilon \notin \bigcap \gamma(B \perp \alpha)$, or in other words, $\bigcap \gamma(B \perp \alpha) \subseteq B \cap (\mathbf{K} \div \alpha)$. From this it follows that $\text{Cn}(\bigcap \gamma(B \perp \alpha)) \subseteq \text{Cn}(B \cap (\mathbf{K} \div \alpha))$. Since $\text{Cn}(B \cap (\mathbf{K} \div \alpha)) = \mathbf{K} \div \alpha$, this is sufficient to show that $\text{Cn}(\bigcap \gamma(B \perp \alpha)) \subseteq \mathbf{K} \div \alpha$. ■

The selection function γ that was used in the postulates-to-construction part of this proof has the completion property (cf. Section 2.17+). To see this, let X be such that $B \sim_\gamma \alpha \subseteq X \in B \perp \alpha$. Then $\text{Cn}(B \sim_\gamma \alpha) \subseteq \text{Cn}(X)$, i.e. $\mathbf{K} \div \alpha \subseteq \text{Cn}(X)$, and it follows from the definition of γ that $X \in \gamma(B \perp \alpha)$.

The corresponding proof for maxichoice contraction can to a large part be based on the foregoing proof. In the construction-to-postulates part, it only remains to show that strong conservativity is satisfied. In the postulates-to-construction part, the same construction can be used as for the general case of partial meet contraction, and it only remains to show that the constructed selection function is maxichoice.

> An operator $\div$ on a consistent belief set $\mathbf{K}$ is generated by an operator of maxichoice contraction for a finite base for $\mathbf{K}$ if and only if $\div$ satisfies *closure*, *inclusion*, *vacuity*, *success*, *extensionality*, *finitude*, *symmetry*, and *strong conservativity*.
> [Theorem 4.9.]

Proof. *Construction-to-postulates*: Let $\div$ be an operation on $\mathbf{K}$ that is generated by an operator $\sim_\gamma$ of maxichoice partial meet contraction on a finite belief base B for $\mathbf{K}$. It follows from Observations 4.21 and 4.22 that *strong conservativity* holds, and from Theorem 4.8 that the rest of the listed posulates are satisfied.

Postulates-to-construction: Since *strong conservativity* implies *conservativity*, the corresponding part of the proof of Theorem 4.8 is applicable, and it only remains to show that $\sim_\gamma$ is maxichoice. This can be done by showing that if $\delta \in B \backslash (B \sim_\gamma \alpha)$, then $B \sim_\gamma \alpha \cup \{\delta\} \vdash \alpha$.

Let $\delta \in B \backslash (B \sim_\gamma \alpha)$. According to the construction of B, $\delta = \&(\mathbf{K} \div \beta)$ for some β.

Suppose that $\&(\mathbf{K}\div\beta) \in \text{Cn}(B\sim_\gamma\alpha)$. Since $B\sim_\gamma\alpha$ is a B-closed subset of B (Observation 1.36), and $\&(\mathbf{K}\div\beta) \in B$, it then follows that $\&(\mathbf{K}\div\beta) \in B\sim_\gamma\alpha$, contrary to our assumption that $\&(\mathbf{K}\div\beta) = \delta \notin B\sim_\gamma\alpha$. We can conclude that $\&(\mathbf{K}\div\beta) \notin \text{Cn}(B\sim_\gamma\alpha)$. From this it follows, by part 4 of the proof of Theorem 4.8, that $\&(\mathbf{K}\div\beta) \notin \mathbf{K}\div\alpha$.

Suppose that $\mathbf{K}\div\beta \subseteq \mathbf{K}\div\alpha$. By *closure*, $\&(\mathbf{K}\div\beta) \in \mathbf{K}\div\beta$, and consequently $\&(\mathbf{K}\div\beta) \in \mathbf{K}\div\alpha$, contrary to what was just shown. We can conclude that $\mathbf{K}\div\beta \not\subseteq \mathbf{K}\div\alpha$.

It follows from $\mathbf{K}\div\beta \not\subseteq \mathbf{K}\div\alpha$, by *strong conservativity*, that $\mathbf{K}\div\beta \cup \mathbf{K}\div\alpha \vdash \alpha$. Since $\mathbf{K}\div\beta = \text{Cn}(\{\&(\mathbf{K}\div\beta)\}) = \text{Cn}(\{\delta\})$ and (by Part 4 of the proof of Theorem 4.8) $\mathbf{K}\div\alpha = \text{Cn}(B\sim_\gamma\alpha)$, we have $B\sim_\gamma\alpha \cup \{\delta\} \vdash \alpha$. This is what we needed in order to prove that $\sim_\gamma$ is maxichoice. ■

The proof for base-generated full meet contraction differs in one important respect from the proofs of the other representation theorems in this chapter: Here, we do not have to construct a contraction operator, since for any given set, there is only one operator of full meet contraction. We only need to construct a base. The standard base can be used here as well.

> An operator $\div$ on a consistent belief set $\mathbf{K}$ is generated by full meet contraction on a finite base for $\mathbf{K}$ if and only if $\div$ satisfies *closure*, *inclusion*, *vacuity*, *success*, *extensionality*, *finitude*, *conservativity*, and *indecisiveness*.
> [Theorem 4.10.]

Proof. *Construction-to-postulates*: Let $\div$ be the operation on $\mathbf{K}$ that is generated by the operator $\sim$ of full meet contraction on a finite belief base B for $\mathbf{K}$. It follows from Observations 4.30 and 4.31 that *indecisiveness* is satisfied, and from Theorem 4.8 that the rest of the listed postulates are satisfied.

Postulates-to-construction: Let $B = \{\&\mathbf{K}' \mid \mathbf{K}' = \mathbf{K}\div\alpha \text{ for some } \alpha\}$. We need to show that (1) B is a finite base for $\mathbf{K}$, (2) for all α, $\text{Cn}(\bigcap(B\bot\alpha)) \subseteq \mathbf{K}\div\alpha$, and (3) for all α, $\mathbf{K}\div\alpha \subseteq \text{Cn}(\bigcap(B\bot\alpha))$. The proof of Part 1 coincides with that of Part 1 of Theorem 4.8.

Part 2: We are first going to prove that $\bigcap(B\bot\alpha) \subseteq \mathbf{K}\div\alpha$. This can be done by showing that if $\zeta \notin \mathbf{K}\div\alpha$, then $\zeta \notin \bigcap(B\bot\alpha)$.

Let $\zeta \notin \mathbf{K}\div\alpha$. If there is no β such that $\zeta = \&(\mathbf{K}\div\beta)$, then it follows by the construction of B that $\zeta \notin \bigcap(B\bot\alpha)$. It remains to prove the principal case, in which $\zeta = \&(\mathbf{K}\div\beta)$ for some β.

Suppose that $\mathbf{K}\div\beta \subseteq \mathbf{K}\div\alpha$. It then follows from *closure* that $\&(\mathbf{K}\div\beta) \in \mathbf{K}\div\beta$, and thus $\&(\mathbf{K}\div\beta) \in \mathbf{K}\div\alpha$, contrary to $\&(\mathbf{K}\div\beta) = \zeta \notin \mathbf{K}\div\alpha$. We can conclude that $\mathbf{K}\div\beta \not\subseteq \mathbf{K}\div\alpha$.

By *conservativity*, there is some δ such that $\mathbf{K}\div\delta \nvdash \alpha$ and $(\mathbf{K}\div\beta)\cup(\mathbf{K}\div\delta) \vdash \alpha$. We have $\mathbf{K}\div\beta = \mathrm{Cn}(\{\&(\mathbf{K}\div\beta)\})$ and, according to Observation 4.36, $\mathbf{K}\div\delta = \mathrm{Cn}(B\cap(\mathbf{K}\div\delta))$. Thus, $\{\&(\mathbf{K}\div\beta)\}\cup(B\cap(\mathbf{K}\div\delta)) \vdash \alpha$.

It follows from $\mathbf{K}\div\delta \nvdash \alpha$ that $B\cap(\mathbf{K}\div\delta) \nvdash \alpha$, and thus from the upper bound property that there is some X such that $B\cap(\mathbf{K}\div\delta) \subseteq X \in B\bot\alpha$. Since we have just proved that $\{\&(\mathbf{K}\div\beta)\}\cup(B\cap(\mathbf{K}\div\delta)) \vdash \alpha$, we can conclude that $\&(\mathbf{K}\div\beta) \notin X \in B\bot\alpha$, and thus $\zeta = \&(\mathbf{K}\div\beta) \notin \bigcap(B\bot\alpha)$.

We have proved that $\bigcap(B\bot\alpha) \subseteq \mathbf{K}\div\alpha$. It follows directly from *closure* that $\mathrm{Cn}(\bigcap(B\bot\alpha)) \subseteq \mathbf{K}\div\alpha$.

Part 3: We are first going to show that $B\cap(\mathbf{K}\div\alpha) \subseteq \bigcap(B\bot\alpha)$. Let $\delta \notin \bigcap(B\bot\alpha)$. We need to prove that $\delta \notin B\cap(\mathbf{K}\div\alpha)$.

If there is no β such that $\delta = \&(\mathbf{K}\div\beta)$, then $\delta \notin B$ and thus $\delta \notin B\cap(\mathbf{K}\div\alpha)$. In the principal case, let $\delta = \&(\mathbf{K}\div\beta)$. It follows from $\&(\mathbf{K}\div\beta) \notin \bigcap(B\bot\alpha)$ that there is some X such that $\&(\mathbf{K}\div\beta) \notin X \in B\bot\alpha$.

According to Observation 1.70, $\{X\} = B\bot\phi$ for some ϕ. We can use Observation 4.37 to obtain $X = B\cap(\mathbf{K}\div\phi)$ and Observation 4.36 to obtain $\mathrm{Cn}(X) = \mathbf{K}\div\phi$.

It follows from $\&(\mathbf{K}\div\beta) \notin X \in B\bot\alpha$ and $X = B\cap(\mathbf{K}\div\phi)$ that $\&(\mathbf{K}\div\beta) \notin B\cap(\mathbf{K}\div\phi) \in B\bot\alpha$. Since $\mathrm{Cn}(B\cap(\mathbf{K}\div\phi)) = \mathbf{K}\div\phi$ we can conclude that $\mathbf{K}\div\phi \nvdash \alpha$. Furthermore since $\&(\mathbf{K}\div\beta) \in B$, it follows from $\&(\mathbf{K}\div\beta) \notin B\cap(\mathbf{K}\div\phi) \in B\bot\alpha$ that $(B\cap(\mathbf{K}\div\phi))\cup\{\&(\mathbf{K}\div\beta)\} \vdash \alpha$, and thus $(\mathbf{K}\div\beta)\cup(\mathbf{K}\div\phi) \vdash \alpha$.

It follows by *indecisiveness* from $\mathbf{K}\div\phi \nvdash \alpha$ and $(\mathbf{K}\div\beta)\cup(\mathbf{K}\div\phi) \vdash \alpha$ that $\mathbf{K}\div\beta \not\subseteq \mathbf{K}\div\alpha$.

Suppose that $\&(\mathbf{K}\div\beta) \in \mathbf{K}\div\alpha$. Then $\mathrm{Cn}(\{\&(\mathbf{K}\div\beta)\}) \subseteq \mathrm{Cn}(\mathbf{K}\div\alpha)$, i.e. by *closure*, $\mathbf{K}\div\beta \subseteq \mathbf{K}\div\alpha$, contrary to what was just shown. We can conclude that $\&(\mathbf{K}\div\beta) \notin \mathbf{K}\div\alpha$, so that $\delta = \&(\mathbf{K}\div\beta) \notin B\cap(\mathbf{K}\div\alpha)$.

With this we have proved that $B\cap(\mathbf{K}\div\alpha) \subseteq \bigcap(B\bot\alpha)$. It follows from Observation 4.36 that $\mathbf{K}\div\alpha \subseteq \mathrm{Cn}(\bigcap(B\bot\alpha))$. ■

The proof of the representation theorem for base-generated kernel contraction is quite similar to that for partial meet contraction, but it also contains several features from the theorems on kernel contraction in Section 2.22+.

> An operator $\div$ for a consistent belief set $\mathbf{K}$ is generated by an operator of kernel contraction for a finite base of $\mathbf{K}$ if and only if $\div$ satisfies *closure, inclusion, vacuity, success, extensionality, finitude, symmetry*, and *weak conservativity*.
> [Theorem 4.7.]

Proof. *Construction-to-postulates*: It follows from Observation 4.4 that *inclusion, vacuity, success*, and *extensionality* are satisfied, and clearly so is *closure*. That *finitude* holds follows directly from the finiteness of the base. That *symmetry* and *weak conservativity* hold follows from Observations 4.21, 4.25, and 4.26.

Postulates-to-construction: Let $\div$ be an operation on $\mathbf{K}$ that satisfies the eight postulates given in the theorem. We are going to show that it is based on a kernel contraction $\approx_\sigma$ on some base B for $\mathbf{K}$. Let B and σ be defined as follows:

$$B = \{\&\mathbf{K}' \mid \mathbf{K}' = \mathbf{K}\div\alpha \text{ for some } \alpha\}$$
$$\sigma(B\perp\!\!\!\perp\alpha) = \{\varepsilon \in B \mid \mathbf{K}\div\alpha \nvdash \varepsilon\}$$

We need to show (1) that B is a finite base for $\mathbf{K}$, (2) that σ is a function, (3) that $\text{Cn}(B\approx_\sigma\alpha) = \mathbf{K}\div\alpha$ for all α, and (4) that σ is an incision function. (It would have been more natural to mention (4) before (3), but it is more practical to prove (3) first since it can be used in the proof of (4).)

Part 1 coincides with the corresponding part of the proof of Theorem 4.8.

Part 2: To show that σ is a function, let $B\perp\!\!\!\perp\alpha = B\perp\!\!\!\perp\beta$. We have to show that $\sigma(B\perp\!\!\!\perp\alpha) = \sigma(B\perp\!\!\!\perp\beta)$.

It follows by Observation 2.84 from $B\perp\!\!\!\perp\alpha = B\perp\!\!\!\perp\beta$ that for all δ, $B\cap(\mathbf{K}\div\delta) \vdash \alpha$ iff $B \cap (\mathbf{K}\div\delta) \vdash \beta$. Furthermore, we know from Observation 4.36 that for all δ, $\text{Cn}(B \cap (\mathbf{K}\div\delta)) = \mathbf{K}\div\delta$. Thus for all δ, $\mathbf{K}\div\delta \vdash \alpha$ if and only if $\mathbf{K}\div\delta \vdash \beta$. By *symmetry*, $\mathbf{K}\div\alpha = \mathbf{K}\div\beta$. It follows from this, by the definition of σ, that $\sigma(B\perp\!\!\!\perp\alpha) = \sigma(B\perp\!\!\!\perp\beta)$.

Part 3: For one direction, let $\beta \in \mathbf{K}\div\alpha$. According to the definition of B, we have $\&(\mathbf{K}\div\alpha) \in B$. Since $\mathbf{K}\div\alpha \vdash \&(\mathbf{K}\div\alpha)$, it follows from the construction of σ that $\&(\mathbf{K}\div\alpha) \notin \sigma(B\perp\!\!\!\perp\alpha)$. According to the definition of B, $\&(\mathbf{K}\div\alpha) \in B$. We therefore have $\&(\mathbf{K}\div\alpha) \in B\backslash\sigma(B\perp\!\!\!\perp\alpha)$. Since $\beta \in \mathbf{K}\div\alpha = \text{Cn}(\{\&(\mathbf{K}\div\alpha)\})$, it follows that $\beta \in \text{Cn}(B\backslash\sigma(B\perp\!\!\!\perp\alpha)) = \text{Cn}(B\approx_\sigma\alpha)$.

For the other direction, let $\beta \notin \mathbf{K}\div\alpha$. By *closure*, $\mathbf{K}\div\alpha \nvdash \beta$. Suppose that $\beta \in \text{Cn}(B\backslash\sigma(B\perp\!\!\!\perp\alpha))$. Since $\mathbf{K}\div\alpha \nvdash \beta$ and $B\backslash\sigma(B\perp\!\!\!\perp\alpha) \vdash \beta$ we have $B\backslash\sigma(B\perp\!\!\!\perp\alpha) \not\subseteq \mathbf{K}\div\alpha$. Thus, there is some $\xi \in B\backslash\sigma(B\perp\!\!\!\perp\alpha)$ such that $\xi \notin \mathbf{K}\div\alpha$. By *closure*, $\mathbf{K}\div\alpha \nvdash \xi$. It follows from $\xi \in B$ and $\mathbf{K}\div\alpha \nvdash \xi$ by the definition of σ that $\xi \in \sigma(B\perp\!\!\!\perp\alpha)$, contrary to $\xi \in B\backslash\sigma(B\perp\!\!\!\perp\alpha)$. We may conclude from this contradiction that $\beta \notin \text{Cn}(B\backslash\sigma(B\perp\!\!\!\perp\alpha))$, i.e. $\beta \notin \text{Cn}(B\approx_\sigma\alpha)$.

Part 4: In order to prove that σ is an incision function for B, we need to show that conditions (i) and (ii) of Definition 2.30 are satisfied.

Ad (i): In order to show that $\sigma(B\perp\!\!\!\perp\alpha) \subseteq \bigcup(B\perp\!\!\!\perp\alpha)$, let $\varepsilon \in \sigma(B\perp\!\!\!\perp\alpha)$. It follows from the definition of σ that $\mathbf{K}\div\alpha \nvdash \varepsilon$. Since $\varepsilon \in B$ there is some λ such that $\varepsilon = \&(\mathbf{K}\div\lambda)$. We then have $\mathbf{K}\div\lambda \not\subseteq \mathbf{K}\div\alpha$. By *weak conservativity* there is some δ such that $\mathbf{K}\div\delta \nvdash \alpha$ and $(\mathbf{K}\div\lambda)\cup(\mathbf{K}\div\delta) \vdash \alpha$. It follows that $\{\&(\mathbf{K}\div\delta)\} \nvdash \alpha$ and $\{\&(\mathbf{K}\div\lambda), \&(\mathbf{K}\div\delta)\} \vdash \alpha$, from which we can conclude that either $\{\&(\mathbf{K}\div\lambda)\}$ or $\{\&(\mathbf{K}\div\lambda), \&(\mathbf{K}\div\delta)\}$ is an element of $B\perp\!\!\!\perp\alpha$. In both cases, $\&(\mathbf{K}\div\lambda) \in \bigcup(B\perp\!\!\!\perp\alpha)$, i.e. $\varepsilon \in \bigcup(B\perp\!\!\!\perp\alpha)$.

Ad (ii): Let $\emptyset \neq X \in B\perp\!\!\!\perp\alpha$. Suppose that $X \cap \sigma(B\perp\!\!\!\perp\alpha) = \emptyset$. Then $X \subseteq B\backslash\sigma(B\perp\!\!\!\perp\alpha)$. Since $X \vdash \alpha$ we then have $B\backslash\sigma(B\perp\!\!\!\perp\alpha) \vdash \alpha$. By Part 3 of the present proof, it follows from this that $\mathbf{K}\div\alpha \vdash \alpha$. It also follows from $\emptyset \neq X \in B\perp\!\!\!\perp\alpha$ that

$\nvdash \alpha$. However, it follows from *success* that $\mathbf{K}\div\alpha \vdash \alpha$ and $\nvdash \alpha$ cannot both hold. We may conclude from this contradiction that $X \cap \sigma(B\bot\alpha) \neq \emptyset$, which concludes the proof. ■

Exercises

198. (a) The proof of Observation 4.35 does not go through if we relax the condition that **K** is consistent. Explain why.
  (b) Prove the following adjusted version of Observation 4.35:
  Let $\div$ be an operator on a belief set **K** that satisfies *inclusion*, *failure*, and *finitude*, and let $B = \{\&\mathbf{K}' \mid \mathbf{K}' = \mathbf{K}\div\alpha \text{ for some } \alpha\}$. Then $\text{Cn}(B) = \mathbf{K}$.

199. What happens if *conservativity* is replaced by *weak conservativity* in the list of postulates that are used above to axiomatically characterize base-generated full meet contraction?

200. [52] Show that the following two conditions on an operation $\div$ on a belief set **K** are equivalent:
  (1) $\div$ is generated by a kernel contraction on a finite base for **K**.
  (2) $\div$ is generated by a smooth kernel contraction on a finite base for **K**.

12+ THE EFFECTS OF DISJUNCTIVE CLOSURE

In Section 1.13+, we learnt that if α_1, α_2, and their disjunction $\alpha_1 \vee \alpha_2$ are all elements of a set A, and $X \in A\bot\beta$ for some sentence β, then:

$$\alpha_1 \vee \alpha_2 \in X \text{ if and only if either } \alpha_1 \in X \text{ or } \alpha_2 \in X.$$

This property of disjunctive elements of remainders is closely connected to the following observation, that provides us with a one-to-one correspondence between remainders from a base and remainders from the disjunctive closure of that base. (Remember that for any set A, $\mathcal{V}(A)$ is the disjunctive closure of A, i.e. the set of sentences that are either elements of A or disjunctions of elements of A.)

OBSERVATION 4.38 ([49]) *Let B be a set of sentences and α a sentence. Then there is a one-to-one correspondence f from $B\bot\alpha$ to $\mathcal{V}(B)\bot\alpha$ such that if $X \in B\bot\alpha$ then $f(X) \in \mathcal{V}(B)\bot\alpha$ and* $\text{Cn}(X) = \text{Cn}(f(X))$.

The following definition will be used in the proof:

DEFINITION 4.39 ([49])

$$\mathcal{V}_A(B) = \mathcal{V}(A \cap B) \cup \{\alpha \vee \beta \mid \alpha \in \mathcal{V}(A \cap B) \& \beta \in \mathcal{V}(B)\}.$$

Thus, $\mathcal{V}_A(B)$ is the set of disjunctions of elements of B such that at least one disjunct is also an element of A. The following observation lists some elementary properties of $\mathcal{V}_A(B)$.

OBSERVATION 4.40

1. $\mathcal{V}(A \cap B) \subseteq \mathcal{V}_A(B) \subseteq \mathcal{V}(B)$
2. *If* $A \subseteq B$, *then* $\mathcal{V}(A) \subseteq \mathcal{V}_A(B)$
3. *If* $A \subseteq B$, *then* $\mathrm{Cn}(\mathcal{V}_A(B)) = \mathrm{Cn}(A)$.
4. *If* $A \cap B = \emptyset$, *then* $\mathcal{V}_A(B) = \emptyset$.

The proof of this observation is left as an exercise to the reader.

Proof of Observation 4.38. Let f be a function such that $f(X) = \mathcal{V}_X(B)$ for all $X \in B\bot\alpha$. We need to prove that: (1) if $X \in B\bot\alpha$, then $f(X) \in \mathcal{V}(B)\bot\alpha$, (2) if $X \in B\bot\alpha$, then $\mathrm{Cn}(X) = \mathrm{Cn}(f(X))$, and (3) for each $Y \in \mathcal{V}(B)\bot\alpha$ there is exactly one $X \in B\bot\alpha$ such that $Y = f(X)$.

Part 1: We are going to show that if $X \in B\bot\alpha$, then $\mathcal{V}_X(B) \in \mathcal{V}(B)\bot\alpha$.

Let $X \in B\bot\alpha$. $\mathcal{V}_X(B)$ is a subset of $\mathcal{V}(B)$, and since $\mathrm{Cn}(X) = \mathrm{Cn}(\mathcal{V}_X(B))$, we also have have $\mathcal{V}_X(B) \nvdash \alpha$. Suppose that $\mathcal{V}_X(B) \notin \mathcal{V}(B)\bot\alpha$. Then there is some β such that $\beta \in \mathcal{V}(B)\backslash\mathcal{V}_X(B)$ and $\mathcal{V}_X(B) \cup \{\beta\} \nvdash \alpha$. It follows from $\beta \in \mathcal{V}(B)$ that there are $\beta_1, \ldots \beta_n \in B$ such that $\beta = \beta_1 \vee \ldots \vee \beta_n$. It follows from $\beta \notin \mathcal{V}_X(B)$ that $\beta_k \notin X$ for all $\beta_k \in \{\beta_1, \ldots \beta_n\}$. Thus, $\{\beta_1, \ldots \beta_n\} \subseteq B\backslash X$.

Since $\mathrm{Cn}(X) = \mathrm{Cn}(\mathcal{V}_X(B))$ it can be concluded from $\mathcal{V}_X(B) \cup \{\beta\} \nvdash \alpha$ that $X \cup \{\beta_1 \vee \ldots \vee \beta_n\} \nvdash \alpha$. However, since $X \in B\bot\alpha$ and $\beta_k \in B\backslash X$ for each β_k, we have $X \cup \{\beta_k\} \vdash \alpha$, i.e. $X \vdash \beta_k \rightarrow \alpha$, for each β_k, so that $X \vdash \beta_1 \vee \ldots \vee \beta_n \rightarrow \alpha$, i.e. $X \cup \{\beta_1 \vee \ldots \vee \beta_n\} \vdash \alpha$, contrary to what we have just shown. It follows from this contradiction that $\mathcal{V}_X(B) \in \mathcal{V}(B)\bot\alpha$.

Part 2: It follows from $X \subseteq B$ that $\mathrm{Cn}(X) = \mathrm{Cn}(\mathcal{V}_X(B)) = \mathrm{Cn}(f(X))$.

Part 3: Let $Y \in \mathcal{V}(B)\bot\alpha$. We are now going to show that (a) $f(Y \cap B) = Y$, (b) $Y \cap B \in B\bot\alpha$, and (c) if $f(X) = Y$ for some $X \in B\bot\alpha$, then $X = Y \cap B$.

Part 3a: We are going to show that $f(Y \cap B) = Y$, i.e. $\mathcal{V}_{Y \cap B}(B) = Y$.

In order to prove that $Y \subseteq \mathcal{V}_{Y \cap B}(B)$, let $\beta \in Y$ and suppose that $\beta \notin \mathcal{V}_{Y \cap B}(B)$. Then β is a disjunction of elements of B, none of which is in $Y \cap B$, i.e. $\beta = \beta_1 \vee \ldots \vee \beta_n$ and $\{\beta_1, \ldots \beta_n\} \subseteq B\backslash Y$. It follows from $\beta \in Y \in \mathcal{V}(B)\bot\alpha$ that $Y \nvdash \beta \rightarrow \alpha$, i.e. $Y \nvdash \beta_1 \vee \ldots \vee \beta_n \rightarrow \alpha$. Thus there is some β_k such that $Y \nvdash \beta_k \rightarrow \alpha$, i.e. $Y \cup \{\beta_k\} \nvdash \alpha$. Since $\beta_k \in B \subseteq \mathcal{V}(B)$ and $\beta_k \notin Y$, this contradicts $Y \in \mathcal{V}(B)\bot\alpha$. We may conclude from this contradiction that $Y \subseteq \mathcal{V}_{Y \cap B}(B)$.

For the other direction, let $\beta \in \mathcal{V}_{Y \cap B}(B)$. Then there are $\beta_1, \ldots \beta_n$ in B such that $\beta = \beta_1 \vee \ldots \vee \beta_n$ and $\beta_1 \in Y \cap B$. Since $Y \vdash \beta$ and $\beta \in \mathcal{V}(B)$ it follows by the $\mathcal{V}(B)$-closure of Y (Observation 1.36) that $\beta \in Y$.

Part 3b: We are going to show that $Y \cap B \in B\bot\alpha$.

Since $Y \in \mathcal{V}(B)\bot\alpha$, $Y \cap B$ is a subset of B that does not imply α. Suppose that $Y \cap B \notin B\bot\alpha$. Then there is some $\beta \in B$ such that $\beta \notin Y \cap B$ and $(Y \cap B) \cup \{\beta\} \nvdash \alpha$, thus $Y \cap B \nvdash \beta \rightarrow \alpha$.

It follows from Part 3a of the present proof that $\text{Cn}(Y) = \text{Cn}(\mathcal{V}_{Y\cap B}(B))$. Thus, according to Part 3 of Observation 4.40, $\text{Cn}(Y) = \text{Cn}(Y \cap B)$. We therefore have $Y \nvdash \beta \rightarrow \alpha$, so that $Y \cup \{\beta\} \nvdash \alpha$. Since $Y \in \mathcal{V}(B)\bot\alpha$ and $\beta \in \mathcal{V}(B)$ it follows that $\beta \in Y$. Since we have assumed that $\beta \in B$ it follows that $\beta \in Y \cap B$, contrary to our assumptions. We may conclude that $Y \cap B \in B\bot\alpha$.

Part 3c: Let $X \in B\bot\alpha$ and $f(X) = Y$, i.e. $\mathcal{V}_X(B) = Y$. We are going to prove that $X = Y \cap B$.

$X \subseteq B$ and $X \subseteq \mathcal{V}_X(B) = Y$ follow directly. It remains to be shown that $Y \cap B \subseteq X$. Let $\beta \in Y \cap B$. It follows from $\beta \in Y = \mathcal{V}_X(B)$ that there are $\beta_1, \ldots \beta_n \in B$ such that $\beta = \beta_1 \vee \ldots \vee \beta_n$ and $\beta_1 \in X$. Since $\vdash \beta_1 \rightarrow \beta$ and $\beta_1 \in B$ it follows from the B-closure of X (Observation 1.36) that $\beta \in X$. ∎

This one-to-one correspondence between the remainders of a base and the remainders of its disjunctive closure can be used to prove the representation theorem for base-generated partial meet contraction from disjunctively closed bases. In the postulates-to-construction part of the following proof, the strategy will be to (1) show that all the required properties hold for a partial meet contraction that is defined in the usual way for the standard base B, and (2) show that these properties also apply to an operator on $\mathcal{V}(B)$ that is defined from the first operator according to the one-to-one correspondence.

> An operator $\div$ on a consistent belief set **K** is generated by partial meet contraction of a finite, disjunctively closed base for **K** if and only if $\div$ satisfies *closure*, *inclusion*, *vacuity*, *success*, *extensionality*, *finitude*, *symmetry*, *conservativity*, and *meet maximality*.
> [Theorem 4.11.]

Proof. *Construction-to-postulates*: It follows from Observations 4.33 and 4.34 that *meet maximality* is satisfied, and from Theorem 4.8 that the rest of the listed postulates hold.

Postulates-to-construction: Let **K** and $\div$ satisfy the postulates. We are going to use the construction for Theorem 4.8. Let $B = \{\&\mathbf{K}' \mid \mathbf{K}' = \mathbf{K}\div\alpha \text{ for some } \alpha\}$, and let γ be is defined as follows:

1. If $B\bot\alpha \neq \emptyset$, then $\gamma(B\bot\alpha) = \{X \in B\bot\alpha \mid \mathbf{K}\div\alpha \subseteq \text{Cn}(X)\}$, and
2. If $B\bot\alpha = \emptyset$, then $\gamma(B\bot\alpha) = \{B\}$.

It follows from the proof of Theorem 4.8 that B is a finite base for **K**, that γ is a selection function for B, and that for all α:$\mathbf{K}\div\alpha = \text{Cn}(\bigcap\gamma(B\bot\alpha))$. As was noted after the proof of that theorem, γ has the completion property.

However, B is not disjunctively closed. We are going to make use of its disjunctive closure $\mathcal{V}(B)$, and of a function γ'' such that:

(I) If $\mathcal{V}(B)\perp\alpha \neq \emptyset$, then
$\gamma''(\mathcal{V}(B)\perp\alpha) = \{Y \in \mathcal{V}(B)\perp\alpha \mid \mathrm{Cn}(X) = \mathrm{Cn}(Y) \text{ for some } X \in \gamma(B\perp\alpha)\}$

(II) If $\mathcal{V}(B)\perp\alpha = \emptyset$, then $\gamma''(\mathcal{V}(B)\perp\alpha) = \{\mathcal{V}(B)\}$

Clearly, $\mathcal{V}(B)$ is a finite and disjunctively closed base for **K**. It remains for us to show (1) that γ'' is a selection function for $\mathcal{V}(B)$, and furthermore (2) that $\mathbf{K}\div\alpha = \mathrm{Cn}(\mathcal{V}(B)\sim_{\gamma''}\alpha)$

Part 1: In order to show that γ'' is a selection function for $\mathcal{V}(B)$, we need to show that if $\mathcal{V}(B)\perp\alpha \neq \emptyset$, then $\gamma''(\mathcal{V}(B)\perp\alpha) \neq \emptyset$. It follows from $\mathcal{V}(B)\perp\alpha \neq \emptyset$ that α is not a tautology, and thus that $B\perp\alpha \neq \emptyset$. Since γ is a selection function, $\gamma(B\perp\alpha)$ is non-empty. Let $X \in \gamma(B\perp\alpha)$. Then, by Observation 4.38, there is some $Y \in \mathcal{V}(B)\perp\alpha$ such that $\mathrm{Cn}(X) = \mathrm{Cn}(Y)$. It follows from the definition of γ'' that $Y \in \gamma''(\mathcal{V}(B)\perp\alpha)$, and thus $\gamma''(\mathcal{V}(B)\perp\alpha) \neq \emptyset$.

Preparatory step for part 2: Before proving part 2, we need to show that $\mathbf{K}\div\beta$ is a maximally preservative α-removal if and only if $B\sim_\gamma\beta \in \gamma(B\perp\alpha)$.

For one direction, let $B\sim_\gamma\beta \in \gamma(B\perp\alpha)$. Since γ is completed, this is equivalent with $B\sim_\gamma\alpha \subseteq B\sim_\gamma\beta \in B\perp\alpha$. It follows that $\mathbf{K}\div\alpha \subseteq \mathbf{K}\div\beta \nvdash \alpha$. Furthermore, it follows that there is no ε such that $B\sim_\gamma\beta \subset B\sim_\gamma\varepsilon \nvdash \alpha$, and thus no ε such that $\mathbf{K}\div\beta \subset \mathbf{K}\div\varepsilon \nvdash \alpha$. We can conclude that $\mathbf{K}\div\beta$ is a maximally preservative α-removal.

For the other direction, let $\mathbf{K}\div\beta$ be a maximally preservative α-removal. Then $\mathbf{K}\div\alpha \subseteq \mathbf{K}\div\beta$, and consequently $B\sim_\gamma\alpha \subseteq B\sim_\gamma\beta$. Suppose that $B\sim_\gamma\beta \notin B\perp\alpha$. Then there must be some $X \subseteq B$ such that $B\sim_\gamma\beta \subset X \in B\perp\alpha$. It follows from Observation 1.70 that there is some δ such that $\{X\} = B\perp\delta$, and thus $B\sim_\gamma\delta = X$, so that $\mathbf{K}\div\delta = \mathrm{Cn}(X)$. It follows from $B\sim_\gamma\beta \subseteq B\sim_\gamma\delta$ that $\mathbf{K}\div\beta \subseteq \mathbf{K}\div\delta$.

Suppose that $\mathbf{K}\div\delta \subseteq \mathbf{K}\div\beta$. Then $\mathrm{Cn}(B\sim_\gamma\delta) \subseteq \mathrm{Cn}(B\sim_\gamma\beta)$, and consequently $B\sim_\gamma\delta \subseteq B \cap \mathrm{Cn}(B\sim_\gamma\beta)$. Since $B\sim_\gamma\beta$ is a B-closed subset of B, it follows that $B\sim_\gamma\delta \subseteq B\sim_\gamma\beta$, contrary to $B\sim_\gamma\beta \subset X = B\sim_\gamma\delta$. We can conclude that $\mathbf{K}\div\delta \nsubseteq \mathbf{K}\div\beta$.

In summary, we have derived $\mathbf{K}\div\beta \subset \mathbf{K}\div\delta \nvdash \alpha$. However, this is impossible since $\mathbf{K}\div\beta$ is a maximally preservative α-removal. It follows from this contradiction that $B\sim_\gamma\beta \in B\perp\alpha$, and we have $B\sim_\gamma\alpha \subseteq B\sim_\gamma\beta \in B\perp\alpha$, i.e. (since γ is completed) $B\sim_\gamma\beta \in \gamma(B\perp\alpha)$, as desired.

Part 2: We have:

$$\begin{aligned}
\mathbf{K}\div\alpha &= \bigcap\{\mathrm{Cn}(B\sim_\gamma\beta) \mid B\sim_\gamma\beta \in \gamma(B\perp\alpha)\} \\
&\qquad\qquad\qquad\qquad (\textit{meet maximality}, \text{preparatory step}) \\
&= \bigcap\{\mathrm{Cn}(X) \mid X \in \gamma(B\perp\alpha)\} \quad (\text{Observation 1.70}) \\
&= \bigcap\{\mathrm{Cn}(Y) \mid Y \in \gamma''(\mathcal{V}(B)\perp\alpha)\} \quad (\text{Observation 4.38}) \\
&= \mathrm{Cn}(\bigcap\{Y \mid Y \in \gamma''(\mathcal{V}(B)\perp\alpha)\}) \quad (\text{Observation 1.34}) \\
&= \mathrm{Cn}(\bigcap\gamma''(\mathcal{V}(B)\perp\alpha)) \\
&= \mathrm{Cn}(\mathcal{V}(B)\sim_{\gamma''}\alpha)). \qquad \blacksquare
\end{aligned}$$

Exercises

201. Prove Parts 1–4 of Observation 4.40.

202. Show that $\mathcal{V}(B)\backslash\mathcal{V}_A(B) \subseteq \mathcal{V}(B\backslash A)$.

203. [49] Let γ be a selection function for B, and let $\simeq_\gamma$ denote *pre-closed partial meet contraction*, defined as follows:
$B \simeq_\gamma \alpha = \bigcap\{\text{Cn}(X) \mid X \in \gamma(B\bot\alpha)\}$
In other words, this is a variant of partial meet contraction in which the elements of $\gamma(B\bot\alpha)$ are closed under consequence before the intersection is formed. (This operation was proposed by Hans Rott. [112; 116]) Show that the following two properties of an operator $\div$ on a belief set **K** are equivalent:

(1.) $\div$ is generated by $\simeq_\gamma$ for some selection function γ for a finite base for **K**.

(2.) $\div$ is generated by $\sim_\gamma$ for some selection function γ for a finite and disjunctively closed base for **K**.

(Hint: Use Observations 1.34 and 4.38.)

13+ THE EFFECTS OF TRANSITIVITY

We have now proved all the representation theorems from Sections 4.4–4.5, except the following:

> An operator $\div$ on a consistent belief set **K** is generated by a TMR partial meet contraction on some finite, disjunctively closed base for **K** if and only if $\div$ satisfies *closure, inclusion, vacuity, success, extensionality, finitude, symmetry, conservativity, conjunctive overlap, conjunctive inclusion,* and *conjunctive trisection.*
> [Theorem 4.12.]

The proof of this theorem is unfortunately quite lengthy, and the reader is referred to the research literature for a full proof [49]. In this section, only a brief outline of the proof will be given.

The construction-to-postulates part of the theorem is as so often the easiest one. Indeed, we have already shown it in pieces (Theorem 4.8 and Observations 4.27, 4.28, 4.29, and 4.32). It is the postulates-to-construction part that makes the proof so long. The same basic strategy can be used as in the proof of Theorem 4.11 in the previous section. Thus, the required properties are first shown to hold for an operator on the standard base. After that, the same properties are shown to hold for a corresponding operator on the disjunctive closure of the standard base.

It is necessary in this proof to specify a marking-off relation. The following definition turns out to do the work:

> $X \sqsubseteq Y$ iff either $X \subset Y$ or there is some β such that $\{X, Y\} = B\bot\beta$ and $\mathbf{K}\div\beta \subseteq \text{Cn}(Y)$.

(It can be shown to make no difference if $\{X, Y\} = B\bot\beta$ is replaced by $\{X, Y\} \subseteq B\bot\beta$ in this definition.)

A selection function γ is defined in the usual way from $\sqsubseteq$ via the marking-off identity (see Section 2.6), i.e.:

1. If $B\bot\alpha \neq \emptyset$, then $\gamma(B\bot\alpha) = \{X \in B\bot\alpha \mid Y \sqsubseteq X$ for all $Y \in B\bot\alpha\}$.
2. Otherwise, $\gamma(B\bot\alpha) = \{B\}$.

In order to verify this construction, it must be shown (1) that B is a finite base for **K** (This is done just as it was done above for Theorem 4.8.), (2) that γ is a selection function for B, (3) that the partial meet contraction $\sim_\gamma$ on B generates the operation $\div$ on **K**, and (4) that γ is transitively, maximizingly relational by $\sqsubseteq$. After that, Observation 4.38 can be used to show (5) that the corresponding properties hold for an appropriately defined selection function on the disjunctively closed base $\mathcal{V}(B)$.

No axiomatic characterization is available for base-generated TMR partial meet contraction in general, i.e. without the requirement that the base is disjunctively closed. However, the following theorem comes close to that, invoking only the additional requirement that the selection function is completed.

THEOREM 4.41 ([51]) *An operation $\div$ on a consistent belief set* **K** *is generated by a TMR partial meet contraction on a finite base for* **K**, *by a completed selection function, if and only if $\div$ satisfies closure, inclusion, vacuity, success, extensionality, finitude, symmetry, conservativity, and the following postulate:*
If $\vdash \alpha \rightarrow \beta$ and the set of β-removals that are also maximally preservative α-removals is non-empty, then it coincides with the set of maximally preservative β-removals. (regularity)

The proof of this theorem is similar in length and structure to that of Theorem 4.12, and the reader is referred to the research literature for the proof [51].

The following negative result confirms that the classes of operations referred to in Theorems 4.12 and 4.41 do not coincide:

> Let the operator $\div$ on the belief set **K** be generated by some TMR partial meet contraction of a finite base for **K**. Then $\div$ does not in general satisfy *conjunctive overlap*.
> [Observation 4.13.]

Proof. Let p, q, and r be logically independent (atomic) sentences. Furthermore, let $B = \{p\&r, q\&r\}$. Let the TMR partial meet contraction $\div$ be based on a marking-off relation $\sqsubseteq$ such that $\{p\&r\} \sqsubseteq \{q\&r\} \sqsubseteq \{p\&r\}$.

We then have $\mathbf{K}\div p = \text{Cn}(\{q\&r\})$, $\mathbf{K}\div q = \text{Cn}(\{p\&r\})$, and $\mathbf{K}\div(p\&q) = \text{Cn}(\emptyset)$. It follows that $r \in (\mathbf{K}\div p) \cap (\mathbf{K}\div q)$ but $r \notin \mathbf{K}\div(p\&q)$, thus contradicting *conjunctive overlap*. ■

Exercises

204. [51] Let the operation $\div$ on the consistent belief set **K** be generated by some TMR partial meet contraction on a finite base for **K**. Show that (even if the base is not disjunctively closed) $\div$ satisfies the following weakened variant of *conjunctive overlap*: If $\mathbf{K}\div\delta \subseteq (\mathbf{K}\div\alpha)\cap(\mathbf{K}\div\beta)$, then $\mathbf{K}\div\delta \subseteq \mathbf{K}\div(\alpha\&\beta)$. (*weak conjunctive overlap*) (Hint: Make use of Observation 2.19.)

14+ PROPERTIES OF BASE-GENERATED REVISION

The proofs of closure-invariance for properties of revision operators are similar to those for properties of contraction operators:

The following revision-postulates are closure-invariant:

1. *Success*: $\alpha \in A * \alpha$
2. *Consistency*: $A * \alpha$ is consistent if α is consistent.

Furthermore, under the assumption that $+$ is interpreted as closing expansion when applied to a belief set and as non-closing expansion when applied to a belief base for that belief set, the following revision-postulates are also closure-invariant:

3. *Inclusion*: $A * \alpha \subseteq A + \alpha$
4. *Inconsistent expansion*: If $\neg\alpha \in \mathrm{Cn}(\emptyset)$ then $A * \alpha = A + \alpha$.
5. *Vacuity*: If $\neg\alpha \notin \mathrm{Cn}(A)$, then $A * \alpha = A + \alpha$.
6. *Superexpansion*: $A * (\alpha\&\beta)) \subseteq (A * \alpha) + \beta$.
7. *Subexpansion*:
   If $\neg\beta \notin \mathrm{Cn}(A * \alpha)$, then $(A * \alpha) + \beta \subseteq A * (\alpha\&\beta)$.

[Observation 4.17.]

Proof. Here, only parts 1, 3, and 6 will be proved. Parts 2, 4, 5, and 7 are left to the reader as an exercise. Let B be a belief base and $\mathbf{K} = \mathrm{Cn}(B)$. Furthermore, let $\circ$ be an operator on B and $*$ the closure of $\circ$.

Part 1: Let $\circ$ satisfy *success*. Then $\alpha \in B \circ \alpha$. It follows from this and $\mathbf{K} * \alpha = \mathrm{Cn}(B \circ \alpha)$ that $\alpha \in \mathbf{K} * \alpha$.

Part 3: Let $\circ$ satisfy *inclusion*. Then:

$$
\begin{aligned}
&B \circ \alpha \subseteq B \cup \{\alpha\}\\
&\mathrm{Cn}(B \circ \alpha) \subseteq \mathrm{Cn}(B \cup \{\alpha\})\\
&\mathrm{Cn}(B \circ \alpha) \subseteq \mathrm{Cn}(\mathrm{Cn}(B) \cup \{\alpha\})\\
&\mathbf{K} * \alpha \subseteq \mathrm{Cn}(\mathbf{K} \cup \{\alpha\})\\
&\mathbf{K} * \alpha \subseteq \mathbf{K} + \alpha
\end{aligned}
$$

Part 6: Let $\circ$ satisfy *superexpansion.* Then:

$$\begin{aligned}
&B \circ (\alpha \& \beta) \subseteq (B \circ \alpha) \cup \{\beta\} \\
&\text{Cn}(B \circ (\alpha \& \beta)) \subseteq \text{Cn}((B \circ \alpha) \cup \{\beta\}) \\
&\text{Cn}(B \circ (\alpha \& \beta)) \subseteq \text{Cn}(\text{Cn}(B \circ \alpha) \cup \{\beta\}) \\
&\mathbf{K} * (\alpha \& \beta) \subseteq \text{Cn}((\mathbf{K} * \alpha) \cup \{\beta\}) \\
&\mathbf{K} * (\alpha \& \beta) \subseteq (\mathbf{K} * \alpha) + \beta \qquad \blacksquare
\end{aligned}$$

We will not have much use for the closure-invariance of superexpansion and subexpansion, since these properties are not satisfied by the operations on bases that we use to generate operations on belief sets. Instead, another proof method is available for revision postulates. We can use the Levi identity to derive properties of (base-generated) revision from properties of (base-generated) contraction. The reason why this can be done is that the Levi identity is itself closure-invariant in the following sense:

OBSERVATION 4.42 *Let* $-$ *and* $\circ$ *be operations on a set B such that for all* α*:*

$$B \circ \alpha = (B - \neg\alpha) \cup \{\alpha\} \textit{ (the Levi identity)}$$

Furthermore, let $\mathbf{K} = \text{Cn}(B)$*, and let* $\div$ *be the closure of* $-$ *and* $*$ *the closure of* $\circ$*. Then:*

$$\mathbf{K} * \alpha = (\mathbf{K} \div \neg\alpha) + \alpha.$$

The proof of this observation is left to the reader.

We can use the Levi identity to show that base-generated TMR partial meet contraction from a finite and disjunctively closed base satisfies disjunctive inclusion:

OBSERVATION 4.43 *Let* $*$ *be an operator on a belief set* **K** *that is generated by some TMR internal partial meet revision on a finite and disjunctively closed base for* **K**. *Then* $*$ *satisfies:*
If $\mathbf{K} * (\alpha \vee \beta) \nvdash \neg\alpha$*, then* $\mathbf{K} * (\alpha \vee \beta) \subseteq \mathbf{K} * \alpha$ *(disjunctive inclusion)*

Proof. Let $\div$ be the base-generated partial meet contraction on **K** that is generated from the same base and with the same selection function as $*$.

Let $\mathbf{K} * (\alpha \vee \beta) \nvdash \neg\alpha$. Then it can be concluded from the Levi identity (Observation 4.42) that $(\mathbf{K} \div (\neg\alpha \& \neg\beta)) \cup \{\alpha \vee \beta\} \nvdash \neg\alpha$, i.e. $\mathbf{K} \div (\neg\alpha \& \neg\beta) \nvdash \alpha \vee \beta \rightarrow \neg\alpha$, or equivalently $\mathbf{K} \div (\neg\alpha \& \neg\beta) \nvdash \neg\alpha$.

We know from Observations 2.19 and 4.27 that $\div$ satisfies *conjunctive inclusion*, and thus $\mathbf{K} \div (\neg\alpha \& \neg\beta) \subseteq \mathbf{K} \div \neg\alpha$. It follows that

$$\text{Cn}((\mathbf{K} \div (\neg\alpha \& \neg\beta)) \cup \{\alpha \vee \beta\}) \subseteq \text{Cn}((\mathbf{K} \div \neg\alpha) \cup \{\alpha\}),$$

so that, again using the Levi identity (Observation 4.42): $\mathbf{K} * (\alpha \vee \beta) \subseteq \mathbf{K} * \alpha$. $\blacksquare$

Disjunctive inclusion and subexpansion, as applied to a belief set, are equivalent in the presence of three of the basic postulates (extensionality, closure, and success, Observation 3.50). Therefore, the above observation can also be used to show that subexpansion holds for base-generated TMR internal partial meet revision, if the base is finite and disjunctively closed.

The other supplementary postulate also has two closely related forms, disjunctive overlap and superexpansion. The latter is easy to handle in the context of base-generated revision. Again, we can use the Levi identity:

OBSERVATION 4.44 *Let $\div$ be an operator on a belief set* **K** *that satisfies closure, extensionality, and conjunctive trisection, and let $*$ be the operator that is generated from $\div$ by the Levi identity, i.e.* $\mathbf{K} * \alpha = (\mathbf{K}\div\neg\alpha) + \alpha$ *for all α. Then $*$ satisfies superexpansion.*

Proof. It follows from *conjunctive trisection* that:

$$\text{If } (\neg\alpha\vee\neg\beta\vee\delta) \in \mathbf{K}\div((\neg\alpha\vee\neg\beta\vee\delta)\&(\neg\alpha\vee\neg\beta\vee\neg\delta))$$
$$\text{then } (\neg\alpha\vee\neg\beta\vee\delta) \in \mathbf{K}\div((\neg\alpha\vee\neg\beta\vee\delta)\&(\neg\alpha\vee\neg\beta\vee\neg\delta)\&(\neg\alpha\vee\beta))$$

Using *closure* and *extensionality*, we obtain:

$$\text{If } \alpha\&\beta\rightarrow\delta \in \mathbf{K}\div(\neg\alpha\vee\neg\beta), \text{ then } \alpha\&\beta\rightarrow\delta \in \mathbf{K}\div\neg\alpha.$$

We can now use the deductive property:

$$\text{If } \mathbf{K}\div(\neg\alpha\vee\neg\beta)\cup\{\alpha\&\beta\} \vdash \delta, \text{ then } \mathbf{K}\div\neg\alpha\cup\{\alpha\&\beta\}\vdash\delta$$
$$\mathrm{Cn}(\mathbf{K}\div(\neg\alpha\vee\neg\beta)\cup\{\alpha\&\beta\}) \subseteq \mathrm{Cn}(\mathbf{K}\div\neg\alpha\cup\{\alpha\&\beta\})$$
$$\mathrm{Cn}(\mathbf{K}\div(\neg\alpha\vee\neg\beta)\cup\{\alpha\&\beta\}) \subseteq \mathrm{Cn}(\mathrm{Cn}(\mathbf{K}\div\neg\alpha\cup\{\alpha\})\cup\{\beta\})$$
$$\mathbf{K} * (\alpha\&\beta) \subseteq (\mathbf{K} * \alpha) + \beta$$

Thus, *superexpansion* holds. ■

OBSERVATION 4.45 *Let $*$ be an operator on a belief set* **K** *that is generated from a TMR internal partial meet revision on a finite and disjunctively closed base for* **K**. *Then $*$ satisfies superexpansion.*

Proof. Let B be the finite and disjunctively closed set and $\mp_\gamma$ the TMR internal partial meet contraction on B from which $*$ is generated. Let $\div$ be the closure of $\sim_\gamma$. It follows from Observation 4.4 that $\div$ satisfies *extensionality* and from Observations 4.28 and 4.29 that it satisfies *conjunctive trisection*. Clearly, it satisfies *closure*. Furthermore, it follows from Observation 4.42 that $*$ is the operator that is generated from $\div$ via the Levi identity. It follows from Observation 4.44 that $*$ satisfies *superexpansion*. ■

Exercises

205. Prove Parts 2, 4, 5, and 7 of Observation 4.17.

206. Show that the following postulate is closure-invariant:
$A * (\alpha \vee \beta) \subseteq \mathrm{Cn}((A * \alpha) \cup (A * \beta))$ (*weak disjunctive inclusion*)

207. Prove Observation 4.42.

15+ CHARACTERIZING BASE-GENERATED REVISION

The results on withdrawals from Section 3.5 can be put to effective use in proving the following result on base-generated revision:

> The following two statements about an operation $*$ on a belief set $\mathbf{K}$ are equivalent:
>
> 1. There is some selection function γ for $\mathbf{K}$ such that for all α:
>
> $$\mathbf{K} * \alpha = \mathbf{K} \mp_{\gamma} \alpha.$$
>
> 2. There is some base B for $\mathbf{K}$ and some selection function γ for B such that for all α:
>
> $$\mathbf{K} * \alpha = \mathrm{Cn}(B \mp_{\gamma} \alpha).$$
>
> [Observation 4.18.]

Proof. *(1) to (2)*: Just let $B = \mathbf{K}$.

(2) to (1): Let $\mathbf{K} * \alpha = \mathrm{Cn}(B \mp_{\gamma} \alpha)$. Then clearly $*$ satisfies *closure*. Since $\mp_{\gamma}$ satisfies *consistency*, *inclusion*, *vacuity*, and *success* (Theorem 3.6 and Observation 3.2), it follows from Observation 4.17 that $*$ also satisfies these postulates.

Next we are going to show that $*$ satisfies *extensionality*. Let $\alpha \leftrightarrow \beta \in \mathrm{Cn}(\emptyset)$. Then $\neg\alpha \leftrightarrow \neg\beta \in \mathrm{Cn}(\emptyset)$, and thus $B \sim_{\gamma} \neg\alpha = B \sim_{\gamma} \neg\beta$. (Note that $\sim_{\gamma}$ satisfies *contraction-extensionality*, cf. Theorem 2.2 and Observation 2.3.) It follows from this and $\alpha \leftrightarrow \beta \in \mathrm{Cn}(\emptyset)$ that $\mathrm{Cn}((B \sim_{\gamma} \neg\alpha) \cup \{\alpha\}) = \mathrm{Cn}((B \sim_{\gamma} \neg\beta) \cup \{\beta\})$, i.e. $\mathbf{K} * \alpha = \mathbf{K} * \beta$.

Thus, $*$ satisfies all the six basic Gärdenfors postulates for partial meet revision. It follows from Theorem 3.14 that (1) is satisfied. ■

Note the indirect method that is used in the (2)-to-(1) direction of the above proof. By showing that an operator satisfies the six characteristic (Gärdenfors) postulates for partial meet revision we can establish that it is a partial meet revision (and this is done without actually exhibiting a selection function). The same method is used in the following proof:

Let $\mathcal{L}$ be finite. Then the following two statements about an operation $*$ on a belief set $\mathbf{K}$ are equivalent:

1. There is some TMR selection function γ for $\mathbf{K}$ such that for all α:
$$\mathbf{K} * \alpha = \mathbf{K}\mp_\gamma\alpha.$$
2. There is some finite and disjunctively closed base B for $\mathbf{K}$ and some TMR selection function γ for B such that for all α:
$$\mathbf{K} * \alpha = \mathrm{Cn}(B\mp_\gamma\alpha).$$

[Observation 4.20.]

Proof. *(1) to (2)*: Let $B = \mathbf{K}$.

(2) to (1): It follows from Observation 4.18 that $*$ satisfies the basic Gärdenfors postulates for revision. In order to show that (1) holds it is therefore sufficient to show that the supplementary postulates, *superexpansion* and *subexpansion*, are also satisfied. (Cf. Theorem 3.25.) Since the closure of $\sim_\gamma$ satisfies *conjunctive trisection* (Theorem 4.12) it follows from Observations 4.42 and 4.44 that *superexpansion* is satisfied. It follows from Observation 4.43 that *disjunctive inclusion* is satisfied, and then from Observation 3.50 that *subexpansion* is satisfied. This completes the proof. ■

In order to prove the negative result on disjunctive overlap, we need to exhibit a counter-example.

Let γ be a TMR selection function on a finite base B for $\mathbf{K}$, and let $*$ be the closure of $\mp_\gamma$, i.e. $\mathbf{K} * \alpha = \mathrm{Cn}(B\mp_\gamma\alpha)$ for all α. Then *disjunctive overlap* is not, in general, satisfied by $*$.
[Observation 4.19.]

Proof. Let p, q, and r be logically independent (atomic) sentences, and let $B = \{\neg p\&r, \neg q\&r\}$. Let $\sqsubseteq$ be the transitive and maximizing marking-off relation for B such that $\{\neg p\&r\} \sqsubseteq \{\neg q\&r\} \sqsubseteq \{\neg p\&r\}$. Let γ be the selection function that is based on $\sqsubseteq$, and let $*$ be the operation on $\mathbf{K} = \mathrm{Cn}(B)$ that is generated by $\mp_\gamma$. We then have:

$$B\mp_\gamma p = \bigcap\gamma(B\bot\neg p)\cup\{p\} = \{\neg q\&r, p\}$$
$$B\mp_\gamma q = \bigcap\gamma(B\bot\neg q)\cup\{q\} = \{\neg p\&r, q\}$$
$$B\mp_\gamma(p\vee q) = \bigcap\gamma(B\bot(\neg p\&\neg q))\cup\{p\vee q\} = \{p\vee q\}$$

Thus $r \in (\mathbf{K}*p)\cap(\mathbf{K}*q) = \mathrm{Cn}(B\mp_\gamma p)\cap\mathrm{Cn}(B\mp_\gamma q)$, whereas $r \notin \mathbf{K}*(p\vee q) = \mathrm{Cn}(B\mp_\gamma(p\vee q))$. We can conclude that *disjunctive overlap* is violated. ■

Exercise

208. Let B be a finite set and $\mathbf{K} = \mathrm{Cn}(B)$. Let $\sim_\gamma$ be an operator of partial meet contraction on B, and let $\div$ be the closure of $\sim_\gamma$. Furthermore, let $\div'$ be the operator such that for all α :
$\mathbf{K}\div'\alpha = \mathbf{K} \cap ((\mathbf{K}\div\alpha) + \neg\alpha)$.
Show that $\div'$ is an operator of partial meet contraction on $\mathbf{K}$.

CHAPTER 5

BELIEVING AND HYPOTHESIZING

In the previous chapters, we have been exclusively concerned with the basic answer modes (doxastic attitudes) as introduced in Section 1.2. Beliefs have been assumed to be expressible in a rudimentary logical language with no other operators than the classical truth-functional ones. Obviously, this language cannot do full justice to the richness and complexity of actual belief systems.

In this chapter, we are going to study two moderate extensions of the language. Section 5.1 introduces expressions for possibility and necessity, and Section 5.2 conditional expressions.

1 NECESSITY AND POSSIBILITY

The language of *modal logic* contains operators for necessity and possibility. The most commonly used symbols are $\Box$ ('box') for necessity and $\Diamond$ ('diamond') for possibility. The interpretations are obvious:

$\Box\alpha$	'α is necessary'
$\Diamond\alpha$	'α is possible'
$\neg\Diamond\alpha$	'α is impossible'

The two operators are commonly taken to be interdefinable, according to the following equivalence:

$$\Box\alpha \leftrightarrow \neg\Diamond\neg\alpha.$$

As an example, to say that it $1+1=2$ is necessarily true is another way of saying that it is not possible that $1+1=2$ is not true.

In this section, we are going to focus on the possibility operator. We will assume that the object language $\mathcal{L}$ contains the possibility operator $\Diamond$. For any sentence α in $\mathcal{L}$, $\Diamond\alpha$ is also an element of $\mathcal{L}$. (This is a very different exercise from the one that we performed in Section 3.18^{+}. In that section, modal concepts were introduced into the *metalanguage* in which we discuss the agent's beliefs. Here, the modal operator $\Diamond$ is introduced into the *object language* in which the beliefs of the agent are represented.)

Actual epistemic agents have standpoints not only on what is and is not the case, but also on what is possible and not possible.

Examples

1. I consider it to be logically possible that someone constructs a perpetual motion machine, but I consider it to be physically impossible.
2. In my view, it it physically possible (compatible with the laws of physics) that a human being survives after one month with no intake of water, but it is in practice impossible.

As these examples show, there are different variants of possibility, such as logical, physical, and practical possibility. In studies of belief change, the variant most commonly referred to is 'serious possibility' as explicated by Isaac Levi. According to Levi, there is a close connection between what we believe and what we count as serious possibilities.

In some sense, it is possible that the moon consists of green cheese. I do not, however, count this as a serious possibility. This is, according to Levi, just another way of saying that I believe that the moon does not consist of green cheese. The belief set represents a 'standard for serious possibility': it consists precisely of those sentences whose negations are not serious possibilities. [73]

This proposal gives rise to a simple formal representation of modal beliefs. For a given belief set **K**, let *Poss*(**K**) be the *modal extension* of the belief set. [72] It can be defined as follows:

DEFINITION 5.1 (Isaac Levi [72]) *For any belief set* **K**, *Poss*(**K**) *is the smallest superset of* **K** *such that:*
$\Diamond\alpha \in Poss(\mathbf{K})$ *if* $\neg\alpha \notin \mathbf{K}$, *and*
$\neg\Diamond\neg\alpha \in Poss(\mathbf{K})$ *if* $\alpha \in \mathbf{K}$.

Once modal sentences have been introduced, it is a natural step to include them in the belief set. Given the interpretation of $\Diamond$ in terms of serious possibility, *Poss*(**K**) consists of those modal sentences that should be validated by **K**. An obvious way to introduce modal sentences into the belief set is therefore to require that *Poss*(**K**) be included in **K**.

DEFINITION 5.2 (André Fuhrmann [22]) *A belief set* **K** *is closed under Poss if and only if* $Poss(\mathbf{K}) \subseteq \mathbf{K}$.

Closure under *Poss* may seem innocuous, but it turns out to have strange consequences.

OBSERVATION 5.3 *Let* $\mathbf{K}_1$ *and* $\mathbf{K}_2$ *be two belief sets that are both closed under Poss. If* $\mathbf{K}_1 \subset \mathbf{K}_2$, *then* $\mathbf{K}_2$ *is inconsistent.*
[Proof: p. 363.]

Another strange consequence of closure under *Poss* was discovered by André Fuhrmann:

THEOREM 5.4 (Fuhrmann's impossibility theorem [22]) *There is no belief set* **K** *that satisfies the following five conditions:*

1. *There is some sentence* α *such that* $\alpha \notin \mathbf{K}$ *and* $\neg\alpha \notin \mathbf{K}$ *(incompleteness)*
2. $Poss(\mathbf{K}) \subseteq \mathbf{K}$ *(closure under Poss)*
3. *For all* $\alpha, \alpha \in \mathbf{K} * \alpha$ *(success),*
4. *For all* α, *if* $\neg\alpha \notin \mathbf{K}$, *then* $\mathbf{K} \subseteq \mathbf{K} * \alpha$ *(preservation)*
5. *If* α *is consistent, then so is* $\mathbf{K} * \alpha$ *(consistency)*

[Proof: p. 363.]

Success and consistency are among the basic Gärdenfors postulates for revision. Preservation follows from the basic postulates. (It is a weaker variant of vacuity.)

There are at least three possible reactions to this impossibility theorem.

First, one may endorse Isaac Levi's standpoint that modal sentences should not be included in the belief set. According to Levi, sentences such as $\Diamond\alpha$ and $\neg\Diamond\neg\alpha$ are not truth-value-bearing, i.e. they cannot strictly speaking be true or false. Therefore, they should not be included in the belief set. Changes in appraisals of serious possibility occur as a consequence of changes of the belief set, but these appraisals are not themselves *in* the belief set. Rather, they are *about* the belief set. [72]

Secondly, we may accept modal sentences as elements of the belief set, but reject the standard of serious possibility (Definition 5.1) as a criterion of validity for such sentences. Possibly, some other criterion might allow us to include modal sentences in belief sets without the paradoxical results presented above. This way out remains to be investigated.

Thirdly, we may follow Fuhrmann in accepting closure under *Poss*, but rejecting the idea that *Poss*-closed belief sets should obey the same laws as non-modal belief sets. In particular, according to Fuhrmann, preservation does not hold for *Poss*-closed belief sets. [22]

2 CONDITIONAL SENTENCES AND THE RAMSEY TEST

Conditional sentences ('if-sentences') cannot be adequately expressed with truth-functional implication ('material implication'). In particular, this applies to counterfactual conditionals, sentences about what would have been, had things been different.

Example
The author believes that if the reader had not opened this book, then the reader would have been miserable and unhappy.

It would not make much sense to evaluate this sentence truth-functionally. Let α denote that the reader has not opened the book and β that the reader is miserable and unhappy. Under truth-functional interpretation, the sentence 'if α then β' is true for the simple reason that α is false, which is obviously the wrong reason.

A sensible interpretation of this and other conditional sentences must be based on some other principle than truth-functional implication. Several such principles have been proposed. [55] One of them, namely the *Ramsey test*, is particularly well suited to the formal framework of belief dynamics.

In a famous footnote in a paper written in 1929, F. P. Ramsey made the following suggestion:

> "If two people are arguing 'If p will q?' and are both in doubt as to p, they are adding p hypothetically to their stock of knowledge and arguing on that basis about q." [106]

This proposal was taken up in 1968 by Robert Stalnaker, who made the following comment:

> "What about the case in which you know or believe the antecedent to be false? In this situation, you cannot simply add it to your stock of beliefs without introducing a contradiction. You must make adjustments by deleting or changing those beliefs which conflict with the antecedent ... This is how to evaluate a conditional:
>
> First, add the antecedent (hypothetically) to your stock of beliefs; second, make whatever adjustments are required to maintain consistency (without modifying the hypothetical belief in the antecedent); finally, consider whether or not the consequent is then true." [122]

Thus, according to the Ramsey test, 'If α then β' is taken to be believed if and only if β would be believed after revising the present belief state by α. Let the symbol $\Box\!\!\rightarrow$ represent conditionality. Then $\alpha \Box\!\!\rightarrow \beta$ means 'if α then β', or more precisely: 'if α were the case, then β would be the case'.

If we want to treat conditional statements on par with statements about actual facts, then we should include them in the belief set:

DEFINITION 5.5 (Ramsey [106], Stalnaker [122]) *A belief set* **K** *satisfies the* Ramsey test *with respect to* $*$ *if and only if for all* α *and* β*:*
$\alpha \Box\!\!\rightarrow \beta \in \mathbf{K}$ *if and only if* $\beta \in \mathbf{K} * \alpha$.

The Ramsey test gives rise to problems quite similar to those created by closure under *Poss*. To see this, let us consider the contraction of belief sets that satisfy the Ramsey test.

If **K** is a non-modal belief set (not containing $\Box\!\!\rightarrow$), and α is a non-tautological element of **K**, then $\mathbf{K} \div \alpha$ is a proper subset of **K**. However, when we contract a belief set **K** that satisfies the Ramsey test, the outcome will not in general be representable as a subset of the original set that satisfies the Ramsey test. The reason for this is that contraction typically provides support for conditional sentences that were not supported by the original belief state.

Examples [47]

1. If I give up my belief that John is mentally retarded, then I gain support for the conditional sentence 'If John has lived 30 years in London, then John understands the English language.'
2. If I give up my belief that my wife has a headache, then I gain support for the sentence 'If it stops raining, then my wife would like to join me for an afternoon walk'.

Expansion of belief sets that satisfy the Ramsey test gives rise to similar problems. When you expand a non-modal belief set **K** by any sentence α such that $\alpha \notin \mathbf{K}$, then the outcome is a proper superset of **K** (i.e., $\mathbf{K} \subset \mathbf{K} + \alpha$). However, if **K** satisfies the Ramsey test, then the outcome is not in general representable as a superset of **K** that satisfies the Ramsey test. The addition of a factual sentence that is compatible with all previously supported factual sentences typically leads to the withdrawal of conditional sentences that were previously supported.

Example [47]
I previously knew nothing about John's profession. Then I acquired the belief that John is a driver by profession. After this, my belief state will no longer support the conditional sentence 'If John goes home from work by taxi every day, then he is a rich man.'

Hence, the dynamics of belief sets that contain $\Box\!\!\rightarrow$ and satisfy the Ramsey test has to be radically different from that of conventional, non-modal belief sets. [47] Belief contraction will not satisfy the postulate of inclusion, since new conditional sentences must be added when a sentence is contracted. Belief expansion, i.e., the incorporation of beliefs that do not contradict previous factual beliefs, does not follow the simple logical rule that holds for non-modal belief sets (i.e. the rule $\mathbf{K}+\alpha = \mathrm{Cn}(\mathbf{K} \cup \{\alpha\})$).

Studies of conditional sentences in belief revision have mainly focused on a puzzling impossibility theorem by Peter Gärdenfors.

THEOREM 5.6 (Gärdenfors's impossibility theorem [33]) *Let $*$ be a global (revision) operator. Then the following conditions are incompatible:*

1. ***K** satisfies the Ramsey test.*
2. $\mathbf{K} * \alpha = \mathrm{Cn}(\mathbf{K} * \alpha)$ *(closure)*
3. $\alpha \in \mathbf{K} * \alpha$ *(success)*

4. *If α is consistent, then so is* $\mathbf{K} * \alpha$. *(consistency)*
5. *If* $\neg\alpha \notin \mathbf{K}$ *then* $\mathbf{K} \subseteq \mathbf{K} * \alpha$. *(preservation)*
6. *If* **K** *is a belief set, then so is* $\mathrm{Cn}(\mathbf{K} \cup \{\alpha\})$. *(closure under expansion* [108]*)*
7. *There are three sentences* α, β, *and* δ, *and a belief set* **K** *such that* $\alpha\&\beta$, $\alpha\&\delta$, *and* $\beta\&\delta$, *are all inconsistent and that* $\neg\alpha \notin \mathbf{K}$, $\neg\beta \notin \mathbf{K}$, *and* $\neg\delta \notin \mathbf{K}$. *(non-triviality)*

[Proof: p. 364.]

The three reactions to Fuhrmann's impossibility theorem that were mentioned above in Section 5.1 are also possible reactions to Gärdenfors's theorem.

First, we may follow Isaac Levi in asserting that conditional statements are not 'objects of belief which bear truth values and are subject to appraisal with respect to epistemic possibility and probability.' Instead, conditionals are 'appraisals of serious or epistemic possibility relative to transformations of the current corpus of knowledge or belief set.' [72] Therefore, conditional sentences should not be included in belief sets. The Ramsey test may nevertheless be retained, in the following modified form:

> A belief set **K** satisfies *Levi's Ramsey test* with respect to $*$ if and only if for all α and β:
> $\alpha \mathrel{\Box\!\!\rightarrow} \beta$ is accepted according to **K** if and only if $\beta \in \mathbf{K} * \alpha$.

This modification blocks the proof of Gärdenfors's impossibility theorem [81].

Sten Lindström and Wlodek Rabinowicz have proposed what may, from a technical point of view, be seen as a weakened version of Isaac Levi's solution [77; 81]. In their approach, conditional sentences are 'thought of as expressing genuine beliefs, but only in a context-sensitive manner, relative to a belief state' [81]. The traditional representation of belief states as sets of sentences (belief sets) is based on the implicit assumption that each sentence in a belief set expresses a truth-value-bearing proposition in a context-independent way. In Lindström's and Rabinowicz's approach, a conditional 'If α then β' may be thought of as an *indexical* statement which expresses a determinate proposition about the world only relative to the subject's belief state and her dispositions to change her belief state. Given that we represent propositions and belief states by sentences and sets of sentences in a formal language that contains no indexical constructions, the agent will accept a conditional statement $\alpha \mathrel{\Box\!\!\rightarrow} \beta$ relative to a belief set **K** just in case a certain sentence $rep(\alpha \mathrel{\Box\!\!\rightarrow} \beta, \mathbf{K})$ is an element of **K**. Here, $rep(\alpha \mathrel{\Box\!\!\rightarrow} \beta, \mathbf{K})$ denotes a sentence that represents the proposition expressed by $\alpha \mathrel{\Box\!\!\rightarrow} \beta$ relative to **K**. The Ramsey test can then be expressed as follows:

$$rep(\alpha \mathrel{\Box\!\!\rightarrow} \beta, \mathbf{K}) \in \mathbf{K} \text{ if and only if } \beta \in \mathbf{K} * \alpha.$$

If $\mathbf{K}_1$ and $\mathbf{K}_2$ are different belief states, then *rep*$(\alpha \mathbin{\Box\!\!\rightarrow} \beta, \mathbf{K}_1)$ and *rep*$(\alpha \mathbin{\Box\!\!\rightarrow} \beta, \mathbf{K}_2)$ need not be the same sentence. For this reason, Gärdenfors's proof does not go through, and the impossibility theorem can be avoided.

Secondly, we may include sentences containing $\Box\!\!\rightarrow$ in the belief set, but reject the Ramsey test as a criterion of validity. Several weakenings of the Ramsey test have been investigated with a view to avoiding the impossibility theorem. It seems difficult to obtain an alternative to the Ramsey test that both avoids the impossibility theorem and corresponds to intuitively reasonable interpretations of conditional sentences [34; 35; 80; 107].

Thirdly, we may accept both the Ramsey test and the inclusion of conditional sentences into the belief set. As we have already seen, this amounts to accepting belief sets with a behaviour under change that is very different from that of non-modal belief sets. This is the solution endorsed by Hans Rott and others [47; 108]. According to Rott, if we accept the Ramsey test, then we must renounce *closure under expansion*. In his view '[e]xpansions are not the right method to "add" new sentences if the underlying language contains conditionals which are interpreted by the Ramsey test' [108].

A fourth avenue has been investigated by some authors, namely to weaken the logic, and let Cn represent some logic weaker than classical truth-functional logic (such as a non-monotonic logic). The impossibility theorem has resisted all attacks on this flank. Krister Segerberg and David Makinson have shown that the theorem can be reconstructed for various substantial weakenings of the logic [84; 120].

As was observed by Lindström and Rabinowicz, the different ways of resolving the paradox need not compete with each other. Instead they might be viewed as corresponding to different uses of conditional constructions in epistemic contexts.[81] The philosophical issues related to Gärdenfors's impossibility theorem are still largely unexplored.

CHAPTER 5+

EXTENDING THE FORMAL LANGUAGE

This chapter contains proofs of the impossibility results for belief sets containing operators that represent serious possibility ($\Diamond$) or Ramsey-test conditionals ($\Box\!\!\rightarrow$).

3+ PROVING THE IMPOSSIBILITY THEOREMS

The two results from Section 5.1 on closure under *Poss* are quite easily proved.

> Let $\mathbf{K}_1$ and $\mathbf{K}_2$ be two belief sets that are both closed under *Poss*. If $\mathbf{K}_1 \subset \mathbf{K}_2$, then $\mathbf{K}_2$ is inconsistent.
> [Observation 5.3.]

Proof. Let $\mathbf{K}_1 \subset \mathbf{K}_2$. Then there is a sentence α such that $\alpha \in \mathbf{K}_2$ and $\alpha \notin \mathbf{K}_1$. It follows by Definition 5.1 from $\alpha \notin \mathbf{K}_1$ that $\Diamond\neg\alpha \in Poss(\mathbf{K}_1)$, and thus due to *closure under Poss*, $\Diamond\neg\alpha \in \mathbf{K}_1$. Since $\mathbf{K}_1 \subseteq \mathbf{K}_2, \Diamond\neg\alpha \in \mathbf{K}_2$. It follows by Definition 5.1 from $\alpha \in \mathbf{K}_2$ that $\neg\Diamond\neg\alpha \in Poss(\mathbf{K}_2)$, and thus due to *closure under Poss*, $\neg\Diamond\neg\alpha \in \mathbf{K}_2$. We can conclude from $\Diamond\neg\alpha \in \mathbf{K}_2$ and $\neg\Diamond\neg\alpha \in \mathbf{K}_2$ that $\mathbf{K}_2$ is inconsistent. ■

> There is no belief set $\mathbf{K}$ that satisfies the following five conditions:
>
> 1. There is some sentence α such that $\alpha \notin \mathbf{K}$ and $\neg\alpha \notin \mathbf{K}$. (*incompleteness*)
> 2. $Poss(\mathbf{K}) \subseteq \mathbf{K}$. (*closure under Poss*)
> 3. For all $\alpha, \alpha \in \mathbf{K} * \alpha$. (*success*)
> 4. For all α, if $\neg\alpha \notin \mathbf{K}$, then $\mathbf{K} \subseteq \mathbf{K} * \alpha$. (*preservation*)
> 5. If α is consistent, then so is $\mathbf{K} * \alpha$. (*consistency*)
>
> [Theorem 5.4, Fuhrmann's impossibility theorem.]

Proof. According to *incompleteness*, we can let α and $\mathbf{K}$ be such that $\alpha \notin \mathbf{K}$ and $\neg\alpha \notin \mathbf{K}$. Since $\alpha \notin \mathbf{K}, \Diamond\neg\alpha \in Poss(\mathbf{K})$, and it follows from *closure under Poss* that $\Diamond\neg\alpha \in \mathbf{K}$. Furthermore, it follows from $\neg\alpha \notin \mathbf{K}$ and *preservation* that $\mathbf{K} \subseteq \mathbf{K} * \alpha$. We can conclude from $\Diamond\neg\alpha \in \mathbf{K}$ and $\mathbf{K} \subseteq \mathbf{K} * \alpha$ that $\Diamond\neg\alpha \in \mathbf{K} * \alpha$.

According to *success*, $\alpha \in \mathbf{K} * \alpha$. so that $\neg\Diamond\neg\alpha \in Poss(\mathbf{K} * \alpha)$. It follows from *closure under Poss* that $\neg\Diamond\neg\alpha \in \mathbf{K} * \alpha$.

Thus, we have both $\Diamond\neg\alpha \in \mathbf{K} * \alpha$ and $\neg\Diamond\neg\alpha \in \mathbf{K} * \alpha$, so that $\mathbf{K} * \alpha$ is inconsistent.

It follows from $\neg\alpha \notin \mathbf{K}$, since $\mathbf{K}$ is logically closed, that $\neg\alpha$ is not a tautology. Thus α is consistent. We have already shown that $\mathbf{K} * \alpha$ is inconsistent. This contradicts *consistency*, and thereby concludes our proof. ■

The following simple but elegant observation was put forward by Gärdenfors as part of the proof of his impossibility theorem:

OBSERVATION 5.7 (Peter Gärdenfors [33]) *If* $*$ *is a global operator on belief sets that satisfy the Ramsey test with respect to* $*$*, then:*
If $\mathbf{K} \subseteq \mathbf{K}'$*, then* $\mathbf{K} * \alpha \subseteq \mathbf{K}' * \alpha$*. (monotonicity)*

Proof. Let $\mathbf{K} \subseteq \mathbf{K}'$ and $\beta \in \mathbf{K} * \alpha$. Since $\mathbf{K}$ satisfies the Ramsey test, we have $\alpha \Box\!\!\rightarrow \beta \in \mathbf{K}$, and since $\mathbf{K} \subseteq \mathbf{K}'$ we have $\alpha \Box\!\!\rightarrow \beta \in \mathbf{K}'$. Since $\mathbf{K}'$ satisfies the Ramsey test it follows that $\beta \in \mathbf{K}' * \alpha$. ■

> Let $*$ be a global (revision) operator. Then the following conditions are incompatible:
>
> 1. $\mathbf{K}$ satisfies the *Ramsey test.*
> 2. $\mathbf{K} * \alpha = \mathrm{Cn}(\mathbf{K} * \alpha)$ (*closure*)
> 3. $\alpha \in \mathbf{K} * \alpha$ (*success*)
> 4. If α is consistent, then so is $\mathbf{K} * \alpha$. (*consistency*)
> 5. If $\neg\alpha \notin \mathbf{K}$ then $\mathbf{K} \subseteq \mathbf{K} * \alpha$. (*preservation*)
> 6. If $\mathbf{K}$ is a belief set, then so is $\mathrm{Cn}(\mathbf{K} \cup \{\alpha\})$. (*closure under expansion*)
> 7. There are three sentences α, β, and δ and a belief set $\mathbf{K}$ such that $\alpha\&\beta, \alpha\&\delta$, and $\beta\&\delta$ are all inconsistent and that $\neg\alpha \notin \mathbf{K}, \neg\beta \notin \mathbf{K}$, and $\neg\delta \notin \mathbf{K}$. (*non-triviality*)
>
> [Theorem 5.6, Gärdenfors's impossibility theorem.]

Proof. Suppose that all seven conditions are satisfied. Let α, β, and δ be the three non-trivial sentences and $\mathbf{K}$ the belief set that exist according to *non-triviality*. It follows from $\neg\alpha \notin \mathbf{K}$, since $\mathbf{K}$ logically closed, that $\neg\alpha$ is not a tautology, and thus that α is consistent. In the same way it follows that β and δ are consistent.

Consider the belief set $(\mathbf{K} * \alpha) * (\beta \vee \delta)$. Since β is consistent, so is $\beta \vee \delta$. It follows from *consistency* that $(\mathbf{K} * \alpha) * (\beta \vee \delta)$ is consistent. It follows from *success* that $\beta \vee \delta \in (\mathbf{K} * \alpha) * (\beta \vee \delta)$. Since a consistent set cannot contain all three of

$\beta\vee\delta, \neg\beta$ and $\neg\delta$, either $\neg\beta \notin (\mathbf{K} * \alpha) * (\beta\vee\delta)$ or $\neg\delta \notin (\mathbf{K} * \alpha) * (\beta\vee\delta)$. Without loss of generality, we may assume that $\neg\delta \notin (\mathbf{K} * \alpha) * (\beta\vee\delta)$.

It follows from *closure under expansion* that $\mathbf{K} + \alpha$ and $\mathbf{K} + (\alpha\vee\beta)$ are both belief sets, and from the definition of expansion that $\mathbf{K} + (\alpha\vee\beta) \subseteq \mathbf{K} + \alpha$. Since $\neg\alpha \notin \mathbf{K}$, it follows from *preservation* that $\mathbf{K} \subseteq \mathbf{K} * \alpha$. *Success* yields $\alpha \in \mathbf{K} * \alpha$, and then *closure* yields $\text{Cn}(\mathbf{K}\cup\{\alpha\}) \subseteq \mathbf{K}*\alpha$, i.e. $\mathbf{K}+\alpha \subseteq \mathbf{K}*\alpha$. We can conclude from $\mathbf{K} + (\alpha\vee\beta) \subseteq \mathbf{K} + \alpha$ and $\mathbf{K} + \alpha \subseteq \mathbf{K} * \alpha$ that $\mathbf{K} + (\alpha\vee\beta) \subseteq \mathbf{K} * \alpha$.

According to Observation 5.7, *monotonicity* holds, and we can therefore conclude from $\mathbf{K} + (\alpha\vee\beta) \subseteq \mathbf{K} * \alpha$ that $(\mathbf{K} + (\alpha\vee\beta)) * (\beta\vee\delta) \subseteq (\mathbf{K} * \alpha) * (\beta\vee\delta)$. Since $\neg\delta \notin (\mathbf{K} * \alpha) * (\beta\vee\delta)$, we can conclude that $\neg\delta \notin (\mathbf{K} + (\alpha\vee\beta)) * (\beta\vee\delta)$.

Next, suppose that $\neg(\beta\vee\delta) \in \mathbf{K} + (\alpha\vee\beta)$. Since by definition $\mathbf{K} + (\alpha\vee\beta) = \text{Cn}(\mathbf{K} \cup \{\alpha\vee\beta\})$, it follows from the deduction property that $\alpha\vee\beta\rightarrow\neg(\beta\vee\delta) \in \text{Cn}(\mathbf{K})$, or equivalently $\neg\beta\&\neg(\alpha\&\delta) \in \text{Cn}(\mathbf{K})$. Since $\alpha\&\delta$ is inconsistent (*non-triviality*), this is equivalent with $\neg\beta \in \text{Cn}(\mathbf{K})$, which violates our application of *non-triviality*. We can conclude that $\neg(\beta\vee\delta) \notin \mathbf{K} + (\alpha\vee\beta)$.

It follows from $\neg(\beta\vee\delta) \notin \mathbf{K} + (\alpha\vee\beta)$, by *preservation*, that $\mathbf{K} + (\alpha\vee\beta) \subseteq (\mathbf{K} + (\alpha\vee\beta)) * (\beta\vee\delta)$. *Success* yields $\beta\vee\delta \in (\mathbf{K} + (\alpha\vee\beta)) * (\beta\vee\delta)$. Using *closure*, we obtain $\text{Cn}((\mathbf{K} + (\alpha\vee\beta)) \cup \{\beta\vee\delta\}) \subseteq (\mathbf{K} + (\alpha\vee\beta)) * (\beta\vee\delta)$.

The definition of $+$ yields $\text{Cn}((\mathbf{K}+(\alpha\vee\beta))\cup\{\beta\vee\delta\}) = \text{Cn}(\mathbf{K}\cup\{\alpha\vee\beta, \beta\vee\delta\})$. Since $\alpha\&\delta$ is inconsistent (*non-triviality*) this is identical to $\text{Cn}(\mathbf{K}\cup\{\beta\})$ and thus to $\mathbf{K} + \beta$. We have shown that $\mathbf{K} + \beta \subseteq (\mathbf{K} + (\alpha\vee\beta)) * (\beta\vee\delta)$. Hence, $\beta \in (\mathbf{K}+(\alpha\vee\beta))*(\beta\vee\delta)$. Since β logically implies $\neg\delta$ (*non-triviality*), it follows that $\neg\delta \in (\mathbf{K} + (\alpha\vee\beta)) * (\beta\vee\delta)$.

In summary, we have shown both that $\neg\delta \notin (\mathbf{K} + (\alpha\vee\beta)) * (\beta\vee\delta)$ and that $\neg\delta \in (\mathbf{K} + (\alpha\vee\beta)) * (\beta\vee\delta)$. This contradiction concludes the proof. ∎

Exercises

209. [22] Prove the following variant of Fuhrmann's impossibility theorem: There is no belief set $\mathbf{K}$ that satisfies the following five conditions:

    (a) There is some sentence α such that $\alpha \notin \mathbf{K}$ and $\neg\alpha \notin \mathbf{K}$. (*incompleteness*)

    (b) $Poss(\mathbf{K}) \subseteq \mathbf{K}$ (*closure under Poss*)

    (c) If $\alpha \notin \mathbf{K}$ then $\mathbf{K}\div\alpha = \mathbf{K}$. (*contraction-vacuity*)

    (d) $\mathbf{K} * \alpha = (\mathbf{K}\div\neg\alpha) + \alpha$ (*Levi identity*)

    (e) If α is consistent, then so is $\mathbf{K} * \alpha$. (*consistency*)

    (Hint: show that there is a belief set $\mathbf{K}$ and a consistent sentence α such that $\mathbf{K} * \alpha = \mathbf{K} + \alpha$ and that both $\Diamond\neg\alpha$ and $\neg\Diamond\neg\alpha$ are elements if $\mathbf{K} + \alpha$.)

210. Replace the *consistency* postulate in Gärdenfors's impossibility theorem by the following weaker variant:
    If both $\mathbf{K}$ and α are consistent, then so is $\mathbf{K} * \alpha$. (*weak consistency*)
    Does the theorem still go through?

CHAPTER 6

AFTERTHOUGHT

What has been achieved? Researchers in belief dynamics have developed quite a few types of formal operations that can be used to perform changes on belief sets or belief bases. A sizable number of postulates have been proposed that can be used to characterize these operations. In spite of all this we are not in a position to answer, unequivocally, the question what it means to change one's beliefs rationally. However, we are able to restate the question with more precision. In particular, we can sort out various aspects of it, that can be treated separately. This is no small achievement, but it cries out for continued research efforts.

From a *philosopher's* point of view, some traditional issues in epistemology (the theory of knowledge) can now be seen in new light. The distinction between coherentist and foundationalist epistemology can be expressed in a more precise manner [14; 36; 53; 102]. The relations between the three notions of epistemic importance (value), vulnerability to change, and probability is in urgent need of clarification, and the formal apparatus of belief dynamics may facilitate such an investigation [73]. More precise accounts of how scientific theories evolve should be attainable with the tools of belief dynamics, perhaps in particular within the framework of non-prioritized belief change [89]. Some issues in the philosophical study of conditional sentences can be reexpressed in a perspicuous way through the application of the Ramsey test to belief sets [33; 55; 72; 74].

Formal studies in belief dynamics have also given rise to new issues of philosophical import: Should rational belief contraction satisfy the demanding postulate of recovery? [35; 83] Should belief-contravening acquisition of new information take place by first accepting the new belief and then expunging old beliefs that contradict it, or should these two suboperations take place in reverse order?[50] What are the relations between information and informational value?[73]

From the *computer scientist's* point of view, one of the most pressing issues should be: To what extent are the rationality postulates satisfied by various models of database updating? The numerous postulates that have been proposed in the last few years provide us with as many tools for characterizing the properties of knowledge-updating systems [58]. Studies of connectionist ('neural') networks indicate that some such networks satisfy some of the fundamental belief revision postulates [6]. Largely, though, these new possibilities for characterizing updating systems remain unexplored.

From the *psychologist's* point of view, a major issue should be: Under what (if any) circumstances does the behaviour of actual persons comply with the various postulates for belief change? It should not be expected that invariable laws of human reasoning can be found among the postulates of belief dynamics. However, it may be possible to find conditions under which some of these postulates are satisfied, and conditions under which they are not. The distinction between internal and external revision should also be useful in cognitive psychology.

We have no reason to expect the ongoing diversification in belief dynamics to abate. And there is no reason why it should. Since no adequate all-embracing model of belief change seems to be in sight, this field of research must, like so many others, progress by the development of different models, each of which mirrors some but not all of the important features of its objects of study.

CHAPTER 6^+

SOME UNSOLVED PROBLEMS

From the *logician's* perspective, belief dynamics is replete with unsolved problems, waiting for a successful attack. The following sample contains some of the more interesting of these problems.

1. Several important classes of operations on belief sets still lack an axiomatic characterization, including:
   - relational partial meet contraction (has been solved for completed selection functions, see p. 149)
   - multiple (package) TMR partial meet contraction
   - safe contraction
   - base-generated TMR partial meet contraction (has been solved for completed selection functions, see p. 348)
   - base-generated operations from an infinite base
2. The same applies to several classes of operations on belief bases, including:
   - relational partial meet contraction
   - TMR partial meet contraction
   - relational (internal and external) partial meet revision
   - TMR (internal and external) partial meet revision
   - cumulative kernel contraction
3. Nothing is known about base-generated external revision and its relation to base-generated internal revision (that we studied in Sections 4.14^+–4.15^+).
4. Neither kernel nor safe contraction has been generalized to multiple contraction.
5. We still lack workable models of changes on belief sets that have been extended to include non-truth-functional operators, such as operators that represent modal and conditional sentences. (See Chapter 5.)
6. Satisfactory constructions for repeated belief change remain to be developed. In particular:
   - What is the best way to revise an entrenchment relation?

- What are the properties of revision in Rabinowicz's approach, that is based on a similarity relation between possible worlds? (Cf. Section 3.9.)
- How can repeated changes on belief bases be characterized on the knowledge level? (Base-generated repeated contraction and revision.)

7. We only have a rudimentary knowledge of the logic of non-prioritized belief change. As an example of this, the consolidation operator referred to in Section 3.12 makes the whole belief base consistent. In practice, our corrections of inconsistencies are often local, i.e., they only make certain parts of the belief base consistent. No model of such local changes seems to be available.

The solution of these problems is left to the reader.

SUGGESTED READINGS

The numbers refer to items in the bibliography.

BIBLIOGRAPHY

Bracketed numbers in the text refer to this bibliography. The numbers appended to previously published definitions and formal results refer, as far as this has been possible, to where they were first published.

[1] Alchourrón, C. E., Gärdenfors, P. and Makinson, D. On the logic of theory change: partial meet contraction and revision functions. *Journal of Symbolic Logic*, **50**, 510–530, 1985.

[2] Alchourrón, C. E. and Makinson, D. Hierarchies of regulation and their logic. In Hilpinen (ed.), *New Studies in Deontic Logic*, pp. 125–148. D. Reidel Publishing Company, 1981.

[3] Alchourrón, C. E. and Makinson, D. On the logic of theory change: contraction functions and their associated revision functions. *Theoria*, **48**, 14–37, 1982.

[4] Alchourrón, C. E. and Makinson, D. On the logic of theory change: safe contraction. *Studia Logica*, **44**, 405–422, 1985.

[5] Alchourrón, C. E. and Makinson, D. Maps between some different kinds of contraction function: the finite case. *Studia Logica*, **45**, 187–198, 1986.

[6] Balkenius, C. and Gärdenfors, P. Nonmonotonic Inferences in Neural Networks. *Lund University Cognitive Studies*, **3**, 1991.

[7] Boutilier, C. On the revision of probabilistic belief states. *Notre Dame Journal of Formal Logic*, **36**, 158–183, 1995.

[8] Brachman, R. J. and Levesque, H. J. What makes a knowledge base knowledgeable? A view of databases from the knowledge level. In Kerschberg (ed.), *Expert Database Systems, Proceeding from the first international workshop*, pp. 69–78. The Benjamin/Cummings Publishing Company, 1986.

[9] Brewka, G. Belief revision in a framework for default reasoning. In Fuhrmann and Morreau (eds.), *The Logic of Theory Change*, pp. 206–222. Springer-Verlag, Berlin, 1991.

[10] Cross, C. B. and Thomason, R. H. Conditionals and knowledge-base update. In Gärdenfors (ed.), *Belief Revision*, pp. 247–275. Cambridge University Press, Cambridge, 1992.

[11] Dalal, M. Investigations into a theory of knowledge base revision: preliminary report. Seventh National Conference on Artificial Intelligence (AAAI-88), St. Paul, pp. 475–479, 1988.

[12] Doyle, J. A truth maintenance system. *Artificial Intelligence*, **12**, 231–272, 1979.

[13] Doyle, J. Rational belief revision (preliminary report). In Allen (ed.), *Principles of Knowledge Representation and Reasoning*, pp. 163–174. Morgan Kaufmann, Los Altos, CA, 1991.

[14] Doyle, J. Reason maintenance and belief revision: Foundations versus coherence theories. In Gärdenfors (ed.), *Belief Revision*, pp. 29–51. Cambridge University Press, Cambridge, 1992.

[15] Dubois, D. and Prade, H. Epistemic entrenchment and possibilistic logic. *Artificial Intelligence*, **50**, 223–239, 1991.

[16] Fagin, R., Kuper, G. M., Ullman, J. D. and Vardi, M. Y. Updating logical databases. *Advances in Computing Research*, **3**, 1–18, 1986.

[17] Fagin, R., Ullman, J. D. and Vardi, M. Y. On the semantics of updates in databases. In *Proceedings of Second ACM SIGACT-SIGMOD*, pp. 352–365, 1983.

[18] Fermé, E. On the logic of theory change: contraction without recovery. *Journal of Logic, Language and Information*, in press.

[19] Foo, N. Observations on AGM entrenchment, *Computer Science Technical Report 389*, Sydney University, 1990.

[20] Freund, M. and Lehmann, D. Belief revision and rational inference. *Technical Report 1994-16*, Leipniz Centre for Research in Computer Science, Hebrew University of Jerusalem, 1994.

[21] Fuhrmann, A. *Relevant Logics, Modal Logics, and Theory Change*. Doctoral thesis, Australian National University, Canberra, 1988.

[22] Fuhrmann, A. Reflective modalities and theory change. *Synthese*, **81**, 115–134, 1989.

[23] Fuhrmann, A. On the modal logic of theory change. In Fuhrmann and Morreau (eds.), *The Logic of Theory Change*, pp. 259–281. Springer-Verlag, Berlin, 1991.

[24] Fuhrmann, A. Theory contraction through base contraction. *Journal of Philosophical Logic*, **20**, 175–203, 1991.

[25] Fuhrmann, A. and Hansson, S. O. A survey of multiple contraction. *Journal of Logic, Language and Information*, **3**, 39–74, 1994.

[26] Fuhrmann, A. and Morreau, M. (eds.) *The Logic of Theory Change*. Springer-Verlag, Berlin, 1991.

[27] Gabbay, D. M. Theoretical foundations for nonmonotonic reasoning in expert systems. In Apt (ed.), *Logics and Models of Concurrent Systems*, pp. 439–457. Springer-Verlag, Berlin, 1985.

[28] Gallier, J. R. Autonomous belief revision and communication. In Gärdenfors (ed.), *Belief Revision*, pp. 220–246. Cambridge University Press, Cambridge, 1992.

[29] Gärdenfors, P. Conditionals and changes of belief. *Acta Philosophica Fennica*, **30**, 381–404, 1978.

[30] Gärdenfors, P. An epistemic approach to conditionals. *American Philosophical Quarterly*, **18**, 203–211, 1981.

[31] Gärdenfors, P. Rules for rational changes of belief. In *Philosophical Essays Dedicated to L. Åqvist*, pp. 88–101, 1982.

[32] Gärdenfors, P. Epistemic Importance and Minimal Changes of Belief. *Australasian Journal of Philosophy*, **62**, 136–157, 1984.

[33] Gärdenfors, P. Belief revision and the Ramsey test for conditionals. *Philosophical Review*, **95**, 81–93, 1986.

[34] Gärdenfors, P. Variations on the Ramsey test: more triviality results. *Studia Logica*, **46**, 321–327, 1987.

[35] Gärdenfors, P. *Knowledge in Flux. Modeling the Dynamics of Epistemic States*, The MIT Press, Cambridge, MA, 1988.

[36] Gärdenfors, P. The dynamics of belief systems: foundations vs. coherence theories. *Revue Internationale de Philosophie*, **44**, 24–46, 1990.

[37] Gärdenfors, P. Belief revision: an introduction. In Gärdenfors (ed.), *Belief Revision*, pp. 1–28. Cambridge University Press, Cambridge, 1992.

[38] Gärdenfors, P. and Makinson, D. Revisions of knowledge systems using epistemic entrenchment. In Moshe Y. Vardi (ed.), *Proceedings of the Second Conference on Theoretical Aspects of Reasoning about Knowledge*, pp. 83–95. Morgan Kaufmann, Los Altos, 1988.

[39] Gärdenfors, P. and Makinson, D. Nonmonotonic Inference Based on Expectations. *Artificial Intelligence*, **65**, 197–245, 1994.

[40] Gärdenfors, P. and Rott, H. Belief revision. In Gabbay, Hogger and Robinson (eds.), *Handbook of Logic in AI and Logic Programming*, Vol. 4, pp. 35–132. Oxford University Press, Oxford, 1995.

[41] Grove, A. Two modellings for theory change. *Journal of Philosophical Logic*, **17**, 157–170, 1988.

[42] Hansson, S. O. New operators for theory change. *Theoria*, **55**, 114–132, 1989.

[43] Hansson, S. O. *Belief Base Dynamics*. PhD Thesis. Uppsala University, Uppsala, 1991.

[44] Hansson, S. O. Belief contraction without recovery. *Studia Logica*, **50**, 251–260, 1991.

[45] Hansson, S. O. A dyadic representation of belief. In Gärdenfors (ed.), *Belief Revision*, pp. 89–121. Cambridge University Press, Cambridge, 1992.

[46] Hansson, S. O. In defense of base contraction. *Synthese*, **91**, 239–245, 1992.

[47] Hansson, S. O. In defense of the Ramsey test. *Journal of Philosophy*, **89**, 522–540, 1992.

[48] Hansson, S. O. Similarity semantics and minimal changes of belief. *Erkenntnis*, **37**, 401–429, 1992.

[49] Hansson, S. O. Changes on disjunctively closed bases. *Journal of Logic, Language and Information*, **2**, 255–284, 1993.

[50] Hansson, S. O. Reversing the Levi identity. *Journal of Philosophical Logic*, **22**, 637–669, 1993.

[51] Hansson, S. O. Theory contraction and base contraction unified. *Journal of Symbolic Logic*, **58**, 602–625, 1993.

[52] Hansson, S. O. Kernel contraction. *Journal of Symbolic Logic*, **59**, 845–859, 1994.

[53] Hansson, S. O. Taking belief bases seriously. In Prawitz and Westerståhl, (eds.). *Logic and Philosophy of Science in Uppsala*, pp. 13–28. Kluwer Academic Publishers, Dordrecht, 1994.

[54] Hansson, S. O. Changes in preference. *Theory and Decision*, **38**, 1–28, 1995.

[55] Hansson, S. O. The emperor's new clothes. Some recurring problems in the formal analysis of counterfactuals. In Crocco *et al.*, (eds), *Conditionals: from Philosophy to Computer Science*, pp. 13–31. Clarendon Press, Oxford, 1995.

[56] Hansson, S. O. Some solved and unsolved remainder equations. *Mathematical Logic Quarterly*, **41**, 362–368, 1995.

[57] Hansson, S. O. Hidden structures of belief. In Fuhrmann and Rott (eds.), *Logic, Actions and Information*, pp. 79–100. de Gruyter, Berlin, 1996.

[58] Hansson, S. O. A test battery for rational database updating. *Artificial Intelligence Journal*, **82**, 341–352, 1996.

[59] Hansson, S. O. and Makinson, D. Applying normative rules with constraint. In M. L. Dalla Chiara *et al.* (eds.). *Logic and Scientific Method*, pp. 313–332. Kluwer, 1997.

[60] Hansson, S. O. and Olsson, E. J. Levi contractions and AGM contractions: A comparison. *Notre Dame Journal of Formal Logic*, **36**, 103–119, 1995.

[61] Hansson, S. O. and Olsson, E. J. Providing Foundations for Coherentism. Manuscript, 1996.

[62] Hansson, S. O. and Rott, H. How not to change the theory of theory change: A reply to Tennant. *British Journal for the Philosophy of Science*, **46** 361–380, 1995.

[63] Harman, G. Change in View. Principles of Reasoning, MIT Press, Cambridge, Mass., 1986.

[64] Harper, W. Rational Conceptual Change. *PSA 1976*, pp. 462-494, 1977.

[65] Katsuno, H. and Mendelzon, A. O. A unified view of propositional knowledge base updates. In *Proceedings of the 11th International Joint Conference on Artificial Intelligence*, pp. 269–276, 1989.

[66] Katsuno, H. and Mendelzon, A. O. Propositional knowledge base revision and minimal change. *Artificial Intelligence*, **52**, 263–294, 1991.

[67] Katsuno, H. and Mendelzon, A. O. On the difference between updating a knowledge base and revising it. In Gärdenfors (ed.), *Belief Revision*, pp. 183–203. Cambridge University Press, Cambridge, 1992.

[68] Keller, A. and Winslett, M. On the use of an extended relational model to handle changing incomplete information. *IEEE Transactions on Software Engineering*, **SE-11:7**, 620–633, 1985.

[69] Kraus, S., Lehmann, D. and Magidor, M. Nonmonotonic reasoning, preferential models and cumulative logics. *Artificial Intelligence*, **44**, 167–207, 1990.

[70] Levi, I. Subjunctives, dispositions and chances. *Synthese*, **34**, 423–455, 1977.

[71] Levi, I. *The Enterprise of Knowledge*. The MIT Press, Cambridge, MA, 1980.

[72] Levi, I. Iteration of conditionals and the Ramsey test. *Synthese*, **76**, 49–81, 1988.

[73] Levi, I. *The Fixation of Belief and Its Undoing*. Cambridge University Press, Cambridge, MA., 1991.

[74] Levi, I. *For the Sake of Argument*. Cambridge University Press, Cambridge, 1996.

[75] Lewis, D. *Counterfactuals*. Harvard University Press, Cambridge, MA, 1973.

[76] Lindström, S. A semantic approach to nonmonotonic reasoning: inference operations and choice, Uppsala Prints and Reprints in Philosophy, 1994, no. 10.

[77] Lindström, S. The Ramsey test and the indexicality of conditionals: a proposed resolution of Gärdenfors' paradox. In Fuhrmann and Rott (eds.), *Logic, Action, and Information. Essays on Logic in Philosophy and Artificial Intelligence*, pp. 208–228. Walter de Gruyter, Berlin, 1996.

[78] Lindström, S. and Rabinowicz, W. On probabilistic representation of non-probabilistic belief revision *Journal of Philosophical Logic*, **18**, 69–101, 1989.

[79] Lindström, S. and Rabinowicz, W. Epistemic entrenchment with incomparabilities and relational belief revision. In Fuhrmann and Morreau (eds.), *The Logic of Theory Change*, pp. 208–228. Springer-Verlag, Berlin, 1991.

[80] Lindström, S. and Rabinowicz, W. Belief revision, epistemic conditionals and the Ramsey test. *Synthese*, **91**, 195–237, 1992.

[81] Lindström, S. and Rabinowicz, W. The Ramsey test revisited. In Crocco *et al.*, (eds.), *Conditionals: from Philosophy to Computer Science*, pp. 147–191, Clarendon Press, Oxford, 1995.

[82] Makinson, D. How to give it up: a survey of some formal aspects of the logic of theory change. *Synthese*, **62**, 347–363, 1985, and **63**, 185–186, 1986.

[83] Makinson, D. On the status of the postulate of recovery in the logic of theory change. *Journal of Philosophical Logic*, **16**, 383–394, 1987.

[84] Makinson, D. The Gärdenfors impossibility theorem in non-monotonic contexts. *Studia Logica*, **49**, 1–6, 1990.

[85] Makinson, D. Five faces of minimality. *Studia Logica*, **52**, 339–379, 1993.

[86] Makinson, D. General patterns in nonmonotonic reasoning. In D. M. Gabbay *et al.* (eds), *Handbook of Logic in Artificial Intelligence and Logic Programming*, Vol. III, pp. 35–110. Oxford University Press, Oxford, 1993.

[87] Makinson, D. On the force of some apparent counterexamples to recovery. In Valdés, *et al.* (eds.), *Normative Systems in Legal and Moral Theory, Festschrift for Carlos Alchourrón and Eugenio Bulygin*, pp. 475–481, Duncker and Humblot, Berlin, 1997.

[88] Makinson, D. and Gärdenfors, P. Relations between the logic of theory change and nonmonotonic logic. In Fuhrmann and Morreau (eds.), *The Logic of Theory Change*, pp. 185–205. Springer-Verlag, Berlin, 1991.

[89] Martin, E. and Osherson, D. Scientific discovery based on belief revision, manuscript, presented at the Fourth International Symposium on Artificial Intelligence and Mathematics, January 3-5, 1996, Ft. Lauderdale, FL, 1996.

[90] Martins, J. P. and Shapiro, S. C. A model for belief revision. *Artificial Intelligence*, **35**, 25–79, 1988.

[91] Morreau, M. Epistemic semantics for counterfactuals. *Journal of Philosophical Logic*, **21**, 33–62, 1992.

[92] Moulin, H. Choice functions over a finite set: a summary. *Social Choice and Welfare*, **2**, 147–160, 1985.

[93] Nayak, A. C. *Studies in Belief Change*. PhD Thesis. University of Rochester, 1993.

[94] Nayak, A. C. Foundational belief change. *Journal of Philosophical Logic*, **23**, 495–533, 1994.

[95] Nayak, A. C. Iterated belief change based on epistemic entrenchment. *Erkenntnis*, **41**, 353–390, 1994.

[96] Nayak, A., Foo, N. Y., Pagnucco, M. and Sattar, A. Entrenchment kinematics 101. In C Zhang (ed.), *Proceedings of the 7th Australian Joint Conference on Artificial Intelligence*, pp. 157–164. World Scientific, 1994.

[97] Nayak, A., Nelson, P. and Polansky, H. Belief change as change in epistemic entrenchment. *Synthese*, **109**, 143–174, 1996.

[98] Nebel, B. A knowledge level analysis of belief revision. In *Proceedings of the 1st International Conference of Principles of Knowledge Representation and Reasoning*, pp. 301–311, Morgan Kaufmann, 1989.

[99] Nebel, B. Syntax based approaches to belief revision. In Gärdenfors (ed.), *Belief Revision*, pp. 52–88. Cambridge University Press, Cambridge, 1992.

[100] Newell, A. The knowledge level. *Artificial Intelligence*, **18**, 87–127, 1982.

[101] Niederée, R. Multiple contraction. a further case against Gärdenfors' principle of recovery. In Fuhrmann and Morreau (eds.), *The Logic of Theory Change*, pp. 322–334. Springer-Verlag, Berlin, 1991.

[102] Olsson, E. J. *Coherence*, PhD Thesis. Uppsala University, Uppsala, 1997.

[103] Quine, W. V. *Philosophy of Logic*. Prentice-Hall, Inc., Englewood Cliffs, N.J., 1970.

[104] Quine, W. V. and Ullian, J. S. *The Web of Belief*, 2nd ed., J. S. Ullian, New York, 1978.

[105] Rabinowicz, W. Global belief revision based on similarities between worlds. In Hansson and Rabinowicz (eds.), *Logic for a Change. Essays Dedicated to Sten Lindström on the Occasion of his Fiftieth Birthday*, pp. 80–105. Uppsala Prints and Preprints in Philosophy 1995:9, Department of Philosophy, Uppsala University, 1995.

[106] Ramsey, F. P. *Foundations of Mathematics and Other Logical Essays*. 2nd ed., Routledge and Kegan Paul, London, 1950.

[107] Rott, H. Ifs, though and because. *Erkenntnis*, **25**, 345–370, 1986.

[108] Rott, H. Conditionals and theory change: revision, expansions, and additions. *Synthese*, **81**, 91–113, 1989.

[109] Rott, H. *Reduktion und Revision: Aspekte des nichtmonotonen Theorienwandels*. Verlag Peter Lang GmbH, Frankfurt am Main, 1991.

[110] Rott, H. Two methods of constructing contractions and revisions of knowledge systems. *Journal of Philosophical Logic*, **20**, 149–173, 1991.

[111] Rott, H. Modellings for belief change: base contraction, multiple contraction, and epistemic entrenchment (preliminary report). In *Logics in AI. European Workshop JELIA'92*, pp. 139–153. Springer-Verlag, Berlin, 1992.

[112] Rott, H. Modellings for belief change: prioritization and entrenchment. *Theoria*, **58**, 21–57, 1992.

[113] Rott, H. A nonmonotonic conditional logic for belief revision. Part 1: Semantics and logic of simple conditionals. In Fuhrmann and Morreau (eds.), *The Logic of Theory Change*. Springer-Verlag, 1992.

[114] Rott, H. On the logic of theory change: more maps between different kinds of contraction function. In Gärdenfors (ed.), *Belief Revision*, pp. 122–141. Cambridge University Press, Cambridge, 1992.

[115] Rott, H. Preferential belief change using generalized epistemic entrenchment. *Journal of Logic, Language and Information*, **1**, 45–78, 1992.

[116] Rott, H. Belief contraction in the context of the general theory of rational choice. *Journal of Symbolic Logic*, **58**, 1426–1450, 1993.

[117] Rott, H. 'Just because': taking belief bases very seriously. In Hansson and Rabinowicz (eds.), *Logic for a Change. Essays Dedicated to Sten Lindström on the Occasion of his Fiftieth Birthday*, pp. 106–124. Uppsala Prints and Preprints in Philosophy 1995:9, Department of Philosophy, Uppsala, 1995.

[118] Schlechta, K. Some results on theory revision. In Fuhrmann and Morreau (eds.), *The Logic of Theory Change*, pp. 72–92. Springer-Verlag, Berlin, 1991.

[119] Schlechta, K. Theory revision and probability. *Notre Dame Journal of Formal Logic*, **32**, 307–319, 1991.

[120] Segerberg, K. A Note on an Impossibility Theorem of Gärdenfors, *Nous*, **23**, 351–354, 1989.

[121] Sosa, E. The raft and the pyramid: coherence versus foundations in the theory of knowledge. *Midwest Studies in Philosophy*, **5**, 3–25, 1980.

[122] Stalnaker, R. A theory of conditionals. In Rescher (ed.), *Studies in Logical Theory*, pp. 98-112. Blackwell, Oxford, 1968.

[123] Tarski, A. On some fundamental concepts of metamathematics. [1930] *Logic, Semantics, Metamathematics. Papers from 1923 to 1938*, translated by J. H. Woodger, pp. 30–36. Clarendon Press, Oxford, 1956.

[124] Williams, M.-A. Two operators for theory base change. In *Proceedings of the 5th Australian Joint Conference on Artificial Intelligence*, pp. 259–265. World Scientific, 1992.

[125] Williams, M.-A. On the logic of theory base change. In MacNish (ed.), *Logics in Artificial Intelligence*, pp. 86–105. Lecture Note Series in Computer Science, No 835, Springer Verlag, 1994.

[126] Williams, M.-A. Iterated theory base change: a computational model. In *Proceedings, Fourteenth International Joint Conference on Artificial Intelligence*, pp. 1541–1550. Morgan Kaufmann, 1995.

[127] Winslett, M. Reasoning about action using a possible models approach. In *Proceedings of the Seventh National Conference on Artificial Intelligence*, pp. 89–93, 1988.

[128] Wobcke, W. Belief revision, conditional logic and nonmonotonic reasoning. *Notre Dame Journal of Formal Logic*, **36**, 55–102, 1995.

[129] Wójcicki, R. *Theory of Logical Calculi*. Kluwer Academic Publishers, Dordrecht, 1988.

SYMBOL INDEX

Selection mechanisms

γ selection function (pp. 13, 105, and 134)
$\hat{\gamma}$ completion of selection function (p. 141)
Γ covering function (p. 136)
σ incision function (p. 89)
s kernel selection function (p. 92)
f propositional selection function (p. 290)
$\sqsubseteq$ marking-off relation (p. 82)
$\sqsubset$ strict part of $\sqsubseteq$ (p. 82)
$\leq$ entrenchment relation (p. 97)
$<$ strict part of $\leq$ (p. 97)
$\equiv$ symmetric part of $\leq$ (p. 97)
$\prec$ hierarchy (p. 93)
$\lhd$ generalized entrenchment (p. 109)
$\lesssim$ ensçoncement relation (p. 103)
$\ll$ strict part of $\lesssim$ (p. 103)
V epistemic value (informational value) (p. 87)
N necessity measure (p. 197)

Operators of change

$\circ$ (any) operator (p. 306)

$\div$ contraction (pp. 11 and 14)
$-$ contraction (p. 305)
$\sim_\gamma$ partial meet contraction (pp. 14, 105, and 134)
$\sim$ full meet contraction (p. 15)
$\sim_\gamma{\perp}$ partial meet consolidation (p. 236)
$\simeq_\gamma$ pre-closed partial meet contraction (p. 347)
$\tilde{\sim}_\gamma$ Nebel's pseudocontraction (p. 318)
$\div_G$ Gärdenfors's entrenchment-based contraction (p. 101)
$\div_R$ Rott's entrenchment-based contraction (p. 101)
$\div_W$ Williams's ensconcement-based contraction (p. 104)
$\approx_\sigma$ kernel contraction (pp. 89 and 107)
$\hat{\approx}_\sigma$ saturated kernel contraction (p. 91)
C_α indeterministic contraction (p. 116)
$\ominus$ propositional contraction (p. 292)

$+$ expansion, closing or non-closing (pp. 15 and 19)
$\oplus$ propositional expansion (p. 289)

$*$ revision (p. 16)
$\mp_\gamma$ internal partial meet revision (pp. 203, 211, and 260)
$\mp$ internal full meet revision (pp. 210, and 214)
$\pm_\gamma$ external partial meet revision (pp. 204, 211, and 260)
$\pm$ external full meet revision (p. 210)
$\mp_G$ Gärdenfors's entrenchment-based revision (p. 226)
$\mp_R$ Rott's entrenchment-based revision (p. 226)
$\circledast$ propositional revision (p. 290)

Functions that transform operations

$\mathbb{R}$ Levi identity function (p. 212)
$\mathbb{C}$ Harper identity function (p. 212)
E function from contraction to entrenchment (p. 197)
C function from entrenchment to contraction (p. 197)

Possible world models

$\mathcal{W}$ proposition (p. 221)
[] propositional representation (p. 52)
g_A Grove's bijection (p. 54)
f propositional selection function (p. 290)
$\mathfrak{S}$ system of spheres (p. 294)
S_α smallest intersecting sphere (pp. 299 and 300)
sim similarity relation (p. 224)

Modal concepts

The Greek alphabet

A α alpha
B β beta
Γ γ gamma
Δ δ delta
E ε epsilon
Z ζ zeta
H η eta
Θ θ, ϑ theta
I ι iota
K κ kappa
Λ λ lambda
M μ mu
N ν nu
Ξ ξ xi
O o omicron
Π π pi
P ρ rho
Σ σ sigma
T τ tau
Y υ upsilon
Φ ϕ, φ phi
X χ chi
Ψ ψ psi
Ω ω omega

NAME INDEX

SUBJECT INDEX

A Textbook of Belief Dynamics

Solutions to exercises

CONTENTS

SOLUTIONS FOR CHAPTER 1^+

1. No. For a counterexample, let α and β be logically independent sentences, and let $A = \{\alpha \vee \beta\}$.

2. We need to show that for all β, $\beta \in \mathrm{Cn}(\{\alpha \vee \neg\alpha\})$ holds if and only if $\beta \in \mathrm{Cn}(\varnothing)$.

By deduction, $\beta \in \mathrm{Cn}(\{\alpha \vee \neg\alpha\})$ holds if and only if $\alpha \vee \neg\alpha \to \beta \in \mathrm{Cn}(\varnothing)$, (since $\alpha \vee \neg\alpha \to \beta$ is equivalent with β) if and only if $\beta \in \mathrm{Cn}(\varnothing)$.

3. Since $\alpha \to \beta$ is equivalent with $\neg\alpha \vee \beta$, we have $\mathrm{Cn}(\{\alpha \to \beta\}) = \mathrm{Cn}(\{\neg\alpha \vee \beta\})$. It therefore follows from Observation 1.17 that $\mathrm{Cn}(\{\neg\alpha \vee \beta\}) = \mathrm{Cn}(\{\neg\alpha\}) \cap \mathrm{Cn}(\{\beta\})$.

4. $\mathrm{Cn}(\{\alpha \to \beta\}) \cap \mathrm{Cn}(\{\beta \to \alpha\}) =$
$= \mathrm{Cn}(\{\neg\alpha \vee \beta\}) \cap \mathrm{Cn}(\{\neg\beta \vee \alpha\})$
$= \mathrm{Cn}(\{\neg\alpha\}) \cap \mathrm{Cn}(\{\beta\}) \cap \mathrm{Cn}(\{\neg\beta\}) \cap \mathrm{Cn}(\{\alpha\})$
$= \mathrm{Cn}(\{\alpha\}) \cap \mathrm{Cn}(\{\neg\alpha\}) \cap \mathrm{Cn}(\{\beta\}) \cap \mathrm{Cn}(\{\neg\beta\})$
$= \mathrm{Cn}(\{\alpha \vee \neg\alpha\}) \cap \mathrm{Cn}(\{\beta \vee \neg\beta\})$ (Observation 1.17)
$= \mathrm{Cn}(\varnothing) \cap \mathrm{Cn}(\varnothing)$ (Exercise 2)
$= \mathrm{Cn}(\varnothing)$

5. Suppose that $A \subseteq D \subseteq B \subseteq \mathrm{Cn}(A)$. It follows by monotony from $D \subseteq B$ that $\mathrm{Cn}(D) \subseteq \mathrm{Cn}(B)$.

It also follows by monotony from $B \subseteq \mathrm{Cn}(A)$ that $\mathrm{Cn}(B) \subseteq \mathrm{Cn}(\mathrm{Cn}(A))$. By iteration, $\mathrm{Cn}(\mathrm{Cn}(A)) = \mathrm{Cn}(A)$, so that $\mathrm{Cn}(B) \subseteq \mathrm{Cn}(A)$. It follows by monotony from $A \subseteq D$ that $\mathrm{Cn}(A) \subseteq \mathrm{Cn}(D)$. From $\mathrm{Cn}(B) \subseteq \mathrm{Cn}(A)$ and $\mathrm{Cn}(A) \subseteq \mathrm{Cn}(D)$ we obtain $\mathrm{Cn}(B) \subseteq \mathrm{Cn}(D)$.

From $\mathrm{Cn}(D) \subseteq \mathrm{Cn}(B)$ and $\mathrm{Cn}(B) \subseteq \mathrm{Cn}(D)$ we may conclude that $\mathrm{Cn}(D) = \mathrm{Cn}(B)$.

6. Suppose that $A \subseteq \mathrm{Cn}(B)$. It follows from inclusion that $B \subseteq \mathrm{Cn}(B)$, so that $A \cup B \subseteq \mathrm{Cn}(B)$. By monotony, $\mathrm{Cn}(A \cup B) \subseteq \mathrm{Cn}(\mathrm{Cn}(B))$. By iteration, $\mathrm{Cn}(\mathrm{Cn}(B)) = \mathrm{Cn}(B)$, so that $\mathrm{Cn}(A \cup B) \subseteq \mathrm{Cn}(B)$.

7. For one direction, let $\mathrm{Cn}(B) = \mathrm{Cn}(D)$. We then have $B \subseteq \mathrm{Cn}(B) = \mathrm{Cn}(D)$ and $D \subseteq \mathrm{Cn}(D) = \mathrm{Cn}(B)$.

For the other direction, let $B \subseteq \mathrm{Cn}(D)$ and $D \subseteq \mathrm{Cn}(B)$. It follows by monotony that $\mathrm{Cn}(B) \subseteq \mathrm{Cn}(\mathrm{Cn}(D))$ and by iteration that $\mathrm{Cn}(\mathrm{Cn}(D)) = \mathrm{Cn}(D)$, so that $\mathrm{Cn}(B) \subseteq \mathrm{Cn}(D)$ can be concluded. In the same way it follows by monotony that $\text{Cn}(D) \subseteq \text{Cn}(\text{Cn}(B))$ and by iteration that $\text{Cn}(\text{Cn}(B)) = \text{Cn}(B)$, so that $\text{Cn}(D) \subseteq \text{Cn}(B)$ can be concluded.

8. We need to show that (I) if Cn is a consequence operator, then the formula given in the exercise is satisfied, and (II) if the formula is satisfied, then Cn is a consequence operator.

Part I: It follows from inclusion and iteration that $X \subseteq \text{Cn}(\text{Cn}(X))$. Furthermore, it follows from iteration that $\text{Cn}(\text{Cn}(X)) \subseteq \text{Cn}(X)$ and from monotony that $\text{Cn}(X) \subseteq \text{Cn}(X \cup Y)$.

Part II: We now assume that the formula given in the exercise is satisfied. In order to show that Cn is a consequence operator, we must prove that it satisfies inclusion, monotony, and iteration.

Inclusion follows directly from $X \subseteq \text{Cn}(\text{Cn}(X)) \subseteq \text{Cn}(X)$.

For monotony, suppose that $X \subseteq Y$. Then $Y = X \cup Y$, so that $\text{Cn}(X) \subseteq \text{Cn}(Y)$ follows direclty from $\text{Cn}(X) \subseteq \text{Cn}(X \cup Y)$.

One direction of iteration, namely $\text{Cn}(\text{Cn}(X)) \subseteq \text{Cn}(X)$, is directly given. The other direction follows from inclusion, that has already been obtained.

9. One direction of the desired equivalence is trivial, namely that if Cn = Cn', then $\text{Cn}(\varnothing) = \text{Cn}'(\varnothing)$. For the other direction, suppose that $\text{Cn}(\varnothing) = \text{Cn}'(\varnothing)$. In order to show that Cn = Cn' we need to prove that for all B and α, $\alpha \in \text{Cn}(B)$ if and only if $\alpha \in \text{Cn}'(B)$. Due to symmetry, it is sufficient to show that for all B and α, if $\alpha \in \text{Cn}(B)$, then $\alpha \in \text{Cn}'(B)$.

It follows by compactness from $\alpha \in \text{Cn}(B)$ that there is a finite subset B'' of B such that $\alpha \in \text{Cn}(B'')$. By repeated use of Observation 1.18, $\text{Cn}(B'') = \text{Cn}(\{\&B''\})$. We therefore have $\alpha \in \text{Cn}(\{\&B''\})$. By deduction, $\&B'' \rightarrow \alpha \in \text{Cn}(\varnothing)$. Since $\text{Cn}'(\varnothing) = \text{Cn}(\varnothing)$, we have $\&B'' \rightarrow \alpha \in \text{Cn}'(\varnothing)$.

Now we can perform the same procedure backwards, but on Cn' instead of Cn: It follows by deduction that $\alpha \in \text{Cn}'(\{\&B''\})$. By repeated use of Observation 1.18, we obtain $\text{Cn}'(B'') = \text{Cn}'(\{\&B''\})$, so that $\alpha \in \text{Cn}'(B'')$. By $B'' \subseteq B$ and monotony, $\text{Cn}'(B'') \subseteq \text{Cn}'(B)$, so that $\alpha \in \text{Cn}'(B)$, as desired.

10. Suppose that $\text{Cn}_0(X) \subseteq \text{Cn}_0(Y)$.

It follows from inclusion for Cn_0 that $X \subseteq \text{Cn}_0(X)$. By monotony for Cn, $\text{Cn}(X) \subseteq \text{Cn}(\text{Cn}_0(X))$.

It follows by monotony for Cn that $\text{Cn}(\text{Cn}_0(X)) \subseteq \text{Cn}(\text{Cn}_0(Y))$.

It follows by the supraclassicality of Cn that $\text{Cn}_0(Y) \subseteq \text{Cn}(Y)$. By monotony for Cn, $\text{Cn}(\text{Cn}_0(Y)) \subseteq \text{Cn}(\text{Cn}(Y))$ and by iteration $\text{Cn}(\text{Cn}(Y)) = \text{Cn}(Y)$. so that $\text{Cn}(\text{Cn}_0(Y)) \subseteq \text{Cn}(Y)$.

We now have $\text{Cn}(X) \subseteq \text{Cn}(\text{Cn}_0(X))$, $\text{Cn}(\text{Cn}_0(X)) \subseteq \text{Cn}(\text{Cn}_0(Y))$, $\text{Cn}(\text{Cn}_0(Y)) \subseteq \text{Cn}(\text{Cn}(Y))$, and $\text{Cn}(\text{Cn}(Y)) \subseteq \text{Cn}(Y)$. They combine to $\text{Cn}(X) \subseteq \text{Cn}(Y)$, as desired.

11. In order to prove that Cn_T is a consequence operator, we need to show that it satisfies inclusion, monotony, and iteration.

Inclusion: By the inclusion and monotony properties of Cn_0, $A \subseteq \mathrm{Cn}_0(A)$ and $\mathrm{Cn}_0(A) \subseteq \mathrm{Cn}_0(T \cup A) = \mathrm{Cn}_T(A)$.

Monotony: Suppose that $A \subseteq B$. Then $T \cup A \subseteq T \cup B$ and, by the monotony of Cn_0, $\mathrm{Cn}_0(T \cup A) \subseteq \mathrm{Cn}_0(T \cup B)$, i.e., $\mathrm{Cn}_T(A) \subseteq \mathrm{Cn}_T(B)$.

Iteration: One direction of iteration follows directly from inclusion. For the other direction of this property, suppose that $\chi \in \mathrm{Cn}_T(\mathrm{Cn}_T(A))$. Then $\chi \in \mathrm{Cn}_0(T \cup \mathrm{Cn}_0(T \cup A))$. By inclusion and monotony for Cn_0, $T \subseteq \mathrm{Cn}_0(T \cup A)$, so that $T \cup \mathrm{Cn}_0(T \cup A) = \mathrm{Cn}_0(T \cup A)$. We thus have $\chi \in \mathrm{Cn}_0(\mathrm{Cn}_0(T \cup A))$ and, by the iteration property for Cn_0, $\chi \in \mathrm{Cn}_0(T \cup A)$, i.e. $\chi \in \mathrm{Cn}_T(A)$.

Supraclassicality: Let $\chi \in \mathrm{Cn}_0(A)$. Then by monotony for Cn_0, $\chi \in \mathrm{Cn}_0(T \cup A)$, i.e., $\chi \in \mathrm{Cn}_T(A)$.

Deduction: $\psi \in \mathrm{Cn}_T(A \cup \{\chi\})$ holds if and only if $\psi \in \mathrm{Cn}_0(T \cup A \cup \{\chi\})$, thus (by deduction for Cn_0) if and only if $(\chi \rightarrow \psi) \in \mathrm{Cn}_0(T \cup A)$, if and only if $(\chi \rightarrow \psi) \in \mathrm{Cn}_T(A)$.

Compactness: Suppose that $\chi \in \mathrm{Cn}_T(A)$, i.e., $\chi \in \mathrm{Cn}_0(T \cup A)$. By the compactness of Cn_0, there are finite subsets S of T and A' of A such that $\chi \in \mathrm{Cn}_0(S \cup A')$. By monotony for Cn_0, $\chi \in \mathrm{Cn}_0(T \cup A')$, i.e. $\chi \in \mathrm{Cn}_T(A')$.

12. We need to show that Cn' satisfies inclusion, monotony, and iteration.

Inclusion: Let $\alpha \in A$. Then $\alpha \in \mathrm{Cn}'(A)$ follows from $\alpha \in \mathrm{Cn}(\{\alpha\})$.

Monotony: Suppose that $A \subseteq B$ and $\alpha \in \mathrm{Cn}'(A)$. Then there is some $\delta \in A$ such that $\alpha \in \mathrm{Cn}(\{\delta\})$. It follows from $A \subseteq B$ that $\delta \in B$, from which we may conclude that $\alpha \in \mathrm{Cn}'(B)$.

Iteration: One direction follows directly from inclusion. For the other direction, let $\alpha \in \mathrm{Cn}'(\mathrm{Cn}'(A))$. Then there is some β such that $\alpha \in \mathrm{Cn}(\{\beta\})$ and $\beta \in \mathrm{Cn}'(A)$. It follows from $\beta \in \mathrm{Cn}'(A)$ that there is some δ such that $\beta \in \mathrm{Cn}(\{\delta\})$ and $\delta \in A$.

From $\{\beta\} \subseteq \mathrm{Cn}(\{\delta\})$ follows by monotony $\mathrm{Cn}(\{\beta\}) \subseteq \mathrm{Cn}(\mathrm{Cn}(\{\delta\}))$ and by iteration $\mathrm{Cn}(\{\beta\}) \subseteq \mathrm{Cn}(\{\delta\})$. From this and $\alpha \in \mathrm{Cn}(\{\beta\})$ follows $\alpha \in \mathrm{Cn}(\{\delta\})$. Since $\delta \in A$. this is sufficient to prove that $\alpha \in \mathrm{Cn}'(A)$.

13. $\alpha \vdash \beta$ if and only if $\beta \in \mathrm{Cn}(\{\alpha\})$, by deduction if and only if $\alpha \rightarrow \beta \in \mathrm{Cn}(\varnothing)$, if and only if $\vdash \alpha \rightarrow \beta$.

14. $\alpha \vdash \beta$ and $\beta \vdash \delta$
$\beta \in \mathrm{Cn}(\{\alpha\})$ and $\delta \in \mathrm{Cn}(\{\beta\})$
$\{\beta\} \subseteq \mathrm{Cn}(\{\alpha\})$ and $\delta \in \mathrm{Cn}(\{\beta\})$
$\mathrm{Cn}(\{\beta\}) \subseteq \mathrm{Cn}(\mathrm{Cn}(\{\alpha\}))$ and $\delta \in \mathrm{Cn}(\{\beta\})$ (monotony)
$\mathrm{Cn}(\{\beta\}) \subseteq \mathrm{Cn}(\{\alpha\})$ and $\delta \in \mathrm{Cn}(\{\beta\})$ (monotony)

$\delta \in \mathrm{Cn}(\{\alpha\})$
$\alpha \vdash \delta$

15. Suppose that $\alpha \vdash \beta$ and $\beta \vdash \alpha$, i.e., $\beta \in \mathrm{Cn}(\{\alpha\})$ and $\alpha \in \mathrm{Cn}(\{\beta\})$. It follows from $\beta \in \mathrm{Cn}(\{\alpha\})$ that $\{\beta\} \subseteq \mathrm{Cn}(\{\alpha\})$, so that by monotony $\mathrm{Cn}(\{\beta\}) \subseteq \mathrm{Cn}(\mathrm{Cn}(\{\alpha\}))$. By iteration, $\mathrm{Cn}(\mathrm{Cn}(\{\alpha\})) = \mathrm{Cn}(\{\alpha\})$, so that $\mathrm{Cn}(\{\beta\}) \subseteq \mathrm{Cn}(\{\alpha\})$.

In the same way we can also prove that $\mathrm{Cn}(\{\alpha\}) \subseteq \mathrm{Cn}(\{\beta\})$. We may therefore conclude that $\mathrm{Cn}(\{\alpha\}) = \mathrm{Cn}(\{\beta\})$. Thus, for all δ, $\delta \in \mathrm{Cn}(\{\alpha\})$ if and only if $\delta \in \mathrm{Cn}(\{\beta\})$, that is $\alpha \vdash \delta$ if and only if $\beta \vdash \delta$.

16. Suppose that $X \vdash \alpha$ and $X \cup \{\alpha\} \vdash \beta$, i.e., that $\alpha \in \mathrm{Cn}(X)$ and $\beta \in \mathrm{Cn}(X \cup \{\alpha\})$. It follows by deduction from $\beta \in \mathrm{Cn}(X \cup \{\alpha\})$ that $\alpha \rightarrow \beta \in \mathrm{Cn}(X)$. Since α and $\alpha \rightarrow \beta$ truth-functionally imply β, it follows by supraclassicality that $\beta \in \mathrm{Cn}(X)$, that is $X \vdash \beta$.

17. a. Suppose to the contrary that $A \vdash \alpha$. Then $X \cup \{\beta \rightarrow \alpha\} \vdash \alpha$, i.e., by the deduction property $X \vdash (\beta \rightarrow \alpha) \rightarrow \alpha$, or equivalently $X \vdash \alpha \vee \beta$, contrary to the conditions.
b. Directly from $\{\alpha \vee \beta, \beta \rightarrow \alpha\} \vdash \alpha$

18. a. $\{p \vee q, \top\}$ **b.** $\{p \rightarrow q, \top\}$ **c.** $\{p, p \vee q, q \rightarrow p, \top\}$ **d.** $\{\top\}$

19. One direction is trivial: if A is logically closed, then there is some B, namely $B = A$ such that $A = \mathrm{Cn}(B)$.

For the other direction, let B be such that $A = \mathrm{Cn}(B)$. By iteration, $\mathrm{Cn}(\mathrm{Cn}(B)) = \mathrm{Cn}(B)$. By substituting A for $\mathrm{Cn}(B)$ we obtain $\mathrm{Cn}(A) = A$, so that A is logically closed.

20. *Part I*: For one direction of the desired equivalence, we are going to show that if $A \cup B$ is logically closed, then either $A \subseteq B$ or $B \subseteq A$. We are going to prove this implication in its converse form. Thus, we are going to show that if it is not the case that $A \subseteq B$ or $B \subseteq A$, then $A \cup B$ is not logically closed. For this purpose, suppose that that $A \nsubseteq B$ and $B \nsubseteq A$. Our task is to prove that $A \cup B \neq \mathrm{Cn}(A \cup B)$.

It follows from $A \nsubseteq B$ that there is some α such that $\alpha \in A$ and $\alpha \notin B$. Similarly, it follows from that $B \nsubseteq A$ that there is some β such that $\beta \in B$ and $\beta \notin A$. We are going to show (1) that $\alpha \leftrightarrow \beta \in \mathrm{Cn}(A \cup B)$, and (2) that $\alpha \leftrightarrow \beta \notin A \cup B$.

For (1): Since $\alpha \in A$, $\alpha \in A \cup B$. Similarly, since $\beta \in B$, $\beta \in A \cup B$. By truth-functional logic, $\alpha \leftrightarrow \beta \in \mathrm{Cn}(\{\alpha, \beta\})$. Since $\{\alpha, \beta\} \subseteq A \cup B$, monotony for

Cn yields $\mathrm{Cn}(\{\alpha,\beta\}) \subseteq \mathrm{Cn}(A\cup B)$. We therefore have $\alpha\leftrightarrow\beta \in \mathrm{Cn}(A\cup B)$, as desired.

For (2): In order to show that $\alpha\leftrightarrow\beta \notin A\cup B$ it is sufficient to show that $\alpha\leftrightarrow\beta \notin A$ and $\alpha\leftrightarrow\beta \notin B$. In order to show that $\alpha\leftrightarrow\beta \notin A$, suppose to the contrary that $\alpha\leftrightarrow\beta \in A$. Since $\alpha \in A$, and β follows by truth-functional logic from α and $\alpha\leftrightarrow\beta$, it would follow that $\beta \in \mathrm{Cn}(A)$, and – since A is closed under logical consequence – that $\beta \in A$, contrary to the conditions. We may conclude from this contradiction that $\alpha\leftrightarrow\beta \notin A$.

The proof that $\alpha\leftrightarrow\beta \notin B$ is similar. We now know that $\alpha\leftrightarrow\beta \notin A\cup B$.

In summary, we have found a sentence $(\alpha\leftrightarrow\beta)$ that is an element of $\mathrm{Cn}(A\cup B)$ but not an element of $A\cup B$. This is sufficient to prove that $\mathrm{Cn}(A\cup B) \neq A\cup B$, i.e., that $A\cup B$ is not logically closed.

Part II: For the other direction of the desired equivalence, suppose that either $A\subseteq B$ or $B\subseteq A$. If $A\subseteq B$, then $A\cup B = B$, and the logical closure of $A\cup B$ follows from that of B. Similarly if $B\subseteq A$, then $A\cup B = A$, and the logical closure of $A\cup B$ follows from that of A.

21. Only c, d and e are $\{p, p\vee q\}$-closed. In a and b, $p\vee q$ is missing.

22. For one direction, let $B_1 \subset B_2$. Then $\mathrm{Cn}(B_1) \subseteq \mathrm{Cn}(B_2)$ follows directly from $B_1 \subseteq B_2$. Suppose that $\mathrm{Cn}(B_1) = \mathrm{Cn}(B_2)$. Since B_1 and B_2 are A-closed, we then have $B_1 = A\cap\mathrm{Cn}(B_1) = A\cap\mathrm{Cn}(B_2) = B_2$, contrary to $B_1 \subset B_2$. It follows from this contradiction that $\mathrm{Cn}(B_1) \neq \mathrm{Cn}(B_2)$, and since we have already proved that $\mathrm{Cn}(B_1) \subseteq \mathrm{Cn}(B_2)$ we can conclude that $\mathrm{Cn}(B_1) \subset \mathrm{Cn}(B_2)$.

The other direction follows from Observation 1.30.

23. Let $c(B_1) = c(B_2)$. We then have $\mathrm{Cn}(B_1) = \mathrm{Cn}(c(B_1)) = \mathrm{Cn}(c(B_2)) = \mathrm{Cn}(B_2)$. Since B_1 and B_2 are A-closed subsets of A, we can therefore derive: $B_1 = A\cap\mathrm{Cn}(B_1) = A\cap\mathrm{Cn}(B_2) = B_2$.

24. Let A_1 and A_2 be B-closed subsets of B. We are going to show that A_1 is A_2-closed, i.e., that $\mathrm{Cn}(A_1)\cap A_2 \subseteq A_1$.

Since $A_2 \subseteq B$, we have $\mathrm{Cn}(A_1)\cap A_2 \subseteq \mathrm{Cn}(A_1)\cap B$. Since A_1 is B-closed, we also have $\mathrm{Cn}(A_1)\cap B \subseteq A_1$. It follows that $\mathrm{Cn}(A_1)\cap A_2 \subseteq A_1$, i.e., that A_1 is A_2-closed. In the same way we can prove that A_2 is A_1-closed. It follows that A_1 and A_2 are mutually closed.

25. Suppose that A and B are closed under implication. We need to show that $A\cap B$ is also closed under implication.

Let α and β be elements of $A\cap B$. Then $\alpha \in A$ and $\beta \in A$, and by the closure under implication of A, $\alpha\rightarrow\beta \in A$. In the same way it follows that

$\alpha \rightarrow \beta \in B$. From $\alpha \rightarrow \beta \in A$ and $\alpha \rightarrow \beta \in B$ we may conclude that $\alpha \rightarrow \beta \in A \cap B$.

26. a. $\{p,q\} \perp p\&q = \{\{p\},\{q\}\}$
b. $\{p,q,r\} \perp p\&q = \{\{p,r\},\{q,r\}\}$
c. $\{q\} \perp p\&q = \{\{q\}\}$
d. $\{p, q \vee r, q \vee \neg r\} \perp p\&q = \{\{p, q \vee r\},\{p, q \vee \neg r\},\{q \vee r, q \vee \neg r\}\}$
e. $\{p\&q, p\&\neg p\} \perp p\&q = \{\varnothing\}$
f. $\{p \vee r, p \vee \neg r, q\&s, q\&\neg s\} \perp p\&q = \{\{p \vee r, p \vee \neg r\},\{p \vee r, q\&s\},\{p \vee r, q\&\neg s\},\{p \vee \neg r, q\&s\},\{p \vee \neg r, q\&\neg s\}\}$
g. $\{p \vee q, p \leftrightarrow q\} \perp p\&q = \{\{p \vee q\},\{p \leftrightarrow q\}\}$
h. $\{p \vee q, p \rightarrow q, q \rightarrow p\} \perp p\&q = \{\{p \vee q, p \rightarrow q\},\{p \vee q, q \rightarrow p\},\{p \rightarrow q, q \rightarrow p\}\}$
i. $\varnothing \perp p\&q = \{\varnothing\}$
j. $\varnothing \perp p \vee \neg p = \varnothing$
k. $\{p\&q\} \perp \{p,q\} = \{\varnothing\}$
l. $\{p \vee q\} \perp \{p,q\} = \{\{p \vee q\}\}$
m. $\{q,r\} \perp \{p,q\} = \{\{r\}\}$
n. $\{p \vee r, p \vee \neg r\} \perp \{p,q\} = \{\{p \vee r\},\{p \vee \neg r\}\}$
o. $\{p \vee q, p \rightarrow q, q \rightarrow p\} \perp \{p,q\} = \{\{p \vee q\},\{p \rightarrow q, q \rightarrow p\}\}$
p. $\{p,q,r\} \perp \varnothing = \{\{p,q,r\}\}$
q. $\{p,\neg p\} \perp \varnothing = \{\{p,\neg p\}\}$
r. $\{p,\neg p\} \perp \{r\} = \{\{p,\},\{\neg p\}\}$
s. $\varnothing \perp \varnothing = \{\varnothing\}$

27. Suppose not. It then follows from $\alpha \in \text{Cn}(X)$ that $\alpha \vee \beta \in \text{Cn}(X)$, contrary to $X \in A \perp (\alpha \vee \beta)$.

28. Let $X \in A \perp B_1 \cap A \perp B_2$. We are going to show that $X \in A \perp (B_1 \cup B_2)$ by showing that the three conditions of Definition 1.35 are satisfied. We have $X \subseteq A$ from $X \in A \perp B_1$, so that (i) is satisfied. For (ii), suppose to the contrary that X implies some element of $B_1 \cup B_2$. Then it either implies some element of B_1, contrary to $X \in A \perp B_1$, or some element of B_2, contrary to $X \in A \perp B_2$. We can conclude from this contradiction that (ii) is satisfied.

For (iii), suppose to the contrary that there is some Y such that $X \subset Y \subseteq A$ and $Y \cap \text{Cn}(B_1 \cup B_2) = \varnothing$. Then $Y \cap \text{Cn}(B_1) = \varnothing$, contrary to $X \in A \perp B_1$. We may conclude from this contradiction that (iii) is also satisfied.

29. Let $X \in A \perp \alpha \cap A \perp \beta$. We are going to show that $X \in A \perp (\alpha \& \beta)$ by showing that the three conditions of Definition 1.35 are satisfied. We have $X \subseteq A$ from $X \in A \perp \alpha$, so that (i) is satisfied. For (ii), suppose to the contrary that $X \vdash \alpha \& \beta$. Then $X \vdash \alpha$, contrary to $X \in A \perp \alpha$. We can conclude from this contradiction that (ii) is satisfied.

For (iii), suppose to the contrary that there is some Y such that $X \subset Y \subseteq A$ and $\alpha\&\beta \notin \text{Cn}(Y)$. Then either $\alpha \notin \text{Cn}(Y)$, contrary to $X \in A\perp\alpha$, or $\beta \notin \text{Cn}(Y)$, contrary to $X \in A\perp\beta$. We may conclude from this contradiction that (iii) is also satisfied.

30. Suppose to the contrary that $X \subset Y$. It follows from $Y \in A\perp\beta$ that $Y \nvdash \beta$, and then from $\vdash \alpha\rightarrow\beta$ that $Y \nvdash \alpha$. We therefore have $X \subset Y \subseteq A$, and $Y \nvdash \alpha$, contrary to $X \in A\perp\alpha$.

31. Suppose to the contrary that $\varnothing \in A\perp B$ and $\{\varnothing\} \neq A\perp B$. Then there is some X such that $\varnothing \neq X \in A\perp B$. But since $\varnothing \subset X$, $\varnothing$ and X cannot be elements of the same remainder set.

32. $\cup(X\perp Y)$ is a subset of X, and each element of $X\backslash\cup(X\perp Y)$ implies some element of Y. By repeated use of Observation 1.40, we obtain $X\perp Y = (\cup(X\perp Y))\perp Y$.

33. *Part I*: Suppose that $X \in (A\cup\{\alpha\})\perp\neg\alpha$. We are going to show (1) that $\alpha \in X$ and (2) that $X \in (A\cup\{\alpha\})\perp\perp$.

For (1), suppose to the contrary that $\alpha \notin X$. It follows from this and $X \in (A\cup\{\alpha\})\perp\neg\alpha$ that $X\cup\{\alpha\} \vdash \neg\alpha$. By deduction this yields $X \vdash \alpha \rightarrow \neg\alpha$, which is truth-functionally equivalent to $X \vdash \neg\alpha$. Since this contradicts $X \in (A\cup\{\alpha\})\perp\neg\alpha$, we may conclude that $\alpha \in X$.

For (2) we need to show that the three conditions of Definition 1.35 are satisfied. We already have $X \subseteq A\cup\{\alpha\}$, so that (i) is satisfied. For (ii), suppose to the contrary that $X \vdash \perp$. Then $X \vdash \neg\alpha$, contrary to $X \in (A\cup\{\alpha\})\perp\neg\alpha$. We may conclude from this contradiction that (ii) is satisfied.

For (iii), suppose to the contrary that there is some X' such that $X \subset X' \subseteq A\cup\{\alpha\}$ and $X' \nvdash \perp$. It follows from $\alpha \in X$ that $\alpha \in X'$. From this and $X' \nvdash \perp$ we may conclude that $X' \nvdash \neg\alpha$. We therefore have $X \subset X' \subseteq A\cup\{\alpha\}$ and $X' \nvdash \neg\alpha$, contrary to $X \in (A\cup\{\alpha\})\perp\neg\alpha$. From this contradiction, it can be concluded that (iii) holds.

Part II: Suppose that $\alpha \in X \in (A\cup\{\alpha\})\perp\perp$. We are going to show that $X \in (A\cup\{\alpha\})\perp\neg\alpha$, and as usual this amounts to showing that conditions (i)-(iii) of Definition 1.35 are satisfied. We already have $X \subseteq A\cup\{\alpha\}$, so that (i) is satisfied. For (ii), suppose to the contrary that $X \vdash \neg\alpha$. Since $\alpha \in X$, we then have $X \vdash \alpha\&\neg\alpha$, i.e., $X \vdash \perp$, contrary to $X \in (A\cup\{\alpha\})\perp\perp$. We can conclude that (ii) is satisfied. For (iii), suppose to the contrary that there is some Y such that $X \subset Y \subseteq A\cup\{\alpha\}$ and $Y \nvdash \neg\alpha$. Then $Y \nvdash \perp$, contrary to $X \in (A\cup\{\alpha\})\perp\perp$. The contradiction is sufficient to establish that (iii) holds, which concludes the proof.

34. Let $X \subseteq A\perp\beta$. It follows from Observation 1.40 that $A\perp\beta = A\perp\{\alpha,\beta\}$, so that $X \in A\perp\{\alpha,\beta\}$. It follows from this by Observation 1.44 that there is some Y such that $X \subseteq Y \in A\perp\alpha$.

35. If $A\perp\alpha = A\perp\beta$, then $X \not\subset Y \not\subset X$ for all $X \in A\perp\alpha$ and $Y \in A\perp\beta$. It follows from Observation 1.46 that $A\perp(\alpha\&\beta) = A\perp\alpha \cup A\perp\beta = A\perp\alpha$.

36. *For one direction*, let $X \in A\perp B$. Then $X \subseteq A$, and since X does not imply any element of B, $X \cap B = \varnothing$. It follows that $X \subseteq A \backslash B$, so that clause (i) of Definition 1.35 is satisfied. Since X implies no element of B, it implies no element of $\text{Cn}(A) \cap B$, and thus (ii) is satisfied.

To see that (iii) is satisfied, let $X \subset X' \subseteq A \backslash B$. Then since $X \in A\perp B$ there must be some $\beta \in B$ such that $X' \vdash \beta$. It follows from this and $X' \subseteq A$ that $\beta \in \text{Cn}(A)$, and consequently $\beta \in \text{Cn}(A) \cap B$. This shows that (iii) is satisfied.

For the other direction, let $X \in (A \backslash B)\perp(\text{Cn}(A) \cap B)$. It follows that $X \subseteq A$, so that clause (i) is satisfied. For (ii), suppose that X implies some element β of B. Then $\beta \in \text{Cn}(X)$ and, since $X \subseteq A$, $\beta \in \text{Cn}(A)$, so that $\beta \in \text{Cn}(A) \cap B$, contrary to $X \vdash \beta$ and $X \in (A \backslash B)\perp(\text{Cn}(A) \cap B)$. We can conclude from this contradiction that (ii) holds.

For (iii), let $\delta \in A \backslash X$. We need to show that $X \cup \{\delta\}$ implies some element of B. If $\delta \in B$, then this follows trivially. If $\delta \notin B$, then $X \subset X \cup \{\delta\} \subseteq A \backslash B$, and it follows from $X \in (A \backslash B)\perp(\text{Cn}(A) \cap B)$ that $X \cup \{\delta\}$ implies some element of $\text{Cn}(A) \cap B$. This is sufficient to show that (iii) holds.

37. a. Conditions (i') and (i) (of Definition 1.35) are the same. To show that (ii') and (ii) coincide for singletons, it is sufficient to note that $\{\beta\} \not\subseteq \text{Cn}(X)$ if and only if $\text{Cn}(X) \cap \{\beta\} = \varnothing$, by set theory. To see that (iii') and (iii) coincide, observe that $\{\beta\} \not\subseteq \text{Cn}(X')$ if and only if $\text{Cn}(X') \cap \{\beta\} = \varnothing$.

b. Let the language consist of the atomic sentences p and q and their truth-functional combinations. Let Cn be purely truth-functional. Then $\{p\} \in \{p,q\}\angle\{p,q\}$, but $\{p\} \notin \{p,q\}\perp\{p,q\}$.

c. Let $\beta = \&(B)$. We are going to show $A\angle B = A\perp\{\&(B)\}$ by proving first $A\angle B \subseteq A\perp\{\&(B)\}$ and then $A\perp\{\&(B)\} \subseteq A\angle B$.

Part I: Let $X \in A\angle B$. We are going to show that $X \in A\perp\{\&(B)\}$. This will be done by showing that the three conditions of Definition 1.35 are satisfied.

It follows from $X \in A\angle B$ that $X \subseteq A$, so that (i) is satisfied.

For (ii), suppose to the contrary that $\text{Cn}(X) \cap \{\&(B)\} \neq \varnothing$, i.e., that $\&(B) \in \text{Cn}(X)$. It follows that $B \subseteq \text{Cn}(X)$, contrary to $X \in A\angle B$. We may conclude that $\&(B) \notin \text{Cn}(X)$, so that (ii) is satisfied.

For (iii), suppose to the contrary that there is some X' such that $X \subset X' \subseteq A$ and $\&(B) \notin \text{Cn}(X')$. It follows that $B \not\subseteq \text{Cn}(X')$. We then have $X \subset X' \subseteq A$

and $B \not\subseteq \mathrm{Cn}(X')$, contrary to $X \in A \angle B$. We can conclude from this contradiction that (iii) is satisfied.

Part II: Let $X \in A \perp \{\&(B)\}$. We are going to show that $X \in A \angle B$. To do this, we need to show that (i'), (ii'), and (iii') are satisfied.

It follows from $X \in A \perp \{\&(B)\}$ that $X \subseteq A$, so that (i') is satisfied.

For (ii'), suppose to the contrary that $B \subseteq \mathrm{Cn}(X)$. Since $\&(B) \in \mathrm{Cn}(B)$ we then have $\&(B) \in \mathrm{Cn}(X)$, contrary to $X \in A \perp \{\&(B)\}$. We may conclude that $B \not\subseteq \mathrm{Cn}(X)$, so that (ii') holds.

For (iii'), suppose to the contrary that there is some X' such that $X \subset X' \subseteq A$ and $B \not\subseteq \mathrm{Cn}(X')$. It follows from $B \not\subseteq \mathrm{Cn}(X')$ that $\&(B) \notin \mathrm{Cn}(X')$. We then have $X \subset X' \subseteq A$ and $\&(B) \notin \mathrm{Cn}(X')$, contrary to $X \in A \perp \{\&(B)\}$. We can conclude from this contradiction that (iii') is satisfied.

38. a. $A \perp (p\&q) = \{\{p, q \to p, p \vee q, \top\}, \{p \leftrightarrow q, q \to p, p \to q, \top\}, \{q, p \to q, p \vee q, \top\}\}$

b. $A \perp p = \{\{p \leftrightarrow q, q \to p, p \to q, \top\}, \{q, p \to q, p \vee q, \top\}\}$

c. $A \perp (p \leftrightarrow q) = \{\{p, q \to p, p \vee q, \top\}, \{q, p \to q, p \vee q, \top\}\}$

d. $A \perp (q \to p) = \{\{q, p \to q, p \vee q, \top\}\}$

e. $A \perp (p \vee q) = \{\{p \leftrightarrow q, q \to p, p \to q, \top\}\}$

f. $A \perp \{p, p \vee q\} = \{\{p \leftrightarrow q, q \to p, p \to q, \top\}\}$

g. $A \perp \{p, q\} = \{\{p \vee q, \top\}, \{p \leftrightarrow q, p \to q, q \to p, \top\}\}$

h. $A \perp \{p \leftrightarrow q, p \vee q\} = \{\{q \to p, \top\}, \{p \to q, \top\}\}$

i. $A \perp \{p, q, p \leftrightarrow q\} = \{\{q \to p, \top\}, \{p \to q, \top\}, \{p \vee q, \top\}\}$

39. It follows from Observation 1.56 that $A \perp (\alpha \vee \beta) = A \perp \alpha \cap A \perp \beta$. We have $A \perp \alpha \cap A \perp \beta \subseteq A \perp \alpha \cup A \perp \beta$, and from Observation 1.55 we obtain $A \perp \alpha \cup A \perp \beta = A \perp (\alpha \& \beta)$.

40. It follows from $X \subseteq A$ and $\alpha \in A$, by the logical closure of A, that $\mathrm{Cn}(X \cup \{\alpha\}) \subseteq A$. For the other direction, we need to show that if $\beta \in A$, then $\beta \in \mathrm{Cn}(X \cup \{\alpha\})$. Let $\beta \in A$. It follows from the corollary of Observation 1.52 (the recovery lemma) that $\alpha \to \beta \in X$. By deduction, $\beta \in \mathrm{Cn}(X \cup \{\alpha\})$.

41. It follows from Observation 1.52 (the recovery lemma) that $\alpha \to \beta \in \mathrm{Cn}(X)$, which is equivalent to $\neg\beta \to \neg\alpha \in \mathrm{Cn}(X)$. The deduction property yields $\neg\alpha \in \mathrm{Cn}(X \cup \{\neg\beta\})$, from which follows $\mathrm{Cn}(X \cup \{\neg\alpha\}) \subseteq \mathrm{Cn}(X \cup \{\neg\beta\})$.

42. Let $\beta \in Y \backslash X$. Then $\beta \in A \backslash X$. It follows from Observation 1.53 that $X \in A \perp \beta$ and from the corollary of Observation 1.52 that $\mathrm{Cn}(X \cup \{\beta\}) = A$. Since $X \cup \{\beta\} \subseteq Y$, we therefore have $Y \subset A = \mathrm{Cn}(X \cup \{\beta\}) \subseteq \mathrm{Cn}(Y)$, so that $Y \subset \mathrm{Cn}(Y)$.

43. It follows from the logical closure of X that if $\beta \in X$ then $\alpha \vee \beta \in X$.

For the other direction, suppose to the contrary that $\alpha \vee \beta \in X$ and $\beta \notin X$. It follows from $\beta \in A \setminus X$ and $X \in A \perp \alpha$ that $X \cup \{\beta\} \vdash \alpha$. Since X is logically closed, we have $\beta \rightarrow \alpha \in X$. Since $\alpha \vee \beta$ and $\beta \rightarrow \alpha$ together imply α, it follows from $\alpha \vee \beta \in X$ and $\beta \rightarrow \alpha \in X$ that $X \vdash \alpha$, contrary to $X \in A \perp \alpha$. This contradiction concludes the proof.

44. *Part I*: We are first going to show that if $X \in A \perp \alpha$, then $\alpha \notin X \in A \perp \kappa$. It follows from $X \in A \perp \alpha$ that $\alpha \notin X$. We are going to show that $X \in A \perp \kappa$.

Since $\alpha \in A$ it follows from $X \in A \perp \alpha$ that $X \subset A$, so that $\kappa \notin X$. We now have $X \in A \perp \alpha$ and $\kappa \in A \setminus X$. It follows from Observation 1.53 that $X \in A \perp \kappa$.

Part II: For the other direction of the observation, suppose that $\alpha \notin X \in A \perp \kappa$. We then have $\alpha \in A \setminus X$, and $X \in A \perp \alpha$ follows directly from Observation 1.53.

45. Let $X \in A \perp \alpha$, and $\beta \in A$. In order to prove that $\alpha \rightarrow \beta \in X$, suppose to the contrary that $\alpha \rightarrow \beta \notin X$.

It follows from $\beta \in A$, by the logical closure of A, that $\alpha \rightarrow \beta \in A$. We therefore have $\alpha \rightarrow \beta \in A \setminus X$. Since $X \in A \perp \alpha$, it follows that $X \cup \{\alpha \rightarrow \beta\} \vdash \alpha$. By the deduction property, this is equivalent with $X \vdash (\alpha \rightarrow \beta) \rightarrow \alpha$, which is truth-functionally equivalent with $X \vdash \alpha$. This, however contradicts our assumption that $X \in A \perp \alpha$. We may conclude from this contradiction that $\alpha \rightarrow \beta \in X$.

46. Suppose to the contrary that $B_1 \subset B_2$, $B_1 \in A \perp \alpha$, and $B_2 \in A \perp \beta$. From Observation 1.55 we have $B_1 \subset B_2$, $B_1 \in A \perp \alpha \& \beta$, and $B_2 \in A \perp \alpha \& \beta$, which is impossible since an element of a remainder set cannot be a proper subset of another element of that same remainder set.

47. If B is logically closed, then $B \cap \mathrm{Cn}(\varnothing) \neq \varnothing$, and it follows by monotony that $B \cap \mathrm{Cn}(X) \neq \varnothing$ for all sets of sentences. It follows from Definition 1.35, clause (ii), that $A \perp B$ is empty.

48. Since $\alpha \leftrightarrow \beta$ is equivalent to $(\alpha \& \beta) \vee (\neg\alpha \& \neg\beta)$, this follows directly from Part 3 of Observation 1.57.

49. $[\alpha] = \{X \mid \alpha \in X \in \mathcal{L} \perp \perp\}$, by Observation 1.58 $= \{X \mid X \in \mathcal{L} \perp \neg\alpha\} = \mathcal{L} \perp \neg\alpha$.

50. Since $A \cap X \subseteq X$, clause (i) of Definition 1.35 is satisfied. Since $X \nvdash \alpha$, $A \cap X \nvdash \alpha$, so that clause (ii) is satisfied.

In order to show that clause (iii) is satisfied, suppose to the contrary that there is some $\beta \in A\backslash(A\cap X)$ such that $(A\cap X) \cup \{\beta\} \nvdash \alpha$. Then $\beta\rightarrow\alpha \notin A\cap X$. Since both α and β are elements of A, so is $\beta\rightarrow\alpha$, and we may conclude that $\beta\rightarrow\alpha \notin X$. Since $X \in \mathcal{L}\perp\perp$, it follows that $\neg(\beta\rightarrow\alpha) \in X$. Furthermore, it follows from $\beta \in A\backslash(A\cap X)$ that $\beta \notin X$, hence $\neg\beta \in X$. We now have $\{\neg\beta,\neg(\beta\rightarrow\alpha)\} \subseteq X$, which is impossible since it requires X to be inconsistent.

51. Let $B = \{\beta_1,...\beta_n\}$. Then:
$X \in [B]$
iff $B \subseteq X \in \mathcal{L}\perp\perp$ (Definition 1.59)
iff $\beta_k \in X \in \mathcal{L}\perp\perp$ for all $1\leq k\leq n$
iff $X \in \mathcal{L}\perp\neg\beta_k$ for all $1\leq k\leq n$ (Observation 1.58)
iff $X \in (\mathcal{L}\perp\neg\beta_1) \cap ... \cap (\mathcal{L}\perp\neg\beta_n)$
iff $X \in \mathcal{L}\perp(\neg\beta_1\vee...\vee\neg\beta_n)$ (Observation 1.56)
iff $X \in \mathcal{L}\perp n(B)$.

52. a. $[\alpha] \subseteq [\beta]$
iff $[\text{Cn}(\{\alpha\})] \subseteq [\text{Cn}(\{\beta\})]$
iff $\text{Cn}(\{\beta\}) \subseteq \text{Cn}(\{\alpha\})$ (Observation 1.61)
iff $\vdash \alpha\rightarrow\beta$.
b. $[\neg\alpha]$
$= \{X \mid \neg\alpha \in X \in \mathcal{L}\perp\perp\}$
$= (\mathcal{L}\perp\perp)\backslash\{X \mid \neg\alpha \notin X \in \mathcal{L}\perp\perp\}$
$= (\mathcal{L}\perp\perp)\backslash\{X \mid \alpha \in X \in \mathcal{L}\perp\perp\}$ (Observation 1.57)
$= (\mathcal{L}\perp\perp)\backslash[\alpha]$.
c. $[\alpha\&\beta]$
$= [\{\alpha,\beta\}]$
$= [\{\alpha\}]\cap[\{\beta\}]$ (Observation 1.61)
$= [\alpha]\cap[\beta]$
d. $[\alpha\vee\beta]$
$= \{X \mid \alpha\vee\beta \in X \in \mathcal{L}\perp\perp\}$
$= \{X \mid (\alpha \in X \in \mathcal{L}\perp\perp) \vee (\beta \in X \in \mathcal{L}\perp\perp)\}$ (Observation 1.57, Part 3)
$= \{X \mid \alpha \in X \in \mathcal{L}\perp\perp\} \cup \{X \mid \beta \in X \in \mathcal{L}\perp\perp\}$
$= [\alpha]\cup[\beta]$.
e. $[\alpha\rightarrow\beta]$
$= [\neg\alpha\vee\beta]$
$= [\neg\alpha]\cup[\beta]$ (Part *d* of this exercise)
$= ((\mathcal{L}\perp\perp)\backslash[\alpha])\cup[\beta]$ (Part *b* of this exercise)
$= (\mathcal{L}\perp\perp)\backslash([\alpha]\backslash[\beta])$

53. a. $X \in A\perp(\alpha\&\beta)$
iff $g_A(X) \in \mathcal{L}\perp(\alpha\&\beta)$

iff $\neg(\alpha\&\beta) \in g_A(X)$
iff $\neg\alpha\vee\neg\beta \in g_A(X)$
iff $\neg\alpha \in g_A(X)$ or $\neg\beta \in g_A(X)$ (Observation 1.57, Part 3)
iff $\alpha \notin g_A(X)$ or $\beta \notin g_A(X)$ (Observation 1.57, Part 2)
iff $g_A(X) \in \mathcal{L}\bot\alpha$ or $g_A(X) \in \mathcal{L}\bot\beta$
iff $X \in A\bot\alpha$ or $X \in A\bot\beta$
iff $X \in (A\bot\alpha \cup A\bot\beta)$
b. $X \in A\bot(\alpha\vee\beta)$
iff $g_A(X) \in \mathcal{L}\bot(\alpha\vee\beta)$
iff $\neg(\alpha\vee\beta) \in g_A(X)$
iff $\neg\alpha\&\neg\beta \in g_A(X)$
iff $\neg\alpha \in g_A(X)$ and $\neg\beta \in g_A(X)$
iff $\alpha \notin g_A(X)$ and $\beta \notin g_A(X)$ (Observation 1.57, Part 2)
iff $g_A(X) \in \mathcal{L}\bot\alpha$ and $g_A(X) \in \mathcal{L}\bot\beta$
iff $X \in A\bot\alpha$ and $X \in A\bot\beta$
iff $X \in (A\bot\alpha \cap A\bot\beta)$

54. No. Let $A = \{\delta,\neg\delta\}$.

55. Let $B = \{\beta_1,\dots \beta_n\}$. Then
$A\Delta B = A\bot\beta_1 \cup\dots\cup A\bot\beta_n$
$= A\bot(\beta_1\&\dots\&\beta_n)$ (Observation 1.55)
$= A\bot(\&B)$.

56. Let $B = \{\beta_1,\dots\beta_n\}$. Then $A\Delta B = A\Delta\{\beta_1,\dots\beta_n\} = (A\bot\beta_1) \cup\dots\cup (A\bot\beta_n)$.

For each $\beta_k \in B$ it follows from $A\bot\beta_k \subseteq A\Delta D$, according to Observation 1.66, that there is some finite subset D_k of D such that $A\bot\beta_1 \subseteq A\Delta D_k$. It follows that
$(A\bot\beta_1) \cup\dots\cup (A\bot\beta_n) \subseteq (A\Delta D_1) \cup\dots\cup (A\Delta D_k)$, thus
$A\Delta B \subseteq (A\Delta(D_1\cup\dots\cup D_k))$.
Let $D' = D_1\cup\dots\cup D_k$. Then D' is a finite subset of D, and $A\Delta B \subseteq A\Delta D'$, as desired.

57. Both equations can be solved if and only if $\mathrm{Cn}(A)\cap B = \varnothing$, and $X = A$ is then a solution.

58. Both equations have a trivial solution for all sets A, since $A\bot\varnothing = \{A\}$ for all A.

59. Clearly, (a) implies (b). In order to see that (b) implies (a), suppose that $\{A_1,\dots A_n\} = X\bot Y$. Then $A_1\cup\dots\cup A_n \subseteq X$.

It follows from the upper bound property that each element of $X\backslash\cup(X\perp Y)$ implies some element of Y. It follows from Observation 1.40 that $X\perp Y = (\cup(X\perp Y))\perp Y$. Furthermore, $(\cup(X\perp Y))\perp Y = (A_1\cup\ldots\cup A_n)\perp Y$, and we are done.

60. The condition is that A and B are mutually closed and that $A\not\subset B\not\subset A$. (Cf. Exercise 24 for the definition of mutual closure.)

Proof that this condition is necessary: Let $\{A,B\} \subseteq X\perp Y$. Then clearly $A\not\subset B\not\subset A$. Suppose that A and B are not mutually closed. Then either A is not B-closed, or B is not A-closed. Without loss of generality, we may assume that A is not B-closed. Since $B \subseteq X$ it follows from Observation 1.29 that A is not X-closed. According to Observation 1.36, this contradicts $A \in X\perp Y$. We may conclude that A and B are mutually closed.

Proof that the condition is sufficient: Suppose that A and B are mutually closed and that $A\not\subset B\not\subset A$. Since A is A-closed, it follows from its B-closure by Observation 1.29 that A is $A\cup B$-closed. Similarly, B is $A\cup B$-closed. The rest follows from Observation 1.68.

61. It follows from Observation 1.70 that there are sentences α_1' and α_2' such that $\{A_1\} = B\perp\alpha_1'$ and $\{A_2\} = B\perp\alpha_2'$. Furthermore, it follows from Observation 1.46 that $\{A_1,A_2\} = B\perp(\alpha_1'\&\alpha_2')$.

62. Given the Corollary of Observation 1.70, it remains to show that $\{A\} = B\perp(\alpha\vee\bigvee(B\backslash A))$. There are two cases, according to whether or not $B\backslash A = \varnothing$.

Case 1, $B\backslash A = \varnothing$: Then $\bigvee(B\backslash A) = \perp$ and $\vdash \alpha\vee\bigvee(B\backslash A) \leftrightarrow \alpha$. We therefore have $A \in B\perp(\alpha\vee\bigvee(B\backslash A))$ directly from $A \in B\perp\alpha$. It follows from $B\backslash A = \varnothing$ and $A \in B\perp\alpha$ that $A = B$. We may conclude that $\{A\} = B\perp(\alpha\vee\bigvee(B\backslash A)$, as desired.

Case 2, $B\backslash A \neq \varnothing$: Let $B\backslash A = \{\xi_1,\ldots\xi_n\}$. Then $\alpha\vee\bigvee(B\backslash A) = (\alpha\vee\xi_1\vee\ldots\vee\xi_n)$. We are first going to show that $A \in B\perp(\alpha\vee\xi_1\vee\ldots\vee\xi_n)$. Again, this will be done by showing that the three conditions of Definition 1.35 are satisfied.

It follows from $A \in B\perp\alpha$ that $A \subseteq B$, so that (i) is satisfied.

In order to prove (ii), we make use of $A \in B\perp\alpha$ to conclude that for each ξ_k, $A\cup\{\xi_k\} \vdash \alpha$ and, by the deduction property, $A \vdash \xi_k\rightarrow\alpha$. Now suppose that (ii) is not satisfied. Then $A \vdash (\alpha\vee\xi_1\vee\ldots\vee\xi_n)$. Since $A \vdash \xi_k\rightarrow\alpha$ holds for every ξ_k, it would follow truth-functionally that $A \vdash \alpha$, contrary to $A \in B\perp\alpha$. We can conclude from this contradiction that $A \nvdash (\alpha\vee\xi_1\vee\ldots\vee\xi_n)$, i.e., that (ii) is satisfied.

For (iii), suppose to the contrary that there is some set X such that $A \subset X \subseteq B$ and $X \nvdash (\alpha\vee\xi_1\vee\ldots\vee\xi_n)$. It follows set-theoretically from $A \subset X \subseteq B$ that there is some $\xi_k \in B\backslash A$ such that $\xi_k \in X$. Since $\xi_k \vdash (\alpha\vee\xi_1\vee\ldots\vee\xi_n)$ we obtain

$X \vdash (\alpha \vee \xi_1 \vee ... \vee \xi_n)$, contrary to our assumption. This contradiction is sufficient to show that (iii) is satisfied.

We have now proved that $A \in B \perp (\alpha \vee \xi_1 \vee ... \vee \xi_n)$. It remains to be shown that $\{A\} = B \perp (\alpha \vee \xi_1 \vee ... \vee \xi_n)$. For that purpose, let $W \in B \perp (\alpha \vee \xi_1 \vee ... \vee \xi_n)$. Our task is to show that $W = A$.

Since all elements of $B \setminus A$ imply $\alpha \vee \xi_1 \vee ... \vee \xi_n$, it follows from $W \in B \perp (\alpha \vee \xi_1 \vee ... \vee \xi_n)$ that $W \cap (B \setminus A) = \varnothing$. Since A and W are subsets of B, it follows set-theoretically that $W \subseteq A$. Since A and W are elements of the same remainder set, we have $W \not\subset A$, and consequently $W = A$. This concludes the proof.

SOLUTIONS FOR CHAPTER 2^+

63. a. By *recovery*, $A \subseteq \text{Cn}((A+(\alpha\vee\beta))\cup\{\alpha\vee\beta\})$. Since $\alpha \in A$, it follows that $\alpha \in \text{Cn}((A+(\alpha\vee\beta))\cup\{\alpha\vee\beta\})$. By the deduction property of Cn, this is equivalent to $(\alpha\vee\beta)\rightarrow\alpha \in \text{Cn}(A+(\alpha\vee\beta))$, i.e., $\beta\rightarrow\alpha \in \text{Cn}(A+(\alpha\vee\beta))$. By *closure*, this is equivalent to $\beta\rightarrow\alpha \in A+(\alpha\vee\beta)$.
b. It follows from *recovery* and $\alpha \in A$ that $\alpha \in \text{Cn}((A+(\alpha\rightarrow\beta))\cup\{\alpha\rightarrow\beta\})$, thus by the deduction propety, $(\alpha\rightarrow\beta)\rightarrow\alpha \in \text{Cn}(A+(\alpha\rightarrow\beta))$, or equivalently $\alpha \in \text{Cn}(A+(\alpha\rightarrow\beta))$. It follows from *closure* that $\alpha \in A+(\alpha\rightarrow\beta)$.

64. Let $\vdash \alpha$. We need to show that $A+\alpha = A$. It follows from *inclusion* that $A+\alpha \subseteq A$. It remains to be shown that $A \subseteq A+\alpha$.

Let $\varepsilon \in A$. By *recovery*, $A \subseteq \text{Cn}((A+\alpha)\cup\{\alpha\})$, so that $\varepsilon \in \text{Cn}((A+\alpha)\cup\{\alpha\})$. By the deduction property of Cn, $\alpha\rightarrow\varepsilon \in \text{Cn}(A+\alpha)$. It follows from $\vdash \alpha$ that $\alpha\rightarrow\varepsilon$ is logically equivalent to ε, and we therefore have $\varepsilon \in \text{Cn}(A+\alpha)$. It follows by *relative closure* from $\varepsilon \in A$ and $\varepsilon \in \text{Cn}(A+\alpha)$ that $\varepsilon \in A+\alpha$. This concludes the proof.

65. Suppose that $\beta \in A+\alpha$. Then $\alpha\vee\beta \in A+\alpha$ follows from *closure*. For the other direction, let $\alpha\vee\beta \in A+\alpha$. Since $\beta \in A$ it follows from *recovery* that $\alpha\rightarrow\beta \in \text{Cn}(A+\alpha)$. Since $\alpha\vee\beta$ and $\alpha\rightarrow\beta$ together imply β, it follows that $\beta \in \text{Cn}(A+\alpha)$, and we can use *closure* to obtain $\beta \in A+\alpha$.

66. a. Let $\delta \in A$ and $\delta \in \text{Cn}(\{\neg\alpha\})$. It follows from $\delta \in \text{Cn}(\{\neg\alpha\})$ that $\vdash\neg\alpha\rightarrow\delta$. It follows by *recovery* from $\delta \in A$ that $\alpha\rightarrow\delta \in \text{Cn}(A+\alpha)$. Since δ follows from $\neg\alpha\rightarrow\delta$ and $\alpha\rightarrow\delta$, we may conclude that $\delta \in \text{Cn}(A+\alpha)$.
b. From Part *a* and Observation 2.12.

67. Suppose to the contrary that $\alpha_1 \notin A+(\alpha_1\&\alpha_2)$, $\alpha_2 \notin A+(\alpha_1\&\alpha_2)$, and $\alpha_1\leftrightarrow\alpha_2 \notin A+(\alpha_1\&\alpha_2)$. It follows by *fullness* from $\alpha_1 \in A$ and $\alpha_1 \notin A+(\alpha_1\&\alpha_2)$ that $\alpha_1\&\alpha_2 \in \text{Cn}(((A+(\alpha_1\&\alpha_2))\cup\{\alpha_1\})$. It follows by the deduction property of Cn that $(\alpha_1 \rightarrow \alpha_1\&\alpha_2) \in \text{Cn}((A+(\alpha_1\&\alpha_2))$. In the same way (substitute α_2 for α_1) it follows that $(\alpha_2 \rightarrow \alpha_1\&\alpha_2) \in \text{Cn}((A+(\alpha_1\&\alpha_2))$, and (substitute $\alpha_1\leftrightarrow\alpha_2$ for α_1) that $(\alpha_1\leftrightarrow\alpha_2 \rightarrow \alpha_1\&\alpha_2) \in \text{Cn}((A+(\alpha_1\&\alpha_2))$.

In summary, we have shown that $\alpha_1 \rightarrow \alpha_1\&\alpha_2$, $\alpha_2 \rightarrow \alpha_1\&\alpha_2$ and $(\alpha_1\leftrightarrow\alpha_2) \rightarrow \alpha_1\&\alpha_2$ are all elements of $\text{Cn}((A+(\alpha_1\&\alpha_2))$. Together, these three expressions imply $\alpha_1\&\alpha_2$, and we may conclude that $\alpha_1\&\alpha_2 \in \text{Cn}((A+(\alpha_1\&\alpha_2))$. It follows from *success* that $\alpha_1\&\alpha_2 \in \text{Cn}(\varnothing)$. However, it follows by *closure* from $\alpha_1 \notin A+(\alpha_1\&\alpha_2)$ that $\alpha_1 \notin \text{Cn}(\varnothing)$, and thus $\alpha_1\&\alpha_2 \notin \text{Cn}(\varnothing)$. This contradiction concludes the proof.

68. Suppose to the contrary that there is some α such that $\alpha \in A$ and $\alpha \notin A{+}\neg\alpha$. It follows from *core-retainment* that there is some set A' such that $A' \subseteq A$, $\neg\alpha \notin \mathrm{Cn}(A')$ and $\neg\alpha \in \mathrm{Cn}(A' \cup \{\alpha\})$. However, $\neg\alpha \in \mathrm{Cn}(A' \cup \{\alpha\})$ implies $\alpha \rightarrow \neg\alpha \in \mathrm{Cn}(A')$ and thus $\neg\alpha \in \mathrm{Cn}(A')$.

69. a. *(i) implies (ii)*: Let X be such that $X \subseteq A$, $X \nvdash \alpha$ and $X \cup \{\beta\} \vdash \alpha$. It follows from the upper bound property that there is some X' such that $X \subseteq X' \in A \perp \alpha$ To see that (ii) is satisfied, it is sufficient to note that $\beta \notin X'$ follows from $X \subseteq X'$, $X' \nvdash \alpha$ and $X \cup \{\beta\} \vdash \alpha$.

(ii) implies (i): Let X be such that $\beta \notin X \in A \perp \alpha$. Then we directly have $X \subseteq A$ and $X \nvdash \alpha$. Since $\beta \in A$, but $\beta \notin X \in A \perp \alpha$, it follows from the maximality of remainders that $X \cup \{\beta\} \vdash \alpha$.

b. Core-retainment has been defined as follows:

(1) If $\beta \in A$ and $\beta \notin A{+}\alpha$, then there is a set A' such that $A' \subseteq A$ and that $\alpha \notin \mathrm{Cn}(A')$ but $\alpha \in \mathrm{Cn}(A' \cup \{\beta\})$.

By Part *a*, this is equivalent to:

(2) If $\beta \in A$ and $\beta \notin A{+}\alpha$, then there is some X such that $\beta \notin X \in A \perp \alpha$.

This is equivalent to:

(3) If $\beta \in A$ and $\beta \notin A{+}\alpha$, then $A \perp \alpha$ is non-empty and $\beta \notin \cap(A \perp \alpha)$.

Since α is not logically true, $A \perp \alpha$ is non-empty, and (3) is equivalent to:

(4) If $\beta \in A$ and $\beta \notin A{+}\alpha$, then $\beta \notin \cap(A \perp \alpha)$.

If $\beta \notin A$, then β is not included in any element of $A \perp \alpha$. Therefore, we can simplify (4) as follows:

(5) If $\beta \notin A{+}\alpha$, then $\beta \notin \cap(A \perp \alpha)$.

(6) $\cap(A \perp \alpha) \subseteq A{+}\alpha$.

70. a. *(i) implies (ii)*: Let X be such that $B \subseteq X \subseteq A$, $X \nvdash \alpha$ and $X \cup \{\beta\} \vdash \alpha$. It follows from the upper bound property that there is some X' such that $X \subseteq X' \in A \perp \alpha$. To see that (ii) is satisfied, it is sufficient to note that $B \subseteq X' \in A \perp \alpha$ and that $\beta \notin X'$. (The latter can be concluded from $X \subseteq X'$, $X' \nvdash \alpha$ and $X \cup \{\beta\} \vdash \alpha$.)

(ii) implies (i): Let X be such that $B \subseteq X \in A \perp \alpha$ and $\beta \notin X$. Then we directly have $B \subseteq X \subseteq A$ and $X \nvdash \alpha$. Since $\beta \in A$, but $\beta \notin X \in A \perp \alpha$, it follows from the maximality of remainders that $X \cup \{\beta\} \vdash \alpha$.

b. Relevance has been defined as follows:

(1) If $\beta \in A$ and $\beta \notin A{+}\alpha$, then there is a set A' such that $A{+}\alpha \subseteq A' \subseteq A$ and that $\alpha \notin \mathrm{Cn}(A')$ but $\alpha \in \mathrm{Cn}(A' \cup \{\beta\})$.

By Part *a*, this is equivalent to:

(2) If $\beta \in A$ and $\beta \notin A{+}\alpha$, then there is some X such that $A{+}\alpha \subseteq X \in A \perp \alpha$ and $\beta \notin X$.

This is equivalent to:

(3) If $\beta \in A$ and $\beta \notin A+\alpha$, then $\{X \mid A+\alpha \subseteq X \in A\bot\alpha\}$ is non-empty and $\beta \notin \cap\{X \mid A+\alpha \subseteq X \in A\bot\alpha\}$

Since *success* is satisfied and α is not logically true, $\{X \mid A+\alpha \subseteq X \in A\bot\alpha\}$ is non-empty, and (3) is equivalent to:

(4) If $\beta \in A$ and $\beta \notin A+\alpha$, then $\beta \notin \cap\{X \mid A+\alpha \subseteq X \in A\bot\alpha\}$

If $\beta \notin A$, then β is not included in any element of $A\bot\alpha$. Therefore, we can simplify (4) as follows:

(5) If $\beta \notin A+\alpha$, then $\beta \notin \cap\{X \mid A+\alpha \subseteq X \in A\bot\alpha\}$

(6) $\cap\{X \mid A+\alpha \subseteq X \in A\bot\alpha\} \subseteq A+\alpha$

Finally, since each element of $\{X \mid A+\alpha \subseteq X \in A\bot\alpha\}$ contains $A+\alpha$, (6) is equivalent to:

(7) $A+\alpha = \cap\{X \mid A+\alpha \subseteq X \in A\bot\alpha\}$.

71. a. If $\alpha \notin \mathrm{Cn}(\varnothing)$ and $AC_\alpha B$, then $\alpha \notin \mathrm{Cn}(B)$.

b. If $AC_\alpha B$, then $B \subseteq A$.

c. If $\alpha\leftrightarrow\beta \in \mathrm{Cn}(\varnothing)$, then it holds for all sets B that $AC_\alpha B$ if and only if $AC_\beta B$.

72. Suppose that $\delta \in A+\alpha$. It follows from *closure* that $\alpha\vee\delta \in A+\alpha$. We also have $\alpha\vee\delta \in \mathrm{Cn}(\{\alpha\})$. By *partial antitony*, $(A+\alpha)\cap\mathrm{Cn}(\{\alpha\}) \subseteq A+(\alpha\&\beta)$, from which we can conclude that $\alpha\vee\delta \in A+(\alpha\&\beta)$.

73. a. Let + be an operation for A that satisfies *success*, *failure*, and *conjunctive inclusion*.

In the limiting case when $\vdash \alpha\&\beta$, we also have $\vdash \alpha$, and it follows from *failure* that $A+(\alpha\&\beta) = A = A+\alpha$, so that conjunctive covering holds.

In the principal case, when $\nvdash \alpha\&\beta$, it follows from *success* that $\alpha\&\beta \notin \mathrm{Cn}(A+(\alpha\&\beta))$. From this we may conclude that either $\alpha \notin \mathrm{Cn}(A+(\alpha\&\beta))$ or $\beta \notin \mathrm{Cn}(A+(\alpha\&\beta))$. It follows from this, by *conjunctive inclusion*, that either $A+(\alpha\&\beta) \subseteq A+\alpha$ or $A+(\alpha\&\beta) \subseteq A+\beta$, so that *conjunctive covering* holds.

b. By set theory from Part *a*.

c. Let $\alpha \notin A+\beta$. It follows from Part *a* that either $A+(\alpha\&\beta) \subseteq A+\alpha$ or $A+(\alpha\&\beta) \subseteq A+\beta$. We need to show that if $A+(\alpha\&\beta) \subseteq A+\beta$, then $A+(\alpha\&\beta) \subseteq A+\alpha$.

It follows from $A+(\alpha\&\beta) \subseteq A+\beta$ and $\alpha \notin A+\beta$ that $\alpha \notin A+(\alpha\&\beta)$. From this it follows, since *closure* is satisfied, that $\alpha \notin \mathrm{Cn}(A+(\alpha\&\beta))$. We can use *conjunctive inclusion* to conclude that $A+(\alpha\&\beta) \subseteq A+\alpha$.

74. Let A be logically closed, and let + be an operator for A that satisfies *closure*, *inclusion*, *extensionality*, *recovery*, and *conjunctive overlap*. In order to show that *conjunctive trisection* holds, let $\alpha \in A+(\alpha\&\beta)$. We are going to show that $\alpha \in A+(\alpha\&\beta\&\delta)$.

Since $\alpha\&\beta\&\delta$ is logically equivalent to $(\alpha\&\beta)\&(\alpha\&\beta\rightarrow\delta)$, it follows from *extensionality* that we can solve our task by proving that $\alpha \in A+((\alpha\&\beta)\&(\alpha\&\beta\rightarrow\delta))$. If we can prove both $\alpha \in A+(\alpha\&\beta)$ and $\alpha \in A+(\alpha\&\beta\rightarrow\delta)$, then $\alpha \in A+((\alpha\&\beta)\&(\alpha\&\beta\rightarrow\delta))$ will follow directly from *conjunctive overlap*. Since $\alpha \in A+(\alpha\&\beta)$ was one of our assumptions, it only remains to show that $\alpha \in A+(\alpha\&\beta\rightarrow\delta)$.

This can be proved from *recovery*. It follows from *recovery* that $A \subseteq \mathrm{Cn}((A+(\alpha\&\beta\rightarrow\delta))\cup\{\alpha\&\beta\rightarrow\delta\})$. It follows from $\alpha \in A+(\alpha\&\beta)$, by *inclusion*, that $\alpha \in A$. We therefore have $(A+(\alpha\&\beta\rightarrow\delta))\cup\{\alpha\&\beta\rightarrow\delta\} \vdash \alpha$. By the deduction property of Cn, we then have $A+(\alpha\&\beta\rightarrow\delta) \vdash ((\alpha\&\beta\rightarrow\delta)\rightarrow\alpha)$. Since $(\alpha\&\beta\rightarrow\delta)\rightarrow\alpha$ is truth-functionally equivalent to α, we then have $A+(\alpha\&\beta\rightarrow\delta) \vdash \alpha$. By *closure*, $\alpha \in A+(\alpha\&\beta\rightarrow\delta)$, as desired.

75. a. Let $\beta \in A+(\alpha\&\beta)$. We are going to show that $A+(\alpha\&\beta) \subseteq A+\alpha$. There are two cases, according to whether or not $\alpha\&\beta$ is logically true.

Case 1, $\vdash\alpha\&\beta$: It follows that $\vdash\alpha$, and by *failure* that $A+(\alpha\&\beta) = A$ and $A+\alpha = A$. From this, $A+(\alpha\&\beta) \subseteq A+\alpha$ follows directly.

Case 2, $\nvdash \alpha\&\beta$: It follows from *success* that $\alpha\&\beta \notin \mathrm{Cn}(A+(\alpha\&\beta))$. From this and $\beta \in A+(\alpha\&\beta)$ we can conclude that $\alpha \notin \mathrm{Cn}(A+(\alpha\&\beta))$. It follows from *conjunctive inclusion* that $A+(\alpha\&\beta) \subseteq A+\alpha$.

b. Let $\beta \in A+(\alpha\&\beta)$. In order to show that $A+\alpha \subseteq A+(\alpha\&\beta)$, let $\varepsilon \in A+\alpha$. Our task is to show that $\varepsilon \in A+(\alpha\&\beta)$. Since $\beta \in A+(\alpha\&\beta)$ and $A+(\alpha\&\beta)$ is logically closed (by *closure*) it is sufficient to show that $\beta\rightarrow\varepsilon \in A+(\alpha\&\beta)$.

It follows from $\varepsilon \in A+\alpha$ by *inclusion* that $\varepsilon \in A$. By *recovery*, $A \subseteq \mathrm{Cn}((A+\beta)\cup\{\beta\})$. It follows from the deduction property of Cn that $\beta\rightarrow\varepsilon \in \mathrm{Cn}(A+\beta)$, and from *closure* that $\beta\rightarrow\varepsilon \in A+\beta$.

Since $\beta\rightarrow\varepsilon$ is a logical consequence of ε it also follows by *closure*, from $\varepsilon \in A+\alpha$, that $\beta\rightarrow\varepsilon \in A+\alpha$. We therefore have $\beta\rightarrow\varepsilon \in (A+\alpha)\cap(A+\beta)$. By *conjunctive overlap*, $\beta\rightarrow\varepsilon \in A+(\alpha\&\beta)$. Since we have assumed that $\beta \in A+(\alpha\&\beta)$, it follows that $\varepsilon \in \mathrm{Cn}(A+(\alpha\&\beta))$. By *closure*, $\varepsilon \in A+(\alpha\&\beta)$, which finishes our proof.

c. Let $\alpha\rightarrow\beta \in A+\beta$. Then it follows from *extensionality* that $\alpha\rightarrow\beta \in A+((\alpha\rightarrow\beta)\&(\alpha\vee\beta))$. It follows from (1) that $A+((\alpha\rightarrow\beta)\&(\alpha\vee\beta)) \subseteq A+(\alpha\vee\beta)$, thus by *extensionality* that $A+\beta \subseteq A+(\alpha\vee\beta)$. Furthermore, it follows from $\alpha\rightarrow\beta \in A+((\alpha\rightarrow\beta)\&(\alpha\vee\beta))$ by (2) that $A+(\alpha\vee\beta) \subseteq A+((\alpha\rightarrow\beta)\&(\alpha\vee\beta))$, and thus by *extensionality* that $A+(\alpha\vee\beta) \subseteq A+\beta$. We can conclude that $A+\beta = A+(\alpha\vee\beta)$.

d. The proof consists of two parts:

(I) Proof that (1) and (2) imply (3): Suppose that (1) and (2) are satisfied. Let $\alpha\rightarrow\beta \in A+\beta$ and $\beta\rightarrow\alpha \in A+\alpha$. Since *extensionality* holds, it follows by Part *c* of the present exercise from $\alpha\rightarrow\beta \in A+\beta$ that $A+\beta = A+(\alpha\vee\beta)$.

Similarly, it follows from $\beta \rightarrow \alpha \in A+\alpha$ that $A+\alpha = A+(\alpha \vee \beta)$. We can conclude that $A+\alpha = A+\beta$.

(II) Proof that (3) implies (1) and (2): Suppose that (3) is satisfied. Let $\beta \in A+(\alpha \& \beta)$. In order to show that (1) and (2) are satisfied, we need to show that $A+(\alpha \& \beta) = A+\alpha$.

Since $\alpha \rightarrow (\alpha \& \beta)$ is a logical consequence of β, it follows by *closure* from $\beta \in A+(\alpha \& \beta)$, that $\alpha \rightarrow (\alpha \& \beta) \in A+(\alpha \& \beta)$. Furthermore, since $\vdash (\alpha \& \beta) \rightarrow \alpha$ it follows by *closure* that $(\alpha \& \beta) \rightarrow \alpha \in A+\alpha$. We can now apply (3) to $\alpha \rightarrow (\alpha \& \beta) \in A+(\alpha \& \beta)$ and $(\alpha \& \beta) \rightarrow \alpha \in A+\alpha$, and obtain $A+(\alpha \& \beta) = A+\alpha$, as desired.

76. a. $A \sim (p \& q) = \{p \vee q\}$ **b.** $A \sim p = \{q, p \vee q\}$ **c.** $A \sim q = \{p, p \vee q\}$ **d.** $A \sim (p \vee q) = \varnothing$ **e.** $A \sim (p \rightarrow q) = \{p, p \vee q\}$

77. a. Success is violated.
b. Inclusion is violated.
c. Relevance is violated.

78. Case 1, $\vdash \beta$: Then $A \sim_\gamma \beta = A$, and since $\beta \in A$ we are done.
Case 2, $\nvdash \beta$: Let $X \in \gamma(A \perp \beta)$. Then $X \in A \perp \beta$, and X is A-closed (Observation 1.36), i.e., $A \cap \text{Cn}(X) \subseteq X$. It follows from $\alpha \in \text{Cn}(\varnothing)$ that $\alpha \in \text{Cn}(X)$, and we have assumed that $\alpha \in A$. We therefore have $\alpha \in A \cap \text{Cn}(X) \subseteq X$. Since this holds for all $X \in \gamma(A \perp \beta)$, we have $\alpha \in \cap \gamma(A \perp \beta)$, i.e., $\alpha \in A \sim_\gamma \beta$.

79. Let $\alpha \vee \beta \in A \sim_\gamma \alpha$ and $Z \in \gamma(A \perp \alpha)$. It follows from $\alpha \vee \beta \in A \sim_\gamma \alpha = \cap \gamma(A \perp \alpha)$ that $\alpha \vee \beta \in Z$. Suppose that $\beta \notin Z$. Since $\beta \in A$ and $Z \in A \perp \alpha$ it then follows that $Z \cup \{\beta\} \vdash \alpha$, i.e. $Z \vdash \beta \rightarrow \alpha$. It follows from this and $\alpha \vee \beta \in Z$ that $Z \vdash \alpha$, contrary to $Z \in A \perp \alpha$. We can conclude from this contradiction that $\beta \in Z$. Since this holds for all $Z \in \gamma(A \perp \alpha)$, we can conclude that $\beta \in \cap \gamma(A \perp \alpha) = A \sim_\gamma \alpha$.

80. Since full meet contraction satisfies recovery, we have $A \subseteq \text{Cn}((A \sim \alpha) \cup \{\alpha\})$. It also follows from $A \sim \alpha \subseteq A+\alpha$ that $\text{Cn}((A \sim \alpha) \cup \{\alpha\}) \subseteq \text{Cn}((A+\alpha) \cup \{\alpha\})$. It follows directly that $A \subseteq \text{Cn}((A+\alpha) \cup \{\alpha\})$.

81. $(A \sim \alpha) \cap (A \sim \neg \alpha)$
$= (A \cap \text{Cn}(\{\neg \alpha\})) \cap (A \cap \text{Cn}(\{\alpha\}))$ (Observation 2.12.)
$= A \cap \text{Cn}(\{\neg \alpha\}) \cap \text{Cn}(\{\alpha\})$
$= A \cap \text{Cn}(\{\alpha \vee \neg \alpha\})$ (Observation 1.17.)
$= A \cap \text{Cn}(\varnothing)$
$= \text{Cn}(\varnothing)$

82. a. We can use Observation 2.12 to obtain: $A\sim\alpha = A \cap \mathrm{Cn}(\{\neg\alpha\}) = \mathrm{Cn}(\{\alpha\}) \cap \mathrm{Cn}(\{\neg\alpha\}) = \mathrm{Cn}(\{\alpha\vee\neg\alpha\}) = \mathrm{Cn}(\varnothing)$. (Cf. Observation 1.17 and Exercise 2 for the last two steps.)
b. $A\sim\beta = A \cap \mathrm{Cn}(\{\neg\beta\}) = \mathrm{Cn}(\{\alpha\}) \cap \mathrm{Cn}(\{\neg\beta\}) = \mathrm{Cn}(\{\alpha\vee\neg\beta\}) = \mathrm{Cn}(\{\beta\rightarrow\alpha\})$. (Cf. Exercise 3.)

83. If α is logically true, then $A+\alpha = A$, and we are done. For the principal case, when α is not logically true, let $\beta \in A$ and $\delta \in A$. We are going to prove the converse form of the postulate, i.e., we are going to show that if $\beta \notin A+\alpha$ and $\delta \notin A+\alpha$, then $\beta\vee\delta \notin A+\alpha$.

Since + is maxichoice, $A+\alpha \in A\bot\alpha$, and it follows from $\beta \in A$ and $\beta \notin A+\alpha$ that $\alpha \in \mathrm{Cn}((A+\alpha)\cup\{\beta\})$. By the deduction property of Cn, $\beta\rightarrow\alpha \in \mathrm{Cn}(A+\alpha)$. In the same way it follows from $\delta \in A$ and $\delta \notin A+\alpha$ that $\delta\rightarrow\alpha \in \mathrm{Cn}(A+\alpha)$. Since $\beta\rightarrow\alpha$ and $\delta\rightarrow\alpha$ together imply $\beta\vee\delta\rightarrow\alpha$, we have $\beta\vee\delta\rightarrow\alpha \in \mathrm{Cn}(A+\alpha)$.

Since maxichoice contraction satisfies the success postulate, we have $\alpha \notin \mathrm{Cn}(A+\alpha)$. From $\beta\vee\delta\rightarrow\alpha \in \mathrm{Cn}(A+\alpha)$ and $\alpha \notin \mathrm{Cn}(A+\alpha)$ we can conclude that $\beta\vee\delta \notin A+\alpha$.

84. a. *Closure*: Since both $A\sim_\gamma\alpha$ and $A\sim_\gamma(\alpha\rightarrow f(\alpha))$ are logically closed, so is $A\sim_\gamma\alpha \cap A\sim_\gamma(\alpha\rightarrow f(\alpha))$.
Inclusion: It follows from $A\sim_\gamma\alpha \subseteq A$ that $A\sim_\gamma\alpha \cap A\sim_\gamma(\alpha\rightarrow f(\alpha)) \subseteq A$.
Vacuity: If $\alpha \notin \mathrm{Cn}(A)$, then if follows from clause (II) of the definition that $A+\alpha = A\sim_\gamma\alpha$. Since vacuity holds for partial meet contraction, we have $A\sim_\gamma\alpha = A$.
Success: Let $\alpha \notin \mathrm{Cn}(\varnothing)$. Since success holds for partial meet contraction, we have $\alpha \notin A\sim_\gamma\alpha$, and since $A+\alpha \subseteq A\sim_\gamma\alpha$ we can conclude that $\alpha \notin A+\alpha$.
Extensionality: From extensionality for partial meet contraction and clause (2) of the definition of *f*.
Failure: Let $\alpha \in \mathrm{Cn}(\varnothing)$. Then it follows from clause (II) of the definition that $A+\alpha = A\sim_\gamma\alpha$. Since partial meet contraction satisfies *failure*, we also have $A\sim_\gamma\alpha = A$, and it follows that $A+\alpha = A$.
b. Let $\alpha \in A\backslash\mathrm{Cn}(\varnothing)$ and $f(\alpha) \notin \mathrm{Cn}(\{\alpha\})$. In order to prove that $A \neq \mathrm{Cn}((A+\alpha)\cup\{\alpha\})$, suppose to the contrary that $A = \mathrm{Cn}((A+\alpha)\cup\{\alpha\})$, i.e., $A = \mathrm{Cn}((A\sim_\gamma\alpha \cap A\sim_\gamma(\alpha\rightarrow f(\alpha)))\cup\{\alpha\})$. Then $A \subseteq \mathrm{Cn}(A\sim_\gamma(\alpha\rightarrow f(\alpha))\cup\{\alpha\})$. Since $f(\alpha) \in A$, it follows that $f(\alpha) \in \mathrm{Cn}(A\sim_\gamma(\alpha\rightarrow f(\alpha))\cup\{\alpha\})$, and hence by deduction $\alpha\rightarrow f(\alpha) \in \mathrm{Cn}(A\sim_\gamma(\alpha\rightarrow f(\alpha)))$ from which it follows that $\alpha\rightarrow f(\alpha) \in \mathrm{Cn}(\varnothing)$, contrary to $f(\alpha) \notin \mathrm{Cn}(\{\alpha\})$.

85. Let $\beta \in A$. Due to the closure of A under implication, $(\alpha_1\rightarrow(\alpha_2\rightarrow\ldots(\alpha_n\rightarrow\beta))) \in A$. (Note that $(\alpha_1\rightarrow(\alpha_2\rightarrow\ldots(\alpha_n\rightarrow\beta)))$ is equivalent to $(\alpha_1\&\ldots\alpha_n)\rightarrow\beta$.)

Suppose that $(\alpha_1 \rightarrow (\alpha_2 \rightarrow ...(\alpha_n \rightarrow \beta))) \notin \cap\gamma(A\perp(\alpha_1\&...\&\alpha_n))$. Then there is some $X \in A\perp(\alpha_1\&...\&\alpha_n)$ such that $(\alpha_1 \rightarrow (\alpha_2 \rightarrow ...(\alpha_n \rightarrow \beta))) \notin X$. From this and $(\alpha_1 \rightarrow (\alpha_2 \rightarrow ...(\alpha_n \rightarrow \beta))) \in A$ follows $X \cup \{(\alpha_1 \rightarrow (\alpha_2 \rightarrow ...(\alpha_n \rightarrow \beta)))\} \vdash \alpha_1\&...\&\alpha_n$. Using the deduction property of Cn, we can obtain $(\alpha_1 \rightarrow (\alpha_2 \rightarrow ...(\alpha_n \rightarrow \beta))) \rightarrow (\alpha_1\&...\&\alpha_n) \in \text{Cn}(X)$, that is, equivalently, $(\alpha_1\&...\&\alpha_n \rightarrow \beta) \rightarrow (\alpha_1\&...\&\alpha_n) \in \text{Cn}(X)$, equivalently $\alpha_1\&...\&\alpha_n \in \text{Cn}(X)$. This contradicts $X \in A\perp(\alpha_1\&...\&\alpha_n)$, and we may conclude from this contradiction that $(\alpha_1 \rightarrow (\alpha_2 \rightarrow ...(\alpha_n \rightarrow \beta))) \in \cap\gamma(A\perp(\alpha_1\&...\&\alpha_n))$. From this the desired result follows directly.

86. Let $A\perp\alpha \neq \varnothing$. It follows from the definition of a selection function that $\gamma(A\perp\alpha)$ is a non-empty subset of $A\perp\alpha$. From this it follows that $\{X \in A\perp\alpha \mid A\sim_\gamma\alpha \subseteq X\}$ is non-empty. Since all of its elements contain $A\sim_\gamma\alpha$, we can conclude that $A\sim_\gamma\alpha \subseteq \cap\{X \in A\perp\alpha \mid A\sim_\gamma\alpha \subseteq X\}$.

For the other direction, i.e., $\cap\{X \in A\perp\alpha \mid A\sim_\gamma\alpha \subseteq X\} \subseteq A\sim_\gamma\alpha$, let $\beta \notin A\sim_\gamma\alpha$. We are going to show that $\beta \notin \cap\{X \in A\perp\alpha \mid A\sim_\gamma\alpha \subseteq X\}$.

It follows from $\beta \notin A\sim_\gamma\alpha$ that there is some $Y \in \gamma(A\perp\alpha)$ such that $\beta \notin Y$. Clearly, $A\sim_\gamma\alpha \subseteq Y$, so that $Y \in \{X \in A\perp\alpha \mid A\sim_\gamma\alpha \subseteq X\}$. It follows from this and $\beta \notin Y$ that $\beta \notin \cap\{X \in A\perp\alpha \mid A\sim_\gamma\alpha \subseteq X\}$, which is what we needed to complete the proof.

87. *Construction-to-postulates*: This follows from Theorem 2.7 and Exercise 83.

Postulates-to-construction: Let A be logically closed, and let $\div$ be an operator for A that satisfies *closure*, *inclusion*, *vacuity*, *success*, *extensionality*, *recovery*, and *primeness*. It follows from Theorem 2.7 that $\div$ is a partial meet contraction, i.e., there is a selection function γ for A such that $\div$ and $\sim_\gamma$ coincide ($A\div\alpha = A\sim_\gamma\alpha$ for all α). We need to show that $\sim_\gamma$ is a maxichoice operator, i.e., that for all α, if $\beta \in A\setminus(A\sim_\gamma\alpha)$, then $\alpha \in \text{Cn}((A\sim_\gamma\alpha)\cup\{\beta\})$. By *closure* and the deduction property of Cn, this is equivalent to showing that if $\beta \in A\setminus(A\sim_\gamma\alpha)$, then $\beta\rightarrow\alpha \in A\sim_\gamma\alpha$.

Let $\beta \in A\setminus(A\sim_\gamma\alpha)$. Since $\beta\vee(\beta\rightarrow\alpha) \in \text{Cn}(\varnothing)$, it follows from *closure* that $\beta\vee(\beta\rightarrow\alpha) \in A\sim_\gamma\alpha$. We have $\beta \in A$, and we can easily obtain $\alpha \in A$. (Since $\beta \in A\setminus(A\sim_\gamma\alpha)$, we have $A \neq A\sim_\gamma\alpha$ and we can use *vacuity* to obtain $\alpha \in A$.) It follows from *closure* that $\beta\rightarrow\alpha \in A$.Therefore, *primeness* can be applied, and it yields that either $\beta \in A\sim_\gamma\alpha$ or $\beta\rightarrow\alpha \in A\sim_\gamma\alpha$. Since the former is precluded by our initial condition for β, it follows that $\beta\rightarrow\alpha \in A\sim_\gamma\alpha$. This is what was required to finish the proof.

88. a. Let γ be defined as follows:
(i) If $A\perp\alpha \neq \varnothing$, then $\gamma(A\perp\alpha) = \{X \in A\perp\alpha \mid A\div\alpha \subseteq X\}$
(ii) If $A\perp\alpha = \varnothing$, then $\gamma(A\perp\alpha) = \{A\}$

We need to show (1) that γ is a function, (2) that γ is a selection function (from which follows that $\sim_\gamma$ is an operator of partial meet contraction), and (3) that $A{+}\alpha \subseteq A{\sim_\gamma}\alpha$ for all α.

Part 1: Let $A\bot\alpha = A\bot\beta$. It follows from *uniformity* and Observation 1.39 that $A{+}\alpha = A{+}\beta$, and thus, according to our definition of γ, $\gamma(A\bot\alpha) = \gamma(A\bot\beta)$.

Part 2: We need to show that if $A\bot\alpha$ is non-empty, then so is $\gamma(A\bot\alpha)$. Suppose that $A\bot\alpha \neq \varnothing$. Then $\nvdash\alpha$, and by *success* $\alpha \notin \mathrm{Cn}(A{+}\alpha)$. By *inclusion*, $A{+}\alpha \subseteq A$. It follows from the upper bound property that there is some set X such that $A{+}\alpha \subseteq X \in A\bot\alpha$. By the construction of γ, $X \in \gamma(A\bot\alpha)$, so that $\gamma(A\bot\alpha) \neq \varnothing$.

Part 3: This follows directly from the definition.

b. We can use Observation 2.4 to conclude that *uniformity* holds. The rest follows as in Part *a*.

89. *Construction-to-postulates*: Let $\sim_\gamma$ be an operation of partial meet package contraction for A.

P-success: Suppose that $B\cap\mathrm{Cn}(\varnothing) = \varnothing$. Then $A\bot B \neq \varnothing$, and it follows from Definition 2.61 that $\gamma(A\bot B)$ is a non-empty subset of $A\bot B$. Let $X \in \gamma(A\bot B)$. Then it follows from $X \in A\bot B$ that $B\cap\mathrm{Cn}(X) = \varnothing$. Furthermore, it follows from $X \in \gamma(A\bot B)$ that $\cap\gamma(A\bot B) \subseteq X$, so that $\mathrm{Cn}(\cap\gamma(A\bot B)) \subseteq \mathrm{Cn}(X)$. We can conclude that $B\cap\mathrm{Cn}(\cap\gamma(A\bot B)) = \varnothing$.

P-inclusion: If $A\bot B$ is empty, then by Definition 2.61 $A{\sim_\gamma}B = A$, and we are done. If $A\bot B$ is non-empty, then by the same definition $\gamma(A\bot B)$ is a subset of $A\bot B$. It follows that every element of $\gamma(A\bot B)$ is a subset of A, and then so is $\cap\gamma(A\bot B)$.

P-relevance: Let $\beta \in A$ and $\beta \notin A{\sim_\gamma}B$. It follows from Definition 2.61 that there is some A' such that $\beta \notin A' \in \gamma(A\bot B)$. Clearly, $A{\sim_\gamma}B \subseteq A' \subseteq A$. It follows from $A' \in A\bot B$ that $B\cap\mathrm{Cn}(A') = \varnothing$. It also follows from $\beta \in A$ and $\beta \notin X \in A\bot B$ that $B\cap\mathrm{Cn}(A'\cup\{\beta\}) \neq \varnothing$.

P-uniformity: Let B_1 and B_2 be two sets such that any subset of A implies B_1 if and only if it implies B_2. It follows from Observation 1.39 that $A\bot B_1 = A\bot B_2$. From this it follows directly by Definition 2.61 that $A{+}B_1 = A{+}B_2$.

Postulates-to-construction: Let $+$ be an operation for A that satisfies *P-success*, *P-inclusion*, *P-relevance*, and *P-uniformity*. Let γ be such that:

(i) If $A\bot B \neq \varnothing$, then $\gamma(A\bot B) = \{X \in A\bot B \mid A{+}B \subseteq X\}$

(ii) If $A\bot B = \varnothing$, then $\gamma(A\bot B) = \{A\}$

We need to show (1) that γ is a (well-defined) function, (2) that γ is a package selection function, and (3) that for all B, $\cap\gamma(A\bot B) = A{+}B$.

Part 1: In order for γ to be a function, it must be the case that for all B_1 and B_2, if $A\bot B_1 = A\bot B_2$, then $\gamma(A\bot B_1) = \gamma(A\bot B_2)$. Suppose that $A\bot B_1 = A\bot B_2$. It then follows from Observation 1.39 that any subset of A implies some element of B_1 if and only if it implies some element of B_2. By *P-uniformity*, $A{+}B_1 = A{+}B_2$. It follows from the definition of γ that $\gamma(A{\perp}B_1) = \gamma(A{\perp}B_2)$.

Part 2: In order to prove that γ is a package selection function, it is sufficient to show that if $A{\perp}B$ is non-empty, then so is $\gamma(A{\perp}B)$. Suppose that $A{\perp}B$ is non-empty. Then $B\cap\mathrm{Cn}(\varnothing) = \varnothing$, and it follows from *P-success* that $B\cap\mathrm{Cn}(A{+}B) = \varnothing$. It follows from *P-inclusion* that $A{+}B \subseteq A$. By the upper bound property, there is some D such that $A{+}B \subseteq D \in A{\perp}B$. By the construction of γ, $D \in \gamma(A{\perp}\alpha)$, which proves that $\gamma(A{\perp}\alpha)$ is non-empty.

Part 3: There are two cases, according to whether or not $B\cap\mathrm{Cn}(\varnothing)$ is empty.

First case, $B\cap\mathrm{Cn}(\varnothing) \neq \varnothing$: It follows that $A{\perp}B = \varnothing$. Our definition of γ yields $\gamma(A{\perp}B) = \{A\}$, and thus $\cap\gamma(A{\perp}B) = A$. It remains to be shown that $A{+}B = A$.

By *P-inclusion*, $A{+}B \subseteq A$. In order to show that $A \subseteq A{+}B$, suppose to the contrary that this is not the case. Then there is some ε such that $\varepsilon \in A$ and $\varepsilon \notin A{+}B$. It follows from *P-relevance* that there is some set A' such that $A{+}B \subseteq A' \subseteq A$ and $B\cap\mathrm{Cn}(A') = \varnothing$ but $B\cap\mathrm{Cn}(A'\cup\{\varepsilon\}) \neq \varnothing$. This, however, is impossible. Since $B\cap\mathrm{Cn}(\varnothing) \neq \varnothing$, it cannot hold that $B\cap\mathrm{Cn}(A') = \varnothing$. From this contradiction we may conclude that $A \subseteq A{+}B$, and thus $A{+}B = A$.

Second case, $B\cap\mathrm{Cn}(\varnothing) = \varnothing$: In this case, $A{\perp}B$ is non-empty, and we have shown in Part 2 of the present proof that $\gamma(A{\perp}B)$ is also non-empty. It follows from our definition of γ that $A{+}B$ is a a subset of every element of $\gamma(A{\perp}B)$, from which we may conclude that $A{+}B \subseteq \cap\gamma(A{\perp}B)$.

In order to show that $\cap\gamma(A{\perp}B) \subseteq A{+}B$, let $\varepsilon \notin A{+}B$. We are going to show that $\varepsilon \notin \cap\gamma(A{\perp}B)$. This is obvious if $\varepsilon \notin A$. In the remaining case, when $\varepsilon \in A$, we have $\varepsilon \in A$ and $\varepsilon \notin A{+}B$. It follows from *P-relevance* that there is some set A' such that $A{+}B \subseteq A' \subseteq A$, $B\cap\mathrm{Cn}(A') = \varnothing$ and $B\cap\mathrm{Cn}(A'\cup\{\varepsilon\}) \neq \varnothing$. It follows by the upper bound property from $A' \subseteq A$ and $B\cap\mathrm{Cn}(A') = \varnothing$ that there is some set D such that $A' \subseteq D \in A{\perp}B$. Clearly, $\varepsilon \notin D$. It follows from $A{+}B \subseteq A' \subseteq D$, by our definition of γ, that $D \in \gamma(A{\perp}B)$. From this and $\varepsilon \notin D$ we can conclude that $\varepsilon \notin \cap\gamma(A{\perp}B)$. This concludes the proof.

90. a. Yes, since $A{\perp}\{\alpha,\alpha\} = A{\perp}\{\alpha\}$.
b. Yes, since if $\beta \notin \mathrm{Cn}(A)$, then $A{\perp}\{\alpha,\beta\} = A{\perp}\{\alpha\}$.
c. Yes. Observation 1.40 yields $A{\perp}\{\alpha\} = A{\perp}\{\alpha\&\beta, \alpha\}$
d. Yes. Observation 1.40 yields $A{\perp}\{\alpha,\beta\} = A{\perp}\{\alpha\&\beta, \alpha, \beta\}$
e. No. It does not hold in general that $A{\perp}\{\alpha\&\beta\} = A{\perp}\{\alpha, \beta\}$. For a counter-example, let $A = \{p,q,p\leftrightarrow q\}$. Then $A{\perp}\{p\&q\} = \{\{p\},\{q\},\{p\leftrightarrow q\}\}$ and $A{\perp}\{p,q\} = \{\{p\leftrightarrow q\}\}$. Let $\gamma(A{\perp}\{p\&q\}) = \{\{p\}\}$ and $\gamma(A{\perp}\{p,q\}) = \{\{p\leftrightarrow q\}\}$. We then have $A{+}\{p\&q\} = \{p\}$ and $A{+}\{p,q\} = \{p\leftrightarrow q\}$.

91. Let Γ be the covering function that generates the subremainder contraction $\div$ for a logically closed set A.

P-closure: $A \div B = \cap\Gamma(B)$ is the intersection of a set of remainders of A. Since A is logically closed set, so are all its remainders (Observation 1.48). The intersection of a set of logically closed sets is logically closed (Observation 1.25).

P-inclusion: Every element of $\Gamma(B)$ is a subset of A, and consequently so is $\cap\Gamma(B)$.

P-vacuity: Let $B \cap \text{Cn}(A) = \emptyset$. It follows that $A \perp \beta = \{A\}$ for every $\beta \in B$, and thus $A \Delta B = \{A\}$, $\Gamma(B) = \{A\}$ and $\cap\Gamma(B) = A$.

P-success: Let $B \cap \text{Cn}(\emptyset) = \emptyset$. It follows from Definition 2.64 that $\Gamma(B)$ is a subset of $A \Delta B$ such that $\Gamma(B) \cap (A \perp \beta) \neq \emptyset$ for all $\beta \in B$.

Let $\beta \in B$. There is then some $X \in A \perp \beta$ such that $X \in \Gamma(B)$ and consequently $\cap\Gamma(B) \subseteq X$. It follows from $\beta \notin X$ that $\beta \notin \cap\Gamma(B)$.

P-failure: Let $B \cap \text{Cn}(\emptyset) \neq \emptyset$. It follows from Definition 2.64 that $\Gamma(B) = \{A\}$, and consequently $\cap\Gamma(B) = A$.

92. a. *(1) implies (2)*: Let X be such that $D \subseteq X \subseteq A$, $B \cap \text{Cn}(X) = \emptyset$, and $B \cap \text{Cn}(X \cup \{\beta\}) \neq \emptyset$. It follows from the upper bound property that there is some X' such that $X \subseteq X' \in A \perp B$. To see that (2) is satisfied, it is sufficient to note that $D \subseteq X' \in A \perp B$ and that $\beta \notin X'$. (The latter can be concluded from $X \subseteq X'$, $B \cap \text{Cn}(X') = \emptyset$, and $B \cap \text{Cn}(X \cup \{\beta\}) \neq \emptyset$.)

(2) implies (1): Let X be such that $D \subseteq X \in A \perp B$ and $\beta \notin X$. Then we directly have $D \subseteq X \subseteq A$ and $B \cap \text{Cn}(X) = \emptyset$. Since $\beta \in A$, but $\beta \notin X \in A \perp B$, it follows from the maximality of remainders that $B \cap \text{Cn}(X \cup \{\beta\}) \neq \emptyset$.

b. *P-relevance* has been defined as follows:

(1) If $\beta \in A$ and $\beta \notin A \div B$, then there is a set A' such that $A \div B \subseteq A' \subseteq A$ and that $B \cap \text{Cn}(A') = \emptyset$ but $B \cap \text{Cn}(A' \cup \{\beta\}) \neq \emptyset$.

By Part *a*, this is equivalent to:

(2) If $\beta \in A$ and $\beta \notin A \div B$, then there is some X such that $A \div B \subseteq X \in A \perp B$ and $\beta \notin X$.

This is equivalent to:

(3) If $\beta \in A$ and $\beta \notin A \div B$, then $\{X \mid A \div B \subseteq X \in A \perp B\}$ is non-empty and $\beta \notin \cap\{X \mid A \div B \subseteq X \in A \perp B\}$

Since *P-success* is satisfied and B contains no logically true sentence, $\{X \mid A \div B \subseteq X \in A \perp B\}$ is non-empty, and (3) is equivalent to:

(4) If $\beta \in A$ and $\beta \notin A \div B$, then $\beta \notin \cap\{X \mid A \div B \subseteq X \in A \perp B\}$

If $\beta \notin A$, then β is not included in any element of $A \perp B$. Therefore, we can simplify (4) as follows:

(5) If $\beta \notin A \div B$, then $\beta \notin \cap\{X \mid A \div B \subseteq X \in A \perp B\}$

(6) $\cap\{X \mid A \div B \subseteq X \in A \perp B\} \subseteq A \div B$

Finally, since $\{X \mid A \div B \subseteq X \in A \perp B\}$ is non-empty, (6) is equivalent to:

(7) $A{+}B = \cap\{X \mid A{+}B \subseteq X \in A\perp B\}$.

93. a. *Construction-to-postulates*: Let $\sim_\gamma$ be an operation of partial meet choice contraction for A.

C-success: For this part of the proof, let $B \not\subseteq \text{Cn}(\varnothing)$. Then $A\angle B$ is non-empty, so that that $\gamma(A\angle B)$ is a non-empty subset of $A\angle B$. Let $X \in \gamma(A\angle B)$. Then it follows from $X \in A\angle B$ that $B \not\subseteq \text{Cn}(X)$. Furthermore, it follows from $X \in \gamma(A\angle B)$ that $\cap\gamma(A\angle B) \subseteq X$, so that $\text{Cn}(\cap\gamma(A\angle B)) \subseteq \text{Cn}(X)$. We can conclude that $B \not\subseteq \text{Cn}(\cap\gamma(A\angle B))$.

C-inclusion: If $A\angle B$ is empty, then $A\sim_\gamma B = A$, and we are done. If $A\angle B$ is non-empty, then $\gamma(A\angle B)$ is a subset of $A\angle B$. It follows that every element of $\gamma(A\angle B)$ is a subset of A, and then so is $\cap\gamma(A\angle B)$.

C-relevance: Let $\beta \in A$ and $\beta \notin A\sim_\gamma B$. It follows that there is some A' such that $\beta \notin A' \in \gamma(A\angle B)$. Clearly, $A\sim_\gamma B \subseteq A' \subseteq A$. It follows from $A' \in A\angle B$ that $B \not\subseteq \text{Cn}(A') = \varnothing$. It also follows from $\beta \in A$ and $\beta \notin X \in A\angle B$ that $B \subseteq \text{Cn}(A'\cup\{\beta\})$.

C-uniformity: Let B_1 and B_2 be such that $B_1 \subseteq \text{Cn}(X)$ iff $B_2 \subseteq \text{Cn}(X)$ for all $X \subseteq A$. We are first going to show that $A\angle B_1 = A\angle B_2$.

Let $X \in A\angle B_1$. It follows directly that (1) $X \subseteq A$, (2) $B_2 \not\subseteq \text{Cn}(X)$, and (3) if $X \subset Y \subseteq A$, then $B_2 \subseteq \text{Cn}(Y)$. Thus, $X \in A\angle B_2$. It follows in exactly the same way that if $X \in A\angle B_2$, then $X \in A\angle B_1$. Thus, $A\angle B_1 = A\angle B_2$.

It follows from $A\angle B_1 = A\angle B_2$ that $\cap\gamma(A\angle B_1) = \cap\gamma(A\angle B_2)$.

Postulates-to-construction: Let + be an operation for A that satisfies *C-success*, *C-inclusion*, *C-relevance*, and *C-uniformity*. Let γ be such that:

(i) If $A\angle B \neq \varnothing$, then $\gamma(A\angle B) = \{X \in A\angle B \mid A{+}B \subseteq X\}$

(ii) If $A\angle \text{B} = \varnothing$, then $\gamma(A\angle B) = \{A\}$

We need to show (1) that γ is a (well-defined) function, (2) that γ is a choice selection function, and (3) that for all B, $\cap\gamma(A\angle B) = A{+}B$.

Part 1: In order for γ to be a function, it must be the case that for all B_1 and B_2, if $A\angle B_1 = A\angle B_2$, then $\gamma(A\angle B_1) = \gamma(A\angle B_2)$. Let $A\angle B_1 = A\angle B_2$. It follows that $B_1 \subseteq \text{Cn}(X)$ iff $B_2 \subseteq \text{Cn}(X)$ for all $X \subseteq A$. By *C-uniformity*, $A{+}B_1 = A{+}B_2$. From this it follows by the definition of γ that $\gamma(A\angle B_1) = \gamma(A\angle B_2)$.

Part 2: For γ to be a selection function, it must be the case that if $A\angle B \neq \varnothing$, then $\gamma(A\angle B) \neq \varnothing$. Let $A\angle B \neq \varnothing$. Then $B \not\subseteq \text{Cn}(\varnothing)$, and it follows by *C-success* that $B \not\subseteq \text{Cn}(A{+}B)$. By *C-inclusion*, $A{+}B \subseteq A$. It follows by the upper bound property (or rather, by its corresponding version for $\angle$) that there is some Z such that $A{+}B \subseteq Z \in A\angle B$. By our definition of γ, $Z \in \gamma(A\angle B)$.

Part 3: There are two cases, according to whether or not $B \subseteq \text{Cn}(\varnothing)$.

First case, $B \subseteq \text{Cn}(\varnothing)$: It follows that $A\angle B = \varnothing$. Our definition of γ yields $\gamma(A\angle B) = \{A\}$, and thus $\cap\gamma(A\angle B) = A$. It remains to be shown that $A{+}B = A$.

By *C-inclusion*, $A+B \subseteq A$. In order to show that $A \subseteq A+B$, suppose to the contrary that this is not the case. Then there is some ε such that $\varepsilon \in A$ and $\varepsilon \notin A+B$. It follows by *C-relevance* that there is some set A' such that $A+B \subseteq A' \subseteq A$ and $B \not\subseteq \text{Cn}(A')$ and $B \subseteq \text{Cn}(A' \cup \{\varepsilon\}) \neq \emptyset$. This, however, is impossible. Since $B \subseteq \text{Cn}(\emptyset)$, it cannot hold that $B \not\subseteq \text{Cn}(A')$. From this contradiction we may conclude that $A \subseteq A+B$, and thus $A+B = A$.

Second case, $B \not\subseteq \text{Cn}(\emptyset)$: In this case, $A \angle B$ is non-empty, and we have shown in Part 2 of the present proof that $\gamma(A \angle B)$ is non-empty as well. It follows by our definition of γ that $A+B$ is asubset of every element of $\gamma(A \angle B)$, from which we may conclude that $A+B \subseteq \cap\gamma(A \angle B)$.

In order to show that $\cap\gamma(A \angle B) \subseteq A+B$, let $\varepsilon \notin A+B$. We are going to show that $\varepsilon \notin \cap\gamma(A \angle B)$. This is obvious if $\varepsilon \notin A$. In the remaining case we have $\varepsilon \in A$ and $\varepsilon \notin A+B$. It follows from *C-relevance* that there is some set A' such that $A+B \subseteq A' \subseteq A$, $B \not\subseteq \text{Cn}(A')$ and $B \subseteq \text{Cn}(A' \cup \{\varepsilon\})$. It follows by (the variant for $\angle$ of) the upper bound property from $A' \subseteq A$ and $B \not\subseteq \text{Cn}(A') = \emptyset$ that there is some set D such that $A' \subseteq D \in A \angle B$. Clearly, $\varepsilon \notin D$. It follows from $A+B \subseteq A' \subseteq D$, by our definition of γ, that $D \in \gamma(A \angle B)$. From this and $\varepsilon \notin D$ we can conclude that $\varepsilon \notin \cap\gamma(A \angle B)$. This concludes the proof.

b. For any finite set B, $B \subseteq \text{Cn}(A)$ if and only if $\&B \in \text{Cn}(A)$. It follows from this that for all finite B, $A \angle B = A \angle (\&B) = A \perp (\&B)$. It is therefore sufficient to let +' be the restriction of + to remainders with singleton rejectors.

94. According to Observation 2.68, $\cap\gamma(A \perp \alpha) = \cap\hat{\gamma}(A \perp \alpha)$. We therefore have $\hat{\hat{\gamma}}(A \perp \alpha) = \{X \mid \cap\hat{\gamma}(A \perp \alpha) \subseteq X \in A \perp \alpha\} = \{X \mid \cap\gamma(A \perp \alpha) \subseteq X \in A \perp \alpha\} = \hat{\gamma}(A \perp \alpha)$.

95. It follows set-theoretically from $\gamma_1(A \perp \alpha) \subseteq \gamma_2(A \perp \alpha)$ that $\cap\gamma_2(A \perp \alpha) \subseteq \cap\gamma_1(A \perp \alpha)$. In the same way it follows from $\gamma_2(A \perp \alpha) \subseteq \hat{\gamma}_1(A \perp \alpha)$ that $\cap\hat{\gamma}_1(A \perp \alpha) \subseteq \cap\gamma_2(A \perp \alpha)$. Since $\cap\hat{\gamma}_1(A \perp \alpha) = \cap\gamma_1(A \perp \alpha)$ (Observation 2.68), we can conclude that $\cap\gamma_1(A \perp \alpha) = \cap\gamma_2(A \perp \alpha)$.

96. It follows set-theoretically from $\gamma(A \perp \alpha) \subseteq \gamma(A \perp \beta)$ that $\cap\gamma(A \perp \beta) \subseteq \cap\gamma(A \perp \alpha)$.

Let $X \in \hat{\gamma}(A \perp \alpha)$. Then $\cap\hat{\gamma}(A \perp \alpha) \subseteq X$. Since $\cap\hat{\gamma}(A \perp \alpha) = \cap\gamma(A \perp \alpha)$ (Observation 2.68), we have $\cap\gamma(A \perp \alpha) \subseteq X$. We can conclude from this and $\cap\gamma(A \perp \beta) \subseteq \cap\gamma(A \perp \alpha)$ that $\cap\gamma(A \perp \beta) \subseteq X$. It follows from $\cap\gamma(A \perp \beta) \subseteq X \in A \perp \alpha$, by Observation 2.69, that $X \in \hat{\gamma}(A \perp \beta)$.

97. a. It follows set-theoretically from $\gamma(A \perp \beta) \subseteq \gamma(A \perp \alpha)$ that $\cap\gamma(A \perp \alpha) \subseteq \cap\gamma(A \perp \beta)$, i.e., $A \sim_\gamma \alpha \subseteq A \sim_\gamma \beta$. For the other direction, let $A \sim_\gamma \alpha \subseteq A \sim_\gamma \beta$ and let $X \in \gamma(A \perp \beta)$. Then $\cap\gamma(A \perp \beta) \subseteq X$, i.e., $A \sim_\gamma \beta \subseteq X$. Since $A \sim_\gamma \alpha \subseteq A \sim_\gamma \beta$ it

follows that $A \sim_\gamma \alpha \subseteq X \in A \perp \beta$. It follows from Part 2 of Observation 2.69 that $X \in \gamma(A \perp \alpha)$.
b. If $(A \sim_\gamma \alpha) \cup (A \sim_\gamma \beta) \nvdash \alpha$, then there is by the upper bound property some X such that $(A \sim_\gamma \alpha) \cup (A \sim_\gamma \beta) \subseteq X \in A \perp \alpha$. By applying Observation 2.69, to $A \sim_\gamma \alpha \subseteq X \in A \perp \alpha$, we obtain $X \in \gamma(A \perp \alpha)$, and by applying it to $A \sim_\gamma \beta \subseteq X \in A \perp \alpha$, we obtain $X \in \gamma(A \perp \beta)$. We have established that $X \in \gamma(A \perp \alpha) \cap \gamma(A \perp \beta)$, and thus $\gamma(A \perp \alpha) \cap \gamma(A \perp \beta) \neq \varnothing$.

98. *I implies II*: Since $\div$ is an operator of partial meet contraction, it is based on some selection function γ, and by Observation 2.68 it is also based on $\hat{\gamma}$, the completion of γ.

Suppose that (I) holds. In order to show that (II) holds for $\hat{\gamma}$, suppose that $\alpha, \beta \in A \backslash Cn(\varnothing)$, $\beta \notin \cap \hat{\gamma}(A \perp \alpha \& \beta)$, and $X \in \hat{\gamma}(A \perp \alpha)$.

It follows from $X \in \hat{\gamma}(A \perp \alpha)$ that $\cap \hat{\gamma}(A \perp \alpha) \subseteq X$. From (I) we have $A \div (\alpha \& \beta) \subseteq A \div \alpha$, i.e., $\cap \hat{\gamma}(A \perp \alpha \& \beta) \subseteq \cap \hat{\gamma}(A \perp \alpha)$. Thus, $\cap \hat{\gamma}(A \perp \alpha \& \beta) \subseteq X$. It follows by Observation 1.53 from $X \in A \perp \alpha$ that $X \in A \perp (\alpha \& \beta)$. We therefore have $\cap \hat{\gamma}(A \perp \alpha \& \beta) \subseteq X \in A \perp (\alpha \& \beta)$, and it follows from the completion property that $X \in \hat{\gamma}(A \perp \alpha \& \beta)$.

II implies I: There are four limiting cases:

Case 1, $\vdash \alpha$: Then $A \div \alpha = A$, so that $A \div (\alpha \& \beta) \subseteq A \div \alpha$ holds.

Case 2, $\vdash \beta$: Then $\beta \in A \div (\alpha \& \beta)$, and (I) is vacuously satisfied.

Case 3, $\alpha \notin A$: Then $A \div \alpha = A$, so that $A \div (\alpha \& \beta) \subseteq A \div \alpha$ holds.

Case 4, $\beta \notin A$: Then (I) holds vacuously.

Case 5, $\alpha, \beta \in A \backslash Cn(\varnothing)$: Suppose that $\beta \notin A \div (\alpha \& \beta)$, i.e., $\beta \notin \cap \gamma(A \perp \alpha \& \beta)$. It follows from (II) that $\gamma(A \perp \alpha) \subseteq \gamma(A \perp (\alpha \& \beta))$, and from this that $\cap \gamma(A \perp (\alpha \& \beta)) \subseteq \cap \gamma(A \perp \alpha)$, i.e., $A \div (\alpha \& \beta) \subseteq A \div \alpha$.

99. a. It follows from Observation 1.55 that $X, Y \in A \perp (\alpha \& \beta)$. Let $Z \in \gamma(A \perp (\alpha \& \beta))$. Then $X \sqsubseteq Z$ and $Y \sqsubseteq Z$.
b. Let $X \in \gamma(A \perp (\alpha \& \beta)) \cap (A \perp \alpha)$. In order to show that $X \in \gamma(A \perp \alpha)$ we need to show that if $Y \in A \perp \alpha$, then $Y \sqsubseteq X$.

Let $Y \in A \perp \alpha$. It follows from Observation 1.55 that $Y \in A \perp (\alpha \& \beta)$. We can conclude from $X \in \gamma(A \perp (\alpha \& \beta))$ that $Y \sqsubseteq X$.

100. a. Let $A \perp \alpha \subseteq A \perp \beta$ and $A \sim_\gamma \beta \nvdash \alpha$. Since $\sim_\gamma$ is maxichoice, $A \sim_\gamma \beta \in \gamma(A \perp \beta)$, and we can conclude from $A \sim_\gamma \beta \nvdash \alpha$, by Observation 1.53 that $A \sim_\gamma \beta \in A \perp \alpha$.

Let $X \in A \perp \alpha$. Since $A \perp \alpha \subseteq A \perp \beta$ we then have $X \in A \perp \beta$. We can conclude from this and $A \sim_\gamma \beta \in \gamma(A \perp \beta)$ that $X \sqsubseteq (A \sim_\gamma \beta)$. Since this holds for all $X \in A \perp \beta$, we can conclude that $A \sim_\gamma \beta \in \gamma(A \perp \alpha)$ and, since γ is maxichoice, that $\{A \sim_\gamma \beta\} = \gamma(A \perp \alpha)$, so that $A \sim_\gamma \alpha = A \sim_\gamma \beta$.

b. It follows from Observation 1.54 that $\vdash \beta \rightarrow \alpha$ holds if and only if $A \perp \alpha \subseteq A \perp \beta$. Furthermore, since $A \sim_\gamma \beta$ is logically closed, $\alpha \in A \sim_\gamma \beta$ holds if and only if $A \sim_\gamma \beta \vdash \alpha$. Using these two equivalences, we can obtain the desired result directly from Part *a*.
c. Suppose to the contrary that $A \sim_\gamma(\alpha \& \beta) \neq A \sim_\gamma \alpha$ and $A \sim_\gamma(\alpha \& \beta) \neq A \sim_\gamma \beta$. It follows from Part *b* that either $\alpha \in A \sim_\gamma(\alpha \& \beta)$ or $A \sim_\gamma(\alpha \& \beta) = A \sim_\gamma \alpha$. Thus, $\alpha \in A \sim_\gamma(\alpha \& \beta)$. It follows in the same way that $\beta \in A \sim_\gamma(\alpha \& \beta)$. We can use *closure* to conclude that $\alpha \& \beta \in A \sim_\gamma(\alpha \& \beta)$. However, since both α and β are elements of $A \setminus \text{Cn}(\varnothing)$, $\alpha \& \beta \notin \text{Cn}(\varnothing)$, and *success* yields $\alpha \& \beta \notin A \sim_\gamma(\alpha \& \beta)$. This contradiction concludes the proof.

101. *Choice-distributivity implies property* α: Suppose that choice-distributivity is satisfied, and that $\alpha, \beta \in A \setminus \text{Cn}(\varnothing)$ and $A \perp \alpha \subseteq A \perp \beta$. We are going to show that $(A \perp \alpha) \cap \gamma(A \perp \beta) \subseteq \gamma(A \perp \alpha)$.

It follows from $A \perp \alpha \subseteq A \perp \beta$, by Observation 1.54, that $\vdash \beta \rightarrow \alpha$. It follows from this that β is equivalent with $\alpha \& (\alpha \rightarrow \beta)$. It follows from choice-distributivity that $\gamma(A \perp (\alpha \& (\alpha \rightarrow \beta))) \subseteq \gamma(A \perp \alpha) \cup \gamma(A \perp (\alpha \rightarrow \beta))$, i.e., $\gamma(A \perp \beta) \subseteq \gamma(A \perp \alpha) \cup \gamma(A \perp (\alpha \rightarrow \beta))$. Intersect both sides of this last expression with $A \perp \alpha$. We obtain:

$$(A \perp \alpha) \cap (\gamma(A \perp \beta)) \subseteq (A \perp \alpha) \cap (\gamma(A \perp \alpha) \cup \gamma(A \perp (\alpha \rightarrow \beta)))$$

and consequently (by set theory)

$$(A \perp \alpha) \cap (\gamma(A \perp \beta)) \subseteq ((A \perp \alpha) \cap (\gamma(A \perp \alpha))) \cup ((A \perp \alpha) \cap \gamma(A \perp (\alpha \rightarrow \beta)))$$

This expression can be simplified. Since $\gamma(A \perp \alpha) \subseteq A \perp \alpha$, we have $(A \perp \alpha) \cap (\gamma(A \perp \alpha)) = \gamma(A \perp \alpha)$. Furthermore, since $A \perp (\alpha \rightarrow \beta) = (A \perp \beta) \setminus (A \perp \alpha)$ (Observation 1.65), $(A \perp \alpha) \cap (A \perp (\alpha \rightarrow \beta)) = \varnothing$, and consequently $(A \perp \alpha) \cap \gamma(A \perp (\alpha \rightarrow \beta)) = \varnothing$. We therefore obtain:

$$(A \perp \alpha) \cap (\gamma(A \perp \beta)) \subseteq \cap \gamma(A \perp \alpha),$$

which finishes this part of the proof.

Property α *implies choice-distributivity*: Suppose that property α is satisfied and that $\alpha, \beta \in A \setminus \text{Cn}(\varnothing)$. Let $X \in \gamma(A \perp (\alpha \& \beta))$. Our task is to show that $X \in \gamma(A \perp \alpha) \cup \gamma(A \perp \beta)$.

It follows from $X \in A \perp (\alpha \& \beta)$ by Observation 1.55 that either $X \in A \perp \alpha$ or $X \in A \perp \beta$.

Case 1, $X \in A \perp \alpha$: According to Observation 1.54, $A \perp \alpha \subseteq A \perp (\alpha \& \beta)$. It follows from $A \perp \alpha \subseteq A \perp (\alpha \& \beta)$, $X \in \gamma(A \perp (\alpha \& \beta))$ and $X \in A \perp \alpha$, by property α, that $X \in \gamma(A \perp \alpha)$.

Case 2, $X \in A \perp \beta$: It follows in the same way that $X \in \gamma(A \perp \beta)$.
Thus, in both cases $X \in \gamma(A \perp \alpha) \cup \gamma(A \perp \beta)$. This finishes the proof.

102. *Part 2*: It follows from $X \sqsubset Y$ that $X \sqsubseteq Y$, and by transitivity from $X \sqsubseteq Y$ and $Y \sqsubseteq Z$ that $X \sqsubseteq Z$.

Suppose that $Z \sqsubseteq X$. Since $Y \sqsubseteq Z$ it then follows by transitivity that $Y \sqsubseteq X$, contrary to $X \sqsubset Y$. We may conclude from this contradiction that $\neg(Z \sqsubseteq X)$. Since we already have $X \sqsubseteq Z$, we may conclude that $X \sqsubset Z$.

Part 3: Let $X \sqsubset Y$ & $Y \sqsubset Z$. We then have $X \sqsubseteq Y$ & $Y \sqsubset Z$, and it follows from Part 1 of the present proof that $X \sqsubset Z$.

103. a. $X \sqsubset Y$ follows from the maximizing property. We therefore have $X \sqsubset Y \sqsubseteq Z$. It follows from the transitivity of $\sqsubseteq$ that $X \sqsubset Z$ (cf. Observation 2.75).
b. $Y \sqsubset Z$ follows from the maximizing property. We therefore have $X \sqsubseteq Y \sqsubset Z$. It follows from the transitivity of $\sqsubseteq$ that $X \sqsubset Z$ (cf. Observation 2.75).
c. There are two cases, $X \subset Y \sqsubset Z$ and $X = Y \sqsubset Z$.

If $X \subset Y \sqsubset Z$, then $X \sqsubset Y$ follows from the maximizing property, and we have $X \sqsubset Y \sqsubset Z$. It follows from the transitivity of $\sqsubseteq$ that $X \sqsubset Z$ (cf. Observation 2.75).

If $X = Y \sqsubset Z$, then $X \sqsubset Z$ follows directly from $Y \sqsubset Z$.
d. There are two cases, $X \sqsubset Y \subset Z$ and $X \sqsubset Y = Z$.

If $X \sqsubset Y \subset Z$, then $Y \sqsubset Z$ follows from the maximizing property, and we have $X \sqsubset Y \sqsubset Z$. It follows from the transitivity of $\sqsubseteq$ that $X \sqsubset Z$ (cf. Observation 2.75).

If $X \sqsubset Y = Z$, then $X \sqsubset Z$ follows directly from $X \sqsubset Y$.
e. There are two cases, $X \subset Y \sqsubseteq Z$ and $X = Y \sqsubseteq Z$.

If $X \subset Y \sqsubseteq Z$, then $X \sqsubseteq Z$ follows from Part *a*.

If $X = Y \sqsubseteq Z$, then $X \sqsubseteq Z$ follows directly from $Y \sqsubseteq Z$.
f. There are two cases, $X \sqsubseteq Y \subset Z$ and $X \sqsubseteq Y = Z$.

If $X \sqsubseteq Y \subset Z$, then $X \sqsubseteq Z$ follows from Part *b*.

If $X \sqsubseteq Y = Z$, then $X \sqsubseteq Z$ follows directly from $X \sqsubseteq Y$.

104. In order to show that $Y \in \gamma(A \perp \alpha)$ we must show that $Z \sqsubseteq Y$ for all $Z \in A \perp \alpha$. Let $Z \in A \perp \alpha$.

It follows from $X \in \gamma(A \perp \alpha)$ that $Z \sqsubseteq X$. Since $\sqsubseteq$ is transitive, we can conclude from $Z \sqsubseteq X$ and $X \sqsubseteq Y$ that $Z \sqsubseteq Y$.

105. a. Let γ be as stated in the theorem, and let $A \sim_\gamma \alpha \in A \perp \beta$ and $A \sim_\gamma \beta \in A \perp \alpha$. Since γ is maxichoice, we have $\gamma(A \perp \alpha) = \{A \sim_\gamma \alpha\}$ and $\gamma(A \perp \beta) = \{A \sim_\gamma \beta\}$. It follows from $A \sim_\gamma \beta \in A \perp \alpha$ and $\gamma(A \perp \alpha) = \{A \sim_\gamma \alpha\}$, by the marking-off identity, that $A \sim_\gamma \beta \sqsubseteq A \sim_\gamma \alpha$.

Next, we are going to show that $A \sim_\gamma \alpha \in \gamma(A \perp \beta)$. Let $X \in A \perp \beta$. Then it follows from $A \sim_\gamma \beta \in \gamma(A \perp \beta)$, again by the marking-off identity, that $X \sqsubseteq A \sim_\gamma \beta$. Since $\sqsubseteq$ is transitive, it follows from $X \sqsubseteq A \sim_\gamma \beta$ and $A \sim_\gamma \beta \sqsubseteq A \sim_\gamma \alpha$ that $X \sqsubseteq A \sim_\gamma \alpha$. We have shown that $X \sqsubseteq A \sim_\gamma \alpha$ for all $X \in A \perp \beta$, and since $A \sim_\gamma \alpha \in A \perp \beta$ it now follows by the marking-off identity that $A \sim_\gamma \alpha \in \gamma(A \perp \beta)$. It can be concluded from $A \sim_\gamma \alpha \in \gamma(A \perp \beta)$ and $\gamma(A \perp \beta) = \{A \sim_\gamma \beta\}$ that $A \sim_\gamma \alpha = A \sim_\gamma \beta$.

b. Let γ be as stated in the theorem, and let $A\sim_\gamma\alpha \nvdash \beta$ and $A\sim_\gamma\beta \nvdash \alpha$.

Case 1, $\alpha \notin A$: Then $A\sim_\gamma\alpha = A$. It follows from $A\sim_\gamma\alpha \nvdash \beta$ that $\beta \notin A$, which in its turn implies $A\sim_\gamma\beta = A$. We therefore have $A\sim_\gamma\alpha = A\sim_\gamma\beta = A$.

Case 2, $\beta \notin A$: Symmetrical with case 1.

Case 3, $\alpha \in A$ and $\beta \in A$: Since $\sim_\gamma$ is maxichoice, we have $A\sim_\gamma\alpha \in A\bot\alpha$. It follows from this, $\beta \in A$ and $\beta \notin A\sim_\gamma\alpha$, that $A\sim_\gamma\alpha \in A\bot\beta$. (Observation 1.53. Note that the logical closure of A is necessary here.) In the same way it follows that $A\sim_\gamma\beta \in A\bot\alpha$, and we can now use the result of Part *a* to obtain $A\sim_\gamma\alpha = A\sim_\gamma\beta$.

106. Let $\sqsubseteq$ be the transitive and weakly maximizing relation on which γ is based. Let $A\sim_\gamma(\alpha\&\beta) \vdash \alpha$. There are four cases.

Case 1, $\vdash \alpha$: It follows directly that $A\sim_\gamma(\alpha\&\beta\&\delta) \vdash \alpha$.

Case 2, $\vdash \beta$: Then $\alpha\&\beta$ and are logically equivalent, and consequently $A\sim_\gamma(\alpha\&\beta) = A\sim_\gamma\alpha$. From $A\sim_\gamma(\alpha\&\beta) \vdash \alpha$, i.e., $A\sim_\gamma\alpha \vdash \alpha$. it follows that $\alpha \in \mathrm{Cn}(\varnothing)$, and we are back in case 1.

Case 3, $\vdash \delta$: Then $\alpha\&\beta\&\delta$ is logically equivalent to $\alpha\&\beta$, so that $A\sim_\gamma(\alpha\&\beta\&\delta) = A\sim_\gamma(\alpha\&\beta)$, from which the desired result follows directly.

Case 4, $\nvdash \alpha$, $\nvdash \beta$ and $\nvdash \delta$: Let $\cap\gamma(A\bot(\alpha\&\beta)) \vdash \alpha$. We are first going to show that if $X \in \gamma(A\bot(\alpha\&\beta\&\delta))$, then $X \vdash \alpha$. Suppose not, i.e., suppose that there is some X such that $X \in \gamma(A\bot(\alpha\&\beta\&\delta))$ and $\alpha \notin \mathrm{Cn}(X)$. It follows from $X \in A\bot(\alpha\&\beta\&\delta)$ and $\alpha \notin \mathrm{Cn}(X)$ that $X \in A\bot(\alpha\&\beta)$.

Suppose that $X \in \gamma(A\bot(\alpha\&\beta))$. Then $\cap\gamma(A\bot(\alpha\&\beta)) \nvdash \alpha$, contrary to the conditions. By this contradiction, $X \notin \gamma(A\bot(\alpha\&\beta))$.

Next, let $Y \in \gamma(A\bot(\alpha\&\beta))$. Then $X \sqsubset Y$. Since $Y \nvdash \alpha\&\beta\&\delta$ there is, by the upper bound property, some Y' such that $Y \subseteq Y' \in A\bot(\alpha\&\beta\&\delta)$. If $Y = Y'$, then $X \sqsubset Y'$ follows directly from $X \sqsubset Y$. If $Y \subset Y'$, then the weak maximizing property yields $Y \sqsubseteq Y'$. It follows by transitivity from $X \sqsubset Y$ and $Y \sqsubseteq Y'$ that $X \sqsubset Y'$. In both cases, we have $X \sqsubset Y'$, $X \in \gamma(A\bot(\alpha\&\beta\&\delta))$ and $Y' \in A\bot(\alpha\&\beta\&\delta)$. This contradiction shows that $\alpha \notin \mathrm{Cn}(X)$ cannot hold. We can conclude that if $X \in \gamma(A\bot(\alpha\&\beta\&\delta))$, then $X \vdash \alpha$. Since $\gamma(A\bot(\alpha\&\beta\&\delta))$ has a finite number of elements, it follows by repeated application of Observation 1.34 that $\cap\gamma(A\bot(\alpha\&\beta\&\delta)) \vdash \alpha$. With this, the proof is finished.

107. a. Let $\sqsubseteq$ be the marking-off relation by which γ is relational. Let $\sqsubseteq'$ be the restriction of $\sqsubseteq$ to the domain $A\Delta\mathcal{L} = \{X \mid X \in A\bot\alpha \text{ for some } \alpha\}$. (Thus, if $X, Y \in A\Delta\mathcal{L}$, then $X\sqsubseteq'Y$ if and only if $X\sqsubseteq Y$, and otherwise $X\not\sqsubseteq'Y$.)

If $X, Y \in A\bot\alpha$, then $X\sqsubseteq Y$ if and only if $X\sqsubseteq'Y$. Therefore, it makes no difference to replace $\sqsubseteq$ by $\sqsubseteq'$ in the marking-off relation.

To see that $\sqsubseteq'$ is reflexive, let $X \in A\Delta\mathcal{L}$. It follows from Observation 1.70 that there is some β such that $\{X\} = A\bot\beta$. It follows from $\gamma(A\bot\beta) = A\bot\beta$, i.e., $\gamma(\{X\}) = \{X\}$, that $X\sqsubseteq X$ and thus $X\sqsubseteq'X$.

b. Suppose that $\sqsubseteq$ is transitive. To see that $\sqsubseteq'$ is transitive, let $X \sqsubseteq' Y \sqsubseteq' Z$. It follows that $X \sqsubseteq Y \sqsubseteq Z$, so that $X \sqsubseteq Z$. Since $X, Z \in A\Delta\mathcal{L}$, we then obtain $X \sqsubseteq' Z$.

108. a. Define $X<Y$ if and only if $\neg(Y \sqsubseteq X)$, and the two identities will be equivalent.

b. $X<Y \rightarrow \neg(Y<X)$
iff $\neg(Y \sqsubseteq X) \rightarrow \neg(\neg(X \sqsubseteq Y))$
iff $\neg(Y \sqsubseteq X) \rightarrow (X \sqsubseteq Y)$
iff $Y \sqsubseteq X \vee X \sqsubseteq Y$

c. Transitivity. Proof:
$X \sqsubseteq Z \rightarrow X \sqsubseteq Y \vee Y \sqsubseteq Z$
iff $\neg(Z<X) \rightarrow \neg(Y<X) \vee \neg(Z<Y)$
iff $\neg(\neg(Y<X) \vee \neg(Z<Y)) \rightarrow \neg(\neg(Z<X))$
iff $Y<X$ & $Z<Y \rightarrow Z<X$
iff $Z<Y$ & $Y<X \rightarrow Z<X$

109. Let the language consist of the logically independent atoms p and q and their truth-functional combinations, and let Cn represent classical truth-functional consequence. Let $A = \mathrm{Cn}(\{p,q\})$. Then $A\perp\{p\} = \{\mathrm{Cn}(\{q\}),\mathrm{Cn}(\{p\leftrightarrow q\})\}$ and $A\perp\{p,p\leftrightarrow q\} = \{\mathrm{Cn}(\{q\}),\mathrm{Cn}(\{q\rightarrow p\})\}$. Let $\gamma(A\perp\{p\}) = \{\mathrm{Cn}(\{q\})\}$ and $\gamma(A\perp\{p,p\leftrightarrow q\}) = \{\mathrm{Cn}(\{q\rightarrow p\})\}$. If γ is relational by $\sqsubseteq$, then $\mathrm{Cn}(\{p\leftrightarrow q\}) \sqsubset \mathrm{Cn}(\{q\}) \sqsubset \mathrm{Cn}(\{q\rightarrow p\})$. If $\sqsubseteq$ is transitive, then $\mathrm{Cn}(\{p\leftrightarrow q\}) \sqsubset \mathrm{Cn}(\{q\rightarrow p\})$. On the other hand, if $\sqsubseteq$ is maximizing, then $\mathrm{Cn}(\{q\rightarrow p\}) \sqsubset \mathrm{Cn}(\{p\leftrightarrow q\})$. Although $\sqsubseteq$ is transitively relational, it is not transitively, maximizingly relational.

110. a. Let B be an A-closed subset of A. Then, by Observation 1.67, there is a set X such that $\{B\} = A\perp X$. By Definition 2.61, $\gamma(A\perp X) = \{B\}$, and by the marking-off identity, $B \sqsubseteq B$, so that $\sqsubseteq$ is reflexive.

b. Let A_1 and A_2 be A-closed subsets of A such that neither of them is a proper subset of the other. Then, by Observation 1.68, there is a set X such that $\{A_1,A_2\} = A\perp X$. By Definition 2.61, either $A_1 \in \gamma(A\perp X)$ or $A_2 \in \gamma(A\perp X)$. By the marking-off identity, in the former case $A_2 \sqsubseteq A_1$ and in the latter $A_1 \sqsubseteq A_2$.

c. Let $\sqsubseteq'$ be defined as follows:

(I) If $A_1 \not\subset A_2 \not\subset A_1$, then $A_1 \sqsubseteq' A_2$ if and only if $A_1 \sqsubseteq A_2$

(II) If $A_1 \subset A_2$, then $A_1 \sqsubset' A_2$

We need to verify (1) that $\sqsubseteq'$ is connected, and (2) that $\sqsubseteq'$ generates the same partial meet contraction as $\sqsubseteq$.

(1) follows from the definition and Part *b*.

For (2), note that if $A_1, A_2 \in A\perp X$, then $A_1 \not\subset A_2 \not\subset A_1$, so that $A_1 \sqsubseteq' A_2$ holds if and only if $A_1 \sqsubseteq A_2$. Therefore, although $\sqsubseteq$ and $\sqsubseteq'$ do not necessarily coincide in general, it makes no difference to replace $\sqsubseteq$ by $\sqsubseteq'$ in the marking-off relation.

111. It follows directly from $A\perp\alpha \subseteq S(A,\alpha)$ that if $S(A,\alpha)$ is empty, then so is $A\perp\alpha$. For the other direction, let $A\perp\alpha = \varnothing$. Then $\vdash\alpha$, and it follows from clause (iii) of Definition 2.24 that $S(A,\alpha) = \varnothing$.

112. Suppose to the contrary that $S(A,\alpha) = S(A,\beta)$ and $A\perp\alpha \neq A\perp\beta$. Without loss of generality, we may assume that there is some X such that $X \in A\perp\alpha$ and $X \notin A\perp\beta$.

It follows from $X \in A\perp\alpha$ by Observation 2.23 that $X \in S(A,\alpha)$ and thus $X \in S(A,\beta)$, so that $\beta \notin X$. From this and $X \in A\perp\alpha$ it follows by Observation 1.53 that $X \in A\perp\beta$. This contradiction concludes the proof.

113. Let $\div$ be a maxichoice AGM-contraction that is based on the selection function γ. Let γ' be the selection function such that for all α, $\gamma'(S(A,\alpha)) = \gamma(A\perp\alpha)$. It follows from Exercise 112 that γ' is a well-defined selection function. Let $\div'$ be the Levi-contraction that is based on γ'. Then clearly $A\div\alpha = A\div'\alpha$ for all α.

114. *(1) implies (2)*: Let $Y \in S(A,\alpha)$. Then $Y = \text{Cn}(Y) \subseteq A$ and $Y \nvdash \alpha$. Let Z be any element of $A\perp\alpha$ such that $Y \subseteq Z$. It remains to be shown that $Z \cap \text{Cn}(\{\alpha\}) \subseteq Y$. Let $\varepsilon \in Z \cap \text{Cn}(\{\alpha\})$. Since $Y \in S(A,\alpha)$ we know that either ε or $\neg\varepsilon$ is an element of $\text{Cn}(Y \cup \{\neg\alpha\})$.

If $\neg\varepsilon \in \text{Cn}(Y \cup \{\neg\alpha\})$, then since $Y \subseteq Z$ we have $\neg\varepsilon \in \text{Cn}(Z \cup \{\neg\alpha\})$, and by deduction $\neg\alpha \rightarrow \neg\varepsilon \in \text{Cn}(Z)$. Since $\varepsilon \in Z$ this implies $\alpha \in \text{Cn}(Z)$, contrary to $Z \in A\perp\alpha$. We can conclude from this contradiction that $\neg\varepsilon \notin \text{Cn}(Y \cup \{\neg\alpha\})$, and thus $\varepsilon \in \text{Cn}(Y \cup \{\neg\alpha\})$.

By deduction, $\neg\alpha \rightarrow \varepsilon \in \text{Cn}(Y)$. Since $\varepsilon \in Z \cap \text{Cn}(\{\alpha\})$, deduction also yields $\alpha \rightarrow \varepsilon \in \text{Cn}(\varnothing)$ and thus $\alpha \rightarrow \varepsilon \in \text{Cn}(Y)$. Since ε can be derived from $\neg\alpha \rightarrow \varepsilon$ and $\alpha \rightarrow \varepsilon$, we obtain $\varepsilon \in \text{Cn}(Y)$, hence $\varepsilon \in Y$. This finishes the proof.

(2) implies (3): Since $Y \subseteq A$ and $Y \nvdash \alpha$ it follows from the upper bound property that that there is some Z such that $Y \subseteq Z \in A\perp\alpha$. It follows from (2) that then $Z \cap \text{Cn}(\{\alpha\}) \subseteq Y$ also holds.

(3) implies (1): Let Y be logically closed, and let $Z \cap \text{Cn}(\{\alpha\}) \subseteq Y \subseteq Z \in A\perp\alpha$. It follows directly that clauses (i) and (ii) of Definition 2.24 are satisfied. It remains to be shown that clause (iii) is satisfied, in other words that $\text{Cn}(Y \cup \{\neg\alpha\}) \in \mathcal{L}\perp\perp$. It follows from $Z \in A\perp\alpha$ that $\text{Cn}(Z \cup \{\neg\alpha\}) \in \mathcal{L}\perp\perp$ (Observation 2.23), so it will be sufficient to show that $\text{Cn}(Y \cup \{\neg\alpha\}) = \text{Cn}(Z \cup \{\neg\alpha\})$.

Since $Y \subseteq Z$ we immediately have $\text{Cn}(Y \cup \{\neg\alpha\}) \subseteq \text{Cn}(Z \cup \{\neg\alpha\})$. In order to show that $\text{Cn}(Z \cup \{\neg\alpha\}) \subseteq \text{Cn}(Y \cup \{\neg\alpha\}$, let $\delta \in \text{Cn}(Z \cup \{\neg\alpha\})$.

Then by deduction $\neg\alpha\rightarrow\delta \in$ Cn(Z), i.e., since Z is logically closed, $\neg\alpha\rightarrow\delta \in Z$. Since $\neg\alpha\rightarrow\delta \in \mathrm{Cn}(\{\alpha\})$, we have $\neg\alpha\rightarrow\delta \in Z \cap \mathrm{Cn}(\{\alpha\})$. Since $Z \cap \mathrm{Cn}(\{\alpha\}) \subseteq Y$ we may conclude that $\neg\alpha\rightarrow\delta \in Y$ and thus, by deduction, $\delta \in \mathrm{Cn}(Y \cup \{\neg\alpha\})$.

115. a. Using the result from the foregoing exercise we obtain:
$A+\alpha = \cap(S(A,\alpha))$
$= \cap\{Y \mid Z \cap \mathrm{Cn}(\{\alpha\}) \subseteq Y = \mathrm{Cn}(Y) \subseteq Z \in A\bot\alpha$ for some $Z\}$
$= \cap\{Y \mid \mathrm{Cn}(Z \cap \mathrm{Cn}(\{\alpha\})) \subseteq Y = \mathrm{Cn}(Y) \subseteq Z \in A\bot\alpha$ for some $Z\}$
$= \cap\{\mathrm{Cn}(Z \cap \mathrm{Cn}(\{\alpha\})) \mid Z \in A\bot\alpha\}$
$= \cap\{Z \cap \mathrm{Cn}(\{\alpha\}) \mid Z \in A\bot\alpha\}$
$= \cap(A\bot\alpha) \cap \mathrm{Cn}(\{\alpha\})$
$= (A\sim\alpha) \cap \mathrm{Cn}(\{\alpha\})$
b. $A+\alpha = (A\sim\alpha) \cap \mathrm{Cn}(\{\alpha\})$ (Part *a* of this exercise)
$= A \cap \mathrm{Cn}(\{\neg\alpha\}) \cap \mathrm{Cn}(\{\alpha\})$ (Observation 2.12)
$= A \cap \mathrm{Cn}(\{\neg\alpha\vee\alpha\})$ (Observation 1.17)
$= A \cap \mathrm{Cn}(\varnothing)$
$= \mathrm{Cn}(\varnothing)$.

116. a. $A{\perp\!\!\perp}p = \{\{p\}\}$
b. $A{\perp\!\!\perp}(p\vee q) = \{\{p\},\{q\},\{p\vee q\}\}$
c. $A{\perp\!\!\perp}(p\&q) = \{\{p,q\}\}$
d. $A{\perp\!\!\perp}(p\rightarrow q) = \{\{q\}\}$
e. $A{\perp\!\!\perp}(p\vee\neg p) = \{\varnothing\}$
f. $A{\perp\!\!\perp}(p\&\neg p) = \varnothing$

117. a. $(\mathrm{Cn}(A)){\perp\!\!\perp}p = \{\{p\}, \{p\&q\}, \{p\leftrightarrow q,q\}, \{p\leftrightarrow q,p\vee q\}, \{q,q\rightarrow p\}, \{p\vee q,q\rightarrow p\}\}$
b. $(\mathrm{Cn}(A)){\perp\!\!\perp}(p\vee q) = \{\{p\},\{p\&q\},\{q\},\{p\vee q\}\}$
c. $(\mathrm{Cn}(A)){\perp\!\!\perp}(p\vee\neg p) = \{\varnothing\}$
d. $(\mathrm{Cn}(A)){\perp\!\!\perp}(p\&\neg p) = \varnothing$

118. a. Let $A\subseteq B$ and $X \in A{\perp\!\!\perp}\alpha$. Then $X \subseteq B$, and X implies α but none of its proper subsets implies α. It follows that $X \in B{\perp\!\!\perp}\alpha$.
b. Let $X \in B{\perp\!\!\perp}\alpha \cap \wp(A)$. $X \in \wp(A)$ is equivalent with $X \subseteq A$. Thus $X \subseteq A$, and X implies α but none of its proper subsets implies α. It follows that $X \in A{\perp\!\!\perp}\beta$.
c. One direction follows from Part *b*. For the other direction, let $A \subseteq B$ and $X \in A{\perp\!\!\perp}\alpha$. Then $X \in B{\perp\!\!\perp}\alpha$ follows from Part *a*. It follows from $X \in A{\perp\!\!\perp}\alpha$ that $X \subseteq A$, or equivalently $X \in \wp(A)$.
d. For one direction, let $X \in A{\perp\!\!\perp}\alpha$. It follows directly that $X \subseteq A$, and by Part *b* of this exercise that $X \in X{\perp\!\!\perp}\alpha$.

For the other direction, suppose that $X \subseteq A$ and $X \in X \perp\!\!\perp \alpha$. It follows by Part *a* of the present exercise that $X \in A \perp\!\!\perp \alpha$.

e. Suppose to the contrary that $\delta \in X \in A \perp\!\!\perp \alpha$ and $X \setminus \{\delta\} \vdash \delta$. Then $\mathrm{Cn}(X \setminus \{\delta\}) = \mathrm{Cn}(X)$, and $X \setminus \{\delta\}$ is a proper subset of X that implies α, contrary to $X \in A \perp\!\!\perp \alpha$.

f. Let $X \in (A \perp\!\!\perp \alpha) \cap (A \perp\!\!\perp \beta)$. Then (i) $X \subseteq A$, (ii) X implies $\alpha \& \beta$, and (iii) no proper subset of X implies α, so that no proper subset of X implies $\alpha \& \beta$. We can conclude that $X \in A \perp\!\!\perp (\alpha \& \beta)$.

g. Let $X \subseteq Y$, $X \in A \perp\!\!\perp \alpha$, and $Y \in A \perp\!\!\perp \beta$. Then (i) $Y \subseteq A$, (ii) Y implies $\alpha \& \beta$, and (iii) no proper subset of Y implies β, so that no proper subset of Y implies $\alpha \& \beta$. We can conclude that $Y \in A \perp\!\!\perp (\alpha \& \beta)$.

119. We first need to show that $Z \vdash \delta \vee \alpha$. Let $Y = \{\psi_1, ... \psi_n\}$. Then $Z = \{\delta \vee \psi_1, ... \delta \vee \psi_n\}$, and thus $Z \vdash \delta \vee (\psi_1 \& ... \& \psi_n)$. It follows by sentential logic from this and $(\psi_1 \& ... \& \psi_n) \vdash \delta \vee \alpha$ that $Z \vdash \delta \vee \alpha$.

Next, suppose that $Z \notin A \perp\!\!\perp (\delta \vee \alpha)$. Then there is some proper subset Z' of Z such that $Z' \vdash \delta \vee \alpha$. It follows from the construction of Z that there is some proper subset Y' of Y such that $Z' = \{\delta \vee \psi \mid \psi \in Y'\}$. Since Z' is logically equivalent with $\delta \vee \& Y'$, we then have $(\delta \vee \& Y') \vdash \delta \vee \alpha$. From this it follows truth-functionally that $\& Y' \vdash \delta \vee \alpha$, so that $Y' \vdash \delta \vee \alpha$, contrary to $Y' \subset Y$ and $Y \in A \perp\!\!\perp (\delta \vee \alpha)$. We can conclude from this contradiction that $Z \in A \perp\!\!\perp (\delta \vee \alpha)$.

120. *Maxichoice to unicity*: Let $\approx_\sigma$ be a maxichoice contraction, i.e., let there be a maxichoice selection function γ for A such that $A \sim_\gamma \alpha = A \approx_\sigma \alpha$ for all α. Let $\beta \in \sigma(A \perp\!\!\perp \alpha)$.

We then have $\beta \in A \setminus (A \approx_\sigma \alpha) = A \setminus (A \sim_\gamma \alpha)$. Since γ is maxichoice, we have $A \sim_\gamma \alpha \in A \perp \alpha$, so that $(A \sim_\gamma \alpha) \cup \{\beta\} \vdash \alpha$.

Using compactness, we can conclude from $(A \sim_\gamma \alpha) \cup \{\beta\} \vdash \alpha$ that there is a finite set Z such that $Z \subseteq A \sim_\gamma \alpha$ and $Z \cup \{\beta\} \vdash \alpha$. There must then be some $Z' \subseteq Z$ such that $Z' \cup \{\beta\} \in A \perp\!\!\perp \alpha$.

It follows from $Z' \subseteq Z \subseteq A \sim_\gamma \alpha = A \approx_\sigma \alpha = A \setminus (\sigma(A \perp\!\!\perp \alpha))$ that $Z' \cap \sigma(A \perp\!\!\perp \alpha) = \varnothing$. Thus, we have $Z' \cup \{\beta\} \in A \perp\!\!\perp \alpha$ and $(Z' \cup \{\beta\}) \cap \sigma(A \perp\!\!\perp \alpha) = \{\beta\}$, which concludes this direction of the proof.

Unicity to maxichoice: Let σ be such that for all $\beta \in \sigma(A \perp\!\!\perp \alpha)$ there is some $X \in A \perp\!\!\perp \alpha$ such that $X \cap \sigma(A \perp\!\!\perp \alpha) = \{\beta\}$.

In order to show that $\approx_\sigma$ is a maxichoice contraction, it is sufficient to show that for all α, $A \approx_\sigma \alpha \in A \perp \alpha$. This can be shown by proving that if $\beta \in A \setminus (A \approx_\sigma \alpha)$, then $(A \approx_\sigma \alpha) \cup \{\beta\} \vdash \alpha$.

Let $\beta \in A \setminus (A \approx_\sigma \alpha)$. Then $\beta \in \sigma(A \perp\!\!\perp \alpha)$. It follows by unicity that there is some $X \in A \perp\!\!\perp \alpha$ such that $X \cap \sigma(A \perp\!\!\perp \alpha) = \{\beta\}$. Since $X \subseteq A$ it follows set-theoretically from $X \cap \sigma(A \perp\!\!\perp \alpha) = \{\beta\}$ that $X \subseteq (A \setminus \sigma(A \perp\!\!\perp \alpha)) \cup \{\beta\} =$

$(A{\approx_\sigma}\alpha)\cup\{\beta\}$. It follows from $X \in A{\perp\!\!\perp}\alpha$ that $X \vdash \alpha$, and we can conclude that $(A{\approx_\sigma}\alpha)\cup\{\beta\} \vdash \alpha$, as desired.

121. a. We are going to assume that $A{\approx_\sigma}\alpha \neq A{\approx_\sigma}\beta$, and show that there is some δ for which it does not hold that $A{\approx_\sigma}\delta \vdash \alpha$ iff $A{\approx_\sigma}\delta \vdash \beta$.

It follows from $A{\approx_\sigma}\alpha \neq A{\approx_\sigma}\beta$ that $A{\perp\!\!\perp}\alpha \neq A{\perp\!\!\perp}\beta$. By Observation 2.84, $A\perp\alpha \neq A\perp\beta$. Without loss of generality we may assume that there is some $X \in A\perp\alpha$ such that $X \notin A\perp\beta$. There are two cases:

Case 1, $X \vdash \beta$: Since $X \in A\perp\alpha$ we can use Observation 1.70 to conclude that there is some δ such that $\{X\} = A\perp\delta$. By Observation 2.86, every element of $A{\perp\!\!\perp}\delta$ has exactly one element. Thus $A{\approx_\sigma}\delta = A\backslash\cup(A{\perp\!\!\perp}\delta)$. It follows from Observation 2.85 that $A\backslash\cup(A{\perp\!\!\perp}\delta) = \cap(A\perp\delta) = X$. We therefore have $A{\approx_\sigma}\delta = X$, so that $A{\approx_\sigma}\delta \nvdash \alpha$ and $A{\approx_\sigma}\delta \vdash \beta$, as desired.

Case 2, $X \nvdash \beta$. Then, since A is finite, there is some X' such that $X \subset X' \in A\perp\beta$. It follows in the same way as in case 1 that there is some δ such that $A{\approx_\sigma}\delta = X'$. It follows that $A{\approx_\sigma}\delta \vdash \alpha$ and $A{\approx_\sigma}\delta \nvdash \beta$.

b. Let $A{\approx_\sigma}\beta \nsubseteq A{\approx_\sigma}\alpha$. It follows that $A{\approx_\sigma}\alpha \neq A$, so that $\nvdash \alpha$. It also follows that there is some ε such that $\varepsilon \in \sigma(A{\perp\!\!\perp}\alpha)$ and $\varepsilon \notin \sigma(A{\perp\!\!\perp}\beta)$. By Definition 2.30, $\varepsilon \in \cup(A{\perp\!\!\perp}\alpha)$, and according to Observation 2.85, $\varepsilon \notin \cap(A\perp\alpha)$. Let X be such that $\varepsilon \notin X \in A\perp\alpha$. By Observation 1.70, there is some δ such that $\{X\} = A\perp\delta$. By Observation 2.86, every element of $A{\perp\!\!\perp}\delta$ has exactly one element, and consequently $\sigma(A{\perp\!\!\perp}\delta) = \cup(A{\perp\!\!\perp}\delta)$ and $A{\approx_\sigma}\delta = A\backslash\cup(A{\perp\!\!\perp}\delta)$. By Observation 2.85, $A{\approx_\sigma}\delta = \cap(A\perp\delta) = X$.

It follows from $\varepsilon \in A$ and $\varepsilon \notin X \in A\perp\alpha$ that $X \cup \{\varepsilon\} \vdash \alpha$. Since $\varepsilon \in A{\approx_\sigma}\beta$, we therefore have $A{\approx_\sigma}\delta \nvdash \alpha$ and $(A{\approx_\sigma}\beta) \cup (A{\approx_\sigma}\delta) \vdash \alpha$, as desired.

122. a. Let $\alpha{\prec}\beta$ and $\beta{\vdash}\delta$. Then either $\beta{\leftrightarrow}\delta \in \mathrm{Cn}(\varnothing)$ or $\mathrm{Cn}(\delta) \subset \mathrm{Cn}(\beta)$. In the former case, $\alpha{\prec}\delta$ follows from intersubstitutivity (Definition 2.43). In the latter case, strict dominance yields $\beta{\prec}\delta$, and $\alpha{\prec}\delta$ can be obtained from transitivity.

b. Let $\alpha{\vdash}\beta$ and $\beta{\prec}\delta$. Then either $\alpha{\leftrightarrow}\beta \in \mathrm{Cn}(\varnothing)$ or $\mathrm{Cn}(\beta) \subset \mathrm{Cn}(\alpha)$. In the former case, $\alpha{\prec}\delta$ follows from intersubstitutivity (Definition 2.43). In the latter case, strict dominance yields $\alpha{\prec}\beta$, and $\alpha{\prec}\delta$ can be obtained from transitivity.

123. Let $\prec$ be a hierarchy that satisfies virtual connectivity, and let $\alpha{\prec}\beta$ and $\beta{\prec}\delta$. It follows from virtual connectivity that either $\alpha{\prec}\delta$ or $\delta{\prec}\beta$. In the latter case, acyclicity is violated. We can conclude that $\alpha{\prec}\delta$.

124. a. *Closure*: It follows from $A{+}\alpha = \mathrm{Cn}(A\backslash\sigma(A{\perp\!\!\perp}\alpha))$ that $\mathrm{Cn}(A{+}\alpha) = \mathrm{Cn}(\mathrm{Cn}(A\backslash\sigma(A{\perp\!\!\perp}\alpha))) = \mathrm{Cn}(A\backslash\sigma(A{\perp\!\!\perp}\alpha)) = A{+}\alpha$.

Inclusion: It follows from $A\backslash\sigma(A\top\!\!\top\alpha) \subseteq A$ that $\mathrm{Cn}(A\backslash\sigma(A\top\!\!\top\alpha)) \subseteq \mathrm{Cn}(A)$, i.e. (since A is logically closed) $A{+}\alpha \subseteq A$.
Vacuity: If $\alpha \notin \mathrm{Cn}(A)$, then $A\top\!\!\top\alpha = \varnothing$ so that $\sigma(A\top\!\!\top\alpha) = \varnothing$ and consequently $\mathrm{Cn}(A\backslash\sigma(A\top\!\!\top\alpha)) = \mathrm{Cn}(A) = A$.
Success: Let B be any subset of A that implies α. Then $B \not\subseteq A\backslash\sigma(A\top\!\!\top\alpha))$. It follows from this that $A\backslash\sigma(A\top\!\!\top\alpha))$ does not imply α, and thus $\alpha \notin \mathrm{Cn}(A\backslash\sigma(A\top\!\!\top\alpha))$.
Extensionality: Directly from the intersubstitutivity of the hierarchy $\prec$. (Definition 2.43.)
b. *Failure*: Let $\tau \in \mathrm{Cn}(\varnothing)$. Then $\tau \in A$. Let α be any element of A. Then $\{\alpha\} \in A\top\!\!\top\tau$, and consequently $\alpha \in s(\{\alpha\}) \subseteq \sigma(A\top\!\!\top\tau)$. It follows that $\sigma(A\top\!\!\top\tau) = A$, and consequently $A{+}\tau = \mathrm{Cn}(A\backslash\sigma(A\top\!\!\top\tau)) = \mathrm{Cn}(\varnothing)$, contrary to *failure*.
c. Suppose that *recovery* is satisfied. It then follows from Part *a* and Observations 2.6 and 2.3 that *failure* is satisfied, contrary to Part *b*. We can conclude that *recovery* does not hold.

125. Suppose to the contrary that $\delta \in \sigma(A\perp\!\!\!\perp\alpha)$ and $\delta \in \mathrm{Cn}(\{\neg\alpha\})$. There is then some $X \in A\perp\!\!\!\perp\alpha$ such that $\delta \in s(X)$.

Let $Y = X\backslash\{\delta\}$. It follows from $Y\cup\{\delta\} \vdash \alpha$ by the deduction property that $Y \vdash \delta\rightarrow\alpha$. It follows from $\delta \in \mathrm{Cn}(\{\neg\alpha\})$ that $\neg\alpha\rightarrow\delta \in \mathrm{Cn}(\varnothing)$ or equivalently $\neg\delta\rightarrow\alpha \in \mathrm{Cn}(\varnothing)$. Since $\delta\rightarrow\alpha$ and $\neg\delta\rightarrow\alpha$ together imply α we have $Y \vdash \alpha$. Since $Y \subset X$ this contradicts $X \in A\perp\!\!\!\perp\alpha$. This contradiction concludes the proof.

126. *Left-to-right*: Let $\delta \in A\backslash\sigma(A\perp\!\!\!\perp\alpha)$. If $\delta \in \mathrm{Cn}(\{\neg\alpha\})$, then clearly $\delta \in A\cap\mathrm{Cn}(\{\neg\alpha\})$. If $\delta \notin \mathrm{Cn}(\{\neg\alpha\})$, then it follows from Observation 2.90 that $\delta \notin \sigma(A\top\!\!\top\alpha)$, and thus $\delta \in A\backslash\sigma(A\top\!\!\top\alpha)$.

Right-to-left: It follows from $A\perp\!\!\!\perp\alpha \subseteq A\top\!\!\top\alpha$ that $\sigma(A\perp\!\!\!\perp\alpha) \subseteq \sigma(A\top\!\!\top\alpha)$ and consequently $A\backslash\sigma(A\top\!\!\top\alpha) \subseteq A\backslash\sigma(A\perp\!\!\!\perp\alpha)$. It follows from Exercise 125 that $A\cap\mathrm{Cn}(\{\neg\alpha\}) \subseteq A\backslash\sigma(A\perp\!\!\!\perp\alpha)$.

127. Since $\prec$ is empty, all elements of all kernels are minimal, i.e., $s(X) = X$ for all $X \in A\perp\!\!\!\perp\alpha$. It follows that $\sigma(A\perp\!\!\!\perp\alpha) = \cup(A\perp\!\!\!\perp\alpha)$, and thus $A{+}\alpha = \mathrm{Cn}(A\backslash\sigma(A\perp\!\!\!\perp\alpha)) = \mathrm{Cn}(A\backslash\cup(A\perp\!\!\!\perp\alpha))$. According to Observation 2.85, $A\backslash\cup(A\perp\!\!\!\perp\alpha)) = \cap(A\perp\alpha)$, and thus $A{+}\alpha = \mathrm{Cn}(\cap(A\perp\alpha))$. Since $\cap(A\perp\alpha)$ is logically closed, we therefore have $A{+}\alpha = \cap(A\perp\alpha)$, as desired.

128. a. From $\alpha\vdash\alpha$ and *dominance*.
b. From Part *a* and *intersubstitutivity* (Observation 2.92).
c. For one direction, let $\alpha\leq\beta$. By *conjunctiveness*, either $\alpha\leq\alpha\&\beta$ or $\beta\leq\alpha\&\beta$. In the first case, we are done, and in the second case, we can apply *transitivity* to $\alpha\leq\beta$ and $\beta\leq\alpha\&\beta$ to obtain $\alpha\leq\alpha\&\beta$.

For the other direction, let $\alpha\leq\alpha\&\beta$. We can apply *dominance* to obtain $\alpha\&\beta\leq\beta$ an then *transitivity* to obtain $\alpha\leq\beta$.
d. Let $\alpha\leq\beta$. It follows from *dominance* that $\alpha\&\delta\leq\alpha$, and then from *transitivity* that $\alpha\&\delta\leq\beta$.
e. Let $\alpha\leq\beta$. It follows from *dominance* that $\alpha\&\delta\leq\alpha$ and $\beta\leq\beta\vee\varepsilon$. We can apply *transitivity* to $\alpha\&\delta\leq\alpha\leq\beta\leq\beta\vee\varepsilon$ and obtain $\alpha\&\delta\leq\beta\vee\varepsilon$.
f. By *conjunctiveness*, either $\alpha\leq\alpha\&\beta$ or $\beta\leq\alpha\&\beta$. In the first case, we can apply *transitivity* to $\delta\leq\alpha$ and $\alpha\leq\alpha\&\beta$ and obtain $\delta\leq\alpha\&\beta$. In the second case, we instead apply *transitivity* to $\delta\leq\beta$ and $\beta\leq\alpha\&\beta$, obtaining $\delta\leq\alpha\&\beta$ in this case as well.
g. Suppose to the contrary that $\alpha\leq\beta$ and $\neg(\alpha\&\delta\leq\beta\&\delta)$. From *connectivity* (Observation 2.48) we obtain $\beta\&\delta<\alpha\&\delta$. Due to *conjunctiveness*, either $\beta\leq\beta\&\delta$ or $\delta\leq\beta\&\delta$.

If $\beta\leq\beta\&\delta$, then we can apply *transitivity* and Observation 2.75 to $\alpha\leq\beta\leq\beta\&\delta<\alpha\&\delta$ and obtain $\alpha<\alpha\&\delta$ and thus $\neg(\alpha\&\delta\leq\alpha)$, contrary to *dominance*. If $\delta\leq\beta\&\delta$, then we can apply *transitivity* and Observation 2.75 to $\delta\leq\beta\&\delta<\alpha\&\delta$ and obtain $\delta<\alpha\&\delta$ and thus $\neg(\alpha\&\delta\leq\delta)$, again contrary to *dominance*. These contradictions conclude the proof.

129. a. Let $\alpha<\beta$. By *dominance*, $\alpha\&\beta\leq\alpha$. Applying *transitivity* (and Observation 2.75) we obtain $\alpha\&\beta<\beta$.
b. Let $\alpha<\beta$. It follows from *dominance* that $\alpha\&\delta\leq\alpha$. We can apply *transitivity* and Observation 2.75 to $\alpha\&\delta\leq\alpha<\beta$ and obtain $\alpha\&\delta<\beta$.
c. Let $\alpha<\beta$. It follows from *dominance* that $\beta\leq\beta\vee\delta$. We can apply *transitivity* and Observation 2.75 to $\alpha<\beta\leq\beta\vee\delta$ and obtain $\alpha<\beta\vee\delta$.
d. Let $\alpha<\beta$.It follows from *dominance* that $\alpha\&\delta\leq\alpha$ and $\beta\leq\beta\vee\varepsilon$. We can apply *transitivity* and Observation 2.75 to $\alpha\&\delta\leq\alpha<\beta\leq\beta\vee\varepsilon$ and obtain $\alpha\&\delta<\beta\vee\varepsilon$.
e. Let $\alpha\&\beta<\beta$. By *conjunctiveness*, either $\alpha\leq\alpha\&\beta$ or $\beta\leq\alpha\&\beta$. However, $\beta\leq\alpha\&\beta$ cannot hold, since $\alpha\&\beta<\beta$. Thus, $\alpha\leq\alpha\&\beta$. It follows from this and $\alpha\&\beta<\beta$, by *transitivity* and Observation 2.75, that $\alpha<\beta$.
f. It follows by *dominance* from $\beta\&\delta\vdash\alpha$ that $\beta\&\delta\leq\alpha$. By *transitivity* and Observation 2.75, $\beta\&\delta\leq\alpha$ and $\alpha<\beta$ yield $\beta\&\delta<\beta$.

It follows from conjunctiveness that either $\beta\leq\beta\&\delta$ or $\delta\leq\beta\&\delta$. Since we have just shown that $\beta\&\delta<\beta$, we can conclude that $\delta\leq\beta\&\delta$. It follows from $\delta\leq\beta\&\delta$ and $\beta\&\delta<\beta$, again with the help of *transitivity* and Observation 2.75, that $\delta<\beta$.
g. Let $\beta\&\delta<\alpha$. Suppose, to the contrary, that $\neg(\beta<\alpha)$ and $\neg(\delta<\alpha)$. From *connectivity* (Observation 2.48) we obtain $\alpha\leq\beta$ and $\alpha\leq\delta$. Due to *conjunctiveness*, either $\beta\leq\beta\&\delta$ or $\delta\leq\beta\&\delta$. In the first case, we can apply *transitivity* to $\alpha\leq\beta\leq\beta\&\delta$ to obtain $\alpha\leq\beta\&\delta$. In the second case, we can apply *transitivity* to $\alpha\leq\delta\leq\beta\&\delta$ to obtain $\alpha\leq\beta\&\delta$. Since $\alpha\leq\beta\&\delta$ contradicts $\beta\&\delta<\alpha$, we are done.

h. Let $\alpha\&\delta<\beta\&\delta$. By *conjunctiveness*, either $\alpha\leq\alpha\&\delta$ or $\delta\leq\alpha\&\delta$. Suppose that $\delta\leq\alpha\&\delta$. We then have $\delta\leq\alpha\&\delta$, $\alpha\&\delta<\beta\&\delta$, and (by *dominance*) $\beta\&\delta\leq\delta$. It follows by *transitivity* and Observation 2.75 that $\delta<\delta$, which is impossible. Thus not $\delta\leq\alpha\&\delta$, thus $\alpha\leq\alpha\&\delta$.

We thus have $\alpha\leq\alpha\&\delta$, $\alpha\&\delta<\beta\&\delta$, and (by *dominance*) $\beta\&\delta\leq\beta$. Again using *transitivity* and Observation 2.75 we obtain $\alpha<\beta$.

i. Let $\alpha<\beta$ and $\delta<\varepsilon$. It follows from *conjunctiveness* that either $\beta\leq\beta\&\varepsilon$ or $\varepsilon\leq\beta\&\varepsilon$.

If $\beta\leq\beta\&\varepsilon$, then we have $\alpha\&\delta\leq\alpha$ (by *dominance*), $\alpha<\beta$, and $\beta\leq\beta\&\varepsilon$. It follows by *transitivity* and Observation 2.75 that $\alpha\&\delta<\beta\&\varepsilon$.

If $\varepsilon\leq\beta\&\varepsilon$, then we can in the same way obtain $\alpha\&\delta\leq\delta$, $\delta<\varepsilon$, and $\varepsilon\leq\beta\&\varepsilon$. Again, we obtain $\alpha\&\delta<\beta\&\varepsilon$.

j. For one direction, let $\neg\alpha < \alpha\rightarrow\beta$. It follows from *conjunctiveness* and intersubstitutivity (Observation 2.92) that either $\alpha\rightarrow\neg\beta\leq\neg\alpha$ or $\alpha\rightarrow\beta\leq\neg\alpha$. The latter cannot hold, since $\neg\alpha < \alpha\rightarrow\beta$. Thus, $\alpha\rightarrow\neg\beta\leq\neg\alpha$. It follows by *transitivity* and Observation 2.75 that $\alpha\rightarrow\neg\beta < \alpha\rightarrow\beta$.

For the other direction, let $\alpha\rightarrow\neg\beta < \alpha\rightarrow\beta$. It follows from *dominance* that $\neg\alpha\leq\alpha\rightarrow\neg\beta$. We can use *transitivity* and Observation 2.75 to obtain $\neg\alpha < \alpha\rightarrow\beta$. This concludes the proof.

130. Since $\vdash\alpha$, it holds for all sentences δ that $\delta\vdash\alpha$ and (due to *dominance*) that $\delta\leq\alpha$. We can use *transitivity* to conclude that $\delta\leq\beta$ for all δ, and then *maximality* to conclude that $\vdash\beta$.

131. It follows from *connectivity* that $\alpha\leq\alpha$. It also follows from *connectivity* that either $\alpha\leq\beta$ or $\beta\leq\alpha$.

If $\alpha\leq\beta$, then we have $\alpha\leq\alpha$ and $\alpha\leq\beta$, and the condition given in the exercise can be used to derive $\alpha\leq\alpha\&\beta$.

If $\beta\leq\alpha$, then $\beta\leq\alpha\&\beta$ follows in the same way.

132. a. To be a hierarchy, $<$ must satisfy *acyclicity* and *intersubstitutivity*. The latter follows from Observation 2.92. For *acyclicity*, suppose that $\alpha_1<...<\alpha_n$. It follows from transitivity that $\alpha_1\leq\alpha_n$, and from this that $\alpha_n<\alpha_1$ does not hold.

b. Let $\alpha<\beta$ and $\beta\vdash\delta$. It follows from *dominance* that $\beta\leq\delta$ and from *transitivity* and Observation 2.75 that $\alpha<\delta$.

c. Let $\alpha\vdash\beta$ and $\beta<\delta$. It follows from *dominance* that $\alpha\leq\beta$ and from *transitivity* and Observation 2.75 that $\alpha<\delta$.

d. This can be shown by proving that if the right-hand side of the implication does not hold, then neither does the left-hand side. Suppose that neither $\alpha<\delta$ nor $\delta<\beta$. Then by *connectivity* (Observation 2.48), $\delta\leq\alpha$ and $\beta\leq\delta$. By *transitivity*, $\beta\leq\alpha$, and thus not $\alpha<\beta$.

133. a. EE1: Since $\top\vdash\top$ it follows from dominance that $\top\leq\top$, hence $\neg(\top<\top)$. EE2↑, EE2↓, EE3↑, and EE3↓: See Exercise 132, parts b and c, and Exercise 129, parts i and e.

b. *Dominance*: Suppose to the contrary that there are sentences α and β such that $\alpha\vdash\beta$ and $\neg(\alpha\leq\beta)$. We then have $\beta<\alpha$, and EE2↑ yields $\alpha<\alpha$.

It can be shown, however, that $\alpha<\alpha$ does not hold. Suppose for contradiction that $\alpha<\alpha$. Since $\top\&\alpha\vdash\alpha$, we can then use EE2↓ to obtain $\top\&\alpha<\alpha$, and EE3↓ yields $\top<\alpha$. Since $\alpha\vdash\top$, we can use EE2↑ to obtain $\top<\top$, contrary to EE1. This contradiction concludes the proof.

Conjunctiveness. Suppose to the contrary that $\neg(\alpha\leq\alpha\&\beta)$ and $\neg(\beta\leq\alpha\&\beta)$. Then $\alpha\&\beta<\alpha$ and $\alpha\&\beta<\beta$. We can use EE3↑ to obtain $\alpha\&\beta<\alpha\&\beta$, contrary to the irreflexivity of < (that was shown in Part *a* of this exercise).

c. EE↑ implies EE2↑: Let $B = \{\beta\}$.

EE↑ implies EE3↑: $B = \{\beta,\delta\}$

EE2↑ and EE3↑ imply EE↑: Let α and B be such that $\alpha<\beta$ for all $\beta\in B$, and let $B\vdash\delta$. It follows from compactness that there is a finite subset $\{\beta_1,...\beta_n\}$ of B such that $\{\beta_1,...\beta_n\}\vdash\delta$. Repeated application of EE3↑ yields $\alpha<\beta_1\&...\&\beta_n$. We can use EE2↑ to obtain $\alpha<\delta$.

d. EE↓ implies EE2↓: If $\alpha\vdash\beta$, then $\{\alpha,\delta\}\vdash\beta$. The conclusion follows directly.

EE↓ implies EE3↓: Let $\alpha\&\beta<\beta$. Clearly, $\{\alpha,\beta\}\vdash\alpha\&\beta$. We can apply EE↓ to $\{\alpha,\beta\}\vdash\alpha\&\beta$ and $\alpha\&\beta<\beta$, and obtain $\alpha<\beta$.

EE2↓ and EE3↓ imply EE↓: Let $\{\alpha,\delta\}\vdash\beta$ and $\beta<\delta$. Since $\delta\&(\delta\rightarrow\beta)\vdash\beta$ and $\beta<\delta$, we can use EE2↓ to obtain $\delta\&(\delta\rightarrow\beta)<\delta$, and then EE3↓ to obtain $\delta\rightarrow\beta<\delta$. It follows from $\{\alpha,\delta\}\vdash\beta$ that $\alpha\vdash\delta\rightarrow\beta$. We therefore have $\alpha\vdash\delta\rightarrow\beta$ and $\delta\rightarrow\beta<\delta$, and EE2↓ yields $\alpha<\delta$.

134. For one direction, let $\alpha\in A$. It follows from *minimality* that there is some β such that $\alpha\leq\beta$ does not hold. Thus, by *connectivity* (Observation 2.48), $\beta<\alpha$, so that $\alpha\in\{\delta \mid \beta<\delta \text{ for some } \beta\}$.

For the other direction, let $\alpha\notin A$. It follows from *minimality* that $\alpha\leq\beta$ for all β, thus there is no β such that $\beta<\alpha$, thus $\alpha\notin\{\delta \mid \beta<\delta \text{ for some } \beta\}$.

135. $\alpha<\beta$ iff $\alpha\leq\beta$ and not $\beta\leq\alpha$

iff ($\alpha\notin A+(\alpha\&\beta)$ or $\vdash\alpha\&\beta$) and not ($\beta\notin A+(\alpha\&\beta)$ or $\vdash\alpha\&\beta$)

iff ($\alpha\notin A+(\alpha\&\beta)$ or $\vdash\alpha\&\beta$) and $\beta\in A+(\alpha\&\beta)$ and $\nvdash\alpha\&\beta$

iff $\alpha\notin A+(\alpha\&\beta)$ and $\beta\in A+(\alpha\&\beta)$ and $\nvdash\alpha\&\beta$

It follows by *closure* from $\alpha\notin A+(\alpha\&\beta)$ that $\nvdash\alpha$ and consequently $\nvdash\alpha\&\beta$. We can continue:

iff $\alpha\notin A+(\alpha\&\beta)$ and $\beta\in A+(\alpha\&\beta)$

136. *Success*: Let $\nvdash\alpha$. We need to show that $\alpha \notin A{+}\alpha$. It follows by *dominance* that $\neg(\alpha<\alpha)$. It follows from this and $\nvdash\alpha$, by (R+), that $\alpha \notin A{+}\alpha$.

Extensionality: Let $\alpha\leftrightarrow\beta \in \mathrm{Cn}(\varnothing)$. We are first going to show that $A{+}\alpha \subseteq A{+}\beta$.

Let $\delta \in A{+}\alpha$. Then, by (R+), $\delta \in A$ and either $\alpha<\delta$ or $\vdash \alpha$. According to *intersubstitutivity* (Observation 2.92), $\alpha<\delta$ holds if and only if $\beta<\delta$.

We have shown that $\delta \in A$ and that either $\beta<\delta$ or $\vdash \alpha$. Again using (R+), we can conclude that $\delta \in A{+}\beta$.

Thus, $A{+}\alpha \subseteq A{+}\beta$. We can prove $A{+}\beta \subseteq A{+}\alpha$ in the same way, and conclude that $A{+}\alpha = A{+}\beta$.

Conjunctive overlap: Let $\delta \in (A{+}\alpha)\cap(A{+}\beta)$. There are two cases:

Case 1, $\vdash\alpha$: Then $\beta\leftrightarrow\alpha\&\beta \in \mathrm{Cn}(\varnothing)$. It follows by *extensionality*, that we have already proved, that $A{+}(\alpha\&\beta) = A{+}\beta$, and thus $\delta \in A{+}(\alpha\&\beta)$, as desired.

Case 2, $\nvdash\alpha$: It follows from *dominance* that $\alpha\&\beta\leq\alpha$. Furthermore, it follows from $\delta\in A{+}\alpha$ that $\alpha<\delta$. We can conclude, using *transitivity* and Observation 2.75, that $\alpha\&\beta<\delta$.

It follows by (R+) from $\delta\in A{+}\alpha$ that $\delta \in A$. We can conclude from $\delta \in A$ and $\alpha\&\beta<\delta$ that $\delta \in A{+}(\alpha\&\beta)$.

Conjunctive inclusion: Let $\alpha \notin A{+}(\alpha\&\beta)$. We have to show that $A{+}(\alpha\&\beta) \subseteq A{+}\alpha$.

Let $\delta \notin A{+}\alpha$. We are going to show that $\delta \notin A{+}(\alpha\&\beta)$. This follows by *inclusion* if $\delta \notin A$, so we may assume that $\delta \in A$.

Using (R+), we can conclude from $\delta \notin A{+}\alpha$ and $\delta \in A$ that $\neg(\alpha<\delta)$ and $\alpha \notin \mathrm{Cn}(\varnothing)$. By *connectivity* (Observation 2.48), $\delta\leq\alpha$.

Since $\alpha \notin A{+}(\alpha\&\beta)$ and $\alpha \in A$ it follows from (R+) that $\neg(\alpha\&\beta<\alpha)$. *Connectivity* yields $\alpha\leq\alpha\&\beta$.

We can now apply *transitivity* to $\delta\leq\alpha$ and $\alpha\leq\alpha\&\beta$ and obtain $\delta\leq\alpha\&\beta$, and thus $\neg(\alpha\&\beta<\delta)$. Since it follows from $\nvdash\alpha$ that $\nvdash\alpha\&\beta$, we can use (R+) to conclude that $\delta \notin A{+}(\alpha\&\beta)$, as desired.

137. a. Let $E(+) = \leq$ and $C(E(+)) = +'$. It follows from Part 1 of Theorem 2.50 that + is a standard entrenchment ordering and from Part 2 of the same Theorem that +' satisfies the eight postulates. We have:

$\beta \in A{+}'\alpha$ iff $\beta \in A$ and either $\vdash\alpha$ or $\alpha<\alpha\vee\beta$

iff $\beta \in A$ and either $\vdash\alpha$ or $((\alpha \notin A{+}\alpha)\&(\alpha\vee\beta \in A{+}\alpha))$ (Exercise 135)

iff $\beta \in A$ and either $\vdash\alpha$ or $\alpha\vee\beta \in A{+}\alpha$ (*success*)

iff $\beta \in A$ and either $\vdash\alpha$ or $\beta \in A{+}\alpha$ (Exercise 65)

iff $\beta \in A{+}\alpha$

b. Let $C(\leq) = +$ and $E(C\leq)) = \leq'$.

$\alpha\leq'\beta$ iff $\vdash\alpha\&\beta$ or $\alpha \notin A{+}(\alpha\&\beta)$

iff $\vdash\alpha\&\beta$ or not ($\alpha \in A$ and either $(\alpha\&\beta)<((\alpha\&\beta)\vee\alpha)$ or $\vdash(\alpha\&\beta)$)

iff $\vdash\alpha\&\beta$ or $\alpha \notin A$ or (not $(\alpha\&\beta)<((\alpha\&\beta)\vee\alpha)$ and $\nvdash(\alpha\&\beta)$)
iff $\vdash\alpha\&\beta$ or $\alpha \notin A$ or ($\alpha\leq(\alpha\&\beta)$ and $\nvdash(\alpha\&\beta)$)
iff $\vdash\alpha\&\beta$ or $\alpha \notin A$ or ($\alpha\leq\beta$ and $\nvdash(\alpha\&\beta)$) (Exercise 128, Part *c*)
(Due to *dominance*, $\vdash\alpha\&\beta$ implies $\alpha\leq\beta$. Due to *minimality*, $\alpha \notin A$ implies $\alpha\leq\beta$. Hence:)
iff $\alpha\leq\beta$

138. a. $\min(N(\alpha),N(\neg\alpha)) = N(\alpha\&\neg\alpha)$ (N2)
$= N(\perp)$ (N3)
$= 0$ (N1)
b. $N(\alpha\vee\beta) \geq \min(N(\alpha\vee\beta),N(\alpha\vee\neg\beta))$
$= N((\alpha\vee\beta)\&(\alpha\vee\neg\beta))$ (N2)
$= N(\alpha)$ (N3)
In the same way, we can obtain $N(\alpha\vee\beta) \geq N(\alpha)$. Since $\max(N(\alpha),N(\beta))$ is either $N(\alpha)$ or $N(\beta)$, it follows that $N(\alpha\vee\beta) \geq \max(N(\alpha),N(\beta))$.
c. Let $\alpha\vdash\beta$. Then:
$N(\alpha) = N(\alpha\&\beta)$ (N3)
$\leq \max(N(\alpha\&\beta),N(\neg\alpha\&\beta))$
$\leq N((\alpha\&\beta)\vee(\neg\alpha\&\beta))$ (Part *b* of this Exercise)
$= N(\beta)$ (N3)
d. Let $\beta \in \mathrm{Cn}(\{\alpha \mid N(\alpha)>0\})$. Then, due to compactness, there is some finite subset A of $\{\alpha \mid N(\alpha)>0\}$ such that $\beta \in \mathrm{Cn}(A)$ and consequently $\beta \in \mathrm{Cn}(\{\&A\})$. It follows from repeated use of (N2) that $N(\&A)>0$. We can use Part *c* of the present exercise to obtain $N(\beta)\geq N(\&A)$, and hence $N(\beta)>0$.
e. *Transitivity*: Immediate.
Dominance: See Part *c* of the present exercise.
Conjunctiveness: Immediate from (N2).
Minimality:
$\alpha \notin \{\alpha \mid N(\alpha)>0\}$ iff $N(\alpha)=0$
iff $N(\alpha)\leq N(\beta)$ for all β
iff $\alpha\leq\beta$ for all β

SOLUTIONS FOR CHAPTER 3^+

139. a. $A\ddagger_\gamma\neg q$
$= \cap\gamma(A\bot q)\cup\{\neg q\}$
$= \cap\gamma(\{\{p\},\{p\rightarrow q\}\})\cup\{\neg q\}$
$= \cap(\{\{p\},\{p\rightarrow q\}\})\cup\{\neg q\}$
$= (\{p\}\cap\{p\rightarrow q\})\cup\{\neg q\}$
$= \{\neg q\}$.
b. $A\ddagger_\gamma(\neg p\vee\neg q)$
$= \cap\gamma(A\bot(p\&q))\cup\{\neg p\vee\neg q\}$
$= \cap\gamma(\{\{p\},\{p\rightarrow q,q\}\})\cup\{\neg p\vee\neg q\}$
$= \cap(\{\{p\rightarrow q,q\}\})\cup\{\neg p\vee\neg q\}$
$= \{p\rightarrow q,q\}\cup\{\neg p\vee\neg q\}$
$= \{p\rightarrow q,q,\neg p\vee\neg q\}$.
c. $A\ddagger_\gamma(\neg p\&\neg q)$
$= \cap\gamma(A\bot(p\vee q))\cup\{\neg p\&\neg q\}$
$= \cap\gamma(\{\{p\rightarrow q\}\})\cup\{\neg p\&\neg q\}$
$= \cap(\{\{p\rightarrow q\}\})\cup\{\neg p\&\neg q\}$
$= \{p\rightarrow q\}\cup\{\neg p\&\neg q\}$
$= \{p\rightarrow q,\neg p\&\neg q\}$.
d. $A\ddagger_\gamma(q\rightarrow p)$
$= \cap\gamma(A\bot(q\&\neg p))\cup\{q\rightarrow p\}$
$= \cap\gamma(\{A\})\cup\{q\rightarrow p\}$
$= \{A\}\cup\{q\rightarrow p\}$
$= \{p,p\rightarrow q,q\}\cup\{q\rightarrow p\}$
$= \{p,p\rightarrow q,q,q\rightarrow p\}$.

140. There are four subsets of A, namely A itself, $\emptyset$, $\{\neg p\}$ and $\{q\}$. Two of these, namely $\emptyset$ and $\{q\}$, retain consistency if p is added, and the same two retain consistency if $p\&r$ is added. It therefore follows from *uniformity* (that holds according to Theorem 3.6) that $A\cap(A\ddagger_\gamma p) = A\cap(A\ddagger_\gamma(p\&r))$.

141. a. Suppose that α is consistent. Then $\neg\alpha$ is not a tautology, and it follows (from the postulate of *contraction–success*) that $\neg\alpha \notin \mathrm{Cn}(A\sim_\gamma\neg\alpha)$. Since $\alpha\rightarrow\neg\alpha$ is logically equivalent with $\neg\alpha$, we have $\alpha\rightarrow\neg\alpha \notin \mathrm{Cn}(A\sim_\gamma\neg\alpha)$. It follows by the deduction property that $\neg\alpha \notin \mathrm{Cn}((A\sim_\gamma\neg\alpha)\cup\{\alpha\})$, i.e., $\neg\alpha \notin A\ddagger_\gamma\alpha$.
b. It follows from $A\sim_\gamma\neg\alpha \subseteq A$ that $(A\sim_\gamma\neg\alpha)\cup\{\alpha\} \subseteq A\cup\{\alpha\}$, i.e., $A\ddagger_\gamma\alpha \subseteq A\cup\{\alpha\}$.
c. $\alpha \in (A\sim_\gamma\neg\alpha)\cup\{\alpha\} = A\ddagger_\gamma\alpha$ follows directly from the definition.

d. Suppose that it holds for all $A' \subseteq A$ that $A' \cup \{\alpha\}$ is inconsistent if and only if $A' \cup \{\beta\}$ is inconsistent. $A' \cup \{\alpha\}$ is inconsistent if and only if $A' \vdash \neg\alpha$. Similarly, $A' \cup \{\beta\}$ is inconsistent if and only if $A' \vdash \neg\beta$. It therefore holds for all $A' \subseteq A$ that $A' \vdash \neg\alpha$ if and only if $A' \vdash \neg\beta$. It follows from Observation 1.39 that $A \bot \neg\alpha = A \bot \neg\beta$. From this we can conclude that $\cap\gamma(A \bot \neg\alpha) = \cap\gamma(A \bot \neg\beta)$, i.e., $A \sim_\gamma \neg\alpha = A \sim_\gamma \neg\beta$. By the Harper identity (Observation 3.11), this is equivalent to $A \cap (A \mp_\gamma \alpha) = A \cap (A \mp_\gamma \beta)$.

142. No. Internal partial meet revision satisfies *consistency*. It follows from *consistency* that if α is consistent and A is inconsistent, then $A * \alpha$ is consistent, and thus $A * \alpha \neq A$.

143. We will do this by showing that $A * \alpha * \neg\alpha \neq A * \neg\alpha * \alpha$, where α is a sentence such that neither α nor $\neg\alpha$ is inconsistent. It follows from *success* that $\neg\alpha \in A * \alpha * \neg\alpha$, and then from *consistency* that $\alpha \notin A * \alpha * \neg\alpha$. It follows from *success* that $\alpha \in A * \neg\alpha * \alpha$.

144. a. $\{p,q\} \mp \neg p$
$= \cap(\{p,q\} \bot p) \cup \{\neg p\}$
$= \cap\{\{q\}\} \cup \{\neg p\}$
$= \{q\} \cup \{\neg p\}$
$= \{\neg p, q\}$
b. $\{p,q\} \mp (\neg p \vee \neg q)$
$= \cap(\{p,q\} \bot (p \& q)) \cup \{\neg p \vee \neg q\}$
$= \cap\{\{p\}, \{q\}\} \cup \{\neg p \vee \neg q\}$
$= \varnothing \cup \{\neg p \vee \neg q\}$
$= \{\neg p \vee \neg q\}$
c. $\{p,q,p \rightarrow q\} \mp (p \& \neg q)$
$= \cap(\{p,q,p \rightarrow q\} \bot (\neg p \vee q)) \cup \{p \& \neg q\}$
$= \cap\{\{p\}\} \cup \{p \& \neg q\}$
$= \{p\} \cup \{p \& \neg q\}$
$= \{p, p \& \neg q\}$
d. $\{p \rightarrow q, q \rightarrow p\} \mp (p \leftrightarrow \neg q)$
$= \cap(\{p \rightarrow q, q \rightarrow p\} \bot (p \leftrightarrow q)) \cup \{p \leftrightarrow \neg q\}$
$= \cap\{\{p \rightarrow q\}, \{q \rightarrow p\}\} \cup \{p \leftrightarrow \neg q\}$
$= \varnothing \cup \{p \leftrightarrow \neg q\}$
$= \{p \leftrightarrow \neg q\}$.

145. Let * be internal full meet revision. Then $\{p,q\} * (\neg p \vee \neg q) = \{\neg p \vee \neg q\}$. Thus, *tenacity* is not satisfied. (To see this, note that $p \in \{p,q\}$, $p \notin \{\neg p \vee \neg q\}$ and $\neg p \notin Cn(\{\neg p \vee \neg q\})$.) It follows from Theorem 3.33 that * is not internal maxichoice revision.

146. *Case 1*, α is consistent: Then $\neg\alpha$ is not a tautology, and thus $A\bot\neg\alpha$ is non-empty. It follows that $\varnothing \neq \gamma(A\bot\neg\alpha) \subseteq A\bot\neg\alpha$, and thus $\cap(A\bot\neg\alpha) \subseteq \cap\gamma(A\bot\neg\alpha)$. We can conclude that $(\cap(A\bot\neg\alpha))\cup\{\alpha\} \subseteq (\cap\gamma(A\bot\neg\alpha))\cup\{\alpha\}$, i.e., $A\ddagger\alpha \subseteq A\ddagger_\gamma\alpha$.

Case 2, α is inconsistent: Then $\neg\alpha$ is a tautology, and thus $A\bot\neg\alpha$ is empty. It follows that $A\sim\neg\alpha = A\sim_\gamma\neg\alpha = A$, and thus $(A\sim\neg\alpha)\cup\{\alpha\} = (A\sim_\gamma\neg\alpha)\cup\{\alpha\}$, i.e., $A\ddagger\alpha = A\ddagger_\gamma\alpha$.

147. *For one direction*, let $\varepsilon \in A+\alpha\ddagger\alpha$. Suppose that $\varepsilon \notin A\ddagger\alpha$. Then ε is not identical to α, and we can conclude from $\varepsilon \in A+\alpha\ddagger\alpha$ that $\varepsilon \in A$. It follows from $\varepsilon \notin A\ddagger\alpha$ that $\varepsilon \notin A\sim\neg\alpha$, i.e., $\varepsilon \notin \cap(A\bot\neg\alpha)$. There must be some X such that $\varepsilon \notin X \in A\bot\neg\alpha$.

We can use Observation 1.41 to obtain $X\cup\{\alpha\} \in (A\cup\{\alpha\})\bot\neg\alpha$. Since ε is not identical to α, and $\varepsilon \notin X$, we have $\varepsilon \notin X\cup\{\alpha\} \in (A\cup\{\alpha\})\bot\neg\alpha$, from which follows that $\varepsilon \notin \cap((A\cup\{\alpha\})\bot\neg\alpha)$, i.e., $\varepsilon \notin \cap((A+\alpha)\bot\neg\alpha)$. Again using the fact that ε is not identical to α, we obtain $\varepsilon \notin (\cap((A+\alpha)\bot\neg\alpha))\cup\{\alpha\}$, i.e., $\varepsilon \notin A+\alpha\ddagger\alpha$. We can conclude from this contradiction that $\varepsilon \in A\ddagger\alpha$. This finishes our proof that $A+\alpha\ddagger\alpha \subseteq A\ddagger\alpha$.

For the other direction, let $\varepsilon \in A\ddagger\alpha$. We are going to show that $\varepsilon \in A+\alpha\ddagger\alpha$. This follows directly if ε is identical to α. It remains to prove the principal case in which $\varepsilon \in (A\ddagger\alpha)\backslash\{\alpha\}$. It follows from $\varepsilon \in (A\ddagger\alpha)\backslash\{\alpha\}$ that $\varepsilon \in \cap(A\bot\neg\alpha)$.

Let $X \in (A\cup\{\alpha\})\bot\neg\alpha$. If $\alpha \in A$, then $X \in A\bot\neg\alpha$, and it follows directly from $\varepsilon \in \cap(A\bot\neg\alpha)$ that $\varepsilon \in X$. If $\alpha \notin A$, then it follows from Observation 1.41 that $X\backslash\{\alpha\} \in A\bot\neg\alpha$, so that we can conclude from $\varepsilon \in \cap(A\bot\neg\alpha)$ that $\varepsilon \in X\backslash\{\alpha\}$ and consequently $\varepsilon \in X$. Thus in both cases, $\varepsilon \in X$.

Since $\varepsilon \in X$ for all $X \in (A\cup\{\alpha\})\bot\neg\alpha$, we have $\varepsilon \in \cap((A\cup\{\alpha\})\bot\neg\alpha)$ and consequently $\varepsilon \in (\cap((A\cup\{\alpha\})\bot\neg\alpha))\cup\{\alpha\}$, i.e., $\varepsilon \in A+\alpha\ddagger\alpha$. This concludes the proof that $A\ddagger\alpha \subseteq A+\alpha\ddagger\alpha$.

148. Let p and q be two logically independent sentences of the language, and let $A = \{\neg p\&q\}$. Then $A\bot\neg p = \{\varnothing\}$, and consequently it holds for all selection functions γ for A that $A\sim_\gamma\neg p = \varnothing$, and thus $A\ddagger_\gamma p = \{p\}$.We then have $q \in \mathrm{Cn}(A)$, but neither $q \in \mathrm{Cn}(A\ddagger_\gamma p)$ nor $\neg q \in \mathrm{Cn}(A\ddagger_\gamma p)$.

149. a. $\{p,q\rightarrow p\}\pm_\gamma\neg p$
$= \cap\gamma(\{p,q\rightarrow p,\neg p\}\bot p)$
$= \cap\gamma\{\{q\rightarrow p,\neg p\}\}$
$= \cap\{\{q\rightarrow p,\neg p\}\}$
$= \{q\rightarrow p,\neg p\}$.
b. $\{p,q\rightarrow r,\neg q\rightarrow r\}\pm_\gamma(\neg p\vee\neg r)$

$= \cap\gamma(\{p,q\rightarrow r,\neg q\rightarrow r,\neg p\vee\neg r\}\perp(p\&r))$
$= \cap\gamma(\{\{p,\neg q\rightarrow r,\neg p\vee\neg r\},\{p,q\rightarrow r,\neg p\vee\neg r\},\{q\rightarrow r,\neg q\rightarrow r,\neg p\vee\neg r\}\}$
$= \cap\{\{p,\neg q\rightarrow r,\neg p\vee\neg r\},\{p,q\rightarrow r,\neg p\vee\neg r\},\{q\rightarrow r,\neg q\rightarrow r,\neg p\vee\neg r\}\} =$
$= \{\neg p\vee\neg r\}$
c. $\{p,q,q\&r\}\pm_\gamma(p\&q)$
$= \cap\gamma(\{p,q,q\&r,p\&q\}\perp(\neg p\vee\neg q))$
$= \cap\gamma(\{\{p,q,q\&r,p\&q\}\})$
$= \cap\{\{p,q,q\&r,p\&q\}\}$
$= \{p,q,q\&r,p\&q\}$
d. $\{p,q,q\&r\}\pm_\gamma\neg(p\&q)$
$= \cap\gamma(\{p,q,q\&r,\neg(p\&q)\})\perp(p\&q))$
$= \cap\gamma(\{\{p,\neg(p\&q)\},\{q,q\&r,\neg(p\&q)\}\})$
$= \cap(\{\{q,q\&r,\neg(p\&q)\}\})$
$= \{q,q\&r,\neg(p\&q)\}$

150. *Consistency*: If α is consistent, then $\neg\alpha$ is not a tautology, and thus (by *contraction-success*) $(A+\alpha)\sim_\gamma\neg\alpha \nvdash \neg\alpha$, i.e., $A\pm_\gamma\alpha \nvdash \neg\alpha$.

Inclusion: It follows from *contraction-inclusion* that $(A+\alpha)\sim_\gamma\neg\alpha \subseteq A+\alpha$, i.e., $A\pm_\gamma\alpha \subseteq A+\alpha$.

Success: Suppose to the contrary that $\alpha \notin A\pm_\gamma\alpha$, i.e., $\alpha \notin (A+\alpha)\sim_\gamma\neg\alpha$ There is then some $X \in \gamma((A+\alpha)\perp\neg\alpha)$ such that $\alpha \notin X$. This is impossible according to Observation 3.30.

Pre-expansion: It follows from $A\cup\{\alpha\}\cup\{\alpha\} = A\cup\{\alpha\}$ that $(A\cup\{\alpha\}\cup\{\alpha\})\sim_\gamma\neg\alpha = (A\cup\{\alpha\})\sim_\gamma\neg\alpha$, i.e.,
$((A+\alpha)+\alpha)\sim_\gamma\neg\alpha = (A+\alpha)\sim_\gamma\neg\alpha$, i.e.,
$(A+\alpha)\pm_\gamma\alpha = A\pm_\gamma\alpha$.

151. If $\alpha \in A$, then it follows from Observation 3.30 that $\alpha \in A\sim_\gamma\neg\alpha$. Therefore, $A\pm_\gamma\alpha = (A\cup\{\alpha\})\sim_\gamma\neg\alpha = A\sim_\gamma\neg\alpha = (A\sim_\gamma\neg\alpha)\cup\{\alpha\} = A\mp_\gamma\alpha$.

152. Let $A\perp\neg\alpha = \{X\}$. It follows that $A\sim_\gamma\neg\alpha = X$ and consequently $A\mp_\gamma\alpha = X\cup\{\alpha\}$.

It follows from Observation 1.41 that $\{X\cup\{\alpha\}\} = (A\cup\{\alpha\})\perp\neg\alpha$, and consequently $A\pm_\gamma\alpha = X\cup\{\alpha\}$.

153. Let p and q be logically independent sentences, and let γ be a maxichoice selection function such that:
$\gamma(\{\{p\vee q,\neg p\},\{p\vee\neg q,\neg p\}\}) = \{\{p\vee q,\neg p\}\}$
$\gamma(\{\{p\vee q,\neg p\&\neg r\},\{p\vee\neg q,\neg p\&\neg r\}\}) = \{\{p\vee\neg q,\neg p\&\neg r\}\}$
Then:
$\{p\vee q,p\vee\neg q\}\pm_\gamma\neg p = \{p\vee q,\neg p\}$
$\{p\vee q,p\vee\neg q\}\pm_\gamma(\neg p\&\neg r) = \{p\vee\neg q,\neg p\&\neg r\}$

Since every subset of $\{p \vee q, p \vee \neg q\}$ is inconsistent with $\neg p$ if and only if it is inconsistent with $\neg p \& \neg r$, this shows that uniformity is not satisfied.

154. Let $A = \{\neg p \vee r, \neg p \vee \neg r\}$ and let γ be a two-place selection function that is based on a relation $\sqsubseteq$ such that:

$\{\neg p \vee r\} \sqsubset \{\neg p \vee \neg r\} \sqsubset \{p, \neg p \vee \neg r\} \sqsubset \{p, \neg p \vee r\}$.

This is compatible with γ being maxichoice and with $\sqsubseteq$ being maximizing and transitive. Then:

$$A \mp_\gamma p = (\cap\gamma(A \perp \neg p)) \cup \{p\}$$
$$= (\cap\gamma(\{\{\neg p \vee r\}, \{\neg p \vee \neg r\}\})) \cup \{p\}$$
$$= \{\neg p \vee \neg r\} \cup \{p\}$$
$$= \{\neg p \vee \neg r, p\}$$

and:

$$A \pm_\gamma p = \cap\gamma((A \cup \{p\}) \perp \neg p)$$
$$= \cap\gamma(\{\{p, \neg p \vee \neg r\}, \{p, \neg p \vee r\}\})$$
$$= \{p, \neg p \vee r\}$$

It follows that $A \mp_\gamma p \not\subseteq A \pm_\gamma p$ and $A \pm_\gamma p \not\subseteq A \mp_\gamma p$

155. a. $\{\perp, \neg\alpha\}$

b. $\neg\alpha$

c. $\{\perp, \neg\alpha, \neg\beta, \neg\delta, \neg\alpha \vee \neg\beta, \neg\alpha \vee \neg\delta, \neg\beta \vee \neg\delta, \neg\alpha \vee \neg\beta \vee \neg\delta\}\}$

d. $\neg\alpha \vee \neg\beta \vee \neg\delta$

156. a. $X = \{\neg p, \neg q\}$

b. $X = \{\neg p \& \neg q\}$

c. This equation has no solution, since for all X, if $p, q \in \neg X$, then $p \vee q \in \neg X$.

157. Let $\varepsilon \in B \cap \neg B$: There are, according to Definition 3.35, three cases:

(1) ε is inconsistent. Then we are done.

(2) ε is equivalent to $\neg\delta$ for some $\delta \in B$: Then $\{\varepsilon, \delta\} \subseteq B$, and B is inconsistent.

(3) ε is equivalent to $\neg\delta_1 \vee \ldots \neg\delta_n$ for some $\delta_1, \ldots \delta_n \in B$. Then $\{\varepsilon, \delta_1, \ldots \delta_n\}$ is inconsistent, and since $\{\varepsilon, \delta_1, \ldots \delta_n\} \subseteq B$, so is B.

158. *For one direction*, let $B \vdash \perp$. Then by compactness there is a finite subset $\{\beta_1, \ldots \beta_n\}$ of B such that $\{\beta_1, \ldots \beta_n\} \vdash \perp$. We have:

$\{\beta_1, \ldots \beta_n\} \vdash \perp$

$\beta_1 \& \ldots \beta_n \vdash \perp$

$\vdash \beta_1 \& \ldots \beta_n \rightarrow \perp$ (deduction property)

$\vdash \neg(\beta_1 \& \ldots \beta_n)$

$\vdash \neg\beta_1 \vee \ldots \neg\beta_n$

$\neg\beta_1 \vee ... \neg\beta_n \in Cn(\emptyset)$

By Definition 3.35, $\neg\beta_1 \vee ... \neg\beta_n \in \neg B$. We can conclude that $\neg B \cap Cn(\emptyset) \neq \emptyset$.

For the other direction, let $\neg B \cap Cn(\emptyset) \neq \emptyset$. Then there is a finite subset $\{\beta_1, ... \beta_n\}$ of B sucht that $\neg\beta_1 \vee ... \neg\beta_n \in Cn(\emptyset)$, i.e., $\vdash \neg\beta_1 \vee ... \neg\beta_n$, i.e., $\vdash \neg(\beta_1 \& ... \& \beta_n)$, i.e., $\vdash \beta_1 \& ... \& \beta_n \rightarrow \perp$, i.e., $\beta_1 \& ... \& \beta \vdash \perp$. Hence, $B \vdash \perp$.

159. a. Suppose to the contrary that $\beta \in A \cap B$ and $\beta \notin X \in A \perp \neg B$. It follows from $\beta \in A \backslash X$ and $X \in A \perp \neg B$ that there is some sentence $\delta \in \neg B$ such that $X \cup \{\beta\} \vdash \delta$. By the deduction property, $X \vdash \beta \rightarrow \delta$, or equivalently $X \vdash \neg\beta \vee \delta$.

It follows from $\beta \in B$ and $\delta \in \neg B$, by the construction of $\neg B$, that $\neg\beta \vee \delta \in \neg B$. It follows from this and $X \vdash \neg\beta \vee \delta$ that $X \notin A \perp \neg B$, contrary to the conditions. This contradiction concludes the proof.

b. Directly from Part *a* since if $B \subseteq A$, then $A \cap B = B$.

160. *For one direction*, let $X \in (A \cup B) \perp \neg B$. It follows from Exercise 159 that $B \subseteq X$. To prove that $X \in (A \cup B) \perp \perp$, suppose to the contrary that this is not so. Since X is a subset of $A \cup B$ that does not imply $\perp$ (note that $\perp \in \neg B$), there must then be some $\varepsilon \in (A \cup B) \backslash X$ such that $X \cup \{\varepsilon\} \nvdash \perp$. However, it follows from $X \in (A \cup B) \perp \neg B$ that ε implies some element of $\neg B$. Since $B \subseteq X$ and every element of $\neg B$ is inconsistent with B (i.e., if $\zeta \in \neg B$, then $B \cup \{\zeta\}$ is inconsistent), we can conclude that $X \cup \{\varepsilon\} \vdash \perp$. This contradiction is sufficient to establish that $X \in (A \cup B) \perp \perp$.

For the other direction, let $B \subseteq X \in (A \cup B) \perp \perp$. Then (again since every element if $\neg B$ is inconsistent with B) $(\neg B) \cap Cn(X) = \emptyset$. Suppose that $X \notin (A \cup B) \perp \neg B$. Since X is a subset of $A \cup B$ that does not imply any element of $\neg B$ there must then be some $\varepsilon \in (A \cup B) \backslash X$ such that $(\neg B) \cap Cn(X \cup \{\varepsilon\}) = \emptyset$. Since $\neg B$ is non-empty, it follows from this that $X \cup \{\varepsilon\}$ is consistent, contrary to $X \in (A \cup B) \perp \perp$. This contradiction concludes the proof.

161. a. Let $B \subseteq A$. It follows from Exercise 159b that if $X \in A \perp \neg B$, then $B \subseteq X$. From this we can conclude that $B \subseteq A \sim_\gamma \neg B$. Therefore: $A \pm_\gamma B = (A \cup B) \sim_\gamma \neg B = A \sim_\gamma \neg B = (A \sim_\gamma \neg B) \cup B = A \mp_\gamma B$.

b. Let B be inconsistent. It follows from Exercise 158 that $\neg B$ contains a tautology, and thus $A \sim_\gamma \neg B = A$, and consequently $A \mp_\gamma B = A \cup B$.

162. a. Let B be consistent. It follows from Exercise 158 that $\neg B \cap Cn(\emptyset) = \emptyset$. It follows (by the contraction-postulate of *P−success*) that $\neg B \cap Cn(A \sim_\gamma \neg B) = \emptyset$, and consequently that $A \mp_\gamma B = (A \sim_\gamma \neg B) \cup \{\varepsilon\}$ is consistent.

b. There are two cases, depending on whether or not B is consistent.

If B is inconsistent, then if follows from Exercise 158 that $\neg B \cap \mathrm{Cn}(\varnothing) \neq \varnothing$. Then $A \perp \neg B$ is empty so that $\gamma(A \perp \neg B) = \{A\}$ and consequently $A \ddagger_\gamma \alpha = \cap\gamma(A \perp \neg B) \cup B = A \cup B$. Thus, there can be no ε such that $\varepsilon \in A$ and $\varepsilon \notin A \ddagger_\gamma B$, and *relevance* is vacuously satisfied.

If B is consistent, let $\varepsilon \in A \setminus (A \ddagger_\gamma B)$. Then $\varepsilon \notin A \sim_\gamma \neg B$, so that there must be some X such that $\varepsilon \notin X \in \gamma(A \perp \neg B)$. It follows that $\neg B \cap \mathrm{Cn}(X) = \varnothing$ and $\neg B \cap \mathrm{Cn}(X \cup \{\varepsilon\}) \neq \mathrm{Cn}(\varnothing)$. It follows from this that $X \cup B$ is consistent and $(X \cup B) \cup \{\varepsilon\}$ is inconsistent. We can also conclude from the definition of internal partial meet revision that $A \ddagger_\gamma B \subseteq X \cup B \subseteq A \cup B$. Hence, *P-relevance* is satified.

163. a. Let $ML\alpha \in m(A_0)$. Then there is some A' such that $A_0 RA'$ and $L\alpha \in m(A')$. It follows that $\alpha \in m(A'{+}B{+}\bot)$ for all B.

Let A'' be any belief base such that $A_0 RA''$. Then we have $\alpha \in m(A'{+}A''{+}\bot) = m(A''{+}A'{+}\bot)$, so that $M\alpha \in m(A'')$. Since this holds for all A'' such that $A_0 RA''$, we may conclude that $LM\alpha \in m(A_0)$.

b–c. As in Observation 3.46.

d. It follows from Part *a* that $MLM\alpha \vDash LMM\alpha$. By $MM\alpha \vDash M\alpha$ (Part *c*) and (DR1) follows $LMM\alpha \vDash LM\alpha$. It follows that $MLM\alpha \vDash LM\alpha$. By Part 3 of Observation 3.44 follows $LM\alpha \vDash MLM\alpha$. We may conclude that $MLM\alpha \dashv\vDash LM\alpha$.

e. Apply Part 1 of Observation 3.44 to $MLM\alpha \dashv\vDash LM\alpha$ that was obtained in Part *d*.

f. In the same way as in Theorem 3.44, we can reduce any formula to either the form $\Pi B\alpha$ or the form $\neg\Pi B\alpha$, where Π is a (possibly empty) sequence of L and M. Using parts b-c of the present exercise we can delete any repetitions of L or M in Π. After that, parts d and e of the present exercise can be used to shorten any sequence of three or more letters L and M. What remains are formulas of the ten mentioned forms.

g. $LB\alpha \vDash MLB\alpha$: From Part 3 of Observation 3.44.
$MLB\alpha \vDash LMB\alpha$: From Part *a* of this exercise.
$LMB\alpha \vDash MB\alpha$: From Part 2 of Observation 3.44.
$LB\alpha \vDash B\alpha$: From Part 2 of Observation 3.44.
$B\alpha \vDash MB\alpha$: From Part 3 of Observation 3.44.

164. Suppose that *success* and *closure* are satisfied, and that $\alpha \vdash \beta$. It follows from *success* that $\alpha \in A*\alpha$, and then from $\alpha \vdash \beta$ that $\beta \in \mathrm{Cn}(A*\alpha)$. By *closure*, $\mathrm{Cn}(A*\alpha) = A*\alpha$, so that $\beta \in A*\alpha$.

165. a. *Vacuity*.
b. One direction: *Preservation* follows from *vacuity* alone.

The other direction: Let $\neg\alpha \notin \text{Cn}(A)$. It follows from *inclusion* that $A*\alpha \subseteq A+\alpha$. It follows from *success* that $\alpha \in A*\alpha$ and from *preservation* that $A \subseteq A*\alpha$; thus $A+\alpha = A*\alpha$, and we are done.

166. Suppose that $*$ satisfies *success, closure*, and *reciprocity*, and let $\alpha\leftrightarrow\beta \in \text{Cn}(\varnothing)$. It follows from *success* that $\alpha \in A*\alpha$. From this and $\alpha\leftrightarrow\beta \in \text{Cn}(\varnothing)$ we can conclude that $\beta \in \text{Cn}(A*\alpha)$. By *closure*, $\text{Cn}(A*\alpha) = A*\alpha$, so that $\beta \in A*\alpha$. It follows in exactly the same way that $\alpha \in A*\beta$, and we can apply *reciprocity* to conclude that $A*\alpha = A*\beta$.

167. There are two cases, according to whether or not $\alpha\vee\beta$ is consistent.

Case 1, $\alpha\vee\beta$ is inconsistent: Then α is inconsistent, and it follows from *success* that $A*\alpha$ is inconsistent, so that $\text{Cn}((A*\alpha)\cup(A*\beta)) = \mathcal{L}$, from which $A*(\alpha\vee\beta) \subseteq \text{Cn}((A*\alpha)\cup(A*\beta))$ follows directly.

Case 2, $\alpha\vee\beta$ is consistent: We are first going to show that either $\neg\alpha \notin A*(\alpha\vee\beta)$ or $\neg\beta \notin A*(\alpha\vee\beta)$. Suppose to the contrary that $\neg\alpha \in A*(\alpha\vee\beta)$ and $\neg\beta \in A*(\alpha\vee\beta)$. Then $\neg\alpha\&\neg\beta \in \text{Cn}(A*(\alpha\vee\beta))$. It follows from *success* that $\alpha\vee\beta \in A*(\alpha\vee\beta)$. Since $\neg\alpha\&\neg\beta$ and $\alpha\vee\beta$ together are inconsistent, it follows that $A*(\alpha\vee\beta)$ is inconsistent. Since in this case $\alpha\vee\beta$ is consistent, this contradicts the postulate of *consistency*. We can conclude from this contradiction that either $\neg\alpha \notin A*(\alpha\vee\beta)$ or $\neg\beta \notin A*(\alpha\vee\beta)$.

If $\neg\alpha \notin A*(\alpha\vee\beta)$, then it follows from *disjunctive inclusion* that $A*(\alpha\vee\beta) \subseteq A*\alpha$, and if $\neg\beta \notin A*(\alpha\vee\beta)$ that $A*(\alpha\vee\beta) \subseteq A*\beta$. In both cases, $A*(\alpha\vee\beta) \subseteq \text{Cn}((A*\alpha)\cup(A*\beta))$, which concludes the proof.

168. a. Let $A*\alpha = A*\beta$. It follows from *success* that $\alpha \in A*\alpha$. It also follows from *success* that $\beta \in A*\beta$, and thus $\beta \in A*\alpha$. Since α and β together imply $\alpha\leftrightarrow\beta$, we can conclude that $\alpha\leftrightarrow\beta \in \text{Cn}(A*\alpha)$, and *closure* yields $\alpha\leftrightarrow\beta \in A*\alpha$.

b. Let $A*\alpha = A*\beta$. We showed in Part *a* that $\alpha\leftrightarrow\beta \in A*\alpha$. By *inclusion*, $A*\alpha \subseteq \text{Cn}(A\cup\{\alpha\})$, and thus $\alpha\leftrightarrow\beta \in \text{Cn}(A\cup\{\alpha\})$. By the deduction property, $\alpha\rightarrow(\alpha\leftrightarrow\beta) \in \text{Cn}(A)$, or equivalently $\alpha\rightarrow\beta \in \text{Cn}(A)$.

It also follows from Part *a* that $\alpha\leftrightarrow\beta \in A*\beta$. By the same argument, we can conclude that $\beta\rightarrow\alpha \in \text{Cn}(A)$.

It follows from $\alpha\rightarrow\beta \in \text{Cn}(A)$ and $\beta\rightarrow\alpha \in \text{Cn}(A)$ that $\alpha\leftrightarrow\beta \in \text{Cn}(A)$, and since A is logically closed we can conclude that $\alpha\leftrightarrow\beta \in A$.

169. We use *inclusion* to obtain $A*\alpha \subseteq \text{Cn}(A\cup\{\alpha\})$ and then set theory to obtain $A*\alpha = (A*\alpha) \cap \text{Cn}(A\cup\{\alpha\})$. By *success* and *closure*, $A*\alpha = \text{Cn}((A*\alpha)\cup\{\alpha\})$. We therefore have:

$$A*\alpha = \text{Cn}((A*\alpha)\cup\{\alpha\}) \cap \text{Cn}(A\cup\{\alpha\})$$

The right-hand side of this expression can be simplified as follows:

$\beta \in \mathrm{Cn}((A*\alpha)\cup\{\alpha\}) \cap \mathrm{Cn}(A\cup\{\alpha\})$
iff $\beta \in \mathrm{Cn}((A*\alpha)\cup\{\alpha\})$ and $\beta \in \mathrm{Cn}(A\cup\{\alpha\})$
iff $\alpha\rightarrow\beta \in \mathrm{Cn}(A*\alpha)$ and $\alpha\rightarrow\beta \in \mathrm{Cn}(A)$ (deduction property)
(By *closure*, $\mathrm{Cn}(A*\alpha) = A*\alpha$, and since A is logically closed $\mathrm{Cn}(A) = A$. We can continue:)
iff $\alpha\rightarrow\beta \in A*\alpha$ and $\alpha\rightarrow\beta \in A$
iff $\alpha\rightarrow\beta \in A\cap(A*\alpha)$
iff $\beta \in \mathrm{Cn}((A\cap(A*\alpha))\cup\{\alpha\})$ (deduction property)
iff $\beta \in (A\cap(A*\alpha))+\alpha$
Thus, $A*\alpha = \mathrm{Cn}((A*\alpha)\cup\{\alpha\}) \cap \mathrm{Cn}(A\cup\{\alpha\}) = (A\cap(A*\alpha))+\alpha$.

170. a. For one direction, let $\alpha \vdash \beta$. It follows from *inclusion* that $A_0*\beta \subseteq \mathrm{Cn}(A_0\cup\{\beta\})$, i.e., $A_0*\beta \subseteq \mathrm{Cn}(\{\beta\})$. Furthermore, it follows from *success* that $\alpha \in A_0*\alpha$, and since $\alpha\vdash\beta$ we can conclude that $\beta \in A_0*\alpha$ and thus $\mathrm{Cn}(\{\beta\}) \subseteq \mathrm{Cn}(A_0*\alpha)$. By *closure*, $\mathrm{Cn}(A_0*\alpha) = A_0*\alpha$, and thus $A_0*\beta \subseteq \mathrm{Cn}(\{\beta\}) \subseteq A_0*\alpha$.

For the other direction, let $A_0*\beta \subseteq A_0*\alpha$. It follows from *success* that $\beta \in A_0*\beta$ and from *inclusion* that $A_0*\alpha \subseteq \mathrm{Cn}(A_0\cup\{\alpha\})$, i.e., $A_0*\alpha \subseteq \mathrm{Cn}(\{\alpha\})$. We therefore have $\beta \in \mathrm{Cn}(\{\alpha\})$, i.e., $\alpha\vdash\beta$.
b. Let p and q be logically independent sentences such that $p\&q$ is consistent. Let $A = \mathrm{Cn}(\{p,\neg q\})$. Without violating the three postulates we may let $A*p = A$. It follows that $\neg q \in A*p$.

It follows from *success* that $p\&q \in A*(p\&q)$, and from *consistency* that $A*(p\&q)$ is consistent. We can conclude from this that $\neg q \notin A*(p\&q)$, and thus $A*p \not\subseteq A*(p\&q)$. Since $\vdash p\&q \rightarrow p$, this is sufficient for the desired negative result.

171. *Case 1*, α is inconsistent: It follows from *success* that both $A*\alpha$ and $(A*\alpha)*\alpha$ are inconsistent, and from *closure* that they are both logically closed. They are therefore both identical to $\mathcal{L}$, so that $A*\alpha = (A*\alpha)*\alpha$.

Case 2, α is consistent: It follows from *success* that $\alpha \in A*\alpha$, and then from *consistency* that $\neg\alpha \notin A*\alpha$ and from *vacuity* that $(A*\alpha)*\alpha = \mathrm{Cn}((A*\alpha)\cup\{\alpha\})$. Due to *success* and *closure*, $\mathrm{Cn}((A*\alpha)\cup\{\alpha\}) = A*\alpha$, and we may conclude that $(A*\alpha)*\alpha = A*\alpha$.

172. a. This can be proved in the same way as Exercise 143.
b. Let p and q be logically independent sentences, and let A be an arbitrary belief set. Suppose that *vacuity*, *consistency*, and *monotonicity* all hold.

It follows from *vacuity* that $\mathrm{Cn}(\{p\})*(\neg p\vee\neg q) = \mathrm{Cn}(\{p,\neg p\vee\neg q\})$ and from *monotonicity* that $\{p,\neg p\vee\neg q\} \subseteq \mathrm{Cn}(\{p,q\})*(\neg p\vee\neg q)$.

In the same way we can show that $\{q,\neg p\vee\neg q\} \subseteq \mathrm{Cn}(\{p,q\})*(\neg p\vee\neg q)$.

It follows from $\{p,\neg p\vee\neg q\} \subseteq \text{Cn}(\{p,q\})*(\neg p\vee\neg q)$ and $\{q,\neg p\vee\neg q\} \subseteq \text{Cn}(\{p,q\})*(\neg p\vee\neg q)$ that $\{p,q,\neg p\vee\neg q\} \subseteq \text{Cn}(\{p,q\})*(\neg p\vee\neg q)$, contrary to *consistency*. This contradiction concludes the proof.

c. Let $A_1 \subseteq A_2$. Then we have:

$A_1*\alpha = (A_1\cap A_2)*\alpha$

$= A_1*\alpha \cap A_2*\alpha$

$\subseteq A_2*\alpha$

so that *monotonicity* holds, which we have shown in Part *b* to be impossible.

d. Suppose to the contrary that the four postulates all hold. Let p and q be logically independent sentences. (Remember that $\top$ denotes a tautology and $\bot$ a contradiction.) We then have:

$\text{Cn}(\{p\}) = \text{Cn}(\{p\})*\top$ (*vacuity*)

$= \text{Cn}(\{p\})*\bot*\top$ (the new postulate)

$= \mathcal{L}*\top$ (*success* and *closure*)

$= \text{Cn}(\{q\})*\bot*\top$ (*success* and *closure*)

$= \text{Cn}(\{q\})*\top$ (the new postulate)

$= \text{Cn}(\{q\})$ (*vacuity*)

so that p and q are logically equivalent, contrary to our conditions. This contradiction concludes the proof.

173. It follows from $\beta\rightarrow\alpha \in A+\alpha$ by *contraction-closure* that $\neg\alpha\rightarrow\neg\beta \in A+\alpha$. We have $A*\neg\alpha = \text{Cn}((A+\neg\neg\alpha)\cup\{\neg\alpha\})$, which is by *contraction-extensionality* equivalent to $A*\neg\alpha = \text{Cn}((A+\alpha)\cup\{\neg\alpha\})$. Since $\neg\alpha$ and $\neg\alpha\rightarrow\neg\beta$ together imply $\neg\beta$, we can conclude that $\neg\beta \in A*\neg\alpha$.

174. It follows from $+ = \mathbb{C}(*)$ that $A+\alpha = A\cap(A*\neg\alpha)$. It follows from the logical closure and inconsistency of A that $\neg\alpha \in A$ and from *revision-success* that $\neg\alpha \in A*\neg\alpha$, so that $\neg\alpha \in A\cap(A*\neg\alpha) = A+\alpha$ as desired.

175. a. We need to show that $\mathbb{R}(+') = \mathbb{R}(+)$, i.e., $\mathbb{R}(\mathbb{C}(\mathbb{R}(+))) = \mathbb{R}(+)$. It follows from Observation 3.54 that $\mathbb{R}(+)$ satisfies all the basic revision-postulates, and thus from Observation 3.57 that $\mathbb{R}(\mathbb{C}(\mathbb{R}(+))) = \mathbb{R}(+)$.

b. Let $\mathbb{R}(+) = *$. We then have $+' = \mathbb{C}(*)$. It follows that $A+'\alpha = A\cap(A*\neg\alpha)$. Using $* = \mathbb{R}(+)$ we obtain $A+'\alpha = A\cap\text{Cn}((A+\neg\neg\alpha)\cup\{\neg\alpha\})$. It follows from *contraction-extensionality* that $A+\neg\neg\alpha = A+\alpha$, and from *contraction-inclusion* that $A+\alpha \subseteq A$. We therefore have:

$A+\alpha \subseteq A\cap\text{Cn}((A+\alpha)\cup\{\neg\alpha\})$

$= A\cap\text{Cn}((A+\neg\neg\alpha)\cup\{\neg\alpha\})$

$= A+'\alpha$.

c. We only need *inclusion* and *extensionality*. *Closure*, *vacuity*, and *success* are not needed for this result.

d. Suppose to the contrary that $A+''\alpha \not\subseteq A+'\alpha$ for some α. Then there is some ε such that $\varepsilon \in A+''\alpha$ and $\varepsilon \notin A+'\alpha$. Since $+''$ satisfies *contraction-inclusion*, it follows from $\varepsilon \in A+''\alpha$ that $\varepsilon \in A$. It follows from Observations 3.54 and 3.55 that $+'$ satisfies *recovery*, and thus $\varepsilon \in \mathrm{Cn}((A+'\alpha)\cup\{\alpha\})$. Furthermore, $+'$ satisfies *contraction-closure*, and we can conclude from $\varepsilon \notin A+'\alpha$ that $\varepsilon \notin \mathrm{Cn}(A+'\alpha)$. It follows from $\varepsilon \in \mathrm{Cn}((A+'\alpha)\cup\{\alpha\})$ and $\varepsilon \notin \mathrm{Cn}(A+'\alpha)$ that $\varepsilon \notin \mathrm{Cn}((A+'\alpha)\cup\{\neg\alpha\})$.

We know from Part *a* of the present exercise that $+$ and $+'$ are revision-equivalent. By assumption, so are $+$ and $+''$, and thus so are $+'$ and $+''$. Thus, $\mathrm{Cn}((A+'\neg\neg\alpha)\cup\{\neg\alpha\}) = \mathrm{Cn}((A+''\neg\neg\alpha)\cup\{\neg\alpha\})$, i.e. (by *contraction-extensionality*) $\mathrm{Cn}((A+'\alpha)\cup\{\neg\alpha\}) = \mathrm{Cn}((A+''\alpha)\cup\{\neg\alpha\})$. This, however, is impossible. We have just shown that $\varepsilon \notin \mathrm{Cn}((A+'\alpha)\cup\{\neg\alpha\})$, and it follows from $\varepsilon \in A+''\alpha$ that $\varepsilon \in \mathrm{Cn}((A+''\alpha)\cup\{\neg\alpha\})$. We can conclude from this contradiction that $A+''\alpha \subseteq A+'\alpha$ for all α.

176. *(a) to (b)*: Let (a) be satisfied, and let $\beta \in A\ddagger_\gamma\alpha$. We need to show that $A\ddagger_\gamma\alpha \subseteq A\ddagger_\gamma(\alpha\&\beta))$

$\beta \in A\ddagger_\gamma\alpha$

$\beta \in \mathrm{Cn}((A\sim_\gamma\neg\alpha)\cup\{\alpha\})$ (Levi identity)

$\alpha\rightarrow\beta \in \mathrm{Cn}(A\sim_\gamma\neg\alpha)$ (deduction property)

$\alpha\rightarrow\beta \in A\sim_\gamma\neg\alpha$ (*contraction-closure*)

$\alpha\rightarrow\beta \in A\sim_\gamma((\neg\alpha\vee\neg\beta)\&(\alpha\rightarrow\beta))$ (*contraction-extensionality*)

$A\sim_\gamma((\neg\alpha\vee\neg\beta)\&(\alpha\rightarrow\beta)) \subseteq A\sim_\gamma(\neg\alpha\vee\neg\beta)$ (from (a))

$A\sim_\gamma\neg\alpha \subseteq A\sim_\gamma(\neg(\alpha\&\beta))$ (*contraction-extensionality*)

$\mathrm{Cn}((A\sim_\gamma\neg\alpha)\cup\{\alpha\}) \subseteq \mathrm{Cn}((A\sim_\gamma(\neg(\alpha\&\beta)))\cup\{\alpha\&\beta\})$ (property of Cn)

$A\ddagger_\gamma\alpha \subseteq A\ddagger_\gamma(\alpha\&\beta)$ (Levi identity)

(b) to (a): Let (b) be satisfied, and let $\beta \in A\sim_\gamma(\alpha\&\beta)$. We need to show that $A\sim_\gamma(\alpha\&\beta) \subseteq A\sim_\gamma\alpha$.

$\beta \in A\sim_\gamma(\alpha\&\beta)$

$\beta \in A\cap(A\ddagger_\gamma\neg(\alpha\&\beta))$ (Harper identity)

$\beta \in A\ddagger_\gamma\neg(\alpha\&\beta)$

$\alpha\rightarrow\beta \in A\ddagger_\gamma\neg(\alpha\&\beta)$ (*revision-closure*)

$A\ddagger_\gamma\neg(\alpha\&\beta) \subseteq A\ddagger_\gamma(\neg(\alpha\&\beta)\&(\alpha\rightarrow\beta))$ (*cautious monotony*)

$A\ddagger_\gamma\neg(\alpha\&\beta) \subseteq A\ddagger_\gamma\neg\alpha$ (*revision-extensionality*)

$A\cap(A\ddagger_\gamma\neg(\alpha\&\beta)) \subseteq A\cap(A\ddagger_\gamma\neg\alpha)$

$A\sim_\gamma(\alpha\&\beta) \subseteq A\sim_\gamma\alpha$ (Harper identity)

177. *(a) implies (b):* Suppose that *reciprocity* holds and that $\beta\rightarrow\alpha \in A\sim_\gamma\alpha$ and $\alpha\rightarrow\beta \in A\sim_\gamma\beta$. It follows from *contraction-closure* that $\neg\alpha\rightarrow\neg\beta \in A\sim_\gamma\alpha$, by the deduction property that $\neg\beta \in \mathrm{Cn}((A\sim_\gamma\alpha)\cup\{\neg\alpha\})$, by *contraction-extensionality* that $\neg\beta \in \mathrm{Cn}((A\sim_\gamma\neg\neg\alpha)\cup\{\neg\alpha\})$, and by the Levi identity that $\neg\beta \in A\ddagger_\gamma\neg\alpha$. In the same way it follows that $\neg\alpha \in A\ddagger_\gamma\neg\beta$, and we can conclude from *reciprocity* that $A_{\mp\gamma}\neg\alpha = A_{\mp\gamma}\neg\beta$. It follows from this that $A\cap(A_{\mp\gamma}\neg\alpha) = A\cap(A_{\mp\gamma}\neg\beta)$, and thus by the Harper identity that $A\sim_\gamma\alpha = A\sim_\gamma\beta$.

(b) implies (a): Let (b) hold. For one direction of *reciprocity*, let $A_{\mp\gamma}\alpha = A_{\mp\gamma}\beta$. It follows from *revision-success* that $\beta \in A_{\mp\gamma}\beta$ and hence $\beta \in A_{\mp\gamma}\alpha$. In the same way, it follows that $\alpha \in A_{\mp\gamma}\beta$. (Note that (2) is not needed for this part of the proof.)

For the other direction of *reciprocity*, let $\beta \in A_{\mp\gamma}\alpha$ and $\alpha \in A_{\mp\gamma}\beta$. We then have:

$\beta \in A_{\mp\gamma}\alpha$ and $\alpha \in A_{\mp\gamma}\beta$

$\beta \in Cn((A\sim_\gamma\neg\alpha)\cup\{\alpha\})$ and $\alpha \in Cn((A\sim_\gamma\neg\beta)\cup\{\beta\})$ (Levi identity)

$\alpha\to\beta \in Cn(A\sim_\gamma\neg\alpha)$ and $\beta\to\alpha \in Cn(A\sim_\gamma\neg\beta)$

$\neg\beta\to\neg\alpha \in Cn(A\sim_\gamma\neg\alpha)$ and $\neg\alpha\to\neg\beta \in Cn(A\sim_\gamma\neg\beta)$

$\neg\beta\to\neg\alpha \in A\sim_\gamma\neg\alpha$ and $\neg\alpha\to\neg\beta \in A\sim_\gamma\neg\beta$ *(contraction-closure)*

$A\sim_\gamma\neg\alpha = A\sim_\gamma\neg\beta$ (from (b))

From this and $\alpha\to\beta \in Cn(A\sim_\gamma\neg\alpha)$ and $\beta\to\alpha \in Cn(A\sim_\gamma\neg\beta)$ (also shown above) it follows that that $\alpha\leftrightarrow\beta \in Cn(A\sim_\gamma\neg\alpha)$. Hence:

$A_{\mp\gamma}\alpha = Cn((A\sim_\gamma\neg\alpha)\cup\{\alpha\})$

$= Cn((A\sim_\gamma\neg\alpha)\cup\{\beta\})$

$= Cn((A\sim_\gamma\neg\beta)\cup\{\beta\})$

$= A_{\mp\gamma}\beta$

178. Let $\mathbb{R}(+_m) = *_m$ and $\mathbb{R}(\sim) = \mp$. It follows from the Levi identity that:

(i) If $\neg\alpha \in A$, then $A*_m\alpha = Cn(\{\alpha\})$.

(ii) If $\neg\alpha \notin A$, then $A*_m\alpha = Cn(A\cup\{\alpha\})$

If follows from Observation 3.21 that $*_m$ coincides with $\mp$.

179. There are three cases.

Case 1, α is inconsistent. Then $\alpha\vee\beta$ is equivalent with β, and it follows from *extensionality* that $A*(\alpha\vee\beta) = A*\beta$.

Case 2, β is inconsistent. It follows in the same way that $A*(\alpha\vee\beta) = A*\alpha$.

Case 3, both α and β are consistent. Then $\alpha\vee\beta$ is also consistent. It follows from Observation 3.22 that $A*\alpha$, $A*\beta$ and $A*(\alpha\vee\beta)$ are all maximally consistent subsets of L, i.e. they are all elements of $L\bot$.

It follows from *success* that $\alpha\vee\beta \in A*(\alpha\vee\beta)$ and from *consistency* that either $\neg\alpha \notin A*(\alpha\vee\beta)$ or $\neg\beta \notin A*(\alpha\vee\beta)$.

If $\neg\alpha \notin A*(\alpha\vee\beta)$, then it follows from *disjunctive inclusion* that $A*(\alpha\vee\beta) \subseteq A*\alpha$. Since both $A*(\alpha\vee\beta)$ and $A*\alpha$ are elements of $L\bot$, $A*(\alpha\vee\beta) \not\subset A*\alpha$ and thus $A*(\alpha\vee\beta) = A*\alpha$.

If $\neg\beta \notin A*(\alpha\vee\beta)$, then it follows in the same way that $A*(\alpha\vee\beta) = A*\beta$.

180. a. Let $W \in \mathcal{L}\perp\perp$. Then it holds for all sentences α that either $\alpha \in W$ or $\neg\alpha \in W$, but not both. (Cf. Observation 1.57). Thus, $W \in [\alpha]$ if and only if $W \notin [\neg\alpha]$.
b. For one direction, let $A \subseteq B$ and $W \in [B]$. Then $B \subseteq W$, and consequently $A \subseteq W$ so that $W \in [A]$.

For the other direction, suppose that $[B] \subseteq [A]$. Then $\cap[A] \subseteq \cap[B]$, i.e., $A \subseteq B$.
c. $X \in [\mathrm{Cn}(A \cup B)]$
iff $\mathrm{Cn}(A \cup B) \subseteq X \in \mathcal{L}\perp\perp$.
iff $\mathrm{Cn}(A) \subseteq X \in \mathcal{L}\perp\perp$ and $\mathrm{Cn}(B) \subseteq X \in \mathcal{L}\perp\perp$
iff $X \in [A]$ and $X \in [B]$
iff $X \in [A] \cap [B]$
d. It follows from Part *b* that $[A] \subseteq [A \cap B]$ and $[B] \subseteq [A \cap B]$.
e. $[\alpha] \subseteq [\beta]$
iff $[\mathrm{Cn}(\{\alpha\})] \subseteq [\mathrm{Cn}(\{\beta\})]$
iff $\mathrm{Cn}(\{\beta\}) \subseteq \mathrm{Cn}(\{\alpha\})$ (Part *b* of this exercise)
iff $\vdash \alpha \rightarrow \beta$
f. $[\alpha \& \beta] = [\mathrm{Cn}(\{\alpha \& \beta\})]$
$= [\mathrm{Cn}(\mathrm{Cn}(\{\alpha\}) \cup \mathrm{Cn}(\{\beta\}))]$
$= [\mathrm{Cn}(\{\alpha\})] \cap [\mathrm{Cn}(\{\beta\})]$ (Part *c* of this exercise)
$= [\alpha] \cap [\beta]$
g. For one direction, let $W \in [\alpha \vee \beta]$. Then $\alpha \vee \beta \in W \in \mathcal{L}\perp\perp$, and we can conclude from Observation 1.57 that either $\alpha \in W$ or $\beta \in W$. In the first case, $W \in [\alpha]$, and in the second case $W \in [\beta]$. Thus, in both cases $W \in [\alpha] \cup [\beta]$.

For the other direction, let $W \in [\alpha] \cup [\beta]$. Then either $W \in [\alpha]$ or $W \in [\beta]$, so that either $\alpha \in W$ or $\beta \in W$, and thus in both cases $\alpha \vee \beta \in W$, so that $W \in [\alpha \vee \beta]$.
h. $[\alpha \rightarrow \beta] = [\neg\alpha \vee \beta]$ (sentential logic)
$= [\neg\alpha] \cup [\beta]$ (Part *g* of this exercise)
i. $[\alpha \rightarrow \beta] \cap [\beta \rightarrow \alpha]$
$= [(\alpha \rightarrow \beta) \& (\beta \rightarrow \alpha)]$ (Part *f* of this exercise)
$= [(\alpha \& \beta) \vee (\neg\alpha \& \neg\beta)]$ (sentential logic)
$= [\alpha \& \beta] \cup [\neg\alpha \& \neg\beta]$ (Part *g* of this exercise)

181. We have $[\mathrm{Cn}(A)] = [\& A]$, and since $\& A$ is logically equivalent to $\neg n(A)$ the rest follows from Part *a* of Exercise 180.

182. a. $\mathcal{W} \circledast [\alpha] = \mathcal{W} \ominus [\neg\alpha] \oplus [\alpha]$.
b. $\mathcal{W} \ominus [\alpha] = \mathcal{W} \cup (\mathcal{W} \circledast [\neg\alpha])$.

183. a. An operator $\circledast$ of propositional revision such that $\mathcal{W} \circledast [\alpha]$ is a singleton (consists of a single possible world) if $\mathcal{W} \subseteq [\neg\alpha]$.

b. The operator $\circledast$ of propositional revision such that $\mathcal{W}\circledast[\alpha] = [\alpha]$ if $\mathcal{W} \subseteq [\neg\alpha]$.

184. a. $[\beta]\cap S_\alpha \neq \varnothing$ means that S_α intersects with $[\beta]$. Since S_β is a subset of all spheres that intersect with $[\beta]$, it follows directly that $S_\beta \subseteq S_\alpha$.
b. It follows from $\vdash \alpha \rightarrow \beta$ that $[\alpha] \subseteq [\beta]$ (Exercise 52), and thus from $[\alpha]\cap S_\alpha \neq \varnothing$ that $[\beta]\cap S_\alpha \neq \varnothing$. We can conclude as in Part *a* that $S_\beta \subseteq S_\alpha$.
c. Directly from Part *a*.

185. We have for all α: $\mathrm{Cn}((A+_R\neg\alpha)\cup\{\alpha\}) \subseteq \mathrm{Cn}((A+\neg\alpha)\cup\{\alpha\}) \subseteq \mathrm{Cn}((A+_G\neg\alpha)\cup\{\alpha\})$. Since $+_R$ and $+_G$ are revision-equivalent (Part 1 of Observation 3.28), it follows that $\mathbb{R}(+) = \mathbb{R}(+_G) = \mathbb{R}(+_R)$, and the desired result therefore follows from Part 2 of Observation 3.28.

SOLUTIONS FOR CHAPTER 4^+

186. *Inclusion* ($A+\alpha \subseteq A$): Suppose that *inclusion* holds for the operator $-$ on B. Let $\mathbf{K} = \text{Cn}(B)$ and let $+$ be the closure of $-$. In order to show that *inclusion* holds for $\mathbf{K}$, we must show that $\mathbf{K}+\alpha \subseteq \mathbf{K}$ holds for all α.

Since *inclusion* holds for B, we have $B-\alpha \subseteq B$, and consequently $\text{Cn}(B-\alpha) \subseteq \text{Cn}(B)$. Since $\mathbf{K}+\alpha = \text{Cn}(B-\alpha)$ and $\mathbf{K} = \text{Cn}(B)$, it follows directly that $\mathbf{K}+\alpha \subseteq \mathbf{K}$.

Success (If $\alpha \notin \text{Cn}(\varnothing)$, then $\alpha \notin \text{Cn}(A+\alpha)$): Suppose that *success* holds for the operator $-$ on B. Let $\mathbf{K} = \text{Cn}(B)$ and let $+$ be the closure of $-$. In order to show that *success* holds for $\mathbf{K}$, we must show that if $\alpha \notin \text{Cn}(\varnothing)$, then $\alpha \notin \text{Cn}(\mathbf{K}+\alpha)$.

Let $\alpha \notin \text{Cn}(\varnothing)$. Since *success* holds for B, we then have $\alpha \notin \text{Cn}(B-\alpha)$, and since $\text{Cn}(B-\alpha) = \text{Cn}(\mathbf{K}+\alpha)$ it follows that $\alpha \notin \text{Cn}(\mathbf{K}+\alpha)$.

Extensionality (If $\alpha\leftrightarrow\beta \in \text{Cn}(\varnothing)$, then $A+\alpha = A+\beta$.): Suppose that *extensionality* holds for the operator $-$ on B. Let $\mathbf{K} = \text{Cn}(B)$ and let $+$ be the closure of $-$. In order to show that *extensionality* holds for $\mathbf{K}$, we must show that if $\alpha\leftrightarrow\beta \in \text{Cn}(\varnothing)$, then $\mathbf{K}+\alpha = \mathbf{K}+\beta$.

Let $\alpha\leftrightarrow\beta \in \text{Cn}(\varnothing)$. Since $-$ satisfies *extensionality*, we then have $B-\alpha = B-\beta$, and consequently $\text{Cn}(B-\alpha) = \text{Cn}(B-\beta)$, i.e., $\mathbf{K}+\alpha = \mathbf{K}+\beta$.

Failure (If $\alpha \in \text{Cn}(\varnothing)$, then $A+\alpha = A$.): Suppose that *failure* holds for the operator $-$ on B. Let $\mathbf{K} = \text{Cn}(B)$ and let $+$ be the closure of $-$. In order to show that *failure* holds for $\mathbf{K}$, we must show that if $\alpha \in \text{Cn}(\varnothing)$, then $\mathbf{K}+\alpha = \mathbf{K}$.

It follows from $\alpha \in \text{Cn}(\varnothing)$, since $-$ satisfies *failure*, that $B-\alpha = B$, and consequently $\text{Cn}(B-\alpha) = \text{Cn}(B)$, i.e., $\mathbf{K}+\alpha = \mathbf{K}$.

187. *Conservativity*: Let $\mathbf{K} = \text{Cn}(B)$ and let $+$ be the closure of the operator $-$ on B. Suppose that $-$ satisfies *conservativity*. In order to show that $+$ satisfies *conservativity*, suppose that $\mathbf{K}+\beta \not\subseteq \mathbf{K}+\alpha$. We need to show that there is some δ such that $\mathbf{K}+\alpha \subseteq \mathbf{K}+\delta \nvdash \alpha$ and $\mathbf{K}+\delta \cup \mathbf{K}+\beta \vdash \alpha$.

It follows from $\mathbf{K}+\beta \not\subseteq \mathbf{K}+\alpha$ that $B-\beta \not\subseteq B-\alpha$. Since $-$ satisfies *conservativity*, there is some δ such that $B-\alpha \subseteq B-\delta \nvdash \alpha$ and $B-\delta \cup B-\beta \vdash \alpha$. It follows that $\mathbf{K}+\alpha \subseteq \mathbf{K}+\delta \nvdash \alpha$ and $\mathbf{K}+\delta \cup \mathbf{K}+\beta \vdash \alpha$.

Strong conservativity: Let $\mathbf{K} = \text{Cn}(B)$ and let $+$ be the closure of the operator $-$ on B. Suppose that $-$ satisfies *strong conservativity*. In order to show that $+$ satisfies *strong conservativity*, suppose that $\mathbf{K}+\beta \not\subseteq \mathbf{K}+\alpha$. We need to show that $\mathbf{K}+\alpha \nvdash \alpha$ and $\mathbf{K}+\beta \cup \mathbf{K}+\alpha \vdash \alpha$.

It follows from $\mathbf{K}+\beta \not\subseteq \mathbf{K}+\alpha$ that $B-\beta \not\subseteq B-\alpha$. Since $-$ satisfies *strong conservativity*, $B-\alpha \nvdash \alpha$ and $B-\beta \cup B-\alpha \vdash \alpha$. It follows that $\mathbf{K}+\alpha \subseteq \nvdash \alpha$ and $\mathbf{K}+\beta \cup \mathbf{K}+\alpha \vdash \alpha$.

188. Let **K** = Cn(B), and let + be the closure of the operator – for B.
a. Since – satisfies *conjunctive covering*, it holds for all sentences α and β that either B–(α&β) ⊆ B–α or B–(α&β) ⊆ B–β. In the first case it follows that **K**+(α&β) = **K**+α and in the second case that **K**+(α&β) = **K**+α.
b. Let – satisfy the postulate, and let β ∈ Cn(**K**+(α&β)). We then have β ∈ Cn(B–(α&β)). Since – satisfies the postulate it follows that B–(α&β) ⊆ B–α, and consequently Cn(B–(α&β)) ⊆ Cn(B–α), i.e., **K**+(α&β) ⊆ **K**+α.
c. Since – satisfies *weak conjunctive inclusion*, we have for all sentences α and β:
B–(α&β) ⊆ Cn((B–α)∪(B–β))
Cn(B–(α&β)) ⊆ Cn((B–α)∪(B–β))
Cn(B–(α&β)) ⊆ Cn(Cn(B–α)∪Cn(B–β))
K+(α&β) ⊆ Cn((**K**+α)∪(**K**+β))

189. For one direction, suppose that *finitude* is satisfied. Then there is a finite set A such that for every α, **K**+α = Cn(A') for some $A' \subseteq A$. Since every subset of A is finite, *finite representability* holds. Since A only has a finite number of subsets, *finite number of contractions* holds as well.

For the other direction, suppose that *finite representability* and *finite number of contractions* hold. Let $\mathbf{K}_1 ... \mathbf{K}_n$ be all the possible outcomes of contractions. For each $\mathbf{K}_k$, with $1 \leq k \leq n$, there is a finite set A_k such that $\mathbf{K}_k$ = Cn(A_k). Let $A = A_1 \cup ... \cup A_n$. Then A is the finite set that is needed for *finitude* to hold.

190. a. Let **K** = Cn(B) and let + be the closure of the operator – on B. Let – satisfy *hyperregularity*. In order to show that + satisfies the same postulate, suppose that ⊢ α→β and **K**+α ⊬β. We then have B–α ⊬β, and since – satisfies *hyperregularity* it follows that B–α = B–β, from which **K**+α = **K**+β follows directly.
b. Let A be a set and $\sim_\gamma$ a TMR maxichoice contraction on A. Let ⊑ be the marking-off relation by which γ is TMR. Furthermore, suppose that ⊢ α→β and $A \sim_\gamma \alpha$ ⊬β. We have to show that $A \sim_\gamma \beta = A \sim_\gamma \alpha$.

Since $\sim_\gamma$ is maxichoice, $A \sim_\gamma \alpha \in A \perp \alpha$. It therefore follows from ⊢ α→β and $A \sim_\gamma \alpha$ ⊬β that $A \sim_\gamma \alpha \in A \perp \beta$.

Let $X \in A \perp \beta$. It follows from ⊢ α→β that X ⊬ α. Therefore, there is some X' such that $X \subseteq X' \in A \perp \alpha$.

It follows from $X' \in A \perp \alpha$ and $A \sim_\gamma \alpha \in \gamma(A \perp \alpha)$ that $X' \sqsubseteq A \sim_\gamma \alpha$. If $X = X'$, then $X \sqsubseteq A \sim_\gamma \alpha$ follows directly. If $X \subset X'$, then it follows by the maximizing property that $X \sqsubseteq X'$, and thus from the transitivity of ⊑ that $X \sqsubseteq A \sim_\gamma \alpha$.

Thus, $X \subseteq A\sim_\gamma\alpha$ for all $X \in A\perp\beta$. Since $A\sim_\gamma\alpha \in A\perp\beta$, we can conclude $A\sim_\gamma\alpha \in \gamma(A\perp\beta)$, and, since $\sim_\gamma$ is maxichoice, that $A\sim_\gamma\alpha = A\sim_\gamma\beta$.

191. Suppose to the contrary that the three conditions are satisfied for α and β with respect to an operator +. Since α and β are elements of the logically closed set **K**, so is α→β. It follows from *recovery* that $\mathbf{K}+(\alpha\rightarrow\beta) \vdash (\alpha\rightarrow\beta)\rightarrow\alpha$, or equivalently $\mathbf{K}+(\alpha\rightarrow\beta) \vdash \alpha$. It follows from $\mathbf{K}+(\alpha\rightarrow\beta) \vdash \alpha$, using the third condition (antecedent of symmetry) that $\mathbf{K}+(\alpha\rightarrow\beta) \vdash \beta$. Since α→β follows logically from α and β, we now have $\mathbf{K}+(\alpha\rightarrow\beta) \vdash (\alpha\rightarrow\beta)$, and *success* yields $\alpha\rightarrow\beta \in \mathrm{Cn}(\varnothing)$.

In the same way it follows that $\beta\rightarrow\alpha \in \mathrm{Cn}(\varnothing)$. Hence, $\alpha\leftrightarrow\beta \in \mathrm{Cn}(\varnothing)$, contrary to the conditions. This contradiction concludes the proof.

192. Since – satisfies *meet identity*, it holds for all sentences α and β that:
$B-(\alpha\&\beta) = (B-\alpha)\cap(B-\beta)$
$\mathrm{Cn}(B-(\alpha\&\beta)) = \mathrm{Cn}((B-\alpha)\cap(B-\beta))$
$\mathrm{Cn}(B-(\alpha\&\beta)) = \mathrm{Cn}(B-\alpha)\cap\mathrm{Cn}(B-\beta))$ (Observation 1.34)
$\mathbf{K}+(\alpha\&\beta) = (\mathbf{K}+\alpha)\cap(\mathbf{K}+\beta)$
(*Inclusion* and *relative closure* are needed for the application of Observation 1.34.)

193. Let $\mathbf{K} = \mathrm{Cn}(B)$, and let + be the closure of the operator – for B.

Since – satisfies *conjunctive factoring*, it holds for all sentences α and β that either (1) $B-(\alpha\&\beta) = B-\alpha$, (2) $B-(\alpha\&\beta) = B-\beta$, or (3) $B-(\alpha\&\beta) = (B-\alpha) \cap (B-\beta)$.

In case (1) it follows directly that $\mathbf{K}+(\alpha\&\beta) = \mathbf{K}+\alpha$, and similarly in case (2) that $\mathbf{K}+(\alpha\&\beta) = \mathbf{K}+\alpha$. In case (3):
$\mathbf{K}+(\alpha\&\beta)$
$= \mathrm{Cn}(B-(\alpha\&\beta))$
$= \mathrm{Cn}((B-\alpha)\cap(B-\beta))$ (by assumption, see above)
$= \mathrm{Cn}(B-\alpha)\cap\mathrm{Cn}(B-\beta)$ (Observation 1.34)
$= (\mathbf{K}+\alpha) \cap (\mathbf{K}+\beta)$

194. a. It follows directly from the definition of closure of operators (Definition 4.1) that if $B-\alpha \subseteq B-\beta$, then $\mathbf{K}+\alpha \subseteq \mathbf{K}+\beta$.

For the other direction, suppose to the contrary that there are α and β such that $\mathbf{K}+\alpha \subseteq \mathbf{K}+\beta$ and $B-\alpha \not\subseteq B-\beta$. It follows from *inclusion* that $B-\alpha \subseteq B$, and thus $B-\alpha \subseteq B\cap(\mathbf{K}+\alpha)$. It follows from *relative closure* that $B\cap(\mathbf{K}+\alpha) \subseteq B-\alpha$. We can conclude that $B-\alpha = B\cap(\mathbf{K}+\alpha)$. In the same way it follows that $B-\beta = B\cap(\mathbf{K}+\beta)$.

We thus have $B\cap(\mathbf{K}+\alpha) \not\subseteq B\cap(\mathbf{K}+\beta)$. However, it follows from $\mathbf{K}+\alpha \subseteq \mathbf{K}+\beta$ that $B\cap(\mathbf{K}+\alpha) \subseteq B\cap(\mathbf{K}+\beta)$. This contradiction concludes the proof.

b. $\mathbf{K}+\alpha = \mathbf{K}+\beta$
iff $\mathbf{K}+\alpha \subseteq \mathbf{K}+\beta$ and $\mathbf{K}+\beta \subseteq \mathbf{K}+\alpha$
iff $B-\alpha \subseteq B-\beta$ and $B-\beta \subseteq B-\alpha$ (Part *a* of this exercise)
iff $B-\alpha = B-\beta$
c. $\mathbf{K}+\alpha \subset \mathbf{K}+\beta$
iff $\mathbf{K}+\alpha \subseteq \mathbf{K}+\beta$ and $\mathbf{K}+\beta \not\subseteq \mathbf{K}+\alpha$
iff $B-\alpha \subseteq B-\beta$ and $B-\beta \not\subseteq B-\alpha$ (Part *a* of this exercise)
iff $B-\alpha \subset B-\beta$

195. Let $(B-\alpha_1)\cap\ldots\cap(B-\alpha_n) \subseteq (B-\beta)$, and $\delta \in (\mathbf{K}+\alpha_1)\cap\ldots\cap(\mathbf{K}+\alpha_n)$ Then:
$\delta \in \mathrm{Cn}(B-\alpha_1)\cap\ldots\cap\mathrm{Cn}(B-\alpha_n)$
$\delta \in \mathrm{Cn}((B-\alpha_1)\cap\ldots\cap(B-\alpha_n))$ (Observation 1.34)
$\delta \in \mathrm{Cn}(B-\beta)$
$\delta \in \mathbf{K}+\beta$

196. If $\vdash \neg\alpha$, then $B\sim_\gamma\neg\alpha = B\overset{\rightarrow}{\sim}_\gamma\neg\alpha$, from which the desired conclusion follows directly.

If $\nvdash \neg\alpha$, then:
$\mathrm{Cn}((B\overset{\rightarrow}{\sim}_\gamma\neg\alpha)\cup\{\alpha\})$
$= \mathrm{Cn}(\cap\gamma(B\bot\neg\alpha) \cup \{\neg\alpha\rightarrow\&B\} \cup \{\alpha\})$
$= \mathrm{Cn}(\cap\gamma(B\bot\neg\alpha) \cup \{\alpha\})$ (since α implies $\neg\alpha\rightarrow\&B$)
$= \mathrm{Cn}((B\sim_\gamma\neg\alpha) \cup \{\alpha\})$

197. We know from Observation 2.12 that $\mathbf{K}\sim\alpha = \mathbf{K}\cap\mathrm{Cn}(\{\neg\alpha\})$.

First step: We are going to show that $\varepsilon \in \mathbf{K}\cap\mathrm{Cn}(\{\neg\alpha\})$ if and only if ε is equivalent with $\alpha\rightarrow\beta$ for some $\beta \in \mathbf{K}$.

One direction: If $\beta \in \mathbf{K}$ then, since $\mathbf{K}$ is logically closed, $\alpha\rightarrow\beta \in \mathbf{K}$. Since $\alpha\rightarrow\beta \in \mathrm{Cn}(\{\neg\alpha\})$, we also have $\alpha\rightarrow\beta \in \mathbf{K}\cap\mathrm{Cn}(\{\neg\alpha\})$, and since $\mathbf{K}\cap\mathrm{Cn}(\{\neg\alpha\})$ is logically closed, it holds for every sentence ε that if ε is equivalent with $\alpha\rightarrow\beta$, then $\varepsilon \in \mathbf{K}\cap\mathrm{Cn}(\{\neg\alpha\})$.

The other direction: Let $\varepsilon \in \mathbf{K}\cap\mathrm{Cn}(\{\neg\alpha\})$. It follows from $\vdash \neg\alpha\rightarrow\varepsilon$ that $\vdash \varepsilon\leftrightarrow(\alpha\rightarrow\varepsilon)$. Let $\beta = \varepsilon$, and we are done.

Second step:
$+$ satisfies *recovery*
iff $\mathbf{K} \subseteq \mathrm{Cn}((\mathbf{K}+\alpha)\cup\{\alpha\})$
iff for all β: if $\beta \in \mathbf{K}$ then $\beta \in \mathrm{Cn}((\mathbf{K}+\alpha)\cup\{\alpha\})$
iff for all β: if $\beta \in \mathbf{K}$ then $\alpha\rightarrow\beta \in \mathrm{Cn}(\mathbf{K}+\alpha)$
iff for all β: if $\beta \in \mathbf{K}$ then $\alpha\rightarrow\beta \in \mathrm{Cn}(B-\alpha)$
iff $\{\alpha\rightarrow\beta \mid \beta \in \mathbf{K}\} \subseteq \mathrm{Cn}(B-\alpha)$
iff $\mathbf{K}\sim\alpha \subseteq \mathrm{Cn}(B-\alpha)$ (here step 1 of the proof is used)

198. a. If $\mathbf{K}$ is inconsistent, then there is no ξ such that $\xi \notin \mathbf{K}$.

b. Let $\xi \in \mathrm{Cn}(\varnothing)$. It follows from *failure* that $\mathbf{K}{+}\xi = \mathbf{K}$ and from *finitude* that $\&(\mathbf{K}{+}\xi) = \&\mathbf{K}$ is well-defined. We therefore have that $\&\mathbf{K} \in B$, and consequently $\mathrm{Cn}(\{\&\mathbf{K}\}) \subseteq \mathrm{Cn}(B)$, i.e., Thus, $\mathbf{K} \subseteq \mathrm{Cn}(B)$.

It follows from *inclusion* that $B \subseteq \mathbf{K}$, and thus $\mathrm{Cn}(B) \subseteq \mathbf{K}$. We can conclude that $\mathrm{Cn}(B) = \mathbf{K}$.

199. The adjusted list is still an axiomatic characterization of base-generated full meet contraction. Where *conservativity* is used in the proof, *weak conservativity* is sufficient.

200. *(1) to (2)*: Suppose that + is generated by the kernel contraction $\approx_\sigma$ on a base B for **K**. According to Definition 2.35, it holds for all α that $B\hat{\approx}_\sigma\alpha = B \cap \mathrm{Cn}(B\approx_\sigma\alpha) = B \cap \mathrm{Cn}(B\setminus\sigma(A\perp\!\!\!\perp\alpha))$. We are going to show that $\mathrm{Cn}(B\hat{\approx}_\sigma\alpha) = \mathrm{Cn}(B\approx_\sigma\alpha)$.

It follows from $B\setminus\sigma(A\perp\!\!\!\perp\alpha) \subseteq B \cap \mathrm{Cn}(B\setminus\sigma(A\perp\!\!\!\perp\alpha))$ that $\mathrm{Cn}(B\setminus\sigma(A\perp\!\!\!\perp\alpha)) \subseteq \mathrm{Cn}(B \cap \mathrm{Cn}(B\setminus\sigma(A\perp\!\!\!\perp\alpha)))$, i.e. $\mathrm{Cn}(B\approx_\sigma\alpha) \subseteq \mathrm{Cn}(B\hat{\approx}_\sigma\alpha)$.

It follows from $B \cap \mathrm{Cn}(B\setminus\sigma(A\perp\!\!\!\perp\alpha)) \subseteq \mathrm{Cn}(B\setminus\sigma(A\perp\!\!\!\perp\alpha))$ that $\mathrm{Cn}(B \cap \mathrm{Cn}(B\setminus\sigma(A\perp\!\!\!\perp\alpha))) \subseteq \mathrm{Cn}(B\setminus\sigma(A\perp\!\!\!\perp\alpha))$, i.e., $\mathrm{Cn}(B\hat{\approx}_\sigma\alpha) \subseteq \mathrm{Cn}(B\approx_\sigma\alpha)$.

Thus, $\mathrm{Cn}(B\hat{\approx}_\sigma\alpha) = \mathrm{Cn}(B\approx_\sigma\alpha)$. According to Theorem 2.36, there is some smooth incision function σ' such that for all α, $B\hat{\approx}_\sigma\alpha = B\approx_{\sigma'}\alpha$.

According to our assumption, it holds for all α that $\mathbf{K}{+}\alpha = \mathrm{Cn}(B\approx_\sigma\alpha)$. We now have $\mathbf{K}{+}\alpha = \mathrm{Cn}(B\hat{\approx}_\sigma\alpha) = \mathrm{Cn}(B\approx_{\sigma'}\alpha)$.

(2) implies (1): Every smooth kernel contraction is a kernel contraction.

201. *Part 1*: $\mathcal{V}(A\cap B) \subseteq \mathcal{V}_A(B)$ followd directly from the definition.

By the definition, every element of $\mathcal{V}_A(B)$ is either (1) an element of $\mathcal{V}(A\cap B)$ and thus of $\mathcal{V}(B)$ or (2) a disjunction of a sentence $\alpha \in \mathcal{V}(A\cap B)$ and a sentence $\beta \in \mathcal{V}(B)$. Since both α and β are elements of $\mathcal{V}(B)$, so is $\alpha\vee\beta$.

Part 2: Let $\alpha \in \mathcal{V}(A)$ and $A\subseteq B$. Since $A\subseteq B$, we have $A\cap B = A$ and thus $\alpha \in \mathcal{V}(A\cap B)$, that is, according to the definition, a subset of $\mathcal{V}_A(B)$

Part 3: Let $A \subseteq B$. It follows from Part 2 that $\mathcal{V}(A) \subseteq \mathcal{V}_A(B)$. Thus $\mathrm{Cn}(\mathcal{V}(A)) \subseteq \mathrm{Cn}(\mathcal{V}_A(B))$. Furthermore, it follows from the construction that every element of $\mathcal{V}_A(B)$ is either an element of $\mathcal{V}(A)$ or a disjunction with at least one element of $\mathcal{V}(A)$ as a disjunct, so that $\mathrm{Cn}(\mathcal{V}_A(B)) \subseteq \mathrm{Cn}(\mathcal{V}(A))$.

Thus $\mathrm{Cn}(\mathcal{V}(A)) = \mathrm{Cn}(\mathcal{V}_A(B))$, and since $\mathrm{Cn}(A) = \mathrm{Cn}(\mathcal{V}(A))$ it follows that $\mathrm{Cn}(\mathcal{V}_A(B)) = \mathrm{Cn}(A)$.

Part 4: If $A\cap B = \varnothing$, then $\mathcal{V}(A\cap B) = \varnothing$, from which it follows that $\mathcal{V}_A(B) = \varnothing$.

202. Let $\beta \in \mathcal{V}(B)\setminus\mathcal{V}_A(B)$. It follows from $\beta \in \mathcal{V}(B)$ that $\beta = \beta_1\vee\ldots\vee\beta_n$ for some $\beta_1,\ldots\beta_n \in B$. Since $\beta \notin \mathcal{V}_A(B)$, none of $\beta_1,\ldots\beta_n$ is an element of $A\cap B$.

It follows that $\{\beta_1,\ldots\beta_n\} \subseteq B\backslash(A\cap B) = B\backslash A$, and consequently that β, the disjunction of $\beta_1,\ldots\beta_n$, is an element of $\mathcal{V}(B\backslash A)$.

203. *PROOF THAT (1) IMPLIES (2)*: Let γ be a selection function such that for all α, $K+\alpha = Cn(B\simeq_\gamma\alpha)$. Since $B\simeq_\gamma\alpha$ is logically closed, it follows that for all α, $K+\alpha = B\simeq_\gamma\alpha$. Let γ'' be such that
(1) If $\mathcal{V}(B)\perp\alpha \neq \emptyset$, then
$\gamma''(\mathcal{V}(B)\perp\alpha) = \{Y \in \mathcal{V}(B)\perp\alpha \mid Cn(X) = Cn(Y) \text{ for some } X \in \gamma(B\perp\alpha)\}$
(2) If $\mathcal{V}(B)\perp\alpha = \emptyset$, then $\gamma''(\mathcal{V}(B)\perp\alpha) = \{\mathcal{V}(B)\}$
Clearly, $\mathcal{V}(B)$ is a finite base for K. We need to show that (I) γ'' is a selection function for $\mathcal{V}(B)$, (II) $K+\alpha \subseteq Cn(\mathcal{V}(B)\sim_{\gamma''}\alpha)$, and (III) $Cn(\mathcal{V}(B)\sim_{\gamma''}\alpha) \subseteq K+\alpha$.

Part I: In order to show that γ'' is a selection function for $\mathcal{V}(B)$, we need to show that if $\mathcal{V}(B)\perp\alpha \neq \emptyset$, then $\gamma''(\mathcal{V}(B)\perp\alpha) \neq \emptyset$. It follows from $\mathcal{V}(B)\perp\alpha \neq \emptyset$ that α is not a tautology, and thus $B\perp\alpha \neq \emptyset$. Since γ is a selection function, $\gamma(B\perp\alpha)$ is non-empty. Let $X \in \gamma(B\perp\alpha)$. It follows from Observation 4.38 that there is some $Y \in \mathcal{V}(B)\perp\alpha$ such that $Cn(X) = Cn(Y)$. It follows from the definition of γ'' that $Y \in \gamma''(\mathcal{V}(B)\perp\alpha)$.

Part II: Let $\beta \in K+\alpha$, i.e., $\beta \in B\simeq_\gamma\alpha$. Then for each $X \in \gamma(B\perp\alpha)$, $X \vdash \beta$. By the definition of γ'', for each $Y \in \gamma''(\mathcal{V}(B)\perp\alpha)$, $Y \vdash \beta$. Since the elements of $\mathcal{V}(B)\perp\alpha$ are closed under disjunction, it follows from Observation 1.34 that $\beta \in Cn(\cap\gamma''(\mathcal{V}(B)\perp\alpha))$, i.e. $\beta \in Cn(\mathcal{V}(B)\sim_{\gamma''}\alpha)$.

Part III: Let $\beta \in Cn(\mathcal{V}(B)\sim_{\gamma''}\alpha)$, i.e., $\beta \in Cn(\cap\gamma''(\mathcal{V}(B)\perp\alpha))$. Then for each $Y \in \gamma''(\mathcal{V}(B)\perp\alpha)$ we have $Y \vdash \beta$. By Observation 4.38 and the definition of γ'', for each $X \in \gamma(B\perp\alpha)$ there is some $Y \in \gamma''(\mathcal{V}(B)\perp\alpha)$ such that $Cn(X) = Cn(Y)$, and thus $X \vdash \beta$. We may conclude
that $\beta \in B\simeq_\gamma\alpha$. Thus, $Cn(\mathcal{V}(B)\sim_{\gamma''}\alpha) \subseteq B\simeq_\gamma\alpha = K+\alpha$.

PROOF THAT (2) IMPLIES (1): Let B be a disjunctively closed base for K and let γ be a selection function for B that gives rise to the operation $+$ on K, i.e.:

$K+\alpha = Cn(B\sim_\gamma\alpha)$

We are going to use the same base B and the same selection function γ. It is clearly sufficient for the proof to show that $Cn(B\sim_\gamma\alpha) = Cn(B\simeq_\gamma\alpha)$ holds for all α.

In order to show that $Cn(B\sim_\gamma\alpha) \subseteq Cn(B\simeq_\gamma\alpha)$, let $\beta \in Cn(B\sim_\gamma\alpha) = Cn(\cap\gamma(B\perp\alpha))$. For every $X \in \gamma(B\perp\alpha)$, $\cap\gamma(B\perp\alpha) \subseteq X$, so that $\beta \in Cn(X)$. It follows that $\beta \in B\simeq_\gamma\alpha$, thus $\beta \in Cn(B\simeq_\gamma\alpha)$.

In order to show that $Cn(B\simeq_\gamma\alpha) \subseteq Cn(B\sim_\gamma\alpha)$, let $\beta \in Cn(B\simeq_\gamma\alpha)$. Then for each $X \in \gamma(B\perp\alpha)$, we have $\beta \in Cn(X)$. It follows from Observation 1.34 that $\beta \in Cn(\cap\gamma(B\perp\alpha))$, i.e., $\beta \in Cn(B\sim_\gamma\alpha)$.

204. Let B be a base for **K** and γ a selection function for B that is transitively maximizingly relational. We know from Observation 2.19 that $\sim_\gamma$ satisfies *conjunctive overlap*, i.e., that $(B\sim_\gamma\alpha)\cap(B\sim_\gamma\beta) \subseteq B\sim_\gamma(\alpha\&\beta)$ for all α and β.

Now let $\mathbf{K}+\delta \subseteq (\mathbf{K}+\alpha)\cap(\mathbf{K}+\beta)$. It follows from $\mathbf{K}+\delta \subseteq \mathbf{K}+\alpha$ that $B\cap(\mathbf{K}+\delta) \subseteq B\cap(\mathbf{K}+\alpha)$, i.e., $B\sim_\gamma\delta \subseteq B\sim_\gamma\alpha$. Similarly, $B\sim_\gamma\delta \subseteq B\sim_\gamma\beta$. Since $(B\sim_\gamma\alpha)\cap(B\sim_\gamma\beta) \subseteq B\sim_\gamma(\alpha\&\beta)$, we have $B\sim_\gamma\delta \subseteq B\sim_\gamma(\alpha\&\beta)$, thus $\mathrm{Cn}(B\sim_\gamma\delta) \subseteq \mathrm{Cn}(B\sim_\gamma(\alpha\&\beta))$, i.e. $\mathbf{K}+\delta \subseteq \mathbf{K}+(\alpha\&\beta)$.

205. Let B be a belief base and $\mathbf{K} = \mathrm{Cn}(B)$. Furthermore, let $\bullet$ be an operator on B and $*$ the closure of $\bullet$.

Part 2: Suppose that $\bullet$ satisfies *consistency*. Let α be consistent. Then $B\bullet\alpha$ is consistent, and hence so is its logical closure $\mathbf{K}*\alpha$.

Part 4: Suppose that $\bullet$ satisfies *inconsistent expansion*. Let $\neg\alpha \in \mathrm{Cn}(\varnothing)$. We then have:

$B\bullet\alpha = B\cup\{\alpha\}$.

$\mathrm{Cn}(B\bullet\alpha) = \mathrm{Cn}(B\cup\{\alpha\})$

$\mathrm{Cn}(B\bullet\alpha) = \mathrm{Cn}(\mathrm{Cn}(B)\cup\{\alpha\})$ (properties of Cn)

$\mathbf{K}*\alpha = \mathrm{Cn}(\mathbf{K}\cup\{\alpha\})$

$\mathbf{K}*\alpha = \mathbf{K}+\alpha$

Part 5: Suppose that $\bullet$ satisfies *vacuity*: Let $\neg\alpha \notin \mathrm{Cn}(\mathbf{K})$. Since $\mathrm{Cn}(\mathbf{K}) = \mathrm{Cn}(B)$, we then have then $B\bullet\alpha = B\cup\{\alpha\}$, and it follows in the same way as in Part 4 that $\mathbf{K}*\alpha = \mathbf{K}+\alpha$.

Part 7: Suppose that $\neg\beta \notin \mathrm{Cn}(\mathbf{K}*\alpha)$. It follows that $\neg\beta \notin \mathrm{Cn}(B\bullet\alpha)$. Since $\bullet$ satisfies *subexpansion*, we then have:

$(B\bullet\alpha)\cup\{\beta\} \subseteq B\bullet(\alpha\&\beta)$

$\mathrm{Cn}((B\bullet\alpha)\cup\{\beta\}) \subseteq \mathrm{Cn}(B\bullet(\alpha\&\beta))$

$\mathrm{Cn}(\mathrm{Cn}(B\bullet\alpha)\cup\{\beta\}) \subseteq \mathrm{Cn}(B\bullet(\alpha\&\beta))$

$\mathrm{Cn}((\mathbf{K}*\alpha)\cup\{\beta\}) \subseteq \mathbf{K}*(\alpha\&\beta))$

$(\mathbf{K}*\alpha)+\beta \subseteq \mathbf{K}*(\alpha\&\beta))$

206. Let B be a belief base and $\mathbf{K} = \mathrm{Cn}(B)$. Furthermore, let $\bullet$ be an operator on B and $*$ the closure of $\bullet$. Suppose that $\bullet$ satisfies *weak disjunctive inclusion*. We then have for all sentences α and β:

$B\bullet(\alpha\vee\beta) \subseteq \mathrm{Cn}((B\bullet\alpha)\cup(B\bullet\beta))$

$\mathrm{Cn}(B\bullet(\alpha\vee\beta)) \subseteq \mathrm{Cn}((B\bullet\alpha)\cup(B\bullet\beta))$

$\mathrm{Cn}(B\bullet(\alpha\vee\beta)) \subseteq \mathrm{Cn}(\mathrm{Cn}(B\bullet\alpha)\cup\mathrm{Cn}(B\bullet\beta))$

$\mathbf{K}*(\alpha\vee\beta) \subseteq \mathrm{Cn}((\mathbf{K}*\alpha)\cup(\mathbf{K}*\beta))$

207. Let $-$ and $\bullet$ be operations on a set B such that $B\bullet\alpha = (B-\neg\alpha)\cup\{\alpha\}$ for all α. Furthermore, let $\mathbf{K} = \mathrm{Cn}(B)$, and let $+$ be the closure of $-$ and $*$ the closure of $\bullet$. Then:

$\mathbf{K}*\alpha = \mathrm{Cn}(B\bullet\alpha)$

$= \mathrm{Cn}((B - \neg\alpha) \cup \{\alpha\})$
$= \mathrm{Cn}(\mathrm{Cn}(B - \neg\alpha) \cup \{\alpha\})$
$= \mathrm{Cn}((\mathbf{K} \div \neg\alpha) \cup \{\alpha\})$
$= (\mathbf{K} \div \neg\alpha) + \alpha$

208. Let $*$ be the operation such that for all β:
$\mathbf{K} * \beta = (\mathbf{K} \div \neg\beta) + \beta$.
Then, since $\div$ is the closure of $\sim_\gamma$, $\mathbf{K} * \beta = \mathrm{Cn}((B \sim_\gamma \neg\beta) \cup \{\beta\}) = \mathrm{Cn}(B \mp_\gamma \beta)$. It follows from Observation 4.18 that $*$ is an operator of partial meet revision on $\mathbf{K}$, and from Observation 3.15 that $\mathbf{K} \cap (\mathbf{K} * \neg\alpha)$ is an operator of partial meet contraction on $\mathbf{K}$. Since $\mathbf{K} \cap (\mathbf{K} * \neg\alpha) = \mathbf{K} \cap ((\mathbf{K} \div \alpha) + \neg\alpha) = \mathbf{K} \div' \alpha$, this is sufficient to prove that $\div'$ is an operator of partial meet contraction for $\mathbf{K}$.

SOLUTIONS FOR CHAPTER 5$^+$

209. According to *incompleteness*, we can let $\alpha \notin$ **K** and $\neg\alpha \notin$ **K**.

It follows from *contraction-vacuity* that **K**$\div\neg\alpha$ = **K**. Applying the *Levi identity* to this, we obtain **K**$*\alpha$ = **K**$+\alpha$. Since $\alpha \in$ **K**$+\alpha$, it follows from *closure under Poss* that $\neg\Diamond\neg\alpha \in$ **K**$+\alpha$.

Applying *closure under Poss* to $\alpha \notin$ **K**, we obtain $\Diamond\neg\alpha \in$ **K**. Since **K** $\subseteq$ **K**$+\alpha$, it follows that $\Diamond\neg\alpha \in$ **K**$+\alpha$.

We have shown that both $\neg\Diamond\neg\alpha$ and $\Diamond\neg\alpha$ are elements of **K**$+\alpha$ and that **K**$*\alpha$ = **K**$+\alpha$; thus **K**$*\alpha$ is inconsistent.

It follows from $\neg\alpha \notin$ **K**, since **K** is logically closed, that $\neg\alpha$ is not logically true. Thus α is consistent. We have already shown that **K**$*\alpha$ is inconsistent. This contradicts *consistency*, and thereby concludes our proof.

210. Yes. In the proof, *consistency* is only applied to prove that (**K**$*\alpha$)$*$($\beta\vee\delta$) is are consistent. It can be replaced by *weak consistency*, as follows:

Since **K** and α are both consistent, it follows from *weak consistency* that **K**$*\alpha$ is consistent. Thus, both **K**$*\alpha$ and $\beta\vee\delta$ are consistent, and it follows from *weak consistency* that (**K**$*\alpha$)$*$($\beta\vee\delta$) is consistent.

APPLIED LOGIC SERIES

1. D. Walton: *Fallacies Arising from Ambiguity.* 1996 ISBN 0-7923-4100-7
2. H. Wansing (ed.): *Proof Theory of Modal Logic.* 1996 ISBN 0-7923-4120-1
3. F. Baader and K.U. Schulz (eds.): *Frontiers of Combining Systems.* First International Workshop, Munich, March 1996. 1996 ISBN 0-7923-4271-2
4. M. Marx and Y. Venema: *Multi-Dimensional Modal Logic.* 1996 ISBN 0-7923-4345-X
5. S. Akama (ed.): *Logic, Language and Computation.* 1997 ISBN 0-7923-4376-X
6. J. Goubault-Larrecq and I. Mackie: *Proof Theory and Automated Deduction.* 1997 ISBN 0-7923-4593-2
7. M. de Rijke (ed.): *Advances in Intensional Logic.* 1997 ISBN 0-7923-4711-0
8. W. Bibel and P.H. Schmitt (eds.): *Automated Deduction - A Basis for Applications.* Volume I. Foundations - Calculi and Methods. 1998 ISBN 0-7923-5129-0
9. W. Bibel and P.H. Schmitt (eds.): *Automated Deduction - A Basis for Applications.* Volume II. Systems and Implementation Techniques. 1998 ISBN 0-7923-5130-4
10. W. Bibel and P.H. Schmitt (eds.): *Automated Deduction - A Basis for Applications.* Volume III. Applications. 1998 ISBN 0-7923-5131-2
(Set vols. I-III: ISBN 0-7923-5132-0)
11. S.O. Hansson: *A Textbook of Belief Dynamics.* Theory Change and Database Updating. 1999 including *Solutions to exercises.* 1999. Hb: ISBN 0-7923-5324-2; Set: (Pb): ISBN 0-7923-5329-3
12. R. Pareschi and B. Fronhöfer (eds.): *Dynamic Worlds.* From the Frame Problem to Knowledge Management. 1999 ISBN 07923-5535-0
13. D.M. Gabbay and H. Wansing (eds.): *What is Negation?.* 1999 ISBN 0-7923-5569-5
14. M. Wooldridge and A. Rao (eds.): *Foundations of Rational Agency.* 1999 ISBN 0-7923-5601-2

KLUWER ACADEMIC PUBLISHERS – DORDRECHT / BOSTON / LONDON